# A COMMENTARY

ON

# The Epistle
# to the Hebrews

BY

## ROBERT MILLIGAN

*Late President of the College of the Bible in Kentucky University*

GOSPEL ADVOCATE COMPANY
NASHVILLE, TENN.
1981

## PREFACE TO REPRINT EDITION

It is now more than seventy years since Milligan's Commentary on Hebrews was first published. During these years it has enjoyed a wide circulation. It has been a blessing to thousands. In the home, in the study, and in the schoolroom it has been recognized as a standard work on the subject.

During the turbulent war years it was allowed to go out of print. Shortages of paper and labor were responsible. Now that the war is over and conditions are somewhat improved, the Gospel Advocate Company is glad to make this treasured volume again available to all who desire it.

This volume is sent forth, without apology, in the hope that it may be instrumental in leading thousands into a better understanding of the Epistle to the Hebrews.

B. C. GOODPASTURE.

# PUBLISHERS' PREFACE

In announcing the volume on Hebrews of the New Testament Commentary, we are pained to state that the author of it did not live till it had passed through the press. Still, we are rejoiced that his work on it was complete before he was called away from this scene of his labors. We doubt not the work will be received as a valuable contribution to Biblical criticism on its own merits. It will be doubly dear to a host of friends of the deceased who had the highest regard for him personally while living, and who, now that he has passed into the spirit-land, hold him in most affectionate remembrance. A brief sketch of his life and character will be found at the end of this volume.

For writing this volume on Hebrews, President Milligan possessed some very rare qualifications. He was a man of most deep and fervent piety. This brought him into close sympathy with our Saviour in his mediatorial and priestly offices. Then his general and accurate scholarship, his practical experience as a teacher, and above all his ardent love for the truth, and nothing but the truth, at once made it impossible for him to fail in a work of this kind. The volume is not burdened with new interpretation or original views. The author has aimed to be safe rather than brilliant; faithful to the Divine Spirit rather than original; and eminently practical rather than novel. Still it shows that he had decided opinions of his own, and these are always freely given when it is thought to be necessary. Nevertheless, the work is decidedly conservative. Everywhere we see stamped upon it this peculiar characteristic of the author's mind. President Milligan was naturally a very prudent man, while his profound reverence for the word of God, and his constant anxiety lest he might lead someone astray, tended to quicken the natural bent of his mind, and shut out all doubtful interpretations, even when the temptation was very great. And it ought to be said, furthermore, that not only his habits of mind, but his studies as well, led him to discredit everything in the new school of criticism, and threw him largely upon the old critics for help. Hence his work from beginning to end has the flavor of the old authors, and may be said to occupy a middle ground between the old and new schools of criticism. While it relies chiefly on the old English commentators as authorities, it is nevertheless well up to the demands of the present times in Biblical criticism.

The plan of this volume does not materially differ from the one on Matthew and Mark, and yet there are some features in this that are specially worthy of mention. It will be noticed that each section is preceded by a very careful and full analysis. This we think will be found valuable to the student as helping him at once to comprehend the whole argument. Besides this, each section is followed by practical reflections which are always interesting and sometimes of great value. These supply largely a homiletical part which we doubt not will be very acceptable to most students and especially preachers of the gospel.

The author had made the study of typology a specialty for many years of his life, and he has freely given us the results of his studies in this volume. And it is believed that his treatment of the types will receive the highest commendation from those who are at all competent to judge. We feel confident that this interesting study will receive new interest from what President Milligan has written, and we do not hesitate to call special attention to this portion of his work.

# INTRODUCTION

The main historical circumstances of this Epistle may be summed up and considered under the following general heads:

I. By whom was the Epistle written?
II. Is it, or is it not, of canonical authority?
III. To whom was it written?
IV. For what purpose was it written?
V. When and where was it written?
VI. In what language was it written?

## SECTION ONE

### BY WHOM WAS THE EPISTLE WRITTEN?

Some have ascribed it to Clement of Rome; some to Barnabas, the companion of Paul; some to Silas or Silvanus; some to Apollos; some to Aquila; some to Mark; and some to Paul the Apostle. These hypotheses have all been maintained by able critics, and with some show of reason, as any one may see by referring to Davidson's Introduction to the New Testament, Alford's Prolegomena, or Stewart's Introduction to this Epistle. But to my mind, it is quite evident that the last of these is the only hypothesis that is really worthy of our consideration, because it is the only one that is sustained by any reliable evidence. The others are all purely conjectural; and hence if it can be shown that Paul did not write the Epistle, then indeed we may as well give up all further inquiry about its authorship, and wait patiently for the revelations of the day of judgment. But that it is one of Paul's genuine Epistles seems, at least, quite probable from the following considerations:

I. *It is ascribed to Paul by many of the Christian Fathers, who, so far as we know, had the best means of information with regard to both its genuineness and its authenticity.*

1. The first of these is Pantaenus, an eminent Oriental scholar, who was for several years President of the Catechetical School of sacred learning in Egypt. He flourished about A.D. 180, and he is

spoken of by Eusebius and Jerome as a man of great learning and influence. None of his writings are now extant; but his testimony with regard to the authorship of the Epistle to the Hebrews is given by Clement of Alexandria in his work called *Hypotyposis* (Institutions). The work itself is now lost, but Clement's testimony, embracing that of Pantaenus, is given in an extract from it, preserved by Eusebius in the fourteenth chapter of the sixth book of his Ecclesiastical History. In this extract, Clement is attempting to explain why it is that Paul did not connect his name with the Epistle, and after giving his own opinion, he says, "But now as the blessed Presbyter [Pantaenus] used to say, Since the Lord, who was the Apostle of the Almighty, was sent to the Hebrews, Paul, by reason of his inferiority, as if sent to the Gentiles, did not subscribe himself an Apostle to the Hebrews, both out of reverence for the Lord, and because he wrote of his abundance to the Hebrews, as a herald and Apostle to the Gentiles."

This testimony is very direct, and comes from one who had rare opportunities of judging correctly about such matters. He had heard, as we learn from Photius, those who had seen the Apostles; and according to Eusebius (Eccl. Hist. B. v. 10), he was, on account of his great learning and piety, sent by Julian, Bishop of Alexandria, as a missionary to the East, even as far as to India. He was also, according to the same historian (Eccl. Hist. B. vi. 14), very highly commended by Alexander, Bishop of Jerusalem, about A.D. 212. And hence it would seem that the testimony of Pantaenus is entitled to very great respect in the settlement of this question. In matters of opinion he was of course liable to err, as we all are, and I do not therefore attach much importance to the reason which he assigns, in explanation of the fact, that Paul did not attach his name to the Epistle.

2. Next to the testimony of Pantaenus comes that of Clement of Alexandria. He was for some time a pupil of Pantaenus, and about A.D. 187 he succeeded him as President of the Catechetical School in Alexandria. His birthplace is uncertain, but in his *Stromata* (Miscellanies), he tells us that he had been instructed by one teacher in Italy, one in Greece, two in the East, and one in Egypt. (Lard. Cred. vol. ii. 22.) He was therefore, no doubt, well acquainted with the prevailing opinions of both the Eastern and Western churches, touching the Canon of the Holy Scriptures.

In his Ecclesiastical History (B. vi. 14), Eusebius has recorded the testimony of Clement with regard to the authorship of our Epistle. Eusebius says, "In his work called *Hypotyposis,* he [Clement] affirms that Paul is the author of the Epistle to the Hebrews; and that, as it was addressed to the Hebrews, it was originally written in their language, and afterward translated by Luke for the Greeks—which is the reason why the coloring of the style is the same in this Epistle and in the Acts of the Apostles. The reason why Paul did not affix his name to the head of it, probably is, because the Hebrews had conceived a prejudice against him, and were suspicious of him. Very prudently, therefore, did he not place his name at the head of the Epistle, so as to divert them from the perusal of it."

In his other works, Clement testifies several times to the same effect, touching the authorship of this Epistle.

3. Our next witness is the celebrated Origen. He was born in Egypt about A.D. 185, and was, from his youth, thoroughly instructed in both religion and philosophy. At the early age of eighteen he was made Principal of the Catechetical School in Alexandria, and in or about A.D. 213, he went to Rome in quest of religious knowledge. Afterward, he also visited Greece, Arabia, and Asia Minor, and in A.D. 231 he left Alexandria in Egypt, and went to Caesarea in Palestine, where he was long honored and respected by Alexander of Jerusalem, and other Bishops of the East. Jerome calls him, "The greatest doctor of the Church since the Apostles." And again he says, that he himself would willingly undergo all the hatred that Origen had endured, if he had only his knowledge of the Holy Scriptures. (Lard. Cred. vol. ii. 38.)

The testimony of this eminent scholar is therefore entitled to very great weight in the settlement of the question before us. This he has given very explicitly in several of his works. In his letter to Africanus, for example, he says, "But possibly some one pressed with this argument will have recourse to the opinion of those who reject this Epistle, as not written by Paul. In answer to such a one, we intend to write a separate discourse *to show that Epistle to be Paul's.*"

Still more full and explicit is his testimony given in the following extract from Eusebius (Eccl. Hist. B. vi. 25). This learned historian says, "Origen decides thus in his Homilies upon it: The character of the style of the Epistle to the Hebrews has not the unpolished cast of the Apostle's language, who professed himself to be a man unlearned in speech; that is, in phraseology. Besides, this Epistle, in the texture of its style, is more conformed to the Greek idiom, as every one must confess who is able to distinguish differences in style. Moreover, the ideas in the Epistle are admirable, and not inferior to those which are confessedly apostolic: and that this is true, every one must concede who has attentively read the writings of the Apostles. A little further on he [Origen] adds, If I were to give my opinion, I would say the phraseology and the texture belong to some one relating the Apostle's sentiments, and, as it were, commenting on the words of his master. If any church, therefore, holds this to be an Epistle of Paul, let it receive commendation on account of this; for it is not without reason that *the ancients have handed it down as Paul's.* Who wrote the Epistle, God only knows with certainty: but the report which has reached us, is that some affirm it to be written by Clement, Bishop of Rome; and some, by Luke, who wrote the Gospel and the Acts."

To some it may seem as if this testimony of Origen, given in his Homilies, is inconsistent with that which is given in his letter to Africanus, for in that he expressed his unqualified conviction that Paul is the author of the Epistle, and he avows his intention to write a discourse in proof of this; but in the extract from his Homilies he says, "Who wrote the Epistle God only knows certainly." By this remark, however, he evidently does not intend to express any doubt as to the authorship of the Epistle, but only as to the person who in this case acted as Paul's amanuensis. He seems to think that as Tertius wrote the Epistle to the Romans (Rom. 16: 22), so also in the present case some skillful rhetorician wrote for him the Epistle to the Hebrews, taking, perhaps, at the same time, with Paul's consent and approval, some liberty with regard to the style and phraseology of the Epistle. But nevertheless in the latter extract, as well as in the former, he seems to agree with "the ancients" that the thoughts are Paul's, and that he is therefore the real and proper author of the Epistle.

4. From the testimony of Origen we pass next to that of The Council of Antioch. This Council first met in A.D. 264, and was composed of about seventy or eighty Bishops, representing the

most enlightened and influential churches in Western Asia. In a synodical letter written by this Council near the close of its second session in A.D. 269, touching the trial and condemnation of Paul of Samosata, the Epistle to the Hebrews is ascribed to the same Apostle that wrote the first and second Epistles to the Corinthians. This is apparent from the following extracts. The Bishops say, "Now the Lord is that Spirit, according to *the Apostle* [2 Cor. 3: 17.] And according to *the same,* For they drank of the spiritual rock, etc. [1 Cor. 10: 4].—And of Moses *the Apostle* writes, Esteeming the reproach of Christ greater riches, etc. [Heb. 11: 26]." See Davidson's Introduction to the New Testament, vol. iii. p. 191. There is scarcely any room to doubt that by "the Apostle" in this extract, the writer of this letter and the other members of the Council meant Paul the Apostle. And, if so, then this testimony shows very clearly what was at that time the general opinion of the Eastern churches with respect to the authorship of the Epistle to the Hebrews; for this Council was composed of many of the most learned Bishops and Presbyters of Western Asia.

5. The next prominent witness in order is Eusebius the historian. He was born in Caesarea in Palestine about A.D. 264; and in A.D. 320, or perhaps sooner, he was made Bishop of the Church in that city. He became greatly distinguished for his piety and his learning, and was inferior to none of his contemporaries in his knowledge of ecclesiastical affairs. There can be no doubt, therefore, that he was well qualified to bear testimony in the case before us. This he has done repeatedly in his Ecclesiastical History. In B. iii. 3, for instance, he says, "Fourteen Epistles are clearly and certainly Paul's: although it is proper to be known that some have rejected that which is written to the Hebrews, alleging that it is spoken against as not belonging to Paul." In B. iii. 25, he classifies "the Epistles of Paul" among those that were received as canonical. And in B. iii. 38, speaking of the epistle of Clement, he says, "In which, inserting many sentiments of the Epistle to the Hebrews, and also using some of the very words of it, he [Clement] plainly manifests that this Epistle is no modern writing, and hence it has not without reason been reckoned among the other writings of the Apostle. For Paul having written to the Hebrews in their own language, some think that the Evangelist Luke, and others that this very Clement, translated it [into Greek];

which last opinion is the more probable of the two, there being a resemblance between the style of the epistle of Clement and of that to the Hebrews; nor are the sentiments of these two writings very different."

From these citations it is manifest that Eusebius received the Epistle to the Hebrews as one of Paul's genuine letters; though, like Origen, he seems to have thought that some other person had translated what Paul had himself originally dictated.

After the age of Eusebius, this Epistle was commonly received throughout the East as an Epistle of Paul. Indeed, it was very generally so regarded from the beginning in the Egyptian, Greek, and Syrian churches. It was chiefly in the West that its Pauline authorship was, for a time, denied or doubted. About A.D. 180, Irenaeus, Bishop of Lyons in Gaul, is supposed to have denied its Pauline origin. We have no direct testimony from him touching this matter; but according to Photius, Bishop of Constantinople, Stephen Gober, a writer of the sixth century, says, "Hyppolytus and Irenaeus say that the Epistle of Paul to the Hebrews is not his." (Lard. Cred. vol. ii., p. 165.)

Soon after this, about A.D. 190 or 200, Tertullian, a learned and noted Presbyter of the Church at Carthage in North Africa, ascribed this Epistle to Barnabas, the friend and companion of Paul. In his defense of the rigid disciplinary views of the Montanists (De Pudicitia, cap. 20), having, as he supposed, sufficiently proved his point from the other Epistles of Paul, and the first Epistle of John, he proceeds as follows: "Nevertheless, I am willing, over and above, to allege the testimony of a companion of the Apostles; a fit person to show, at the next remove, what was the sentiment of the masters. For there is an Epistle of Barnabas, inscribed To the Hebrews, written by a man of such authority that Paul has placed him with himself in the same course of abstinence: Or I only and Barnabas, have not we power to forbear working (1 Cor. 9: 6)? And certainly the Epistle of Barnabas [by which he means the Epistle to the Hebrews] is more generally received by the churches than the apocryphal Pastor of adulterers [the Shepherd of Hermas]. Admonishing then his disciples, he exhorts them to leave all first principles, and rather to go on to perfection, and not to lay again the foundation of repentance from the works of the dead. For it is impossible, he says, for those who were once enlightened, and have tasted of the heavenly gift, and were made partakers of the Holy Spirit, and have tasted of the sweet word of God, if they shall fall away now at the end of the world, to recall them again to repentance, since they crucify again the Son of God to themselves, and put him to an open shame. He who learned this from the Apostles, and taught with the Apostles, never knew that a second repentance had been promised by the Apostles to an adulterer and a fornicator. For he excellently interprets the law, and shows its figures in the truth." (Lard. Cred. vol. ii., p. 27.)

About the same time, or perhaps a little later, Caius, a learned Presbyter of Rome, seems to have also doubted the apostolic origin of this Epistle; so, at least, the case is represented to us by Eusebius. This historian says (Eccl. Hist. B. vi. 20), "There is, besides, a discussion that has come down to us, of Caius, a most eloquent man, held at Rome in the time of Zephyrinus, against Proclus, who contended exceedingly for the Phrygian heresy [Montanism]; in which, while he censures the rashness and daring of his opponents in composing new scriptures, he makes mention of thirteen Epistles of the holy Apostle, not reckoning that to the Hebrews with the rest. And indeed, to this very time, by some of the Romans, this Epistle is not thought to be the Apostle's."

Several other Latin writers of the third century are often cited as witnesses against the Pauline authorship of this Epistle; such as Cyprian, Bishop of Carthage; Novatian, a Presbyter of Rome; and Victorinus, Bishop of Pettau in Pannonia. But the testimony of these writers is chiefly negative, implying doubt or uncertainty, rather than opposition. And this uncertainty prevailed in the West till about the middle of the fourth century. Then the tide of popular sentiment began to change; and soon after that the Epistle was acknowledged to be one of Paul's genuine works by Hilary, Bishop of Poictiers; Lucifer, Bishop of Milan, and several other Western writers of some note.

6. But it was not till after the time of Jerome, A.D. 392, that the apostolic origin of the Epistle to the Hebrews was generally acknowledged in the Western churches. Jerome himself believed with the Greek Fathers that it was one of Paul's genuine Epistles. But many of his Latin contemporaries still entertained doubts concerning it. This is evident from sundry passages found in the writings of this most learned of all the Latin Fathers. But the fol-

lowing extract from his letter to Dardanus will suffice for illustration at present. He (Jerome) says, "This much must be said by ours, that this Epistle which is inscribed To the Hebrews, is received as the Apostle Paul's, not only by the churches of the East, but by all the ecclesiastical writers of former times; though most [of the Latins?] ascribe it to Barnabas or Clement; and that it makes no difference whose it is, since it belongs to an ecclesiastical man, and is daily read in the churches. But if the Latins do not commonly receive it among the canonical Scriptures, the Greek churches do the same with the Apocalypse of John. We, however, receive both; not following the usage of the present time, but the authority of *the ancient writers,* who for the most part quote both; not as they were wont to quote sometimes apocryphal books, but as canonical."

7. Contemporary with Jerome was Augustine, Bishop of Hippo in North Africa. Among the Latin Fathers, he stood next to Jerome in point of scholarship; and in his profound and discriminating judgment of men and things, he was inferior to none of them. In his Commentary on the Epistle to the Romans he says, "Paul had a like salutation at the beginning of all his Epistles, with the exception of that which he wrote to the Hebrews; where he is said to have omitted his ordinary salutation designedly, lest the Jews who were obstinately opposed to him, taking offense at his name, should either read with an unfriendly mind, or neglect altogether to read what he had written respecting their salvation. For which reason, some have been afraid to receive that Epistle into the Canon of Scripture."

Soon after this, the Epistle to the Hebrews was received, as a genuine Epistle of Paul, by the Council of Hippo and also by the third Council of Carthage. Other churches in the West soon acquiesced in the more enlightened judgment of their brethren in the East; so that from about the beginning of the fifth century to the time of the Protestant Reformation in the sixteenth, the Pauline authorship of this Epistle was almost universally acknowledged in the Western as well as in the Eastern churches.

From these premises, then, it seems quite evident,

1. That in the East, where the Epistle to the Hebrews was first received, and where of course its historical circumstances were

best understood, it was from the beginning indorsed by the most enlightened ecclesiastical writers, as an Epistle of Paul.

2. That for a time, many of the Western Fathers were in doubt concerning it. But that after more mature investigation, the churches of the West, as well as those of the East, were constrained to admit its Pauline authorship.

From all of which, it follows with a very high degree of probability, if indeed not with absolute certainty, that the Epistle to the Hebrews is one of Paul's genuine Epistles.

II. *This conclusion is, I think, corroborated by the internal evidence of the Epistle.* I am aware that many writers do not think so. Luther, Bertholdt, Schultz, Eichhorn, De Wette, Ullmann, Wieseler, Bunsen, Tholuck, Alford, and others, appeal to this source of evidence with much confidence, to prove that the Epistle was not written by Paul. They allege,

1. That the style of this Epistle is very unlike that of Paul, as we find it given and illustrated in his other writings. And I am willing to admit, that there is some force in this objection. Indeed, it is to my mind much the strongest argument that has ever been urged against the Pauline authorship of this Epistle. For it must be conceded, that its periods are generally more regular, ornate, and oratorical than those which are found in the other writings of Paul. This was felt and acknowledged by the ancients; as it is now, by most modern writers. But nevertheless I am constrained to think that the force of this argument has been greatly overrated; and that the evidence brought forward in support of it, falls far short of what is really necessary to produce conviction in an unprejudiced mind. For be it observed,

(1.) That the time, place, and circumstances, have a very great influence over the thoughts, feelings, and expressions of an author. How very different, for instance, is the style of Deuteronomy from that of Leviticus; and how very unlike the style of John's Epistles is the style of the Apocalypse. But we know that Moses wrote both Leviticus and Deuteronomy; and that the same beloved disciple who wrote the Epistles of John, composed also the Apocalypse. The difference of style in these works arises, therefore, chiefly out of the various circumstances under which they were written. But who can rightly estimate the force and influence of all the impressive and peculiar circumstances under which Paul wrote this most tender, sublime, and pathetic letter to his Hebrew brethren? And who can say how much they may have differed from the circumstances under which he wrote his Epistle to the Romans or to the Galatians? It seems to me that until we can do this, it is not becoming in us to dogmatize on the peculiarities of style that are found in this Epistle.

(2.) It is also further conceded, that the style of an author should always correspond with the nature and character of his work. The style of Virgil's Bucolics differs very materially from that of his Georgics; and the style of his Georgics differs still more from that of his Aeneid. And this is to some extent true of all the Greek, Roman, and English classics. We do not expect to find in an epistle the stately and oratorical style of a regular treatise. But to this day, it is still a question with the critics, whether the so-called Epistle to the Hebrews possesses more of the characteristics of the former or of the latter. It is evidently of a mixed character; a unique sort of composition; without an exact parallel in all the other writings of Paul. It begins like a treatise, but it ends like an epistle. And hence we would naturally expect that its style would be somewhat more elevated and oratorical than that of an ordinary and formal epistle.

These two considerations, relating first to the influence of circumstances, and secondly to the character of the composition, are perhaps sufficient to account for all that is peculiar in the style of this Epistle: especially if we give to Luke or Clement, as Paul's amanuensis, some liberty of choice with regard to its phraseology. But as this cannot well be demonstrated, and as some may think otherwise, I would further suggest, as another *possible* modifying element in the composition of this Epistle, that the Holy Spirit may itself in this case have exercised a more than ordinary control over the style of the writer. If, for wise and benevolent reasons, it constrained Paul to withhold his name from his suspicious and prejudiced Jewish brethren; then why may it not, for like reasons, have also somewhat modified his style and phraseology? See 1 Cor. 2: 6, 13. For my own part, I know of no other limit to the influence of the Holy Spirit, in the work of inspiration, than the limit of sufficiency. God never does, either personally or by his Spirit, what is unnecessary to be done. But the Holy Spirit was given to the writers of both the Old and the New Testament, for the purpose of enabling them to make a perfect book; and with the view of *perfectly adapting it* to the capacity, wants, and circumstances of all. Why, then, should it be thought incredible by any one, that God by his Spirit, should, in some cases, exercise an influence over even the style of the inspired writers?

2. It is further alleged by some, that neither Paul nor any other Apostle could have written this letter; because in 2:4, the author says that the things pertaining to the great salvation had been handed down to himself and his contemporaries by those who had heard the Lord Jesus. And from this it is inferred by Bleek, Alford, and others, that the writer had neither seen nor heard Jesus; and consequently that he could not have been an Apostle.

But does this fairly follow from the premises? Does not an author often associate himself with his readers for the purpose of more effectually winning their hearts and softening his own admonitions? In the sixth chapter of this same Epistle, the author says, "Wherefore leaving the first principles of the doctrine of Christ, let *us* go on to perfection; not laying again the foundation of repentance from dead works, and of faith toward God, of the doctrine of baptisms, and of the laying on of hands, and of the resurrection of the dead, and of eternal judgment. And this *we* will do, if God permit." Now are we to infer from this, that the writer of this Epistle was as delinquent as were those to whom he wrote? Must we infer from this that he, as well as they, needed to be urged and admonished to go on to perfection in Christian knowledge; and that he, as well as his readers, was really in danger of apostatizing in consequence of his inexcusable neglect of the word of God? Surely not. The Epistle itself is a full and perfect refutation of any and every such allegation. But by a common figure of speech, the Apostle here associates himself with his readers, for the purpose of softening his admonitions; and referring the more delicately to their common trials, interests, and prospects.

And just so it is in the second chapter. By the same figure of rhetoric, the author here uses the first person plural instead of the second, for the purpose of more delicately and impressively contrasting the relations, prospects, and obligations of his Hebrew brethren in Christ, with those of the Israelites under Moses. He refers first to their greater responsibilities, as the recipients of the revelations which God had so graciously given them, through his own dear Son. "We" [Christians], he says, "ought to give the more earnest heed to the things which *we* have heard," etc. And then, still keeping up the same figure of thought for the sake of giving more tenderness and efficacy to his appeal, he asks the question, "How shall *we* escape if *we* neglect so great salvation; which at the first began to be spoken by the Lord, and was confirmed unto *us* by them that heard him; God also bearing them witness both with signs, and wonders, and divers miracles, and gifts of the Holy Spirit, according to his will?"

Manifestly, then, it was not the intention of the writer in all this to say that he was not an Apostle; that he had not seen and heard Jesus; and that he was now merely retailing to his brethren the secondhand reports of those who had been eyewitnesses of his majesty. Nay verily. This is but one of those masterly strokes of rhetoric in which the Epistle abounds from its alpha to its omega.

It should also be borne in mind that, in this instance, the writer may, and probably does, refer simply to Christ's personal ministry on earth. And if so, then Paul might speak even literally as he does, without in any way renouncing his claims to be an Apostle of Jesus Christ. See Notes on 2:4.

3. It is urged as a third objection against the Pauline author-ship of our Epistle, that the writing partakes somewhat of "the Al-exandrian hue;" and that the Epistle must therefore have been composed by someone belonging to the Alexandrian School. Be-cause, forsooth, the author uses some words and phrases which occur in the writings of Philo; and because, like this learned Jew, he interprets the law of Moses somewhat after the manner of an allegory, it is confidently inferred by Eichhorn, Bleek, Alford, and others, that he and Philo must have been educated in the same school of literature and philosophy. But did it never occur to these learned critics, that on this hypothesis all the writers of the New Testament, and especially Paul himself, must have been edu-cated with Philo in the Alexandrian School? See, for instance, 1 Cor. 10: 1-12, and Gal. 4: 19-31. Compare also John 1: 1-14, with Philo *Quis Div. Rer. Haer.,* Section 26. Surely, it would have been more reasonable, had these writers inferred that the au-thor of our Epistle must have been very thoroughly educated in the School of Moses and of Christ.

Sundry other objections are frequently urged against the Pauline authorship of this Epistle. It is alleged, for instance, that Paul would not have written an anonymous letter; that he would not have written a letter to his persecutors; that he would have spoken more frequently of the Kingdom of God, the resurrection of the dead, and the final judgment. But all such allegations are without weight, and seem to have been invented merely for the purpose of sustaining a favorite hypothesis.

And such, it must be confessed, are also some of the arguments that are sometimes urged in favor of the Pauline authorship of the Epistle. Who, for instance, that is honestly and earnestly seeking for the truth, and that has proper views of the unity of the Scriptures and the plenary inspiration of the sacred writers, would ever think of ascribing this Epistle to Paul, on the ground that its *doctrine* is in harmony with his other Epistles? In these investigations, we should never forget that the Holy Spirit is really in a paramount sense the author of the whole Bible; and consequently that the sixty-six books of which it is composed, are all in perfect harmony with each other: for "holy men of God spoke as they were moved by the Holy Spirit." (2 Pet. 1:21.) And hence we may feel perfectly sure, that the Epistle to the Hebrews would correspond in doctrine with all the other Epistles of Paul, whether it were written by him or by any other inspired man. The above allegation is pertinent, therefore, so far as it may serve to determine, whether or not the Epistle was written by an inspired man; but no further. A writer must indeed be hard pressed, who will resort to such sophistry on either side of the question. The truth needs no such arguments for its support.

Is there, then, any evidence in the Epistle itself that it was written by Paul? I think there is some; though I am willing to admit that it is not in and of itself wholly conclusive. But,

1. The simple fact that the Epistle is anonymous, is presumptive evidence that it was written by Paul. For surely the author, whoever he was, had some valid reason for withholding his name from a portion of those for whose benefit the Epistle was written. But what other reason can be assigned for this extraordinary omission, that so well accords with all the known facts of the case, as that which was alleged by Clement, Origen, Eusebius, Augustine, and other Christian Fathers: viz., that Paul did not prefix his name to the Epistle, lest its appearance might prevent many of his

Jewish brethren from reading it, and judging of it by its own merits? Certain it is, that no better reason than this has ever been assigned for the omission of the author's name; and it is moreover equally certain, that in the light of all history, this reason applies to no one else so well as to the Apostle Paul, against whom a very strong and general prejudice existed among both the converted and the unconverted Jews of that age.

2. There is certainly much in the style, phraseology, and logical structure of the Epistle, which very much resembles the other writings of Paul. That the style is somewhat more elevated and rhetorical than that of his other Epistles, is of course conceded. But after making every reasonable abatement, it must, I think, be admitted that there is still much remaining, especially in the logical structure of the Epistle, which is essentially Pauline. For instance, Paul's manner of leaving for a time the regular and direct train of thought, and of returning to it again in the course of his argument, is very frequently and forcibly illustrated in this Epistle. An instance of this occurs in the beginning of the second chapter, where the writer breaks off from his regular line of argument, and returns to it again in the fifth verse. And again in the fifth chapter, we have a still more striking and characteristic example of this Pauline peculiarity. Here the author breaks off at the word *Melchisedek* in the tenth verse, and does not return to his main subject, till he reaches the beginning of the seventh chapter. Other examples and illustrations will occur to the reader.

3. There are some expressions in the Epistle which seem to indicate that it was written by Paul. Such, for example, as the following:

(1.) In 13: 23, our author says, "Know ye that our brother Timothy is set at liberty; with whom if he come shortly, I will see you." The word *apolelumenon* in this verse is somewhat ambiguous. It may mean, either that Timothy had been released from imprisonment, as in our English Version; or that he had been sent away on an errand. In either case, the remark seems to favor the Pauline authorship. For it is well known to all readers of the New Testament, that from the beginning of Timothy's ministry (Acts 16: 3) to the time of Paul's martyrdom (2 Tim. 4: 9-21), he (Timothy) was a constant helper and companion of Paul. That he was with Paul in Rome, during the Apostle's first imprisonment, is evident from Phil. 2 : 19; and also from the fact that Paul in his letters to the Philippians, Colossians, and Philemon, has associated Timothy with himself in his several salutations. And hence it is much more probable, that he, rather than anyone else, would accompany Paul in his proposed journey to Palestine. Indeed, it seems quite probable that none but Paul would presume to speak for Timothy, as our author does in this case.

(2.) In 13 :24, the author says to his Hebrew brethren, "They of Italy (apo tees Italias) salute you." From this remark, Lardner, Hug, Stewart, and others, infer that Paul was most likely the author of the Epistle. Stewart says, "Paul writing from Rome, which had communication of course with all parts of Italy, and with the Italian churches; more or less of whose members, we may well suppose to have been often in Rome, may very naturally be supposed to have sent such a salutation. Indeed, the circumstances render this quite probable."

Such, then, are some of the main reasons drawn from the Epistle itself, which seem to favor the opinion that it was written by Paul. That they are not of themselves sufficient to produce entire conviction is an unprejudiced mind, I readily grant. But still, it seems to me, they should have considerable weight in settling this question; and that they serve to corroborate very materially the conclusion drawn from the external evidence: viz., that the Epistle to the Hebrews is in all probability one of Paul's genuine Epistles. That Luke may have served as Paul's amanuensis in composing it; and that, as an inspired man, he may with Paul's consent have modified in some measure the style of the Apostle, is not at all improbable. But unless we wholly ignore the testimony of the Christian Fathers, we are constrained to believe that Paul himself is the real author of this Epistle.

## SECTION TWO

### IS THIS EPISTLE ENTITLED TO A PLACE IN THE CANON OF THE HOLY SCRIPTURES?

This is by far the most important of all the questions involved in the discussion of the historical circumstances of this Epistle. It matters but little to us, who wrote the Epistle; provided, that it can be proved from clear and satisfactory evidence, that the Epistle itself is entitled to a place in the Canon of the Holy Scriptures. And on this point, it gives me pleasure to say, the evidence is full, clear, and conclusive. For,

I. *It is almost, if indeed it is not quite, certain that Paul himself, assisted perhaps by Luke, composed the Epistle.* And hence we may justly infer that it is also almost, if not quite, certain that the Epistle is both inspired and canonical. The latter conclusion is just as valid as the former. For let it be first clearly proved, that Paul either wrote or indorsed this letter, and then of course there can be no doubt as to its canonical authority. And that Paul is its author, has, I think, been proved with such a degree of probability as falls but little short of absolute certainty.

II. *This Epistle was quoted as Scripture, and used as such in the churches, for many years previous to the cessation of miraculous gifts; proving beyond a doubt that it was written by an inspired man, and that it was also frequently used and indorsed by those who had the gift of inspiration.* For a full discussion of this proposition, I must refer the reader to my work on Reason and Revelation, Revised Edition, pp. 220-256. But for our present purpose, the following is, I think, quite sufficient. In A.D. 96, Clement of Rome wrote a very able and copious letter, in behalf of the Church of Rome to the Church of Corinth. In this letter, he frequently refers to our Epistle, and sometimes he quotes from it *verbatim.* This will appear from the following parallels:

### HEBREWS

1. *Who being the brightness of his glory, and the express image of his person.—Being made so much better than the angels, as he hath by inheritance obtained a more excellent name than they. For unto which of the angels said he, at any time, Thou art my Son, this day I have begotten thee? And of the angels he saith, Who maketh his angels spirits, and his ministers a flame of fire.—But to which of the angels said he at any time, Sit on my right hand, until I make thine enemies thy footstool?* 1: 3, 5, 7, 13.

2. *As also Moses was faithful in all his house. And verily Moses was faithful in all his house as a servant.* 3: 2, 5.

### CLEMENT

1. *Who being the brightness of his majesty, is by so much greater than the angels, as he hath by inheritance obtained a more excellent name than they. For it is written, Who maketh his angels spirits, and his ministers a flame of fire. But of his Son thus saith the Lord, Thou art my Son, this day have I begotten thee. Ask of me and I will give thee the heathen for thine inheritance, and the uttermost parts of the earth for thy possession. And again he saith unto him, Sit on my right hand until I make thy enemies thy footstool.* Ch. 36.

2. *When also Moses, that blessed and faithful servant in all his house.* Ch. 43. *Moses was called faithful in all his house.* Ch. 18.

3. *And is a discerner of the thoughts and intents of the heart.* 4 : 12.

4. That by two immutable things, in which it was impossible for God to lie. 6 : 18.

5. *By faith Enoch was translated that he should not see death, and was not found, because God had translated him.* 11 : 5.

6. *By faith Noah being warned of God, of things not seen as yet, moved with fear prepared an ark for the saving of his house.* 11 : 7.

7. *By faith Abraham, when he was called to go out into a place which he should after receive for an inheritance, obeyed; and went out, not knowing whither he went.* 11 : 8.

8. *By faith the harlot Rahab perished not with them that believed not, when she had received the spies with peace.* 11 : 31.

9. *And others had trials of cruel mockings and scourgings; yea, moreover, of bonds and imprisonments. They were stoned; they were sawn asunder; were tempted: were slain with the sword.* 11 : 36, 37.

10. *They wandered about in sheep-skins and goat-skins.* 11 : 37.

11. *Wherefore seeing we also are compassed about with so great a cloud of witnesses, let us lay aside every weight and the sin which doth so easily beset us, and let us run with patience the race that is set before us: looking unto Jesus, the author and finisher of our faith; who for the joy that was set before him, endured the cross, despising the shame, and is set down at the right hand of the throne of God.* 12 : 1, 2.

12. *For whom the Lord loveth he chasteneth; and scourgeth every son whom he receiveth. Furthermore, we have had fathers of our flesh*

3. *For He is a searcher of the intents and thoughts.* Ch. 21.

4. *For nothing is impossible with God but to lie.* Ch. 27.

5. Let us take Enoch for an example, *who, by obedience being found righteous, was translated, and his death was not found.* Ch. 9.

6. *Noah being found faithful, did by his ministry preach regeneration to the world.* Ch. 9.

7. *This man [Abraham] by obedience went out of his own country,* and from his kindred, and from his father's house; that so forsaking a small country, a weak affinity, and a little house, he might inherit the promises of God. Ch. 10.

8. *By faith and hospitality was Rahab the harlot saved. For when the spies were sent by Joshua the son of Nun to Jericho, the hospitable Rahab received them, hid them on the top of her house, under stalks of flax.* Ch. 12.

9. *The righteous were persecuted; but it was by the wicked. They were cast into prison; but it was by the impious. They were stoned by transgressors. They were killed by the polluted, and by those who had conceived unjust envy. When they suffered these things, they endured them gloriously.* Ch. 45.

10. Let us be imitators of those *who went about in goat-skins and sheep-skins,* preaching the coming of Christ. Ch. 17.

11. *Having therefore many great and precious examples, let us return to the mark of peace, which from the beginning was set before us; and let us look up steadfastly to the Father and Creator of the whole world.* Ch. 19.

12. *Let us receive correction, at which no man ought to repine. The reproof and correction which we exercise toward one another are good*

*who corrected us, and we gave them reverence; shall we not much more be in subjection to the Father of spirits and live? For they verily for a few days chastened us after their own pleasure; but he, for our profit, that we might be partakers of his holiness. Now no chastening, for the present, seemeth to be joyous, but grievous; nevertheless it afterward yieldeth the peaceable fruits of righteousness unto them that are exercised thereby.* 12: 6, 9, 10, 11.

*and exceedingly profitable; for they closely unite us to the will of God.* For so says the sacred word: *Whom the Lord loveth he chasteneth; and scourgeth every son whom he receiveth.* Ye see, beloved, there is a defense for those who are corrected by the Lord. *For being a good instructor, he is willing that we should be admonished by his holy discipline.* Ch. 56.

After Clement, we meet with no more very clear and direct references to the Epistle, till we come down to the time of Justin Martyr, who flourished about A.D. 140. In his Dialogue with Trypho the Jew, he makes several allusions to it. But it is not necessary that we should further multiply either quotations from it, or references to it. Those already cited from the epistle of Clement, are quite sufficient for our present purpose. They prove beyond all doubt,

1. That the Epistle to the Hebrews had been in existence for some time previous to A.D. 96. For Clement does not introduce it, or speak of it, as a novelty; but he refers to it, and quotes from it, as a well known document.

2. It is also perfectly evident from the given citations, that Clement himself received the Epistle, as canonical. For he quotes from it just as he quotes from other canonical books: not always, indeed, *verbatim;* for it was not the custom of the Christian Fathers to do so. For the most part, they no doubt quoted from memory; and they aimed therefore to give the substance, rather than the very words, of the Living Oracles. But they always appealed to the Holy Scriptures, as writings of paramount authority on all questions of faith and piety. And just so does Clement repeatedly appeal to our Epistle in his letter to the Church of Corinth. *"As it is written,"* he says, "who maketh his angels spirits; and his ministers a flame of fire." It will not do to say with Bleek, Tholuck, and others, that Clement refers here to Psalm 104. The context is clearly opposed to such an allegation. That the author of our Epistle quotes from this Psalm, is of course admitted. But it is quite evident from what precedes and follows this citation, that Clement quotes directly from the Epistle itself: and furthermore,

that he quotes from it just as he quotes from the other inspired and canonical books. Indeed, if we may judge from the number of his quotations, it would seem that he had a partiality for this Epistle.

3. It seems but just to conclude also from the given quotations, that the canonical authority of this Epistle, was, in A.D. 96, acknowledged also by at least the leading members of the Church of Corinth, as well as by those of the Church of Rome. Clement certainly acted on this assumption; for surely he would not, in so grave a matter, have so often quoted from a document, the canonical authority of which was not generally acknowledged by his Corinthian brethren.

But can we believe that the Overseers of the Church of Rome and the Church of Corinth, would receive as canonical an Epistle which had not the approval of their inspired contemporaries? That there were then still living in at least all the principal churches of Christendom, men who were supernaturally qualified to distinguish between what was spurious and what was dictated by the Holy Spirit, may be proved from both the Holy Scriptures and the testimony of the Christian Fathers. In the "First Epistle General of John," for example, a document which was also written about A.D. 96, the aged and venerable author cautions and admonishes his readers, to be on their guard as to what they should receive as the word of God. In 4: 1, he says to them, "Beloved, believe not every spirit; but try the spirits whether they are of God: because," he says, "many false prophets are gone out into the world." And in 2: 20, he says, "But ye have an unction [referring to the gifts of the Holy Spirit] from the Holy One, and ye know all things." And again in 2: 27, he says, "But the anointing which ye have received of him abideth in you; and ye need not that any man teach you; but as the same anointing teacheth you of all things, and is truth, and is no lie, and even as it hath taught you, ye shall abide in him."

I need not multiply witnesses on this point. From the testimony here given, it is abundantly evident, that in A.D. 96 or about the close of the first century, there were still living in the churches many who were, by the gifts of the Holy Spirit, specially qualified to distinguish between what was inspired and what was spurious in the literature of the times: and moreover, that these men were charged with the duty of exercising their spiritual gifts for this very purpose; so that the churches might not be imposed on by the craft and cunning devices of wicked and deceitful men. And hence it follows, that if the Epistle had not been inspired and given to the Church as a part of her Creed, it would have been at once condemned and rejected as spurious, by the spiritual men of that age; and it never would have been received and quoted as canonical by any of the Christian Fathers. But we have seen that it was so received and so quoted by at least one of the most pious and enlightened of the Apostolic Fathers; and who, if he were not himself inspired, had at least the very best opportunity of knowing what was the judgment of his inspired contemporaries with regard to it. And hence, we think, there is no room to doubt the canonical authority of the Epistle.

III. *This Epistle is found in the oldest Versions of the New Testament.* The first or earliest of these, now extant, is the Peshito, or Old Syriac Version; which, according to Prof. Gauson and many other able critics, was made about the close of the first century. Others fix the date of this translation at the beginning of the second century; and others again at or about A.D. 150. It contains all the books of the New Testament, except the second Epistle of Peter, the second and third of John, the Epistle of Jude, and the Revelation; and it contains no others. This, then, shows very clearly, that the Epistle to the Hebrews was received as canonical in Syria, and indeed I may say in the Eastern churches generally, about the close of the first century or the beginning of the second. The oldest Latin Versions made, according to our best authorities, about the same time as the Peshito, seem to have also contained this Epistle. At least there is no intimation to the contrary given by Jerome, Augustine, or any of the other Christian Fathers.

IV. *It is found also in all the ancient Catalogues of the canonical Books of the New Testament;* such as that of Origen, published about A.D. 220; that of Eusebius, A.D. 315; that of Athanasius, A.D. 326; that of Cyril, Bishop of Jerusalem, A.D. 348; and that of the Council of Laodicea, A.D. 363. These Catalogues are but an expression of the common sentiment of the Christian Fathers, resting of course primarily on the judgment and authority of the Apostles and other inspired men. On no other hypothesis, can we account for the marvelous unanimity with which the primitive Christians received and adopted the books of the New Testament, as their only rule of faith and practice.

V. *This Epistle contains within itself, so far as we are competent to judge, full and satisfactory evidence of its own canonicity.* For,

1. Its doctrine is in perfect harmony with that which is contained in all other parts of the Holy Scriptures. Not the slightest discrepancy, in this respect, has ever been found between this Epistle and the other canonical Books of the Old and New Testaments.

2. There is in it an air of authority, dignity, and majesty, which is wholly peculiar to the Sacred Writings. The reader, while perusing and studying it, *feels* that he is dealing with that which is "quick and powerful, and sharper than any two-edged sword, piercing even to the dividing asunder of the soul and spirit, and of the joints and marrow, and which is a discerner of the thoughts and intents of the heart."

3. It has also a depth of meaning which is peculiar to the Holy Scriptures. When we read the works of Plato, Aristotle, Bacon, Locke, Newton, and Leibnitz, we meet with many things which require much thought and patient investigation. But with due preparation and proper perseverance, we may overcome all difficulties. We feel at length that we have really become master of these works. We become conscious that we have, after much effort, finally fathomed their greatest depths; and that we have learned all that is in them, and that can be learned from them.

But not so with the Holy Scriptures. They have a depth and fullness of meaning which is wholly inexhaustible; so that after we have studied them, with the greatest care and diligence, for ten, twenty, or even fifty years, we are still conscious that we have as yet come far short of sounding their greatest depths, or of comprehending the immense fullness of their meaning. And hence it is that we return to them again and again, with even increasing interest, to explore still further the new fields of beauty, glory, and sublimity which are constantly rising before our enraptured vision. This is to the diligent student of the Bible one of the strongest evidences of its Divine origin; and this he discovers in the Epistle to the Hebrews, as well as in all other parts of the Living Oracles.

We conclude, then, that the Epistle to the Hebrews is canonical,

1. Because it was in all probability written by the Apostle Paul.

2. Because it was quoted by the Apostolic Fathers in such a way as to clearly indicate that it was written by an inspired man; and that it was so received and indorsed by their inspired contemporaries.

3. Because it is found in all the ancient Versions of the New Testament.

4. Because it is contained in all the most ancient Catalogues of the canonical Books of the New Testament.

5. And finally, because it has within itself all the internal evidences which serve to distinguish the Bible from other books, as the inspired word of God.

## SECTION THREE

### TO WHOM WAS THE EPISTLE FIRST ADDRESSED?

On this question the critics are still much divided. Nearly all of them agree that the Epistle was written primarily for the benefit of certain Jews who had become followers of Christ, and who were then in danger of apostatizing, through the manifold trials and temptations which they were at that time enduring. But from this one point of agreement, they then diverge in all possible directions. Some think that it was written for all Jewish believers in Christ, wherever found. Others are of the opinion that it was written for the special benefit of those converted Jews who were then in Galatia, or who had been scattered abroad through the several provinces of Asia Minor. Others suppose that it was intended chiefly for those living in Greece; others, for those in Italy; others, for those in Spain; and others again, for those of them who were in Egypt. But the majority of writers believe that it was intended primarily for those Jewish converts to Christianity who were then living in Palestine. This is the opinion of Beza, Capellus, Mill, Pearson, Lardner, Michaelis, Hallet, Bertholdt, Hug, Schott, Bleek, Hofmann, Macknight, Davidson, Stewart, and many others. This, then, is the prevailing hypothesis; and that it is the correct one seems probable for the following reasons:

I. *It is most in harmony with the title, "To the Hebrews," which was at a very early date prefixed to the Epistle.* Some, indeed, are of the opinion that this title was prefixed to the Epistle by the author himself. But this is not probable. The inspired writers generally indicate in their introductory addresses the persons to whom they write. Thus, for instance, Paul says in the beginning of his letter to the Romans, "Paul a servant of Jesus Christ, a called Apostle, —to all that are in Rome, beloved of God, called saints," etc. And in like manner are commenced nearly all the other Epistles. And hence it is not probable, that the inspired writers would prefix to their several letters what they were accustomed to express in their salutations.

But this much is certain, that the title was prefixed to our Epistle at a very early date, and most likely before the close of the Apostolic age; so that it, in all probability, received the sanction and approval of some of the inspired men of the primitive churches. For we know that it was quoted by some of the Christian Fathers in the second century; and that it is found in the oldest versions of the New Testament, as well as in the oldest Greek manuscripts. And hence we must, in any event, regard it as a prefix of a very early date. And when we remember the jealous care with which the primitive Christians watched over their sacred writings; and their extreme unwillingness to allow any rash hand to interfere with them in any way, we are constrained to think that this title was most likely prefixed to the Epistle by those who were fully acquainted with the facts of the case; and that, as it denotes, the Epistle was in all probability first transmitted to the Hebrews.

But who were the Hebrews? Was this name used, like the name *Israelite,* to denote all the descendants of Jacob; or was it given to those Jews only who lived in Palestine and who spoke the Hebrew language?

The word *Hebrew* occurs first in Gen. 14: 13, where the Septuagint has *peratēs,* that is, *one who passes over.* It seems to have been first given to Abraham by the Canaanites, because he had come from *the region beyond* the Euphrates. This is the opinion of Origen, Chrysostom, Jerome, Theodoret, Munster, Grotius, Scalliger, Selden, Eichhorn, Gesenius, Fürst, Jones, and others, though Josephus, Suidas, Bockhart, Drusius, Vossius, Buxtorf, Leusden, and some others derive the name from *Eber* (*one that passes over*), the great grandson of Shem, from whom Abraham was a descendant of the sixth generation. But whatever may be true of the origin of the name *Hebrew,* this much at least is certain, that it is generally used in the Old Testament with reference to the *external* relations of God's chosen people; and not like the patronymic *Israelite,* to denote their *domestic* relations and the fact of their descent from a common ancestry. And hence the name *Hebrew* is commonly used whenever foreigners are introduced as the speakers; or when the Iraelites are speaking of themselves to foreigners; or when they are in any way contrasted with foreigners.

And this, too, is very nearly its use in the New Testament, save that it is here used in a more limited sense. In the Old Testament, the name *Hebrew* was used co-extensively with the name *Israelite* to denote all the descendants of Jacob. But not so in the New Testament. As the name *Hebrew* was used to distinguish God's ancient people from foreigners; and of course to eliminate from them everything that was foreign or exotic; it so happened that when a portion of them migrated into foreign countries, and there learned to speak the Greek language, they were, in consequence of this, no longer called *Hebrews* but *Hellenists (Hellanistai).* They were still regarded and recognized as Jews and Israelites, but not as Hebrews: the mere use of a foreign language serving, as it would appear, to eliminate them in some measure from the native stock. And hence in the New Testament, the name *Hebrew* seems to have always some reference to the language, as well as to the many other boasted rights and privileges of the seed of Abraham. See Acts 6 : 1 ; 2 Cor. 11 : 22 ; and Phil. 3 : 5.

If we are right in this view of the matter, and the title, *"To the Hebrews,"* was correctly applied by the ancients, then it follows that the Epistle was, as is generally supposed, addressed to the Jewish Christians in Palestine. For they were the only body of Christians in that age who spoke the Hebrew language (or rather the Aramaic, which was a corruption of the Hebrew) ; and who habitually used the Hebrew Scriptures, and these only, in their public assemblies. "No traces," says Delitzsch, "are found of the existence of any such purely Jewish churches in the Dispersion, as the recipients of this Epistle must have been ; while the Church of Jerusalem actually bore the title, *'The Church of the Hebrews' (ton Hebraion ekklesia)"*—(Clementis Epis. ad Jacob. hom. 11 : 35.)

II. This view of the matter is supported by the testimony of the Christian Fathers. So far as they have expressed any opinion on the subject, it is to the effect, that the Epistle was addressed to the Jewish believers in Palestine. On this point, Dr. Lardner says, "It may be taken for granted that this was the opinion of Clement of Alexandria, and Jerome, and Euthalius, who supposed this Epistle to have been first written in Hebrew, and afterward translated into Greek. It may be allowed to have been also the opinion of many others who quote this Epistle as written to the Hebrews, when they say nothing to the contrary. Nor do I recollect any ancients, who say, it was written to Jews living out of Judea. Chrysostom says that the Epistle was sent to the believing Jews of Palestine; and he supposes that the Apostle afterward made them a visit. Theodoret, in his preface to the Epistle, allows it to have been sent to the same Jews. And Theophylact, in his argument of the Epistle, expressly says as Chrysostom, that it was sent to the Jews of Palestine. So that this was the general opinion of the ancients. (Lard. Cred. vol. 6, 12, 14.)

III. *The internal evidence of the Epistle harmonizes best with the supposition that it was addressed primarily to the Jewish believers in Palestine.*

1. There are some considerations growing out of the general scope and tenor of the Epistle, which seem to favor this view of the matter. Such, for example, as the following:

(1.) It is implied throughout the entire Epistle, that the persons addressed were perfectly familiar with all the rites and ceremonies of the Mosaic Economy; and, in this respect, it seems to look to Palestine as the place of its destination. For there, the people generally observed, with great care and tenacity, at least all the ceremonial requirements of the Law. There, the daily sacrifices were still regularly offered; and there, all the males went up regularly to Jerusalem, at least three times a year, to celebrate their annual festivals. But it was quite different outside of Palestine. There, they had no daily sacrifices or other Temple services. And but few, comparatively, of the foreign Jews were in the habit of going up to Jerusalem to attend the yearly festivals. The natural and necessary consequence of all this was, of course, a growing indifference for the laws and ordinances of Moses; and a want of that familiarity with the rites and services of the Temple, which is implied in this Epistle.

(2.) There is no allusion in this Epistle, as there often is in the

other writings of Paul, to the controversies which were then prevalent between the Jews and the Gentiles, outside of Palestine: but
on the contrary, it is everywhere implied in this letter, that the
trials and temptations of the persons addressed, arose wholly from
the opposition of the unconverted Jews. And hence it is most
likely, that the Church to which this Epistle was sent, was composed wholly or at least chiefly of Jewish converts; and that they
were then in the midst of an unbelieving and persecuting Jewish
population. But these conditions existed only in Palestine; where
Paul himself was most violently persecuted during the last visit
that he had made to Jerusalem, about five years previous to the
time of his writing this Epistle.

(3.) The main fear of our author seems to have been, that the
persons addressed were in danger of renouncing Christ, and falling
back again to Judaism. But the danger of this was far greater in
Palestine, and especially in Jerusalem than in any other place. In
other provinces of the Roman Empire, the disciples of Christ were
in quite as much danger of being misled by the tenets of Plato and
Aristotle, as by the rites and ceremonies of Moses. But not so in
Palestine. There the people were all zealous for the Law. (Acts
21 : 20.) And there occurred in fact, through the influence of Judaizing teachers, the first schism in the Church of Christ. Early
in the second century, and immediately after the second destruction of Jerusalem by the Emperor Hadrian, those so-called Jewish
Christians, known as Ebionites, who maintained the necessity of
observing the Mosaic Law in order to the enjoyment of eternal salvation, withdrew from other Christians, and set up other congrega-
tions of their own. They denied the divinity of Christ; rejected
the Epistles of Paul; and maintained the universal and perpetual
obligations of the Law of Moses. See Mosh. Eccl. Hist. vol. 1, p.
96. It would seem, therefore, that Paul was moved by the Holy
Spirit to write this most convincing and heart-searching Epistle to
his brethren in Palestine; many of whom were even then in great
danger of apostatizing from the faith.

2. There are also some expressions in the Epistle, which go to
show that it was written to the Jewish Christians in Palestine, and
most likely to the Church in Jerusalem. Such, for example, are
the following:

(1.) In 10: 32-34, our author says, "But call to remembrance the former days, in which, after ye were illuminated, ye endured a great fight of afflictions; partly, whilst ye were made a gazing-stock both by reproaches and afflictions; and partly, whilst ye became companions of them that were so used. For ye both sympathized with them who were in bonds, and ye took joyfully the spoiling of your goods, knowing in yourselves that ye have in Heaven a better and an enduring substance." These remarks all apply well to the Christians who were then living in Palestine; and, so far as we know, to no others. For previous to the date of this Epistle, believers in the Holy Land had suffered much from the violent opposition of their unconverted brethren. After the death of Stephen, we are told (Acts 8 : 1) that "at that time there was a great persecution against the Church which was at Jerusalem; and they were all scattered abroad throughout the regions of Judea and Samaria, except the Apostles." And again in Acts 12, we have given an account of the persecution of the same Church by Herod Agrippa. But outside of Judea, previous to the persecution of Nero in A.D. 64, the Roman emperors and the magistrates were generally opposed to persecution. See Acts 18: 12-17 and 19: 35-41. And hence it is most likely that the persecuted ones to whom the author refers in the tenth chapter of this Epistle, were the believers in Christ, in and around Jerusalem.

(2.) Again, from what is contained in 13: 12-14, we would infer that the persons addressed were living in a "city," and that they were familiar with *"the gate:"* the same probably through which criminals had to pass on their way to Golgotha, and through which Christ himself was led to the cross. The author says, "Wherefore Jesus also that he might sanctify the people with his own blood suffered without the gate. Let us go forth, therefore, unto him without the camp, bearing his reproach. For here we have no continuing city, but we seek one to come." In all this, there is no attempt at explanation. The writer evidently thought that a mere allusion to these matters was sufficient; which of course implies that the persons addressed were quite familiar with the facts and topographical circumstances to which he refers.

On the whole, then, I cannot but think with the ancients, that this Epistle was written for the benefit of the Hebrew Christians in Palestine; and that it was most likely addressed to those of them who were then living in Jerusalem. That it was addressed to some one congregation, seems probable from such expressions as occur in 13: 19, 23, etc. And if so, then to what other congregation would our author be so likely to address it as to that in the city of Jerusalem? *There* was the seat of all the adverse influences, against which the whole Epistle is directed; and from that city, as from a radiating center, would be most likely to go out into all parts of Palestine and the surrounding provinces, the very salutary influences of this Divine communication to the churches.

## SECTION FOUR

### FOR WHAT PURPOSE WAS THE EPISTLE WRITTEN?

The primary object of our author in writing this Epistle, was manifestly to persuade his Hebrew brethren in Christ to persevere to the end in their begun Christian course; and not to fall back again to Judaism. They had all been educated under the laws and institutions of Moses; their minds had been thoroughly molded in the form of doctrine which he had delivered to them; and all their religious habits and early impressions served to attach them to the imposing rites and ceremonies of the Law. And to these educational predilections in favor of Judaism, there were added also many other causes of discontent and discouragement in their Christian course. The same spirit of envy and malice which had moved the unbelieving Jews to put to death the Lord of life and glory, still prompted and excited them to harass and annoy in every conceivable way his innocent and unoffending followers. The scribes and rulers exercised all their powers of logic, rhetoric, and sophistry, against the disciples of the despised Nazarene, as they were wont to call our Immanuel; and when the force of argument was unavailing, they had recourse to persecution. Some of them they killed; some, they put into prison; and others, they despoiled of their goods:—and all this they did with the view of putting a stop to the progress of Christianity, and inducing all to follow Moses as their leader.

This was of course very discouraging to the followers of Christ in Palestine; and especially to those of them who lived in Jerusalem, under the very shadow of the Temple, and in the midst of the most violent opposition from their unconverted brethren. The knees of many of them became feeble; their hands hung down; and their faith greatly wavered. (12: 12, 13.) They needed help; and it pleased God to send it to them through the agency of him who once thought that he ought to do many things contrary to the name of Jesus of Nazareth. (Acts 26:9.) Having himself but recently suffered so much from the hand of Jewish persecutors, he knew well how to sympathize with those who were still suffering from the same cause; and how, with the help of the Holy Spirit, to give to his afflicted brethren that comfort and consolation which they so much needed under the circumstances.

For this purpose, he wrote to them this admirable Epistle; in the course of which he clearly demonstrates the infinite superiority of Christianity over Judaism; and shows, moreover, that the Gospel plan is really the only plan by which any sinner can be saved. He begins the first section of the Epistle (1: 1-2: 4), by acknowledging the sublime fact, that God had in ancient times spoken to the Fathers by the Prophets. But then he goes further, and assures us that he has also "in the last of these days" spoken unto us by his Son, who is himself the heir of all things; the maker and upholder of all things; the effulgence of the Father's glory and the express image of his essence; and who after he had by his own blood made expiation for our sins, sat down forever at the right hand of the Majesty in the Heavens, all the angels, principalities, and powers being made subject to him. In the second section (2: 5, 18), the author dwells chiefly on the humanity of Christ. He shows particularly that it is through the death, sufferings, and sympathies of the Lord Jesus, *as a man,* that the dominion of Satan will be brought to an end; the enslaved captives of his power set at liberty; and that the earth itself, purified by fire, will be again restored to the saints of the Most High. In the third section (3: 1-4: 13), he contrasts Christ, as the Apostle of the New Covenant, with Moses, the Apostle of the Old. And while he concedes that Moses was a faithful servant in the house of God, he maintains that Christ is now faithful over God's house as a Son; and that he is in fact as much superior to Moses, as the builder of a house is superior to the house. In the second and third paragraphs, he notices the interesting fact to which David, speaking by the Spirit, refers in the ninety-fifth Psalm: viz., that Christ, as the Apostle of the New Institution, has provided for all his faithful followers *a rest* which far surpasses in interest and duration all the rests which the Jews enjoyed under the Law of Moses. He then closes the section, by giving to his readers an admonition with reference to the heart-searching character of the word of God. In the fourth section (4: 14-5: 10), he introduces the priesthood of Christ; speaks encouragingly of him as our great and sympathetic High Priest, who has gone up for us through the heavens, and through whom we may at all times approach God as suppliants, and ask for seasonable help. For he assures us that Christ did not usurp this office; but that, like Aaron, he was by God himself duly appointed to it; and that, like Melchisedek, he remains a Priest forever, having through his own death and mediation become the author of eternal salvation to all them that obey him. In the fifth section (5: 11-6: 20), he makes a digression from his main line of thought, for the purpose of admonishing and exciting his Hebrew brethren to greater diligence in the study of God's word. He here warns them against the great danger of apostasy; and then encourages them to hope and persevere to the end, trusting in the mercy and fidelity of God; who by both his word and his oath, has given great encouragement to all who have fled to Christ for refuge. In the sixth section (7: 1-8: 5), he resumes the consideration of Christ's priesthood; and by a series of arguments, he shows that it is in all respects greatly superior to the priesthood of Aaron. In the seventh section (8: 6-13), he takes up and considers particularly the two covenants. And from the testimony of Jeremiah, who was by the Jews acknowledged to be a true Prophet, he first proves that it had long been God's purpose to give to the people a better covenant than the Sinaitic: and then he proceeds to notice the points of contrast between the two, and to show wherein the New is superior to the Old. In the eighth section (9: 1-10: 18), he speaks particularly of the sacrifice and mediation of Christ; and by a great variety of illustrations, he shows in many ways the immense superiority of his offering and administration over all the offerings and services of the Mosaic Economy. This section is one of the most profoundly interesting portions of the whole Bible. In the ninth section (10: 19-39), he makes a practical application of the leading points involved in the preceding discussions: dwelling particularly on the greater privileges and obligations of Christians, warning his brethren against the dangers of apostasy; and encouraging them by a reference to the sacrifices which they had voluntarily endured for the sake of Christ, and by the fact that their deliverance was then near at hand. In the tenth section (ch. 11), he discusses and illustrates very fully the nature, power, and influence of faith, both as a principle of endurance and as a means of enjoyment. In the eleventh section (ch. 12), he still further encourages his brethren to persevere in their Christian course, by referring to the example of Christ and many other illustrious witnesses of faith; reminding them, moreover, that God's chastisements were all for their good; that there is no place of repentance for the apostate; that the privileges of the New Covenant are greatly superior to those of the Old, involving, of course, greater responsibilities; and that the Kingdom of Christ is steadfast and enduring. In the twelfth section (ch. 13), the author concludes with a brief notice of sundry matters, chiefly of a local and personal nature; devoutly praying for the perfection and welfare of those to whom he writes, and promising to make them a visit as soon as practicable.

Such is, in brief, a statement of the general scope and primary object of this very profound, comprehensive, and intensely interesting Epistle. It was written primarily, as I have said, for the purpose of persuading and encouraging the Hebrew Christians to persevere in their begun course, and not to yield to the false suggestions and evil designs of their persecutors. But the Epistle has also an ulterior design. It was evidently intended by the Holy Spirit that it should form part of the Canon: and it was therefore written also for *our* comfort, encouragement, and consolation, as well as for the benefit of the persecuted and desponding Hebrew Christians.

That it is well adapted to our wants, and indeed to the wants and circumstances of the Church in all ages and in all countries, must be obvious to every one who properly understands it. For,

1. It is preeminently a book of motives. In composing it, the author had in view, not only the reason of man and his understanding, but also all the active and emotional principles of his nature. Every chord that can influence the human will, and incline it to what is honest, just, pure, lovely, holy, and of good report, is perceived by the author, and touched with the hand of a master. And this is done, not by means of what is merely transient and circumstantial; but it is done by presenting to the understanding and to the heart, motives high as Heaven, deep as Hell, and enduring as eternity. And hence it follows that while the world stands, this

Epistle will be to the Church as an anchor of the soul, both sure and steadfast. No other portion of the written word is better calculated to encourage all Christians to persevere in the Divine life, and to perfect holiness in the fear of God.

2. In this Epistle, we have also most clearly set forth the relations subsisting between the Old and the New Covenant; a proper understanding of which is of immense importance to the whole body of Christ. This is a subject which very greatly agitated the primitive churches, outside as well as inside of Palestine; and it is a subject on which Paul has said much in his other Epistles. But in this one, it is his main theme. Here, he virtually demonstrates in every section what he has plainly and formally stated in the eighth; viz., that the Law or Old Covenant was, in fact, but a shadow of the New; and that there was therefore really nothing in it to take away the sins of any man. It simply offered to the people typical or relative pardon, through a typical Mediator; a typical High Priest; and typical sacrifices; until the Seed should come to whom the promise was made. True, indeed, the promise which God made to Abraham, before he left Ur of Chaldea, was of a twofold nature. It contained within itself, in a sort of embryonic state, the germs of both the Old and the New Covenant. The one related to the family of Abraham according to the flesh; and the other to his family according to the Spirit. The one had reference to the type; and the other to the antitype. The one was the basis of that which Paul describes as the shadow; and the other was the basis of that which he characterizes as the substance.

During the Patriarchal age, these two elements were so closely united, and so intimately blended together, that, to the eye of human reason, they seemed to be but as one. And even after the carnal element was fully developed in the Sinaitic Covenant, the spiritual element was still associated with it, and was even then pregnant with blessings to all who were of the seed of Abraham. But though the Law was very closely connected with the spiritual element of the promise, and though for a time it served to support and preserve it, as the oak supports and preserves the tender vine which clings to its branches, it was nevertheless at all times essentially separate and distinct from it. For "the Law is not of faith." (Gal. 3: 11.) Faith belonged to the other side of the Abrahamic promise. But the Law speaketh on this wise, "The man that doeth these things shall live by them." (Rom. 10:50.) And hence the Law could save no one from his sins. (Rom. 3:20.) It was given for typical and other temporary purposes, till Christ should come; and it served, moreover, as a schoolmaster to bring us to Christ. (Gal. 3:19, 24.) But when the time came for the full development of that element of the Abrahamic promise which related to Christ, then the Sinaitic Covenant was no longer necessary. As a religious institution, it had then accomplished its purpose; and it was therefore taken out of the way to make room for the introduction of "a better Covenant which was established on better promises." So reasons the Apostle; evidently for our sake, as well as for the sake of his Hebrew brethren.

## SECTION FIVE

### WHEN AND WHERE WAS THE EPISTLE WRITTEN?

From some expressions in the Epistle, we would infer that it was written some considerable time after the opening of the Kingdom of Christ, on the day of Pentecost A.D. 34. Such, for example, as the following: "For when for the time ye ought to be teachers, ye have need that one teach you again which be the first principles of the Oracles of God." (5:12.) By which the author evidently means, that so great a length of time had elapsed since their conversion to Christ, that they should, at the time of his writing, have been able to instruct others in the truths of the Gospel. And again in 10:32, 33, he says, "But call to remembrance the former days, in which after ye were illuminated, ye endured a great fight of afflictions; partly, whilst ye were made a gazing-stock, both by reproaches and afflictions; and partly, whilst ye became companions of them that were so used." Here, the author clearly refers to a period of persecution, which had occurred at some considerable time previous to the date of his writing.

From other passages, it is equally plain that the Epistle was written before the destruction of Jerusalem; while the Temple was standing, and while the daily sacrifices were still offered. In 8:4, for example, the author says, "For if he [Jesus] were on earth, he could not be a Priest; seeing there are Priests who offer gifts according to the Law." And again in 10:11, he says, "And every Priest standeth daily ministering and offering oftentimes the same sacrifices which can never take away sins." In both of these passages, the Apostle clearly refers to the Temple services, as being still in existence. And hence we conclude that the Epistle was written before the destruction of Jerusalem in A.D. 70.

But from some other passages it is equally obvious, that the fall of Jerusalem and the destruction of the Jewish commonwealth were then very near at hand. In 10: 24, 25, our author says, "Let us consider one another, to provoke unto love and good works; not forsaking the assembling of ourselves together as the manner of some is: but exhorting one another, and so much the more as ye see the day approaching." The word *day* is here used with reference to some well known time of trial, which was manifestly then near at hand; and to which the Hebrew brethren were all looking forward with much anxiety. But so far as we know, there is no other event in their history to which this reference so well applies, as to the siege and destruction of Jerusalem. For against the dangers of that short but eventful period, Christ had himself previously and solemnly warned his disciples. "When ye therefore," he says, "shall see the abomination of desolation spoken of by Daniel the Prophet, stand in the holy place; then let them who be in Judea flee into the mountains; and let him who is on the house-top not come down to take any thing out of his house; neither let him who is in the field return back to take his clothes. And woe unto them that are with child, and to them that give suck in those days. But pray that your flight may not be in the winter, neither on the Sabbath-day: for then shall be great tribulation, such as was not since the beginning of the world to this time; no, nor ever shall be. And except those days should be shortened, there should no flesh be saved; but for the elect's sake those days shall be shortened." (Matt. 24: 15-22.)

In 10: 37, our author again refers to the same events, as then near at hand. He says, "For yet a little while, and he that shall come, will come, and will not tarry." The *coming One* is manifestly Christ himself; and the *coming* that is here spoken of, is not his coming in person to judge the world; but it is his coming in providence for the destruction of Jerusalem and the removal of the Jewish commonwealth. Of these matters he himself speaks in Matt. 24: 29-34, as follows: "Immediately after the tribulation of those days [referring to the distress of the siege], shall the Sun be darkened, and the Moon shall not give her light, and the stars shall fall from heaven, and the powers of the heavens shall be shaken. And then shall appear the Son of man in heaven; and then shall all the tribes of the Earth mourn; and they shall see the Son of man *coming* in the clouds of heaven, with power and great glory. And he shall send his angels with a great sound of a trumpet; and they shall gather together his elect from the four winds, from one end of heaven to the other. Now learn a parable of the fig-tree; When its branch is yet tender and putteth forth leaves, ye know that summer is nigh. So likewise ye, when ye shall see all these things, know that it is near, even at the doors. Verily I say unto you, *This generation shall not pass, till all these things be fulfilled."* In this highly symbolical passage, there is probably reference also to Christ's second personal coming to destroy the Earth and to judge the world: but certainly the primary reference is to his coming in providence to destroy Jerusalem, and so to put an end to the persecuting power of the Jewish nation. And to this, the author of our Epistle also manifestly refers in 10: 37; showing that the fall of Jerusalem was then very near at hand.

From Phil. 1: 21-26, and 2: 24, we learn, moreover, that while Paul was a prisoner at Rome, in A.D. 62, he fully expected to be delivered from his confinement, and to make another visit to Philippi. "And having this confidence," he says, "I know that I shall abide and continue with you all, for your furtherance and joy of faith; that your rejoicing may be the more abundant in Jesus Christ for me by my coming again unto you." And again, it seems probable from 13: 23, of this Epistle, that when it was written, Paul was then actually at liberty; and that it was his purpose to visit Jerusalem very soon in company with Timothy.

Putting these facts together, then, it seems most likely that the Epistle to the Hebrews was written at Rome, in A.D. 63, soon after the end of Paul's first imprisonment. This is the opinion of Lardner, Mill, Davidson, and many others.

## SECTION SIX

### IN WHAT LANGUAGE WAS THE EPISTLE WRITTEN?

Some of the ancients thought that it was written in Hebrew, or rather in the Aramaic, which, at that time, was the vernacular language of Palestine. This was the opinion of Clement of Alexandria, Eusebius, Theodoret, Euthalius, Theophylact, and probably also of Jerome.

But this opinion does not rest on any historical basis. It does not appear that any of these Fathers had ever seen a copy of it in the Hebrew language; nor do they say that any one else had ever seen a copy. They knew that Paul had written a letter to the Hebrew brethren; and they would of course naturally suppose that he would write it in their own vernacular. On this ground, it is alleged, the report was first circulated in certain quarters that the Epistle was written in Hebrew. And afterward, it is thought, that this opinion was adopted by others, as a plausible hypothesis, in order to account for the diversity of style that is supposed to exist between this and the other Epistles of Paul.

But, so far as we know, the opinion of these Fathers, touching the original language of the Epistle, was wholly conjectural. And it is now very generally believed by the most eminent critics, that the Epistle was originally written in Greek. This is the view of Lightfoot, Whitby, Mill, Basnage, Wetstein, Lardner, Hug, Bleek, Stewart, Davidson, Ebrard, Alford, and many others who have carefully weighed the evidence on both sides. Alford says, "This has been the opinion of almost all moderns: of all, we may safely say, who have handled the subject impartially and intelligently."

In support of this hypothesis, it may be alleged,

1. That there is a strong presumption in favor of the Greek original, arising out of the circumstances of the case. For,

(1.) The Greek was then not only the most perfect of all languages, but it was also most generally used throughout the civilized world. And hence it was properly chosen by God, as the language of the New Testament Canon: as the medium through which to communicate the good news to every kindred, and people, and nation. Even the Gospel of Matthew, which was written for the benefit of Jewish converts in Palestine, seems to have been composed in Greek, as well perhaps as in Hebrew; and the Epistle to the Romans, though addressed to a Latin Church, was nevertheless written in Greek.

(2.) The Greek was, on the whole, best adapted to the wants and circumstances of the Hebrew Christians. On this point Davidson well remarks as follows: "Since the first Gospel had been composed by Matthew in Hebrew, about twenty years had elapsed, during which the Greek tongue was rapidly acquiring greater currency among all classes in Palestine. It had encroached much on the vernacular dialect of the Hebrews. The destruction of Jerusalem was now approaching. Within a very few years, the metropolis was to be laid waste, and with it Judaism, as a system, was doomed to fall. The Hebrew polity was near its close; and under such circumstances, it would have been almost superfluous to compose the letter before us in Hebrew. The Jewish Christians were soon to be incorporated more closely with the Gentiles in one body, and with one common tongue. To write in Greek was therefore to facilitate an amalgamation of all believers, both Jews and Gentiles; especially, as the Apostle saw that Judaism was virtually extinct. Hence he wisely consulted at once the benefit of Jewish Christians in Palestine; and of all future believers, by writing the letter in Greek.

2. It is thought that there are in the Epistle reasons sufficient to prove that it was written in Greek. Such, for instance, as the following:

(1.) Nearly all the quotations from the Old Testament are taken from the Septuagint, and not from the original Hebrew. This, it is presumed, would not have been the case, had the author been writing in Hebrew.

(2.) In the beginning of the seventh chapter, the author pauses to explain the Hebrew name *Melchisedek:* a circumstance which renders it probable that he was writing in Greek. True, indeed, a translator, as well as an author, may sometimes explain foreign words. But in this case, the explanation occurs in the regular course of the argument; and forms, in fact, a part of the author's premises.

(3.) In 9: 15-18, the author makes use of the double meaning of the word *diathēkē,* which means both a *covenant* and a *will.* The corresponding Hebrew word *berceth* always means *a covenant;* and is never used in the Old Testament in the sense of *a will.*

(4.) The general construction of the Epistle favors the idea that it was written in Greek. "The construction of the periods," says Alford, "is such, in distinction from the character of Oriental languages, that if it is a translation, the whole argumentation of the original must have been broken up into its original elements of thought; and all its connecting links recast; so that it would not be so much a translation, as a rewriting of the Epistle.

For these reasons mainly, we concur with Alford and others, that the Epistle to the Hebrews is not a translation; but that, like all other parts of the New Testament, it was originally composed in Hellenistic Greek.

## SECTION SEVEN
### EXPLANATIONS

In preparing the following Commentary, I have endeavored,

1. To present to the reader such an analysis of each section as will best enable him to comprehend its logical bearings and relations. The connection of thought is carefully traced in each of these divisions; and at its close is given, as briefly as possible, the special scope of each of the several paragraphs of which it is composed.

2. To give such an explanation of the text as will best serve to make the meaning plain and obvious to the common class of English readers; endeavoring at the same time to meet, as far as practicable, all such difficulties as are likely to embarrass young Preachers, Teachers or Bible classes, etc. For this purpose I have tried (1) to keep constantly ,before the reader the main scope of the whole Epistle; and to show, at the same time, the relative bearings of the several sections, paragraphs, and clauses of which it consists; (2) to explain the design of Judaism, and its relations to Christianity, as an introductory part of the scheme and economy of redemption; (3) to show the perfect harmony of the Old and New Testaments, and their relations to each other as essential parts of the one complete and perfect revelation of God to man; (4) to explain the principles on which citations are made from the Old Testament Scriptures, in the course of this Epistle; and (5) to give to the classical student, as far as possible, without embarrassment to the English reader, the grounds of all the leading criticisms.

3. To lead and incline the reader to reflect on the infinite riches, beauties, and perfections of the inspired word: to help him look into it, as a mirror, where he may see reflected in their true colors and proportions the wants of his own character, and also God's own appointed means of supplying them. For this purpose each section is followed with a few such leading reflections as, it is

hoped, will incline and enable the reader to look deeper and deeper into the infinite fullness of God's grace, as it is revealed to us in the Gospel.

The Text used in this Commentary is that of Bagster's Critical English New Testament; in which are presented at one view the Authorized Version and the results of modern criticism. The design of the Publishers in preparing this edition of the New Testament was to make our Common English Version "a groundwork on which to exhibit the results of the criticism of the original text, for the use of the general reader. For this purpose they have taken the following critical Texts to furnish the readings which have been thus exhibited: those, namely, of Lachmann; of Tischendorf, in his last completed edition; of the Twofold New Testament, slightly altered in some places, on a careful review; of Alford, as finally given in the abridgment of his larger work; and of Tregelles, as far as it has been already published. With each variation from the common reading, those of the above-named critical texts are cited in which such variation has been adopted; and, in addition, the principal documents by which it is supported, whenever such citation has been deemed material."

*Omissions* from the common text are marked by brackets, as in 1 : 3; *insertions* are printed in italics and inclosed in brackets, as in 1 : 8; and *variations* are indicated by inclosing between two vertical lines both the common reading and the proposed substitute, the latter being always written in italics, as in 4 : 7.

The following are the principal Manuscripts referred to in the critical and explanatory Notes.

Aleph—Codex Sinaiticus. The entire New Testament, with a few chasms. Century IV.

A—Codex Alexandrinus. The New Testament, wanting Matthew to 25 : 6, and John 6 : 50 to 8 : 52. Cent. V.

B—Codex Vaticanus. The New Testament, wanting Hebrews from 9 : 14, 1 and 2 Timothy, Titus, Philemon, and Revelation. Cent. IV.

C—Codex Ephræmi. Fragments of the New Testament, amounting to about two-thirds of the whole. Cent. V.

D—Codex Claromontanus. The Epistles of Paul. Cent. VI.

E—The Epistles of Paul. A later transcript of D.

F—Codex Augiensis. The Epistles of Paul. Cent. IX.

G—Codex Boernerianus. The Epistles of Paul. Cent. IX.

H—Fragments of the Epistles of Paul. Cent. VI.

K—The Epistles. Cent. IX.

L—Codex Angelicus Romanus. The Epistles of Paul. Cent. IX.

M—Codex Uffenbachianus. Fragments, embracing a part of Hebrews. Cent. X.

P—Codex Porphyrii. Acts, Epistles, and Revelation. Cent. VIII.

These manuscripts are all written in uncial or capital letters; and are considered of more value than those which are written in cursive characters. The latter are generally of less antiquity, and are commonly designated by the Arabic numerals. Copies of the Old Latin versions are indicated by the letters a, b, c, d, e, f, g, etc. *Rec.* denotes the "Received Text" (Textus Receptus) of Elzevir. It was first published in A.D. 1633, and was afterward slightly modified by several editors.

The *references* have been selected with much care; and, it is hoped, they will greatly assist the diligent student in his efforts to gain a more profound and comprehensive knowledge of the economy of redemption, as it is discussed and illustrated in this Epistle.

KENTUCKY UNIVERSITY, December 27, 1874.

# A COMMENTARY ON THE
# EPISTLE TO THE HEBREWS

## SECTION ONE
### 1: 1 to 2: 4

### ANALYSIS

In this section, the Apostle endeavors to persuade and encourage his Hebrew brethren in Christ to persevere to the end in their begun Christian course, by presenting to them sundry motives drawn chiefly from the Divine nature, glory, and dignity of Christ, considered as the Creator, Preserver, and Governor of all things.

I. He concedes that God had in ancient times, in divers parts and ways, spoken to the Fathers by the Prophets. But then he claims that the same God did in the end of these days, or at the close of the Jewish age, speak to us by his own Son (verse 1).

But who is this Son of God? There is by the common consent of all, a very close and intimate connection between the character of the messenger and the weight and importance of his message. And hence the Apostle next proceeds to answer this question: to speak particularly of the incomparable majesty, glory, and perfections of Jesus Christ, as the Son of God. He says,

1. That he is the heir, or Lord, of all things (verse 2).

2. That through him, God made the worlds (verse 2).

3. That he is the effulgence of the Father's glory (verse 3).

4. That he is the exact image or likeness of the Father's essence (verse 3).

5. That he supports all things by the word of his power (verse 3).

6. That by means of his own blood, he has made purification for our sins (verse 3).

7. And that having done this, he now sits, as King of kings and Lord of lords, on the right hand of the Majesty in the heavens (verse 3).

II. In the remaining portion of the first chapter, the Apostle further expands and amplifies this subject, by comparing Christ with angels. He proves chiefly from the Old Testament Scriptures, that he (Christ) is superior to the angels.

1. In that he has obtained by inheritance a more excellent name than they (verses 4, 5).

2. The angels are all required to worship him (verse 6).

3. True, indeed, the angels are very powerful and exalted beings. Before them the enemies of Jehovah melt away, as wax or stubble before the flame. And endowed, as they are, with all the strength and purity indicated by the symbolic use of the word *spirit,* they are of course far removed from all the infirmities and imperfections of the flesh. But by the appointment of the Father, as well as by his own essential Divinity, the Son is exalted far above all the angels of Heaven. As *God,* he sits on the throne of the universe, judging and governing it in truth and in righteousness (verses 7, 8).

4. He has been anointed with the Holy Spirit and with power, far above all kings and princes (verse 9). "The Father giveth not the Spirit by measure unto him."

5. He is from everlasting to everlasting. By him the foundations of the Earth were laid, and the heavens are the work of his hands. They will all finally perish; and he will roll them up and recast them, as a worn-out garment; but he is himself still the same, yesterday, today, and forever. This cannot, of course, be said of the angels, or of any other creature (verses 10-12).

6. The angels are all ministering spirits, sent forth under Christ to minister to the heirs of salvation. But Christ sits on the right hand of God, waiting until, according to the promise of the Father, his enemies shall be made his footstool (verses 13, 14).

III. From these premises, then, our author concludes that we Christians, whether we be Jews or Gentiles, should give the more earnest heed to the things which we have heard from God through Christ and his holy Apostles and Prophets; lest at any time we should be carried away from them by the evil influences of the world, and so making shipwreck of our faith, we should finally come short of the eternal inheritance. For,

1. It is a principle of the Divine government, as well indeed as of all just human governments, that wherever much is given, there also much is ever expected and required (2: 1, 2).

*2.* But even under the Law, in an age of comparative darkness, there was no pardon for the willfully disobedient (verse 2).

*3.* And hence it follows that there is no possible way of escape for those who now *neglect* the great salvation that is offered to us in the Gospel (verses 3, 4).

From this analysis, it is obvious that the whole section may be properly divided into the three following paragraphs:

I. 1:1-3. The fact that God has spoken to us through his Son, with a statement of the Son's rank and dignity.

II. 1:4-14. The Son of God compared with angels.

III. 2:1-4. Danger of neglecting what God has revealed to us through his Son.

*Title.*—In the oldest manuscripts, such as the Sinaitic, the Vatican, the Alexandrian, etc., the title is simply, *"To the Hebrews."* In the editions of Stephens, it is, "The Epistle of Paul the Apostle to the Hebrews"; and in the "Received text" of Elzevir, it is, "The Epistle to the Hebrews." Some other slight variations occur in a few of the manuscripts; but the first form, "To the Hebrews," is sustained by the best authorities; and was probably prefixed to the Epistle in the Apostolic age, by some of the inspired Fathers; or, at least, with their consent and approval. See Introduction 3:1.

## 1. THE FACT THAT GOD HAS SPOKEN TO US THROUGH HIS SON, WITH A STATEMENT OF THE SON'S RANK AND DIGNITY
### 1:1-3

1 God, who [1]at sundry times and [2]in divers manners spake in time past unto [3]the fathers by the prophets,

[1]Gen. iii. 15; xii. 1-3; xxvi. 2-5; 1 Pet. i. 10-12.
[2]Num. xii. 6-8; Joel ii. 28.
[3]Luke i. 55, 72; John vii. 22; Acts xiii. 32.

---

1 **God who**—This is a very striking and remarkable introduction. Full of his subject, and earnest in his desires to communicate to his desponding Hebrew brethren the word of life, the author indulges in no unnecessary preliminaries, but enters at once on the discussion of his sublime theme. He concedes what had indeed been often demonstrated, and what the Jews then all confidently believed, that God had anciently (*palai*) spoken to the Fathers by the Prophets: but then he also claims with equal confidence and on equal authority, that the *same* glorious and infinitely perfect Being did, "at the end of these days," or near the close of the Jewish age, speak unto us by his own Son. True, indeed, he had, for some time previous to Paul's writing this Epistle, been generally known by a name that would have appeared somewhat barbarous to the ancient Hebrews. To them he was primarily revealed as Eloheem, a word in the plural number which means *powerful ones; persons of great authority and influence;* because in the beginning, the power of the Father, and of the Son, and of the Holy Spirit, was most eminently displayed and illustrated in creating and garnishing the heavens and the earth. This is therefore the only name by which the Deity is made known to us in the first chapter of Genesis. But in the second and following chapters, he is called also Jehovah, *the existing One; the Being absolute;* because he only has life and immortality in himself; all other being is derived from him and depends on him. These are the proper names by which the Deity is commonly designated in the Old Testament. But in the New he is called Theos, which, according to Herodotus, means *one who places, disposes, or arranges* (from *titheemi, to place*); because, says he, the gods were supposed to have fixed all things in the world, in their proper places. According to Plato, *theos* means *one who runs* (from *theo, to run*); because the Sun, Moon, and stars, which he regarded as the primary gods, run their course

daily from east to west, as if exercising a watch-care over the Earth and its inhabitants. But it is now generally believed by the ablest critics, that both Herodotus and Plato were in error; and that the Greek word *theos* and the Latin *deus* are of the same family as *Zeus,* and cognate with the Sanscrit *dyu,*—a word which means *splendor, brightness, the bright sky.* Any and all of these Greek conceptions would, of course, for a time, seem somewhat barbarous and repulsive to the pious and superstitiously sensitive Hebrews. But a change of names does not of necessity imply a change of nature, essence, or character. The Creator, Preserver, and Governor of the universe, whether known as Eloheem, Jehovah, Theos, Deus, Dyu, or God, is ever the same, yesterday, today, and forever; without any variableness or shadow of change. (James 1: 17.) The Author of the Old Testament is the Author of the New. And hence it follows that the Bible is a unit; and that it is throughout perfectly consistent in all its parts. For "all Scripture is given by inspiration of God, and is profitable for doctrine, for reproof, for correction, for instruction in righteousness; that the man of God may be perfect, thoroughly furnished for every good work." (2 Tim. 3: 16, 17.)

**at sundry times**—The word that is here rendered, *at sundry times"* (*polumezos*), means properly *in many parts.* It refers to the well known fact, that God's plan of mercy through Jesus Christ, was revealed to the ancients gradually and in fragments. To Eve, it was promised indirectly, that through her Seed the Old Serpent should be crushed (Gen. 3: 15); to Abraham directly, that through his Seed all the nations of the Earth should be blessed (Gen. 12: 1-3); to Judah, that Shiloh (*the Pacificator*) should come, before the scepter should depart from him (Gen. 49: 10); and to all Israel, that God would raise up to them, from among themselves, a Prophet like unto Moses, to whom he would require all to hearken (Deut. 18: 18). David, in one of his Psalms (22: 11-21), speaks of the sufferings of the Messiah; in another (16: 7-11), of his resurrection, and his deliverance from the power of Hades; and in another (110), of his priesthood, reign, and triumphs. And so also it may be said of all the other Prophets. Through them, God gave to his people, as their wants and circumstances required, "precept upon precept, precept upon precept; line upon line, line upon line; here a little, and there a little." (Isa. 28:

10-14.) But when in the fullness of time, He came, who is himself the Light of the world (John 8: 12, and 9: 5), then the whole plan of redemption was speedily revealed to mankind in all its fullness. This was done, partly through his own personal ministry, and partly through the ministry of his Apostles; "God also bearing them witness, both with signs, and wonders, and with divers miracles, and gifts of the Holy Spirit, according to his own will."

**and in divers manners**—This expression denotes the *various ways* (*polutzopos*) in which God made his will known to the ancients. This he did sometimes by dreams; sometimes by visions; sometimes, by symbols; sometimes, by Urim and Thummim; sometimes, by audible voices; and sometimes, by inspiration or prophetic ecstasy: all of which served to mark, in some measure, the comparative imperfection of the Old Economy. They severally indicate that so long as it continued, there was a wide breach—an unhappy state of alienation and separation between man and his Maker. (Num. 12: 6-8.) But in Christ, God and man are united. He (Christ) has slain the enmity, and taken it out of the way, by the blood of his cross (Col. 1: 20-22), so that through him, not only can God now consistently speak more freely and directly to man, but man can also speak with more freedom and confidence to God. See 4: 16; 10: 19-22. In this respect, then, there is a very great contrast between the Old and the New Economy. God never before spoke to the people, even from the Mercy-seat of the Tabernacle, as he did in and through his own Son during his earthly ministry.

**spake in time past unto the fathers**—This phrase is understood differently by commentators. Some think that it embraces all time, from Adam to Christ, including even the ministry of John the Baptist. But it is most likely, that the Apostle has here in view only the revelations of God to the Hebrew fathers, from Abraham to Malachi; or perhaps to Simon the Just. This explanation accords best with the context and also with Hebrew usage. The Jews all looked upon Abraham, as the father and founder of their nation; and Malachi wrote the last book of the Old Testament; though it seems probable, that the spirit of prophecy did not wholly cease among the Jews, till the time of Simon the Just, about 300 years B.C. He is called by the Jews "One of the remnants of the Great Synagogue," said to have been founded by Ezra for the

2 Hath in ¹these last days ²spoken unto us by his Son, whom he hath ³appointed heir of all things, ⁴by whom also he made the worlds;

¹Isa. ii. 2; Mich. iv. 1; Acts ii. 17; Gal. iv. 4.
²John i. 18; iii. 34; vii. 16; viii. 28, 40.
³Psa. ii. 6-9; Isa. liii. 10-12; John iii. 35; xiii. 3; xvi. 15; Col. i. 46.
⁴John i. 3; 1 Cor. viii. 6; Eph. iii. 9; Col. i. 16, 17.

revision and completion of the Old Testament Canon. See "Reason and Revelation," p. 207-219, by the author. The word here rendered, "in time past" (*palai*), means properly *in ancient times;* and it can therefore hardly have reference to the ministry of John.

**by the prophets;**—literally, *in the Prophets.* God first worked in the Prophets, and then through them, in making known to the Hebrew Fathers the various messages of his grace. The English word *prophet* is now generally used to denote *one who foretells future events.* And this is sometimes the meaning of the original word (*propheroph*) in Hellenistic Greek. But in Classic Greek it means *one who speaks for another;* and especially, one who speaks for a god and interprets his words to men. Thus, for instance, Mercury is called the prophet of Jupiter; and in the same sense, the poets are called the prophets of the Muses. The corresponding Hebrew word is *nâvee* (from the root, *to boil up as a fountain*), and means literally *one who boils over.* The name was given to the ancient prophets, because, under the influence of the Holy Spirit, they seemed to pour out their inspired utterances, as a fountain pours out its waters. (Psalm 45: 1.) And hence it was always God who spoke in and by the Prophets: for says Peter, "No prophecy of the Scripture is of private interpretation; but holy men of old spake as they were moved by the Holy Spirit." (2 Pet. 1: 20, 21.)

**2 in these last days**—or rather, according to our best authorities, *at the end of these days* (*epi eschatou ton heemeron touton*). This is the reading given in MSS. A, B, D, K, L, and M. Three different views have been taken of these words. It is alleged (1) that they refer simply to the closing period of the Jewish age (Moll); (2) that they refer exclusively to the Christian age (Stuart); and (3) that they refer to the closing period of the prophetic era, embracing both the ministry of Christ and of his Apostles (Luther). The first of these hypotheses is favored (a) by the use of the aorist tense of the verb (*elaleesen*) *he spoke,* not he has spoken; (b) by the fact that during the last three and a half years of the Jewish age, God did actually speak to the people in the person of his own Son; and (c) by the current use of this phrase among the Jews. They were wont to divide all time into two ages, viz., *"the present age"* (*ho aion houtos*) and *"the coming age"* (*ho aion mellon*). By the former, they meant the age then existing before the coming of Christ; and by the latter they meant the age subsequent to his coming. (Matt. 12:32.) And hence it was, that in the Hebrew dialect *"these days"* came to signify the Jewish age; and *"the last days,"* the coming age. The dividing line of these two ages was never drawn very distinctly by the Jews. But as Christ put an end to the Law, nailing it to his cross (Col. 2:14), his death, of course, serves to define this boundary, fixing definitely the end of the Jewish age, as well as the beginning of the Christian age. So that the days of Christ's personal ministry on earth, previous to his death, were according to the Hebrew "usus loquendi," the end of "these days." The second hypothesis is favored by the reading of the "Textus Receptus," and also by several of the ancient versions, which have *"in these last days"* (*epi eschaton ton heemeron*). That "the last days" is a phrase in Hebrew literature, equivalent to "the coming age," is plain from sundry passages in both the Old and the New Testament. See, for example, Isa. 2:2; Jer. 23:20; Micah 4:1; and Acts 2:17. The third hypothesis is supposed to receive some support from the fact conceded in 2:3; viz., that the things "which at the first began to be spoken by the Lord" himself, were afterward confirmed unto us by his Apostles and Prophets, during the opening period of the Christian age. The *fact* here stated, no one of course denies who believes the Bible to be the word of God; but whether it has any bearing on the question before us, may be doubted. On the whole, it seems most probable that the Apostle is speaking here simply of Christ's personal ministry on Earth; and that he refers only, as the tense of the verb indicates, to the last days of the Jewish age.

**by his Son,**—literally, *in Son* (*en hui*); the word *son* being used without the article or possessive pronoun, as a quasi-proper name. So also the word *son* is used without any limiting epithet in Psalm 2:12. But our English idiom requires an article or a possessive pronoun before the word *son,* as in our Common Version.

But why is Christ called the Son of God? To this question, three answers have been given: (1) Because of his supernatural birth by the virgin Mary.  (2) Because of his being begotten from the grave, as the first-fruits of them that slept.  And (3) because of his being eternally begotten of the Father.

In proof of the first hypothesis, we have the direct testimony of the angel Gabriel.  According to Luke, this ambassador of God, when sent to announce to Mary the birth of the coming Messiah, said to her, "The Holy Spirit shall come upon thee, and the power of the Highest shall overshadow thee; therefore also that holy thing which shall be born of thee, shall be called the Son of God." (Luke 1 : 35.)  And in proof of the second, we have given the testimony of Paul in Acts 13 : 33.  Speaking by the Spirit, he says, "And we declare unto you the glad tidings, that the promise which was made unto the Fathers, God hath fulfilled the same unto us their children, in that he hath raised up Jesus again; as it is also written in the second Psalm, Thou art my Son, this day I have begotten thee"; that is, this day I have begotten thee from the dead. (Rev. 1 : 5.)

That Jesus Christ, then, is called the Son of God, because he was miraculously begotten by the Holy Spirit of the virgin, and also because he was the First-begotten from the dead, there can be no doubt.  But is it true that he is called also the Son of God, because he was eternally begotten of the Father?  So many believe and testify (Origen, Athanasius, Augustine, etc.).  And in proof of their position, they appeal with much confidence to what is said of the Son in this connection. (1 : 2, 3.)  For how, say they, could God make the worlds by his Son, if he had no Son for thousands of years after the worlds were created?  But in reply to this, it may perhaps be enough to say, How could God create all things by Jesus Christ (Eph. 3 : 9), four thousand years before the Word became incarnate?  And how could Jesus say to his disciples (John 6 : 62), "What, and if ye shall see the Son of man ascend up where he was before?"  Was the Logos known as the Son of man before he became incarnate?  Surely not.

Here, then, we might pause, relying on the correctness of the old logical adage, that "Whatever proves too much, proves nothing." But the question is of easy solution.  We all know that it is very common to use names and titles acquired at a later period of life, to designate the same persons even in their childhood, youth, and early manhood.  We say, for example, that Abraham left Ur of

Chaldea and went to Haran, when he was seventy years of age; though he was really not called Abraham, but Abram, until about twenty-nine years after his departure from Ur. And just so it is, with respect to the titles given to the eternal Logos after he became incarnate. These may all be used, in like manner, to designate his Divine personality before he became flesh and dwelt among us. Thus we say with all propriety, that in the beginning the Logos created all things; that Jesus Christ created all things; that the Son of God created all things; and that the Son of man created all things. And hence we conclude that whatever may be true of Christ's eternal sonship, the doctrine is not taught in this passage of Scripture.

It does not follow, however, as, some have erroneously supposed, that the name, *Son of God,* is applied to Christ in the Scriptures, with reference merely to his human nature. Certainly not. On the contrary it is always used with special reference to his Divine nature, in the new relations which he sustains to the Father, as our Immanuel. This is the sense in which the name *son*, as applied to Christ, is used throughout this entire chapter. This is the sense in which Christ himself speaks of his sonship in relation to the Father (John 5: 17-27); and this is the sense in which Paul uses the term *son,* when he contrasts the human nature of Christ with his Divine nature (Rom. 1: 4). He (Christ), says Paul, "was made of the seed of David, according to the flesh [that is, according to his human nature]; and declared to be the Son of God, with power, according to the Spirit of holiness [that is according to his holy spiritual or Divine nature], by his resurrection from the dead." See also Matt. 16: 16.

**whom he hath appointed heir of all things,**—Here again the verb (*etheeken*) is in the aorist (the indefinite past): whom he *appointed* Heir of all things. But when did God appoint or consti- tute his Son the Heir of all things? No doubt this was done *in purpose,* when in the eternal counsels of Jehovah, it was also de- creed that the Logos should become the Son of God, incarnate. So it appears from the second Psalm, in which reference is made to this appointment. "I will declare the decree," says the Messiah, speaking by the Psalmist, "Jehovah hath said unto me, Thou art my Son; this day I have begotten thee. Ask of me, and I will give thee the heathen for thine inheritance; and the uttermost parts of the earth for thy possession." It is manifest from this passage, that the heirship of Christ is made to depend on his sonship; and that both are the result of God's eternal purpose (Eph. 3: 11); though it was not until after Christ's resurrection, that he assumed *in fact,* the dignity, glory, and dominion, which belong to him as the Son of God and the Heir of all things (Isa. 9: 6, 7; Matt. 28: 47; Acts 2: 36; Phil. 2: 5-11).

The Greek word (*kleeronomos*) here translated *heir,* means (1) one who acquires anything by lot; and (2) one who inherits anything by the will and appointment of another. In this latter sense, that is, by the appointment of God, Christ, as our elder brother, is made Heir of the universe. And as he has made us (Christians) heirs with himself (Rom. 8: 17), we too may be said to inherit all things (1 Cor. 3: 21-23).

**by whom also he made the worlds;**—that is, by his Son, the Logos, before he became incarnate. (John 1: 2.) It would be vain and useless to speculate here, as many commentators have done, on the relations which the Father, the Son, and the Holy Spirit, sustained to each other in the work of creation. Such themes are too high for us; and we must not therefore pretend to be wise concerning such matters, beyond what is written. "Secret things belong unto the Lord our God; but those things which are revealed belong unto us and to our children." (Deut. 29: 29.)

The proper meaning of the word here rendered *worlds* (*aiones*) is still a matter of controversy. The singular number *aiōn* means (1) endless duration; (2) any age or period of time; and (3) by metonymy, anything that lives or exists forever. Some have taken the word, as it occurs here, in its second or metaphorical sense; and they suppose that it means simply the several ages of the world, such as the Patriarchal, the Jewish, and the Christian. But this meaning does not well accord with the context; and in 11: 3, it is clearly inadmissible. We must therefore look to the third or metonymical meaning of this word, for a sense that will harmonize with the conditions of the context, and the design of the writer. What, then, are the *aiōnes,* or *aeons,* to which Paul here refers? The ancient Gnostics used this word to denote certain emanations from the Deity, of which they supposed that Christ himself was the chief. The Christian Fathers applied it to the angels, both good and bad. And even the Greek philosophers were wont to desig-

3 Who being ¹the brightness of his glory, and ²the express image of his person, and ³upholding all things by the ⁴word of his power, when ⁵he had [by himself] purged [our] sins, ⁶sat down on the right hand of the ⁷Majesty on high:

¹John i. 14, 18; xiv. 9, 10.
²2 Cor. iv. 4; Col. i. 15.
³Acts xvii. 28; Col. i. 17.
⁴Gen. i. 3, 6, 9; Psa. xxxiii. 6, 9.
⁵Chap. vii. 27; ix. 12, 14, 26; John i. 29; 1 John i. 7; iii. 5.
⁶Psa. cx. 1; Acts ii. 33; vii. 56; Rom. viii. 34; Eph. i. 20-22.
⁷Micah v. 4; 2 Pet. i. 16, 17; Jude 25.

nate by it their demigods and other beings superior in rank to man. (Mosh. Eccl. Hist. vol. 1, p. 63.)  And hence some commentators, as Wolf and Frabicius, suppose that by the word *aeons*, in this connection, the Apostle means simply the higher created spiritual intelligences.  But in 9:3, this word manifestly embraces the material universe.  The author says, "By faith we understand that the worlds (*aiones*) were framed by the word of God; so that things which *are seen* were not made of things which *do appear*."  That is, God did not, by his Son, make the material and visible universe, as a carpenter makes a house, out of preexisting materials; but, *ex nihilo,* out of nothing.  From this passage, then, it is manifest that the *aeons*, or at least some of them are visible to the eye.  And hence it seems most probable that under this word, the Apostle intends to embrace the entire created universe, both rational and irrational, material and immaterial.  But it is the universe, not as the mere aggregate of all things (*ta panta*); nor even as the beautifully adorned and organized cosmos (*kosmos*); but as a system of powers and agencies which will endure forever.  If this view is correct, then our author not only says with John (1: 1), that through Christ all things began to be (*egeneto*), but he goes even further, and indicates the comparative perfection and perpetuity of his works.  For he has not only created all things "which are in Heaven and on Earth, visible and invisible, whether they be thrones or dominions, principalities or powers" (Col. 1:16), but he has also made them *aeons*, the imperishable elements of a system which, under certain modifications, will endure forever.

3 **Who being the brightness of his glory,**—This has reference to the Son of God, incarnate; in whom dwells all the fullness of the Godhead bodily (Col. 2: 9); and through whom the glories of the Father are now so fully revealed to mortals.  The word *apaugasma* means *radiance, effulgence,* light beaming from a luminous body:

and it is here used by the Holy Spirit, as a very beautiful and expressive metaphor, to indicate an existing relation between the Father and the Son. The analogy may be stated thus: as the radiance of the Sun is to the Sun itself, so is Christ, the Son of God, to the Father. And hence we see the Father through the Son (John 14: 9), just as we see the Sun itself through its effulgence. For "no man," says John, "hath seen the Father at any time; [but] the only begotten Son, who is in the bosom of the Father, he hath declared him." (John 1: 18.)

This, then, is but a partial presentation of the doctrine of Christ's mediation between God and man; a doctrine which abounds in all parts of the Holy Scriptures. Previous to his fall, man, no doubt, sustained to his Maker the most direct and intimate relations. He often saw him, and conversed with him as friend with friend. But sin broke off all such intercourse, and drew a veil of impenetrable darkness between them. Now, no man can see God in his essential glory and live. (Ex. 33: 20.) But, nevertheless, through Christ, who is the way, the truth, the resurrection, and the life (John 11: 25, and 14: 6), God has graciously given us such a display of his own glorious perfections, as our sinful nature can bear; and such as is, in all respects, best adapted to our present wants and circumstances.

**and the express image of his person,**—This, in connection with the last expression, forms a sort of Hebrew parallelism, both the members of which have reference to the *Divine nature* of Christ. But they serve to describe him, not as the Logos, but as the Son of God incarnate. This view is most in harmony with the object of the Apostle, which is to encourage his brethren to persevere to the end in their fidelity to Christ. And this he does by presenting Christ to us, not as he was in the beginning, but as he is now, "God manifest in the flesh." (1 Tim. 3: 16.)

The word *charaktēr means* (1) an engraver, an engraving or stamping instrument; (2) the figure or image made by such an instrument, as on coins, wax, or metals; (3) the features of the face or countenance; and (4) any characteristic mark by which one thing is distinguished from another. The word *hupostasis,* here rendered *person*, means (1) a foundation, that which stands under and supports a superstructure; (2) well grounded trust, firmness, confidence; (3) the subject-matter of a discourse or narrative; and

(4) the essence or substance of anything; that which underlies and supports its phenomena. Previous to the Arian controversy, in the beginning of the fourth century, this word was seldom used in the sense of person (*prosopon*). But then, Athanasius and other leaders of his party so explained it, because they thought it necessary to make a distinction between the *ousia* (*esence, being*) of the Deity, and his *hupostasis*. They alleged that in the Godhead there could be but one essence, that the essence of the Son is of necessity the same as the essence of the Father and of the Holy Spirit, though they supposed that each might have his own proper personality. And hence they inferred that it is the personality, and not the essence or substance, of Christ which is here compared with that of the Father. But it is now very generally conceded that in this they were in error; and that the word *hupostasis* here means the *essence* or *substance* of the Father; and consequently that the word *charakter* expresses the exact likeness of the Son to the Father in all the essential elements of his being, as well as of his personality. When the Father is represented as a Sun, then Christ is called his radiance or effulgence. But when the former is represented to us as a substance whose essential being underlies all the pure and unsullied phenomena of the universe, then the latter is represented as the exact likeness of that substance, being in his own person all the essential marks and characteristics of the Deity. Is the Father represented as being omnipotent, omniscient, omnipresent—infinitely wise, holy, just, and good; so also is the Son. For, says Christ, "I and my Father are one" (John 10: 30); and again he says, "He that hath seen me, hath seen the Father" (John 14: 9).

**and upholding all things by the word of his power,**—It is difficult to say what is the exact meaning of the word *upholding* in this connection. Christ, by the word of his power, created all things in the beginning. "He spake, and it was done; he commanded, and it stood fast." (Psalm 33: 6, 9; compare with Gen. 1: 3, 6, 9, and John 1: 2.) Is the word *upholding* used here to denote that Christ, by his word, so supports all things as to keep them still in existence? Does it mean that unless supported by his word, all things would at once sink into annihilation? Or does it mean simply that, by his word, he still maintains the order, harmony, and well-being of the whole creation, so as to bear all things forward to

their appointed destiny? The influence, whatever it is, is all-pervading and universal. It extends to all things created, whether
they be angels, men, suns, moons, stars, comets, systems, or
atoms; so that by it the hairs of our head are numbered (Matt. 10:
29, 30), and the revolutions of the planets are constantly regulated.
This much is certain. But is this all? What is it to create, and
what is it to annihilate? What is it to give life, and what is it to
take it away? By what means and agencies are the flowers caused
to bloom, and the fields to yield an abundant harvest? Who can
properly estimate the mediate and immediate energies and influences by which Christ preserves, upholds, regulates, and governs
all things throughout his vast dominions? If he is himself the
fountain of life (Psalm 36: 9; John 4: 14; 5: 26), then who can say
how much and how constantly all things animate depend on him
for life, and breath, and all things? If we live, and move, and have
our being in him (Acts 17: 28), then who is able to estimate
aright the degree and the extent of that influence by and through
which our adorable Redeemer supports every creature and even
every atom to which he has given being? The context does not
enable us to answer these questions; and none of the parallel passages throw much light on the subject. True, it is said in Col. 1:
16, 17, that "by him [Christ] were all things created that are in
Heaven and that are in Earth, visible and invisible; whether they
be thrones, or dominions, or principalities, or powers—all things
were created by him and for him; and he is before all things, and
by him all things consist." But what, again, is the meaning of the
word consist (*sunesteeke*)—or, as it may be rendered *subsist, held
together?* Manifestly, this is a subject which rises far above the
conception of finite minds.

The expression, "*word of his power,*" is commonly regarded as
a Hebraism for "his powerful word." But any change in the arrangement of these words would very greatly weaken the force of
the expression. It is not by his word in the *abstract,* but in the
*concrete* as it proceeds from and is supportd by his omnipotent
power and energy, that Christ upholds, sustains, and governs all
things. The word of God is but an expression of his will, and
must always be taken in connection with the power which gave it
utterance. God said, "Let there be light," because he so willed
it; and instantly his creative power was exercised in harmony with

his will, as expressed in his word. And just so it is still. Christ has but to speak, and the rains are withheld, the flowers wither, and all nature languishes. Again he speaks, and "the wilderness and solitary parts of the earth are made glad, and the very deserts rejoice and blossom as the rose."

What further need, then, have we of testimony to prove that Christ is Divine? If he upholds all things by the word of his power; then, indeed, beyond all doubt, he is "God with us."

**when he had by himself purged our sins,**—Or as it may be more literally rendered, *Having by himself made purification for sins.* In reading this Epistle, we should never forget that it was written primarily for the Hebrew Christians; and that its words and phrases should therefore be generally interpreted according to Hebrew usage. But in the law of Moses, nothing is made to stand out more prominently than the fact, that moral defilement could be removed only by means of sacrifice; and that without the shedding of blood there could be really no "purification of sins." In the law prescribing and regulating the services of the day of atonement, for instance, it is said, "Then shall he [the High Priest] kill the goat of the sin-offering, that is for the people, and bring his blood within the Veil; and do with that blood as he did with the blood of the bullock, and sprinkle it upon the Mercy-seat, and before the Mercy-seat; *and he shall make an atonement for the Holy Place, because of the uncleanness of the children of Israel,* and because of their transgressions in all their sins; and so shall he do for the Tabernacle of the congregation, that remaineth among them in the midst of their uncleanness." (Lev. 16: 15, 16.) And again, in the twenty-ninth and thirtieth verses of the same chapter, it is said, "And this shall be a statute forever unto you; that in the seventh month, on the tenth day of the month, ye shall afflict your souls, and do no work at all, whether it be one of your own country, or a stranger that sojourneth among you: for on that day shall the Priest *make an atonement for you, to cleanse you,* that ye may be clean from all your sins before the Lord."

So God testified to the people through Moses. Without the shedding of blood there could be no atonement (Lev. 17: 11); and without an atonement there could be no purification from sin (Lev. 16: 30). But the atonement made by the High Priest, under the Law, was but a shadow of the atonement which Christ made by the

offering of his own blood for the sins of the people. (Col. 2: 16;
Heb. 10: 1.) "For what the law [of Moses] could not do, in that
it was weak through the flesh, God [has done by] sending his
own Son, in the likeness of sinful flesh, and [by an offering] for
sin, has condemned sin in the flesh; that the righteousness required
by the law might be fulfilled in us who walk, not after the flesh, but
after the Spirit." (Rom. 8: 3, 4.) And hence says John, "If we
walk in the light, as he [God] is in the light, we have fellowship
one with another, and the blood of Christ, his Son, cleanses us
from all sin." (1 John 1: 7.) And again he says, that Jesus has
washed us from our sins in his own blood. (Rev. 1: 5.) It was
not, then, as the Socinians allege, merely by his moral example
and his very instructive teachings, but by "his own blood," that
our blessed Savior made expiation and purification for the sins of
the people.

On this point the following very just remarks of Ebrard will be
instructive to the reader, and serve to develop still further the profound significance of the words of our text. He says, "They are
entirely wrong who understand the words, *to make purification
(katharismou poiein)*, to denote simply moral amelioration; as if
the author wished to set forth Christ here as a moral teacher, who,
by precept and example, excited men to amendment. . . . The
whole law of purification, as given by God to Moses, rested on the
assumption, that our nature, as sinful and guilt-laden, is not capable of coming into immediate contact with our holy God and
Judge. The mediation between man and God, in that Most Holy
Place separated from the people, was revealed in three forms : (1)
in sacrifices; (2) in the priesthood; and (3) in the Levitical laws
of purity. Sacrifices were typical acts or means of purification
from guilt; priests were the agents for accomplishing these acts,
and were not themselves accounted purer than the rest of the people, having consequently to bring offerings for their own sins, before they offered for those of the people. And lastly, Levitical
purity was the condition which was attained positively by sacrifice
and worship; and negatively by avoiding Levitical pollution—the
condition in which the people were enabled, by means of the
priests, to come into relation with God without dying (Deut. 5 :
26) : the result of the cultus which was past, and the postulate of
that which was to come. So that that which purified was sacrifice;

and the purification was the removal of guilt. . . . And hence a Christian Jew would never, on reading *katharismou poiein* (to make purification), think of what we call *moral amelioration*; which if not springing out of the living ground of a heart reconciled to God, is mere self-deceit, and only external avoidance of evident transgression. But the purification (*katharismos*) which Christ brought in, would, in the sense of our author and his readers, be understood only of that gracious atonement for all guilt of sin of all mankind, which Christ, our Lord and Savior, has completed for us by his sinless sufferings and death; and out of which flows forth to us, as from a fountain, all power to love in return, all love to Him our heavenly pattern, and all hatred of sin which caused his death."

It matters not, then, whether the words *"by himself"* (*dia heautou*) are genuine or spurious. If they were not expressed in the original, they are at least fairly and necessarily implied in it. This may be clearly shown by a reference to many parallel passages in both the Old and New Testaments. See, for instances, 7: 27; 9: 12, 26; 10: 10; John 1: 29; 1 Peter 2: 24; 1 John 3: 5.

**sat down on the right hand of the Majesty on high:**—The word *majesty* is used here to denote God himself; it means simply the Majestic One. *"On the right hand"* is a phrase indicating the place of highest honor and authority. See 1 Kings 2: 19; Psalm 45: 9; 80: 17; 110: 1; Matt. 20: 20-23; 26: 64, etc. And *"on high"* denotes a sphere far above all created heavens (Eph. 4: 10), where now dwells our Elder Brother filled with all the fullness of the Godhead (Col. 2: 9). In the beginning, "he was in the form of God, and thought it not robbery to be equal with God"; but, for the sake of redeeming mankind from the dominion of sin, death, and the grave, "he made himself of no reputation, and took upon him the form of a servant, and was found in the likeness of men; and being found in fashion as a man, he humbled himself and became obedient unto death, even the death of the cross. Wherefore God also hath highly exalted him, and given him a name which is above every name; that at the name of Jesus every knee should bow, of things in Heaven, and things in Earth, and things under the Earth; and that every tongue should confess that Christ is Lord to the glory of God the Father." (Phil. 2: 6-11.) Now, therefore, all authority in Heaven and on Earth is given to him (Matt. 28:

18) ; and he will reign over the entire universe (God the Father
only excepted), until he shall have put down all rule and all authority and power (1 Cor. 15 : 24). Then, and not till then, will he
deliver up the kingdom to the Father, "that God may be all and in
all."

How infinitely glorious, then, is the Son of God, our Immanuel,
through whom the Father has spoken to us "in the last of these
days"!  He is the Heir of all things; the Creator of all things; the
effulgence of the Father's glory, and the exact likeness of his substance.  He upholds all things by the word of his power.  And having in infinite condescension and love made expiation and purification for our sins by the sacrifice of himself, he now reigns over the
entire universe as King of kings and Lord of lords.  These are all
plain and simple words; but who is able to comprehend their full
and proper import?  Under such thoughts of the Infinite, the brain
staggers, and the mind itself becomes bewildered as it tries in vain
to comprehend the extent and magnitude of their immeasurable
fullness.  But here, as in other cases, "the Spirit helps our infirmities."  Knowing our incapacity to comprehend these matters
aright, it has still further amplified and explained them in the following paragraph.

## 2. THE SON OF GOD COMPARED WITH ANGELS
### 1 : 4-14

4 Being made ¹so much better than the angels, as he hath ²by inheritance
obtained a more excellent name than they.

¹Eph. i. 21; Col. i. 18; 1 Peter iii. 22.
²Psa. ii. 7, 8; Phil. ii. 9-11.

The object of the Apostle in this paragraph is twofold: (1) to
develop and illustrate still further the infinite perfections of Jesus
as the Son of God; and (2) to show as a consequence of his many
excellencies, the paramount obligations that we are all under to observe and respect the revelation which God has so graciously made
to us through him.  This will appear more obvious as we proceed
with the consideration of the several points that are brought out in
the following comparisons.

4 **Being made so much better than the angels,—**This clause
is very nearly related to the last part of the preceding verse; and it
is added for the purpose of defining and illustrating more fully the

5 For unto which of the angels said he at any time, ¹Thou art my Son, this day have I begotten thee? And again, ²I will be to him a Father, and he shall be to me a Son?

¹Chap. v. 5; Psa. ii. 7; Acts xiii. 33.
²2 Sam. vii. 14; 1 Chron. xvii. 13; xxii. 10; xxviii. 6; Psa. lxxxix. 26, 27.

---

infinite power, majesty, and dominion of our Redeemer. The reference here is still of course chiefly, though not exclusively, to the Divine nature of Christ. It is not of the man Jesus alone, nor of the Logos alone, but of the Logos incarnate, that our author speaks in this, and in the following verses of this chapter. And be it observed that here, as well as in the clause immediately preceding, the exaltation of Christ is spoken of as a result and consequence of his humiliation and his obedience unto death. The idea of the Apostle is, not that he was made better than the angels by his incarnation, but that having by himself made purification for our sins, and having been raised from the dead, the first-fruits of them that slept, he then *became* (*genoemnos*) in rank, dignity, and authority, superior (*kreitton*) to them: he was then exalted to a sphere of glory, dignity, and authority, which is as far above that of the highest angels, as the name which he inherited is superior to theirs.

**as he hath by inheritance obtained a more excellent name than they.**—Whenever God gives a name to anyone, he gives it in harmony with the rank and character of the person so designated. Previous to his incarnation, Jesus was called the Logos (John 1: 1), because he was himself both the medium and the substance of all the revelations which God had ever made to fallen man. But after his resurrection, when by virtue of his sufferings and death he was made the Heir of all things, it became necessary that he should receive a name corresponding with his new rank and official dignity, as the First-born from the dead (Col. 1: 18), the Beginning of the creation of God (Rev. 3: 14)—then it was that by right of inheritance he was called the Son of God. This name, as the Apostle proceeds to show, indicates that Christ, in his new relations, is far superior to the angels.

5 **For unto which of the angels said he at any time, Thou art my Son, this day have I begotten thee?**—That God the Father said this to Christ, when he raised him from the dead, and set him at his own right hand in the heavenly realms (Eph. 1: 20),

is evident from the second Psalm, and also from Paul's address at Antioch in Pisidia (Acts 13: 33, 34). But never was this name given in its full and proper meaning (John 5: 18) to any of the angels. True, indeed, they are all called sons of God (Job 33: 7); and so also are pious men and women called "the sons and daughters of the Lord God Almighty" (2 Cor. 6: 18). But no mere creature, however pure and exalted, was ever so singled out and distinguished from all others, by the Father of spirits. This is the peculiar honor of Him who is, not only one with the Father (John 10: 30), and who is himself God equal with the Father (John 5: 18), but who is also the First-begotten from the dead, the Prince of the kings of the Earth" (Rev. 1: 5). On him this title was repeatedly bestowed by the Father, with reference to both his incarnation and his resurrection. See Psalm 2: 7; Matt. 3: 17; 17: 5; Acts 13: 33, etc. But in this case, the Spirit refers particularly to his resurrection from the dead, when the Father not only gave him a name indicative of his Divinity and oneness with himself, but also at the same time exalted him "far above all principality, and power, and might, and dominion, and every name that is named, not only in this world, but also in that which is to come; and put all things under his feet, and give him to be the Head over all things to the Church, which is his body, the fullness of Him that filleth all in all" (Eph. 1: 21-23); angels, and authorities, and powers being made subject unto him" (1 Pet. 3: 22).

**And again, I will be to him a Father, and he shall be to me a Son?**—This is a quotation from 2 Samuel 7: 14, introduced here for the purpose of illustrating the very near, dear, and intimate relations which exist between the Father and the Son; with the view of showing still further the very great superiority of the Son over the angels. But there is an apparent difficulty in applying this passage to Christ; for it is quite obvious from the context, that primarily it had reference to Solomon. David, it seems, had purposed in his heart to build a house for the Lord God of Israel. But while he was meditating on the matter, God sent Nathan the Prophet to him, saying, "When thy days are fulfilled, and thou shalt sleep with thy Fathers, I will set up thy seed after thee, who shall proceed out of thy bowels, and I will establish his kingdom. He shall build a house for my name, and I will establish the throne of his kingdom forever. I will be his Father, and he shall be my

Son. If he commit iniquity, I will chasten him with the rod of men, and with the stripes of the children of men; but my mercy shall not depart from him, as I took it from Saul, whom I put away before thee." There can be no doubt, then, that this whole passage refers to Solomon; and so Solomon himself understood it, as we learn from 1 Kings 8: 17-21. How, then, can it with propriety be applied to Christ?

It is usual with many commentators to explain such passages on the principle of accommodation. But this will not do. No exposition of this passage of Scripture is at all admissible which does not make its meaning extend through and beyond Solomon to him who is, par excellence, the Seed of David according to the flesh; and who, as such, is to sit on David's throne, "to order it, and to establish it, with justice and with judgment, from henceforth even forever." (Isa. 9:7.) And hence the only way of explaining it properly is on the principle of double reference.

As a knowledge of this principle is essential to a proper understanding of much that is contained in this Epistle, the learned reader will excuse the following attempt to make it plain and intelligible to even mere beginners in the study of sacred literature. It is one of the very few principles of interpretation, which are peculiar to the Holy Scriptures. Generally, the Bible is to be interpreted like other books. But in the use of this principle, it is unlike any and every other document. The nearest approach to it may be found in the instructions which a skillful educator gives to his pupils by means of pictures and diagrams. For the purpose of illustrating the unknown or the abstract, he draws a visible outline or representation of it, by means of which he is enabled to impart to his pupils a more accurate knowledge of the object to be illustrated than he could possibly communicate to them by any mere combination of words and sentences. In his verbal remarks and explanations, he may sometimes refer exclusively to the pictorial illustration; and sometimes he may refer only to the object or thing that is to be illustrated; but not unfrequently he will purposely so arrange his remarks as to make them applicable to both the sign and the thing signified. He presents the picture to the eye of sense, as a sort of medium through which the eye of the understanding may perceive more clearly and distinctly the various qualities and properties of what he wished to describe and illustrate.

Very much in this way has God explained to mankind the more abstract and recondite realities of the economy of redemption. To do this successfully in the early ages of the world, in any way and by any means, was a very difficult problem; a problem which God alone was then capable of solving. But all things are possible with him. He resolved to give to mankind a revelation of his purpose of mercy concerning them; and he resolved to do it in such a way as would not only be best adapted to the purposes of instruction; but also, it would seem, in such a way that it could never be successfully imitated or counterfeited by any impostor.

For this purpose, he called Abraham out of Ur of Chaldea, and made him the Father of two families; the one according to the flesh, and the other according to the Spirit. The former was related to the latter, as the type is related to the antitype; or as the picture is related to the reality which it is designed to represent. And hence it is that many things said of the former in the Old Testament, have reference also to the latter. Sometimes, indeed, there are promises of an exclusive nature, made in reference to each of these. But not unfrequently what is said of the type, has reference also in a still higher sense, to the antitype. Of this we have many impressive examples in nearly all the books of the Old Testament. In the seventy-second Psalm, for example, David has given us a most graphic and interesting description of the peaceful and prosperous reign of Solomon; but throughout this beautiful ode there is also constant reference to a greater than Solomon.

And just so it is in the quotation made from 2 Sam. 7: 12-16. The primary reference here is to Solomon; and in part of the narrative it is to Solomon only; for certainly God would never, even hypothetically, impute iniquity to Christ. But in the expression, "I will be to him a Father, and he shall be to me a Son," God speaks both of Solomon as a type and of Christ in a far higher sense as the antitype. The relation of Solomon's sonship was, in fact, to that of Christ, just as the shadow is to the substance (Col. 2: 17) ; so that the meaning of the passage, properly understood, is in perfect harmony with the sentiment of the preceding clause. They both serve to present to us our blessed Savior in a relation that is peculiar to himself.

6 And again [1]when he bringeth in the firstbegotten into the world, he saith, And let all the angels of God worship him.

[1]Matt. x. 23; xvi. 28; Mark ix. 1; Luke ix. 27; Acts ii. 1-36; xi. 15.

6 **And again, when he bringeth, etc.**—To what does the adverb *again* (*palin*) here refer? Is it used here, as in the last part of the fifth verse, merely to indicate that this is another citation from the Old Testament? Or does it refer to a second introduction of the First-born into the world? On this point the critics are about equally divided. It is, however, generally conceded that the latter view is most in harmony with the Greek idiom and construction: and on this ground it is advocated by De Wette, Lünemann, Tholuck, Delitzsch, Alford, and most of the ancient interpreters.

But it is urged as an objection to this interpretation, that our author has not spoken elsewhere, in the preceding verses, of the *first* introduction of the First-born into the world; and that it is therefore not probable that he would here refer to the second, as such. And hence the former view (that the adverb *again* serves merely to introduce another quotation) is, on the whole, preferred by Luther, Calvin, Beza, Bleek, Ebrard, Stuart, and others, who think that there is really nothing in the Greek construction which seriously militates against this interpretation. According to their notion, the passage may be freely rendered as follows: "But when, on another occasion, God speaks of bringing the First-begotten into the world, he saith, And let all the angels of God worship him." And according to the second mode of constructing the adverb, the meaning runs thus: "But when God speaks of bringing the First-born a second time into the world, he saith, And let all the angels of God worship him." To my mind there is nothing in the latter rendering which is in any way inconsistent with either the Apostle's reasoning in the case, or with the general tenor of the Psalm from which he quotes. And I therefore see no reason for departing from what is generally conceded to be the most simple and natural construction of the Greek text.

**The First-born** refers of course to Christ. The same word (*prototokos*) occurs in Col. 1: 18 and Rev. 1: 5; in both of which passages, it means "the First-born from the dead"; having reference to the fact that Jesus was the first who rose from the dead to die no more. Others, as Lazarus (John 11), had risen before him; but not as he rose, above death and superior to it. They were still under the dominion of death, and soon returned again to the dust to see corruption. But Jesus rose a conqueror over death, and also over him who has the power of death. (2: 14.) And to this same thought there may be some allusion in our text, and also in such parallel passages as Psalm 89: 27; Rom. 8: 29; and Col. 1: 15. But in these cases, the primary reference is to the laws and customs of primogeniture; according to which the first-born was entitled to preeminence in all things. "For it pleased the Father that in him should all fullness dwell"; and "that in all things he should have the preeminence." (Col. 1: 18, 19.)

**into the world,**—The term *world* (*oichoumenee*) means properly *the inhabited earth; the habitable globe.* But to what bringing in of the First-born does the Apostle here refer? Some say to his incarnation (Chrysostom and Calvin); some to his entering on his public ministry, after his baptism, when the Holy Spirit descended on him like a dove, and the Father himself proclaimed from Heaven in the audience of the people, "This is my beloved Son, in whom I am well pleased"; some say that the reference is to his resurrection from the dead (Brentius and A. Clark); some, to his coming in power to set up his Kingdom on Earth, on the Pentecost which next followed after his resurrection (Grotius and Wetstein); and some again, to his second personal coming, when he will raise the dead, purify the Earth by fire, judge the world, and deliver up the Kingdom to the Father (De Wette, Lünemann, Tholuck, Hofmann, Delitzsch, Alford, etc.).

These several hypotheses, save perhaps the second, have all been maintained by men of learning and ability, and I therefore think it proper to introduce them to the reader. But to my mind, it is evident that it is to Christ's coming in power to set up his Kingdom and begin his reign on Earth, on the fiftieth day after his resurrection; and that it is to this alone, that the Holy Spirit here refers. To this view, I am led chiefly by the following considerations:

(1.) It is most in harmony with the construction and scope of both the text and the context. The adverb *again* (*palin*), as we have seen, indicates most naturally a return of the First-born into the world. And the scope of the Apostle's argument clearly indicates, that this second manifestation of the Lord Jesus would be with great power and authority. When he came into the world the first time (10: 5), he came in humility and weakness (Luke 2) ; for then it was necessary that he should by his own death make purification for sins (1: 3). But having done this once for all, it was then fit that he should enter on his mediatorial reign over Heaven and Earth; which he did on the Pentecost which next followed after his resurrection. To this reign our author has constant reference in this part of his argument. His object here is, not to show what Christ *was* previous to his coronation; nor is it to show what he *will be* after that he shall have delivered up the Kingdom to the Father (1 Cor. 15: 24) ; but it is to show what he *is now,* and what are now our obligations to love, serve, and obey him in all things. And hence we are required by the force of the Apostle's argument to understand this second coming of Christ as having reference to the beginning of his mediatorial reign.

(2.) This view is most in harmony with the scope of the ninety-seventh Psalm, from which this citation, in proof of Christ's superiority over the angels, is made. The Psalmist begins by calling on the whole Earth, even on the isles of the Gentiles, to be glad and rejoice on account of the universal reign of Jehovah (verse 1). In the second paragraph (verses 2-5), he describes the majesty of Jehovah as the Lord of the whole Earth; speaks of the justice and righteousness of his administration, and of the awful manifestations of his power and judgments, before which the Earth melts and his enemies are consumed. In the third (verses 6, 7), he speaks of the manifestations of God's glory, as it were, from the very heavens; predicts the embarrassment and confusion of all idolaters; and then calls on all in authority, all Eloheem, whether men or angels, to fall down and worship him. In the fourth (verses 8, 9), he speaks of the joy of all the saints, on witnessing the judgments and the glorious exaltation of their sovereign Lord. And finally (verses 10-12), he admonishes the pious to abstain from all evil; and encourages them to trust in the Lord and give thanks to him, on account of his gracious care over them, and the great abundance of the provisions which he has made for them. The whole Psalm, therefore, clearly indicates that it has reference to the long expected reign of the Messiah. And this is the view that was taken of it by many of the ancient Rabbis, as well as by most Christian expositors. Raschi and Kimchi say that all the Psalms, from 93 to 101, refer to the reign of the Messiah.

It is no objection to this interpretation, that the universal reign of Jehovah is the proper subject of this beautiful and triumphal ode; and that the name of the Messiah does not, in fact, occur in it. This is equally true of many other passages in the Old Testament, which, in the New, are applied directly to Christ. Take, for example, the following from Isa. 40: 3-5: "The voice of him that crieth in the wilderness, Prepare ye the way of the Lord; make straight in the desert a highway for our God. Every valley shall be exalted, and every mountain and hill shall be made low; and the crooked shall be made straight, and the rough places plain; and the glory of the Lord shall be revealed, and all flesh shall see it together; for the mother of the Lord hath spoken it." Here, too, as well as in the ninety-seventh Psalm, it is Jehovah Eloheem that is spoken of by the Prophet. And yet, in Matt. 3: 3, this passage is applied to Christ; who, in Jer. 23: 6, is called Jehovah our righteousness.

But it is alleged by some, that our author cannot have reference here to the ninety-seventh Psalm; because, say they, the proper rendering of the last clause of the sixth verse is, "Worship him all ye gods, and not all ye angels (*angeloi*)." This is plausible; but it is by no means a valid objection against the view taken. For in the Septuagint the word *Eloheem* is rendered *angels* in this very passage; and better still the same word *Eloheem* in Psalm 8: 5, is by the author of our Epistle rendered *angels* in 2: 7. "Thou hast made him a little lower," he says, "than the angels." Here the word rendered angels is in the Hebrew *Eloheem*, the same as that which occurs in Psalm 97: 7. So also Philo says, "The angels are the servants of God; and they are esteemed actual gods by those who are in toil and slavery." (Philo on Fugitives, Section 38.)

It is wholly unnecessary, therefore, to refer to Deut. 32: 43, for the quotation given in our text. True, indeed, the identical words, "Let all the angels of God worship him," are there found in the Septuagint; but they are wholly wanting in the original Hebrew; and are of course without canonical authority.

(3.) The view taken of the passage is also most in harmony with other portions of Scripture which relate to the coming and reign of the Messiah. Our Savior himself speaks of the inauguration of his reign on Earth, as his second coming into the world. "Verily, verily," says he, "I say unto you, there are some standing here who

shall not taste of death, till they see the Son of man coming in his
kingdom." (Matt. 16:28.) In this passage Christ has reference,
most likely, to both his transfiguration, which occurred eight days
afterward (Matt. 17: 1-13), and to his coming in power to set up
his Kingdom and begin his reign on earth, as he did on the day of
Pentecost which next followed after his resurrection (Acts 2: 1-
38). But if so, the former was but the shadow, while the latter
was the reality of what is here promised. And hence when Peter
had, on the latter occasion, submitted to his astonished auditors the
evidence of Christ's resurrection, he closed his address with the assurance that God had made Jesus, the lately crucified One, both
Lord and Christ; that is, the anointed Sovereign of the universe.
And, accordingly, from that day forward his right to universal dominion is everywhere conceded. See, for example, Acts 10: 36; 1
Cor. 15: 27; Eph. 1: 22; and Phil. 2: 9-11. The binding obligation of the decree of Jehovah with regard to the homage that is due
to his Son, as our anointed and mediatorial Sovereign, commenced,
therefore, with his coronation; and will continue, until having put
down all adverse power and authority, he shall deliver up the
Kingdom to the Father. Till then, every knee in Heaven and
Earth must bow to him, and every tongue must confess that he "is
Lord to the glory of God the Father" (Phil. 2:11).

**let all the angels of God worship him.**—This is, at least to us,
the main point of the argument. All that precedes this in the sixth
verse is only circumstantial; and does not in any way, however
construed, materially affect the sense of this clause. Even if we
should have mistaken the proper grammatical use of the word
*"again";* the chapter and verse of the Old Testament from which
the citation is made; and also the time of Christ's introduction
into the world as here spoken of; still the fact remains indisputable, that by the decree of Jehovah all the angels of glory are required to bow down and worship him who is the First-begotten
from the dead, the First-born of the whole creation. This is
enough for us. Resting as it does on apostolic authority, this one
declaration is, of itself, sufficient to prove, beyond all doubt, not
only that Jesus is infinitely exalted above all angels, but also that it
is now right and proper that all created intelligences should adore
and worship the Son, even as they also adore and worship the
Father.

7 And of the angels he saith, [1]Who maketh his angels spirits, and his ministers a flame of fire.

[1]2 Kings ii. 11; vi. 17; Psa. civ. 4; Ezek. i. 13, 14.

**7 And of the angels he saith,**—That is, while he speaks thus and so of the angels, he speaks in immeasurably higher terms of the Son. This will appear clear in the sequel. But what does he say of the angels?

**Who maketh his angels spirits, and his ministers a flame of fire.**—This is another instance of Hebrew parallelism taken from Psalm 104: 4. The words *angels* and *ministers* refer to the same class of persons, and their predicates "spirits" and "a flame of fire" are both used for a like purpose. But what do those clauses severally mean? Some commentators have proposed to change the order of the words, so as to make the clauses read thus: "Who maketh spirits [or winds] his angels; and a flame of fire his ministers." But this is scarcely allowable even in the Hebrew. To say that a flame of fire is the ministers of God, is not in harmony with the laws of propriety in any language. But in our Greek text the absurdity of this rendering is still more obvious. For (1) the proper subject of the parallelism is *angels*. The object of the Apostle is to contrast these high celestial intelligences, and not spirits, or winds, or a flame of fire, with Christ. (2) The use of the Greek article before *angels* (*tous angelous*) and *ministers* (*tous leitourgous*), and not before *spirits* (*pneumata*) and a *flame of fire* (*puror phloga*), clearly indicates that the former words are to be taken as the subjects, and the latter as the predicates of the phrases in which they severally stand. And hence we are compelled to accept the arrangements of these words as given in our English Version.

But what is the meaning of the word *pnūmata* (*pneumata*) in the first clause? Does it mean *spirits,* as in our Common Version, or does it mean *winds*, as some have alleged? This must be determined by the scope of the passage, which evidently is, not to degrade, but to exalt the angels as far as possible, with the view of exalting the Son still higher by the comparison. To say, then, that God makes his angels as strong and as irresistible as winds and

tempests, would harmonize very well with the Apostle's design;
and also with the scope and construction of the next clause in
which God's ministers are compared, not merely with fire, but with
a flame of fire. But in this case, though the word *ruach* might have
been used in the Hebrew, it is most likely that it would have been
rendered by the Greek *anemos*, as in Ex. 10: 13, 19; 14: 21, etc.,
and not by *pnūma,* the current meaning of which in both classic
and sacred literature, is *breath* or *spirit.* Seldom, if ever, does it
denote a violent wind or tempest, unless when used figuratively, as
in Ex. 15:8, 10, for the breath of Jehovah.

Much more, then, in harmony with the context and general
usage is the word *spirit* as given in our English Version.
Throughout the entire Bible, the word *spirit* often stands in antithesis with the word *flesh;* the latter being used symbolically for
whatever is weak, frail, depraved, and corruptible; and the former,
in like manner; for what is strong, pure, and incorruptible. "That
which is born of the flesh," says Christ, "is flesh; and that which is
born of the Spirit is spirit." (John 3: 6.) And again he says,
"God is spirit; and they that worship him must worship him in
spirit and in truth." (John 4: 24.) And again, "It is the Spirit
that quickeneth; the flesh profiteth nothing." (John 6: 63.) In no
other way, therefore, could our author more effectually exalt the
angels in the estimation of his Hebrew brethren than by calling
them *spirits;* that is, beings "who excel in strength," and who are
wholly removed from all the weaknesses, impurities, and imperfections of the flesh.

This, too, corresponds well with the history of these pure celestial intelligences, so far as it is given in the Holy Scriptures.
They have always served as God's ministers (*leitourgoi*), before
whom the enemies of Jehovah have often melted away as wax or
stubble before a flame of fire. This is abundantly proved and illustrated by the overthrow of Sodom and Gomorrah (Gen. 19: 1-
26); the destruction of the first-born of the Egyptians (Ex. 12:
29, 30); the punishment of the Israelites under David (2 Sam. 24,
15-17); the discomfiture of the hosts of Benhadad, King of Syria
(2 Kings 6: 8-23); and the overthrow of the army of Sennacherib
(2 Kings 19: 35).

8 But unto the Son he saith, [1]Thy throne, [2]O God, is [3]forever and ever; [and,] [4]a scepter of righteousness is the scepter of thy kingdom.

[1]Psa. xlv. 6, 7.
[2]Isa. ix. 6, 7; Jer. xxiii. 6; John i. 1-3; v. 18; x. 30, 33.
[3]Dan. ii. 44; 1 Cor. xv. 25; 2 Pet. i. 11.
[4]Psa. lxxii. 1-4; Isa. ix. 7; xxxii. 1, 2.

8 **But unto the Son he saith, etc.**—The quotation which follows in this verse and the next, is taken from the forty-fifth Psalm; on the meaning of which commentators are still much divided. Many suppose that this Psalm was designed primarily to celebrate the marriage of Solomon with the daughter of Pharaoh or some other foreign princess; and secondarily to foreshadow and illustrate, by means of this conjugal alliance, the union that exists between Christ and his Church. But it is difficult to see how this Psalm could with any propriety be applied to Solomon. He was not "blessed forever" as was the hero of this ode (verse 2); nor was he in any sense distinguished for his victories (verses 3-5); neither was his administration throughout one of justice and equity (verses 6, 7); nor did he ever make his sons princes in the Earth (verse 16). It is extremely doubtful also whether what is said of the queen and her companions (verses 9-15) can with truth and propriety be applied to any of the wives and concubines of Solomon. And hence it is most likely that the forty-fifth Psalm is a simple allegory designed to celebrate, primarily and exclusively, the perfections, conquests, and righteous administration of Christ; to illustrate the intimate and sanctified union which exists between himself and his Church; and to set forth, in the most pleasing and impressive manner, the happy and eternal consequences of this very holy and endearing relationship. That the marriage of Solomon, or some other king of Israel, may have suggested the form and much of the imagery of the Psalm, is quite probable. But it is most likely that the protasis of this allegory, like that of the parable of the ten virgins, was constructed from the conceptions of the writer. It is an ideal representation of certain realities in the grand drama of redemption which could not be so well illustrated by any one chapter of real history.

The Psalmist begins with a brief statement of the effect which, under the influence of the Holy Spirit, his great theme was having on his own mind and heart. My heart, he says, is overflowing. I am saying a good word. My works are for the King. My tongue

9. Thou hast ¹loved righteousness, and ²hated iniquity; therefore God,

¹Chap. vii. 26; Psa. xxxiii. 5; xl. 8, 9; xlv. 7.
²Rom. xii. 9; Rev. ii. 6, 15.

is the pen of a ready writer. Next, he describes the personal loveliness, grace, and blessedness of the royal Bridegroom. Beautiful,
beautiful, art thou, above the sons of men. Grace is poured upon
thy lips. Therefore, God hath blessed thee forever. In the third,
fourth, and fifth verses, he speaks of the King as a great military
hero. Gird thy sword on thy thigh, O mighty One; [put on] thy
honor and thy majesty; and in thy majesty go forward, ride on,
for the sake of truth, humility, and righteousness; and thy right
hand shall teach thee terrible things. Thy arrows are sharp in the
heart of the King's enemies; nations shall fall under thee. Next in
order is the given quotation from which our author infers the great
superiority of Christ over the angels: "Thy throne, God, is forever
and ever; a scepter of righteousness is the scepter of thy kingdom."

9 **Thou hast loved righteousness, etc.**—The inspired Psalmist,
whoever he was, spoke of course the words of God; and hence our
author justly ascribes these stanzas to God himself as their author.
Viewed in this light they clearly indicate the superior rank and exaltation of Christ, in the following particulars: (1) He is here
called God by the Father himself; and that, too, not as angels and
magistrates are sometimes called gods, in a metaphorical sense, but
in the literal and proper sense of this word as it is applied to the
uncreated, eternal, and omnipresent Deity. The context fairly admits of no other meaning in this case. And this interpretation is
fully sustained by many parallel passages. See remarks on verses
third, fifth, and sixth. (2) His reign is eternal. The word *throne*
indicates power, rule, and dominion. And hence to say that the
throne of the Messiah "is forever and ever" is but to say that "his
dominion is an everlasting dominion." (Dan. 7 : 4.) True, in one
sense, his reign will terminate "when he shall have put down all
rule, and all authority, and power." Then, we are told, "he will
deliver up the Kingdom to the Father, that God may be all in all."
(1 Cor. 15 : 24.) But this is spoken of his mediatorial reign over
the universe for the redemption and recovery of mankind. In another sense, however, "he will reign over the house of Jacob forever; and of his Kingdom there shall be no end." (Luke 1 : 33.)

even ¹thy God, hath ²anointed thee with the ³oil of gladness above ⁴thy fellows.

¹John xx. 17; 1 Pet. i. 3.
²Psa. ii. 2. 6; Isa. lxi. 1; Luke iv. 18; Acts iv. 27; x. 38.
³Psa. xxiii. 5; Isa. lxi. 3.
⁴Isa. ix. 7; Hos. iii. 5.

And hence, Peter speaks of "the everlasting Kingdom of our Lord and Savior Jesus Christ." (2 Pet. 1 : 11.) (3) His administration is throughout one of absolute justice and rectitude. The word rendered *scepter* (*rabdos*) originally meant a rod or staff. But in the hands of the ancient patriarchs and shepherds, this scepter soon became a badge of their authority; and in the hands of kings it afterward became an emblem of royal authority. (Esth. 4 : 11.) And hence the word is used in our text to denote Christ's power and authority over all. And as his entire administration is carried on in justice and in judgment, his scepter is called "a scepter of rectitude." (4) In consequence of his exalted rank, immaculate holiness, and the righteous character of his administration, God has himself anointed him with the oil of joy and gladness above his associates. *"The oil of joy"* is a figurative expression derived from the Oriental custom of anointing the head at important festivals (Psalm 23 : 5). Here, the reference is to the joyful effects of Christ's coronation. But who are his *fellows?* Some say the angels (Bleek, Lünemann, Pierce); others think that the reference is to his disciples, all of whom are in fellowship with him (Braun, Cranmer); but as Christ is here described as a king, it is most likely that the Psalmist refers to kings as the associates of Christ (Ebrard, Alford, etc.). These were anointed with oil (1 Sam. 9 : 16; 16 : 3; 1 Kings 1 : 34); but Christ was anointed with the Holy Spirit and with power (Isa. 61 : 1-3; Acts 10 : 38). They were anointed simply as kings; but Christ was anointed as a Prophet and as a Priest, as well as a King.

From these facts and illustrations, it is now easy to see the bearing of the whole passage on the Apostle's argument. The angels, he admits, are beings of very high rank and of very great power and influence. But they are not gods, save in a metaphorical sense. Neither are they kings, like our Immanuel, reigning over the universe. On the contrary, as our author now proceeds to show, they are all but ministering spirits, sent forth under Christ to do his will in ministering to the heirs of salvation.

10 And, ¹Thou, Lord, ²in the beginning ³hast laid the foundation of the
earth; and ⁴the heavens are the works of thine hands:

¹Psa. cii. 25-27.
²Gen. i. 1; John i. 1.
³Isa. xlviii. 13; li. 13; Jer. xxxii. 17.
⁴Psa. viii. 3; xix. 1.

10 **And, Thou, Lord, in the beginning**—The word *"and"* is
used here by the author to connect the three following with the
two preceding verses; so that the tenth, eleventh, and twelfth
verses, as well as the eighth and ninth, are to be taken and construed as the testimony of God the Father, speaking by the mouth
of one of his holy Prophets concerning his Son Jesus Christ.

But here again there is an apparent difficulty in applying these
words to the Son of God. The citation is made from Psalm 102:
25-27; and seems to refer primarily, not to the Son of God, as such,
but to God himself absolutely considered. Some, I know, are of a
different opinion. They think that there are in this Psalm sundry
indications that it is a complaint of the Church, in her afflictions,
addressed directly to her ever living and exalted Head, in the person of our adorable Redeemer. And this may be so. Certainly
some of the expressions contained in this Psalm (see particularly
verses 18-22) appear to be spoken of the reign of the Messiah over
all the Earth. But the first impression of all who read this Psalm
without prejudice, is, that it was primarily addressed to Eloheem
Jehovah, the Lord God absolute.

On what principle, then, is it here applied to Christ? Some say
again, "On the principle of accommodation." But this is manifestly wrong. The argument of the Apostle clearly requires more
than this. His object here is, not to teach us what might be said of
the Lord Jesus, but rather what the Father himself has actually
said of him in the writings of the holy Prophets. On no other hypothesis would our author be justified in quoting and applying this
passage as he does.

How, then, is this matter to be explained? Will it do to say
with some that "whatever is predicated of God the Father may also
in like manner be predicated of the Son and of the Holy Spirit?"
Certainly not; save within certain well defined limits. The Father
has his own proper personality, and performs his own proper work
in creation, providence, and redemption. And this is also true of
the Son and of the Holy Spirit. The Father sent the Son to be the

Savior of the world. (1 John 4: 14.) The Son, by the grace of
God, tasted death for every man; and so made it possible for God
to be just in justifying everyone who believes in Jesus. (John 3:
16; Rom. 3: 25, 26.) He also sent the Holy Spirit to convince the
world of sin, of righteousness, and of judgment (John 16: 8-11) ;
and to be in all his saints as a well of water springing up into everlasting life (John 4: 14; 7: 38, 39). In some respects, therefore,
the Father, Son, and Holy Spirit are essentially distinct from each
other, and perform different functions in the economy of grace.
But in other respects they are identical, one and essentially the
same. "I and my Father," says Christ, "are one." (John 10: 30;
14: 9-11.) And hence it is that in the Old Testament especially,
they are all commonly included in the one name Eloheem Jehovah
(Deut. 6: 4) ; and that the same works are often ascribed equally
to each of the three. In Gen. 1: 1, for example, it is said that God
(Eloheem) created the heavens and the Earth; that is, the whole
material universe. But in Rev. 4: 8-11, the creation of all things
is ascribed to the Father; in John 1: 1-3, it is ascribed to the Son;
and from sundry other passages, such as Gen. 1: 2; Job 26: 13;
Psalm 104: 30; Matt. 12: 28; Luke 1: 35; John 6: 63; and Rom.
8: 11, it seems clear that the Holy Spirit has an agency in the
working of all miracles.

On the principle of identity in the Godhead, then, it seems to
me, our author here applies to the Son language which, in its first
intention, had reference to the entire Eloheem—the Father, the
Son, and the Holy Spirit. As on another occasion Eloheem said,
Let *us* make man in *our* image, after *our* likeness; so also it was in
the beginning. It was not the Father alone, nor the Son alone, nor
the Spirit alone; but it was the three in one, and the one in three,
that created and garnished the heavens and the Earth. And hence
it is perfectly legitimate to say as our author has said here, "Thou,
Lord, in the beginning, didst lay the foundation of the Earth, and
the heavens are the works of thy hands."

But whatever may be true of the principle on which this language is applied to the Son of God, the fact itself, as here stated, is
indisputable. Guided by the Spirit of God, the author of our Epistle here deposes, that this is the testimony of God the Father himself with respect to his Son. This, then, is enough. All who
admit the inspiration and canonical authority of the Epistle, must

11 They ¹shall perish; but ²thou remainest; and they all ³shall wax old as doth a garment;

¹Isa. lxv. 17; 2 Pet. iii. 7-10; Rev. xxi. 1.
²Psa. xc. 2; Rev. i. 11, 17, 18; ii. 8.
³Isa. l. 9; li. 6-8.

also admit, that our Redeemer is the Creator of the heavens and of the Earth. And if he is, then it follows that he is Divine, "God with us."

The words of these two clauses are, in the main, quite simple and easily understood. The word *Lord* is not expressed in the original Hebrew, but it is clearly implied. *"In the beginning"* (*kata archas*) means simply *of old.* The phrase is not so definite as the expression in Gen. 1 : 1 (*en archee*); but it is here equivalent to it; and it means simply that at a certain epoch in past eternity, the Son, in connection and cooperation with the Father and the Holy Spirit, did actually create the whole material universe. To found the Earth, is equivalent to creating it. Christ is here presented to us as the great architect of nature. In this capacity, he is represented as laying the foundations of the Earth; not, however, as a human architect, out of preexisting materials: but *ex nihilo,* out of nothing: for things which are seen were not made out of things which do appear. (11 : 3.) The word *heavens* is in the plural number, and in connection with the word *earth* means at least the whole material universe. In the words, "thy hands," we have an example of anthropomorphism.

11 **They shall perish;**—That is, most likely, both the heavens and the Earth shall perish. But what is meant by the word *perish* (*apollumi*)? Does it mean that the heavens and the Earth will hereafter be annihilated? Or does it mean simply that they will be destroyed with respect to their present state? The latter is most likely all that is here intended by the Holy Spirit. Neither the Hebrew word nor the Greek ever means to annihilate, so far as we know. Nor have we any evidence either from the book of nature, or from the Holy Scriptures, that God will ever annihilate any substance to which he has given being. This he, of course, can do; and this he may do. No creature can foretell what changes God will work in nature, in the course of coming ages. But it is most likely from all the evidence of the context, as well as from parallel passages, that our author refers here only to those changes of form

and state which will be necessary in order to refit and readjust the material universe to the wants and progressive developments of the spiritual.   Such changes often have taken place; and it is quite probable that they will often occur hereafter; perhaps indeed while the cycles of eternal ages shall continue to roll on.

It is now, for instance, generally conceded by geologists, that the Earth was originally created in a state of igneus fusion; and that by the cooling process were formed vast quantities of granite, porphyry, and other kinds of unstratified rocks.   But at the proper time, God effected a change on the whole surface of the Earth; and so adapted it to the growth of vegetables and animals.   Another period of immense duration passed by, during which vast deposits of various kinds were laid up for the use of man; and then the Earth with all its living tenantry was again destroyed.   And this occurred again and again; until finally out of the preadamic chaos God prepared the heavens and the Earth which now are; and which Peter says "are kept in store, reserved unto fire against the day of judgment"; when, he says, "the heavens shall pass away with a great noise, and the elements shall melt with fervent heat; the Earth also and the works that are therein shall be burnt up." But he adds, "Nevertheless we, according to his promise, look for new heavens and a new Earth, wherein dwelleth righteousness." (2 Pet. 3: 7, 10, 13.) See also Isa. 65: 17 and Rev. 21: 1-8.

By the word *heavens* in 2 Pet. 3: 10, the Apostle most likely means only the aerial heavens, as does Moses in Gen. 1: 8; and not the sidereal heavens to which the Psalmist and our author manifestly refer in our text.   The object of Peter is to describe the final change which will take place in our own mundane system, "when the Lord Jesus shall be revealed from Heaven with his mighty angels, in flaming fire, taking vengeance on them that know not God, and that obey not the Gospel of our Lord Jesus Christ." (2 Thess. 1: 7, 8.)   But changes analogous to those wrought in our own planet, may also occur in every other planet and system throughout the vast empire of Jehovah.   Indeed we are not wholly without evidence that such is the fact.   Astronomers tell us that changes are now taking place in the Moon, similar to those which occurred in the preadamic Earth.   And the history of astronomy records instances of celestial configurations, not unlike that which, according to the Apostle Peter, awaits our own world.   A very re-

12 And as a vesture shalt thou fold them up, and they shall be changed: but [1]thou art the same, and [2]thy years shall not fail.

13 But to which of the angels said he at any time, [3]Sit on my right hand, [4]until I make thine enemies thy footstool?

[1]Ch. xiii. 8; Ex. iii. 14; John viii. 58; Jas. i. 17; Rev. i. 8, 11.
[2]Psa. cx. 4.
[3]Psa. cx. 1; Matt. xxii. 44.
[4]Psa. xxi. 8, 9; 1 Cor. xv. 25, 26; Rev. xix. 11-21; xx. 15.

---

markable instance of this kind occurred in A.D. 1572, when suddenly a star shone forth in the constellation Cassiopeia, exceeding in brilliancy the largest of the planets; and after blazing for some months, it gradually disappeared forever. Another example of the same kind occurred in A.D. 1604, in the constellation Ophiuchus. The flame, at first, was of a dazzling white color; then of a reddish yellow; and finally it was of a leaden paleness. These phenomena are not so rare as many suppose. Dr. Good says, "During the last century, not less than thirteen stars seem to have utterly perished; and ten new ones have been created."

These facts may serve to illustrate what seems to be here revealed to us by the Holy Spirit: viz., that all the suns, and moons, and stars, and systems, composing the sidereal heavens, are destined to undergo changes similar to those through which our own little mundane system is passing; and that in the course of ages, they will all wax old as doth a garment; and that our Redeemer will roll them up and recast them, as men are wont to change and recast worn-out vestments. But throughout all these changes and revolutions, he himself will remain unchanged; "the same yesterday, to-day, and forever." (13 : 8.)

12 **And as a vesture shalt thou fold them up,**—This verse is but an amplification of what is given in the preceding. The Psalmist, in order to give intensity to the thought, repeats the sentiment that while the material universe becomes old, and changes as a garment, Christ, the Creator of all things, will endure forever, without even the shadow of change.

Here, then, it is clearly taught (1) that Christ is the Creator of all things; (2) that he is the immutable Lord and Governor of all things; and consequently, that he is infinitely superior to the angels.

13 **But to which of the angels, etc.**—Our author now proceeds to lay the keystone of his argument, in vindicating the superiority

14 Are they not all ¹ministering spirits, ²sent forth to minister for them who shall be ³heirs of salvation?

¹Psa. ciii. 20, 21; Matt. xiii. 41, 49, 50; xviii. 10.
²Psa. xxxiv. 7; xci. 11, 12; Dan. vi. 22; Matt. xxiv. 31; Luke xvi. 22; Acts v. 19; x. 3, 4.
³Matt. xxv. 34; Rom. viii. 17; Gal. iii. 29; 1 Pet. i. 4; iii. 7.

of Christ over the holy angels. For this purpose he refers to Psalm 110: 1, where David speaking by the Spirit says, "Jehovah said to my Lord, Sit on my right hand, until I make thine enemies thy footstool"; that is, until through your administration I shall have completely vanquished all who resist my authority, whether they be men or angels. It was a custom with ancient kings and princes to tread on the necks of their vanquished enemies, in token of their complete victory over them. See Josh. 10: 22-25. This symbol of conquest is often found in the paintings of the ancient Egyptians.

The word *Lord* (*Kurios*) in this citation refers to the Messiah. This is obvious from the scope and structure of the Psalm itself, and also from the repeated references that are made to it in the New Testament. See Matt. 22: 41-46; Mark 12: 35-37; Luke 20: 41-44; Acts 2: 34; 1 Cor. 15: 25; Heb. 5: 6; 7: 17, 21; 10: 13. Indeed, the first of these references, Matt. 22: 41-46, is quite sufficient to satisfy every unprejudiced mind, that this is a Messianic Psalm; and that the address of Jehovah, given in the first verse, was made directly to his Son. "While the Pharisees were gathered together," says Matthew, "Jesus asked them, saying, What think ye of Christ? whose son is he? They say unto him, The son of David. He said unto them, How then doth David in Spirit call him Lord, saying, Jehovah said to my Lord, Sit on my right hand, till I shall have put thy enemies beneath thy feet? If David then calls him Lord, how is he his son?"

It is evident, therefore, that God has honored his Son by assigning to him the place of highest honor and authority, until he shall have completely subjugated all his and our enemies. But no such honor as this was ever conferred on an angel. On the contrary, as he says,—

14 **Are they not all ministering spirits, etc.?**—The interrogative mode of expression, as it occurs in this verse, is not used to indicate any doubt or uncertainty on the part of the writer, but just the reverse. It is a figure of speech, often used in all writings, sacred and profane, to express an obvious truth in the most

pointed and forcible manner. See, for example, Balaam's reply to Balak, Num. 23 : 19, and God's reply to Job, given in chapters 38, 39, 40, and 41. There can be no doubt, then, that all the angels, of whatever rank and order, are now ministers of Christ; and that they are sent forth, under him, to minister in behalf of those who are about to inherit salvation. The Apostle does not mean to say that the angels have all actually left the realms of light, and come to this world to minister to the saints. This is no doubt true of many of them. But the words of the Apostle do not of necessity imply that it is true of them all. His meaning is more general. What he intends to say is simply this: that under Christ, it is now the business of all angels, from the highest to the lowest, to aid in the work of redeeming man; and in carrying out this work to its final consummation. Some of them may be sent to frustrate the wiles and devices of Satan and his fallen compeers (Jude 6); some, to punish wicked men (Gen. 19: 1-26; 2 Kings 19: 35; Acts 12: 23); some, to preside over the councils and courts of princes (Dan. 10: 20, 21; 11: 1; 12: 1); some, to aid providentially in bringing men to repentance (Acts 10: 1-8); some, to take care of the living saints (2 Kings 6: 15-23; Psalm 34: 7; 91: 11; Dan. 3; 25-28; 6: 22; Matt. 18: 10; Acts 5: 19; 12: 7-10); some, to comfort dying saints and to bear their spirits home to glory (Luke 16: 22); some may peradventure remain in Heaven to minister to the spirits of the just made perfect; and some may go, as Christ's ambassadors, to other worlds, to assist in there executing his decrees and purposes. But as the mediatorial reign of Christ, though extending over all worlds, is designed primarily and chiefly for the redemption of man, so also is the ministration of the countless myriads of angels that serve under him. They are all sent forth to minister in some way, directly or indirectly, for the benefit of those who are the heirs of salvation.

This is the end of our author's first argument drawn from the exalted rank and character of our blessed Lord and Redeemer. He has yet much to say of him in many respects. But being himself deeply impressed with a sense of the obligations which all men are under to love, honor, and obey such a Savior; and perceiving at the same time the dreadful consequences of their neglecting to do so; he suddenly breaks off from his direct line of argument, and draws from his submitted premises the conclusion which follows.

### 3. DANGER OF NEGLECTING WHAT GOD HAS
### REVEALED TO US THROUGH HIS SON
### 2 : 1-4

1 [1]Therefore we ought to give [2]the more earnest heed to the things which we have heard, lest at any time [3]we should let them slip.

[1]Ch. xii. 25, 26.
[2]Deut. iv. 9, 23; Prov. ii. 1-6.
[3]Ch. iv. 1; Matt. xiii. 18-22.

1 **Therefore we ought, etc.**—The word *therefore* (*dia touto*) is illative, and forms the hinge of the Apostle's argument. It is the connecting link between the conclusion which follows, and all that he has said in the preceding chapter, touching the revelation which God has made to us through his only begotten Son. He argues that since it is an indisputable fact, that God has spoken to us by his Son, who is himself the Heir of all things, the Creator of all things, and the Upholder of all things; the brightness of the Father's glory and the express image of his essence; and since he is himself the expiator of our guilt, endowed with all the attributes of Divinity, and infinitely exalted above all angels, it follows, of course, that "we should give the more earnest heed to the things which we have heard" from the Father through him and concerning him. The Apostle proceeds here on the assumption that wherever much is given, there also much is always justly expected and required. (Luke 12 : 47, 48; Matt. 11 : 20-24.) And hence he measures the greater extent of our obligations to give heed to the things spoken, both by the greater fullness of these revelations and also by the greater dignity of him through whom they have been made to us. According to our author, there is resting on every man who hears the Gospel, an obligation to receive and obey it, that is commensurate with the infinitely exalted character of Christ.

**the things which we have heard,**—By these are meant simply the facts, precepts, promises, warnings, and threatenings of the Gospel. They are of course very numerous; but the following brief summary of the main points may suffice for illustration. It seems, then, (1) that God made man upright, in his own image and after his own likeness; pure, holy, and happy. (Gen. 1 : 26, 27; Eccles. 7 : 29; Eph. 4 : 24; Col. 3 : 9, 10.) (2) That Adam fell by disobedience, bringing death upon himself and on his entire posterity. (Gen. 3 : 1-19; Rom. 5 : 12, 18, 19; 1 Cor. 15 : 21, 22.) (3)

That in this fallen condition, man was morally helpless, unable to do anything whatever either to please God (Rom. 8: 8), or to save himself from the incurred penalty of God's violated law. (Rom. 3: 20; 8: 13-25.) (4) That while mankind were all in this deplorable and helpless condition, God mercifully interposed in their behalf, and provided for them a remedy; a remedy perfectly suited to their wants; and which at the same time meets the requirements of his own government so far that he can now be just in justifying everyone who truly believes in Jesus. (John 3: 16; Rom. 3: 21-31.) (5) That for the purpose of perfecting this plan of Divine mercy, and carrying it into effect for the salvation of the world, the Son of God himself became incarnate (John 1: 14); tasted death for every man (2 Cor. 5: 14, 15; 1 Tim. 2: 6); was buried and rose again the third day, according to the Scriptures (1 Cor. 15: 1-4); reascended to the heavens (Acts 1: 9); offered his own blood in the Holy of holies not made with hands (9: 12, 24); and was then crowned Lord of all, "angels, and authorities, and powers being made subject to him" (1 Pet. 3: 22). (6) That he then, according to his promise, sent the Holy Spirit to qualify the Apostles for the work of their mission (John 16: 13; Acts 1: 8); to convince the world of sin, and of righteousness, and of judgment (John 16: 7-11); and to dwell in his saints as their comforter and sanctifier (Rom. 8: 11; 1 Cor. 6: 19; Gal. 4: 6; Eph. 4: 18), helping their infirmities (Rom. 8: 26), and strengthening them with might even into the inner man (Eph. 3: 16). (7) That salvation from all past personal transgressions is now promised to all who truly believe in Christ; confess his name before men, repent of their sins; and who, in obedience to the authority of Christ, are baptized into the name of the Father, and of the Son, and of the Holy Spirit. (Mark 16: 16; Acts 2: 38; Rom. 10: 10.) (8) That all who are thus received into the Kingdom of Heaven on Earth, and who continue to give all diligence in walking soberly and righteously and godly in this present world, will ultimately be admitted into the everlasting Kingdom of our Lord and Savior Jesus Christ. (2 Pet. 1: 5-11.) (9) That those who neglect the Gospel, and obey not the truth, but obey unrighteousness, will be finally banished with an everlasting destruction from the presence of the Lord and from the glory of his power. (2 Thess. 1: 9; Rev. 20: 11-15.) Such is a very brief summary of

2 For if ¹the word spoken by angels was steadfast, and ²every transgression and disobedience received a just ³recompense of reward;

¹Deut. xxxiii. 2; Psa. lxviii. 17; Acts vii. 53; Gal. iii. 19.
²Ex. xxxii. 27, 28; Lev. x. 1, 2; Num. xi. 33; xiv. 28-37; xv. 32-36; xvi. 31-35;
1 Cor. x. 5-12.
³Ch. x. 35; xi. 26.

the things which we have heard from God through his Son and his
own chosen Apostles; and to which our author would have us give
the more earnest heed.

**lest at any time we should let them slip.**—Or rather, lest
perchance we should be drifted away from them (*pararruomen*
aor. 2, sub. pass); "as a ship," says Luther, "shoots away into destruction." Our author represents us all as on a stream, the natural tendency of which is to carry us downward to ruin. If it is any
one's purpose to go there with the devil and his angels, it is an
easy matter for him to do so. No exertion on his part is at all
necessary. Like a man that is afloat above the falls of Niagara, he
has but to fold his arms, give himself up to the natural current, and
very soon he will be beyond the reach of mercy. But the man who
would reach the haven of eternal rest must of necessity make an
effort. He must lay hold of all the means and helps which God
has graciously provided and offered to him in the Gospel; or otherwise, he must soon perish forever. "Strive," says Christ, "to enter
in at the strait gate; for many, I say unto you, will seek to enter in
and shall not be able." (Luke 13: 24.) Why not? Because they
do not strive until it is too late; until they have allowed themselves
to be carried away beyond the proper limits of safety and security.
"When once the Master of the house," he says, "is risen up, and
has shut the door," then all cries for help and mercy will be in
vain. See Luke 13: 25-28; Prov. 1: 24-28; and Matt. 25: 11-13.
And hence the necessity of making our calling and election sure (2
Pet. 1: 10) by now giving diligent heed to the things which we
have heard.

2 **For if the word spoken by angels was steadfast,**—The
Apostle now proceeds to give a reason for what he has so strongly
urged in the preceding verse, viz., that we should give the more
earnest heed to the things which we have heard from God through
his own well beloved Son. This he insists we should all do in view
of our greater responsibilities. For if the law which God gave to
the Israelites through the ministration of angels was steadfast, and

3 [1]How shall we escape, if we neglect [2]so great salvation; which at the

[1]Ch. xii. 25; Matt. xxiii. 33; 1 Pet. iv. 17, 18.
[2]Ch. v. 9; vii. 25; John iii. 16-18; Acts iv. 12; 1 Tim. i. 15; Titus ii. 11.

every positive transgression (*parabosis*) of it, and even every mishearing or neglect (*parachioee*) of it received a just recompense (*misthopodosia, a paying off of wages,* a requital in the sense of either reward or punishment), then, how, he asks, can we escape unpunished, if we neglect the fuller and more gracious means of salvation which God has offered to us in the Gospel? This mode of reasoning is what logicians call "a minori ad majus;" from the less to the greater. The argument rests on the assumption that an increase of light and privileges implies also an increase of responsibility on our part.

That "the word spoken by angels" means the Sinaitic Law, is quite obvious from sundry other passages of Scripture as well as from the context. Paul, for example, writing to the Galatians, says, the Law "was ordained by angels in the hand of a mediator" (Gal. 3: 19); that is, it was promulgated through the intervention of angels, and by the hand of Moses acting as a mediator between God and the people. See also Deut. 33: 2; Psalm 68: 17; and Acts 7: 53. It is evident, therefore, that angels were present at the giving of the Law from Mount Sinai, and that they performed some part in its promulgation, as the Jewish Doctors believed and taught. (Joseph. Ant. 15: 5, 3). But in what that part consisted is not so clear. Nor is it at all necessary that we should understand this. (Deut. 29: 29.) It is revealed that the angels served as God's ministers, in some capacity, in the giving of the Law from Sinai; and it is further revealed that every objective transgression of that Law, and even every subjective neglect of it, received its just punishment. The man, for instance, who was found gathering sticks on the Sabbath-day, was stoned to death (Num. 15: 32-36); and the man who would presumptuously neglect to hear the instructions and warnings of the Priest, touching the requirements of the Law, even that man was to be put to death (Deut. 17: 12, and 27: 26). This, then, being so, how fearfully great are our responsibilities under the superior light of the Gospel; and how very penetrating and heart-searching is the following interrogatory.

3 **How shall we escape, etc.**—In what way, and by what means shall we escape the just recompense of our neglect? If there was

first ³began to be spoken by the Lord, and ⁴was confirmed unto us by them that heard him;

³Matt. iv. 17; Mark i. 14; John i. 18.
⁴Matt. xxviii. 19, 20; Acts ii. 14-40; iii. 12-26.

no way by which the Jews could escape under the Old Economy, then how shall we escape under the superior light and increased responsibilities of the New? This question has been on file for the last eighteen hundred years; but as yet no satisfactory answer has been given to it. Indeed, the Apostle did not propose it as a problem for solution. It is another case of *erotesis* in which the author affirms with strong emphasis the utter impossibility of any one's being saved who neglects the means of salvation which God has so graciously offered to us in the Gospel. The pronoun *"we"* in this clause is emphatic, and comprehends all who have heard and received the offer of salvation through Christ. The object of the Apostle here is, not to contrast any one class of Jews with another, or any one class of Christians with another, but to contrast all Jews as subjects of the Old Covenant with all Christians as subjects of the New Covenant; and that, too, for the purpose of showing the greater obligations of the latter, and the consequent dangers of neglecting the provisions of the Gospel. And hence he includes in this strong interrogation all the professed followers of Christ, whether they be of Jewish or of Gentile origin.

**if we neglect so great salvation;**—It is not necessary that we should positively reject or despise God's offers of mercy and means of grace, in order to seal our final condemnation. To effect this, it is enough that we simply *neglect* (*ameleesantes*) the means of salvation which God has provided. "He that believeth not on me," says Christ, "is condemned already, because he has not believed on the only-begotten Son of God." (John 3: 18.) And again he says, "He that believeth not the Son shall not see life; but the wrath of God abideth on him." (John 3: 36.) In all such passages the word believe implies not only faith subjectively considered, but also the obedience of faith as illustrated in the eleventh chapter of our Epistle. And hence Christ says on another occasion, "He that is not with me is against me; and he that gathered not with me, scattereth abroad." (Matt. 12: 30.) A strict observance of all the commandments and ordinances of God, is therefore indispensable, not as a means of *procuring* salvation, but as a condition of *enjoy-*

*ing* what Christ has himself freely purchased for us with his own blood.

There is an implied contrast here between the salvation which was offered to the Jews, on the conditions of legal obedience; and that which is now offered to all, on the conditions of Gospel obedience. The former was relative; but the latter is absolute. The former was procured through carnal ordinances imposed on the people till the time of reformation; but the latter has been procured for us through the blood of Christ. The former was temporal; the latter is eternal. And hence it is properly called a "great salvation," involving as it does the free and full pardon of sin; the justification and sanctification of the sinner; the redemption of the body from the corruption of the grave; and the eternal glorification of both the soul and the body in the everlasting Kingdom of our Lord and Savior Jesus Christ.

**which began to be spoken by the Lord.**—The author does not mean that this salvation was wholly unknown to the ancients. The good news of redemption through Jesus Christ was enigmatically suggested even to our first parents before they were expelled from Eden (Gen. 3: 15); and the subject was afterward more fully revealed to Abraham (Gen. 12: 3; Gal. 3: 8) and the Prophets (Isa. 53; 1 Pet. 1: 10-12.) Nevertheless, it is certainly true in a very important sense that Christ by his appearing "brought life and immortality to light through the Gospel." (2 Tim. 1: 10.) He was the first to reveal to the people by his teachings, his sufferings, and his triumphs, the true economy of the grace of God which "bringeth salvation to all men." And hence it is that the most ignorant subject of his Kingdom knows more of the way of life and salvation through the atoning blood of Christ and the renewing influence of the Holy Spirit, than did even John the Baptist. (Matt. 11: 11.) How far Christ himself, while on Earth, revealed to his disciples the plan of redemption, it may be difficult to say. But from sundry passages of Scripture (Matt. 28: 20; John 14: 26), it seems probable that he instructed them in nearly all, if not in quite all of the laws and principles of his Kingdom. And hence our author says that this salvation which "at the first began to be spoken by the Lord" was afterward *"confirmed* unto us by them that heard him"; that is, by the Apostles and Prophets who were eye

4 ¹God also bearing them witness, both with signs and wonders, and with divers miracles, and gifts of the Holy Ghost, ²according to his own will?

¹Acts ii. 32, 33; iii. 15; iv. 10; xiv. 3; xix. 11, 12.
²Matt. xi. 26; Luke x. 21; xii. 32; Rom. ix. 11-16; Eph. i. 5, 9, 11.

and ear witnesses of his personal ministry. (Acts 1: 8, 21, 22; 1 John 1: 1-3.)

From this remark, it is inferred by Bleek, Alford, and others, that Paul is not the author of this Epistle. For it is manifest, they say, that the writer classifies himself with those who had not heard the Lord, in contrast with those who had heard him. But it appears from Gal. 1: 11-24, that Paul had not only heard and seen Jesus, but that he had also actually received from him his commission and all his qualifications as an Apostle.

This is a plausible objection against the Pauline authorship of the Epistle; but that it is not valid, will appear from the following considerations: (1) It seems probable that in the above remark, the author has reference only to Christ's personal ministry on Earth; and consequently that he speaks here only of those who saw Christ, heard him, handled him, and conversed with him, during the period of his earthly ministry. If so, then Paul may in fact have belonged to that class of Christ's ministers who did not hear and see him during the period to which our author refers. At all events, he certainly did not hear him in the full and pregnant sense in which the word *hear* is used in this connection. (2) It is not the author's purpose here to vindicate his own authority as an Apostle, or to give prominence to himself in any way; but just the reverse. He aims simply to vindicate the claims and the authority of the Gospel, and while doing so to keep himself in the background as much as possible. And hence by a common figure of rhetoric (*anacoenosis*), he seems to have purposely associated himself with his readers, as he often does in other parts of the Epistle (3: 14; 4: 1, 2, 3, 11, 14, 15, 16; 6: 1, 3, etc.), in order that he might have as strong a hold on their sympathies as possible. See Introduction Section I. Div. 2: 2.

4 **God also bearing them witness,**—God himself is ever present with whatever agents or ministers he employs to work out any given end or purpose. "My presence," said he to Moses, "shall go with thee, and I will give thee rest." (Ex. 33: 14.) "I am not alone," says Christ (John 8: 16) ; "the Father that dwelleth in me,

he doeth the works" (John 14:10). So also God was ever present with the Apostles, confirming their testimony with signs, and wonders, and divers miracles, and distributions of the Holy Spirit, according to his own will. There are not so many different kinds of miracles, wrought by God in attestation and confirmation of the truth; but they are rather the same miracles viewed under different aspects. It is plain, as Ebrard says in substance, that miracles may be regarded in a fourfold aspect; first, with regard to their *design*, as signs (*seemeia*), miraculous testimonies in behalf of the truth; secondly, with respect to their *nature*, as wonders (*terata*), supernatural acts calculated to excite wonder and amazement in the minds of those who witnessed them; thirdly, with respect to their *origin*, as manifestations of supernatural powers (*dunameis*); and finally, in their specifically *Christian* aspect, as gifts and distributions of the Holy Spirit (*pneumatos hagios merismoi*) imparted to the original witnesses and proclaimers of the truth, according to the will of God. (1 Cor. 12; Eph. 4:11.)

## REFLECTIONS

These might be multiplied almost indefinitely. But it is hoped that the few suggested under each section will be sufficient to induce the thoughtful reader to reflect and meditate on the text for himself; and to draw from it such lessons of comfort and consolation, as are best adapted to his own immediate wants and circumstances. The following are given but as a specimen:

1. God has certainly spoken to fallen man (1:1). Of this we have very strong evidence in this first section of our Epistle; the thoughts of which are as far above the conceptions of the most gifted heathen poets and philosophers, as Heaven is above the Earth. Compare, for instance, the theology of this section with the theology of Homer and Hesiod; and mark the infinite contrast.

2. But just as certain as God spoke to the ancients, first by the Prophets and afterward by his Son, so certain it is that he now speaks to us in and through every book, chapter, and verse of the Holy Scriptures. "For whatsoever things were written aforetime, were written for our learning, that we through patience and comfort of the Scriptures might have hope." (Rom. 15:4.) The canon of Holy Writ was framed for our benefit, on whom the end of the ages has come. And hence we should receive every word of the

Bible as the living voice of Jehovah; for "all Scripture is given by inspiration of God, and is profitable for doctrine, for reproof, for correction, for instruction in righteousness; that the man of God may be perfect, thoroughly furnished for every good work." (2 Tim. 3: 16, 17.)

3. The harmony of the Old and New Testament Scriptures is complete. As the Christian Fathers taught, "The New Testament lies concealed in the Old; and the Old Testament lies patent in the New." The one is but the complement of the other. The revelations of the New Testament are fuller and simpler, and consequently more encouraging than those of the Old; but together they serve to develop and illustrate one plan of mercy and grace for the salvation of the world.

4. The Eloheem Jehovah of the Old Testament, is the Father, Son, and Holy Spirit of the New. Sometimes, indeed, these names are ascribed to the Father alone (Psalm 2:2, 7; 45:7; 110: 1, 2, 4); and sometimes to the Son alone (Psalm 45:6; Jer. 23: 6); but generally, as in Gen. 1: 26; 3: 22, 23, they each comprehend the whole Godhead; the former expressing the infinite power, and the latter the essential being and eternity of the Deity. And hence it follows that the Father, the Son, and the Holy Spirit, are the one eternal, immutable and omnipresent God. "Hear, O Israel, Jehovah our Eloheem is one Jehovah." (Deut. 6: 4.)

5. The evidence of Christ's Divinity given in this section is full and complete. He is the Creator of all things; the Upholder of all things; the effulgence of the Father's glory and the exact likeness of his substance. He is associated with the Father in the government of the universe; is called God by the Father himself; and as God he is worshiped by all the holy angels. His throne is eternal; and though he will roll up the heavens as a curtain, and change and readjust them as a worn-out garment, he himself is still the same, "yesterday, to-day, and forever." If these facts are not sufficient to prove beyond all doubt the Divinity of the Lord Jesus, then will our Socinian friends have the kindness to tell us what evidence would be sufficient for this purpose?

6. We have also in this section abundant evidence of God's willingness to save sinners. The obstacles that lay in the way of his doing so were of course very great. Great indignity had been cast on himself as well as on his government, by the sin of man. All

mankind had become enemies to him by wicked works (Col. 1: 20, 21), and the human heart had itself become desperately wicked and polluted (Jer. 17:9; Matt. 15:19). To remove these obstacles out of the way, was of course a very difficult problem. But "all things are possible with God." He so loved the world, even when it was dead in trespasses and sins, that he gave his Son, his only Son, to make expiation and propitiation for the sins of mankind. (John 3: 16; Rom. 5: 8; 8: 32.) He sent the Holy Spirit to convince the world of sin, and righteousness, and of judgment (John 15: 26; 16: 8-11); and also to dwell in the hearts of his children as their Comforter and Advocate (John 14: 16, 17; 16: 7; Rom. 8: 26). He sent holy angels to minister to the heirs of salvation; and he has given to us the Holy Bible as the rule of our faith and practice. He created the Church and furnished it with all that is necessary for our edification and growth in the Divine life. Who, then, can doubt, that as a Father pities and loves his children, so also the Lord pities and loves those who earnestly endeavor to serve him?

7. How transcendently great are our obligations to love and serve God, through Christ, for his abounding goodness to us poor miserable sinners. (2: 1-4.) If, to redeem us from death, he spared not his own Son, but delivered him up for us all; if he has sent his Holy Spirit to enlighten, comfort, and sanctify us; if he watches over us with even more than a Father's care; and if he has promised to save us from our sins, to deliver us from the corruption of the grave, and to crown us with honor, glory and immortality in the everlasting Kingdom of our Lord and Savior Jesus Christ, on the simple condition that we give him our poor hearts, and consecrate our lives to his service—then who can estimate the extent of our obligations to do this? And who can estimate the infinite remorse and agonies of those who live and die in the neglect of this great salvation! May Heaven save us from the folly and destiny of all such.

## SECTION TWO
### 2: 5-18

#### ANALYSIS

The main object of the Apostle in this section is to encourage the believing Hebrews to persevere in their Christian course, by presenting to them sundry motives drawn chiefly from the humanity of Christ; from his oneness with us, and his great love, condescension, sympathy, and sufferings for us.

Having presented the origin and greatness of the salvation that is offered to us in the Gospel, as a reason why we should give the more earnest heed to the things which we have heard, the Apostle now passes with consummate skill to the consideration of some other matters looking in the same direction. He insists particularly that we should give the more earnest heed to the things which we have heard:

I.  Because, he says, it is through the man Jesus and that system of grace of which he is author and the finisher, that we will regain our lost dominion over the world (verses 5-9).

1.  When man was created, God said to him, "Have dominion over the fish of the sea, and over the fowl of the air, and over every living thing that moveth upon the Earth." (Gen. 1: 28.)

2.  But in consequence of sin, man has, in a great measure, lost this dominion. (Gen. 3: 15-24.) Satan for a time got possession of this world (Psalm 68: 18; John 12: 31; 14: 30; 16: 11; 2 Cor. 4: 4; Eph. 2: 2; 1 John 5: 19; Rev. 12: 9) ; and by his cunning artifice and hellish malice, he not only enslaved man, but actually turned many of the elements of the world against him. Even the worm and the insect now luxuriate on his fallen remains.

3.  That this state of things is, however, only temporary, and that, according to God's purpose, man will again have at his command the dominion of the world, is manifest from the eighth Psalm, in which David says, "What is man, that thou art mindful of him? or the son of man, that thou visitest him? For thou hast made him a little lower than the angels, and hast crowned him with glory and honor. Thou madest him to have dominion over the works of thy hands; thou hast put all things under his feet; all sheep and oxen, yea, and the beasts of the field; the fowl of the air,

and the fish of the sea, and whatsoever passeth through the paths of the seas."

4. From this passage, then, it is quite evident that God intends that man shall possess and hold the world as his lawful and rightful patrimony. But this, says Paul, has not yet been accomplished: "We do not yet see all things put under him."

5. But what do we see? "We see Jesus," says he, "who was made a little lower than the angels, so that he by the grace of God might taste death for every man, crowned with glory and honor for the suffering of death." All things are put under him as our Leader and Captain. And this is therefore to us a sure pledge that in due time the dominion of the world will be restored to man; that he will enjoy the whole habitable Earth as his home, and that he will rule over it as his rightful patrimony, even as Adam ruled over Eden before he fell.

II. But just here arises another thought that requires further development and illustration; the consideration of which occupies the remainder of this section (verses 10-18). The Apostle has said in the ninth verse that Jesus was made a little lower than the angels, so that he by the grace of God might taste death for every man. The question, then, naturally occurs here, Why was this? Why did the Logos assume a nature that is a little lower than that of the angels, with the view of tasting death for every man?

1. The reason assigned by our author is, that it *became* God the Father, in bringing many sons unto glory, to make the Captain of their salvation perfect through sufferings (verse 10). The full meaning of this remark he does not stop to develop. But in the light of what follows in this section, and what is clearly taught in many parallel passages, it is evident—

(1.) That this was required by the nature and government of God. Without an atonement adequate to meet and satisfy all the claims of Divine Justice against man, there could be no pardon; no emancipation from the dominion of sin and Satan; no recovery of man's lost dominion over the world; and of course no bringing of many sons unto glory.

(2.) This was required by the nature, wants, and circumstances of mankind. None but a suffering, bleeding, dying Savior, uniting in his own person all the elements of humanity, as well as all the attributes of Divinity, could take hold of the affections and so control the hearts and lives of men as to bring them back again to God, and make it possible for him to restore to them their forfeited inheritance.

(3.) When Christ became a man, it was then necessary that, *as a man,* he should be educated and qualified for the great work that was before him. He had to grow in knowledge and in experience, like other men. (Luke 2:52.) And hence we see that it became God to make Jesus perfect through sufferings—(a) with reference to the claims of his own government on man; (b) with reference to the condition and wants of mankind; and (c) with reference to the educational wants and requirements of Christ's human nature.

2. And now to show that this was no new device, but that God had so decreed from the beginning, the Apostle makes sundry quotations from the Old Testament Scriptures, clearly demonstrating that even under the Law, it was God's revealed purpose that the Messiah should be one with his brethren (verses 11-13).

3. And hence it was that, in harmony with God's ancient purpose, the Logos became flesh; and thus, *as a man,* was made a little lower than the angels; so that by his death he might be able (1) to destroy Satan, who has the power of death; and (2) that he might deliver those who had been made captives by Satan, and who through the fear of death were all their lifetime subject to bondage (verses 14, 15).

4. The necessity of Christ's being made a little lower than the angels by becoming a man—a suffering, bleeding, sorrowful man —is still further amplified and illustrated by the fact that he came to help fallen men, and not angels. And hence it behooved him to become like unto his brethren in all things (sin only excepted), so that, as their officiating High Priest, he may the more readily and fully sympathize with them in all their trials, temptations, and sufferings (verses 16-18).

This section, therefore, comprises the two following subdivisions:

I. 2:5-9. Man's lost dominion over the world to be restored through Jesus.

II. 2:10-18. Why the Word became flesh and dwelt among us.

## 1. MAN'S LOST DOMINION OVER THE WORLD
## TO BE RESTORED THROUGH JESUS
### 2:5-9

5 For unto the angels hath he not put in subjection [1]the world to come, whereof we speak.

[1]Chap. i. 6; vi. 5; Matt. xii. 39.

5 **For unto the angels**—The logical connection here is not very clear; and hence the critics are not agreed as to what is the proper antecedent clause of the conjunction *"for"* (*gar*). Some find it in 1:13; and others in 2:4. But it seems most probable that the object of the Apostle is to introduce another line of argument co-ordinate with that which is given in the first chapter, and leading to the same general conclusion found in 2:4. And hence he beautifully and with great rhetorical skill and propriety, makes the exhortation given in 2:1-4, the connecting link between the two. In view of what is stated in the first chapter, he says, "We ought to give the more earnest heed to the things which we have heard, lest haply we should be drifted away from them." And this, he says by implication, we should do also from the further consideration, that God has made it the business of Christ, and not of angels, to restore to mankind their lost dominion over the world.

**the world to come, whereof we speak.**—The world to come (*hee oikoumenee hee mellousa*) means, not the coming age (*ho aion ho mellon*) as in Matt. 12:39, etc., but *the habitable world* under the reign and government of the Messiah. (1:6.) It is the world in which we now live; and in which, when it shall have been purified from sin, the redeemed will live forever. For man, it was at first created (Gen. 1:28-31); and to man, it still belongs by an immutable decree of Jehovah. This is manifest, as the Apostle here shows, from what is recorded in the eighth Psalm, to which in the popular style of his age, our author here elegantly refers. It consists of two parts; in the first of which (verses 1, 2), David celebrates the praises of God for the marvelous manifestations of his wisdom, power, and goodness, displayed in all his works. These manifestations of the Divine perfections are so very plain that even babes and sucklings perceive and acknowledge them (Matt. 11:25; 21:16), and thus put to silence the profane scoffings of ignorant and foolish men, who say in their hearts, "No God." (Psalm 14:1.)

6 But ¹one in a certain place testified, saying, ²What is man, that thou
art mindful of him? or ³the son of man, that thou ⁴visitest him?

7 Thou ⁵madest him a little lower than the angels; thou crownedst him
with glory and honor, [and didst set him over the works of thy hands:]

¹Ch. iv. 4; v. 6.
²Job vii. 17, 18; xv. 14; Psa. viii. 4; cxliv. 3.
³Job xxv. 6; Psa. cxliv. 3, 4; Isa. li. 12.
⁴Gen. l. 24; Luke i. 68, 78.
⁵Psa. viii. 5; John vi. 7.

In the second part (verses 3-9), the author speaks particularly
of God's favor and goodness to man: "When I consider thy heavens, the work of thy fingers, the Moon and the stars which thou
hast ordained," then he says I am constrained to exclaim,

6 **What is man, that thou art mindful of him?**—That this has
reference to mankind in general, and not to Jesus Christ personally
considered, as some have alleged, is evident from the Psalm itself,
as well as from the scope of the Apostle's argument. It is God's
care for the human race, as such, and not for any one person in
particular, which so much excites the wonder and admiration of
the Psalmist. When he looked upon the heavens as the work of
God's fingers, and thought of the Moon and the stars which he
(God) had created, he was amazed that a Being so exalted, so excellent, and so glorious, should ever condescend to think of man
and to supply his numerous wants.

**or the son of man, that thou visitest him?**—This, in connection with the preceding clause, is a case of synonymous parallelism.
*"Son of man" (huios anthropou)* in the latter clause is equivalent
to *"man" (anthropos)* in the first; and each of these terms is used
generically for the race. The word *visit*, according to Hebrew
usage, means to manifest one's self to another, for the purpose of
either blessing (Gen. 1: 1; Ex. 3: 16) or punishing (Job 35:
15; Psalm 89: 32). In this connection, both the words, *visit* and
*remember,* are used in a favorable sense, indicating God's special
care over man, in that he provides for him, and, as Christ says,
numbers even the hairs of his head. (Matt. 10: 10.)

7 **Thou madest him a little lower than the angels,**—Or as the
Hebrew may be more literally rendered, Thou hast made him fall
but little short of Eloheem; or, Thou has lowered him a little beneath Eloheem. The word *Eloheem* in this passage means the angels. It is so rendered in the Septuagint, no doubt in harmony
with Hebrew usage, and most likely on the authority of some of

the ancient Prophets; and it is, moreover, so rendered by the author of our Epistle.

It is still a question with the critics whether the word *little* (*Brachu ti*) is expressive of time or of degree. Those who take this as a Messianic Psalm, and refer the words *"man"* and *"son of man"* to Christ, generally construe the word *"little"* as a particle of *time* (Bleek, Lünemann, Macknight, Clarke); and so also do some others, as Ebrard, who take these words as referring to mankind generally. But I agree with Delitzsch, Alford, Moll, and others, that both the Psalmist and our author refer here simply to the *rank* which God has assigned to man in the scale of creation. He has made him, they say, a little inferior to the angels; and there is no intimation given here or elsewhere, that he will ever make him their superior. That man redeemed by the blood of Christ, will, in his glorified state, occupy a place of more tender care and solicitude than the angels, is quite probable. This is in harmony with several scenes in the Apocalypse (Rev. 5: 11, 12; 7: 9-12); and it is in harmony also with the teachings of Christ in the parables of the lost sheep, the lost piece of money, and the prodigal son (Luke 15). But in none of these passages is there any evidence that man will ever rise in rank above the angels. As a lost and recovered child, he will ever be an object of wonder and sympathy throughout the universe; and the angels will doubtless often lean on their harps, and listen in rapture to the more tender and transporting songs of the redeemed. But I know of no evidence in the Scriptures that the present rank of men and angels will ever be reversed.

**thou crownedst him with glory and honor,**—The two words here rendered *glory* and *honor* (*doxee kai timee*) are nearly synonymous in both the Hebrew and the Greek; and they are used, according to a well known Hebrew idiom, for the sake of emphasis. Together, they express royal dignity; and in this instance, they indicate the fullness of the regal power and authority which God has bestowed, not on the first or on the second Adam merely, but on the race; or rather, on the loyal portion of it. By a decree as immutable as the laws of gravitation, God has ordained that man shall inherit the Earth and have dominion over it.

**and didst set him over the works of thy hands:**—This clause is now generally rejected by the critics as spurious. See critical

8 Thou ¹hast put all things in subjection under his feet. For in that he
put all things in subjection under him, he left nothing that is not put under
him. ²But now we see not yet all things put under him.

¹Gen. i. 26-28; ix. 2; Jas. iii. 7.
²Job xxxix. 1-12; xli.

note above given by Bagster. But it is found in the original Hebrew, in the Septuagint, and also in manuscripts, A, C, D, M¹,
etc.; and I am therefore inclined to retain it as genuine.

8 **Thou hast put all things in subjection under his feet.**—
This, with the last clause, is another instance of Hebrew parallelism. It is not, however, synonymous, but constructive parallelism,
which occurs here. The Psalmist first expresses the general
thought, that God has placed man over the work of his hands.
But he does not stop with this. To indicate still further the degree
of man's sovereignty over the world, he adds, "Thou hast put all
things in subjection under his feet." The latter clause is, therefore, more expressive than the former, as it indicates the perfect
and entire subjection of all things earthly to the will of man; and
so the Apostle reasons in what follows.

**For in that he put all things in subjection under him, he left
nothing that is not put under him.**—In these words, there is no
reference whatever to angels, or to other worlds or systems. It is
of the Earth, and of the Earth only, that the Holy Spirit here
speaks. This is obvious from what follows in the latter part of the
eighth Psalm. After saying that all things are by the decree of Jehovah put under the feet of man, the Psalmist immediately adds,
by way of explanation, the following specifications: "all sheep and
oxen, yea, and the beasts of the field; the fowl of the air, and the
fish of the sea, and whatsoever passeth through the paths of the
seas." It is to *this world* as it was, as it is, and especially as it will
be hereafter, that both the Psalmist and the Apostle have reference. When God had renovated the Earth and filled it, as a vast
storehouse, with all that was necessary for the well-being and happiness of its intended sovereign, he said, "Let us make man in our
image, after our likeness; and let them have dominion over the fish
of the sea, and over the fowl of the air, and over the cattle, and
over all the Earth, and over every creeping thing that creepeth
upon the Earth. So God created man in his own image; in the
image of God created he him; male and female created he them.

9 But we see Jesus, [1]who was made a little lower than the angels [2]for the
[1]Isa. liii. 2-11; John i. 14; Phil. ii. 7-9.
[2]Isa. liii. 12.

And God blessed them and said unto them, Be fruitful, and multiply, and replenish the Earth, and subdue it; and have dominion
over the fish of the sea, and over the fowl of the air, and over
every living thing that moveth upon the Earth." (Gen. 1 : 26-28.)
This is the perpetual decree of Jehovah with respect to the domain
and the dominion of man.    True, indeed, Satan has for a time
usurped the dominion of this world; and man has by transgression
forfeited all claims upon it.    The crown of glory and honor has
fallen from his head because of sin; and now he is exposed and
assailed by a thousand obstacles in earth, air, and sea.    And hence
the Apostle adds:

**we see not yet all things put under him.**—From this, it is evident that the eighth Psalm is prophetic.    The Psalmist looks
rather at the decree and purpose of Jehovah touching the final allotment of this world, than to the state of things which actually existed at the time in which he wrote.    He means to say, that although man's scepter is now broken, the decree of Jehovah concerning it is not broken.    His purpose is unchangeable.    And
hence there can be no doubt but that mankind will yet regain their
lost dominion over the Earth.    How far this will be accomplished
before the Earth shall have been renovated by fire (2 Pet. 3), it
may be now difficult to say.    When Satan shall be bound for a
thousand years (Rev. 20: 1-6), and the saints of the Most High
possess the Kingdom (Dan. 7: 14, 18, 22), the prophecy of Isaiah
(11: 6-9) may be more literally fulfilled than we now anticipate.
But whatever may be true of this blissful era, so long and so often
foretold by the Apostles and Prophets, it is not at all probable that
man's dominion over the world will be fully restored, until the new
heavens and the new Earth appear, in which righteousness will
forever dwell. (Rev. 21.)

9 **But we see Jesus,**—The Apostle here makes a very striking
contrast between "Jesus" and "man," to whom by the decree of Jehovah, the world is to be subjected.    "We do not yet," he says,
"see all things put under man"; but in the coronation of Jesus, as
Lord of all, we see that the work is in progress; and this is, of

suffering of death, [1]crowned with glory and honor; that he [2]by the grace of God should [3]taste death [4]for every man.

[1]Chap. i. 2-4; Acts ii. 33, 36; v. 31; Eph. i. 20-23; Phil. ii. 9-11.
[2]John iii. 16; Rom. v. 8; viii. 32; 2 Cor. v. 21; Titus iii. 4-6.
[3]Matt. xvi. 28; John viii. 52.
[4]John i. 29; iii. 16; Rom. v. 18, 19; 1 Cor. xv. 22; 2 Cor. v. 14, 15; 1 Tim. ii. 6.

course, to all Christians a sure pledge that in due time it will be fully consummated.

**who was made a little lower than the angels**—We learn from the seventeenth verse of this chapter, that "in all things it behooved Christ to be made like unto his brethren." But they are all "a little lower than the angels" (verse 7); and hence it was necessary that he too should, as a man, be made "a little lower than the angels." For otherwise, indeed, he would not be a *man;* would not be capable of suffering death for every man; and would not be such a merciful and faithful High Priest, as we all need to sympathize with us in our infirmities. That he is God, the Creator of both men and angels, is clearly taught in the first chapter; and that he is also a man is just as clearly taught in the second. Perfect Divinity and perfect humanity are both perfectly united in the person of the Lord Jesus. Nothing short of this, it seems, would make him just such a Savior as we need.

**for the suffering of death,**—It is still a question with expositors, whether this phrase is grammatically connected with what precedes, or with what follows. As rendered in our Common Version it is most naturally connected with what precedes; and seems intended to express the *end* or *purpose* for which Jesus was made a little lower than the angels: viz., in order that he might be capable of suffering death. If this is the proper rendering, then it follows that this expression forms a sort of parallelism with the last clause of the verse, and the whole sentence may be construed as follows: "But we see Jesus (who was made a little lower than the angels, for the purpose of suffering death, so that he by the grace of God might taste death for every man) crowned with glory and honor." This construction is in harmony with the Apostle's argument; but it does not altogether harmonize with the laws of grammatical arrangement. Had our author intended to express a parallelism by means of these two expressions, it is not probable that he would have separated them, as he has done in the original, by the intervening words, "crowned with glory and honor." And

hence I am inclined to think with Delitzsch, Alford, and most
modern expositors, that the words in question stand connected
with what follows, and that the passage should be rendered thus:
"But we see Jesus, who was made a little lower than the angels,
crowned with glory and honor, for (*dia, because of, on account of*)
the suffering of death"; that is, on account of, and as a reward for,
his sufferings. To this rendering there can be no grammatical objection whatever; and in sense it harmonizes well with the following and other parallel passages: "Let this mind be in you which
was also in Christ Jesus; who being in the form of God, thought it
not robbery to be equal with God; but made himself of no reputation, and took upon him the form of a servant, and was made in
the likeness of men; and being found in fashion as a man, he humbled himself, and became obedient unto death, even the death of
the cross. *Wherefore* God also hath highly exalted him, and given
him a name which is above every name; that at the name of Jesus
every knee should bow, of things in Heaven, and things in Earth,
and things under the Earth; and that every tongue should confess
that Jesus Christ is Lord, to the glory of God the Father." (Phil.
2: 5-11.)

**crowned with glory and honor,**—The best explanation of these
words may be found in the above passage from the Epistle to the
Philippians. God had long before promised that Christ should be
abundantly rewarded for his sufferings. (Isa. 53: 12.) And hence
as we are told by Luke (Acts 1: 1-11), after that he had borne the
pains and agonies of the cross, and after he had risen from the
dead and instructed his disciples for forty days in matters pertaining to the Kingdom of God, he was then taken up into Heaven,
and in the presence of adoring millions (1: 6) crowned Lord of
all; "angels, and authorities, and powers being made subject unto
him" (1 Pet. 3: 22). This was first announced to the people, as
a fact, by the Apostle Peter, on the following Pentecost (Acts 2:
36); and afterward it was proclaimed to every kindred, and
tongue, and people, and nation under heaven. See Acts 4: 10-12;
5: 30-32; 10: 36-42; Eph. 1: 20-23; Col. 1: 23, etc.

There can be no doubt, therefore, that Christ is now the
anointed Sovereign of the universe; and that he will reign over all
creatures in Heaven, and on Earth, and under the Earth, until he

shall have restored to the saints their lost dominion over this world.

**that he by the grace of God should taste death for every man.**—Instead of the phrase *"by the grace of God"* (*chariti. Theou*), we have in a few manuscripts, *"without God"* (*choris Theou*). This reading was preferred by Theodoret, Theodore of Mopsuestia, and the Nestorians. But the evidence, both internal and external, is against it; and it is therefore now generally rejected by the critics, as a marginal gloss.

Conceding, then, that the common reading is genuine, let us next consider what is the proper grammatical connection of this clause with the rest of the sentence. It is manifestly a subordinate and dependent clause; but on what does it depend? What was done so that (*opos*) Jesus "might by the grace of God taste death for every man"? Was he crowned with glory and honor for this purpose? Surely not. His death preceded his coronation; and he was crowned, as we have seen, in consequence of it. What then? Was he made a little lower than the angels, so that he might by the grace of God taste death for every man? Clearly, to my mind, this is the meaning of the passage. And I would therefore prefer the following arrangement of this very complex sentence, as being more in harmony with the less flexible rules of English syntax: "But we see Jesus (who was made a little lower than the angels, so that he might by the grace of God taste death for every man) crowned with glory and honor, on account of the suffering of death."

The several words of this clause need but little explanation. The phrase, *"by the grace of God,"* means simply that the incarnation, death, atonement, and mediation of the Lord Jesus, are all the offspring of Divine love. "For," as Christ says, "God so loved the world that he gave his only-begotten Son, that whosoever believeth in him should not perish, but have eternal life." (John 3 : 16.) To *"taste death,"* is the same as to experience death, or to suffer death. And the phrase *"for every man"* is as plain as it can be made; clearly indicating that the atonement of Jesus Christ is for every human being, and that all men may therefore be saved by it. We have but to comply with the very plain and reasonable conditions on which salvation is offered to all, and then we will finally receive "an abundant entrance into the everlasting Kingdom of our Lord and Savior Jesus Christ." (2 Pet. 1 : 11.)

From the given explanations, then, it is quite obvious that the main object of the Apostle in this paragraph (verses 5-9), is to remind his Hebrew brethren, that by an irrevocable decree of Jehovah this world belongs to man; and that although it has been forfeited by sin, and its dominion usurped by Satan, it is nevertheless God's purpose to redeem it for the benefit of his saints; not, however, through angels, nor through the law given by angels (2 : 2) ; but through that scheme of grace, mercy, and truth of which Jesus is the Author and the Finisher. And so also this same Apostle testifies to his Roman brethren. Speaking of this very matter, he says, "For the promise that he [Abraham] should be heir of the world (*Kleeronomos Kosmou*), was not to Abraham or to his seed through the Law, but through the righteousness of faith. For if they who are of the Law be heirs, faith is made void, and the promise made of none effect. Because the Law worketh wrath; for where there is no law, there is no transgression. Therefore it is of faith, that it might be by grace; to the end that the promise might be sure to all the seed; not to that only which is of the Law, but to that also which is of the faith of Abraham; who is the Father of us all." (Rom. 4 : 13-16.) The promise that his posterity according to the flesh should inherit the land of Canaan, was given to Abraham and to his seed through law. But all these legal, carnal, and temporal arrangements were but a type or shadow of the more gracious provisions of the economy of redemption through Jesus Christ; according to which it seems that Abraham and the whole family of the faithful will yet inherit the entire Earth, after that it shall have been purified by fire, and prepared for the descent of the New Jerusalem. See Psalm 37 : 9-11 ; Matt. 5 : 5 ; 2 Pet. 3 : 10-13 ; Rev. 5 : 10 ; 21.

How very important it is, then, that we should all give the more earnest heed to the things which we have heard, lest perchance we should be drifted away from them. For into this renovated Earth nothing can ever come that is impure or unholy. For "the fearful, and unbelieving, and the abominable, and murderers, and whoremongers, and sorcerers, and idolaters, and all liars, shall have their part in the lake that burneth with fire and brimstone." (Rev. 21 : 8.) How then, shall we escape if we neglect the great salvation

offered to us in the Gospel, "which at the first began to be spoken
by the Lord, and was confirmed unto us by them that heard him"?

## 2. WHY THE WORD BECAME FLESH AND
## DWELT AMONG US
### 2 : 10-18

10 For [1]it became him, [2]for whom are all things, and by whom are all
things, in bringing [3]many sons unto [4]glory, to make the [5]captain of their salvation [6]perfect through sufferings.

[1]Luke xxiv. 26, 46.
[2]Rom. xi. 36; 1 Cor. viii. 36; 2 Cor. v. 18; Rev. iv. 11.
[3]Hos. i. 10; Rom. viii. 14-17; 2 Cor. vi. 18; Gal. iii. 26.
[4]Col. iii. 4; 2 Tim. ii. 10; 1 Pet. v. l. 10.
[5]Isa. lv. 4; Jer. xxx. 9; Acts iii. 15; v. 31.
[6]Chap. v. 8, 9; Isa. liii. 2-11; Luke xxiv. 26, 46.

10 **For it became him,**—The Apostle aims here to meet and refute a Jewish objection founded on the humiliation and sufferings
of Christ. "We have heard out of the law," said the Jews on one
occasion, "that Christ abideth forever." (John 12: 34.) This
opinion was founded on such passages as Psalm 72: 7, 17; 89: 36,
37; 110: 4; Isa. 9: 7; Ezek. 37: 24, 25; Dan. 2: 44; 7: 13, 14;
Mic. 4: 7; in which the Kingdom of the Messiah is described as
an everlasting Kingdom; and his reign, as enduring throughout all
generations. To many of the Jews, these passages of Scripture
seemed wholly inconsistent with the humble life and the ignomin-
ious death of the Lord Jesus. And it was therefore eminently
proper to remove this objection as far as possible, by showing just
at this point of the argument that the humiliation, sufferings, and
death of Christ are, in fact, an essential part of the scheme of redemption. This, our author does with great force and tenderness
in the remaining portion of this chapter. He begins by saying that
it "became (*eprepen*) Him for whom are all things, and by whom
are all things, in bringing many sons unto glory, to make the Captain of their salvation perfect through sufferings." God is here
represented both as the final cause (*dia on*) and also as the
efficient cause (*dia ou*) of all things. The universe is, in fact, but a
manifestation and development of his infinite perfections. And
hence its government is not with him a matter of caprice, or of arbitrary choice, but of divine propriety. As it became God to adapt
means to ends in the work of creation, so also it becomes him to do
the same in the works of providence and redemption. When he
resolved to bring many sons unto glory, there was then imposed on

him (if I may say it with reverence) a moral necessity, deep and profound as his own nature, to qualify Jesus for the great work that was before him: and this, it seems, could be done only by means of his incarnation, sufferings, and death.

**in bringing many sons unto glory,**—To whom does the participle *"bringing"* (*agagonta*) refer? To God the Father, represented by the pronoun *"him"* (*auto* in the dative case), or to Jesus, represented by *"captain"* (*archeegon* in the accusative case)? The grammatical agreement is in favor of the latter; but the scope of the passage and the general construction of the sentence are in favor of the former. And hence this is now generally regarded as a case of *anacoluthon*. See Winer's Gram. Section 63.

The heirs of salvation are here called *"sons,"* in relation to God as their Father and supreme Leader; just as in the following verse they are called *"brethren,"* in relation to Christ who is our Elder Brother and also our Leader by the Father's appointment. To bring many sons unto glory is the same as to bring them to Heaven. This world now abounds in sin and suffering, misery and death. But in Heaven all is light, and life, and love. (Rev. 21.)

**the captain of their salvation**—The word here rendered *captain* (*archeegos*) means properly *a leader;* one who at the head of an army or other company leads them onward to the goal or place of their destination. The word is applied by Philo to Adam, who, as Paul says, "was a type of him that was to come." (Rom. 5:14.) These are both captains or leaders of the entire race. But they lead to different goals, and in opposite directions. The first Adam led all to death; whereas the second Adam leads all to life. "For as in Adam all die, even so in Christ shall all be made alive." (1 Cor. 15: 22.) "For as by one man's disobedience the many were made sinners; so by the obedience of one shall the many, be made righteous." (Rom. 5:19.)

The phrase, *"many sons,"* as used in our text, is not, however, strictly equivalent to *"the many"* in Rom. 5:19. The latter includes the whole human race; but the former includes only those "who by patient continuance in well going," follow Christ wherever he goes. The latter, it is true, will all be raised from the dead, and forever saved from all the effects of the Adamic sin; but many of them will, on account of their own personal transgressions, be raised "to the resurrection of damnation" (John 5: 29), and banished "with an everlasting destruction from the presence of the Lord, and from the glory of his power" (2 Thess. 1: 9). The former, however, will all, without the loss of one, be brought home to the full enjoyment of honor, glory, and immortality. And these, be it observed, will not be a few, but a vast multitude which no man can number, out of every kindred, and tongue, and people, and nation. (Rev. 7: 9, 10.)

**perfect through sufferings.**—The word here rendered *to make perfect* (*teleioo*—from *telos, an end, termination*) means properly to be full, complete, wanting in nothing; and as applied to Christ in this connection, it means simply that he was by God fully qualified for the work that was before him; that in this respect he was complete and entire, wanting in nothing.

In what this perfection consisted, it may be difficult for us to explain. Perhaps none but God can understand this matter fully. But this much we may say in general:

(1.) That it consisted in Christ's being fully prepared to honor God and to magnify his government, by making an adequate atonement for the sins of the world. God, be it reverently spoken, cannot without full satisfaction pardon any sin or transgression of his law. By an eternal moral necessity, the soul that sinneth must die, unless by adequate means the claims of Divine Justice can be fully satisfied. (Ex. 34: 7.) Any attempt, therefore, to bring many sons unto glory without a ransom sufficient to atone for all their transgressions, would of necessity be a failure. And hence it was, that when no other means were found adequate, God set forth Jesus Christ, as a propitiatory sacrifice, for a demonstration of his justice in passing by the sins of his ancient people; and to show also how it is that he can now be just in justifying every one who believes in Jesus. (Rom. 3: 25, 26.) It became God the Father, therefore, to make his Son a perfect Savior by the shedding of his blood, so that by means of it an adequate atonement might be made for the sins of the world.

(2.) The perfection of Christ, as the Captain of our salvation, consisted also in his being relatively adapted to the nature, wants, and circumstances of those whom he came to redeem. It was not enough that he should come with a ransom sufficient to meet and satisfy all the claims of the Divine Government on the sinner. He had to look at the human, as well as at the Divine, side of the question. He had to lay hold of human nature as it was, and adapt himself to it in such a way as would best serve to enlighten the understanding, renew the heart, and control the will and the life of our sin-ruined race. But it is a law of the universe that "Like loves its like." And hence it is, that God has generally clothed himself and his angelic ambassadors in human form, whenever he has sought to manifest them and himself to mankind in compassion, tenderness, and love. (Gen. 18: 1, 2; 19: 1, 12, etc.) But in the case of Jesus, the mere form of humanity was not enough. In order to reach the heart of a race at enmity with God by their own wicked works, and to change that enmity into love, it was necessary that the Word should become flesh, and by the grace of God taste death for every man. (Col. 1: 21, 22.) In no other conceivable way could the love of God be sufficiently manifested to our rebellious race. True, indeed, the benevolence, as well as the wisdom and power of God, is revealed in every law and ordinance of nature. It is seen in every star that twinkles in the firmament; it is seen in every flower that blooms on the landscape; and it is seen in every organ, and even in every element, of the human body. Nevertheless, our experience, as well as the light of history, goes to prove that in all nature there is not power sufficient to convert a single soul. We love God because he first loved us, and manifested his love to us in giving his own dear Son to weep, and bleed, and die for us. (1 John 4: 10, 19.) This, then, is manifestly another reason why it became God the Father, in bringing many sons unto glory, to make the Captain of their salvation perfect through sufferings.

(3.) When Jesus became a man, he had to be perfected, *as a man*. He was, in his infancy, endowed with every element and attribute of human nature in its sinless state; and consequently these elements of humanity in the person of the Lord Jesus had all to be educated by a severe course of discipline and experience, such as is common to man. And hence Luke says, "he [Jesus] increased in wisdom and stature, and in favor with God and man." (Luke 2: 52.) But no man is fully qualified to visit the sick, and to administer to the wants of the afflicted, who has not himself drunk deep of the cup of human sorrow and of human suffering; and hence it was that Christ had to drink of it to its very dregs. And now that

11 For both ¹he that sanctifieth and they ²who are sanctified are
¹all of one: for which cause ²he is not ashamed to call them brethren,

¹Chap. x. 10, 14; xiii. 12; John xvii. 19.
²Acts xxvi. 18; 1 Cor. i. 2; vi. 9-11; Eph. v. 26; 1 Pet. i. 15, 16.
¹Acts xvii. 26; 1 Cor. viii. 6; Gal. iv. 4.
²Matt. xii. 48-50; xxv. 40; John xx. 17; Rom. viii. 29.

"he himself hath suffered being tempted, he is able to succor them
that are tempted."

11 **For both he that sanctifieth, etc.**—The sanctifier is Christ
himself; and the "sanctified" are the same as the "many sons" spoken of in the tenth verse. These and Christ, our author means to
say, are very nearly related, being together properly called *sons*,
"for" they are all of one Father. The word *sanctify* (*hagiazo*)
means (1) to make clean, to purify, to make holy; and (2) to consecrate, or set apart from a common to a sacred use. In the latter
sense, it is applied both to persons and things; in the former, only
to persons. In the latter sense, it has reference to state or condition; in the former, to character. In the latter sense there are properly no degrees and no progress; but in the former, we may and
we should make constant progress. Very frequently this word is
used in one of these two senses to the exclusion of the other; but
in our text, it is used in its most comprehensive sense, so as to include the idea of both consecration and moral purification; each of
which is effected through the death and mediation of the Lord
Jesus, "who of God is made unto us wisdom, and justification, and
sanctification, and redemption." (1 Cor. 1 : 30.)

**are all of one:**—One what? Some say, One race (*ex henos
genous*); some, One blood (*ex henos haimatos*); some, One seed
or offspring (*ex henos spermatos*). But the idea that they are all
of one Father (*ex henos patros*), not Adam or Abraham, but God,
"from whom, and through whom, and to whom, are all things,"
seems to accord best with all the terms and conditions of the context.

**for which cause he is not ashamed to call them brethren,**—If
the Sanctifier and the sanctified are all sons of God, having one
and the same Father, they have also of course one common
brotherhood, of which Jesus is not ashamed; and which, as our author now proceeds to show, had long before the date of this Epistle
been symbolically set forth in the types and shadows of the Old
Testament.

12 Saying, ³I will declare thy name unto my brethren, ⁴in the midst of the church will I sing praise unto thee.

³Psa. xxii. 22, 25.
⁴Psa. xl. 10; cxi. 1; John xviii. 20.

12 **Saying, I will declare thy name, etc.**—This is a quotation from the twenty-second Psalm, in the course of which, David, as a type of Christ, pleads for help (1) on the ground of his very near and intimate relations to God (verses 1-10); and (2) on the ground of his imminent danger and intense sufferings (verses 11-21). After this he changes his tone from the deepest despondency, and breaks out into exclamations of gratitude and praise to God for his signal deliverance and the many mercies bestowed on him (verses 22-31). In all this, David refers primarily to his own personal experience, under the severe trials and persecutions which he endured from Saul. During the last seven or eight years of Saul's reign, he (David) was surrounded by enemies as by wild beasts; and his way to the throne was through the most violent and unreasonable opposition. But, trusting in God, he was delivered from all his foes; and afterward, on many joyful occasions, he declared the name of Jehovah to his brethren; and in the midst of the Church, or congregation of Israel, he often celebrated the praises of his Deliverer.

And just so it was with Christ, the great antitype of David, to whom also the words of this Psalm have special reference, and to whom they are, in fact, several times applied in the New Testament. Compare, for instance, the first verse of this Psalm with Matt. 27: 46; the eighth, with Matt. 27: 43; the fifteenth, with John 19: 28; the sixteenth, with John 20: 25; and the eighteenth, with John 19: 23, 24. It is therefore, beyond doubt, a typical Psalm having reference primarily to David and secondarily to Christ. See notes on 1: 5. But as Delitzsch justly remarks, "David's description of personal experience and suffering goes far beyond any that he had known in his own person; his complaints descend into a lower deep than he had sounded himself; and his hopes rise higher than any realized reward. Through his hyperbolical character, the Psalm became *typico-prophetic*. David, as the sufferer, there contemplates himself and his experience in Christ;

and his own, both present and future, thereby acquires a background which, in height and depth, greatly transcends the limits of his own personality."

That this Psalm, then, has a double reference, relating in its highest and fullest sense to the humiliation, sufferings, deliverance, and final triumphs of the Messiah, as the antitype of David, is very obvious. But why does our author refer to it? For what purpose does he quote from it the words of our text? His object, as we have seen, in this part of his argument, is to show the very intimate relation that exists between Christ and his people; it is to remind his Hebrew brethren in Christ and to convince others, that the Messiah was to be *a man;* a man of sorrows; one in nature and sympathy with the "many sons" whom he is bringing home to glory. This he might have done so far as to satisfy the more enlightened portion of his readers, by referring to such passages of Scripture as Matt. 12 : 48, 49; 25 : 40, etc., in which Jesus speaks to and of the children of God as his brethren. But he very wisely pursues a different course. He was writing for the Hebrews, all of whom had the most implicit confidence in the Divine origin and plenary inspiration of the Old Testament Scriptures. And by appealing to these sacred Oracles, he not only establishes the fact of Christ's oneness with the sons of God, but he furthermore shows that this was all in harmony with God's ancient purpose. To us the narratives of Matthew, Mark, Luke, and John are, of course, just as authoritative as any other parts of the Holy Scriptures. But not so with many of those for whose benefit the Epistle was written. And hence it is that the Apostle so often draws his proofs and arguments from the Old Testament, demonstrating at the same time the sublime unity of God's gracious plans and purposes in all ages and dispensations.

The word *church* (*ekkleesia*), in its Jewish sense, means the nation of Israel assembled in Jerusalem; where David and his brethren often celebrated the praises of Jehovah; but, in its Christian sense, as it is here used and applied by the Apostle, it means the united body of believers under the mediatorial reign of the Messiah. The former was a type of the latter, just as David himself was a type of Christ.

13 And again, ¹I will put my trust in him. And again, ²Behold I and the children which God hath given me.

¹2 Sam. xxii. 3; Psa. xvi. 1; xviii. 2; Isa. viii. 17; xii. 2; Matt. xxvii. 43.
²Isa. viii. 18; John xvii. 6-12.

13 **And again, I will trust in him.**—Words equivalent to these occur in 2 Sam. 22: 3; Psalm 18: 2; Isa. 8: 17; and 12: 2. In the first two instances, David is the speaker, and represents Christ in his relations as the King of God's people; and in the last two, Isaiah is the speaker, and represents Christ in his prophetic relations. It is still a question with the critics, to which of these our author refers. Many think that he refers to Isa. 8: 17; but it is more probable that the quotation is taken from 2 Sam. 22:3, or Psalm 18: 2. In either case, the object of our author in making the citation is simply to show that according to God's will and purpose as revealed in the Old Testament, the Messiah was to be *a man,* endowed with all the attributes and sympathies of our nature. And this he does here by showing that, as a man, Christ, like David, felt his dependence on God and trusted in him.

**Behold I and the children which God hath given me.**—That this clause is taken from Isa. 8: 18, is very evident. But what is its meaning, and what bearing has it on the argument of the Apostle? How can words which in their first intention have a clear reference to Isaiah and his children be applied to Christ and his disciples? The proper answer to this question is to be found in the typical relations which Isaiah and his children sustained to Christ and the children of God. As every divinely appointed high-priest under the Theocracy represented Christ in his priestly office; and as every king of the royal line of David represented him in his kingly office; so also did every true prophet represent him to some extent in his prophetical office. And whatever, therefore, was said of Isaiah and his sons, *as types,* has reference also to Christ and the children which God has given him, *as antitypes.* See notes on 1: 5.

This is further indicated by the names which God gave to this illustrious Prophet and his two sons, to whom reference is made in this section of prophecy. (Isa. 7: 1-9: 7.) The name *Isaiah* means *salvation of Jehovah,* and is nearly equivalent to the name *Joshua* or *Jesus,* which means "Jehovah's salvation," or Jehovah is his salvation. The original name was Hoshea, salvation (Num. 13: 8);

but Moses changed it to Jehoshua, Jehovah's salvation (Num. 8: 16). After their return from captivity, the Jews contracted the name to Jeshua, as in Neh. 8: 17, etc. From this, is derived the Greek name Jesus (*Ieesous*), which is from the same root as the name Isaiah. The eldest son of Isaiah named in the Scriptures is called *Shear-Jashub*, which means, *A remnant shall return*. (Isa. 7: 3.) This, then, as well as the name *Isaiah*, was prophetic, and was manifestly intended by God to be a sign and an assurance to his suffering people, that he had still merciful designs in reserve for those of them who would remain faithful to the end. The next son mentioned was to be called *Immanuel*, which means *"God with us."* This name, it seems, was given to the first-born son of Isaiah by a second wife, to indicate that God was still among his people for their protection and deliverance. (Isa. 7: 13-16.) And as evidence of this, Isaiah was directed to announce the speedy fall of the two kings, Rezin and Pekah, who were then threatening to overthrow Jerusalem. "Before the child [Immanuel]," said God by the Prophet, "shall know to refuse the evil and choose the good, the land that thou abhorrest shall be forsaken of both her kings." (Isa. 7: 16.) And in order to impress this matter still more deeply on the minds and hearts of the people, God further instructed Isaiah to call the same child *Maharshalal-Hashbaz, Haste-to-the-spoil—Speed-to-the-prey:* indicating by this name that in a very short time, even "before the child should know to cry, My father and my mother, the riches of Damascus and the spoil of Samaria would be taken away by the king of Assyria." (Isa. 8: 1-4.) This was all fulfilled, as predicted, within the short space of three years after the delivery of the prophecy.

But there is also in this prophecy, as in many others, a double reference, first to the type and then to the antitype. This is evident from the application which Matthew makes of the fourteenth verse of the seventh chapter. See Matt. 1: 23. If, then, under the inspiration of the Holy Spirit, Matthew could say with propriety, "Now all this was done that it might be fulfilled which was spoken by the prophet, saying, Behold, a virgin shall be with child, and shall bring forth a son, and they shall call his name Immanuel," why may not Paul also say, speaking by the same Spirit, that Christ became a man, and suffered for us, as a man, that it might be fulfilled which was spoken by the Prophet Isaiah, saying, "Be-

14 Forasmuch then as ¹the children are partakers of ²flesh and blood,

¹John xi. 52; Rom. viii. 14-17; ix. 26; Eph. i. 5.
²Matt. xvi. 17; 1 Cor. xv. 50; Gal. i. 16; Eph. vi. 12.

hold I and the children which God hath given me"? Manifestly, the application which is here made of the words of Isaiah, in the latter case, is just as plain, direct, and authoritative, as in the former.

Care must be taken, however, in both cases, not to press the analogies too far. The name *Immanuel,* as applied to the son of Isaiah, was to the chosen people of that age a sign that God was still among them as their guardian and protector; but as applied to Christ, it is indicative of his Divinity, implying that he is himself God manifest in the flesh. There is a difference also between the relation which Isaiah bore to his children, according to the flesh, and that which Christ sustains to his disciples, as the children of God. But the resemblance between the two is sufficient to indicate that Christ and the "many sons" that he is leading on to glory, are all of the same family, and that they are bound together by cords of the deepest and tenderest human sympathy. This is all that the Apostle aims to prove by these citations from the Old Testament.

14 **Forasmuch then**—(*epei oun*) *since then.* In the context preceding, the Apostle has shown that it was a part of God's gracious will and purpose, as revealed in the Old Testament, that Christ and the children of the covenant (Gal. 3: 7, 9, 29) should all be of one Father, and of one family. But according to the established laws and ordinances of nature, the children have all been made partakers (*kekoinoneeke*) of flesh and blood. And hence it was that, in compliance with God's will and purpose, Christ also partook of the same. "Though he was in the form of God, and thought it not robbery to be equal with God, yet he made himself of no reputation, and took upon him the form of a servant, and was made in the likeness of men." (Phil. 2: 6, 7.) The expression, "flesh and blood," says Bleek, "betokens the whole sensuous corporeal nature of man, which he has in common with the brutes, and whereby he is the object of sensuous perception and corporeal impressions; whereby also he is subjected to the laws of infirmity, decay, and transitoriness of material things, in contrast with purely spiritual and incorporeal beings." Frequently it is used by synecdoche in a more comprehensive sense for *human nature;* as, for

¹he also himself likewise took part of the same; that ²through death he might ³destroy him that had the power of death, that is, ⁴the devil; 15 And

---

¹John i. 14; Rom. viii. 3; Gal. iv. 4; Phil. ii. 7, 8; 1 Tim. iii. 16.
²Ch. ix. 15; Isa. liii. 12; John xii. 24, 31-33; Rom. xiv. 9; Col. ii. 14, 15; Rev. i. 18.
³Isa. xxv. 6-8; Hos. xiii. 14; 1 Cor. xv. 54, 55; 2 Tim. i. 10; 1 John iii. 8.
⁴John viii. 44; xiv. 30; xvi. 11; 2 Cor. iv. 4; Eph. ii. 2.

---

example, in Matt. 16: 17; Gal. 1: 16; Eph. 6: 12. And there can be no doubt that in becoming incarnate, the Logos assumed human nature in all its fullness, including every element of our spiritual, as well as of our physical and sensuous being. But in this instance, as in 1 Cor. 15: 50, the words seem to be used in a more limited sense. The Apostle does not say that the children *are* flesh and blood, but that they have been made *partakers* of flesh and blood; thereby making a distinction between what constitutes the essential and eternal part of man's nature, and what is merely accidental, and in which we now live as in a clay tabernacle. (2 Cor. 5: 1.) Even this sensuous part of our nature was put on by Christ, so that he might in every particular, "be made like unto his brethren," and "through death destroy him that has the power of death."

**that is, the devil;**—The word *devil* (*diabolos*—from *diaballo, to calumniate*) means properly a calumniator, a traducer, an accuser, or a slanderer. The corresponding Hebrew word is *Satan,* meaning one that hates, an enemy. Our knowledge of this wonderful being is quite limited. But from the Scriptures we may learn (1) that like man he was at first created upright; and that like man he afterward sinned and fell. Christ says of him in John 8: 44, that "he abode not in the truth"; which implies very clearly that he was once in it. And Jude says (verse 6), "The angels who kept not their first estate, but left their own proper habitation, he has reserved in everlasting chains under darkness unto the judgment of the great day." See also 2 Pet. 2: 4. From a comparison of these passages, it is very manifest that Satan was one of those angels who, not being satisfied with their "first estate," or original condition (*archee*), were cast down to Tartarus on account of their rebellion. (2) There is but little said in the Bible in reference to the particular occasion and circumstances of Satan's fall. But it is pretty evident from 1 Tim. 3: 6, that it was occasioned by pride. Paul here admonishes Timothy not to appoint to the Bish-

op's office "a new convert, lest being lifted up with pride he fall
into the condemnation of the devil"; that is, lest he fall into the
same condemnation into which the devil fell. That this is the
meaning of the Apostle, is evident from the fact that it is not the
prerogative of the devil to condemn anyone. He ensnares (1
Tim. 3: 7); but it is Christ that condemns (Rom. 8: 34). How
pride or any other sin could enter Heaven, may be a mystery
above our comprehension. But it seems that in some way (perhaps by comparing himself too much with his inferiors, instead of
duly considering the Infinite), pride got possession of Satan's
heart, begetting in him, and through him in others, an unhallowed
ambition to rise still higher among the principalities and powers of
the heavenly realms. They "left their own proper habitation"; and
as a consequence were cast down to Hades. (3) After he was cast
out of Heaven, he successfully plotted and effected the fall of man.
Why Satan was allowed to come to this world and tempt our first
parents, as he did, is a question too high for us. God alone may be
capable of fully understanding this mystery. But the fact is indisputable. God had said to Adam: "But of the tree of knowledge of
good and evil, thou shalt not eat of it; for in the day that thou
eatest thereof, thou shalt surely die." (Gen. 2: 17.) Satan, whose
intellect is marvelously great, next it may be to that of the Infinite,
was not long, it seems, in perceiving how he might turn this ordinance of God to his own advantage and to man's ruin. He knew
that so long as man was loyal to his Maker, he and all his fallen
compeers, though numerous it may be as the leaves and flowers of
Eden, could do nothing to his injury. But Satan had no doubt
well weighed and considered the awful, mysterious, and comprehensive import of the word *death* in the threatened penalty. He
saw that there was in this thing death, a power, the possession of
which would make him the prince of the world (John 12: 31; 14:
30; 16: 11), and make man his most abject slave (John 8: 34).
He resolved if possible to secure it; and succeeded but too well in
his diabolical designs. Through his influence, Adam sinned and
fell; and humanity sinned and fell in him. (Rom. 5: 12, 18, 19.)

the power of death,—What is it, and in what does it consist?
This is a question which we can now answer but in part. Until we
understand perfectly what death is, we cannot of course fully understand its power. But such matters are above our weak capac-

ity. We know, however, that it has, in a very important and comprehensive sense, separated man from his Maker (Eph. 2: 12,
13) ; robbed him of his highest spiritual power and enjoyment
(Eph. 2: 1, 5) ; filled his heart with enmity to God (Gen. 3: 8;
Col. 1: 21) ; made him the willing slave of sin and Satan (John 8:
44; Rom. 1: 28-31; 2 Cor. 4: 4; Eph. 2: 2; 1 John 3: 8; 5:
19) ; and greatly deranged all his physical as well as his spiritual
powers, resulting in a separation of soul and body (Rom. 5: 12;
6: 23; 1 Cor. 15: 21, 22). Its power is therefore immensely
great; and it is all used by Satan for the purpose of promoting his
own diabolical ends and purposes.

But "the Word became flesh" in order that, by means of his
death, "he might destroy him that has the power of death." The
word *destroy* (*katargeo*) does not mean to annihilate, but simply
to render useless, to bring to naught. The Apostle John expresses
the same thought in his first Epistle (3: 8) where he says, "For
this purpose was the Son of God manifested that he might destroy
(*lusee*) the works of the devil." The mere destruction of Satan
himself would not accomplish God's purpose. Had Christ annihilated him, as he doubtless might have done, this alone would not
have relieved mankind from their woes and misfortunes. For death,
be it observed, is not wholly an invention of the devil. It was of
course brought about by his hellish craft and cunning; for if man
had never sinned, he would never have died. Nevertheless, death itself, under the circumstances, springs up out of a moral necessity;
a necessity which is as immutable as the truth and justice of God.
And consequently, whatever may become of Satan, death cannot
be destroyed, until all the claims of the Divine government on man
are fully satisfied, and man himself is again made holy and so reconciled to his Maker. To effect these ends, as we have seen in our
exegesis of the tenth verse, it was indispensable that Christ should
become a man, and, as such, be made perfect through suffering.
And now having by his own blood made purification for the sins of
mankind, he has sat down on the right hand of the Majesty on
high; there to reign until the works of Satan shall be destroyed,
and the dominion of the world shall be restored to the "many
sons" whom he is leading on to glory.

¹deliver them ²who through fear of death were all their lifetime ³subject to bondage.

¹Isa. lxi. 1-3; Luke i. 74, 75.
²Job xviii. 11, 14; Psa. lxxiii. 19; 1 Cor. xv. 50-57.
³Rom. viii. 15, 21; Gal. iv. 3, 21-31; 2 Tim. i. 7.

15 **And deliver them**—The Apostle does not mean, that all men will actually be delivered from the bondage brought upon them by sin and the fear of death; but only that through Christ all may be delivered. In partaking of flesh and blood, it was his purpose to open up "a new and living way," through which all might come to God, obtain the pardon of their sins, and be made heirs of the eternal inheritance.

**through the fear of death**—This fear is natural and universal. Men fear death (1) because of the pain, misery, and dissolution, which attend it; (2) because of the darkness and corruption of the grave which follow it; and (3) because of the uncertainty of their condition and destiny beyond it. It is the terminus of our probationary state, beyond which there is no place for repentance. The man who passes this solemn bourn, in union, communion, and fellowship with God, will die no more. (Luke 20: 36.) But for those who are then disloyal and unholy, there remains nothing but the horrors and torments of the second death. (Rev. 20: 14, 15.) See Matt. 25: 46; 26: 26; Heb. 10: 26, 27; Rev. 22: 11.

No wonder, then, that death has been called "the King of terrors." (Job 18: 14.) It must be so to every man in his senses who has not been delivered from its enslaving influences through the Lord Jesus. Nothing but a strong, firm, and unfaltering faith in Christ—a faith which "works by love, purifies the heart, and overcomes the world,"—can ever save and deliver those who through the fear of death are all their lifetime subjects of bondage (*enochoi douleias*). But faith in Christ saves us from all such fears and torments; knowing, as we do, that "if our earthly house of this tabernacle were dissolved, we have a building of God, a house not made with hands eternal in the heavens." (2 Cor. 5: 1.) Under the sustaining and strengthening influence of this faith, we can exclaim with Paul, even in the face of Death, "O Death, where is thy sting? O Grave, where is thy victory?" Or with David we can calmly say, "Though I walk through the valley of the shadow of death, I will fear no evil; for thou [Jehovah] art with me; thy

16 For verily he took not on him the nature of angels; but ¹he took on
him the seed of Abraham.

¹Matt. viii. 17; xiv. 13; 2 Cor. viii. 9.

rod and thy staff, they comfort me." (Psalm 23 : 4.) And hence
we feel that it is even better to depart and to be with Christ. (Phil.
1 : 23.)

16 **For verily he took not on him the nature of angels;**—Or
more literally, *For not indeed of angels doth he take hold; but he
taketh hold of the seed of Abraham.*  The Greek word (*eplambo-
netai*) means (1) to take hold of any thing as one's own; and (2)
to take hold of any person with the view of helping him.  In this
latter sense the word is used here by our author.  His object is,
not as was generally supposed by the ancient commentators to
reassert the fact that Christ took on himself our nature, but rather
to assign a reason for his having done so.  Christ's mission, he
says, was not to take hold of angels and deliver them from slavery;
but it was to take hold of man, and to free him from the bondage
of sin and death.  And hence, as our author has shown in the
preceding context, it was becoming that he (Christ) should be
made a partaker of flesh and blood, so that by means of his death
he might destroy him that has the power of death, and deliver
those (men, not angels) who through fear of death were all their
lifetime subjects of bondage.

**but he took on him the seed of Abraham.**—Or rather as
above explained, *he taketh hold of the seed of Abraham.*  As the
Apostle was writing for the special benefit and encouragement of
the Hebrews, there was certainly no impropriety in his using terms
so very limited.  But in doing so he does not mean to exclude all,
save the seed of Abraham, from the benefits of Christ's death,
atonement, and intercession.  Certainly not; for in the ninth verse
of this chapter, he assures us that Jesus had by the grace of God
tasted death for every man.  This shows beyond all doubt that the
benefits of Christ's death are applicable to all men who will humbly
submit to the terms and conditions on which salvation is so graciously offered to us in the Gospel.  But in this saying there is a
rhetorical propriety which could not be so well expressed by any
terms that are more general and comprehensive.

17 Wherefore in all things [1]it behooved him to be made like unto his
brethren, that he might be [2]a merciful and faithful high priest in things pertaining to God, [3]to make reconciliation for the sins of the people.

[1]Luke xxiv. 26, 46; Rom. iii. 25, 26; Phil. ii. 7, 8.
[2]Ch. iii. 2; iv. 15; v. 1, 2; Isa. xi. 5.
[3]Lev. vi. 30; viii. 15; Dan. ix. 24; Rom. v. 10; 2 Cor. v. 18-21; Eph. ii. 16; Col. i.
21.

17 **Wherefore it behooved him**—As Christ came to help the
seed of Abraham (and all the rest of mankind), it behooved him to
be made like them. The word here rendered *behooved* (*opheilen*)
is different from that which is rendered *became* (*eprepen*) in the
tenth verse; and also from that which is rendered *ought* and *behooved* (*edei*) in Luke 24 : 26, 46. The last of these (*edei*) denotes moral necessity growing out of God's decrees and purposes;
the second (*eprepen*), as previously explained, denotes an intrinsic
fitness and propriety in conformity with the Divine attributes; but
the first (*opheilen*) expresses an obligation which arises out of any
work or enterprise already undertaken. The Apostle means to
say, therefore, that since Christ had voluntarily undertaken the
work of redeeming the seed of Abraham from the bondage of sin
and Satan, he thereby incurred the further obligation of being
made like them.

**in all things**—That is, in all things (*kata panta*) essential to
perfect humanity. This does not of course include the depravity
which we have incurred by sin. See notes on 4 : 15. Christ had
none of the evil lusts and propensities which now defile human nature (Matt. 15 : 18-20) ; enslave the unregenerate (Rom. 7 : 23) ;
and from which even we who have the first-fruits of the Spirit are
not wholly freed while we live in these clay tabernacles (Rom. 8 :
10). He was "without sin" (*choris hamartias*) in the fullest and
widest sense. But he had every faculty, power, and susceptibility
which belongs to human nature in its sinless state; and he was
therefore subject to all the sufferings, perils, temptations, toils, and
conflicts which we endure. Thus far it behooved him to be made
like unto his brethren, so that he might be fully qualified for the
great work which he had undertaken.

**that he might be a merciful and faithful high priest**—Or
rather, that he might *become* (*geneetai*) a merciful and faithful
High Priest. For as Alford very justly remarks in his commentary on this passage, "The High-priesthood of Christ in all its full-

ness, and especially in its work of mercy, and compassion, and succor, was not inaugurated till he entered into the heavenly place.
His being in all things like unto his brethren, sufferings and death
included, was necessary for him in order to his becoming, through
those sufferings and death, our High Priest. It was not the death
(though that was of previous necessity, and is therefore often spoken of as involving the whole), but the bringing the blood into the
Holy Place, in which the work of sacerdotal expiation consisted."
This is all just and right so far as it goes. Care, however, must be
taken not to press this view of the matter so far as to exclude
everything of a sacerdotal character from Christ's earthly ministry. This would be inconsistent with both the types of the Old
Testament and the subsequent teachings of our Epistle. For on
the Day of Atonement, the High Priest had first to slay the victim,
and then carry its blood into the Most Holy Place to make reconciliation for the sins of the people. (Lev. 16: 15.) And so also
Christ is said to have offered himself on the cross, so that he might
afterward enter Heaven with his own blood, and there make expiation for our sins according to the Scriptures. Christ was therefore
the Priest as well as the victim in the offering of himself on Calvary. But this offering on Calvary was only a preliminary part of
the one great offering of Christ which was consummated in
Heaven; and it was, moreover, an essential part of the preparatory
discipline through which he had to pass before he could be fully
qualified to officiate as the great High Priest of our confession.
See notes on 7 : 17, 27. And hence the High-priesthood is not im-
properly presented here as the goal which he had to reach through
his many trials and sufferings; and especially through his sufferings on the cross. "Before reaching it, he had to walk the path of
human suffering down to this deep turning-point, in order to acquire the requisite qualifications for the exercise of high-priestly
functions, extending thenceforth from Heaven to Earth" (*Del. in
loc.*). The idea of the Apostle, then, is this: that it was necessary
for Christ to become a man—a man of sorrows; a man in all respects like ourselves, but without sin—in order that he might be
the better qualified to have compassion on the erring and the ignorant; and to discharge with fidelity, as a High Priest, all his
duties both to God (3 : 2, 6) and to man (10 : 23).

   **in things pertaining to God,**—The High Priest under the law

was wholly consecrated to God.  Holiness to Jehovah was inscribed on the golden plate of his miter, as an indication that he
was set apart to minister to the Lord in the services of his Sanctuary.  And so also Christ, as the High Priest of the New Economy,
has been called and set apart to minister in "the Sanctuary and the
true Tabernacle which the Lord pitched and not man." (8 : 2.)  As
a King, he rules over Heaven and Earth; and supports all things
by the word of his power.  But the functions of his sacerdotal office
are more limited, having special reference to the wants of man and
the relations which we sustain to God and to his government.
This will become more apparent as we proceed with the exegesis of
the Epistle.

**to make reconciliation for the sins of the people.**—These
words indicate the main purpose of Christ's Priesthood.  He became such a Priest, as he is, in order to expiate by means of his
death the sins of the people.  The word here rendered "to make
reconciliation for" (*hilaskomai*), means, in classic Greek, to appease or to propitiate; as, for instance, when Homer, Hesiod, and
others, speak of appeasing the wrath of the gods by means of sacrifices.  But it is a significant fact, that neither this nor the corresponding Hebrew word is ever so used in the sacred writings.
God is never made the direct object of this or any other word of
like import in either the Old or the New Testament.  In no part of
the inspired word do we find such an expression as, to appease
God's wrath or to reconcile him to man by means of sacrifice.
The whole tenor of the inspired word goes to show that God had
compassion on the world, and sent his Son to redeem it. (1 John 4 :
9, 10.)

Caution is necessary, however, just here lest perchance we fall
into the extreme of supposing with some that Christ came into the
world merely for the purpose of showing forth the love of God to
man.  There is certainly a sense in which it may be truthfully said
that the atonement of Christ has rendered God propitious to man.
For it must not be forgotten that we were all by nature the children of God's wrath (Eph. 2 : 3), and that it is only through
Christ that this wrath has been, or can be, averted.  "He that believeth not the Son shall not see life, but the wrath of God abideth
on him." (John 3 : 36.)  There is therefore no reasonable ground
to doubt that the sacrifice of Christ has an influence on the mind of

18 For in that he himself ¹hath suffered being tempted, ²he is able to succor ³them that are tempted.

¹Ch. iv. 15, 16; v. 7-9; Matt. iv. 1-10; xxvi. 36-46; Luke xxii. 53.
²Ch. vii. 25, 26; 2 Cor. xii. 7-10; Phil. iii. 21; 2 Tim. i. 12.
³1 Cor. x. 13; 2 Pet. ii. 9; Rev. iii. 10.

God toward the sinner, as well as on the sinner himself. But it is not such an influence as many have supposed. It may be properly illustrated by the case of a wise, just, and benevolent father; who though insulted by an ungrateful son, still loves and pities him; and while vindicating his own authority as a father, does at the same time all that he can to reclaim his son. In like manner, God was insulted; his government was dishonored; and man had become an enemy to him by wicked works. (Col. 1: 21.) Nevertheless, God had pity and compassion on his erring and prodigal children. He so loved and pitied them, even when they were dead in trespasses and sins, "that he gave his only-begotten Son, so that whosoever believeth in him should not perish, but have everlasting life." (John 3: 16.) Thus "God was in Christ reconciling the world unto himself, not imputing their trespasses unto them." (2 Cor. 5: 19.) "Herein," then, "is love; not that we loved God, but that he loved us, and sent his Son to be the propitiation (*hilasmos*) for our sins." (1 John 4: 10.)

The whole plan of redemption, therefore, including the work of atonement, is an arrangement of the Godhead, embracing the Father, the Son, and the Holy Spirit; and is designed (1) to meet and satisfy the claims of the Divine government against man, so that God's mercy might justly flow to penitent sinners; (2) to reconcile man to God, by removing enmity from his heart and filling it with gratitude and love; and (3) to actually blot out and forever cancel the sins of all such as become obedient to the Divine will. But in order to effect all this, it was necessary, as the Apostle here shows, that Christ should become a man, in all respects like unto his brethren, so that he might be a merciful and faithful High Priest in things pertaining to God. Thus, and thus only, could he make expiation for our sins; and so render it possible for God's abounding mercy and love to flow out freely and fully to all who love and obey him.

18 **For in that, etc.**—In this verse, the Apostle explains how it is, that Christ's being made like unto his brethren in all things

serves to make him a more faithful and compassionate High Priest. "For in that," he says, "he himself hath suffered being tempted, he is able to succor them that are tempted." As God, he knows of course all our wants, and is ever able and willing to supply them. But as a man, he had to experience all the trials, temptations, privations, sorrows, and sufferings, which are common to our race, in order to fully qualify him for the duties of his mediatorial office: and these, as the Divine record shows, he endured to the uttermost. Born in a stable, cradled in a manger, and brought up in the humble condition of a peasant, he entered upon his public duties under the most trying and discouraging circumstances. Satan tempted him; the scribes and Pharisees derided and persecuted him; and even his own friends and brethren forsook him. But he faltered not in his purpose. His course was ever onward toward the sublime goal of his earthly mission. Amidst the lowering tempests and gathering storms of demoniacal fury and satanic malice, he marched directly onward, until baptized in sufferings, his oppressed and care-worn frame sunk under the tremendous pressure of his mental agonies, and his great heart literally burst under the crushing and overwhelming influence of his incurred responsibilities. See notes on 5: 7. He could endure no more; but calmly said, "It is finished"; and then expired.

## REFLECTIONS

1. God has provided a home for his children. (2:5-9.) "The meek," says Christ, "shall inherit the Earth." For ages, the domination of the world has been a matter of strife and contention; and ambitious men have waded through seas of blood to obtain it. But it is all in vain. They will never, except by temporary usurpation, enjoy even so much as a foot-breadth of it; for to Abraham and his seed it has all been given by an irrevocable decree of Jehovah, as their everlasting inheritance. (Rom. 4: 13.) It matters not how humble and how destitute we may now be, if we have the earnest of the Spirit (Eph. 1: 14); "then indeed are we Abraham's seed, and heirs according to the promise" (Gal. 3: 29). I do not say that we will always be confined to this world, as we now are while living in these "houses of clay whose foundation is in the dust." This is not probable. With bodies like unto that of the Son of God (1 John 3: 2), purified and spiritualized (1 Cor. 15: 44, 50),

we may, like angels, pass from world to world, and from system to system, to behold the works of the Lord and to make known to others the mysteries of redemption. But wherever we go, and on whatever errand we may be sent, our object finished, we will return again on joyful wing to this renovated earth to behold with increasing wonder and delight the beauty and the glory of the Lord in the New Jerusalem, "the city of our God, the mountain of his holiness." There with David we will often exclaim, with wonder and amazement, "Lord, what is man that thou art mindful of him, or the son of man that thou visitest him?" When we see the countless myriads of suns, and moons, and stars that compose the vast empire of Jehovah, and the higher sons of light who inhabit them, and who from so many centers of creation swell the lofty praises of their Creator in everlasting anthems— feeling our own nothingness and unworthiness, we will be filled with wonder and amazement that God, in his infinite condescension, mercy, and love, should have provided such a home for us as the New Heavens and the New Earth, filled and illuminated with his own glorious and eternal presence. See Rev. 21 and 22.

2. The atonement made by Christ is for all men, and its benefits are in some measure unconditionally extended to all. Even the lives that we now live in the flesh, we live through the forbearance of God in Christ (1 Tim. 4: 10) ; and the removal of the effects and consequences of the Adamic transgression will be as wide and as comprehensive as the human race. For "as in Adam all die, even so in Christ shall all be made alive." (1 Cor. 15:22.) And "as by means of one trespass, the righteous sentence of God came upon all men to condemnation ; so also by means of one righteous act, the favor of God will come on all men to justification of life [from the penalty of death incurred through Adam]. For as by the disobedience of one man [Adam] the many [all men] were made sinners ; so also by the obedience of the one [Christ], the many [all men] shall be made righteous [so far as it respects the sinfulness incurred through Adam]." (Rom. 5: 18, 19.) Nor is this all : for where sin abounded, grace superabounded. Through the infinite merits of the one offering of Christ, the justice of God has been satisfied, and ample provision has been made for pardoning the many personal offenses of all men who repent of their sins and humbly bow to the will and authority of God. And hence the

cry of Mercy now is, "Ho, every one that thirsteth, come ye to the waters: and he that hath no money; come ye, buy and eat; yea, come buy wine and milk without money and without price."

3.  The scheme of redemption through Christ is not an arbitrary scheme (verse 10). It is a scheme prompted by the love of God; founded in justice, judgment, and equity; and administered throughout in infinite wisdom. The nature of God is its constitution, in harmony with which all its laws and ordinances have been enacted. And hence it became God in bringing many sons unto glory, to look not only to the qualifications of their Captain, but also to the rightful demands of his own nature and government. Until these were satisfied, it were all vain to talk of saving any sinner. By an eternal moral necessity, deep and profound as the Divine nature, the soul that sinneth must die; unless an adequate ransom can in some way be provided. This has been done through the one offering of the Lord Jesus Christ. He, by his death and incarnation, has magnified God's law and made it honorable (Isa. 42: 21); he has by the offering of his blood, once for all, brought in everlasting righteousness (Dan. 9: 24); and under his peaceful and glorious reign, "Mercy and Truth have met together, Righteousness and Peace have kissed each other" (Psalm 85: 10). No wonder, then, that angels desired to look into these things, and to study with profound reverence the economy of redemption. (1 Pet. 1: 12.) There is here nothing of fatality, nor of arbitrary will and caprice; but there is here a system of rectitude, broad, deep, and profound as the Divine government; every element of which is marked by that "wisdom which is first pure, then peaceable, gentle, and easy to be entreated; full of mercy and good fruits, without partiality and without hypocrisy." (James 3: 17.)

4.  How wonderful are the condescension and the love of Christ in assuming our nature and being made like unto his brethren in all things; so that he might by the grace of God taste death for every man, destroy the works of Satan, and "deliver those who through fear of death were all their lifetime subjects of bondage" (verses 9-18).

> "He left his radiant throne on high,
>     Left the bright realms of bliss,
> And came to Earth to bleed and die:
>     Was ever love like this?"

"Scarcely for a righteous man will one die; yet peradventure for a good man some would even dare to die. But God commendeth his love toward us, in that while we were yet sinners, Christ died for us." (Rom. 5: 7, 8.)

5. Perhaps, then, it should not excite our surprise, that this marvelous condescension of the Lord Jesus has always proved to be one of the chief stumblingblocks in the way of unbelievers. There is nothing in the depraved and selfish nature of man that will at all compare with it. And hence to those who are wont to estimate the motives of others by their own, it seems wholly incredible that "he who was in the form of God, and thought it not robbery to be equal with God" should make himself of no reputation, and take upon himself the form of a servant, that he might become obedient to death, even the death of the cross. But as the heavens are higher than the Earth, so are God's ways higher than our ways, and his thoughts above our thoughts. (Isa. 55: 9.)

6. To me, therefore, it seems far more strange and remarkable that any who profess to believe the testimony which God has given to us concerning his Son, should at any time refuse to obey any of his precepts. When we think of the condescension of Jesus; the sufferings of Jesus; and the many benefits which he has procured for us through the rich merits of his own precious blood, we feel as if we could never do enough, or suffer enough for such a Savior. And yet, alas, how many who profess to believe the Gospel are still hardened through the deceitfulness of sin! How many such are still slaves to "the lusts of the flesh, the lusts of the eye, and the pride of life"! Nor is perfection found even in us who have the first-fruits of the Spirit, "which God has given to them that obey him." We, too, fall far short of that perfect obedience which the law of God requires, and which our own hearts approve. To know this is, of course, very painful to every true child of God; and makes us long for that perfect state where we will no longer grieve our Father and our Redeemer.

7. In the meantime, how very encouraging and delightful is the thought that our blessed Savior sympathizes with us in all our griefs, trials, and temptations; and that if we only rely on him, trust in him, and struggle on in our imperfect way for a little while, he will soon take us to that brighter and better world, where we will sin no more (verse 18).

## SECTION THREE
### 3:1 to 4:13

### ANALYSIS

Near the close of the last section (2:17), the Apostle, while discussing the question of Christ's humanity, refers for the first time to his priesthood. And hence we might reasonably expect that this would be made the next topic of discussion. But connected with this, and naturally and historically antecedent to it, is the apostleship of Christ. Moses preceded Aaron in the economy of the Old Testament; and Christ appeared as the Leader of God's people, before he entered on the duties of his priesthood. And hence while our author blends together in some measure the discussion of these two functions of Christ's mediatorial office, he devotes the next section mainly to the consideration of his apostleship and such other matters as depend essentially on it. The following are the main points which he makes in the discussion and development of this part of his subject:

I. He shows the great superiority of Christ over Moses, as the Apostle of God. (3: 1-6.)

1. In making this comparison between Christ and Moses, our author shows no disposition to disparage the latter in any way. He concedes that Moses was faithful to God in all his house (verse 2).

2. But then he argues that according to the Divine arrangement, Christ is as much superior to Moses as he who builds a house is superior to the house itself (verse 3). This argument may be briefly stated as follows: God built all things, including, of course, both the Jewish house and the Christian house. But Christ is God, one with the Father. (1:8.) And hence it follows, that Christ is as much superior to the Jewish or Old Testament house of God, including Moses himself and every other member of the Theocracy, as he who builds a house is superior to it (verses 4, 5).

3. Furthermore, Moses was but a servant in the symbolical house of God; but Christ as a Son presides over the real house of God; which is to the symbolical house of the Old Testament economy, as the substance is to the shadow (verse 6).

II. From this subject, the transition to the pilgrimage of the Israelites under Moses and ours under Christ, is easy and natural (verses 7-19).

1. According to Moses (Num. 2: 32, 33), about six hundred thousand (603,550) Israelites, besides the Levites and the women and children, left Egypt with the fairest and most encouraging prospects of entering Canaan.

2. But, nevertheless, very few of them ever reached the Promised Land. They provoked God in the wilderness, till he finally swore in his wrath that they should never enter into his rest. (Num. 14: 22-30.)

3. From this chapter of sacred history, the Apostle therefore solemnly warns his Hebrew brethren, and through them also all the followers of Christ, of their many dangers, and of the necessity of their giving all diligence in order to make their calling and election sure during their earthly pilgrimage (verses 12-18).

4. It is true that our advantages and privileges are now, in many respects, greatly superior to those of the ancient Israelites. But human nature is still the same; our greatest enemies are still the same; the deceitfulness of sin is the same; many of our trials and temptations are the same; and hence what was "written aforetime was written for our learning, that we through patience and comfort of the Scriptures might have hope." It becomes all Christians, therefore, to exhort and admonish one another daily (verse 13).

III. From the pilgrimage of the Jews under Moses and ours under Christ, the Apostle is next led to consider the *rest* which remains for the people of God. (4: 1-10.)

1. The idea of rest was a very pleasant and consoling thought to the Israelites. They had long been accustomed to reflect on the many pleasures and advantages of a sanctified rest.

(1.) From the regular observance of the weekly Sabbath.

(2.) From the habit of sanctifying many other days to the Lord; as, for example, the first day of every month; the first and last day of the feast of Unleavened Bread, etc.

(3.) From celebrating the Sabbatical Year and the Year of Jubilee.

(4.) From the ease and repose which they enjoyed in Canaan, compared with the many toils and trials which their fathers had endured in the wilderness. From all of which it is manifest, that in an argument designed for the encouragement of the Hebrew brethren, it was particularly necessary to dwell on this element of the Christian religion, and to show that there is a rest remaining for the people of God, that far transcends in importance any earthly rest that was ever enjoyed by the seed of Abraham according to the flesh.

2. But just here the Apostle seems to have anticipated an objection which might peradventure be urged by the judaizing party. That most of the Old Testament references to the heavenly rest were made through types and shadows there can be no doubt. And with some it might, therefore, be a question, whether in such portions of Scripture there is really anything more intended or implied than the mere temporal rest to which the ancient Prophets primarily referred.

3. To this question he makes the following reply:

(1.) He refers to Psalm 95:7, from which he proves that God in his wrath had sworn to the Israelites under Moses, that they should not enter into his rest. And hence he argues that this could not be the Sabbatical rest, because it was instituted in the beginning when God finished the work of creation (Gen. 2:2), and had been enjoyed by the Israelites throughout all their journeyings (Ex. 16:22-31). And hence it follows that there must be another rest for the people of God: a rest into which the rebellious Israelites under Moses never entered (verses 3-6).

(2.) But lest it might be supposed that the promise of God guaranteeing rest to his people, was fulfilled in its fullest and ultimate sense when the Israelites under Joshua entered Canaan, the Apostle refers again to the ninety-fifth Psalm, and proves from it that even in the time of David, after the children of Israel had possessed the land of Canaan for nearly five hundred years—even then there was danger that the living generation would, like their fathers, be excluded from the promised rest. From all of which, it clearly follows that there is still a rest remaining for the people of God. For as our author says, if Joshua had given the people rest in the land of Canaan, then most assuredly God would not afterward have spoken of another rest by the mouth of his servant David (verses 7-9).

IV. The section closes with a renewed exhortation to labor earnestly to enter into the rest of God, especially in view of the heart-searching character of his word by which we are all to be judged at the last day (verses 11-13).

1. Here we may often deceive one another; and sometimes we may even deceive ourselves; but nothing can escape the eye of God and the all-permeating power of his word.

2. And hence the necessity of the most careful and constant self-examination, lest, like the Israelites, we too fall short of the promised rest.

Under this section, we have therefore the four following paragraphs:

I. 3 : 1-6. Christ superior to Moses.

II. 3 : 7-19. Exhortations and warnings drawn from the example of the Israelites under Moses.

III. 4 : 1-10. Concerning the rest which remains for the people of God.

IV. 4 : 11-13. Renewed exhortation to strive earnestly to enter into God's rest, in view especially of the all-penetrating and heart-searching character of God's word.

## 1. CHRIST SUPERIOR TO MOSES
### 3 : 1-6

1 Wherefore, [1]holy brethren, [2]partakers of the [3]heavenly calling, consider the [4]apostle and [5]high priest of our [6]profession, [Christ] Jesus;

[1]Col. iii. 12; 1 Pet. ii. 9.
[2]Ver. 14; Rom. xi. 17; Eph. iii. 6; Col. i. 12; 1 Pet. v. 1.
[3]Rom. i. 6; Eph. iv. 1, 4; Phil. iii. 14; 1 Pet. v. 10; 2 Pet. i. 10.
[4]Isa. lxi. 1-3; John xiii. 20; xx. 21.
[5]Ch. ii. 17; iv. 14, 15; v. 1-10; vi. 20; vii. 26; viii. 1-3; ix. 11; x. 21; Psa. cx. 4; Zech. vi. 13.
[6]Ch. iv. 14; x. 23; 1 Tim. vi. 12. 13.

1 **Wherefore,**—We have here a very beautiful illustration of the easy and natural manner in which our author passes from one subject to another. The word *"wherefore"* (*hothen*) is illative, and shows the very close and intimate connection of what follows in this verse, with what has been said of Christ in the two preceding chapters; and especially in the last paragraph of the second chapter. But what is here introduced as a consequence from premises considered, is made also a ground of transition to another subject.

**holy brethren,**—These were the Hebrew Christians. They are addressed here by the Apostle, not as Jews, nor as brethren of Christ, but as his own brethren in Christ. And they are called *holy* brethren, not because they were all in possession of that holiness of heart which the Gospel requires, but because they had all professed to believe in Christ, to put on Christ (Gal. 3 : 27), and to be separated from the world as the peculiar people of God. In this sense, the Corinthian brethren are all called *saints* (*agioi*, 1 Cor. 1: 2) ; though we are assured by Paul in both his letters to the Corinthian Church, that some of them were very impure men. See references, and notes on 2: 11.

**partakers of the heavenly calling,**—The word rendered *calling* (*kleesis*), means properly a call, a summons, an invitation ; and hence by metonymy it means also the *state* or *condition* into which anyone is called. In 1 Cor. 7: 17-20, for example, Paul says to the Corinthian brethren, "As the Lord hath called every one, so let him walk ; and so I ordain in all the churches. Is any man called being circumcised? let him not be uncircumcised. Is any called in uncircumcision? let him not be circumcised. Circumcision is nothing, and uncircumcision is nothing, but the keeping of the commandments of God. Let every man abide in the same calling wherein he was called." In this passage, the word *calling* evidently refers to the social rank and secular condition of each individual when he was called of God to partake of the "heavenly calling" ; some were Jews and some were Gentiles, some were slaves and some were freemen. The "heavenly calling," according to Paul, is not designed to nullify and set aside arbitrarily and unconditionally all such distinctions. The Jew, though converted to Christ, might nevertheless consistently remain in circumcision ; and the Gentile, in uncircumcision. In this metonymical sense the word *calling* is used in our text to denote, not merely God's gracious invitation to sinners, but also and more particularly the benefits of this invitation ; having special reference to the present state and condition of those who, in obedience to God's call, have put on Christ as he is offered to us in the Gospel. It is the high and holy calling of God in Christ Jesus (Phil. 3: 14), to which our author here refers. And this is denominated a *heavenly* calling because it comes from Heaven, leads to Heaven, and fills with heavenly joys the hearts of all who are made partakers of it.

**consider the apostle and high priest**—Meditate carefully and profoundly (*katanoeesate*) on the nature and character of Jesus, the Apostle and High Priest of our confession. Our author makes here an earnest appeal to his Hebrew brethren to consider well all that he had said, and all that he was about to say, concerning Christ ; to think of his Divinity, his humanity, his sufferings, his death, his burial, his resurrection, his ascension, his glorification, his universal dominion, his love, his sympathies, and every other attribute and perfection of his character. And this he does for the purpose of confirming and strengthening their faith, increasing their love, and guarding them against the sin of apostasy.

The word *apostle* (*apostelos*) means *one who is sent:* a messenger of any kind. In this sense it is here applied to Christ, as the one sent by God for the redemption of mankind. "The Father sent the Son to be the Savior of the world." (1 John 4 : 14.) Christ is then the Apostle of God under the New Economy as Moses was his Apostle under the Old Economy. True, indeed, Moses is nowhere called the Apostle of God in the Holy Scriptures; but words equivalent to these occur frequently in the Old Testament. In Ex. 3 : 10, for example, God says to Moses, "Come, now, therefore, and I will send thee unto Pharaoh, that thou mayest bring forth my people the children of Israel out of Egypt." And in the twelfth verse of the same chapter he says, "And this shall be a token unto thee, that I have sent thee." See also Ex. 3 : 13-15; 4 : 28; 5 : 22; 7 : 16, etc. It is evident, therefore, that our author here applies this term to Christ as the Apostle, or Messenger, of the New Covenant (Mal. 3 : 1), for the purpose of comparing him in this capacity with Moses the renowned and honored Apostle of the Old Covenant. They were both sent by God; and were therefore the Apostles of God. But the ministry of Christ, as Paul now proceeds to show, was far superior to that of Moses. In the fourth, sixth, and eighth sections of the Epistle, the priesthood of Christ is compared with that of Aaron, and shown to be superior to it in every respect.

**of our profession,**—The Greek word here rendered *profession* (*homologia*) means (1) an agreement or compact; and (2) an admission, acknowledgment, or confession. It is God's prerogative to speak (*legein*), and it is man's duty and privilege to acknowledge (*homologein*) the justice and propriety of what he says. Thus God spoke the words of the Old Covenant from Mount Sinai (Ex. 20-23), and the people then acknowledged his words, and consented to observe and do all that he had commanded (Ex. 24 : 3). In like manner God has made known to us all the terms and stipulations of the New Covenant; and to these he requires us to give a hearty and unreserved assent and acknowledgment. But as

2 Who was ¹faithful to him that appointed him, ²as also Moses was faithful in ³all his house.

¹Ch. ii. 17; John vi. 38-40; viii. 29; xvii. 4.
²Num. xii. 7; Deut. iv. 5.
³Eph. ii. 22; 1 Tim. iii. 15; 1 Pet. ii. 5.

Christ is himself the central truth, the Alpha and the Omega, of the New Covenant, it follows of course that all things pertaining to it are briefly summed up in the confession that *"Jesus is the Christ, the Son of the living God."* (Matt. 16:16.) "On this rock," says Christ, "I will build my Church, and the gates of Hades shall not prevail against it." (Matt. 16:17.) This soon became publicly known as "The Confession" of the primitive Christians; and hence it is that the Greek article is always prefixed to the noun which is used to express it. In Paul's first Epistle to Timothy, for example, he says to him, "Fight the good fight of faith, lay hold on eternal life to which thou wast called, and didst confess the good confession (*teen kaleen homologian*) before many witnesses." (6:12.) And in the next verse he says, "I charge thee in the sight of God who quickeneth all things, and before Jesus Christ who before Pontius Pilate testified the good confession, that thou keep this commandment without spot and without reproach until the appearing of our Lord Jesus Christ." See also Heb. 4:14; 10:23; 2 Cor. 9:13. In all these passages the Greek article is used before the noun (*homologia*), as in 1 Tim. 6:12, to denote that the confession made by Christ and Timothy was the common and well-known confession that was then required of all, as a condition of church-membership. For as Paul says to the Roman brethren, "with the heart man believeth unto righteousness; and with the mouth confession is made unto salvation" (Rom. 10:10). And Christ says, "Whosoever therefore shall confess me before men, him will I confess before my Father who is in Heaven." (Matt. 10:32.)

When the confession is made publicly in the presence of witnesses, it may also be called, as in our text, a *profession* (professio); which means simply a public avowal of one's belief and sentiments. But the word *confession* or *acknowledgment* better expresses the meaning of the Apostle, and is also more in harmony with Greek usage.

2 **Who was faithful to him that appointed him,**—More literally, *as being faithful to him that made him.* The present partici-

ple *being* (*onta*) indicates that fidelity to God is an abiding and perpetual characteristic of Christ in his whole sphere of labor. He came to do the will of him that sent him. (John 4:34.) This he did while he tabernacled with us here on Earth; and this he is now doing in the discharge of the higher functions of his mediatorial reign. In his hands, the government of God and the interests of mankind are alike perfectly secure. Sooner will Heaven and Earth pass away, than even one jot or one tittle of the Divine law fail in his hands.

He that appointed or made (*to poieesanti*) him, is, of course, God the Father. The reference here is not, as some think, to Christ's being eternally begotten of the Father (Bleek, Lünemann); nor is it, as others allege, to his incarnation (Athanasius, Ambrose); but it is simply to his being officially appointed by the Father (De Wette, Delitzsch, etc.); to his being made the Apostle and High Priest of our confession. "It is the Lord," says Samuel, "that advanced Moses and Aaron, and brought your fathers up out of the land of Egypt." (1 Sam. 12:6.) Here the Hebrew word rendered *advanced* means, literally, *made,* and it is so rendered in the Septuagint. (*ho poieesan ton Mouseen kai ton Aaron.*) It is, however, quite manifest that Samuel refers here, not to the creation of Moses and Aaron as men, but to their official appointment as the Apostle and High Priest of the Old Covenant. See Mark 3:14. And so also the word (*poieo*) is used in our text. God has made Jesus both the Apostle and High Priest of our confession; and in the discharge of all the duties appertaining to these sacred functions, he (Jesus) has always been faithful.

**as also Moses was faithful in all his house.**—That Moses was faithful in the discharge of all the duties of his office, God has himself borne witness. "If," says he in his admonition to Aaron and Miriam, "there be a prophet among you, I the Lord will make myself known to him in a vision, and I will speak unto him in a dream. My servant Moses is not so, who is faithful in all my house. With him I will speak mouth to mouth, even apparently, and not in dark speeches; and the similitude of the Lord shall he behold." (Num. 12:6-8.)

This much, then, is evident, that Moses was faithful to him that appointed him, in the discharge of all his official duties. But what

is the meaning of the word *house* (*oikos*) in this connection? and
to whom does the pronoun *his* (*autou*) refer?

A house is a dwelling-place; and the word is manifestly used
here to designate the Church of the Israelites, as God's ancient
dwelling place. This is obvious (1) from the context. We learn
from the sixth verse of this chapter, that the house over which
Christ now presides and in which he officiates, is the Christian
Church; which, as Paul says in his Epistle to the Ephesians (2:
20-22), is a holy temple, fitly framed together, and designed as a
habitation or dwelling-place of God through the Spirit. See also 1
Cor. 3: 16, 17; 6: 19; 2 Cor. 6: 16; 1 Tim. 3: 15; 1 Pet. 2: 5, etc.
(2) The same thing is made evident also from the consideration of
sundry other parallel passages, in which God is represented as actually dwelling among the ancient Israelites. In Ex. 25: 8, for example, God says to Moses, "Let them [the Israelites] make me a
Sanctuary that I may dwell among them." And in Ex. 29: 45, he
says, "I will dwell among the children of Israel, and I will be their
God." See also Lev. 26: 12; 1 Kings 6: 11-13, etc. There can be
no doubt, therefore, that the house in which Moses was faithful as
the steward of God, was the house of Israel; the same as the
Church of God in the wilderness. (Acts 7: 38.)

Let us, then, next inquire for the proper antecedent of the pronoun *his* (*autou*) in this connection. What is it? Some think that
the word *his* is used here to represent Christ; and that the Apostle
means to say that Moses was faithful in the house of Christ. This
is Bleek's opinion; but it is forced and unnatural, and scarcely de-
serves to be mentioned. Others make the pronoun refer to Moses,
regarding it, not as a genitive of possession, but of locality.
According to this construction the meaning of the Apostle is simply this: that Moses was faithful in the house to which he belonged
and in which he served. This opinion, supported by Ebrard and
others, is thought to be plausible and in no way inconsistent with
the context. But others again, as Delitzsch and Alford, maintain
with more probability that this pronoun refers to God as its proper
antecedent; to him who appointed both Moses and Christ to their
official positions; the one as a servant in the Old Testament house,
and the other as a Son over the house of the New Testament.
This construction is favored by the reference which our author
makes to Num. 12: 7, where God says as above, "My servant

3 For ¹this man was counted worthy of more glory than Moses, inasmuch as he who hath builded the house hath more honor than the house.

¹Deut. xviii. 18, 19; Matt. xvii. 3.

Moses . . . is faithful in all mine house." This view is also most in harmony with New Testament usage. See references.

Whatever may be thought of these minor points of grammatical construction, the general scope of this verse is very plain and obvious. Our author, wishing to compare Christ with Moses, refers first with great delicacy and propriety to one point in which they may within certain limits be regarded as equal. They were both faithful to him who appointed them, in their proper spheres of labor. But having conceded so much, the Apostle now proceeds to show that the difference between them is really infinite.

3 **For this man, etc.**—This verse in connection with the three following, has long been a stumbling-block in the way of many commentators. And it must be confessed that the passage is very elliptical, and that the construction is therefore somewhat obscure. But the argument of the Apostle manifestly implies that Christ sustains to Moses the same relation that the person who builds and furnishes a house sustains to the house itself. Consider well, he says, Jesus the Apostle and High Priest of our confession; for though he and Moses were both faithful to him who appointed them, he has nevertheless been counted worthy of more glory than Moses, in proportion as he who has builded and furnished a house has more honor than the house. Why so? Manifestly, because Christ is here regarded as the builder and furnisher of the whole house of Israel, of which Moses himself was but a member.

But how, it is asked, could this be, since Jesus was not born for fifteen hundred years after the birth of Moses? And how, we may ask in reply and with equal propriety, could God by his Son make the worlds many ages before the Logos became his Son? See note on 1: 2. How could Paul say to the Colossians (1: 16-18), "By him [God's dear Son] were all things created that are in Heaven and that are in Earth, visible and invisible, whether they be thrones, or dominions, or principalities, or powers; all things were created by him and for him; and he is before all things, and by him all things consist; and he is the head of the body, the Church; that in all things he might have the preeminence"? And how could the

4 For every house is builded by some man; but [1]he that built all things is God.

[1]Gen. i. 1; Ex. xxxi. 17; Psa. viii. 3; Acts xiv. 15; xvii. 24.

beloved John say, "In the beginning was the Word, and the Word was with God, and the Word was God; all things were made by him; and without him was not any thing made that was made"? How could the Word be God and be also with God? The truth is, we often confound ourselves and our readers by endeavoring to comprehend and explain, not indeed what is contrary to our reason, but what is infinitely above it. The sublime truth is, however, clearly taught in the Holy Scriptures, and in no part of them more clearly than in the first chapter of our Epistle, that the Father and the Son are both God; both included in the Eloheem Jehovah of the Old Testament, and the Lord God Omnipotent of the New; and that each of them, as well as the Holy Spirit, has an agency in all that pertains to the redemption of mankind. Jesus, as our author avers in 12 : 2, is both "the Author and the Finisher of the faith." The laws and ordinances of the Patriarchal and the Jewish age, as well as those of the Christian age, are all the product of his wisdom and benevolence, as well as of the wisdom and benevolence of the Father. And hence it may be truthfully said, that he, as God, was the builder and furnisher (*ho kataskeuasas*) of the whole house of Israel, including Moses and everything else that pertained to it.

4 **For every house is builded by some man;**—This is a sort of axiomatic expression which the Apostle throws in here for the purpose of connecting more clearly and distinctly the more remote links on his chain of argument. The nation of Israel under the Theocracy was a house, a dwelling-place of the Most High. And as such it must of course have had a builder and furnisher: "for every house is builded by some one." A design always implies a designer; and the building of every house implies a chief architect. Under him there may of course be many subordinates; but in order to secure unity of design there must of necessity be a chief designer. And just so it was with the house of Israel. It was built, and its affairs were administered through the agency of both men and angels. But still, God himself (including the Father, the Son, and the Holy Spirit) was the Supreme Architect in building the house of Israel, as well as in building the universe. And hence

5 And ¹Moses verily was faithful in all his house, as ²a servant, ³for a testimony of those things which were to be spoken after ;

¹Num. xii. 7.
²Ex. xiv. 31; 1 Cor. iv. 2.
³Ch. viii. 5; Luke xxiv. 27, 44; John v. 45-47; Acts iii. 22, 23.

it follows, as before stated, that Jesus in his entire personality, including his Divine as well as his human nature, is as much superior to Moses, as the builder of a house is to the house itself.

I am aware that their is in the human mind a tendency to think
of Christ merely as a man; and so to bring him down in our conceptions to an equality with creatures of high and exalted intelli-
gence. And I am also aware that with such opinions concerning
him, no one can understand the reasoning of Paul in this connection. No Socinian or Arian can ever give us a fair and consistent
explanation of this short paragraph. But surely the Apostle never
intended to call on his Hebrew brethren or any one else to consider
Jesus, the Apostle and High Priest of our confession, merely as a
man. For if so, then why does he present to us so fully the evidence of his Divinity in the first chapter of this Epistle? To my
mind it is quite evident that he purposely discusses the leading
questions relating to both the Divinity and the humanity of Christ,
before he attempts to compare him with Moses, the Apostle of the
Old Covenant. And then he calls on us to consider him as the
Creator and Founder of all things, including the Jewish Theocracy
as well as the Christian Church. In this view of the matter, all is
plain and simple.

5 **And Moses verily was faithful in all his house as a servant,**—In this and the following verse, the Apostle proceeds to
state two other points in which Moses was inferior to Christ: (1)
Moses was but a *servant* (*therapon*) a waiting-man in the house
of God; but Christ as a Son presides over the house of his Father.
(2) The house in which Moses served was far inferior to that over
which Christ presides. True, indeed, each of them is called the
house of God; but the former was to the latter as the type is to the
antitype, or as the shadow is to the subsance. (Col. 2 : 17; Heb.
10 : 1.) The Law was given through Moses on account of transgression, till the Seed should come (Gal. 3 : 19) ; and it was designed to serve (a) as a code of rules and regulations for the polit-
ical government of the Israelites (1 Tim. 1 : 9). (b) It was given
to convict men of sin; and thus to make them feel the necessity of a

6 But Christ as ¹a Son over his own house; ²whose house are we, ³if we hold fast the confidence and the ⁴rejoicing of the hope [firm unto the end].

¹Ch. i. 2; Psa. ii. 6, 7; Isa. ix. 6, 7; John iii. 35.
²Matt. xvi. 18; 1 Cor. iii. 16; 2 Cor. vi. 16; Eph. ii. 21, 22; 1 Tim. iii. 15; 1 Pet. ii. 5.
³Verse 14; ch. iv. 11; vi. 11; x. 35; Matt. x. 22; Gal. vi. 9; Col. 1. 23; Rev. ii. 25; iii. 11.
⁴Rom. v. 2; xii. 12; 1 Thess. v. 16; 1 Pet. i. 3-6, 8.

better covenant established on better promises. (Rom. 7:7.) (c) It was designed to restrain transgression, and so to prevent the universal spread of idolatry previous to the coming of the Messiah. (Dan. 9:24.) But (d) the main design of the Sinaitic Covenant in its fullest and widest sense, embracing its subjects, ordinances, rites, and services, was to furnish to the world clear and unmistakable evidence as to the Divine origin of the Church of Christ and all that pertains to it. The ministry of Moses was therefore intended to be "for a testimony of those things which were to be spoken after," concerning Christ and his Church. (John 5:45-47.) And hence the particularity with which Moses was instructed to make the "Tabernacle of witness" and all that belonged to it. "See," said God to him, "that thou make all things according to the pattern showed to thee in the mount." (8:5.) Had Moses possessed the spirit of Cain or of some modern Rationalist, he might have so far departed from his received instructions, that there would really be now but little, if any, resemblance between the ordinances of the Old and the New Economy. But not so. He was faithful to the trust committed to him. He made "all things according to the pattern showed to him in the mount"; and so the intended harmony between the Old and New Institutions has been fully preserved. Anyone may now easily perceive not only that there are many existing analogies between the Church of God under the Old Covenant and the Church of Christ under the New, but if he carefully examine the evidence submitted he will see further that these analogies were all designed and preordained by him who sees the end from the beginning, and who does all things according to the counsel of his own will. And hence no amount of sophistry can now fairly set aside the evidence given through the writings of Moses that the same all-wise and benevolent Being who anciently spoke unto the Fathers by the Prophets, has also in these last days spoken unto us by his Son and his Apostles.

6 **But Christ as a Son over his own house, etc.**—Or rather,

*But Christ as a Son is faithful over his* [*God's*] *house.* Moses was faithful in the Old Testament house of God, as a servant; but Christ is faithful over the New Testament house of God, as a Son. There is no authority whatever for the use of the word *"own"* in this connection. The Greek pronoun rendered *his* (*autou*) is of the same form and import in the second, fifth, and sixth verses, refer- ring, no doubt, to God in every case. See note on verse 2. And ac- cordingly in 10: 21, 22, our author says in the conclusion of his argument on the priesthood, "Having [then] a High Priest [Jesus Christ] over the house of God, let us draw near with a true heart, in full assurance of faith, having our hearts sprinkled from an evil conscience, and our bodies washed with pure water." Th expres- sion, *house of Christ,* does not occur in the Bible; but the phrase, *"house of God,"* is of frequent occurrence. See references.

**whose house are we,**—The Apostle here evidently intends to make a distinction between the Old Testament house of God in which Moses officiated as a servant, and the New Testament house of God over which Christ presides as a Son and High Priest. The former was composed of Israelites according to the flesh; but the latter is composed of Christians, or Israelites according to the Spirit. The former was an earthly, transitory, and typical house; but the latter is a heavenly, imperishable, and spiritual house. The former was the shadow, and the latter is the substance. The former was constructed and its services were performed for a testimony of the good things which were to be spoken afterward; but the latter is the sublime and glorious reality itself, concerning which Moses and all the other Prophets have borne witness.

**if we hold fast the confidence, etc.**—The present tense in the first member of this clause, "whose house are (*esmen*) we," is used for both the present and the future. As if the Apostle had said, We are now of the spiritual house of God, and we will ever belong to it, if we hold fast the confidence and the boasting of hope firm to the end of life. This use of the present tense for both the present and future, and indeed for all time, is of frequent occurrence in the New Testament. In John 12: 26, for example, Jesus says to his disciples, "If any man serve me let him follow me; and where I *am* (*eimi*) there shall also my servant be." And in John 14: 3, he says, "And if I go and prepare a place for you, I will come again, and receive you unto myself, that where I *am* (*eimi*) there ye may be also." See Winer's Gram. Section 40, 2, *a*.

The Greek word rendered *confidence* (*parreesia*) means (1) freeness and boldness of speech, and (2) that confidence which prompts any one to the use of such freedom of speech. In the Gospels and Acts, it is generally used in the former sense; but in the Epistles, it always means an inward state of full and undisturbed confidence. See, for example, 6: 11; 10: 19, 35. The word rendered *rejoicing* (*kaucheema*) means properly boasting, or a matter of boasting. And *hope* (*elpis*) is used here, not to denote an affection of the mind, but rather the object of our hope, as in Rom. 8: 24.

The object of the Apostle, then, in the use of this clause, is simply to encourage his Hebrew brethren to hold fast their confession, by assuring them that as they were then members of the house of God, so also they would ever continue to be members of it on condition that they would be faithful to the end of life. In that event, as he assures his Roman brethren, God would make all things work together for their good, so that "neither death, nor life, nor angels, nor principalities, nor powers, nor things present, nor things to come, nor height, nor depth, nor any other creature" would be able to separate them "from the love of God which is in Jesus Christ our Lord." (Rom. 8: 28-39.)

**firm unto the end:**—That is, to the end of life; at which time ends also our state of probation. These words are supposed by some to be an interpolation from the fourteenth verse of this chapter, and as such are rejected by Tischendorf, Green, and Alford, on the authority of the Vatican Manuscript, the Aethiopic Version, and certain citations made by Ambrose and Lucifer. But as they are found in manuscripts A, C, D, K, L, M, and also in the Latin Vulgate, it is not surprising that they should be retained and defended as genuine by Tholuck, Lünemann, and others.

## 2. EXHORTATIONS AND WARNINGS DRAWN FROM THE EXAMPLE OF THE ISRAELITES UNDER MOSES
### 3:7-19

7 Wherefore [1](as the Holy Ghost saith, [2]To-day if [3]ye will hear his voice,

[1]Matt. xxii. 43; Acts i. 16; xxviii. 25; 2 Pet. i. 21.
[2]Psa. xcv. 7-11; Prov. xxvii. 1; Eccl. ix. 10; Isa. lv. 6; 2 Cor. vi. 2.
[3]Psa. lxxxi. 11-13; John x. 3, 16, 27.

7 **Wherefore as the Holy Ghost saith,**—The Apostle now proceeds to make a personal application of the important truths elicited in the course of the preceding paragraph; and to warn his Hebrew brethren against the dangers of apostasy, by referring to God's dealings with their fathers. His words may be briefly paraphrased as follows: Since it is true, he says in substance, that Jesus as the Apostle of God is so much superior to Moses; and since it is also true, that your belonging to the house of God under him, and your enjoying the blessings of the New Covenant through him, depend on your holding fast the confidence and the boasting of your hope even to the end of life, you should now take as a warning to yourselves the following solemn admonition made by God to your fathers; and beware lest there be also in any of you an evil heart of unbelief. The quotation is made from the ninety-fifth Psalm, in which David earnestly invites his brethren to worship Jehovah (verses 1, 2); (1) on the ground that he is above all gods, the Creator of all things, and the good Shepherd of Israel (verses 3-7); and (2) on the ground that the neglect of God's word and his ordinances had cost a whole generation of their fathers the loss of Canaan (verses 8-11). This last portion of the Psalm, our author here quotes and applies as a part of his own exhortations and warnings. Observe that these words of David are ascribed to the Holy Spirit; for "holy men of God spake [in ancient times] as they were moved by the Holy Spirit." (2 Pet. 1: 21.) See also 2 Tim. 3: 16, 17.

**To-day, if ye will hear his voice,**—Or rather, *if ye hear his voice. Now* is the acceptable time; *now* is the day of salvation. God never says to anyone, Hearken to my voice and obey my precepts tomorrow. His command is, Do it now; at the very moment that you hear his voice and know his will. And hence the order of the primitive Church was (1) to preach the Gospel to sinners; (2) to receive the confession of such as became penitent believers; and

8 ¹Harden not your hearts, ²as in the provocation, in the day of ³temptation in the wilderness:

¹Ex. viii. 15; 1 Sam. vi. 6; 2 Kings xvii. 14; Matt. xiii. 15; Acts xix. 9; Rom. ii. 5, 6.
²Num. xiv. 11, 22, 23; Deut. ix. 22-24.
³Ex. xvii. 7; Num. xx. 13; Deut. vi. 16; Psa. lxxxi. 7.

(3) to baptize them on the same day, or even at the same hour of the night. See Acts 2: 41; 16: 33; 18: 8, etc. And after their baptism the converts continued steadfast in the Apostle's teachings, giving all diligence to make their calling and their election sure. But now, how very different is the practice of the Church. It is amazing how both saints and sinners now procrastinate and trifle with the word and the ordinances of God.

8 **Harden not your hearts,**—To harden the heart, is to render it insensible in any way. Here, the admonition of the Apostle to his Hebrew brethren is, not to harden their hearts by neglecting even for a day the voice of Jehovah, however expressed. His commands have all respect to the present; and any unnecessary delay in obeying them has always of necessity a hardening influence on the heart. Men who hear the Gospel in their youth or early manhood, and do not then obey it, seldom do so afterward. It is to all who hear it a savor either of life unto life or of death unto death. (2 Cor. 2: 16.) Under its influence, no man can long remain stationary in the Divine life. He must by the laws and impulses of his own nature become either better or worse, as the current of life flows onward. If he does not soften and purify his heart by obeying the truth, he will of necessity harden it by his disobedience. And hence the great concern of the Apostle that all who hear the voice of God should obey it promptly and heartily, even while it is called To-day, lest any should be hardened through the deceitfulness of sin.

**as in the provocation, etc.**—The Hebrew rendered literally is as follows: *Harden not your heart; like Meribah, like the day of Massah in the wilderness.* That is, harden not your hearts, as your fathers did at Meribah; as they did on the day of Massah in the wilderness. These names were both given to a place near Mount Horeb, where the children of Israel murmured for water. (Ex. 17: 1-7.) And when Moses had supplied their wants, "he called the name of the place Massah [temptation] and Meribah [strife], because of the chiding of the children of Israel, and be-

9 When your fathers tempted [me] | proved me: *by proof* | and [1]saw my
works [2]forty years. 10 Wherefore [3]I was grieved with that generation, and

[1]Ex. xix. 4; xx. 22.
[2]Num. xiv. 33; Deut. viii. 2, 4; Josh. v. 6; Acts vii. 36; xiii. 18.
[3]Gen. vi. 6; Psa. lxxviii. 40.

cause they tempted the Lord, saying, Is the Lord among us or
not?" The name *Meribah* was given also to Kadesh (most likely
the same as Kadesh Barnea) in the wilderness of Zin (Num. 27:
14); "because [there] the children of Israel strove with the Lord
and he was sanctified in them." See Num. 20: 1-13. Whether
David, in Psalm 95: 8, refers to one or both of these places is a
question on which expositors are not wholly agreed. It seems
most likely, however, that he has in view only the place of strife
and temptation near Mount Horeb; as the strife at Kadesh did not
occur until about thirty-seven years after that God had sworn in
his wrath that the rebellious generation which came out of Egypt
under Moses should never enter into his rest. (Num. 14: 20-35.)
This view is corroborated by the Greek translation of our author,
which is identical with that of the Septuagint, and may be literally
rendered into English as follows: Harden not your hearts as in the
bitterness, on the day of temptation in the wilderness. It seems,
therefore, that the excessive provocation of the people, here elegantly rendered *bitterness* by the Apostle, occurred on the day of
temptation; and of course at the same place, near Mount Horeb.

9 **When your fathers tempted me**—The Hebrew of this verse
is literally rendered into English as follows: Where [expressive of
either the place where or the time when] your fathers tempted me,
proved me, and saw my work. The Textus Receptus of Elzevir
runs thus: Where [*hou,* where or when] your fathers tempted me,
proved me, and saw my works forty years. This differs from the
Hebrew only in the two following unimportant particulars: (1) in
the Hebrew, the noun *work* is singular; but in the Greek, the corresponding word is plural; (2) in the Hebrew, the expression,
*forty years,* is, according to the Masoretic pointing, connected with
what follows, as in the seventeenth verse of this chapter; but in the
Greek, it qualifies the preceding verb *saw.* These slight differences do not, however, in any way affect the sense of the passage,
the meaning being obviously the same in both the Hebrew and the
Greek. Nor does the reading of Bagster as given in our best man-

said, [4]They do always err in their heart; and [5]they have not known my ways.

[4]Psa. lxxviii. 8; Isa. xxviii. 7; John iii. 19, 20; viii. 45; Rom. i. 28.
[5]Psa. cxlvii. 20; Jer. iv. 22.

uscripts differ in meaning from the Hebrew text. Literally rendered it stands thus: Where your fathers made trial by proof, and saw my works forty years. See critical notes on this verse.

10 **Wherefore I was grieved with that generation,**—That is to say, Because your fathers so often provoked and tempted me in the wilderness, I was sorely grieved and vexed with them. The word rendered, *grieved* (*prosochizo*) is Hellenistic, and like the corresponding Hebrew word means properly to feel a loathing; to be disgusted with any person or thing. The meaning is, that the generation of the children of Israel contemporary with Moses and Aaron, had by their multiplied transgressions become loathsome to God; and, speaking after the manner of men, he was disgusted with them. Many manuscripts have *this* (*toutee*) instead of *that* (*ekeinee*) generation. In the Hebrew, the word answering to generation has no qualifying epithet. It is, however, sufficiently defined by the context; and evidently means the generation which came out of Egypt under Moses, whose carcasses fell in the wilderness.

**and said, They do always err in their heart;**—The Greek word rendered *err* (*planao*), as well as the corresponding Hebrew word means to wander, to go astray. There is perhaps in the use of this word an allusion to the wanderings of the Israelites in the desert; but it is of their heart-wanderings that Jehovah here complains. These, he says, were constant. They do *always* (*aei*) wander in heart. The word *heart* (*kardia*) means properly the central organ of the blood-vessels, situated in the thorax, and supposed to be the seat of animal life. But figuratively it means the seat of the affections, comprehending also not unfrequently the seat of the will and the understanding; as when we speak of a willing heart, an understanding heart, an obedient heart, etc. But in all such cases, the reference is primarily and chiefly to man's moral and emotional nature. As, for instance, when the fool says in his heart, *"No God,"* he expresses a sentiment of his depraved heart, rather than a judgment of his darkened and perverted understanding; though both his heart and his intellect are involved and impli-

11 So ¹I sware in my wrath, They shall not enter into ²my rest.)

¹Num. xiv. 20-35; xxxii. 10-13; Deut. i. 34, 35; ii. 14.
²Ch. iv. 1, 3, 5, 9; Psa. xcv. 7-11; Isa. xi. 10; lvii. 2; Matt. xi. 28-30; Rev. vii. 14-
17; xiv. 13; xxi. 4.

---

cated in the enormous falsehood. Blinded and hardened by the love of sin, he first wishes there were no God; and then, perchance, he is led to believe what he so ardently desires. See Rom. 1 : 28, and 2 Thess. 2 : 10-12.

**and they have not known my ways.**—The children of Israel were quite as ignorant of the ways of God, as they were of the meandering paths of the desert. Like benighted wanderers, they were lost in the mazes of their own follies; and had as yet learned but little of the gracious designs of God in his dealings with them. They were still extremely sensuous; and their hearts were set on worldly pleasures and enjoyments. When they failed to reach Canaan as soon as they expected, they then turned back in their affections, and began to long for the leeks, onions, and flesh-pots of Egypt. They seemed willing to endure Egyptian servitude, or almost anything else, rather than submit to that Divine discipline which was necessary to qualify them for the promised rest.

11 **So I sware in my wrath,**—This is of course a figurative expression, and means simply that when the Israelites murmured and rebelled against God at Kadesh Barnea, he then resolved that they should never enter into his rest. Previous to this they had often provoked and dishonored him by their murmurings against him and his servant Moses. This they did before they crossed the Red Sea, when they were closely pursued by Pharaoh and his hosts. (Ex. 14: 10-12.) Another like provocation occurred at Marah in the wilderness of Shur (Ex. 15: 22-26); another in the wilderness of Sin (Ex. 16: 1-3); another, at Massah and Meribah near Rephadim (Ex. 17: 1-7); another, at Sinai, where they made and worshiped the golden calf (Ex. 32: 1-29); another, at Taberah in the wilderness (Num. 11: 1-3); another at Kibroth-Hattaavah (Num. 11: 4-34); and still another, at Kadesh Barnea, where the people believed the evil report of the ten spies, and refused to go up at the command of God and take possession of the land of Canaan (Num. 14: 1-4). On this last occasion, that wicked and perverse generation filled up the cup of their iniquity; and the Lord said, "Because all these men who have seen my glory and my mir-

acles which I did in Egypt and in the wilderness, have tempted me now these ten times and have not hearkened to my voice; surely they shall not see the land which I sware unto their fathers, neither shall any of them that provoked me see it. . . . I have heard the murmurings of the children of Israel which they murmur against me. Say unto them, As truly as I live, saith the Lord, as ye have spoken in mine ears so will I do unto you; your carcasses shall fall in the wilderness; and all that are numbered of you, according to your whole number, from twenty years old and upward, who have murmured against me, doubtless ye shall not come into the land concerning which I sware to make you all dwell therein, save Caleb, the son of Jephunneh and Joshua the son of Nun." (Num. 14: 22-30.) After this they wandered through the desert in unknown paths, for about thirty-seven years; at the close of which we find them again at Kadesh in the wilderness of Zin, murmuring for water; in consequence of which the place was called Meribah Kadesh. (Num. 20: 1-13.) These places can be traced on any good map of the exodus and wanderings of the Israelites.

**They shall not enter into my rest.**—This clause is best explained by referring to the passage just cited from Num. 14. Up to this time, for about eighteen months after their departure from Egypt, the Lord had borne with the people. But this last act of rebellion was intolerable; and God therefore now swore in his wrath that they should never enter into his rest. The word *rest* (*katapausis*) has in this connection a double reference, as will appear in our exegesis of the next chapter. Primarily, it means the rest of Canaan; and secondarily, it means the heavenly rest, of which the rest in Canaan was but a type. See note on 1: 5. From this rest, in its twofold sense, it seems that most of that wicked and perverse generation were excluded. That there were some exceptions in each case, must of course be conceded. Of this we have the most clear and reliable evidence given in the Old Testament. Joshua and Caleb entered Canaan and enjoyed God's rest in its typical sense; and Moses and Aaron, with doubtless some others, though excluded from Canaan, entered into the heavenly rest. But it is not in harmony with the design of the Apostle to notice these exceptions. He purposely leaves all such out of view, and affirms simply what was true of the masses. They, it would seem, were

12 ¹Take heed, brethren, lest there be in any of you ²an evil heart of unbelief, ³in departing from the ⁴living God.

¹Ch. ii. 1-3; Matt. xxiv. 4.
²Gen. viii. 21; Jer. iii. 17; vii. 24; xi. 8; xvi. 12.
³Ch. vi. 4-6; x. 26-29; xii. 15-17; Prov. i. 24-32; Jer. ii. 13; xvii. 5.
⁴Ch. x. 31; xii. 22; Deut. v. 26; 2 Cor. vi. 16; 1 Tim. iv. 10.

excluded from God's rest in its twofold significance.  See notes on
4 : 3, 6.

12 **Take heed, brethren, etc.**—As if he had said, Beware,
brethren, of an evil unbelieving heart such as the Israelites had in
the wilderness, lest like them you too apostatize from the living
God, and perish on your way to the Promised Land.   Three things
are clearly implied in the words of our text: viz. (1) that the Hebrew Christians were in great danger of apostatizing from the living God, as their fathers had done.   And if so, then it follows that
a Christian may fall from grace; for to apostatize from God is simply equivalent to falling away finally and forever from the grace of
God.   See notes on 6: 4-6.   (2) That this danger arises wholly
from "an evil heart of unbelief."   So long as we have an unwavering trust in God and in his word, all is well.   Nothing can, under
such circumstances, separate us from the love of God which is in
Jesus Christ our Lord. (Rom. 8: 39.)  But let the heart at once
become evil and distrustful, and then his condition becomes at once
awfully alarming. (3) It is further implied in the words of our author, that every Christian may, through the grace of God, avoid
the dangers of apostasy, by keeping his heart with all diligence.
(Prov. 4: 23.)  It is true that without the grace of God we can do
nothing by way of saving ourselves or anyone else (John 15: 5);
and it is also true, that even with this promised grace we can accomplish comparatively but little (1 Cor. 3: 6, 7).   The work is of
God and not of us.   Nevertheless, it has pleased God in the exercise of his wisdom and love to give to every man an agency in the
work of redemption commensurate with his capacity and means of
doing good.   And, consequently, the man who "looketh into the
perfect law of liberty and continueth therein, he being not a forgetful hearer, but a doer of the work, this man shall be blessed in his
doing." (James 1: 25.)  And hence the following earnest exhortations to constant watchfulness and perseverance in the Divine life.

13 But ¹exhort one another daily, ²while it is called To-day; lest any of
you be hardened through ³the deceitfulness of sin.

¹Ch. x. 24, 25; Acts xi. 23; 1 Thess. ii. 11.
²Psa. xcv. 7, 8; 2 Cor. vi. 2.
³Prov. xxviii. 26; Rom. vii. 11; Eph. iv. 22; Jas. i. 14.

---

13 **But exhort one another daily,**—This admonition is not addressed merely to the Elders of the Church, but to every member
of it. All are required to exhort and admonish one another daily
as members of the family of God, and "as joint heirs of the grace
of life." And yet, how very generally is this duty neglected.
"How often," says Mr. Barnes, "do church-members see a fellow-
member go astray without any exhortation or admonition. How
often do they hear reports of the inconsistent lives of other members, and perhaps contribute to the circulation of these reports
themselves, without any pains taken to inquire whether they are
true. How often do the poor fear the rich members of the Church,
or the rich despise the poor, and see one another live in sin, without any attempt to entreat and save them. I would not have the
courtesies of life violated. I would not have any assume a dog-
matic or dictatorial air. I would have no one step out of his proper
sphere of life. But the principle which I would lay down is this:
that the fact of church membership should inspire such confidence
as to make it proper for one member to exhort another whom he
sees going astray. Belonging to the same family; having the same
interests in religion; and all suffering when one suffers, why
should they not be allowed tenderly and kindly to exhort one another to a holy life?"

**while it is called To-day;**—Do not procrastinate, or put off till
tomorrow what should be done today. Much may depend in such
cases on prompt and proper action; and it is to be feared that
thousands are eternally lost through the neglect of it. If the members of every congregation of disciples, would all watch over one
another, not as censors, but as members of the body of Christ, how
many errors might be corrected in their incipiency. But as it is,
how very different are the results. How many delinquent Christians are allowed to become hardened in sin, before even the Elders
of the Church call on them and admonish them! How very unlike
these Elders are to the Good Shepherd that careth for the sheep.

**through the deceitfulness of sin.**—That sin (*hamartia*) is very

14 For ¹we are made partakers of Christ, ²if we hold the beginning of our confidence steadfast unto the end;

¹John xv. 1-7; Rom. xi. 17; 1 Pet. iv. 13; v. 1; 2 Pet. i. 4; 1 John i. 3.
²See refs. verse 6.

deceptive is well known to everyone who has examined carefully the workings and operations of his own heart. It has by the fall of man been implanted as a principle in human nature; so that it is now *natural* for man to follow after its "deceitful lust." (Eph. 4: 22.) "For to will," says Paul, speaking as a representative of those under law without the helps and consolations of the Gospel, "is present with me; but how to perform that which is good, I find not. For the good that I would I do not; but the evil which I would not, that I do. Now if I do that I would not, it is no more I that do it, but *Sin that dwelleth in me.* I find then a law, that when I would do good, evil is present with me. For I delight in the law of God after the inward man; but I see another law in my members, warring against the law of my mind, and bringing me into captivity to the law of Sin which is in my members." (Rom. 7: 18-23.) True, indeed, in and through the process of regeneration the body of Sin is destroyed (Rom. 6: 6); so that we Christians are not now, as formerly, its slaves; its has no longer dominion over us (Rom. 6: 14, 17, 18); for we are not now under law but under grace. But though the body of Sin has been destroyed, its animus still remains as a thorn in the flesh of every Christian; so that unless we are constantly on our guard, and, like Paul, keep our bodies in subjection (1 Cor. 9: 27), we are ever liable, as were the ancient Israelites, to be misled by the deceitfulness of Sin which is in our members. Its promises to us are all pleasure and happiness, but its rewards are misery and death. (Rom. 6: 23.) And hence the necessity of exhorting one another daily, even while it is called To-day, lest any of us "be hardened through the deceitfulness of sin."

14 **For we are made partakers of Christ, etc.**—The Apostle assigns here as another reason for constant perseverance and watchfulness, that our being finally partakers of Christ and his benefits, will depend on our holding fast to the end of life the beginning of our confidence in him. We have not yet reached the end of our course. We are still in a state of trial; and we are therefore ever liable to lose through our neglect or disobedience

15 While it is said, ¹To-day if ye will hear his voice, harden not your hearts, as in the provocation.

¹See refs. verses 7 and 8.

that of which we have already to a certain extent become partakers; but which, for the present, we hold on certain conditions. "For whosoever hath, to him shall be given, and he shall have more abundance; but whosoever hath not, from him shall be taken away even that which he hath." (Matt. 8: 12.) See note on verse 6.

The word rendered *confidence* (*hupostasis*) is of different etymology from that which is so rendered (*parreesia*) in the sixth verse. The former looks rather to the ground of our confidence in Christ; and the latter to our free and open confession of it. They are, however, used here by our author as synonymous terms, to denote simply that firm and well-grounded confidence in Christ, which if held fast to the end of life, will secure for us an abundant entrance into his everlasting Kingdom. Of this confidence the Hebrews were then partakers; they were then in possession of that faith which purifies the heart. And hence the Apostle requires of them simply that they continue to hold fast the beginning of their confidence firm even to the end of life. "Hold fast that which thou hast, that no man take thy crown." (Rev. 3: 11.)

15 **While it is said, To-day, etc.**—The proper grammatical connection of this verse is still a matter of dispute among the critics. Some of them, as Ebrard and Alford, maintain that it stands properly connected with what immediately precedes; and that the object of our author in the use of this clause is simply to give strength to the affirmation made in the fourteenth verse, that our being made partakers of Christ is conditioned on our holding fast "the beginning of our confidence steadfast unto the end." As if he had said, "For we are made partakers of Christ, if we hold the beginning of our confidence steadfast unto the end; [as is clearly implied] in the saying, To-day if ye hear his voice, harden not your hearts, as in the provocation." Others, as Tholuck and Delitzsch, make it the beginning of a sentence, and so connect it with the sixteenth verse as follows: "In the saying, To-day if ye hear his voice harden not your hearts, as in the provocation [it is implied that the provokers to whom the Psalmist refers, were themselves redeemed of the Lord, and yet fell under his wrath, and came short

16 For ¹some, when they had heard, did provoke: howbeit not all that came out of Egypt by Moses.

¹Num. xiv. 11; xxvi. 65; Psa. lxxviii. 17.

---

of the promised rest]. For who were they that having heard gave provocation? Was it not indeed all who under Moses' leadership came out of Egypt?" Others, as Bengal and Michaelis, connect the fifteenth verse with the thirteenth, and include the fourteenth in parentheses. And others again, as Chrysostom and Erasmus, connect it with the beginning of the fourth chapter, making verses 16-19 parenthetical.

On the whole, I think it best to combine the first two. hypotheses. It seems to me that the fifteenth verse is logically connected with both what precedes and what follows: though it does not, as Delitzsch supposes, form the beginning of a sentence. I would therefore render verses 14-19 as follows: For we have been made partakers of Christ, if we hold the beginning of our confidence steadfast unto the end; [as implied] in its being said, To-day if ye hear his voice harden not your hearts as in the provocation. [As if the Apostle had said, It is not enough that you have been redeemed, and that you have commenced your march for the heavenly rest: you must persevere in your begun course to the end of life, or otherwise you will all fall short of the promised rest, as did your fathers in the wilderness.] For who were they that having heard did provoke? Was it not indeed all who came out of Egypt by means of Moses? And with whom was he displeased forty years? Was it not with those that sinned, whose carcasses fell in the wilderness? And to whom did he sware that they should not enter into his rest, but to the disobedient? So we see that they could not enter, on account of unbelief.

16 **For some, when they had heard, did provoke:**—The original manuscripts of the New Testament were written without any accents and also without any marks of punctuation. As early as 240 B.C. Aristophanes of Byzantium introduced into the School of Alexandria an imperfect system of both accents and punctuation; chiefly, it would seem, for the benefit of teachers and scholars of rhetoric. But accents were not generally used by Christian writers till after the middle of the fifth century; and it was not till about the beginning of the tenth century that the custom of using them

became universal. And so also of the system of Greek punctuation. It too was gradually introduced with sundry changes and
modifications. About the middle of the fifth century, Euthalius, a
Deacon of Alexandria, divided the New Testament into *lines* (*sti-
choi*), each line containing as many words as were to be read without any pause or interruption of the voice. In the eighth century,
the comma (,) was invented; and the Greek note of interrogation
(;) in the ninth. But it was not till after the invention of the art
of printing, about the middle of the fifteenth century, that the present system of Greek punctuation was universally adoped by Greek
scholars.

It is obvious, therefore, that no authority is to be attached to
these marks of accent and punctuation, except so far as they are
supported by the conditions of the context and the well-known
laws and principles of the Greek language. And it may therefore be
still a question whether the word *tines* (*tines*) in our text should
be accented on the first or on the second syllable. If on the first
(*tincs*), then it is equivalent to the interrogative pronoun *who,* and
requires a mark of interrogation at the close of the sentence in
which it stands. But if on the second (*tines*), it is an indefinite
pronoun equivalent to *some*, as in our English Version, and requires that the sentence shall close with a period.

What, then, is the proper meaning of this word? Is it an interrogative or an indefinite pronoun? Is it equivalent to *who* or to
*some*? That it should be rendered *who* in the seventeenth and
eighteenth verses, is conceded by all: for here, indeed, the context
will admit of nothing else. But is it not almost, if not quite, as obvious, from the scope of the author's argument, that it must have
the same meaning in the sixteenth verse? Having, in the verses
immediately preceding, solemnly warned his brethren against the
dangers of apostasy from Christ, and having illustrated the whole
matter by a general reference to the fortunes of their fathers in the
wilderness, and also by God's subsequent warnings and admonitions through David, our author now makes a more sweeping and
definite application of Old Testament history. Lest any should attempt to avoid the force of his general argument, on the ground of
its seeming indefiniteness; and should be disposed to take refuge in
the vain hope that though some of the less enlightened of their
brethren might fall, they themselves would nevertheless escape—

17 But ¹with whom was he grieved forty years? ²was it not with them that had sinned, ³whose carcasses fell in the wilderness? 18 And ⁴to whom sware he that they should not enter into his rest, ⁵but to them that believed not?

¹Num. xiv. 43; Deut. viii. 4; Josh. v. 6; Acts vii. 36.
²Num. xxvi. 64, 65; 1 Cor. x. 1-13.
³Num. xiv. 29-33; Deut. ii. 14. 15.
⁴See refs. verse 11.
⁵Num. xiv. 11; xx. 12; Deut. i. 26-32; ix. 23.

fearing this, the Apostle makes another more definite and heart-searching appeal to the well known facts of Old Testament history. He reminds his readers by an appeal to their own knowledge of the facts, that it was not merely a few of the most ignorant and super-stitious of their fathers that fell in the wilderness on account of their disobedience; but that it was in fact the whole redeemed na-tion who came out of Egypt under Moses. The few exceptions, consisting of Joshua, Caleb, Eliezer, and perhaps a few more of the Levites, are purposely and with strict rhetorical propriety kept in the background; and the great mass of the people who had been once enlightened and consecrated to God, are brought forward as persons doomed to destruction, in order to make a more vivid and lasting impression on the minds and hearts of the Hebrew breth-ren. For who, says the author, were they that having heard did provoke? Were they the children and servants of your fathers? Or were they a few of the most ignorant and depraved of that gen-eration? Nay indeed, were they not all of the six hundred thou-sand who came out of Egypt by Moses? The force of this appeal could not be avoided; and it must have made a very deep impres-sion on the mind and heart of every Hebrew Christian who read this Epistle.

17 **But with whom was he grieved forty years?**—With what sort of persons was God displeased for the space of forty years? Was it with babes and slaves and such other persons as were igno-rant of God's will? Nay indeed; was it not with them that sinned, whose carcasses fell in the wilderness? They were persons who knew God's will and transgressed his law. They were all *sinners*. And their sin so provoked God that he caused their *members* (*chola*), such as their arms, legs, etc., to be scattered as fragments through the wilderness; leaving them there as a monument of his righteous displeasure, and as a warning to all subsequent genera-tions. See Num. 26: 64, 65.

19 So we see that [1]they could not enter in because of unbelief.

[1]Mark xvi. 16; John iii. 18. 36; 1 John v. 10.

18 **And to whom did he sware, etc?**—The history of Israel's provocations and of God's dealings with them, was so fully recorded in the Old Testament and so generally believed by the Hebrew Christians, that any formal presentation of evidence in the case was wholly unnecessary; and our author therefore again, with great rhetorical effect, employs the interrogative style of address. By means of a series of questions addressed to their understanding, he brings home with great power to their hearts and consciences what they were all forced to concede, that the six hundred thousand full-grown men who came out of Egypt under Moses, perished in the wilderness through their unbelief. They once believed in God and confided in his servant Moses: for how indeed could they do otherwise? They had seen God's judgments on Pharaoh and on his hosts in Egypt and in the Red Sea; they had seen the manna rained down from heaven, and they had beheld the waters flowing from the rock at the command of God; they had heard his voice from the top of Sinai, and they had witnessed many other manifestations of his power and Divinity, for the space of eighteen months, before they came to the plains of Kadesh. But after all this, through an evil heart of unbelief, they there rebelled against him, and so provoked him on the very borders of Canaan, that he was constrained to swear in his wrath, that they should not enter into his rest. See Num. 14 : 20-35. All this the Hebrews well understood and readily conceded. And hence without further argument, Paul simply concludes in harmony with their own convictions, that owing to practical infidelity a whole generation of God's chosen people were excluded from the promised rest.

19 **So we see, etc.**—In this verse, the Apostle states the result of the whole matter. It was not owing to any unforeseen or fortuitous circumstances, nor to the superior strength of their enemies, that the Israelites were unable to enter the land of Canaan; but it was owing simply to their own infidelity and disobedience. And this is given as a warning to all Christians to beware, lest they too fall after the same example of unbelief.

### 3. CONCERNING THE REST WHICH REMAINS
### FOR THE PEOPLE OF GOD
#### 4 : 1-10

1 [2]Let us therefore fear, lest, a promise being left us of entering into his rest, [3]any of you should seem to come short of it.

2 For [1]unto us was the gospel preached, as well as unto them: but the

[2]Ch. ii. 1-3; xii. 15, 25; Prov. xiv. 16; Rom. xi. 20; 1 Cor. x. 12.
[3]Matt. vii. 21-27; xxv. 1-13; 1 Cor. ix. 27.
[1]Gal. iii. 8; 1 Pet. i. 12.

1 **Let us therefore fear,**—The proper object of fear is danger. And as the Hebrew Christians were then in danger of falling away, the Apostle very properly appeals here to their sense of fear, for the purpose of exciting them to greater diligence in the Divine life. For he well knew that everything depended on their attaining to that rest which remains for the people of God. If they failed in this, they failed in everything. In that event, their confession would be all in vain, and life itself would be worse than an abortion.

**lest a promise being left us of entering into his rest,**—The participle *being left* (*kataleipomenees*) is in the present tense, implying that the promise of entering God's rest is made sure to all Christians who, like Joshua and Caleb, continue faithful to the end of life. This the Apostle here assumes, for the present, on the grounds already stated. But lest anyone should doubt the reality of such a rest, he immediately takes up the consideration of this subject, and makes it his main theme in this paragraph.

**any of you should seem to come short of it.**—Or more exactly, Lest any of you may seem (*dokee*) to have come short of it (*hustereekenai*). That is, lest it may appear at the end of your course or on the day of final reckoning, that any of you shall have failed to reach the heavenly rest, the sabbatism that remains for the people of God. The Apostle would, in a word, have his Hebrew brethren in Christ take heed, lest while there is remaining to them a promise of entering into God's rest, any of them should, like their fathers in the wilderness, fall short of it through their own obstinate unbelief.

2 **For unto us was the gospel preached, etc.**—This is a very inaccurate translation of the original, and conveys to the English reader quite an erroneous impression. Literally rendered the pas-

word preached did not profit them, ²not being mixed with faith in them that heard it.

²Ch. iii. 18, 19; xi. 6; 1 Thess. ii. 13; 2 Thess. ii. 12, 13; Jas. i. 21.

sage stands thus: For we are evangelized (*esmen eueengelis-menoi*) as well as they. That is, the promise of entering into rest, on given conditions, has been made to us Christians, as well as to the ancient Hebrews. The assertion is designed to set forth more directly and categorically what is assumed in the first verse, viz., that there is really left to us a promise of entering into God's rest. The Apostle means to say that the joyful promise of entering into rest, made first to the Israelites, has respect to us as well as to them. Primarily, it had reference to the possession of Canaan; and secondarily, to that better rest of which the rest in Canaan was but a type. This same promise, in its second intention, still remains for the encouragement and consolation of all God's people. Into it they will all finally enter; unless, like the Israelites, they fall by the way on account of their own practical infidelity.

**but the word preached did not profit them,**—Literally, *the word of hearing* (*ho logos tees akoees*) did not profit them. They heard the message which God delivered to them through Moses, but they were not profited by it.

**not being mixed with faith in them that heard it.**—Or as rendered by Erasmus and others: "not having been mingled by means of faith with them that heard it." The word rendered *mixed* (*sugkekramenos*) is used metaphorically, and seems to have reference to the mixing of food with the digestive fluids, in order to its being appropriated to the wants of the body; or, according to the above version of Erasmus, it may refer to the food's being incorporated with the tissues of the body by means of these fluids. In both cases the meaning is substantially the same. Food taken into the stomach, unless it be properly digested and appropriated, is of no benefit whatever to the physical organs, but rather an injury. And just so it is with the word of hearing. If it is received as seed on the highway, or on stony ground, or among thorns, it is of no service whatever to those who hear it. But when it is well understood, and received into good and honest hearts, it then becomes as food to the soul, and gives life, and health, and strength to the whole inner man. Then indeed it is more to be desired than

3 For [1]we who have believed do enter into rest, as he said, [2]As I have sworn in my wrath, if they shall enter into my rest: although [3]the works were finished [4]from the foundation of the world.

[1]Isa. xxviii. 12; Jer. vi. 16; Matt. xi. 28, 29; Rom. v. 1, 2.
[2]Num. xiv. 20-30; Deut. i. 34, 35; ii. 14; Psa. xcv. 11.
[3]Gen. ii. 1-3; Ex. xx. 8-11.
[4]Matt. xiii. 35; Eph. i. 4; 1 Pet. i. 20.

gold, yea than much fine gold; and it is "sweeter also than honey and the honey-comb."

The Israelites were mostly of the stony-ground hearers. They at first received the word with all readiness of mind and promised obedience to its requirements. See Ex. 19: 7, 8, and 24: 3. But they had no root in themselves; and hence when trials and tribulations came, they stumbled and fell. And just so it is with thousands of nominal professors in our own day and generation. Under, it may be, the judgments of God or the exciting influences of a protracted meeting, they receive the word with gladness. For a time they are very zealous for the glory of God and the salvation of souls; and many of them are no doubt honest in their professions. But they lack stability. They have no root in themselves. And before the soul is sufficiently nourished, even while the food is in process of digestion, they stumble and fall, as did the Israelites in the wilderness. But others, like Joshua and Caleb, receive the word into good and honest hearts, "and bring forth fruit with patience."

According to the reading of the Common English Version and also that of Erasmus, the perfect passive participle *sunkekramenos* relates to *logos* in the nominative singular. But many manuscripts have the accusative plural (*sunkekramenos*); according to which the reading would be as follows: "Nevertheless the word of hearing did not profit them, unmingled as they were in faith with its hearers"; or more freely, "but the word preached did not profit them, because they did not believingly associate with those who obeyed it, such as Joshua and Caleb." This reading is on the whole preferred by Alford, but it is now very properly rejected by most expositors; being, as they say, inconsistent with the plain and obvious thought of the writer, that "the word did not profit because it was not received in faith."

3 **For we who have believed do enter into rest:**—*into the rest*; that is, the promised rest. In verse first, our author speaks

of a promise being left us of entering into God's rest; and in the second verse, he says, the good news of entering into God's rest on given conditions, was proclaimed to us as well as to the ancient Israelites. And now in the third, he further categorically affirms that all believers in Christ do actually enter into this rest: and as evidence of this, he again quotes from the ninety-fifth Psalm. The exclusion of some on the ground of their unbelief, implies the admission of others on the ground of their belief.

**if they shall enter into my rest:**—The word here rendered *if* (*ei*) should be rendered *not,* as in 3:11. The form of the expression is elliptical, being borrowed from the usual mode of taking an oath among the Hebrews, and is equivalent to a strong negative. Thus in 2 Sam. 3:35, David says, "So do God to me, and more also, if I taste bread or aught else, till the sun be down." This is but a solemn and emphatic way of expressing his purpose not to eat anything till after sunset. And so also in this connection, God is here represented as declaring with the solemnity of an oath, that the disobedient Israelites who rebelled against him at Kadesh Barnea, should never enter into his rest.

**although the works were finished from the foundation of the world.**—The logical connection of this clause is somewhat obscure in consequence of the passage being so very elliptical. But the Apostle refers here manifestly to the sabbatical rest, which had been sanctified for the glory of God and the good of mankind even from the foundation of the world, or from the time that God finished the work of creation. (Gen. 2:2.) For, to say that the works were finished from the foundation of the world, is equivalent to saying that the Sabbath, commemorative of God's rest, was sanctified and observed from the same ever memorable epoch. Such is the law of all commemorative institutions. The Passover, for example, the Pentecost, the Lord's Day, and the Lord's Supper, were all established in close connection with the events which they were severally intended to celebrate. And hence it is obvious that the oath of God at Kadesh Barnea could not have reference to the sabbatical rest; for this, the Hebrews with others had long enjoyed. But in making this oath Jehovah must have had reference to a future rest; a rest into which the apostate Israelites never entered. That this is the meaning of this very elliptical passage, is plain from what follows.

4 For he spake ¹in a certain place of the seventh day on this wise, ²And God did rest the seventh day from all his works. 5 And in this place again, ³If they shall enter into my rest.

¹Ch. ii. 6.
²Gen. ii. 2; Ex. xxxi. 17.
³Psa. xcv. 11.

**4 For he spake, etc.**—The allusion here is to Gen. 2 : 2; and the object of the Apostle in referring to it, is merely to amplify and illustrate still further what he has with characteristic brevity spoken of in the preceding verse. He here very clearly intimates that the sabbatical rest was instituted by God, at the close of the Adamic renovation, when on the seventh day "he rested from all his works which he had made." And hence it follows, as before stated, that this rest cannot be identical with that from which a whole generation of the Israelites were forever excluded.

**5 And in this place again,**—In what place? Evidently, in the place which our author has under consideration, and to which he refers in the third verse. But what is this? Most expositors agree that the reference is to Psalm 95 : 11; for here the very words of our text occur in the Septuagint, and they are a fair and literal rendering of the original Hebrew. But in the seventh verse, our author clearly refers to Psalm 95 : 7, 8; and as he cites this in proof of a new proposition relating to a much later period, it is alleged by some that in the former case the reference must be to Num. 14 : 28-30. There is no difficulty, however, in supposing that in both cases the Apostle refers to the ninety-fifth Psalm. But the citation made in the third and fifth verses is applied only to those Israelites who rebelled against God under Moses, and who on this account were not allowed to enter the land of Canaan; whereas the citation in the seventh verse applies to those of a later period. The argument of the Apostle may, then, be briefly stated as follows: He shows first by referring to Gen. 2 : 2, that the sabbatical rest was instituted from the foundation of the world, when God had finished the work of creation. And then he proves from Psalm 95 : 11, that twenty-five hundred years after that important epoch, when the Israelites rebelled at Kadesh Barnea, God made oath concerning a rest which was then in the future and from which that perverse and rebellious generation were forever excluded. And hence he infers that this rest could not be the rest of the seventh day, which

6 Seeing therefore [1]it remaineth that some must enter therein, and [2]they to whom it was first preached entered not in because of unbelief:

7 Again, he limiteth a certain day, [1]saying in David, [2]To-day, [3]after so long a time; as | it is said: *has been said before* | To-day if ye will hear his

[1]Num. xiv. 12, 31; Matt. xxi. 43; xxii. 9, 10; Luke xiv. 21-24; Acts xiii. 46, 47.
[2]See refs. ch. iii. 18, 19.
[1]2 Sam. xxiii. 2; Matt. xxii. 43; Acts ii. 25-31.
[2]Psa. xcv. 7.
[3]1 Kings vi. 1; Acts xiii. 20-23.
[4]Josh. i. 15; xxii. 4; xxiii. 1; Psa. lxxviii. 55; cv. 44.

from the beginning had been enjoyed by all the true worshipers of Jehovah.

6 **Seeing therefore it remaineth that some must enter therein,**—The argument of the Apostle is simply this: A rest was provided and offered to the Israelites. But those to whom it was first offered in the time of Moses failed to enter it, on account of their waywardness and unbelief. God, however, provides nothing in vain. He makes no experiments; and he is never disappointed in any of his plans and purposes. The rest provided remains, therefore, for all true Israelites, who, like Joshua and Caleb, have faith in God and rely on his promises. And hence it follows, as stated in the first and third verses, that there is a rest remaining for the people of God; and that we who believe do enter into it.

But here again there is seeming ground for another objection. Though the first generation of the Israelites redeemed from Egyptian bondage, failed to enter the land of Canaan, it was not so with the second. Under Joshua, they crossed the Jordan, and took possession of the promised inheritance. And hence it might be inferred by some that this was a fulfillment of the promise in its fullest sense; and consequently that outside of Judaism there is really no promised rest for the believer. To the refutation of this objection the Apostle therefore next turns his attention.

7 **Again, he limiteth a certain day,**—The object of the Apostle in this verse is to refute the objection just stated. This he does by referring to the fact that in Psalm 95 : 7-11, David by the Spirit warns the people of his own generation against the sin of unbelief, lest they too should, like their fathers under Moses, fail to enter into the enjoyment of the promised rest. "To-day," he says, "if ye hear his voice, harden not your heart as at Meribah, as on the day of Massah in the wilderness, where your fathers tempted me, proved me, and saw my work. Forty years long was I grieved

voice, harden not your hearts. 8 For if ⁴Jesus had given them rest, then would he not afterward have spoken of another day. 9 There ⁵remaineth therefore a rest to the people of God.

⁵Isa. xi. 10; lvii. 2; Matt. xi. 28-30; Rev. vii. 14-17; xiv. 13; xxi. 4.

with that generation, and said, It is a people that do err in their heart, and they have not known my ways. So I sware in my wrath, They shall not enter into my rest." The Psalmist refers back to the time when the Israelites were invited to go up from Kadesh Barnea, and take possession of the land of Canaan. (Num. 13.) But they refused to do so, and were on account of their disobedience condemned to die in the wilderness. (Num. 14.) And from these well known historical facts David warns and admonishes his own contemporaries, and through them all subsequent generations, not to do as the rebellious Israelites had done under Moses; but to promptly enter God's rest whenever invited to do so. If ye hear his voice today, obey it today. And hence it is clearly implied, that even in the time of David, the Israelites, though in the possession of Canaan, had really not entered into God's rest. The expression, "after so long a time," means the time that had intervened between Moses and David: and in the phrase, "as has been said before," the Apostle refers back to what he had said in 3 : 7, 8.

8 **For if Jesus, etc.**—Our translators have here very greatly and unnecessarily perplexed the English reader by using the name *Jesus* instead of *Joshua*: though it should be observed that these names are identical in Greek. The name *Jesous* (*Ieesious*) is always used in Hellenistic Greek for the Hebrew *Y'hoshua* in the earlier books of the Old Testament, and for *Yeshua* in the later books. See note on 2 : 13. There can be no doubt, however, that Paul refers here to Joshua the son of Nun, who, after the death of Moses, conducted the Israelites across the Jordan into the promised land. There, the people enjoyed comparative rest. See Josh. 1 : 15; 22 : 4, etc. But it was not the true rest—the rest of God. For had it been so, then, as our author says, God would not afterward have spoken through David of another day of entering into his rest.

9 **There remaineth therefore a rest to the people of God.**— This is the Apostle's conclusion logically deduced from all the premises. Over and above the sabbatical rest and the rest of Ca-

10 For ¹he that is entered into his rest, he also hath ceased from his own works, as ²God did from his.

¹Luke xvi. 22; 2 Cor. v. 8; Phil. i. 23.
²Gen. ii. 2; Ex. xxxi. 17.

naan, there still remains a rest, a sabbatism (*sabbatismos*), for every child of God. It is God's rest; a rest which he has provided, and such as that which he himself enjoys; a rest from all the toils and ills of this sinful and wearisome life. Of this the Christian has even now a foretaste in the Kingdom and patience of God's dear Son. "Come unto me," says Christ, "all ye that·labor and are heavy laden, and I will give you rest. Take my yoke upon you, and learn of me; for I am meek and lowly in heart; and ye shall find rest unto your souls." (Matt. 11: 28, 29.) You shall even now be released from the oppressive burdens of sin, and find rest to your souls, through the belief of the truth and the consolations of the Holy Spirit. But it is of the heavenly rest, the eternal sabbatism, of which our author here speaks particularly: for in the eleventh verse of this chapter he exhorts even his Christian brethren to labor now so as to finally enter the promised rest.

We have here, then, another beautiful illustration of the symbolical nature and character of the Old Testament economy. As soon as God had finished the work of creation he instituted the Sabbath —(1) for the purpose of commemorating his rest; (2) for the benefit of mankind, by giving them rest from physical labor, and leading them also to higher measures of spiritual culture and enjoyment (Mark 2: 27); and (3) that it might be a means of foreshadowing the heavenly rest, which even then he had in his eternal counsels provided for his faithful and obedient children. Nor was this the only Old Testament symbolical representation of God's rest. The idea of a future sabbatism was afterward greatly intensified by sundry legal observances, such as the rest of the seventh year and the year of Jubilee. And even in the promise of Canaan to Abraham and to his seed for an everlasting possession, there was implied also a promise of Heaven and of a heavenly rest to all who have the faith of Abraham. See Gen. 12: 7; 13: 14-17; 15: 18; 17: 8; 24: 7; 26: 4; Ex. 33: 1, etc. And hence it is that in Psalm 95: 11, the word *rest* is substituted for *land,* as in the original form of the oath given in Num. 14: 28-30.

10 **For he that is entered into his rest,**—To whom does the

Apostle here refer as having entered into rest? To Christ, say some, as Owen, Stark, Ebrard, and Alford; and to any and every departed saint, say others, as Bleek, Lünemann, Stuart, Delitzsch, and others. Which is right? Manifestly the latter, for the following reasons: (1) Because this view is most in harmony with the context. The object of our author in this verse is to assign a reason for calling the rest which remains for God's people a sabbatism; such a rest as God himself has enjoyed ever since he laid the foundations of the Earth, and of which the weekly Sabbath was but a symbol. There is, he says, remaining for the people of God, and of course for every one of them, not merely *a rest* (*katapausis*); such as the Israelites enjoyed in Canaan, but *a keeping of a sabbath* (*sabbatismos*), such as God himself now enjoys. For he (every saint) who enters into God's rest, ceases from his labors and keeps a sabbath, just as God did after he had finished the work of creation. The bearing of all this on the Apostle's argument is therefore very plain and obvious. But what could be the object of the writer in referring here to Christ? And if it was his purpose to do so, then why did he not name him? Why should he refer in this very general and indefinite way to one whose name does not appear in the entire paragraph? (2) The view which we have taken of this matter is also most in harmony with the known facts of the case. It is not true that Christ has yet finished his proper work of regeneration, and entered into his rest, as God did when he had finished the work of creation. That he has finished the work of his earthly mission and made an atonement for our sins, is of course joyfully conceded. But these labors were only preparatory to the great work of recreating the world; a work which is still in progress. Indeed, the whole Christian era is, by Christ himself, called the period of regeneration. (Matt. 19: 28.) And hence the work of Christ will continue until he shall have renovated the heavens and the Earth and delivered up the Kingdom to the Father. Then, and not till then, will he keep a sabbath. But now every saint, who, like Joshua and Caleb, is faithful to the end of life, enters then into the enjoyment of God's rest; which in a subordinate sense is also his own rest. For "blessed are the dead who die in the Lord from henceforth; yea, saith the Spirit, that they may rest from their labors; and their works do follow them." (Rev. 14: 13.)

It is not to be inferred from this, however, that the spirits of the just made perfect are in a state of slumber, or of slothful inactivity. By no means. The four living creatures and the twenty-four Elders are, throughout the vision of the Apocalypse, represented as worshiping God day and night, and participating even with rapture in the joys of Heaven, as they behold from time to time the triumphs of him who by his own blood has redeemed them to God "out of every kindred, and tongue, and people, and nation" (Rev. 4: 6-11; 5: 5-14; 6: 1, 3, 5, 7, etc.) And so Lazarus was, after death, carried by angels into Abraham's bosom (Luke 16: 22); and the penitent thief went immediately with Christ into paradise (Luke 23: 43). To the same effect is also the testimony of Paul. Speaking of Christians, he says, "To be absent from the body is to be present with the Lord" (2 Cor. 5: 8); and to be present with the Lord is to be unspeakably happy (Phil. 1: 23). These passages are therefore wholly inconsistent with the doctrine of soul-sleeping. They severally imply a state of conscious activity and enjoyment after death, as well as of freedom from the toils and sorrows of this eventful life. There can be no doubt, then, that we will be all actively employed after death. But we will be no more wearied by our exertions: for the redeemed, though serving God day and night in his temple, will "hunger no more, neither thirst any more; neither shall the Sun light on them, nor any heat. For the Lamb that is in the midst of the throne shall feed them, and shall lead them into living fountains of waters; and God shall wipe away all tears from their eyes." (Rev. 7: 16, 17.)

### 4. FURTHER EXHORTATION TO STRIVE EARNESTLY TO ENTER INTO GOD'S REST, IN VIEW ESPECIALLY OF THE ALL PENETRATING AND HEART-SEARCHING CHARACTER OF GOD'S WORD
#### 4: 11-13

11 [1]Let us labor therefore to enter into that rest, [2]lest any man fall after the same example of unbelief.

[1]Ch. vi. 11; Matt. vii. 13; Luke xiii. 24; John vi. 27; Phil. ii. 12; 2 Pet. i. 5-11.
[2]See refs. ch. iii. 18, 19.

**11 Let us labor therefore to enter into that rest.**—That is to say, since it is an established fact that there is remaining for the people of God a sabbatical rest; and since it is true that we are all invited to enter into that rest; it therefore becomes us *to strive earnestly (spoudasomen)* to do so; lest we too, like the Israelites under Moses, fall short of it through unbelief and disobedience. For them the symbolical rest of Canaan was freely provided; and God himself was present and ready to lead them into it. But they disobeyed him, and rebelled against him; and as a consequence they perished in the wilderness, short of the promised land. And just so, says Paul, it will be with us, if we follow their example. See 1 Cor. 10: 1-12. In order to gain admission into God's ever-lasting Kingdom, we must give all diligence in adding to our "faith virtue; and to virtue knowledge; and to knowledge temperance; and to temperance patience; and to patience godliness; and to god-liness brotherly-kindness; and to brotherly-kindness love." (2 Pet. 1: 5-11.)

Care must be taken, however, that in all our efforts to enter the promised rest we strive lawfully; and with constant reference to that purity of heart and perfection of character which God re-quires; and without which, no one will ever enjoy his presence or keep a sabbath with him. (12:14.) It is not always the man who works most that will finally receive and enjoy most; for there are first that shall be last; and there are last that shall be first. (Matt. 19:30.) It should never be forgotten that by the deeds of law no flesh is justified in the sight of God. (Rom. 3:20.) There is noth-ing in these legal acts and observances to purify the soul and fit it for the rest of God: "for Christ is the end of the law for righteous-ness to every one that believeth." (Rom. 10:4.) It is only through the rich merits of his blood, the indwelling and sanctifying influence of the Holy Spirit, and the constant use of all the means which Heaven has provided for our growth in grace and progress in the Divine life, that we can be prepared for the promised rest. The whole inner man must be cleansed from every mark of sin and from every stain of iniquity, before we can have that full and per-fect communion with God which the redeemed will finally enjoy, and which is in fact the consummation of all happiness. And hence he says to everyone who would enter into his rest, "Become ye holy, for I am holy." (1 Pet. 1: 16.)

And hence we see the duty of constant self-examination while we are endeavoring to work out our salvation with fear and trem-bling (2 Cor. 13: 5) ; for it is God that works in us (Phil. 2: 13). His word tries us, and proves us, and searches us even to the very

12 For ¹the word of God is quick, and powerful, and ²sharper than any
two-edged sword, piercing even to the dividing asunder of soul and spirit,
and of the joints and marrow, ³and is a discerner of the thoughts and intents
of the heart.

¹Psa. cxix. 130; Eccl. xii. 11; Isa. lv. 11; Jer. xxiii. 29; Luke viii. 11; John vi. 63;
Acts xx. 32; Rom. i. 16; 1 Thess. ii. 13; James i. 18; 1 Pet. i. 23; Rev. xi. 3-16.
²Psa. cxlix. 6; Prov. v. 4; Isa. xi. 4; xlix. 2; Acts ii. 37; v. 33; Eph. vi. 17; Rev.
i. 16; ii. 12; xix. 15, 23.
³1 Cor. xiv. 24, 25; Rev. xx. 12, 13.

center of our being.  This, our author very beautifully and forcibly
illustrates in the two following verses.

12 **For the word of God is quick, and powerful,**—In this
verse, the Apostle gives a reason why we should all be so very earnest and particular in our endeavors to prepare and qualify ourselves, through Divine grace, for the enjoyment of the rest which
remains for the people of God.  A single mistake here may prove
fatal.  For though we keep the whole law, save that we offend only
in one point, we are guilty of all. (James 2 : 10.) Though, like Naa-
man, we dip ourselves seven times in the waters of the Jordan, and
though our persons may seem to be all pure and holy in the eyes of
men and angels, there may, nevertheless, be some secret sin cherished in our hearts, that will wholly unfit us for the fellowship of
God and the society of Heaven.  And if so, it will not escape the
eye of him who searches the hearts of the children of men.  For
the judgment of God is according to truth (*kata aletheian*) in all
cases (Rom. 2 : 2) ; and his word, by which we are to be judged at
the last day, is, like its Author, "living and powerful."

It has long been a question with expositors, whether "the word"
that is here spoken of is the personal Word, the Logos that became
flesh and dwelt among us (John 1 : 14), or the "word of hearing"
(4 : 2), called also "the word of salvation" (Acts 13 : 26).  Many
of the ancients and some of the moderns understand by it the personal Word; who, as they say, "is living and powerful, and his
judgment is sharper and more penetrating than any two-edged
sword."  But it is far more simple and natural, as most modern
commentators concede, to understand by this the instrumental
word, which, as a sharp, two-edged sword, proceeds out of the
mouth of the personal Word (Rev. 1 : 16; 2 : 12; 19 : 15, 23), with
which he now smites the nations; and by means of which he will
finally judge all who hear it.  This word "is living and powerful,"
because it is always supported by him who is himself the fountain

of life (Psalm 36 : 9) and the source of all power (Rom. 13 : 1). It is not a lifeless abstraction, but a living concrete embodiment of God's will, going wherever he pleases, and doing whatever he requires. "For as the rain cometh down, and the snow from heaven, and returneth not thither, but watereth the Earth, and maketh it bring forth and bud, that it may give seed to the sower, and bread to the eater: so," says Jehovah, "shall my word be that goeth forth out of my mouth; it shall not return unto me void, but it shall accomplish that which I please, and it shall prosper in the thing whereto I sent it." (Isa. 55 : 10, 11.) See references.

**and sharper than any two-edged sword,**—Or "more cutting than any two-mouth sword." This can scarcely be predicated, with propriety, of the personal Word; but it applies well to the instrumental word, the sword of the Spirit (Eph. 6 : 17), which goeth out of the mouth of him that sits upon the horse, and with which he smites the nations (Rev. 19 : 15).

**piercing even to the dividing asunder of soul and spirit, etc.** —This passage has given rise to an almost endless number and variety of queries and explanations; the consideration of many of which would be of but little service to the reader. I will therefore confine my remarks on it to such matters as seem necessary in order to a fair understanding of the mind of the Spirit. And (1) What is the meaning of *soul* and *spirit* in this connection? From the days of Pythagoras (500 B.C.), and more especially from the time of Plato (350 B.C.), the doctrine of a trinity in human nature became somewhat prevalent. These philosophers both taught, in substance, that man consists of a material body (*soma*), an animal soul (*psuche*), and an immortal spirit (*tineuma*). The soul was by them regarded as the seat of animal life, together with its several instincts, passions, and appetites; and the spirit was supposed to be the seat of the higher intellectual and moral faculties. In this sense, Paul manifestly uses these terms both in our text and also in 1 Thess. 5 : 23. But whether he aims here to speak of man as he really is, or merely to use by way of accommodation the current phraseology of the Greeks, is not so clear. In either case he would equally accomplish his main purpose, which is simply to indicate to his readers by the use of these terms the whole incorporeal nature of man. (2) What does our author mean by the *joints* (*harmoi*) and the *marrows* (*mueloi*)? Does he use these words in a literal sense to denote the inner and more concealed parts of the body? or does he use them metaphorically to denote the most secret and recondite recesses of the soul and the spirit? The critics are much divided on this point; and it must be confessed that it is not an easy matter to arrive with absolute certainty at the exact meaning of the passage. But after a careful examination of both the text and the context, I am constrained to think with Bengel, Bleek, DeWette, Tholuck, Lünemann, Moll, Alford, and others, that these words are used figuratively to denote the inmost essence of man's spiritual nature. This view of the matter is favored (a) by the use of the single conjunction *and* (*kai*) between the words *soul* and spirit, and the compound conjunction *both and* (*te kai*) between the words *joints* and marrows; thus indicating that these two sets of words are not coordinate, but that the latter phrase is subordinate to the former. Literally rendered, the passage reads as follows: piercing through even to the dividing asunder of soul and spirit, both of joints and marrows; and is a discerner of the thoughts and purposes of the heart. The phrase, *joints and marrows,* seems to be a proverbial expression, indicative of the inmost parts of anything; and it is used here to denote the extreme thoroughness of the dividing process effected in the soul and in the spirit by means of the word of God. (b) This view is also most in harmony with the ascending climax at which the writer evidently aims in the construction of this sentence. The word of God is, first, living; then it is full of power and energy; then it divides and lays bare the soul and the spirit even to the extent of their joints and their marrows; and then rising above the essence of man's nature, it enters inquisitively and judicially into the realms of his ideas, affections, and desires, and passes judgment on the thoughts and purposes of his heart. Nor does our author stop even here; but passing now from the word of God to God himself as its author, he caps the climax by representing all created things as being naked and fully exposed to the eyes of him to whom we are responsible, and to whom we shall have to render a final account. This is all very beautiful and in perfect harmony with the highly rhetorical character of the Epistle. But who does not feel the inconsistency of passing, in the course of this climax, from the soul and spirit of man to even the most concealed parts of his physical organization?

13 [1]Neither is there any creature that is not manifest in his sight: but all things [2]are naked and opened unto the eyes of [3]him with whom we have to do.

[1] Sam. xvi. 7; Psa. xc. 8; cxxxix. 11, 12; Prov. xv. 3, 11; Jer. xvii. 10; xxiii. 24; 1 Cor. iv. 5; Rev. ii. 23.
[2]Job xxvi. 6; xxxiv. 21, 22; Prov. xv. 3.
[3]Eccl. xii. 14; Matt. vii. 21, 22; xxv. 31-46; John v. 22-29; Acts xvii. 31; 2 Cor. v. 10; Rev. xx. 11-15.

If the view taken of this passage is correct, then it follows that the once prevalent notion of a separation of the soul from the spirit, and of the joints from the marrows, is incorrect. The separation takes place within the region of the soul and the region of the spirit; not between them. The living word cleaves and lays bare all parts of the soul and all parts of the spirit, even to the extent of their joints and their marrows; so that all the perfections and imperfections of man's spiritual nature are made perfectly manifest. And not only so, but even the thoughts and purposes of his heart are, by this infallible Judge, fully analyzed and perfectly classified.

13 **Neither is there any creature, etc.**—There is here a manifest transition from the word of God, as his efficient and soul-penetrating instrument, to God himself, in whose presence all things are *naked* (*gumna*), presenting themselves as they really are, without any kind of covering; and *opened* (*tetrachelimena*), with their heads thrown back, and their faces and necks exposed to full view. This is the proper meaning of the word; but from what is the metaphor taken? Some say, from the ancient custom of offering sacrifice. The victim was first slain; then it was flayed, cut open, and exposed to the eye of the priest for inspection. Others think that the Apostle refers here to the Roman custom of bending back the necks of criminals, so as to expose their faces more fully to the eyes of the public. To this Pliny refers in his panegyric on the emperor Trajan. Speaking of the emperor's endeavors to promote virtue and suppress vice, he says, "There is nothing, however, in this age, that affects us more pleasingly and deservedly than to see from above the supine faces and reverted necks of the informers. We thus know them, and are pleased when, as expiating victims of public disquietude, they are led away to lingering punishments and sufferings more terrible than even the blood of the guilty." (Panegyr. xxxiv. 3.) Others again suppose that there is an allusion here to the custom of wrestlers who were wont to

seize their antagonists by their throats, and bend back their heads and necks for the purpose of more easily effecting their overthrow. On the whole, it seems most probable that the expression had reference primarily to the exposure of criminals; and that Paul used it in its then current sense to denote simply that all creatures stand before God with their necks, as it were, bent backward, and their faces fully exposed to the all-seeing "eyes of him with whom we have to do."

## REFLECTIONS

1. Christians are all of one holy brotherhood. (3: 1.) It matters not how much they may differ from one another in wealth, talents, learning, and social advantages, they are nevertheless all one in Christ Jesus. The rich should not therefore despise the poor, nor should the poor envy the rich. But all should strive to maintain "the unity of the Spirit in the bond of peace"; and to promote each other's good, as heirs of the grace of life and joint heirs of the eternal inheritance.

2. To think much about Christ as the Apostle and High Priest of our confession, will be of great service to us in many ways (verse 1). It will serve, for instance, to increase our faith in him and our confidence in the perfection and efficacy of the gospel plan of salvation through him. It will increase our love for God, who has so tenderly loved us as to send his own Son to redeem us. It will correct and restrain our selfishness, and make us more zealous for the glory of God and the salvation of the world. And, in a word, it will make us all more humble, more prayerful, and more earnest in our endeavors to "live soberly, and righteously, and godly."

3. How much, how very much may depend on the fidelity of God's ministers (verse 5). Had the servants of Christ all acted as did Moses, and observed faithfully the more full and encouraging instructions of the Holy Spirit that are given to us in the New Testament, how very different would be both the Church and the world today. How many that are now idolaters would be Christians; and how many of those that are now eternally lost, might today be rejoicing among the spirits of the just made perfect.

4. God still dwells with his people (verse 6). The Church of God is the house of God, as it is written, "I will dwell in them, and

walk in them; and I will be their God, and they shall be my people." (2 Cor. 6: 16.) Why, then, do we not draw nigh to him who has come so very near to us? Why not, like Enoch and Moses, walk with him, as seeing him who is invisible? Why not avoid everything that is offensive in his sight, such as the lusts of the flesh, the lusts of the eye, and the pride of life? And why not, like Christ, humbly endeavor to do the will of God in all things? Surely this is but our highest happiness, as it is also our most reasonable service.

5. Fidelity to the end of life is essential in order to the final enjoyment of the great salvation (verses 6, 14). With such warnings and admonitions before us as those which are given in this section, it is all folly to rely for happiness on the imaginary "unconditional decrees" of God; or on the once prevalent doctrine of "final perseverance." "He that endures to the end shall be saved." (Matt. 10: 22.) Without this actual perseverance on our part, through the abounding grace of God, nothing can save us from the torments of the damned. It is not enough that God has sent his Son into the world to save it; and that Christ has sent the Holy Spirit to convince mankind "of sin, and of righteousness, and of judgment." It is not enough that we have confessed Christ, and that we have been actually washed from our past sins in his blood. We must also continue to persevere in well-doing, seeking for honor, and glory, and immortality, if we would enjoy eternal life. (Rom. 2: 7.) "For if we sin willfully, after that we have received the knowledge of the truth, there remaineth no more [a] sacrifice for sins." (10: 26.) "Let him [then] that thinketh he standeth, take heed lest he fall." (1 Cor. 10: 12.)

6. Let no one, then, trifle with the commands of God, and with the promptings of an enlightened conscience; no, not even for a day or an hour (verses 7, 13). "To-day, if ye hear his voice, harden not your hearts, as at Meribah, as on the day of Massah in the wilderness." All unnecessary delay is dangerous, because it is sinful and serves to harden the hearts of those who yield to its seductive influence. And hence the law of the Kingdom of Heaven is (1) to hear; (2) to believe; and (3) to obey from the heart that form of doctrine which is delivered to us in the Gospel. The primitive Christians did this; and then went on their way rejoicing. See Acts *passim*.

7. But the power of sin over the human heart is very great (verse 13). The unregenerate are slaves to its influence. See Rom. 6: 6, 7, 17, 20; 7: 13-23. And even the Christian, enlightened and assisted as he is by the Holy Spirit, has need to be constantly on his guard, lest he too be ensnared and hardened through its deceitfulness. (1 Cor. 9: 27.) And hence the great importance and necessity of that mutual exhortation and encouragement which our author so earnestly recommends. "Exhort one another daily," he says, "while it is called To-day, lest any of you be hardened through the deceitfulness of sin." And again he says to the Galatian brethren, "Bear ye one another's burdens, and so fulfill the law of Christ." (Gal. 6: 2.) God has made us all fellow-helpers one of another, by committing to us the word of reconciliation and exhortation.

8. Why, then, are we so very unfaithful to the trust which God has committed to us in this particular? Why do we not exhort one another daily? Why are we so prone to talk about anything and everything else rather than about the one thing needful? When we meet with our brethren, we are all wont to ask for their welfare. We inquire very particularly about their prosperity in business, and also about their physical health, comforts, and enjoyments. But how many of us are in the habit of inquiring after the state and condition of their souls? How many mutual inquiries are made about one another's progress in the Divine life; and about the peculiar trials, difficulties, and dangers that beset us, and against which we have to contend in our feeble efforts to reach the heavenly rest? That there is a great want of fidelity among Christians in this respect, admits, I think, of no doubt. But why is it so? Has it ceased to be true that "Out of the abundance of the heart the mouth speaketh"? Or does this habit of worldly conversation about secular matters, indicate an alarming want of spirituality in our own poor unbelieving hearts? That public sentiment is a great barrier in the way of religious conversation in the social circle, I freely admit. It is really amazing to what an extent the Devil has succeeded in persuading the people, that it is impolite to speak of God, or of Christ, or of Heaven, in the parlor or on the public highway. And the fear of giving offense, no doubt, often constrains many a Christian to withhold his lips from speaking good, even when the fire of God's grace is burning in his soul.

(Psalm 39: 1-3.) But after making all due allowance for the binding obligations of public sentiment within proper limits, it must, I fear, be conceded that this general delinquency on the part of Christians is fearfully indicative of our own want of faith in God and in the word of his grace. Christ, it is true, never cast pearls before swine; and in some cases he refrained from working miracles on account of the extreme wickedness and infidelity of the people. See Matt. 13: 58, and Mark 6: 5, 6. But still, the main burden of his conversation, wherever he went, was "the Kingdom of God and his righteousness." May God grant us all grace to walk in his footsteps.

9. Our greatest want has always been a want of faith in God and in the word of his grace (verses 18, 19). It was this that first brought sin into the world. (Gen. 3: 6.) It was this that filled the antediluvian earth with violence, and brought in a flood of waters on the ungodly. It was this that caused the dispersion from Babel, and that soon after filled the world with idolatry. It was this that brought down fire and brimstone from Heaven on Sodom and Gomorrah, and made these cities of the plain a monument of God's hatred of sin. It was this that so often brought down God's judgments on even his own chosen people in the wilderness and in Canaan, and that has made their descendants a proverb and a byword in every nation under Heaven. It was this that divided the Church of God, and that filled the dwelling-place of the Most High with all manner of Jewish and Gentile abominations. And it is this that now deprives us all of a thousand spiritual enjoyments, and that will hereafter shut the gates of Heaven against millions who, like the rebellious Israelites, will seek to enter into God's rest when it is too late. (Luke 13: 24-30.) No wonder, then, that our blessed Savior so often sums up all sin under the head of unbelief. "When he [the Comforter] is come," says Christ, "he will convict the world of sin, because they believe not on me." (John 16: 9.) See also John 3: 18-21; 5: 39-47; 8: 24; 15: 22-25, etc. Let us, then, all beware, lest there be also in any of us an evil heart of unbelief in apostatizing from the living God.

10. The main business of life is to labor to enter into God's rest. (4: 11.) Here we are all but strangers and pilgrims, traveling, like the Israelites in the wilderness, to the promised inheritance. What folly it is, then, to build costly mansions and monuments on

these sandy foundations in the desert over which we are now passing so rapidly on our way to the everlasting Zion! What folly it is
to call our lands by our own names. (Psalm 49: 11), and to lay
up treasures here on Earth, where moth and rust are constantly
corroding and corrupting. Let us all look rather to the end of our
pilgrimage; and labor to enter into the everlasting rest which is
now in reserve for every child of God. And let us rejoice, as did
Paul, that it is better to depart and to be with Christ in those heavenly mansions.

11. How utterly vain are all the hopes and deceits of the hypocrite; and with what shame and confusion of face he will stand finally before God, naked and exposed to the all-penetrating eye of
him with whom we have to do (verses 11-13). Then, every refuge of lies in which he trusted will be swept away; and all the
deep, dark, and hidden recesses of his whole spiritual being will be
made manifest in the light of God's countenance, by means of the
living energies of that word which pierces through to the dividing
asunder of the soul and of the spirit, even to the extent of their
joints and their marrows! May God save us all from such an ordeal on the day of his final reckoning.

## SECTION FOUR
### 4: 14 to 5: 10

#### ANALYSIS

In 3: 1, the Apostle calls on his Hebrew brethren to consider
attentively Jesus, the Apostle and High Priest of our confession.
He then takes up the consideration of his apostleship, and speaks
of it and other matters subordinate to it, to the close of the third
section. (4: 13.) But in doing so, he of course develops and illustrates also, in some measure, the perfections of Christ as a High
Priest. Indeed all that is said of Christ's Divinity in the first section, of his humanity in the second, and of his apostleship in the
third, has some bearing also on his priesthood. And hence it is
that, in the fourth section, he is at once presented to us so encouragingly as our great prevailing and sympathetic High Priest.

In the course of this section, the Apostle—

I. Encourages his brethren to hold fast their confession; and
relying on Jesus as their great and sympathizing High Priest, to

approach the Throne of grace, and ask for help with all confidence. (4: 14-16.) This he exhorts and encourages them to do—

1. On the ground that Jesus is a great High Priest; far above all created intelligences (verse 14).

2. That he has gone up through the heavens, to appear in the presence of God for us (verse 14).

3. That he is himself, as was shown in the first chapter, the Son of God, the only-begotten of the Father, full of grace and truth (verse 14).

4. That he is a tender and sympathetic High Priest, having been tempted in all respects even as we are, but without sin (verse 15).

II. He next shows for what purpose a high priesthood was appointed among men; and specifies some of the principal qualifications that were required in all who would perform its sacred functions. (5: 1-4.)

1. Every such priest taken from among men, is, he says, ordained to officiate for men in things pertaining to God; and especially to offer both gifts, and sacrifices for sins. The office was never intended to be a sinecure. But it was created and sustained for the benefit and encouragement of those who desired to worship and serve God acceptably (verse 1).

2. It was necessary, therefore, that every High Priest should himself be a man of experience and sympathy; so that he might at all times be able to encourage, comfort, and instruct the erring and the ignorant (verse 2).

3. That he should receive his appointment from God as did Aaron (verse 4).

III. After stating the object of the priesthood, and specifying some of the leading duties and qualifications of every High Priest chosen from among men, the Apostle next proceeds to encourage his brethren still further, by showing them how eminently Christ is qualified for all the duties of the sacerdotal office (verses 5-10).

1. He was constituted a High Priest by God himself, as David testifies in Psalm 110: 4 (verses 5, 6).

2. He was, while in the flesh, a man of great sorrow and affliction (verse 7).

3. He was a man of prayer (verse 7).

4. He was heard and delivered from his greatest fears, showing that he had power with God (verse 7).

5. His experience far transcended that of every other man. Though honored and exalted as the Son of God, he nevertheless went down into the lowest depths of human sorrow and suffering (verse 8).

6. And being thus made perfect, as a High Priest, he is now able and willing to save with an everlasting salvation all who believe and obey him (verse 9).

From the preceding analysis it is manifest, that this section may be divided into the three following paragraphs:

I. 4: 14-16. Encouragement to persevere in the Christian life, and to approach with confidence the Throne of grace, drawn from the exalted position and the sympathetic love of Jesus, the great High Priest of our confession.

II. 5: 1-4. Encouraging and benevolent design of the priesthood; and the necessary qualifications of those who would minister acceptably in the High Priest's office.

III. 5-10. Preeminent qualifications of Jesus to officiate as our High Priest; with further encouragements to believe and obey him.

1. ENCOURAGEMENT TO PERSEVERE IN THE CHRISTIAN
LIFE, AND TO APPROACH WITH CONFIDENCE THE
THRONE OF GRACE, DRAWN FROM THE EXALTED
POSITION AND THE SYMPATHETIC LOVE OF JESUS,
AS THE HIGH PRIEST OF OUR CONFESSION
4: 14-16

14 Seeing then that we have [1]a great high priest, [2]that is passed into the heavens, [3]Jesus the Son of God, [4]let us hold fast our profession.

[1]Ch. ii. 17; iii. 1; v. 6; vi. 20; vii. 3, 15, 17; Psa. cx. 4; Zech. vi. 13.
[2]Ch. i. 3; vi. 20; vii. 25, 26; viii. 1; ix. 12; x. 12; Acts i. 11; iii. 21.
[3]See refs. ch. i. 2, 8.
[4]Ch. iii. 6, 14; vi. 11; x. 23, 35; Matt. x. 22; Col. i. 23.

14 **Seeing then that we have a great high priest,**—The main discussion of Christ's priesthood is to be found in what follows to the close of the eighth section. (10: 18.) But in the first three sections there is enough said of him to warrant the conclusion that we have a great High Priest who has gone up through the heavens into the Holy of holies, there to appear in the presence of God for us. And hence it is that the Apostle makes this the ground of another ear-

nest exhortation to his Hebrew brethren to hold fast their confession.

The title *high priest* (*hiereus megas*) occurs first in Lev. 21: 10, where it is used to designate Aaron and his successors, upon whose heads the anointing oil was poured, and who were severally consecrated to put on the holy garments. The corresponding word in the New Testament (*archiereus*) is used to designate (1) the High Priest proper; (2) the deputy of the High Priest; (3) anyone who had ever borne the office; and (4) the head of each of the twenty-four courses of the priesthood. (1 Chron. 24.) But here, as well as in 2: 17; 3: 1; 5: 5, 10; 6: 20; 7: 26; 8: 1; 9: 11, 25, it refers to Christ, who, as a Priest upon his throne (Zech. 6: 13), is ever ready to receive and bless those who come unto God by him. The adjective *great* (*megas*) is used here, not in its technical sense, as it often is, to distinguish Aaron and his successors in office from Priests of the common order, but in its proper sense to denote the real, personal, and official greatness of Christ, who, as our author shows, is superior even to the angels, as well as to Moses and all the Priests of the Old Covenant.

**that is passed into the heavens,**—More literally, *who has passed through* (*dieleluthota*) *the heavens*. That is, through the aerial and sidereal heavens, on his way to the Heaven of heavens, the Most Holy Place, not made with hands; where, as a Priest, Christ offered his own blood once for all, and then sat down at the right hand of the Majesty on high (1: 3); "a minister of the Sanctuary and of the true Tabernacle which the Lord pitched and not men" (8: 2).

**Jesus the Son of God,**—These words are added by way of explanation, to denote more definitely the power, glory, and dignity of our great High Priest. He is not of the house of Aaron; but he is the Son of God, by whom all things were created, and for whom all things were created; "the brightness of the Father's glory and the express image of his person." See notes on 1: 2, 3, 8.

**let us hold fast our profession.**—Rather, *our confession* (*homologia*). See note on 3: 1. As Jesus is himself the subject of this confession (Matt. 16: 16), we cannot renounce it without renouncing him also as our Savior. And to renounce Christ is to seal forever our own condemnation (6: 4-6): "for there is none other

15 For ¹we have not a high priest which can not be touched with the feeling of our infirmities; but ²was in all points tempted like as we are, ³yet
without sin.

¹Ch. ii. 17, 18; Isa. liii. 4, 5; Matt. viii. 16, 17; Phil. ii. 7, 8.
²Ch. v. 7-9; Matt. iv. 1-11; Luke iv. 1-13; xxii. 28, 39-46.
³Ch. vii. 26; Isa. liii. 9; John viii. 46; 2 Cor. v. 21; 1 Pet. ii. 22; 1 John iii. 5.

name under heaven given among men whereby we must be saved"
(Acts 4: 12).

15 **For we have not a high priest which can not, etc.**—Our
High Priest is not only great in power, glory, and majesty, having
in his hands all authority in Heaven and on Earth (Matt. 28: 19),
but he is also full of love and compassion for us. See notes 2: 17,
18.

**but was in all points tempted like as we are, yet without
sin.**—What is meant here by our Savior's being tempted? On this
point Ebrard very justly remarks as follows: "Being tempted is,
on the one hand, something different from being seduced; and, on
the other hand, it is something different from mere physical suffering. He who is seduced, stands not in a purely passive relation,
but with his own will acquiesces in the will of seducer; but he who
is tempted, is, as such, purely passive. This, however, is not
merely physical passivity; headache, as such, is no temptation.
But there is a moral obligation lying upon every man, not to let
himself be mastered by his natural affections, which in themselves
are altogether sinless, but rather to acquire the mastery over
them. . . . That a poor man loves his children, and cannot bear
that they perish of hunger, is in itself a natural and sinless affection; but let him be so placed as that, without danger of discovery,
he could steal a piece of money, then that natural affection becomes
to him a temptation. Now it is quite clear that a man may in this
way find himself in a situation of being tempted, without its being
necessary to suppose that there is therefore an evil inclination.
The poor man may be a truly honest Christian man; the temptation is there; the thought is present to his mind in all the force of a
natural affection, If I were at liberty to take this gold, how I might
appease the hunger of my children; but at the same time he has an
immediate and lively sense of his duty, and not a breath of desire
moves him to take the gold. He knows that he dare not do this: it
is a settled thing with him that he is not a thief. . . . So it was in

16 Let us therefore ¹come boldly unto ²the throne of grace, that we may ³obtain mercy, and find grace to help in time of need.

¹Ch. x. 19-23; Rom. viii. 15-17; Eph. ii. 18.
²Ch. ix. 5; Ex. xxv. 17-22; Lev. xvi. 2.
³Isa. lv. 6, 7; Matt. vii. 7-11; Eph. vi. 18. 19; Phil. iv. 6, 7; Col. iv. 2; 1 Thess. v. 17.

reference to the temptation of Christ.  He was tempted in every respect, in joy and sorrow, in fear and hope, in the most varied situations, but without sin; the being tempted was to him purely passive; purely objective."  No inclination to evil ever defiled his pure spirit.  The lusts of the flesh, the lusts of the eye, and the pride of life, had no place in his affections.  And hence, though tempted by the Devil through all the avenues and natural desires of the human heart, he was still "without sin."

16 **Let us therefore, etc.**—Since it is true that we have a great High Priest who has gone up through the heavens, even into the very Heaven of heavens; and since it is also true, that though so highly exalted he nevertheless sympathizes with us in all our temptations, trials, and afflictions, we should on their account all be encouraged to approach the Throne of grace with confidence.  It is generally thought that the Apostle here makes allusion to the Mercy-seat, on which rested the Shekinah, the visible symbol of God's presence in the ancient Tabernacle.  And this is most likely true, if in connection with the Mercy-seat be taken also the Ark of the covenant.  But it should be observed that the golden lid of the Ark is, in no part of the inspired word called a throne.  Its Hebrew name is simply *kapporeth*, which means a *lid* or *cover;* and its Greek name is *hilasterion,* a propitiatory.  This lid could not therefore, in any proper sense, be called by itself a throne of grace. But the whole Ark, including the lid, was a symbol of God's throne. (Jer. 3: 16, 17.)  And hence the allusion of the Apostle here is, not merely to the Mercy-seat, but to the entire Ark, from the lid of which, sprinkled as it was with blood once every year (Lev. 16: 14, 15), God was pleased to make known his gracious will to the people (Ex. 25: 22).  Any reference, however, to the Ark of the covenant in this connection, is merely for the sake of illustration, for there can be no doubt that by the Throne of grace is here meant the Throne of God; which in 8: 1, is called "the throne of the Majesty in the heavens"; because from it the infinitely Majestic One gives his laws and mandates to the universe.  But it is here, with

equal propriety, called also "the Throne of grace"; because from it
God dispenses grace, mercy, and peace, to all who come to him and
ask for help in the name of Jesus. For being justified by faith, we
can now, through our Lord Jesus Christ, approach God as our
Father, feeling fully assured that if we ask anything according to
his will, he will hear and answer us. (1 John 5: 14.) See also
Matt. 7: 7-11; John 14: 13; 15: 7; 16: 24. How very reasonable,
then, is the exhortation that we should approach the Throne of
grace with confidence (*parresia*), so that we may obtain mercy and
find grace for seasonable help. That is, for such constant help as
our trials and circumstances require. And hence we are encouraged to pray always; to pray without ceasing; and to be careful for
nothing, but in everything by prayer and supplication with
thanksgiving to let our requests be made known unto God. See
Eph. 6: 18; Phil. 4: 6; 1 Thess. 5: 17.

### 2. ENCOURAGING AND BENEVOLENT DESIGN OF THE PRIESTHOOD; AND THE REQUISITE QUALIFICATIONS OF THOSE WHO WOULD MINISTER IN THE HIGH PRIEST'S OFFICE
#### 5: 1-4

1 For [1]every high priest taken from among men [2]is ordained for men in
things pertaining to God, that he may [3]offer both gifts and sacrifices for sins:

[1]Ex. xxviii. 1; Lev. viii. 2.
[2]Num. xvi. 46-48; xviii. 1-3.
[3]Ch. viii. 3, 4; ix. 9; x. 11; Lev. ix. 7, 15-21.

1 **For every high priest, etc.**—The object of the Apostle in this
paragraph, as above indicated, is to further encourage his Hebrew
brethren to draw near at all times to the Throne of grace, and
there, in the name of Jesus, to seek for seasonable help. This he
insists we should feel encouraged to do from the fact that God has
himself appointed the priesthood for the very purpose of aiding
and supporting us in the discharge of our religious duties. For
every High Priest, he says, being taken from among men, is appointed for men in things pertaining to God, that he may offer both
gifts and sacrifices for sins; being able to have compassion for the
ignorant and erring, since he himself is compassed with infirmity;
and on this account, he is under obligation, as for the people, so
also for himself to offer for sins. Since, then, it was God's benevolent intention in the ordination of the priesthood to comfort and

2 ¹Who can have compassion on the ignorant, and on them that are out
of the way; for that he himself also ²is compassed with infirmity.

¹Ch. ii. 18; iv. 15; Ex. xxviii. 12, 29; Lev. x. 11; Deut. xxx. 10; Mal. ii. 7.
²Ch. vii. 28; Ex. xxxii. 21-24; Num. xii. 1-9; xx. 9-12.

support us in the discharge of our religious duties, we should especially feel encouraged to approach the Throne of grace in the name
of Jesus, who, as our ever living High Priest, is so eminently qualified to help our infirmities, bear our weaknesses, and procure for
us through the sacrifice of himself the pardon of our sins, and that
full measure of grace which is necessary for our support under all
the trials, temptations, and conflicts of life.

**is ordained for men**—It was not for the benefit of God, but of
men, that the priesthood was instituted. God does not need any
such help, so far as it respects himself. He was infinitely happy
before the sacerdotal office was created, and he would still be so,
even if all the laws and ordinances of the priesthood were forever
abrogated. Nevertheless, he so loved and pitied our poor, lost, and
ruined race, that he gave his own Son to die for it; and in order to
make the benefits of Christ's death available to all, God instituted
the priesthood and many other ordinances as media of blessings to
mankind. Surely, then, it is not the will of God that any should
perish, but that all should be brought to repentance and to the enjoyment of the great salvation. "He that spared not his own Son,
but delivered him up for us all, how shall he not with him also
freely give us all things?"

**in things pertaining to God,**—That is, in religious matters.
Aaron and his son were not appointed to any secular calling. It
was not their province to cultivate the soil, to carry on commerce,
or even to investigate the laws and ordinances of nature. They
were called to minister in holy things; and especially to "offer gifts
and sacrifices for sins." The words *gifts* (*dora*) and *sacrifices*
(*thusiai*) are sometimes used interchangeably, as in Gen. 4: 3-5.
But when contrasted, as they are in this case, and also in 8: 3; 9:
9, the former is used for bloodless offerings, and the latter for such
as required the life of the victim.

2 **Who can have compassion on the ignorant,**—The word
rendered *have compassion* (*metriopatheo*) means to feel moder-
ately. "It comes," says Delitzsch, "from the mint of Greek ethical

philosophy; and it was employed by Academics, Peripatetics, and Skeptics, to indicate the right mean between a slave-like passion-ateness and a stoical apathy. It is used by Philo to describe Abra-ham's sober grief on the loss of Sarah (volume ii. 37), and Jacob's imperturbable patience under afflictions (volume ii. 45). Trans-ferred from the language of the schools to general literature, it signifies the disposition of mind which keeps the right mean be-tween excessive feeling and sheer indifference; and here it indi-cates a pathetic judgment which is neither too severe nor too le-nient; but reasonable, sober, indulgent, and kind."

Such a quality of head and heart was peculiarly necessary in every High Priest; for to him it belonged to decide, in any given case, whether or not a sacrifice could be legally offered for the sin committed. See Lev. 10: 8-11; Deut. 17: 8-13; 24: 8; 33: 10; Mal. 2: 7. If a man sinned through ignorance or in error, that is, either without a knowledge of God's will in the case, or under such temptations as might serve to obscure for the time being his con-sciousness of guilt, then in that event and under such circumstances a sacrifice might be offered, and the sin might be forgiven. (Num. 15: 22-29.) But not so if the sin was committed with a high hand, that is, in a spirit of haughty insolence and open rebellion against God and his government. In that event, there was no room for repentance, and none for sacrifice. The presumptuous sinner was always to be put to death, "at the mouth of two or three witnesses." (Num. 15: 30, 31; Deut. 17: 6.) See notes on 6: 4-6. But in many cases it might be difficult to determine the exact nature and character of the offense. What the Jews were wont to call, by a species of euphemism, a sin of ignorance, might under some cir-cumstances seem, for a time at least, to be a presumptuous sin. And hence the necessity under the Law, as well as under the Gos-pel, of using all lawful means to bring the offending party to re-pentance. This was especially the duty of the High Priest, who, as the head of the sacerdotal order, was charged, on the one hand, with faithfully executing the law of God against all high-handed transgressors; and, on the other, with exercising all due forbear-ance and compassion towards the ignorant and the erring.

**for that he himself also is compassed with infirmity.**—A proper sense of our own infirmities enables us to bear with more becoming patience the infirmities of others. "I have," says Paul,

3 And by reason hereof ¹he ought, as for the people, so also for himself, to offer for sins.

¹Ch. vii. 27; ix. 7; Ex. xxix. 10-21; Lev. iv. 3-12; xvi. 6-22.

"great heaviness and continual sorrow in my heart for my brethren, my kinsmen, according to the flesh; for I myself was once, like them, wishing to be accursed from Christ." (Rom. 9: 2, 3.) And just so it was with Aaron and his successors. They, too, like their brethren, were compassed about, and, as it were, clothed with all the weaknesses and infirmities common to our fallen nature. Aaron's folly in making the golden calf (Ex. 32: 1-6) was to himself, no doubt, a source of much grief and painful experience; but it served, nevertheless, to make him deal more tenderly with others who were afterward overcome by similar temptations.

3 **And by reason hereof, etc.**—On account of the infirmity which constantly beset him, and which rendered imperfect even his most solemn services, the High Priest was required to offer sacrifices for his own sins, as well as for the sins of the people. This he did not only on special occasions and for special offenses (Lev. 4: 3-12), but also in all the regular daily, weekly, monthly, and yearly sacrifices that were offered for the sins of the nation; in all these there was an acknowledgement of his own guilt, as well as of the guilt of his brethren. And on the Day of atonement, he was required to go into the Most Holy Place, and there make an offering for his own sins, before he was allowed to offer for the sins of the people. This of course served to make him deal more tenderly and compassionately with the ignorant and the erring.

Much of what is said in this paragraph is very beautifully and impressively illustrated by the symbolical dress of the High Priest; several parts of which indicate very clearly the holy and representative character of his office, and also the righteous and benevolent design of his administration. These articles of clothing were (1) a pair of Drawers; (2) a long Coat or Tunic; (3) a Girdle; (4) a Mitre; (5) the Robe of the Ephod; (6) the Ephod; (7) the Breastplate; and (8) the Plate of the Mitre. The first four of these were called "linen garments," because they were made of fine white linen, which in all ages has been regarded as a symbol of purity and holiness. See 1 Chron. 5: 12; Rev. 19: 8. And hence these were called also "holy garments." (Lev. 16: 4.) The four other pieces were also called "holy garments" (Ex. 28: 2, 4) ; and by the Jews they were frequently designated as "The golden garments," because they all consisted more or less of gold, either plated or interwoven with their texture. See Ex. 28. The first of these, the Robe of the Ephod was a long, sky-blue robe, without a seam, and was worn directly under the Ephod. Around its lower border were tassels made of blue, and purple, and scarlet, in the form of pomegranates, alternating with golden bells. The Rabbis say there were seventy-two of each. See Ex. 28: 31-35. The Ephod (from to bind) was a short coat worn over the Robe, and with its "curious girdle" was made of "gold, and blue, and purple, and scarlet, and fine twined linen, with cunning work." To the shoulder pieces were attached two onyx stones, on which were engraved the names of the twelve sons of Jacob, "according to their birth." (Ex. 28: 10.) This phrase, "according to their births," is differently understood by the Jewish Rabbis, as well as by Christian writers. Some place the names of the six oldest sons on the right shoulder, and the names of the six youngest on the left, as follows :

| LEFT | RIGHT |
|---|---|
| Gad | Reuben |
| Asher | Simeon |
| Issachar | Levi |
| Zebulun | Judah |
| Joseph | Dan |
| Benjamin | Naphtali |

Others arrange them alternately on the right and left; placing first in order the six sons of Leah (Reuben, Simeon, Levi, Judah, Issachar, and Zebulun) ; next, the two sons of Bilhah, Rachel's maid (Dan and Naphtali) ; next, the two sons of Zilpah, Leah's maid (Gad and Asher), and lastly, the two sons of Rachel (Joseph and Benjamin), as follows :

| LEFT | RIGHT |
|---|---|
| Simeon | Reuben |
| Judah | Levi |
| Zebulun | Issachar |
| Naphtali | Dan |
| Asher | Gad |
| Benjamin | Joseph |

The Breastplate was a sort of pouch or bag, half a cubit square. It was made of gold, and blue, and purple, and scarlet, and fine-twined linen. To each of the four corners was attached a gold ring by means of which it was, fastened to the Ephod. On the inside of its face were four rows of precious stones set in sockets of gold, through which they were exposed to view on the outside. And on the external faces of these stones were engraved the names of the Twelve Tribes of the children of Israel, most likely according to their birth, as follows:

| Carbuncle<br>Levi | Topaz<br>Simeon | Sardius<br>Reuben |
|---|---|---|
| Diamond<br>Naphtali | Sapphire<br>Dan | Emerald<br>Judah |
| Amethyst<br>Issachar | Agate<br>Asher | Ligure<br>Gad |
| Jasper<br>Benjamin | Onyx<br>Joseph | Beryl<br>Zebulun |

In this Breastplate were placed the Urim and Thummim (Lights and Perfections); names which seem to have been given to the twelve stones, because of their being made, in some miraculous

The High Priest in his Linen Garments.          The High Priest in his Full Dress.

4 And ¹no man taketh this honor unto himself, but he that is called of
God as was Aaron. 5 So also ²Christ glorified not himself to be made an
high priest; but he that said unto him, ³Thou art my Son, to-day have I begotten thee.

¹Ex. xxviii. 1; Lev. viii. 2; Num. xvi.; xvii. 1-11.
²John vii. 18; viii. 54.
³Ch. i. 5; Psa. ii. 7; John iii. 16; Acts xiii. 33; Rom. i. 4; viii. 3.

way, the medium through which God made known his will to the
High Priest.  See Num. 27: 21; Judges 20: 27, 28; 1 Sam. 23: 9;
28: 6; Ezra 2: 63; and Joseph. Ant. iii. 8, 9.  The fourth and last
article of the High Priest's golden attire was the plate of gold
which was fastened to the Mitre by a blue fillet.  On this Plate
was inscribed Holiness to Jehovah.

These articles of clothing are all visibly represented in the
preceding engravings, except the drawers, which are of course concealed by the outer garments.

4 **And no man taketh this honor unto himself, etc.**—Our author refers here to another essential qualification of every High
Priest.  He must be "called of God, as was Aaron."  And the man
who claims this honor for himself as did Korah (Num. 16),
though sustained by the highest human authority, is really not a
High Priest, but a usurper (Acts 23: 5).  It is hardly necessary to
add that the honor which is here spoken of is simply the honor of
being a High Priest, and that it has no reference whatever to the
calling of the Christian ministry.

### 3. PRE-EMINENT QUALIFICATIONS OF CHRIST TO OFFICIATE AS OUR HIGH PRIEST, WITH FURTHER ENCOURAGEMENTS TO BELIEVE AND OBEY HIM.
#### 5: 5-10

5 **So also Christ glorified not himself, etc.**—He took not on
himself the honor and glory of becoming a High Priest.  This
honor was bestowed by God the Father, when he raised him from
the dead, and set him at his own right hand in heavenly places,
thus demonstrating to the world that he was the Son of God, and
of course also the promised Prophet, Priest, and King, who was to
bring in everlasting righteousness and reign over the house of
David forever.  See Deut. 18: 18; Psalm 110: 4; Zech. 6: 13; Isa.
9: 6, 7; Dan. 9: 24-27.  That the citation from Psalm 2: 7 has
reference to the resurrection of Christ, as the first-born from the

6 As he saith also in another place. ¹Thou art a priest forever after the order of ²Melchisedec.

¹Ch. v. 10; vi. 20; vii. 3, 15, 17; Psa. cx. 4.
²Gen. xiv. 18, 19.

dead, is manifest 'from the application which Paul makes of it in Acts 13 : 33. See note on 1 : 5. And it seems to follow, therefore, from our premises, that the beginning of Christ's priesthood, as well as the beginning of his mediatorial reign, was subsequent to his resurrection. Before he could be thus honored, he must by the grace of God taste death for every man. He must go down into the lowest depths of human suffering, before he could be raised to the royal and sacerdotal honors of the kingdom of grace which he came to inaugurate through the medium and efficacy of his own blood. These honors were in fact bestowed on him as the rewards of his sufferings; and must therefore of necessity come after them. But as already intimated in our notes on 2 : 17, it will not do to infer hence that he had never, in any case, previous to his resurrection, acted as a King or a Priest. We often embarrass ourselves by prescribing for the Father, the Son, and the Holy Spirit the same narrow and technical formulae which govern us in our imperfect operations. It must not be forgotten that Christ was God, one with the Father, and that his whole earthly ministry was, in fact, but a preparation for his mediatorial reign and everlasting priesthood. During this period of preparation he performed some acts involving of necessity the exercise of both his royal and sacerdotal prerogatives. But these acts were all preparatory and extraordinary, so that we may still without doing violence to the Scriptures, assume the resurrection of Christ as the beginning of those honors which resulted in his being made both the High Priest, and the King of the new Institution. See notes on 7 : 17, 27.

6 **As he saith also in another place, etc.**—In quoting as above from Psalm 2 : 7, the Apostle makes no special reference to the honors of the priesthood. His object is more general. He aims simply to prove that God had honored Christ, as his own Son, by raising him from the dead and placing him at his own right hand as the anointed Sovereign of the universe. And from this it might, of course, be fairly inferred that the office of the priesthood, as well as all the other honors of the Son, was bestowed on him by the

7 Who in ¹the days of his flesh, ²when he had offered up prayers and sup-

¹Ch. ii. 14; John i. 14; 1 John iv. 3; 2 John 7.
²Psa. xxii. 1-21; Isa. liii. 3, 4, 11; Matt. xxvi. 38-44; Luke xxii. 41-44.

Father.  But the special proof of this, the Apostle now brings forward in a quotation from Psalm 110, where David says, "Jehovah said to my Lord, Sit on my right hand till I make thy enemies thy footstool."  Then addressing the Messiah whom he here calls his Lord, he says, Jehovah shall send the rod of thy strength out of Zion; rule thou in the midst of thy enemies.  Thy people shall be free-will offerings in the day of thy power; in ornaments of holiness; from the womb of the morning shall be to thee the dew of thy youth.  And then he adds, "Jehovah has sworn, and will not repent, Thou art a priest forever after the order of Melchisedec."  That this is a Messianic Psalm, and that the Holy Spirit speaks here of the priesthood of Christ, is manifest from the scope of the Psalm itself, as well as from the several references which are made to it in the New Testament.  See note on 1: 13.  And hence the evidence is conclusive, that Christ glorified not himself by assuming the honors of the priesthood, but that he has been made both a King and a Priest by the decree of Jehovah.

The word *forever* means here, as in many other passages of Scripture, *while time endures*.  As the duration of the Aaronic priesthood was coextensive with the Jewish age (Ex. 40: 15; Num. 25: 13), so also is the duration of Christ's priesthood to be coextensive with the Christian age.  But at the close of the Christian dispensation, when he shall have delivered up the Kingdom to the Father (1 Cor. 15: 24), then also he will doubtless cease to act as a Priest; for then the object of his priesthood, as well as of his mediatorial reign, will have been accomplished.  In the New Jerusalem there will be no sin, and of course no more need of a sin-offering.

**after the order of Melchisedec.**—The proper import of this expression is more fully and clearly set forth in the seventh chapter.  Suffice it to say in this connection, that as Melchisedec was a king upon his throne, as well as a priest so also is Christ. (Zech. 6: 13.)  In this respect, as well as in several others, the rank (*taxis*) of Melchisedec was superior to that of Aaron.  See notes on 7: 1-10.

7 **Who in the days of his flesh,**—That the pronoun *"who"* in

plications with strong crying and tears ³unto him that was able to save him from death, and ⁴was heard in that he feared;

³Matt. xxvi. 52, 53; Mark xiv. 36.
⁴Psa. xviii. 16-19; xxii. 21, 24; Matt. xxvi. 53; Luke xxii. 43; John xii. 27.

this connection refers to Christ, as the proper subject of the discourse, and not to Melchisedec, is quite obvious. But what is its proper predicate? What did Jesus do, when, in the days of his flesh, he offered up prayers and supplications with strong crying and tears to him who was able to save him from death? The proper answer to this question is given in the eighth verse, as will be seen by simply omitting the pleonastic *"he"* of the English Version. Thus, "Who . . . though he was a Son, yet learned obedience by the things which he suffered." The object of the Apostle in these verses, is manifestly to show that Jesus was not only called of God from among men to officiate as a High Priest for men in things pertaining to God; but that having passed also through the deepest scenes of human suffering, and having thereby learned lessons of practical obedience and submission to the will of his Father, he is now most eminently qualified to sympathize with us, and also to aid and comfort us in all our trials, temptations, and afflictions. But let us now look more narrowly into the meaning of the several words and phrases of this profoundly interesting passage. *"In the days of his flesh"* means simply the period of his humiliation, while he appeared here on Earth as a man. "Flesh and blood," we are told (1 Cor. 15: 50), "can not inherit the Kingdom of God." Christ's body is now glorified and freed from all the weaknesses and infirmities of the flesh. (Phil. 3: 21.) But it was not so while he tabernacled here on Earth. Then, he had a body in all respects such as we now have, save that it was in no sense defiled and corrupted by sin.

**when he had offered up prayers and supplications, etc.**— This expression restricts the meaning of the preceding remark to a particular period of Christ's earthly mission. True, indeed, during his whole life, and particularly during the period of his public ministry, he learned obedience from what he suffered. But it is evident that the Apostle has special reference here to his final sufferings, beginning with his agony in Gethsemane and ending with his greater agony on the cross. From these especially, he learned obedience. And while suffering in the garden, he poured out his

prayers and supplications, no doubt, with strong crying and tears
"to Him who was able to save him from death." Such at least is
the natural inference from the following testimony of Luke. He
says, "when he [Jesus] was at the place [Gethsemane], he said
unto them [his disciples], Pray that ye enter not into temptation.
And he was withdrawn from them about a stone's cast, and
kneeled down and prayed, saying, Father, if thou be willing remove this cup from me; nevertheless not my will but thine be
done. And there appeared an angel unto him from heaven
strengthening him. And being in an agony, he prayed more earnestly; and his sweat was, as it were, great drops of blood falling
down to the ground." (Luke 22: 40-44.) From this it seems that
his mental agony was so intensely great as to cause both his sweat
and blood to issue from the pores of his oppressed body.
Instances of a like nature, under excessive passion, are mentioned
by Aristotle, Diodorus, Siculus, Galen, Sir John Chardin, Voltaire,
and others. And hence it is reasonable to suppose, that under the
extreme agony of the hour, the prayers and supplications of Christ
would be mingled, as our author says, with loud exclamations and
tears of the deepest anguish.

The Greek words rendered *prayers* and *supplications* (*deeseis te
kai hiketerias*) are often used interchangeably for prayers in general. But when used together, as in this instance, the former denotes such petitions as flow from a sense of our wants; and the
latter, such as are prompted by a deep sense of our own helpless-
ness. The word *hiketeria* is properly an adjective; and with the
noun *elaia* expressed or understood, it was used by the Greeks to
denote the olive branch, borne by supplicants in token of their very
humble and earnest entreaties. And hence it came, by metonymy,
to signify the prayer of anyone, who, in an humble and servile
manner, asks help of another. The following brief extract from
Livy will serve to illustrate this passage: "Ten delegates from the
Socrians, squalid and covered with rags, came into the hall where
the consuls were sitting, holding out in their hands olive branches
covered with wool, according to the custom of the Greeks; and
prostrated themselves on the ground before the tribunal with a
lamentable cry." (L. xxix. 16.) Their supplications were availing.
By a decree of the Roman Senate, the consul, Q Pleminius, the op-

pressor of the Socrians, was arrested, loaded with chains, and confined in a dungeon, where he finally expired.

**to him who was able to save him from death,**—These words are well explained by a remark which Jesus made to Peter, when he drew his sword to defend Jesus from the violence of the multitude. (Matt. 26: 53, 54.) "Thinkest thou," said he. "that I can not now pray to my Father, and he shall presently give me more than twelve legions of angels? But how then shall the Scriptures be fulfilled that thus it must be?" Ah, yes, that was the difficulty. "How then shall the Scriptures be fulfilled?" Jesus well knew that either he himself must die for mankind, or otherwise that the whole race must perish forever. There seems to have been no other possible alternative. And therefore, bitter as the cup was, he did not hesitate to drink it to its very dregs.

**and was heard in that he feared;**—This has long been a perplexing passage to most expositors. Delitzsch renders the Greek text as follows: "and having been heard because of his piety"; Alford, thus: "and he was heard by reason of his reverent submission." With these learned authors, agree substantially many other able commentators. But to my mind this rendering is not satisfactory. For (1) it gives a very unusual meaning to the Greek preposition *apo*, which generally corresponds with the Latin *ab* or *abs*, and means *from*. Winer says, "It is used to denote simply the point from which motion or action proceeds; and hence it implies distance or separation." (2) While it is, of course, conceded that the word *eulabia* may mean "piety" or "reverent submission," I cannot think but that the rendering "godly fear," or "reverential fear," is more suitable to the occasion, and that it better harmonizes with the terms and conditions of the context. This, too, corresponds well with the etymology of the word and also with Greek usage. *"Eulabeia,"* says Prof. Trench, "which occurs only twice in the New Testament (Heb. 5: 7; 12: 28) and on each occasion signifies piety contemplated on the side on which it is *a fear of God,* is of course from *eu lambanesthai*; the image underlying the word being that of a careful taking hold of, the cautious handling of some precious yet delicate vessel, which with ruder or less anxious handling might be broken. But such a carefulness and cautiousness in the conducting of affairs, springing as no doubt it does in part from a fear of miscarriage, easily lies open to the charge of

timidity. Thus Demosthenes claims for himself that he was only
*eulabes* [cautious], where his enemies charged him with being
*deilos* [timid] and *atolmos* [cowardly]. It is not wonderful then
that *fear* should have come to be regarded as an essential element
of *eulabeia;* though, for the most part, no dishonorable fear; but
such as a wise and good man might not be ashamed to entertain."
(Syn. of the N. Test.) (3) I am at a loss to see why the piety of
Christ should be assigned as a reason for his being heard on this or
any other particular occasion. This sounds too much as a mere
truism. Who that believes in Christ as the Son of God ever
doubted this? "I know," said he, addressing his Father, "that
thou hearest me always." (John 11 : 42.)

For these reasons chiefly I am constrained to think with Calvin,
Beza, Erasmus, Bengal, Hammond, Wetstein, Storr, Ernesti,
Kuinoel, DeWette, Stuart, Tholuck, Ebrard, and others, that the
expression should be rendered substantially as in our Common
Version, "he was heard from his pious fear"; that is, he was heard
and so delivered from 'his pious and reverential fear. The word
*heard* (*eisakoustheis*) is used in a pregnant sense, as in Psalm 22 :
21; where David, speaking as a type of Christ, says in reference to
his last sufferings, "Thou hast heard me from the horns of the unicorns"; which is equivalent to saying, Thou hast heard my supplications, and delivered me from the horns of the unicorns. Such
instances of brachylogy occur very frequently in the Holy Scriptures.

We conclude, then, that Christ's prayers and supplications were
heard, and that he was in a measure delivered from his reverential
fear. But what was the object of this fear? Not death, as Calvin
and others suppose; for from this he was not delivered in the sense
of the context. He had to meet and suffer death in its most appalling forms, soon after his agony in the garden. But be it remembered (1) that Christ was a man; and that, as a man, he possessed
all the sinless feelings and propensities of our nature. As a man,
he had a heart to fear and tremble, like other men, in view of great
undertakings and responsibilities. (2) That while in the garden,
he was on the eve of incurring, not merely physical death, for that
was only a circumstance, but a degree of mental agony, arising
from his feelings of moral obligation, at which even the angels
might have stood appalled. He was about to stand between God

and man, and meet in his own person the claims of the Divine government against the sinner. He knew that in a little while his Father's face would be hid from him; and that his frail human nature would be literally crushed under the tremendous weight of the responsibilities which he had incurred. And (3) it should also be remembered, that the hour of his adversaries had come, and that he was then delivered up to be most severely tried and tempted by the Evil One. (Luke 22: 53.) Christ knew this; and he earnestly warned his disciples to be vigilant and to pray, lest indeed they should all be overcome by the Tempter. (Matt. 26: 41; Mark 14: 38; Luke 22: 40.) But it was of course against Christ himself that Satan was about to direct most of his fiery darts. The Tempter came, and doubtless presented every motive that Hell could invent that might serve to terrify him; to weaken his trust and confidence in God; to make him apprehensive that he might not be equal to the occasion; and to induce him to shrink back from the appalling scene that was before him. The temptation to do so was no doubt very great, and his agony became most alarming. His whole physical frame was so impressed by his mental emotions that sweat and blood, as we have seen, issued from the pores of his oppressed body. But his prayers were heard. An angel was sent to strengthen him. (Luke 22: 43.) He was now in a measure delivered from his pious and fearful apprehensions; and he rose from the ground, returned to his disciples, and calmly met the ruthless mob that were coming to lead him to the cross.

But there a still more intense agony awaited him. Though somewhat relieved from his pious yet fearful apprehension that, as a man, he would not be equal to the occasion; and that he might peradventure fail to so meet and satisfy the claims of the Divine government on man as to make it possible for God to justify penitent believers, he had nevertheless now to meet and endure the solemn and awful reality. He had to pass through such a spiritual ordeal as no creature had ever before experienced. The nails that pierced his hands and his feet were but as nothing. Persons of ordinary strength generally lived on the cross from one to four or five days, and sometimes even longer. But Jesus, though in the prime of manhood, survived but six hours after his crucifixion. The weight of our indebtedness to the Divine government fell like a mountain avalanche on his soul. The light of God's countenance was with-

8 Though ¹he were a Son, yet ²learned he obedience by the things which he suffered;

9 And ¹being made perfect, ²he became the author of eternal salvation ³unto all them that obey him; 10 ⁴Called of God an high priest after the order of Melchisedec.

¹Ch. i. 5; iii. 6; Psa. ii. 7.
²Ch. x. 5-9; Isa. liii. 5, 7, 8; John iv. 34; vi. 38; Phil. ii. 8.
¹Chap. ii. 10; John xix. 30.
²Ch. ii. 3; ix. 12, 15; xii. 2; Acts iii. 15; iv. 12.
³Isa. lv. iii; Matt. vii. 21, 24-27; Acts v. 32; Rom. i. 5; ii. 6, 7, 10; vi. 17; 2 Cor. x. 5; 1 Pet. i. 22.
⁴Ch. vi. 20; Psa. cx. 4.

held; and a horror of appalling darkness overwhelmed his spirit. He could bear no more. He said, "It is finished." His heart broke under the weight of his mental agony; and he meekly bowed his head and expired! See Dr. Stroud's treatise "On the Physical Cause of the Death of Christ."

8 **Though he were a Son, etc.**—Though he was the Son of God, he claimed no special privileges on that account; but as a loyal subject of the Divine government, he submitted willingly to all that was required of him as the Redeemer of the world. And thus he not only magnified God's law and "made it honorable"; but he also, as a man, learned experimentally both the duty and the necessity of obedience, from what he suffered.

9 **And being made perfect,**—By means of these sufferings, he was made a *perfect Savior;* that is, he was thereby fully qualified in every respect to become the Redeemer of mankind. See note on 2: 10. And now he offers salvation freely to all them that obey him. It is not his purpose to save men in their sins, but to save them from their sins. And hence, though he has by the grace of God tasted death for every man and so made an atonement for all, he nevertheless bestows salvation only on those who obey him. "Not every one," says he, "that saith unto me, Lord, Lord, shall enter into the kingdom of heaven; but he that doeth the will of my Father who is in heaven." (Matt. 7: 21.)

10 **Called of God an high priest**—This is the title of honor which the Father bestowed on the Son, when he set him at his own right hand in the heavenly realms. There he will reign as a King, and there he will intercede for his people as a Priest upon his throne, until he shall have perfected the redeemed, and delivered up the Kingdom to the Father. After that there will be no more need of either a Mediator or an Intercessor.

There can be no doubt, therefore, that Jesus is eminently qualified to act as a merciful and faithful High Priest in things pertaining to God.    For (1) he has received his appointment directly
from God as did Aaron.    (2) Being the Son of God, he occupies a
rank far above all created intelligences; and is able therefore to
save to the uttermost all who come unto God by him.    (3) He has
borne temptations, trials, and afflictions, incomparably greater than
those endured by any other man.    And hence he knows well how
to sympathize with the afflicted, and how to support and deliver
those that are tempted. (4) He has by his own obedience unto
death learned the necessity of a strict compliance with all the requirements of the Divine law.    And hence he knows how to support and save those that obey him.

## REFLECTIONS

1.  How very encouraging is the thought that we have now a
great High Priest in the heavens, through whose efficacious atonement and intercession, the throne of the universe has become a
throne of grace to all penitent believers. (4: 14-16.)   Though in
and of ourselves utterly unworthy of the least of all God's mercies,
we can nevertheless now approach him in the name of Jesus, and
through the rich merits of his atoning blood, find grace sufficient to
supply all our wants.    "For this is the confidence that we have in
him, that if we ask any thing according to his will he heareth us."
(1 John 5: 14.)   "He that spared not his own Son, but delivered
him up for us all, how shall he not also with him freely give us all
things?"    "Ask," then, "and it shall be given you; seek, and ye
shall find; knock, and it shall be opened unto you."

2.  What a marvelous thing it is, then, that all men do not, in
obedience to the Divine Call, approach the Throne of grace; and in
the name of our ascended High Priest seek for those blessings
which we all so much need.    Like the poor thoughtless wayward
prodigal, millions are perishing in a strange land, for want of the
bread of life; while in our Father's house there is enough for all
and to spare.    "Come now," says God to his erring children,
"come, and let us reason together; though your sins be as scarlet,
they shall be as white as snow; though they be red like crimson,
they shall be as wool." (Isa. 1: 18.)   And again he says, "Ho, every one that thirsteth, come ye to the waters; and he that hath no

money [come]; come ye, buy and eat; yea, come, buy wine and milk without money and without price." (Isa. 55: 1.) And yet the poor demented sinner goes on in his follies, as careless and indifferent as if no blood had been shed for him, and as if no Throne of grace had been provided for his benefit! What a marvelous illustration we have in all this of the exceeding sinfulness and deceitfulness of sin.

3. Religion has been provided for the benefit of mankind. (5: 1-4.) Not only is every High Priest, taken from among men, ordained for men, in things pertaining to God; but the whole scheme of redemption has been provided for a like purpose. It is for our sake that Jesus became incarnate. For us, he suffered, and bled, and died. For us, he ascended to the heavens, and paid the ransom price of our redemption. For us, he sent the Holy Spirit to be in us as a well of water springing up into everlasting life. For us, he has founded the Church, and endowed it with all the ordinances of his grace. For us, he has provided the Holy Scriptures and all things else pertaining to life and godliness. And hence it follows, that if we are straitened in any respect, it is simply in ourselves, and not in God, nor in the bountiful provisions of his grace. "Ye will not come unto me," says Christ, "that ye may have life." (John 5: 40.)

4. How infinitely great must have been the sufferings of Christ for us. (5: 5-10.) These we shall never be able to comprehend fully. The claims of the Divine government on fallen man is a question that far transcends the reach and capacity of our finite reason. And hence we can never compute the ransom that was paid for our redemption. But we may form some faint conception of what Jesus suffered on our account from what is recorded in the last few pages of his memoirs. How very significant, for instance, were the loud exclamations which he uttered, and the briny tears which he shed in the garden of Gethsemane! How expressive were the drops of bloody sweat which then and there fell from his oppressed body to the Earth! And above all, what a world of mental agony is indicated by the rupture of his heart! Remember, dear sinner, that all this was endured for us. For what the Law of Moses could not do, in that it was weak through the flesh, God has done by sending his own Son in the likeness of sinful flesh, and by an offering for sin has condemned sin in the flesh; so that the righ-

teousness required by the Law might be fulfilled in us, who walk not after the flesh, but after the Spirit. (Rom. 8: 3, 4.) Who, then, can withhold his heart and his affections from such a Savior? Who that understands this matter as he should, is not constrained to give up his soul, his life, and his all to the service of him who has done so much for our redemption?

5. And this, be it observed, is just what every man is required to give, who would enjoy the great salvation that has been so freely procured for us through the atoning sacrifice of the Lord Jesus. He has become "the author of eternal salvation to all them that *obey* him" (verse 9). We are of course saved by grace through faith; and that not of ourselves, it is the gift of God. (Eph. 2: 8.) But nevertheless, it has pleased God to make our enjoyment of the purchased blessings depend on a willing observance of all that is required of us in the Gospel. Thus it is that God permits and enables us to show our loyalty to him and to his government; to educate and prepare ourselves for Heaven; and at the same time, to do good to all men as we may have opportunity.

## SECTION FIVE
### 5: 11 to 6: 20

#### ANALYSIS

In the preceding section, the Apostle has fully introduced and partially considered the priesthood of Christ, as one of the great and leading themes of the Epistle. On this point, he tells us, that he has still much to say. But there was a difficulty in the way of his doing so. The subject is in itself one of the most profound topics pertaining to the economy of redemption; and its full consideration is therefore adapted only to those who have made considerable progress in the study of Divine things. But here was the trouble: many of the Hebrew Christians, though in the school of Christ for some considerable time, were nevertheless still quite ignorant of the more sublime and difficult themes of the Gospel. They had become slothful in the study of God's revealed will; and had now to be instructed again in even the elementary principles of the Christian Religion. And hence our author makes another digression just here from his main line of argument, and devotes this section to the giving of such admonitions, warnings, reproofs, and encouragements, as he saw were most needed under the circumstances.

I. He begins by admonishing his readers, in pretty severe terms, on account of their inertness and slothfulness in the study of God's word; and their consequent incapacity to receive and understand aright the revelations which he was about to make concerning the priesthood of Christ. (5: 11-14.)

1. On this subject, he tells us, that he had much to say, which was hard to be explained on account of their dullness of hearing (verse 11).

2. In order to amplify and illustrate this thought, he further adds, that while, in view of the length of time that had elapsed since their conversion, they should really have become teachers of others, they had, on the contrary, become, as it were, babes in Christ; and had need to be again instructed in the rudiments of the Gospel; or as he goes on to explain it metaphorically, to be fed on the milk rather than on the solid food of the Divine word (verses 12-14).

II. Having thus severely rebuked his Hebrew brethren for their neglect of God's word, he next exhorts them to go on from first principles even to perfection in the study of the Christian Religion, and not to be like a man who is forever laying the foundation of a house, without attempting to complete its superstructure. (6: 1-3.) The elements here enumerated are (1) repentance from dead works, (2) faith toward God, (3) the doctrine of baptisms, (4) the laying on of hands, (5) the resurrection of the dead, and (6) eternal judgments. These are not of course to be wholly neglected at any time; but they should be left behind, as we leave the alphabet and the spelling book behind when we advance to the study of the higher branches of English literature.

III. As a motive to his readers to do as requested, the Apostle now warns them of the dangers and consequences of apostasy (verses 4-8).

1. It seems that in Paul's estimation there is no safety for the followers of Christ but in going on to perfection—slothfulness and inertness tending always to apostasy.

2. But from apostasy there is no deliverance (verses 4-6). If a Christian through his neglect of God's word or any other cause, allows his heart to be so far alienated from Christ, that he ceases to

trust in him, and treats him as an impostor—for such a one there is no repentance. His doom is sealed; and nothing remains for him "but a certain fearful looking for of judgment and fiery indignation which shall devour the adversaries."

3. This, the Apostle further illustrates by a reference to husbandry. "Land," he says, "which has drunk in the rain which cometh often upon it, and produceth herbage meet for them on whose account it is also cultivated, partaketh of blessing from God; but bearing thorns and thistles it is rejected, and is nigh unto a curse; whose end is for burning" (verses 7, 8).

IV. From this gloomy aspect of things, our author now turns to what is more encouraging (verses 9-12).

1. He does not, he says, regard his Hebrew brethren as apostates; and he furthermore expresses the hope that they will never become such (verse 9).

2. This hope is founded on the conviction that God will remember and reward their many acts of charity (verse 10).

3. But Paul is anxious that they shall show the same zeal in everything else pertaining to the full assurance of hope, that they were wont to show in their works of benevolence; so that they might in fact be imitators of those who through faith and patience are now inheriting the promises (verses 11, 12).

V. For the purpose of encouraging his readers still further, the Apostle now refers particularly to the case of Abraham, and to the oath of God as the sure foundation of the Christian's hope (verses 13-20).

1. God, it seems, being anxious to give to Abraham a sure ground of hope, confirmed his promise to him with an oath (verses 13, 14).

2. Abraham relied on these two immutable things; trusted fully and confidently in the promise and oath of God; and finally, at the close of his earthly pilgrimage, he obtained the promised blessing, so far as it related to himself personally (verse 15).

3. And just so, Paul argues, it will also be with everyone who, like Abraham, proves faithful to the end of life. For the promise and oath of God are still the ground of our hope, which, like that of Abraham, reaches within the Vail, into the Holy of holies, whither Jesus has for us entered, and where as our great High Priest he ever lives to make intercession for us (verses 16-20).

The main points and divisions of this section are, therefore, as follows:

I. 5: 11-14. An admonition addressed to the Hebrew Christians, on account of their inattention to the study of God's word.

II. 6: 1-3. An exhortation to go on from the study of the rudiments of Christianity, to perfection in the knowledge of Christ.

III. 6: 4-8. Danger and fearful consequences of apostasy.

IV. 6: 9-12. Encouragement to greater zeal in striving after the full assurance of hope, drawn chiefly from the known justice of God and their own deeds of charity.

V. 6: 13-20. Further encouragement from the example of Abraham, and from the promise and oath of God made to him and all his spiritual seed.

### 1. AN ADMONITION ADDRESSED TO THE HEBREW BRETHREN ON ACCOUNT OF THEIR INATTENTION TO THE STUDY OF GOD'S WORD
#### 5: 11-14

11 Of whom [1]we have many things to say, and hard to be uttered, seeing ye are [2]dull of hearing.

[1]Ch. vii. 1-10; John xvi. 12; 2 Pet. iii. 16.
[2]Isa. vi. 9, 10; Matt. xiii. 15; Luke xxiv. 25; Acts xxviii. 26, 27.

---

11 **Of whom**—(*peri hou*) *concerning which.* These words have been variously applied (1) to Melchisedec, (2) to Christ, and (3) to the priesthood of Christ after the order of Melchisedec, as the leading and proper subject of the discourse. The last of these views is adopted by Hofmann, Delitzsch, Moll, and others: and it is certainly the view which harmonizes best with the context. The reference to Christ, as Delitzsch justly remarks, is too remote; and the reference to Melchisedec is too narrow. It is not of Christ personally, nor is it of Melchisedec personally, that our author has so much to say; but is of the priesthood of Christ, the subject of the last section, about which he wishes to say much to his readers. This is obvious from what immediately follows this digression, in the course of the seventh, eighth, ninth, and tenth chapters.

**hard to be uttered,**—(*dusermeneutos*) *difficult of interpretation.* There is no profounder theme, nor is there any one that is more difficult of interpretation, than the priesthood of Christ. To treat of it fully involves the consideration of man's fallen and sinful

12 For when for the time ¹ye ought to be teachers, ye have need that one ²teach you again which be the first principles of ³the oracles of God; and are become ⁴such as have need of milk, [and] not of strong meat.

¹Ezra vii. 10; 1 Cor. xiv. 19; Col. iii. 16; Titus ii. 3, 4.
²Phil. iii. 1; 2 Pet. iii. 1.
³2 Sam. xvi. 23; Acts vii. 38; Rom. iii. 2; 1 Pet. iv. 11.
⁴Isa. xxviii. 9, 10; 1 Cor. iii. 1-3; 1 Pet. ii. 2.

state; his indebtedness to the Divine government; the shedding of Christ's blood and all that he endured for the sins of the world; the ransom which he paid for our redemption; the efficacy of his blood and his intercessions, through which the gates of Heaven have been opened wide for the reception of every poor penitent sinner who comes to God by him.

**dull of hearing.**—The word rendered *dull* (*nothroi*) means sluggish, indolent, slow to move; and that which is rendered *hearing* (*tais akoais*) means the ears or perceptive faculties of the soul. These were sluggish and inert. Instead of quickening the powers of their understanding and the susceptibilities of their heart, by the regular and systematic study of God's word, many of the Hebrew Christians had become (*gegonate*) dull in their apprehension of spiritual things.

12 **For when for the time**—From what is said in this verse, Mynster, Ebrard, and some others, confidently infer that the Epistle was not sent to the Church of Jerusalem. For this, we know, was the mother of all the churches; and as she enjoyed for some time the instruction of all the Apostles, and the instruction of James the Less, son of Alphaeus, till about A.D. 62, according to Josephus (Ant. xx. 9, 1); or even to A.D. 69, according to Hegesippus and Eusebius (Eccl. Hist. ii. 23); it is thought that such ignorance of the word of God, as is here implied, could not be fairly ascribed to this most favored of all the primitive churches. This is certainly a very plausible objection against the commonly received hypothesis that the Epistle was addressed primarily to the saints living in and around Jerusalem. But be it observed (1) that there had evidently been a backward movement among the disciples for whom this Epistle was written. Ye *have become* (*gegonate*) dull in your hearing, says the Apostle; and ye have become such as have need of milk and not of solid food. They had evidently seen and known more prosperous times; but they had ceased to be diligent students of the word of God, and had there-

fore relapsed somewhat into the darkness and errors of the judaizing party. (2) This is not at all wonderful, when we consider the
very unfavorable state of affairs that was then prevailing in Jerusalem, and indeed throughout Palestine. The same spirit of persecution that seized and imprisoned Paul in A.D. 58, continued to rage
in Judea, until Jerusalem was destroyed in A.D. 70. And hence it
is not at all remarkable that, under such circumstances, many of
the weaker brethren should become somewhat disheartened. (3)
We are not to suppose that the Apostle here describes the actual
condition of all the disciples to whom the Epistle was written.
Perhaps no more than a minority of them are really included in
this severe admonition. Paul often speaks in this general way,
when he has really reference to only a part of those that are addressed. See, for example, 1 Cor. 3: 1-3; 5: 2; 6: 5, 6. This, he
manifestly does in this instance. Some of the Hebrew converts
had become discouraged. Their hands were hanging down, and
their knees were feeble. (12: 12, 13.) They were almost ready to
abandon the Christian conflict, and fall back again into the embrace
of Judaism. Others were daily becoming more and more slothful;
and there was therefore great need just at this crisis, of the severe
rebuke which the Apostle here administers to them, as well as of
the many encouragements with which he labors to sustain and support them. But that many of his readers were still strong in the
faith, and fully prepared to comprehend even the highest mysteries
of the Gospel, when properly unfolded and illustrated, is evident
from the fact, that after making this brief digression, he proceeds
at once to the regular and systematic discussion of Christ's priesthood. There seems, therefore, to be no just ground for the above
allegation of Ebrard and others, that the Epistle was not addressed
to the Hebrew Christians living in and around Jerusalem.

**ye ought to be teachers,**—The Apostle does not mean by this,
that the Hebrew brethren should all be teachers in a public and official sense; but simply that they should be able to explain the Gospel to others in their several places and relations, as parents, neighbors, and friends. The Church of Christ is a school for the improvement of all its members; and while it is certainly impossible
for everyone to become an efficient Elder or Evangelist, it is nevertheless the duty of all to "grow in grace, and in the knowledge of
our Lord and Savior Jesus Christ." (2 Pet. 3: 18.)

13 For every one that useth milk is unskillful in ¹the word of righteousness; for ²he is a babe.

¹Psa. cxix. 123; 2 Cor. iii. 9; 2 Tim. iii. 16.
²Matt. xi. 25; Mark x. 15; 1 Cor. xiii. 11; xiv. 20; Eph. iv. 14; 1 Pet. ii. 2.

**ye have need, etc.**—Instead of going forward, they had, it
seems, rather gone backward in their knowledge of Divine things;
so that they had need to be instructed again in the very elements of
the Christian Religion. Our author does not mean to say, as in
our English Version, that his readers had need to be instructed
again as to "which be [are] the first principles of the Oracles of
God." It is not of their incapacity to distinguish between the rudiments of the Gospel and its more profound and mysterious principles, but of their ignorance of the rudiments themselves, that the
Apostle here complains. And hence with Luther, Calvin, Bleek,
Alford, etc., I would render the passage as follows: "Ye again
have need that some one teach you the rudiments of the beginning
of the Oracles of God." The word *oracle* (*logion*) means simply a
Divine utterance, a communication from God. It occurs but four
times in the New Testament (Acts 7: 38; Rom. 3: 2; Heb. 5: 12;
1 Pet. 4: 11), in all of which it clearly means the inspired utterances of God. In this instance, it has reference to the communica-
tions of God made known to us in the Gospel; the elements of
which are given in 6: 1, 2.

13 **For every one that useth milk, etc.**—This language is of
course metaphorical. As newborn babes in the kingdom of nature
need to be fed on milk, so also it is with babes in the Kingdom of
Christ. They, too, must be fed with "the pure milk of the word"
that they may grow thereby. (1 Pet. 2: 2.) And hence Paul says
to the brethren in Corinth, "I have fed you with milk, and not
with meat [solid food]; for hitherto ye were not able to bear
it; neither yet now are ye able." (1 Cor. 3: 2.) And so also he
says here to the Hebrew brethren, "Ye are become such as have
need of milk [the mere rudiments, or elementary lessons, of the
Christian Religion], and not of solid food [the more difficult and
profound instructions of the Gospel]. "For every one," he says,
"that partakes of milk is unskillful in the word of righteousness;
for he is but a babe in Christ." By the *"word of righteousness,"*
the Apostle means simply the word of the Gospel, in which God's
plan of righteousness by faith is revealed in order to faith (Rom.

14 But strong meat belongeth to them that are of full age, even those who
by reason of use have [3]their senses exercised [4]to discern both good and evil.

[3]Job vi. 30; xii. 11; Psa. cxix. 103; Eph. i. 18.
[4]Gen. iii. 5; 2 Sam. xiv. 17; 1 Cor. ii. 14, 15; Phil. i. 9, 10; 1 Thess. v. 21.

1 : 17) ; so that being justified by faith we may attain to the righteousness that is required of every believer.

14 **But strong meat belongeth, etc.**—In both this and the
preceding verse, there is a blending together of the literal and the
figurative; but not to such an extent as to obscure in any way the
sense of either passage. Indeed, the meaning is so very plain in
both cases, that our author does not deem it necessary to complete
the allegory; but having introduced his subject by means of an illustrating metaphor, he very beautifully and with laconic brevity
combines the literal and the figurative in the same clause. The
analogy may be stated fully as follows: As solid food belongs only
to those who are of full age, and who, by reason of habitual exercise, have their senses so perfectly educated, as to be able to discern through them the physical properties of bodies; so also the
more profound and abstruse principles of the Christian Religion,
such as the priesthood of Christ, his atonement, etc., are suitable
only for those, who, from long study and experience in the school
of Christ, have their inward senses so trained as to be able to dis-
criminate accurately between the right and the wrong, the good
and the evil. The idea is, that discipline of both head and heart is
essentially necessary in order to qualify Christians for the right
apprehension and just appreciation of the more difficult parts of the
Christian system. Every faculty of man's intellectual and moral
nature, as well as every part of his physical organization, is developed, strengthened, and quickened, by means of a judicious
course of exercise. And the disciple who habitually neglects this
course of discipline, can never attain to the stature of a perfect man
in Christ Jesus. By the necessities of his own nature, he will ever
remain but, as it were, a babe in Christ; if indeed he does not utterly fall away from all the hopes and consolations of the Gospel.
This neglect of study and moral discipline was the great error and
misfortune of the Hebrews. Many of them, it would seem, had
never progressed beyond the mere alphabet of the Christian Religion. And hence they were but illy prepared to enter with the

Apostle on the consideration of the many difficult and sublime
themes that are discussed in the following chapters.

The word rendered *senses* (*aistheteria*) means properly the
physical organs of sensation, such as the eyes, the ears, and the fingers, through which we perceive the qualities and properties of
things that are material. But metaphorically, it signifies, as in this
connection, the faculties of the soul, by means of which we dis-
criminate between those things which differ in their moral qualities.

## 2. AN EXHORTATION TO GO ON FROM THE STUDY
## OF THE RUDIMENTS OF CHRISTIANITY, TO
## PERFECTION IN CHRISTIAN KNOWLEDGE
### 6 : 1-3

1 Therefore, ¹leaving the principles of the doctrine of Christ, ²let us go on
unto perfection; not ³laying again the foundation of ⁴repentance from ⁵dead
works, and of ⁶faith toward God,

---

¹Ch. v. 12; Phil. iii. 12-14.
²Ch. vii. 11; xii. 13; Matt. v. 48; 1 Cor. xiii. 10; 2 Cor. vii. 1; Eph. iv. 12; Phil.
iii. 12-15; Col. i. 28; iv. 12; James i. 4.
³Matt. vii. 24-27; Luke vi. 48, 49; 1 Tim. vi. 19.
⁴Matt. iii. 2; iv. 17; xxi. 29, 32; Acts ii. 38; iii. 19; xi. 18; xvii. 30; xx. 21;
xxvi. 20; 2 Cor. vii. 9-11.
⁵Ch. ix. 14; Gal. v. 19-21; Eph. ii. 1-5.
⁶John v. 24; xii. 44; xiv. 1; 1 Pet. i. 21; 1 John v. 10.

---

1 **Therefore, leaving the principles of the doctrine of Christ,**
—The word *therefore* (*dio*) is *illative,* showing the connection of
what precedes with what follows. In the last paragraph, the Apostle avers that none but the perfect (*teleioi*) are capable of receiving, digesting, and duly appropriating the more abstruse and difficult themes of the Gospel. And hence he exhorts his Hebrew
brethren to become perfect; to be no longer babes in Christ, but to
go on with him to perfection in the knowledge of Divine things.

**not laying again the foundation, etc.**—The first thing necessary in building, is to lay a foundation, and to lay it well. And the
man who neglects this, and who, without a proper foundation, begins to build an edifice, will never accomplish much in the way of
architecture. But equally puerile and absurd is the course of the
man who keeps forever laying the foundation, and proceeds no further. The foundation is of course necessary; but the superstructure is equally necessary to complete the building. And just so it
is with regard to the spiritual edification of individuals, families,
churches, and communities. There are certain fundamental princi-

ples belonging to the Religion of Christ, a clear and correct understanding of which is essential to all future progress in the Divine
life; just as a foundation is necessary to a building, or as a knowledge of the English alphabet is essential to the study of the higher
branches of English literature. But having once properly understood these elementary principles of the Christian Religion, we
should henceforth go on to perfection in the knowledge of Christ.

These elementary principles of Christianity, as here laid down
by our author, are:

(1) **Repentance from dead works,**—The word rendered *repentance* (*metanoia*) means properly a change of mind. It implies, therefore, that the sinner has obtained new views of Christ,
of sin, and of holiness. He is made to realize that it was for him
that Jesus wept, and bled, and died. And this conviction begets in
his heart a godly sorrow for his sins. As he now looks on him
who was pierced for his transgressions and bruised for his iniquities, he is himself greatly grieved in spirit; and he resolves that
with the help of God he will henceforth "cease to do evil, and learn
to do well." The resolution is no sooner formed than the change of
life begins. His simple inquiry now is, "Lord, what wilt thou
have me to do?" And having obtained an answer to this question,
he no longer confers with flesh and blood; but with an humble,
loyal, loving, prayerful, and obedient heart, he at once takes upon
him the yoke of Christ, and submits in all things to his will and
government.

Here then we have (1) a change of the understanding, arising
through Divine grace from the force of the testimony submitted;
(2) a change of feeling, a deep sense of conviction wrought in the
heart, by the aforesaid change of the understanding; (3) a change
of the will, effected by the antecedent change of the heart; and (4)
a change of conduct, growing out of the change of the will. Which
of these four elementary changes constitutes what is properly
called true and genuine repentance? They are all essential links in
the same chain of causation; and it may therefore be conceded that
they are all implied in the word *repentance*. But the question is,
not what is implied in this word, but rather what is expressed by it
in the inspired writings. That it denotes a change, subsequent to
that which is effected in the understanding by means of testimony,
and even to that which follows as an immediate effect of this in the

region of the affections, is manifest from such passages as the following: "Now I rejoice," says Paul, "not that ye were made sorry, but that ye sorrowed to repentance (*eis metanoian*) ; for ye were made sorry after a godly manner, that ye might receive damage by us in nothing. For godly sorrow worketh repentance to salvation not to be repented of; but the sorrow of the world worketh death. For behold this self-same thing, that ye sorrowed after a godly sort, what carefulness it wrought in you; yea, what clearing of yourselves; yea, what indignation; yea, what fear; yea, what vehement desire; yea, what zeal; yea, what revenge. In all things, ye have approved yourselves to be clear in this matter." (2 Cor. 7: 9-11.) From this, it seems that Paul had, by a prudent and judicious presentation of facts and arguments in his first Epistle to the Corinthians, wrought a logical change in their understanding; and this change of judgment produced in turn a corresponding change in their feelings. Their hearts were now filled with godly sorrow. But neither of these changes constitutes repentance. It is something which follows after all this in the chain of causation. For says Paul, *"Ye sorrowed to repentance."* And again he says, *"Godly sorrow worketh repentance."* Godly sorrow, then, is essential to repentance, as an antecedent cause is always necessary to an effect. But repentance follows godly sorrow, as godly sorrow itself follows a certain class of our moral judgments.

Does repentance then consist in a change of the will, or in a change of conduct, or in both? Peter answers this question in Acts 3: 19, where he says to the multitude, "Repent then, and turn, in order that your sins may be blotted out, that there may come times of refreshing from the presence of the Lord." Here the word *turn* (*epistrephate*) expresses all that appertains to the required change of conduct; and as repentance is antecedent to this, it follows as a logical necessity from our premises that *repentance consists essentially, in a change of the will.* That the word repentance is often used in a more comprehensive sense, so as to include godly sorrow and also reformation of life is, I think, quite obvious from sundry passages of Scripture. The latter of these (reformation of life) is, indeed, clearly implied in the expression, "repentance from dead works." But the essential element of repentance, in every case, is a change of the will. It consists simply in a perfect and unreserved submission of the will of the sinner to the will of God. This change is always the legitimate effect of godly sorrow in the heart, and always leads to a change of conduct, or a reformation in the life of the penitent believer.

"Dead works" are by many supposed to be the works of the Law. They are so called, it is alleged, because of their utter ineffi-ciency in the way of procuring life and salvation for the sinner. But is not this using the phrase in too limited a sense? Are not all required to repent and turn from everything that is sinful and that leads to death, such as the works of the flesh enumerated in Gal. 5: 19-21? The Apostle here seems to use the phrase "repentance from dead works" in its widest sense, embracing everything from which the sinner is required to turn in his conversion from dark-ness to light, and from the service of Satan to the service of God.

(2) **Faith toward God.**—"Faith," we are told, "comes by hear-ing, and hearing by the word of God." (Rom. 10: 17.) And hence John says, "These [things] are written that ye may believe that Jesus is the Christ, the Son of God; and that believing, ye might have life through his name." (John 20: 31.) It is evident, there-fore, that the first element of Gospel faith is *belief,* a firm in-tellectual conviction, resting on the evidence submitted, that Jesus of Nazareth is the Messiah, the Son of the living God; and that there is, in fact, "no other name under heaven, given among men, whereby we must be saved." (Acts 4: 12.) Under favorable cir-cumstances, this conviction begets, as we have seen, godly sorrow in the heart; and, at the same time, some degree of *confidence and trust* in Christ, as the Son of God and Savior of sinners. But however strong may be the belief, or intellectual conviction of the sinner, touching the person and character of Jesus as the Son of God, his *trust* (which may be regarded as the second element of faith) both in God and in Christ will of necessity be comparatively weak until he repents. This arises necessarily out of the condi-tions of offered pardon. The promise of salvation is to those who believe, repent, and reform. How, then, can the *impenitent* sinner trust confidently in God or in Christ? Manifestly, this is impossi-ble. He may indeed under the firm persuasion that Jesus has by the grace of God tasted death for every man, cherish some degree of hope, and repose some degree of trust in God, even before he fully repents of his sins, and resolves to reform his life; nay, in-deed, this he must do, if he ever repents. But it is not until the

2 Of ¹the doctrine of baptisms, and of ²laying on of hands, and of ³resurrection of the dead, and of ⁴eternal judgment.

¹Matt. iii. 11, 12; xx. 22, 23; xxviii. 19; Acts i. 5; 2 Pet. iii. 7, 10; Rev. xx. 14, 15.
²Acts vi. 6; viii. 17, 18; ix. 17; xiii. 3; xiv. 23; 1 Tim. iv. 14; v. 22; 2 Tim. i. 6.
³Ch. xi. 35; Matt. xxii. 23-32; John v. 28, 29; Acts iv. 2; xvii. 18; 1 Cor. xv. 13-57; 1 Thess. iv. 14-18.
⁴Matt. xxv. 31-46; Acts xvii. 31; Rom. ii. 5-10, 16; 2 Pet. iii. 7; Jude 14, 15; Rev. xx. 10-15.

will of the sinner is wholly subjected to the will of God, that he can fully trust in God, and rely on him for every needed blessing. And hence it is that faith and repentance have a mutual and reflex influence on each other. Faith leads to repentance; while repentance again serves very greatly to increase our faith; and especially, that element of it which relates to the heart, and which we call *trust* in God. And hence it is perhaps, that in this summary of the rudiments of the Christian Religion, faith is placed after repentance; because it is the faith of the heart, to which the Apostle has here special, though not exclusive, reference—his main object in the whole Epistle being to persuade his brethren to repent from all dead works, and to trust in God through Christ for every needed blessing. As he says also in Rom. 10: 10, "For with the heart man believeth unto righteousness, and with the mouth confession is made unto salvation." And again he says in the same Epistle, "But to him that worketh not but believeth on him that justifieth the ungodly, his faith is counted for righteousness." (Rom. 4: 5.)

It is scarcely necessary to add, that faith in God implies also faith in the Lord Jesus Christ and in the Holy Spirit; for the Father, Son, and Holy Spirit are one God (Deut. 4: 4) ; so that he who honoreth not the Son, honoreth not the Father who sent him (John 5: 23) ; and he who blasphemes against the Holy Spirit blasphemes against God (Matt. 12: 31, 32; Acts 5: 4). It is all folly to profess to believe in God, while we reject the claims of Christ as the Savior of the world. "This is life eternal, that they might know thee the only true God and Jesus Christ whom thou hast sent." (John 17: 3.)

2—(3) **Of the doctrine of baptisms,**—This is given as the third elementary principle of the Christian Religion. But why does our author speak of *baptisms* (*baptismoi*) in the plural number? And how is this to be reconciled with what he says in Eph. 4: 5: "[There is] one Lord, one faith, *one baptism*"? In answer to these queries, it is alleged (a) that the Apostle refers here not only to

Christian baptism, as in Eph. 4: 5, but also to the baptism of John, the baptism of Jewish proselytes, and the divers Jewish washings referred to in 9: 10. (Bleek, Hofmann, Delitzsch, Alford). But with what propriety could all these be ranked under the head of *Christian doctrine?* Why should the baptism of John and the various Jewish washings be treated as elementary principles of the *Christian* Religion? On the same principle, it seems to me, we might arrange and classify all the rites and ceremonies of the Law, as elements of the doctrine of Christ. (b) Some think that the plural is used here for the singular; and that nothing more is really intended than the one ordinance of Christian baptism, as in Eph. 4: 5. (Syr. Version, Stuart.) But if so, why does our author use the plural number, when he might have so readily used the singular? Such an arbitrary use of words is not in harmony with the usual accuracy of the inspired writers. (c) Others suppose that our author has reference to the several acts of baptism, three thousand of which were performed on the day of the opening of Christ's reign on Earth. (Theodoret, Storr.) But in reply to this, it is enough to say that it is not of any special acts of faith, repentance, baptism, etc., that our author is here speaking, but of certain elementary and fundamental principles and elements of the kingdom of Christ. (d) Others again think that the allusion is to trine-immersion, or the threefold dipping of confessing penitents. (DeWette, etc.) But of such an ordinance, the New Testament knows nothing. The practice of trine-immersion is post-apostolic, and has no sanction whatever in the word of God.

Is there then a plurality of baptisms under the reign and administration of the Lord Jesus, and which may therefore be ranked with the rudiments of the doctrine of Christ? If so, what are they?

That every believing confessing penitent is required to be baptized, or immersed, in water, is manifest from such passages as the following: Matt. 28: 19; Acts 2: 38; 8: 12, 36, 37; 10: 47, 48, etc. This is always to be done, as appears from these Scriptures, in the name of the Lord Jesus; and the candidate is in all cases baptized into (*eis*) the name of the Father, and of the Son, and of the Holy Spirit. It is therefore one baptism, and but one. And hence Paul argues from this the necessity of there being but one body, animated by one Spirit, and governed by one supreme Head. (Eph. 4:

3-16.) There is then unquestionably one baptism in water, and but one, in which all penitent believers put on Christ (Gal. 3 : 27), and are all immersed into the one body (1 Cor. 12 : 13). But is this all? Is there no other baptism to be administered under the reign of Christ? In Matt. 3 : 12, we have the testimony of John the Baptist, that Christ would be a Baptizer, as well as himself. Speaking to the vast multitudes that came to be baptized by him, he said, "I indeed baptize you in (*en*) water unto repentance; but he that cometh after me is mightier than I, whose shoes I am not worthy to bear; he shall baptize you in (*en*) the Holy Spirit and in fire; whose fan is in his hand, and he will thoroughly purge his floor, and gather his wheat into the garner; but he will burn up the chaff with unquenchable fire." (Matt. 3 : 11, 12.) John did not, and could not, unerringly know the hearts of the people. He was ever liable to be deceived; and he no doubt baptized some very unworthy persons. But not so with the Baptizer who was to come after him. He would thoroughly separate the good from the bad; and the former, here represented by the wheat, he would baptize in the Holy Spirit (John 7 : 37-39; Acts 2 : 38; Eph. 5 : 18); but the latter, represented by the chaff, he would baptize in fire. See 2 Thess. 1 : 7-10; 2 Pet. 3 : 7, 10; Rev. 20 : 15.

We have then under the reign of Christ, as elementary ordinances of the New Economy (1) a baptism in water, in which all penitent believers who confess Christ are introduced into his body; (2) a baptism in the Holy Spirit, administered by Christ himself to all who are really begotten by the Spirit and born of water; and (3) a baptism in fire, by means of which the wicked will all be finally overwhelmed in sufferings. See references. Are not these, then, the baptisms of which our author here speaks? If so, it may be asked, Then why does he not use the word *baptisma* instead of *baptismos?* The former is the common term used for baptism in the New Testament; and the latter is used in both Mark 7 : 4, 8, and Heb. 9 : 10, for Jewish washings. There seems therefore to be some weight in this objection; but it is perhaps only in appearance, as these words are both derivatives from *baptizo* and each signifies a dipping or an immersion. And besides, Josephus uses *baptismos* in speaking of John's baptism. (Ant. xviii. 5, 2). I am therefore, on the whole, inclined to the opinion, that it is to these three baptisms that our author here refers. If this is not his meaning, then I think we must accept the first hypothesis as advocated by Bleek, Hofmann, and others.

(4) **And of laying on of hands,**—The laying on of hands is a natural sign, indicating the bestowment of any gift, trust, or blessing. And hence we find that in the primitive Church, hands were imposed (a) in imparting spiritual gifts (Acts 8: 17); (b) in healing the sick (Acts 28: 8); and (c) in ordaining men to the work of the ministry (Acts 6: 6; 13: 3; 14: 23; 1 Tim. 4: 14; 5: 22). The last only is an established ordinance of the Church. It is to be observed throughout the entire period of the regeneration, while the Son of man shall sit on the throne of his glory, and while the Apostles shall sit on twelve thrones judging the redeemed Israel of God. And hence it is manifest that the doctrine of this ordinance involves also the whole subject of ordination and church organization. For the command to lay hands suddenly on no man (1 Tim. 5: 22), implies of necessity the consideration of the several classes of church officers, together with their prescribed functions and scriptural qualifications, as well as the condition of the Church itself, and the special fitness or unfitness of the individual for the work to which he is about to be consecrated. Most appropriately therefore is this ordinance ranked among the rudiments of Christian doctrine.

(5) **And of resurrection of the dead,**—In the original Greek, the word answering to *resurrection* (*anastasis*) is anarthrous, being sufficiently defined by the adjunct which follows. But the article is required by our English idiom, and the whole phrase should be rendered, "And of the resurrection of the dead." This elementary doctrine of the Christian Religion was denied by the Sadducees (Matt. 22: 23), and by the heathen philosophers generally (Acts 17: 32); but the Apostles often dwell on it as a fundamental doctrine of the Gospel, showing that through Christ all will be raised from the dead, to be judged for the deeds done in the body. See references.

(6) **And of eternal judgment.**—Many of God's judgments are now of only temporary duration; because they are designed for our

## 3. DANGER AND AWFUL CONSEQUENCES OF APOSTASY
### 6: 4-8

3 And this will we do, [1]if God permit.
4 For [2]it is impossible for those [3]who were once enlightened, and have [4]tasted of the heavenly gift, and [5]were made partakers of the Holy Ghost,

[1]Acts xviii. 21; Rom. xv. 32; James iv. 15.
[2]Ch. x. 26-29; xii. 15-17; Matt. xii. 31, 32; 2 Pet. ii. 20-22; 1 John v. 16.
[3]Ch. x. 32; Acts xxvi. 18; Eph. v. 8.
[4]John iii. 36; iv. 10; v. 24; vi. 47-58; Rom. vi. 23; Eph. ii. 8; 1 John iii. 14, 15; v. 11-13.
[5]John vii. 37-39; xiv. 16, 17; Acts ii. 38; Rom. v. 5; viii. 9-11; 1 Cor. vi. 19; 2 Cor. i. 22; Gal. iv. 6; Eph. iv. 30; v. 18.

correction and discipline. (2 Cor. 4: 17; Heb. 12: 6-11.) But not so with the final and general judgment. It will never be reversed; and hence it will in its effects and consequences endure forever. The decree of Jehovah touching the character and destiny of mankind after the judgment, is given by the Holy Spirit as follows: "He that is unjust, let him be unjust still; and he that is filthy, let him be filthy still; and he that is righteous, let him be righteous still; and he that is holy, let him be holy still." (Rev. 22: 11.) And accordingly, Christ closes his description of the general judgment, by saying that the wicked shall go away into everlasting (*aionios*) punishment; but the righteous, into everlasting (*aionios*) life. (Matt. 25: 46.)

3 **And this will we do, etc.**—That is, we will, with the help of God, go on to perfection. The Apostle well knew that without God's help, they could accomplish nothing. (John 15: 5.) And hence while urging his brethren, by all the high motives of the Gospel, to greater diligence in making their calling and election sure, he is careful to remind them of the necessity of submitting to the will of God, and looking to him for help in all things.

4 **For it is impossible**—The word *"for"* (*gar*) connects the main thought of the preceding paragraph with what follows. The object of the Apostle is to set before his readers the fearful import of the dangers to which they were exposed; and his idea is simply this: we must with the help of God strive earnestly to go on to perfection; for otherwise, we are in constant danger of apostatizing, and so of placing ourselves beyond the possibility of recovery. For it is impossible, he says, to renew and save those who were once in covenant with Christ, but who have apostatized from him.

Various attempts have been made, but in vain, to soften the

meaning of this expression. The fact is as plainly taught as it can be, both in the Scriptures and in history, that it is morally impossible to bring some men to repentance. Their hearts have been so hardened by sin, that no power consistent with the will and government of God can soften them. These persons may have been once truly converted to Christ, or they may not. To some of the latter class, Christ refers in Matt. 12: 31, 32. These clearly showed the desperate depravity of their hearts on that occasion by openly blaspheming the Holy Spirit; for which sin, Christ says, there is no forgiveness. But it is obviously of the former class, of those who had been once truly converted and afterward apostatized, that our author here speaks. This will appear more obvious as we proceed with the exegesis of the several clauses of this paragraph.

**those who were once enlightened,**—In John 8: 12, Christ says to the Jews, "I am the light of the world; he that followeth me shall not walk in darkness, but shall have the light of life." And hence it is, that to be enlightened, is often given in the New Testament as a characteristic mark of the true followers of Christ. Thus, for instance, our author reminds his Hebrew brethren, that after they were enlightened they endured a great fight of afflictions. (10: 32.) And to the Ephesians he says, "Ye were once (*pote*) darkness; but now are ye light in the Lord: walk as children of light." (Eph. 5: 8.) There can be no doubt therefore that the Apostle refers here to those who had been once translated from darkness to light, and from the power of Satan to God. See also Col. 1: 12; 1 Thess. 5: 5; 1 Pet. 2: 9; 1 John 2: 9-11.

**and have tasted of the heavenly gift,**—The word *tasted* (*geusamenous*) means here as in 2: 9, to experience, to partake of. But what is the heavenly gift, of which our author speaks? Some say that it is Christ himself; some, that it is the Holy Spirit; some, the remission of sins; and some, the Lord's Supper. But to me it seems most probable, that it is *the new life* which we enjoy in Christ; including of course remission of sins, justification, and all in fact that pertains to our present salvation. This view accords well with the context and also with many parallel passages. Thus, for example, in John 6: 33, Christ says, "The bread of God is he who cometh down from Heaven, and giveth *life* unto the world." And in 20: 31, of the same narrative, John himself bears witness saying, "These things are written that ye might believe, and that believing ye might have *life* through his name."

In some passages, the believer is said to *have* eternal life (John 3:36; 5:24; 6:47) ; and hence it is inferred by some that he can never die. And this is certainly true, if he continue to hold fast the beginning of his confidence steadfast even to the end of this mortal life. The true believer never dies; that is, he never dies while he is a true believer. For Christ says, "Whosoever liveth and believeth in me shall never die." (John 11:26.) So long as we continue faithful, "Neither death, nor life, nor angels, nor principalities, nor powers, nor things present, nor things to come, nor height, nor depth, nor any other creature, shall be able to separate us from the love of God which is in Christ Jesus our Lord." (Rom. 8:38, 39.) But be it observed, that it is only by metonymy that the Christian is now said to *have* eternal life. For this life is in Christ; and hence, as John says, "He that hath the Son hath life." (1 John 5:12.) And in the verse immediately preceding, he says, "This is the record that God hath given to us eternal life, and this life is in his Son." Beyond all doubt, then, there is eternal life in Christ; and everyone therefore who has the Son has also the life that is in him. But if he let go the Son, he is then himself cast off as a branch, and withers. (John 15:1-5.) And hence, as we learn, the actual enjoyment of eternal life is a matter that belongs to the future, and is an object of hope even with the Christian. It is the gift of God, through Jesus Christ, to be bestowed on all who persevere in well doing to the end of their earthly pilgrimage. So Christ and his Apostles both testify in many passages of the inspired word. In Mark 10:29, 30, for example, Christ says to his disciples, "Verily I say unto you, there is no man that hath left house, or brethren, or sisters, or father, or mother, or wife, or children, or lands, for my sake and the Gospel's, but he shall receive an hundredfold now in this time, houses, and brethren, and sisters, and mothers, and children, and lands, with persecutions: *and in the world to come, eternal life.*" And in like manner Paul says to Timothy, "Godliness is profitable unto all things, having the promise of the life that now is, and of that which is to come." (1 Tim. 4:8.) And again he exhorts Timothy to "lay hold on eternal life." (1 Tim. 6:12). See also Matt. 25:46; Luke 18:30; John 12:25; Tit. 1:5; 3:7; 1 John 2:25.

So long, then, as a man abides in him who is himself the fountain of all life, he has life; and in a metonymical sense, he may be
said to have eternal life. But if, by apostasy, he ever separates
himself from Christ, then of course death is inevitable. (John 15:
6; Col. 3: 3, 4.) On any other hypothesis, the argument of the
apostle in this paragraph, and indeed throughout this whole Epistle, is not only pointless, but it is also deceptive. If there is no
possibility of falling from grace, and so forfeiting our claims to
eternal life, then for what purpose was this Epistle written? And
why all the warnings and admonitions to Christians that abound,
not only in this Epistle, but also throughout the whole Bible? God
does not so deceive his children. He is too kind, too merciful, too
benevolent, and too just, to allow anyone, speaking by the Holy
Spirit, to alarm and terrify his people by either false representa-
tions or delusive arguments. "By grace ye are saved through
faith; and that not of yourselves, it is the gift of God," bestowed
freely on all them who persevere in well-doing to the end of life.

**and were made partakers of the Holy Ghost.**—To be made a
partaker of the Holy Spirit is the peculiar favor of God vouchsafed
to the Christian. The world cannot receive it, says Christ. (John
14: 17.) But it is freely promised to all who by faith and obedience put on Christ, and so walk in him. Thus, for instance, Paul
says to the Galatians, "Because ye are sons, God hath sent forth
the Spirit of his Son into your hearts, crying, Abba, Father." (Gal.
4: 6.) And again he says to the Roman brethren, "but ye are not
in the flesh, but in the Spirit, if so be that the Spirit of God dwell
in you. Now if any man have not the Spirit of Christ, he is none
of his. And if Christ be in you, the body is dead because of sin;
but the Spirit is life because of righteousness. But if the Spirit of
him that raised up Jesus from the dead dwell in you, he that raised
up Christ from the dead shall also quicken your mortal bodies by
his Spirit that dwelleth in you." (Rom. 8: 9-11.) This partaking
of the Holy Spirit is therefore quite different from its enlightening
and vivifying influences spoken of in the preceding context; and
also from "the good word of God," and the miraculous gifts and
demonstrations of the Spirit referred to in the following context.
The Apostle here speaks manifestly of the indwelling of the Spirit
itself in the soul of the believer, according to the promise of Christ
given in John 7: 37-39, and the promise of Peter as recorded in

5 And have ¹tasted ²the good word of God, and ³the powers of ⁴the world
to come.

¹Ch. ii. 9; Matt. xvi. 28.
²Psa. xix. 10; cxix. 103; Matt. iv. 4; Eph. vi. 17.
³Ch. ii. 4; Matt. vii. 22; Acts viii. 13; xix. 11; 1 Cor. xii. 10.
⁴Ch. ii. 5; Isa. ii. 2; Matt. xii. 32.

---

Acts 2 : 38. And hence we are again constrained to believe that
the writer has reference here to persons who were once in covenant with God, and who for a time enjoyed all the blessings and
benefits of his church on earth.

5 **And have tasted the good word of God,**—The Greek word
for *taste*, (*geuomai*), is followed in the fourth verse by a noun in
the genitive case; but here it is followed by a noun in the accusative. These two constructions do not differ essentially from each
other; and hence we sometimes find the genitive, as in 2 : 9, where
we would naturally expect the accusative. But when the two cases
are used, as here, in connection with each other, a difference of
meaning would seem to be intended by the author. And hence it
is probable that the accusative case is used after the verb in this
instance to denote the full and experimental enjoyment of "the
good word of God," and of the powerful demonstrations of the
Holy Spirit, which none but the obedient believer in the kingdom
of Christ is able to realize. (John 7 : 17; Rom. 12 : 2.) To him, the
good word of God sustained, as it is by the demonstrations of the
Holy Spirit, is the food of the soul; sweeter to his taste than
honey, yea, than the honey-comb.

**and the powers of the world to come.**—(*mellontos aionos*) *of
the coming age.* The word *powers* (*dunameis*) has manifest reference to the works of the Spirit in revealing the truth, supporting
the truth, and carrying forward the work of redemption to its full
and perfect consummation. The coming age is therefore identical,
at least in part, with the Christian age, or the period of Christ's
mediatorial reign. Whether it extends beyond this limit, so as to
embrace also the era of the New Earth, is worthy of consideration.
See note on 2 : 5. But certain it is that the writer embraces in this
remark the whole Gospel dispensation.

There is therefore here, as Albert Barnes justly remarks, "a regular gradation from the first elements of piety in the soul to its
highest developments; and whether the Apostle so designed it or
not, the language describes the successive steps by which the true

6 If they <sup>5</sup>shall fall away, <sup>1</sup>to renew them again unto repentance: seeing <sup>2</sup>they crucify to themselves the Son of God afresh, and <sup>8</sup>put him to an open shame.

<sup>5</sup>Ch. x. 26-30; 2 Pet. ii. 20-22.
<sup>1</sup>Psa. li. 10; Col. iii. 10; 2 Tim. ii. 25; Titus iii. 5.
<sup>2</sup>Ch. x. 26-29.
<sup>8</sup>Ch. xii. 2; Matt. xxvii. 38-44; Luke xxiii. 35-39.

Christian advances to the highest stage of Christian experience. The mind is (a) enlightened; then (b) it tastes of the heavenly gift, or has some experience of it; then (c) it is made to partake of the influences of the Holy Spirit; then (d) there is experience of the excellence and loveliness of the word of God; and (e) finally there is a participation, of the full powers of the new dispensation; of the extraordinary energy which God puts forth in the Gospel to sanctify and save the soul." And hence it seems evident that the persons referred to by the Apostle, had the fullest evidence, both external and internal, as well as experimental, that the Gospel is the power of God for salvation to everyone that believes and obeys it.

6 **If they shall fall away,**—(*kai parapesontas*) *and having fallen away.* On this expression, Dr. Macknight remarks as follows: "The verbs *photisthentas, geusamenous,* and *genethentas,* being all aorists, are rightly rendered by our translators in the past time; who were enlightened, have tasted, and were made partakers. Wherefore, *parapesontas,* being an aorist, ought likewise to have been translated in past time, *have fallen away.* Nevertheless, our translators following Beza, who without any authority from ancient manuscripts, inserted in his version the word *si* (if), have rendered this clause, 'if they shall fall away'; that this text might not appear to contradict the doctrine of the perseverance of the saints. But as no translator should take upon him to add to or to alter the Scriptures for the sake of any favorite doctrine, I have translated *parapesontas* in the past time, *have fallen away,* according to the true import of the word as standing in connection with the other aorists in the preceding verses." It is therefore possible that a man may have been once enlightened, and have tasted of the heavenly gift, and been made a partaker of the Holy Spirit, and that he may have experienced the blessed sanctifying influences of the good word of God, sustained and supported by the powerful demonstrations of the reign of Heaven, and nevertheless fall away

beyond the reach of recovery. "Let him [then] that thinketh he standeth, take heed lest he fall."

**to renew them again to repentance:**—To do this in the case of those who have apostatized from Christ is simply impossible. When the cord of life and love that binds the true believer to Christ, has been once completely severed, the parties so separated can never again be reunited. The case of the apostate is as hopeless as is that of Satan himself. Nothing remains for him but "a certain fearful looking for of judgment and fiery indignation which shall devour the adversaries." This is so clearly taught both here and in 10: 26-29, that of the fact itself there can be no question. But why is it so? Is it owing simply to the fact that the heart of the apostate becomes so hardened by sin that no moral power can renew it? Or does God then also withdraw his converting and renewing power from every such abandoned sinner? That both are true seems very evident from such passages as the following: Gen. 6: 3; Num. 15: 30, 31; Prov. 1: 24-32; Isa. 55: 6; Hos. 4: 17; Rom. 1: 24, 26, 28; 2 Thess. 2: 11, 12.

**seeing they crucify, etc.**—We have given in this clause the characteristic spirit of that class of persons to whom the Apostle refers in our text. They would crucify, if they could, the Son of God afresh, and put him to an open shame. The mere *backslider,* though fallen, has still faith in Christ. It may be very weak, and almost ready to perish. But with proper care it may be revived and strengthened, and the poor repenting sinner will then mourn over his sins and transgressions, as one that mourns for an only son, or as "one that is in bitterness for his first-born." But not so with the hardened apostate. He has no longer any trust and confidence in Christ. Hatred has taken the place of love in his heart, and esteeming the blood of the covenant wherewith he was sanctified an unholy thing, he tramples it under his feet in contempt, and if it were possible he would even crucify again the Son of God, and expose him to public reproach.

On this whole subject, Dean Alford makes the following very just and critical remarks: "In later times the great combat over our passage has been between the Calvinistic and Armenian expositors. To favor their peculiar views of indefectibility, the former have endeavored to weaken the force of the participial clauses as implying any real participation in the spiritual life. So Calvin,

Beza, Owen, Tait, etc. Owen says, 'The persons here intended are not true and sincere believers:—for (1) in their full and large description there is no mention of faith or believing, etc.'—But all this is clearly wrong, and contrary to the plainest sense of the terms here used. The writer even heaps clause upon clause to show that no such shallow tasting, no 'primoribus tantum labris gustasse [no mere tasting with the top of the lips] is intended. And the whole contextual argument is against the view, for it is the very fact of these persons having veritably entered into the spiritual life, which makes it impossible to renew them afresh if they shall fall away. If they have never entered it, if they are unregenerate, what possible logic is it, or even common sense at all, to say that their shallow taste and partial apprehension, makes it impossible to renew them? And what again to say that it is impossible *palin anakainizein* [to renew again] persons in whose case no *anakainismos* [renewal] has ever taken place? If they never have believed, never have been regenerated, how can it be more difficult to renew them to repentance, than the heathen or any unregenerate person? Our landmark of exegesis must be to hold fast the plain simple sense of the passage, and recognize the fact that the persons are truly the partakers of the spiritual life—regenerate by the Holy Spirit."

These critical reasonings and observations are not to be gainsayed; they are, in fact, wholly unanswerable. But how painful it is after all this to hear from the same learned author such unauthorized remarks as the following: *"Elect,* of course, they are not, or they could not fall away, by the very force of the term. But this is one among many passages, wherein the Scripture, as ever from the teaching of the church, we learn that *elect* and *regenerate* are not convertible terms. All elect are regenerate; but all regenerate are not elect. The regenerate may fall away; the elect never can." Here the learned author certainly attempts to make a groundless distinction. Where in the Scriptures is it taught that some of the regenerate are not elect?! Dean Alford was an able critic; but in his theological speculations he frequently errs.

Equally strange and absurd is the hypothesis of the good and venerable Albert Barnes. He says, "The passage proves that if true believers should apostatize, it would be impossible to renew and save them. If then it should be asked whether I believe that

7 For ¹the earth which drinketh in the rain that cometh oft upon it, and bringeth forth herbs meet for them by whom it is dressed, ²receiveth blessing from God:

8 But that ³which beareth thorns and briers is rejected, and is nigh unto cursing; ⁴whose end is to be burned.

¹Deut. xxviii. 11, 12; Psa. xlv. 9-13; civ. 11-13, Isa. lv. 10-13; Joel ii. 21-27.
²Gen. xxvii. 27; Lev. xxv. 21; Psa. lxv. 10.
³Gen. iii. 17. 18; Prov. xxiv. 31; Isa. v. 1-6; Mark xi. 14, 21.
⁴Deut. xxix. 22, 23; Isa. xxvii. 10, 11; Matt. iii. 10; vii. 19; John xv. 6; Rev. xx. 15.

any true Christian ever did or ever will fall from grace, and wholly lose his religion, I would answer unhesitatingly *no."* Why, then, all this earnest warning about a matter which never did occur, and which from the very nature of the case never can occur?! Why spend our time in solemnly warning the people to beware lest the heavens fall, if by the decrees and ordinances of Jehovah it is made absolutely impossible that they ever can fall?!

7 **For the earth, etc.**—The word *"for"* introduces a comparison, the object of which is to show still further the necessity of *growing* in grace and in the knowledge of our Lord and Savior, and also to illustrate at the same time the awful consequences of not striving to bring forth in our lives the required fruits of the Gospel. Land, says our author, which has drunk in the rain which comes often upon it, and brings forth herbage fit for them on whose account it is also tilled, partakes of blessing from God; but bearing thorns and thistles, it is rejected as worthless, and is nigh unto a curse, whose end is for burning. In this passage the apostle refers for illustration to two kinds of land: the soil of the one is good, and imbibing the rain which falls frequently upon it, it brings forth herbs and plants suitable for those on whose account it is cultivated. And hence, as a consequence of this, it is blessed of God after the manner of the primitive blessing, by being made more fruitful. (Gen. 1 : 28.) See references. This soil represents the fruit-bearing Christian, who, as Hosea says, "shall grow as the lily, and cast forth his roots as Lebanon. His branches shall spread, and his beauty shall be as the olive tree, and his smell as Lebanon." (Hos. 14: 5, 6.) And again Christ says, "Every branch that beareth fruit he purgeth, that it may bring forth more fruit." (John 15: 2.)

8 **But that which beareth thorns, etc.**—There is some land which no ordinary cultivation can render productive. It may be plowed deep, and sowed with the best of seed; the rains and the

dews may descend upon it, and the sunshine of heaven may warm
and cherish it, but it is all in vain. Bringing forth nothing but
thorns and thistles, it is rejected as unfit for cultivation, and is
burned over, not to prepare it for future tillage, but, it may be, for
the beasts of the field, or to prevent its injurious effects on the
lands around it. This land represents those nominal Christians
who bring forth no fruit to perfection. God will finally treat them
as the farmer treats the barren soil. They are even now nigh unto
cursing, like the barren fig-tree (Mark 11: 21); and their *end* is
for burning. They will all finally have their part in the lake of
fire, "where their worm dieth not, and their fire is not quenched."

### 4. ENCOURAGEMENT TO GREATER ZEAL IN STRIVING AFTER THE FULL ASSURANCE OF HOPE, DRAWN CHIEFLY FROM THE KNOWN JUSTICE OF GOD, AND THEIR OWN DEEDS OF CHARITY
#### 6: 9-12

9 But, beloved, we are persuaded better things of you, and [1]things that accompany salvation, though we thus speak.

10 For God is not unrighteous to forget your [2]work and [labor of] love, which ye have shown toward his name, in that ye have ministered to the saints, and do minister.

[1]Matt. xxv. 34-40; 2 Cor. vii. 10; Gal. v. 22, 23.
[2]Matt. x. 42; xxv. 40; Acts iv. 34, 35; xi. 29, 30; Rom. xii. 13; xv. 25-27; 1 Cor. xvi. 1-3; 2 Cor. viii. 1-9; ix. 11-15.

9 **But, beloved, we are persuaded better things of you,**—The apostle having solemnly warned the Hebrew Christians against the threatening dangers and fearful consequences of apostasy, now speaks a word for their encouragement. They were still his "beloved" brethren, much endeared to him by their many Christian excellences, as well as by the ties of consanguinity, and he felt assured that a better destiny awaited them than that which he had just described and illustrated by the case of the barren and reprobate land, the *end* of which is for burning.

**and things that accompany salvation,**—Things that stand in immediate connection with salvation, indicating that the Hebrews were still in a saved state; and, furthermore, giving hope and promise that they would persevere in well doing, even to the end of life. Some of these things the Apostle specifies in the following verse.

10 **For God is not unrighteous**—It seems from 5: 12 that the

11 And ³we desire that every one of you do show the same diligence
¹to the full assurance of ²hope unto the end:

³Rom. xii. 8, 11; Gal. vi. 9; Phil. i. 9-11.
¹Ch. x. 22; 2 Cor. v. 1; Col. ii. 2; 1 Thess. i. 5; 1 John iii. 14. 19.
²Vers. 18-20; Rom. v. 2-5; viii. 24, 25; 1 Cor. xiii. 13; Gal. v. 5; Col. i. 5, 23;
1 Pet. i. 3.

Hebrew brethren had been culpably negligent in the study of God's
word; but, as we learn from our text, they had notwithstanding
this been diligent in works of benevolence. They had faithfully
ministered to the saints, and they were still continuing to do so.
This, when done in the name of God and for the sake of Christ, is
always a favorable indication of vital piety. See references. And
hence the Apostle expresses his conviction that God would be
mindful of them, and that he would sustain them in all their works
of faith and labors of love.

The word *labor* (*tou kopou*) is now generally acknowledged to
be an interpolation from 1 Thess. 1: 3. Literally rendered, according to our best authorities, the passage stands thus: For God
is not unrighteous [so as] to forget your work, and the love
which you have shown for his name, [in] having ministered to the
saints, and [in still] ministering. The *name* of God is here equivalent to God himself as revealed to us in his Holy Oracles. He
himself was the supreme object of this love, and whatever was
done for the saints was done therefore for the sake and glory of his
name. "Inasmuch as ye have done it unto one of the least of these
my brethren," says Christ, "ye have done it unto me." (Matt. 25:
40.)

11 **And we desire**—Or, rather, *But* (*de*) *we earnestly desire
that every one of you do show the same diligence with regard to
the full assurance of your hope until the end.* It is our earnest
wish that every one of you should even to the end of life show
forth the same diligence in all things that appertain to the full assurance of hope, that you have so far manifested in your deeds of
charity; that you show, for example, the same degree of diligence
in the study of the Holy Scriptures, in prayer, praise, and medita-
tion; and also in whatever else is required of you in order to the
full enjoyment of the great salvation. This will serve to increase
your faith (John 7: 17; Rom. 12: 2); and this again will perfect
your hope and love (Rom. 5: 1-5).

*Hope* is a complex emotion of the human mind consisting of a

12 That ye be not slothful, but followers of [a]them who through faith and patience inherit the promises.

[a]Ch. x. 36; xi. 4-38; Matt. xxii. 32; Luke xvi. 22; 1 John ii. 25.

desire for some known object, and an expectation of receiving and enjoying it. The object of the Christian's hope is, of course, eternal life. And the full assurance (*plerophoria*) of this hope is simply the hope itself so increased and intensified, as to leave in our minds no doubt whatever that by the grace of God we will finally attain to the enjoyment of the object. This is to be reached only through the diligent use of all the means which God has himself ordained for our perfection in knowledge, righteousness, and holiness. And hence Paul's anxiety that his Hebrew brethren should give all diligence to make their calling and election sure.

12 **That ye be not slothful,**—Or, rather, That ye *become* (*genesthe*) not slothful, but imitators of them who through faith and endurance inherit the promises: such as Abraham, Isaac, Jacob, Moses, Joshua, Samuel, David, Isaiah, Jeremiah, Daniel, Stephen the first Christian martyr, and James the Apostle who was slain with the sword of Herod Agrippa. These, and many other Patriarchs, Jews, and Christians, had through faith and patience persevered in well doing to the end of life, and then they all entered upon the enjoyment of the blessings which are promised to those who die in the Lord. See Ex. 3: 6; Dan. 12: 13; Luke 16: 22, 25; 2 Cor. 5: 1-9; Phil. 1: 21-23; Rev. 2: 10; 14: 13.

To this blessed state of the spirits of the just made perfect, all the promises of the Bible may be said to have reference either directly or indirectly. In this they all concentrate as in one common focus. And hence they may all be regarded either as one or as many according to circumstances, just as we call the whole Bible the Scripture (*he graphe*), when we contemplate it as one book; or the Scriptures (*hai graphai*), when we consider it with reference to its several parts. In 1 John 2: 25, everything appertaining to the future state of the redeemed, seems to be summed up in the one promise of eternal life. But in our text, the Apostle evidently looks at the promises of God to his redeemed saints distributively; having reference to the promise of a future rest (4:

## 5. FURTHER ENCOURAGEMENT DRAWN FROM THE EXAMPLE OF ABRAHAM, AND ALSO FROM THE PROMISE AND OATH OF GOD MADE TO HIM AND TO ALL HIS SPIRITUAL SEED
### 6: 13-20

13 For when God made promise to Abraham, because he could swear by no greater, [1]he sware by himself,

[1]Gen. xxii. 15-18; Ex. xxxii. 13; Psa. cv. 9, 10; Isa. xlv. 23; Jer. xx. 5; xlix. 13; Micah vii. 20; Luke i. 73.

9) ; the promise of houses not made with hands, eternal in the heavens (2 Cor. 5: 2) ; the promise of God's presence (2 Cor. 5: 6, 8), etc.

**13 For when God made promise to Abraham,**—Between this and the preceding paragraph there is a very close connection. Having exhorted the Hebrews not to be slothful, but to be imitators of those who having finished their earthly course, were then partaking of the blessings promised to the faithful, our author very naturally reverts to Abraham as the most illustrious of these, and to the promise which God made to him and to his seed after him. The particular promise to which the apostle here refers, was made to Abraham immediately after the very remarkable manifestation of his faith in the offering of his son Isaac, and it is found recorded in Gen. 22: 15-18, as follows: "And the angel of the Lord called unto Abraham out of heaven the second time, and said, By myself have I sworn, saith the Lord, for because thou hast done this thing, and hast not withheld thy son, thine only son; that in blessing I will bless thee, and in multiplying I will multiply thy seed as the stars of the heaven, and as the sand which is upon the seashore; and thy seed shall possess the gate of his enemies, and in thy seed shall all the nations of the earth be blessed; because thou hast obeyed my voice." In this promise, confirmed by an oath, about twenty-five years probably after the birth of Isaac (Joseph, Ant. i. 13, 2), there are several elements which claim our consideration. (1) It is evidently implied in this promise that Abraham himself would be personally blessed; (2) that he would have a very numerous posterity according to the flesh (Ex. 1: 7; Deut. 1: 10) ; (3) that through his seed the Messiah would come and bless all the nations (Gal. 3: 16) ; and (4) that his mystical family, the family of the faithful, would also be very numerous (Rom. 4: 11,

14 Saying, Surely blessing I will bless thee, and ¹multiplying I will multiply thee.

¹Ch. xi. 12; Ex. i. 7; xxxii. 13; Deut. i. 10; Neh. ix. 23; Isa. x. 22.

16). It is obvious that this promise had no reference whatever either to the birth of Isaac or to his rescue from the altar, but as
Ebrard says, it is clearly implied in the promise itself that its fulfillment "was to be looked for at some *future time*. For there can
be no need of conforming with an oath the promise of a gift which
is forthwith and immediately bestowed: an oath is then only necessary when the fulfillment is so remote as to make it possible that
doubts might spring up in the mind of the receiver of the promise,
from the long delay."

**because he could swear by no greater,—**In this paragraph
the apostle has in view a twofold object. (1) He aims to
show by the example of Abraham that faith and perseverance
in well-doing will, in the end, certainly receive their reward.
"Though it tarry, wait for it; because it will surely come."
(2) He wishes to remind his readers that their hope rests on
the same secure foundation as that on which the hope of
Abraham rested; and that if they will like him persevere to
the end in the way of obedience, they, too, as well as he, will
certainly obtain the promised blessing. The first of these is
the leading thought in verses 13-15, and the second is brought
out more prominently in what follows. The subject of the
oath is mentioned incidentally in the thirteenth verse merely
for the purpose of showing on what ground the patient endurance of Abraham rested; and its consideration will therefore
fall more appropriately under the exegesis of verses 16-18,
where it becomes the principal subject of the discourse.

14 **Saying, Surely blessing I will bless thee,—**We have in this
clause a Hebraism expressive of *intensity,* both in blessing and in
multiplying. For the purpose of expressing any thought with emphasis and energy, the Hebrews were wont to place the infinitive
absolute before the finite verb, as in the expression, "To die thou
shalt die": that is, "Thou shalt surely die." (Gen. 2: 17.) This
Hebrew idiom is expressed in Hellenistic Greek by placing sometimes a cognate noun (as in Gen. 2: 17; Luke 22: 15), and sometimes a participle before the finite verb. The latter construction

15 And so, ²after he had patiently endured, he obtained the promise.
16 For men verily ³swear by the greater; and ⁴an oath for confirmation is
to them an end of all strife.

²Ex. iii. 6; Matt. xxii. 32; Luke xvi. 22.
³Gen. xiv. 22; xxi. 23; Lev. xix. 12; Deut. vi. 13; x. 20.
⁴Gen. xxi. 30, 31; xxxi. 53; Ex. xxii. 11; Josh. ix. 14-18.

occurs in this instance both in our text and in the Septuagint.
The Hebrew literally rendered stands thus: To bless, I will bless
thee, and to multiply I will multiply thy seed; that is, I will very
greatly bless thee, and I will very greatly multiply thy seed. It is
obvious, therefore, that the expression, "multiplying I will multiply
thee," is equivalent to "multiplying I will multiply thy seed." The
form is changed perhaps merely for the sake of brevity and uni-
formity.

15 **And so after he had patiently endured, he obtained the
promise.**—What promise? Manifestly the promise confirmed by
the oath (Gen. 22: 15-18) ; but not in either its fullest extension or
comprehension. Its fulfillment will not be entirely consummated
until the spirits of all the redeemed, united with their glorified bodies, shall enter upon the full enjoyment of the eternal inheritance.
(Eph. 1: 14; 2 Pet. 3: 13; Rev. 21.) But after patiently waiting
for about fifty years, he obtained the promise so far as it related to
his own personal enjoyment of the promised rest. He then quit the
scenes of this mortal life, and joined "the spirits of the just made
perfect." (12: 23.) That this is the meaning of the Apostle is clear
from the fact that Abraham is here mentioned as one of those who
in the twelfth verse are said to be "inheriting the promises." See
notes on 11 : 39, 40.

16 **For men verily swear by the greater;**—The custom of
swearing on solemn and important occasions is of very ancient
date. The first recorded instance of it is found in Gen. 14: 22, 23,
where Abraham is represented as saying to the King of Sodom, "I
have lifted up my hand unto the Lord, the Most High God, the
possessor of heaven and earth, that I will not take from a thread
even to a shoe-latchet, and that I will not take any thing that is
thine, lest thou shouldest say I have made Abram rich." Compare
Ex. 6: 8; Deut. 32: 40; Dan. 12: 7; Rev. 10: 5, 6. Here we have
implied all that is essential to an oath, which consists (1) of an
invocation, in which God is called on to witness the truth of what

17 Wherein God, willing more abundantly to show unto ¹the heirs of promise ²the immutability of his counsel, confirmed it by an oath:

¹Ch. xi. 7, 9; Rom. viii. 17; Gal. iii. 29; James ii. 5; 1 Pet. iii. 7.
²Job xxiii. 13, 14; Psa. xxxiii. 11; Prov. xix. 21; Jer. xxxiii. 20-26; Rom. xi. 29;
James i. 17.

is sworn; and (2) of an imprecation, in which God is called on to
punish falsehood. Many, indeed, define an oath simply as "an appeal to God for the truth of what is testified or promised." But
even in this there is implied the element of imprecation, as well as
that of invocation, for if God is a witness he is also a judge and an
avenger of all perjury and falsehood. And hence an oath may be
defined as "an ultimate appeal to Divine authority, in order to ratify an assertion." I speak here of course only of the civil and religious oaths of what are commonly called Christian nations.
Among the Jews, Greeks, and Romans, there came to be a familiar
distinction between their greater and their lesser oaths. These
less solemn forms of adjuration included oaths by sacred objects,
or by things peculiarly dear to those who employ them. Thus the
Jews swore by Jerusalem and by the Temple; the Greeks, as well
as the Romans, by the souls of the dead, by the ashes of their fathers, by their life or the lives of their friends, by their heads, and
by their right hands." (Amer. Cyc.) But on all very grave occasions, the Jews appealed to God, and the heathen to their superior
divinities, such as Jupiter, Neptune, and Pluto. And accordingly,
as our author says, it has ever been the custom of mankind, on all
grave and important occasions, to swear by the greater; that is, by
some being or beings supposed to be superior to themselves.

and an oath for confirmation is to them an end of all strife.
—The Apostle here states a general truth. It is a remarkable fact
that in all ages and in all nations, men have commonly reposed
great confidence in a declaration made under the solemnities of an
oath, and hence it is generally an end of all strife. Of the truth of
this we have much evidence given in the Bible, as well as in civil
history. Abimelech seems to have rested with confidence in the
oath of Abraham (Gen. 21: 22-32); and Jacob, in the oath of Joseph (Gen. 47: 31). See references.

17 **Wherein God willing, etc.**—The meaning is, Since it is an
acknowledged fact that men everywhere place so much confidence
in an oath, God therefore (*en o*, on this account), in condescension

18 That by ¹two immutable things, in which it was impossible for God to lie, ²we might have a strong consolation, ³who have fled for refuge ⁴to lay hold upon ⁵the hope set before us:

¹Num. xxiii. 19; Psa. lxxxix. 34, 35; Isa. xl. 8; lv. 11; 2 Cor. i. 20; 2 Tim. ii. 13; Titus i. 2; 1 Pet. i. 25.
²Isa. lxvi. 10-14; 2 Cor. i. 5-7; Phil. ii. 1.
³Gen. xix. 22; Ex. xxi. 12-14; Num. xxxv. 9-15; Josh. xx. 1-6; Matt. iii. 7; 1 Thess. i. 10.
⁴1 Kings i. 50; ii. 28; 1 Tim. vi. 12.
⁵Ch. iii. 6; Col. i. 5, 23, 27; 1 Tim. i. 1; Titus i. 2; ii. 13.

to human weakness and human custom, being anxious to show to the heirs of the promise (*tes epangelias*) that it was his fixed and unchangeable purpose to bestow on them all that he had promised to their father, Abraham, became, as it were, a third party between them and himself, and so interposed as a covenanter with an oath. Primarily, this assurance was intended for the consolation and encouragement of both the families of this illustrious Patriarch. It was to Jacob and his sons a sure pledge that, in due time, their literal descendants would inherit Canaan, and enjoy the promised rest. But before our author wrote this Epistle, the Old Covenant had been nailed to the cross. (Col. 2: 14.) The typical rights and privileges of the family according to the flesh, were all abrogated with the death of Christ, and henceforth the promise has reference only to the family of the faithful. "For," says Paul in his Epistle to the Galatians, "ye are all the children of God by faith in Christ Jesus. For as many of you as have been baptized into Christ, have put on Christ. There is neither Jew nor Greek, there is neither bond nor free, there is neither male nor female; for ye are all one in Christ Jesus. And if ye be Christ's, then are ye Abraham's seed, and heirs according to the promise." (Gal. 3: 26-29.)

18 **That by two immutable things,**—His promise and his oath. We may, I think, safely affirm that God can do anything that is consistent with his own nature, and nothing that is contrary to it. He can create a universe, and he can raise the dead, but he cannot lie or deny himself (2 Tim. 2: 13), because he is himself the truth absolute (John 14: 6, 17; 1 John 5: 6). And hence his promises are all yea and amen in Christ Jesus. (2 Cor. 1: 20.) "Heaven and earth shall pass away," says Christ, "but my words shall not pass away." (Matt. 24: 35.) Every promise of God is, like himself, absolutely unchangeable. With an oath or without an oath, it remains the same until it is accomplished. (Matt. 5: 18.) No opposing power in Heaven, Earth, or Hell, can ever nullify or set

19 Which hope we have as ¹an anchor of the soul, both sure and steadfast, and which ²entereth into that within the vail ;

¹Acts xxvii. 29, 40; Rom. iv. 16; v. 5-10; viii. 28-39.
²Ch. iv. 16; ix. 3, 7, 24; x. 20; Lev. xvi. 2, 15; Matt. xxvii. 51; Col. iii. 1.

aside a decree or promise of Jehovah. But God deals with men, as men. He humbles himself to behold the things that are in heaven and that are in the earth. (Psalm 113 : 6.) And hence, in order that he might give to the heirs of the promise every possible ground of encouragement, he, as it were, ratified his promise with an oath ; thus making it, as we are wont to say doubly sure that he will bless all the seed of Abraham, and bring them into the enjoyment of the inheritance which is "incorruptible, and undefiled, and which fadeth not away." (1 Pet. 1 : 4.)

**who have fled for refuge, etc.**—This remark includes the whole family of the faithful in Christ Jesus, every one of whom has fled from "coming wrath" to lay hold on the hope of eternal life offered to us in the Gospel (Tit. 1 : 2) ; just as the guilty sinner, under the Law, was wont to flee to one of the cities of refuge, or to lay hold on the horns of the altar (1 Kings 1 : 5; 2 : 28). It is worthy of remark that there is but one hope for fallen man, even as there is also but one Spirit, "one Lord, one faith, one baptism, one God and Father of all, who is above all, and through all, and in all." (Eph. 4 : 6.)

19 **Which hope we have as an anchor of the soul,**—The hope of the believer is to his soul what a "sure and steadfast" anchor is to a ship. The storm may rage and the billows may rise like mountains, but so long as the anchor holds, the ship rides prosperously and triumphantly over the troubled waters. And so it is with the soul of the Christian. So long as his hope is "sure and steadfast," so long he is perfectly secure. But when his hope is lost, all is lost. He is then like a ship driven by a tempest.

This figure does not occur elsewhere in the Bible, but in the Greek and Roman classics, and also on the ancient coins, an anchor is often used as an emblem of hope. Socrates says, for example, "To ground hope on a false assumption, is like trusting in a weak anchor."

**and which entereth into that within the vail ;**—By that within the vail is obviously meant Heaven itself, of which the Most

20 Whither ¹the forerunner is ²for us entered, even Jesus, made an ³high priest forever after the order of Melchisedec.

¹Ch. ii. 10; John xiv. 2, 3.
²Ch. i. 3; iv. 14; viii. 1; ix. 12, 24; xii. 2; Rom. viii. 34; Eph. i. 20-23; 1 Pet. iii. 22.
³Ch. v. 6, 10; vii. 3, 15, 17; Psa. cx. 4.

---

Holy Place in the ancient Tabernacle was but a type. See notes on 9: 8, 12, 24. But what is it that entereth into that within the vail? Is it the hope or is it the anchor? Grammatically, the present participle *entering* (*eiserchomenen*) may refer to either. And, accordingly, Bleek, Storr, Kuinoel, Bloomfield, and others, refer it to *hope* (*elpida—hen*), supposing that the figure is dropped with the adjectives *sure* and *steadfast*. But it is more natural to continue the figure, or rather to introduce a second figure by a change of the imagery, and refer the participle *"entering,"* as well as the adjectives *"sure* and *steadfast"* to the word anchor (*agkuran*). So the passage is construed by Beza, DeWette, Ebrard, Lünemann, Delitzsch, Alford, Moll, etc. On this point Ebrard happily remarks as follows: "Two figures are here not so much mixed as elegantly combined. The author might compare the world to a sea, the soul to a ship, the future still concealed glory to the covered bottom of the sea, the remote firm land stretching beneath the water and covered by the water. Or he might compare the present life upon earth to the fore-court, and the future blessedness to the heavenly Sanctuary, which is still, as it were, concealed from us by a vail. He has, however, combined the two figures. The soul, like a shipwrecked mariner, clings to an anchor, and sees not where the cable of the anchor runs to, where it is made fast. It knows, however, that it is firmly fixed behind the vail which conceals from it the future glory, and that if it only keeps fast hold of the anchor, it will in due time be drawn in with the anchor, by a rescuing hand, into the Holiest of all. Thus there is in the hope itself that which the fulfillment of it certainly brings about." "The image," says Delitzsch, "is a bold and noble one, selected from natural things to portray those above nature. The iron anchor of the seaman is cast downward into the deep of the sea, but the hope-anchor of the Christian is thrown upward into the deep of Heaven, and passing through the super-celestial waters, finds there its ground and fast-holding."

20 **Whither the forerunner is for us entered,**—A forerunner

(*prodromos*), is properly one who runs before. In the Septuagint
the word is twice applied to the first-ripe fruit. (Num. 13:21; Isa.
28:4); and in the Greek classics it is often used to denote scouts
of calvary or infantry sent before an army. Here it is very appropriately applied to Christ as the one who has gone before his people to prepare mansions for them. "I go," he says, "to prepare a
place for you." (John 14:2.) As our great High Priest, he has
gone into Heaven itself, there to appear in the presence of God for
us. (9:24.) And hence it is that our hope-anchor rests also within
the vail. While Christ is there, and our hope in him is steadfast,
there is no danger. We have only to work on, and trust in him to
the end, and then when he who is our life shall appear, we, too, will
appear with him in glory. (Col. 3:4.)

**made a high priest forever after the order of Melchisedec.**
—In these words we have a beautiful and natural transition from
the previous digression to the main theme of the Epistle.   The
Apostle having sufficiently admonished his readers, and prepared
their minds and hearts for the consideration of his subject, now
gracefully returns to the point from which he suddenly broke off in
5:11; and proceeds at once to show the superiority of Christ's
priesthood over that of Aaron and his successors.

## REFLECTIONS

1. Dullness of hearing in things sacred and Divine has always
been a great obstacle in the way of religious instruction. (5:
11.) It was so under the Old Testament economy; it was so in
the time of Christ and his Apostles, and it is so in our own day
and generation. How many are even now keen to discern all that
is good and excellent in secular literature, who have no relish
whatever for the Oracles of God. In this respect, their hearts have
become gross; "their ears are dull of hearing, and their eyes they
have closed." (Matt. 12:15.) Light has come into the world, but
alas! how many there are who still "love the darkness rather than
the light, because their deeds are evil." (John 3:19.) Oh that
God would take away our hard and stony hearts, and give us
hearts of flesh (Ezek. 11:19); hearts inclined to hear the truth, to
understand it, to receive it, and to obey it.

2 It is the duty of all Christians to make constant progress in
the knowledge of our Lord and Savior Jesus Christ (verse 12).

The word of God is the good *seed* of the Kingdom, without which it is altogether vain to look for the fruits of righteousness in the lives of professing Christians. True, indeed, our piety is not always commensurate with our knowledge. Various hindrances may concur to prevent the word from having its proper and legitimate effect on the lives of those who hear it. (Matt. 13: 18-23.) But as a rich harvest was never gathered without the sowing of seed, so also it is folly to look for the fruits of the Spirit in the lives and hearts of those who are destitute of the word of life. It can no longer be pleaded that "ignorance is the mother of devotion." The mother of superstition and fanaticism it may be, but certainly not of that holy spiritual devotion which is acceptable in the sight of God. "God is spirit; and they that worship him must worship him in spirit and in truth." And hence Paul says to the Colossians, "Let the word of Christ dwell in you richly in all wisdom, teaching and admonishing one another in psalms, and hymns, and spiritual songs, singing with grace in your hearts to the Lord." (Col. 3: 16.) And again he says to Timothy, "All Scripture is given by inspiration of God, and is profitable for doctrine, for reproof, for correction, for instruction in righteousness, that the man of God may be perfect, thoroughly furnished for every good work." (2 Tim. 3: 16, 17.)

3. It is the duty of all Christians to become teachers of the word of God (verse 12). They cannot, of course, all become Elders and Evangelists, but they may all with the blessing of God soon qualify themselves to tell the simple story of the cross to their friends, neighbors, and fellow-citizens. And hence the last commission given by Christ to his disciples embraces every one of them. (Rev. 22: 17.) "Let him that heareth, say Come," is one of the last and most solemn admonitions of Christ to all his faithful followers. If, then, all would act faithfully under this last commission of our blessed Lord, and would labor earnestly to instruct others in even the rudiments of the Christian Religion, what a powerful influence it would have in promoting the cause and kingdom of Christ. How soon under such circumstances the wilderness and the solitary places of the earth would be made glad, and the very deserts of the world be made to "rejoice and blossom as the rose." Who can doubt that the very best consequences would follow if every Christian would labor as God gives him opportunity, to in-

struct the young and the ignorant in the way of life. But alas, of how many it may still be said, that while for the time they ought to be teachers of others, they have need that some one instruct them again in even the "first principles of the Oracles of God."

4. Christianity, like every other department of knowledge, has its elementary and its more advanced and recondite principles. (6: 1-3.) And hence care should always be taken to adapt our instructions to the age and capacity of our readers, and also of our hearers, as the case may be. It is all folly to attempt to instruct in the principles of Grammar and Rhetoric children who have not studied even the alphabet, or to drill in the Calculus those who are ignorant of even the common rules of Arithmetic. And no less absurd is the practice of attempting to instruct in many things pertaining to the decrees of God, the priesthood of Christ, and the work of the Holy Spirit, such babes in Christ as have not mastered even the elementary lessons of Christianity relating to repentance from dead works, faith toward God, the doctrine of baptisms, the laying on of hands, the resurrection of the dead, and eternal judgment. Much time and labor are vainly spent in attempting to feed the infants of God's family on the solid food of Christian doctrine rather than on the pure and simple milk of the word of truth. (1 Pet. 2: 2.)

5. It is dangerous to rest satisfied with a knowledge of the mere rudiments of Christianity or to stop short of perfection in the knowledge of Christ. (6: 1-3.) Our course should be ever onward and upward in all that pertains to holiness and happiness. The time is short, the work is great, and the prize to be won or lost, is of infinite value. It becomes us, therefore, to give all diligence while life lasts, in adding to our faith knowledge, as well as temperance, patience, godliness, brotherly-kindness, and love. And after we shall have done this, to even the utmost extent of our ability, how little we shall know of the length and breadth, the depth and height of the love of God which passes all understanding. But small as our attainments may be; we have nevertheless the satisfaction to know that they will be quite sufficient to prepare us for a joyful admission into the everlasting Kingdom of our Lord and Savior Jesus Christ. (2 Pet. 1: 11.) After that, when with Prophets and Apostles we stand on the heights of the everlasting Zion,

we will be better qualified to make further and higher advances in the knowledge of Divine things.

6. How very dreadful and alarming is the condition of the apostate (verses 4-8). Once enlightened and comforted by the good word of God, a partaker of the heavenly gift and of the Holy Spirit, but now fallen; dead in trespasses and in sins, without God and without hope; beyond the reach of mercy, even through the blood of the everlasting covenant wherewith he was once sanctified! "Oh wretched state of deep despair!" What mind can fathom the abyss of woe that awaits such an abandoned reprobate? And yet to think that such a doom may perchance be ours! The very thought of even such a possibility should constrain us to put forth every energy of body, soul, and spirit, to make our calling and election sure. To be banished from God as unfit for the society of Heaven; to have our portion with the devil and his angels; to weep forever, "but not in Mercy's sight!" And all this for what? Simply because we would not accept of the great salvation, by ceasing to do evil, and learning to do well. Because we would not humbly, and in reliance on Divine grace, even try to do the will of him who made us, preserved us, and gave his own Son to redeem us. May God save us from such folly and madness by helping and enabling us to work out our salvation with fear and trembling.

7. Any evidence of spiritual vitality is always encouraging (verses 9, 10). The sick may be revived, but the condition of the dead is hopeless. Every possible effort should therefore be made, and made speedily, to raise up the hands that hang down, and to strengthen the feeble knees. God never abandons any of his erring children while there is even a spark of spiritual life in their souls. It is only when they wholly apostatize from him, by going so far in sin as to sever the last cord of their spiritual union with him, that he gives them up to blindness of mind and hardness of heart. Till then he follows them with even more than a father's care and a mother's love. "Return, thou backsliding Israel, saith the Lord, and I will not cause mine anger to fall upon you. For I am merciful, saith the Lord, and I will not keep anger forever. Only acknowledge thine iniquity, that thou hast transgressed against the Lord thy God, and hast scattered thy ways to the strangers under every green tree, and ye have not obeyed my voice, saith the Lord.

Turn, O backsliding Israel, saith the Lord, for I am married unto you; and I will take you, one of a city and two of a family, and will bring you to Zion." (Jer. 3:12-14.) While, then, God labors to reform and restore his backsliding children, we should feel encouraged to do likewise, for God is not willing that any should perish, but that all should be brought to repentance. (2 Pet. 3:9.) See also Matt. 18:12-15; Luke 15:4-7; 22:32; Gal. 6:1; Heb. 12:13; James 5:19, 20; 1 John 5:16; Jude 22, 23.

8. The departed saints are now happy (verses 12, 15). They are inheriting the promises in a far higher and fuller sense than they did during their earthly pilgrimage (verse 12). True, indeed, it is said of Abraham, as well as of many of his children, that he was greatly blessed during his sojourn on earth. (Gen. 24:1, 35.) But all this was but as nothing in comparison with the blessing which he received after that he had patiently waited even to the end of his pilgrimage (verse 15). For "he sojourned in the land of promise, as in a strange country, dwelling in tabernacles with Isaac and Jacob, the heirs with him of the same promise," that is, of the same heavenly inheritance. (11:16.) "For he looked for a city which hath foundations, whose builder and maker is God." (11:9, 10.) And just so it was also with Isaac, and Jacob, and all the Prophets, Apostles, and other holy men of old, "who through faith subdued kingdoms, wrought righteousness, obtained promises, stopped the mouths of lions, quenched the violence of fire, escaped the edge of the sword, out of weakness were made strong, waxed valiant in fight, and turned to flight the armies of the aliens." (11:33, 34.) "These all died in faith, not having received the promises, but having seen them afar off, and embraced them, and confessed that they were strangers and pilgrims on the earth." (11:13.) These have all entered into the rest of God (4:10), and are now heirs of God and joint-heirs with Christ (Rom. 8:17). The entire universe is now theirs, so far as they are now capable of enjoying it. (1 Cor. 3:22, 23.) Heaven is now their home, and the earth, when purified from sin, will be added to their possessions, and become the place of their abode. See notes on 2:5-9. There, invested as they will be with their glorified bodies, they will probably enter on still higher degrees of enjoyment. There God will lead them to fountains of living water, and there he will make all things abound to their everlasting felicity. Surely,

then, it is better to depart and be with Christ (Phil. 1:23); for "while we are at home in the body, we are absent from the Lord." (2 Cor. 5:6).

9. It is right to make oath on grave and momentous occasions (verses 13, 17). This, it seems, has ever been a custom among men, and God himself is here represented as having acted in harmony with this custom. But surely he would not have done so had the custom been in itself sinful, as some allege. That the practice of swearing has been carried to very great excess, even in our civil courts, I readily grant; and that there is in our depraved hearts a lamentable tendency to take the name of God in vain, is, alas, but too evident. All such profane trifling with the name and attributes of God is sinful (Ex. 20:7); and so also is the habit of swearing by Heaven, or by the earth, or by any other creature. All such profanity is wholly inconsistent with the spirit of our holy religion, and is most emphatically forbidden by Christ (Matt. 5:33-37), and also by the Apostle James (James 5:12). But to swear by God when the occasion requires it, that is, when nothing else would serve to remove doubt and give to society the necessary confidence, seems to be in harmony with the example of God himself on sundry occasions. See references.

10. How wonderfully deep and profound are the counsels of Jehovah (verses 13-18). Who without the aid of the Holy Spirit would ever have supposed that God's promise to Abraham comprehended all that has been developed from it in the history of God's dealings with mankind? Who would have thought, for instance, that in that promise there was given to Abraham and to his seed a pledge that they should be the heirs of the world (Rom. 4:13), and partakers of all the rights and privileges of the everlasting kingdom (Gal. 3:29)? But it is even so. God's ways are not as our ways, nor are his thoughts as our thoughts. (Isa. 55:8, 9.) Well may we exclaim with Paul, in view of the whole plan of redemption, "Oh the depth of the riches, and of the wisdom, and of the knowledge of God! How unsearchable are his judgments, and his ways past finding out! For who hath known the mind of the Lord? Or who hath been his counselor? Or who hath first given to him, and it shall be recompensed unto him again? For of him, and through him, and to him, are all things; to whom be glory forever. Amen."

11. The hope of the Christian rests on a sure foundation (verse 19). Unlike the hopes of the world, it will never make us ashamed by disappointing us; for even now we have here a fore-taste of the joys and felicities of Heaven, through "the love of God that is shed abroad in our hearts by the Holy Spirit which is given to us." (Rom. 5:10.) This is a sure earnest of what is to follow. (Eph. 1:14). And besides, Jesus as our forerunner has for us entered into that within the vail. There he has made an atonement for us with his own blood; there he has provided for us heavenly mansions, and there he ever lives and reigns to make intercession for us, and to supply all our wants. Surely this is sufficient ground of encouragement for those "who have fled for refuge to lay hold on the hope set before us." For if when we were enemies to God by wicked works, we were reconciled to him by the death of his Son, much more being now reconciled by his death, we shall be saved by his life. (Rom. 5:10.)

## SECTION SIX
### 7:1 to 8:5

### ANALYSIS

Having by the admonitions and warnings given in the preceding section, excited his Hebrew brethren to greater diligence in the study of God's word, the Apostle again resumes the consideration of Christ's priesthood. His main object in this section is to set forth clearly and prominently its great superiority over that of Aaron and his successors. This he does—

I. By showing that the priesthood of Melchisedec was of a higher order than that of Aaron. And as the priesthood of Mel-chisedec was only a type of the priesthood of Christ, it follows of necessity that the latter is even more than the former superior to that of Aaron. (7:1-10.) That the priesthood of Melchisedec was superior to that of the Levitical order, he proves—

1. From the fact that Melchisedec was a king as well as a priest (verses 1, 2).

2. From the fact that Abraham, the father of the Jewish nation, paid tithes to him (verse 2).

3. From the fact that, as a priest, Melchisedec appears on the typical canvas alone, without predecessors and without successors.

In this, the unity, immutability, and general perfection of Christ's priesthood are beautifully illustrated (verse 3).

4. From the fact that Abraham himself acknowledged the superiority of Melchisedec (1) by giving him a tithe of the spoils, and (2) by receiving his blessing (verses 2, 7).

5. From the fact that on the principle of federal representation, even Levi himself paid tithes to Melchisedec through Abraham (verses 9, 10). From all of which it follows that the priesthood of Melchisedec is of a higher order than that of Aaron, and consequently that the priesthood of Christ is greatly superior to the Levitical.

II. The Apostle further demonstrates the superiority of Christ's priesthood over that of Levi, from the fact that God had promised by David that he would introduce a new order of priesthood. This, as our author shows, implies an imperfection in the Levitical order, and also in the whole law of Moses (verses 11-19). For

1. If the Levitical priesthood had reached the end of God's benevolent purposes, then certainly he would not have thought of introducing another of a different order (verse 11).

2. But this he has done. For in Psalm 110: 4, as our author has shown in 5: 5, 6, God promised to make his Son Jesus a High Priest forever after the order of Melchisedec. And as Jesus is not of the tribe of Levi but of Judah, it follows that the Levitical priesthood is abolished, and with it also the whole law of Moses, of which the Levitical priesthood was the basis (verses 12-14).

3. This is further and still more manifestly implied in the stipulated terms and conditions of the new order of priesthood. Christ holds his office, not as did the Levitical Priests "after the law of a carnal commandment, but after the power of an endless life." He is a priest forever according to the decree of Jehovah as given in Psalm 110: 4.

4. The whole law of Moses, then, embracing the carnal commandment relating to the Levitical priesthood is abrogated, being, as it was, incapable of perfecting anything, and a new and better ground of hope is now brought in through the priesthood of Christ; so that we can now, at all times, draw near to God, as children to a father, and obtain from him seasonable help (verses 18, 19).

III. The Apostle makes a third argument in proof of the superi-

ority of Christ's priesthood on the ground that it was instituted
with an oath. "Jehovah has sworn, and will not repent," says
David, addressing the Messiah, "thou art a priest forever after the
order of Melchisedec." But no such solemnities were observed in
inaugurating the Levitical priesthood (verses 20-22). Now when
it is understood that God never makes oath, save on the most solemn occasions and in reference to the most important matters this
argument is of very great force.

IV. The fourth argument is drawn from the frequent changes
that occurred in the Levitical priesthood, occasioned by the death
of the high priest (verses 23-25).

1. From the inauguration of the Levitical priesthood to the
birth of Christ, sixty-seven different persons held the office of high
priest, and from the same epoch to the destruction of Jerusalem,
eighty-one persons ministered in this office (verse 23).

2. But no such imperfection exists in the priesthood of Christ;
he ever lives to intercede for his people, and to save even to the
uttermost those who come unto God by him (verses 24, 25).

V. In the next place he proves the superiority of Christ's
priesthood from his perfectly holy and sinless nature (verses 26-
28).

1. The Levitical high priests were all sinners like other men,
and hence they had to offer sacrifices daily for themselves as well
as for the people.

2. But Christ being without sin, had no need to offer sacrifice
for himself. And so perfect was the one offering of himself which
he made for the sins of the people that no further offering is required. God can now be just in justifying all who believe in Jesus.

VI. Finally and chiefly, the Apostle proves the superiority of
Christ's priesthood from his exalted position and his official dignity (8: 1-5).

1. He sits enthroned on the right hand of the Majesty in the
heavens (verse 1).

2. He is a minister of the Sanctuary and also of the true Tabernacle, of which Jehovah himself is the supreme architect. In these
archetypes of both the tabernacle of Moses, and the temple of Solomon, Jesus ever ministers as our high priest, dealing not with
shadows as did the priests under the Law, but with the sublime
realities of the economy of redemption (verses 2-5).

It appears, then, from the preceding analysis that the main thoughts and divisions of this section may be briefly summed up as follows:

I. 7: 1-10. The Melchisedecian order of priesthood superior to the Levitical.

II. 7: 11-19. The Levitical priesthood and law of Moses both abrogated on account of their insufficiency, and a better ground of hope brought in through the priesthood of Christ.

III. 7: 20-22. The superiority of Christ's priesthood proved from the fact that, unlike the Levitical, it was inaugurated with an oath.

IV. 7: 23-25. The frequent changes in the Levitical priesthood occasioned by the death of the high priest, contrasted with the ever-enduring and unchangeable character of Christ's priesthood.

V. 7: 26-28. The great superiority of Christ's priesthood proved and illustrated from his own pure and spotless character, and from the perfection of the one offering which he made for the sins of the world.

VI. 8: 1-5. The superiority of Christ's priesthood further demonstrated from the higher and more exalted sphere of his ministry.

### 1. THE MELCHISEDECIAN ORDER OF PRIESTHOOD SUPERIOR TO THE LEVITICAL
#### 7: 1-10

1 For ¹this Melchisedec, king of ²Salem, priest of ³the most high God, who met Abraham returning from ⁴the slaughter of the kings, and blessed him;

¹Ch. v. 6; vi. 20; Gen. xiv. 18-20; Psa. cx. 4.
²Psa. lxxvi. 2.
³Psa. lvii. 2; lxxvii. 56; Dan. v. 18, 21; Acts xvi. 17.
⁴Gen. xiv. 14-20.

1 **For this Melchisedec,**—The Apostle expresses here in one compact sentence the main characteristics of Melchisedec as a type of Christ. His object is to amplify and illustrate the closing remark of the last section that Christ is "made a high priest forever after the order of Melchisedec." This he goes on to say is true, for Melchisedec being king of Salem, etc., abides a priest continually, and so also does Christ.

Who this Melchisedec was, has long been a question of interest with both the learned and the unlearned. Some say that he was

Christ himself (Ambrose, Hottinger) ; some, that he was the Holy
Spirit (Hieracas, Epiphanius) ; some, that he was an angel (Origen, Didymus) ; some, that he was Enoch (Hulsius, Calmet) ;
some, that he was Shem (Jerome, Luther) ; and some have conjectured that he was an extraordinary emanation from the Deity
which suddenly appeared for a little while on the stage of action,
and was then as suddenly removed from it.  But all such notions
are purely hypothetical, and are wholly inconsistent with the manifest purpose of God in making Melchisedec an extraordinary type
of his own Son as the great high priest of our confession.  For it is
very obvious that the Holy Spirit has intentionally thrown an impenetrable veil over both the birth and the death of Melchisedec,
over both his parentage and his posterity, for the purpose of making him a more perfect type of Christ.  He now stands before us
on the typical canvas alone, without father, without mother, without genealogy, having neither beginning of days nor end of life.
He appears in the sacerdotal drama by himself, and in the prime of
manhood, honored and respected by the most eminent servants of
God "as a priest upon his throne," thus beautifully illustrating in
his own person the royal dignity and the perpetual character of
Christ's priesthood.  But let it be once clearly demonstrated that
he was Shem, the son of Noah, or any other person of known
genealogy, and that moment the analogy fails, and he forever
ceases to be a fit type of Christ.  It was not, therefore, a matter of
chance, or of accident, but of real design on the part of God, that
so little is said in history of this truly great and mysterious person.
He comes out suddenly from the dark, invisible background of the
drama of human redemption; appears for a little while as a royal
priest, and then retires forever without leaving behind him the
slightest recorded evidence that he had either predecessors or successors; that he had either beginning of days or end of life.  And
hence it is really more than folly to ransack the archives of antiquity with the view of discovering anything more concerning him
than what is recorded in the fourteenth chapter of Genesis.
Josephus, after the manner of Moses, represents him simply as the
king of Salem, and says that "he supplied Abraham's army in a
hospitable manner, and gave them provisions in abundance." (Ant.
i. 10, 2.) So also Philo speaks of him as a real person. He says,
"God made him king of Salem," and he calls him "the priest of the

Most High God." (Legg. Alleg. Section 25, 26.) The name *Melchisedec,* as our author defines it, means simply king of righteousness.

**King of Salem,**—Some expositors, as Böhme and Bleek, think that we have in these words, as in Melchi-tsedek, a mere title (Melek-Salem) of this illustrious personage, and that there is really here no reference to any locality. Others, as Jerome and Ewald, suppose that the Salem of our text is the same as the Salim of John 3 : 23, near to which John was baptizing. But the common opinion of both Jewish and Christian writers has always been that the Salem of our text is the same as Jerusalem. This was the view of Josephus (Ant. i. 10, 2; vii. 3, 2; Bell. vi. 10), and is probably correct for the following reasons: (1) the name Salem is manifestly given to Jerusalem in Psalm 76 : 2. (2) The name *Jerusalem* is composed as some think of Jebus-Salem (Judges 19 : 10), or as others with more probability, suppose, of *Jeru-Salem,* which means foundation of peace. (3) The situation of Jerusalem corresponds well with the facts recorded in Gen. 14 : 17-20. (4) The name Melchi-tsedek is formed after the same analogy as Adoni-tsedek (lord of righteousness) the name of another king of Jerusalem. (Josh. 10 : 1.) And (5) since it was God's purpose to make Jerusalem prominent above all other places in bringing about the reign of the Prince of Peace (Isa. 9 : 6), it is most likely that he would select it in preference to any other locality for the sacerdotal reign of the king of righteousness.

**priest of the most high God,**—The Hebrew word *kohen,* rendered *priest,* occurs about seven hundred times in the Old Testament, and like the Greek *hiereus,* is always used to denote one who offers sacrifice and ministers in other sacred things. It is first of all applied to Melchisedec in Gen. 14 : 18, who is there, as well as in our text, called "priest of the Most High God." The title "Most High," is given to God, as Philo says, "not because there is any other God who is not most high, for God being one is in Heaven above, and the earth beneath, and there is none other beside him." (Legg. Alleg. Section 26.)

**who met Abraham, etc.**—The account of this meeting is given in the fourteenth chapter of Genesis, to which the reader is referred for all necessary details. Suffice it to say here, that after Abraham had completely routed and vanquished the four kings

2 To whom also Abraham gave ¹a tenth part of all; first being by interpretation ²King of righteousness, and after that also King of Salem, which
is King of peace:
 3 Without father, without mother, without descent, having neither beginning of days, nor end of life; but made like unto the Son of God, ³abideth a
priest continually.

¹Gen. xxviii. 22; Lev. xxvii. 30-32; Num. xviii. 20-32; Deut. xiv. 22-29; 1 Sam. viii.
15-17.
²Psa. xlv. 4-7; lxxii. 1-7; Isa. ix. 6, 7; Jer. xxiii. 5, 6; xxxiii. 15, 16; Rom. iii. 26.
³Vers. 17, 23-28; Psa. cx. 4.

whose names and places are there recorded, and was returning,
laden with the spoils of victory to Hebron, the place of his sojourn
about twenty miles south of Jerusalem, he was met on his way
thither by Melchisedec, who refreshed him and his servants with
bread and wine, and, as the priest of the Most High God, he
blessed Abraham, saying, "Blessed be Abram of the Most High
God, possessor of heaven and earth, and blessed be the Most High
God who hath delivered thine enemies into thine hand."

 2 **To whom also Abraham gave a tenth part of all,**—This act
of devotion on the part of Abraham, as well as the vow of Jacob
(Gen. 28: 22), clearly indicates that the custom of paying tithes to
God for the maintenance of his worship and the support of true
religion, was of very remote antiquity.  Indeed, there is no reason
to doubt that the paying of tithes, as well as the offering of sacrifice, was of Divine origin, and that a law to this effect was given to
Adam and his family soon after the fall. And accordingly we find
traces of its observance not only among the Patriarchs, but also
among many of the most ancient nations, such as the Babylonians,
the Greeks, the Romans, and the Carthaginians.  And hence
Moses does not introduce tithing as a novelty, but finding it, as he
found sacrifice, already in vogue, he merely gave new laws and
regulations concerning it, making that now obligatory which was
perhaps before somewhat voluntary. While, therefore, the offerings of Abraham to Melchisedec were most likely voluntary on the
part of this illustrious Patriarch, it is but reasonable to suppose
that he made them in harmony with what he knew to be an existing religious ordinance, and also on account of the great respect
which he had for Melchisedec as a priest of the Most High God.

 3 **Without Father, etc.**—The Greeks and Romans were wont
to apply the epithets "without father" (*apator*) and "without
mother" (*ametor*), (1) to their gods; (2) to orphans; and (3) to

persons of unknown or obscure parentage. Thus, for instance, Livy says of Servius Tullius, that "he was born of no father." (Lib. iv. 3.) So also the Jews were accustomed to use these terms of persons, the names of whose parents were not given in the Holy Scriptures or in their genealogies. Philo, for example, speaking of Sarah, the wife of Abraham, says, "She is said not to have had a mother, having received the inheritance of relationship from her father only" (De Ebriet, Section 14) : meaning evidently that her mother's name is not found in the sacred records. And to the same effect is the Rabbinical maxim which says of the Gentile proselyte that "He has no father," after his conversion to Judaism. In this popular sense, the Apostle manifestly uses these negative epithets in our text, to denote simply that the parentage of Melchisedec is unknown; that so far as the record goes, he was without father and without mother, and furthermore that he was without descent, or rather, without genealogy (*agenealogetos*). Nothing concerning either his ancestry or his posterity is recorded in the Holy Scriptures. There, he appears on the page of typical history isolated and alone. See note on verse 1.

**having neither beginning of days nor end of life ;**—This is but a part of the constructive parallelism which the Apostle frames here with the view of amplifying his description of Melchisedec in his typical relations to Christ as the great high priest of our confession. Christ, in the sense in which he is here contemplated by our author, had no predecessors, and he will have no successors. He himself will continue to officiate as our royal high priest during the entire period of his mediatorial reign. And so it was with Melchisedec. So far as the record goes, his priesthood, as well as that of Christ, was unbroken, uninterrupted by any changes of succession. All that is here meant by his being made like unto the Son of God, and abiding a priest perpetually (*eis to dienekes*) is simply this: that like Jesus he completely fills up the entire era of his royal priesthood in his own proper person. This period, however short, is intended to serve as a typical representation of the era of Christ's priesthood, and Melchisedec is thus made a more perfect type of Christ than was Aaron or any of his successors. The word *perpetually* (*dienekes*) and *forever* (*aion*) are relative terms, and are simply exhaustive of the period to which they are severally applied, whether it be long or short. And all that is

4 Now consider how great this man was, unto whom [even] the [1]patriarch Abraham [2]gave the tenth of the spoils.

[1]Acts ii. 29; vii. 8, 9.
[2]Gen. xiv. 20.

---

therefore implied in the words of the text is simply this: that as the shadow, however small it may be, corresponds with the substance which forms it, so also did the priesthood of Melchisedec correspond with that of Christ. Each of them was unbroken, uninterrupted, and relatively perfect in itself. Great care is therefore necessary in dealing with these relative terms and expressions, lest peradventure we give them an extension which is wholly beyond what was intended by the Holy Spirit.

4 **Now consider how great this man was,**—The Apostle aims here to exalt the character of Melchisedec with the view of still further exalting the character and priesthood of Christ, of whom Melchisedec was an eminent type. This he does by comparing Melchisedec with Abraham, who, at that time, had apparently reached the very summit of human greatness. "Of his own free-will, he had, from motives of pure benevolence, engaged in an enterprise which resulted in the overthrow of four kings and the deliverance of five, and now he was returning to his quiet home covered with glory and the spoils of victory. But just at this moment, when raised above his fellow-men in deeds of prowess and works of mercy, he encounters the venerable form of the king of Salem, who steps forth for an instant from his mysterious seclusion, and as speedily retires again, but not before Abraham, at his highest exaltation, has acknowledged in Melchisedec one superior to himself" (*Del. in loc.*). This Abraham did (1) by paying to Melchisedec the tenth of all the spoils which he had taken, and (2) by receiving the blessing of Melchisedec as the priest of the Most High God.

The Greek word rendered *spoils* (*akdrothinion*), means literally the top of the heap. It generally occurs in the plural number, and is variously used to denote the first fruits of the harvest, taken as they usually were from the top of the heap of corn, and also the best of the spoils of war, which the heathens generally consecrated to the honor and worship of their gods. In our text it means not the whole of the booty taken, but only those choice articles of it

5 And verily they that are of the sons of Levi, [1]who receive the office of the priesthood, have a commandment [2]to take tithes of the people according to the law; that is, of their brethren, though they [3]come out of the loins of Abraham:

[1]Ex. xxviii. 1; Num. xvii. 1-11; xviii. 7.
[2]Lev. xxvii. 30-33; Num. xviii. 26-32; Deut. xii. 6, 17; xiv. 22-29; xxvi. 12-15.
[3]Gen. xxxv. 11; xlvi. 26; Ex. i. 5.

which Abraham selected and offered to Melchisedec as the tenth of all.

5 **And verily they that are of the sons of Levi, etc.**—The Apostle goes on to demonstrate still further the very exalted personal and official dignity of Melchisedec. This he does in the first place by drawing a broad line of distinction between Melchisedec and the Levitical priests. These, he concedes, were in official rank superior to the laity, as is clearly indicated by their receiving tithes from them. But this difference of rank between the priests and the people, is modified by the fact that they were all brethren, descendants of the common stock of Abraham, and also by the fact that the priests had a legal right to tax the people as a reward for services rendered. But not so in the case of Melchisedec and Abraham. Melchisedec bore no such relation to Abraham; he was not of the same kindred, nor had he, so far as we know, any legal right to tax Abraham for his services. And yet, so great was his personal and official dignity, that even Abraham, the honored father of the whole stock of Israel, including the priesthood as well as the people, paid tithes to him and received his blessing. The whole sentence is well rendered by Delitzsch as follows: "And, indeed, while the sons of Levi receiving the priesthood, have a commandment to take tithes from the people, according to the law, that is, from their own brethren, although issued like themselves from the loins of Abraham; he, on the other hand, who hath no part in their genealogy, hath received tithes from Abraham himself, and bestowed his blessing on the possessor of the promises."

**have a commandment to take tithes of the people**—The Apostle speaks here not of all the sons of Levi, but of those only "who receive the office of the priesthood"; that is, of the house of Aaron. (Ex. 28:1; Num. 17:1-11.) These, he says, have a command to tithe the people. But we learn from Num. 18:22-32, that the people were required to pay a tithe of all their increase to the Levites, and that the Levites were in turn required to pay a tithe

6 But he whose descent is not counted from them [1]received tithes from Abraham, and blessed [2]him that had the promises.

7 And [3]without all contradiction, [4]the less is blessed of the better.

[1]Gen. xiv. 17-20.
[2]Gen. xii. 2, 3; xiii. 14-17; xvii. 4-8; xxii. 17, 18; Acts xiii. 25; Rom. iv. 13; Gal. iii. 16.
[3]1 Tim. iii. 16.
[4]Gen. xxvii. 27-40; xlviii. 15-20; xlix. 28; Num. vi. 22-27; Luke xxiv. 50, 51; 2 Cor. xiii. 14.

of this tithe to the priests. And hence some allege that there is a discrepancy between the requirements of the law and the statement that is here made by our author. But this, as in other cases, is only in appearance. It is owing simply to the very great brevity with which the Apostle makes reference to the provisions of the law. Had his object been to give us a critical analysis of the law, touching the mutual relations, duties, and obligations of the priests, Levites, and people, the case would have been very different. We would then have reason to expect that every point would be stated and discussed with clearness and precision. But in a general reference, such as our author here makes to the law, it is perfectly legitimate to say, as he does, that the priests "have a commandment to tithe the people"; that is, *indirectly* through the Levites. The priests tithed the Levites, and the Levites tithed the people. But in reality it was all done for the sake of the priesthood, for the Levites were the servants of the priests. (Num. 18: 2-6.)

6 **But he whose descent is not reckoned from them**—that is, from the sons of Levi. In this verse the Apostle brings out fully the great contrast between Melchisedec and the Levitical priests. These, indeed, tithed their brethren, a fact which may well excite our surprise when we remember that these brethren were all the children of Abraham, the honored heirs of the promises. But stranger still by far is the fact that Melchisedec, of a wholly different stock, and without any legal authority, tithed Abraham himself, and blessed him who had the promises. In all this, the transcendent dignity of Melchisedec, as the honored priest of the Most High God, is abundantly manifested.

7 **And without all contradiction, the less is blessed of the better.**—The words rendered *less* (*elatton*) and *better* (*kreitton*) are both in the neuter gender, thus indicating the general and proverbial character of the proposition. The Apostle expresses here a sort of axiomatic truth; a truth which is so very plain in

8 And here men that die receive tithes; but there he receiveth them, of
whom it is witnessed that ¹he liveth.

¹Ver. 3; Gen. xiv. 17-20; Psa. cx. 4.

---

itself, and which is so generally acknowledged that it is really beyond dispute. "Now beyond all controversy," he says, "the inferior is blessed by the superior." The one who blesses is to the one
who receives the blessing as the giver is to the receiver. So it was
in the case of Isaac and Jacob (Gen. 27 : 27-29) ; so it was in the
case of Christ and his Apostles (Luke 14: 50, 51) ; and so also it
was in the case of Melchisedec and Abraham (Gen. 19: 17-20).

8 **And here men that die receive tithes, etc.**—The word
*"here"* (*hode*) refers to the Levitical economy; and *"there"*
(*ekei*), to the administration of Melchisedec, as given in the fourteenth chapter of Genesis. Under the Law, the death of the high
priest was always made a matter of record; and so also was the
inauguration of his successor. Aaron died and left his office to his
son Eleazar; Eleazar, to Phinehas; Phinehas, to Abishua; Abishua, to Bukki; Bukki, to Uzzi, etc. (1 Chron. 6: 50-52.) And
hence it came to pass, that under the Mosaic economy, the mortality of the priesthood was one of its most prominent features. But
not so in the inspired representation which is given us of the
priesthood of Melchisedec. When we look at it as a pictorial delineation of the priesthood of Christ, we see no signs of death or
mortality in it, or about it. Every feature of it beams with life and
durability. It has in appearance neither beginning nor ending.
And hence so far as the inspired representation goes, Melchisedec
lives forever. He can never die. As Delitzsch very forcibly and
justly remarks on this point, "The witness of the Scripture concerning him is simply that he liveth. The actual historical Melchisedec no doubt died; but the Melchisedec of the second narrative does nothing but live,—fixed, as it were, by the pencil of inspiration in unchangeable existence; and so made the type of the eternal Priest, the Son of God. The sacred writer has here still only
Genesis 14: 17-20 in view: the abrupt and absolute way in which
Melchisedec is there introduced is for him a testimony that he liveth." This, and nothing more than this, I am constrained to think
is the meaning of the author. True, indeed, there is a sense in
which the type may be said to live in the antitype. David still lives

9 And as I may so say, [2]Levi also, who receiveth tithes, paid tithes in Abraham:

10 For he was yet [1]in the loins of his father when Melchisedec met him.

[2]Gen. xiv. 20; Rom. v. 12.
[1]Gen. xxxv. 11; xlvi. 26; 1 Kings viii. 19.

---

in the person of Christ; and thus it is that his throne endures throughout all generations. (Psalm 89: 19-37.) And so also Melchisedec, as a royal Priest, still lives in Christ, and his priesthood endures forever. But to this view of the matter, I do not think our author makes any reference in this connection. He is here contemplating Melchisedec as a type of Christ, not with the view of exalting Melchisedec through Christ, but rather with the view of exalting the priesthood of Christ through that of Melchisedec. And hence he speaks of Melchisedec in his official relations, simply as a type of Christ.

9 **And as I may so say,**—(*kai hos epos eipein*) and "as the saying is"; or "so to speak." This phrase is often used by Greek writers to modify or soften a paradoxical or apparently harsh expression, which is liable to be pressed too far; and so the Apostle clearly uses it in this connection. So far as he has gone, his argument might seem to be applicable only to Abraham. He has yet made no direct comparison between Melchisedec and the Levitical priesthood. But now for the purpose of covering the whole ground, so that no room might be left for Jewish objections, he proceeds to show still further that his reasoning applies to Levi and his descendants, as well as to Abraham. For, as he says, Levi also, so to speak, paid tithes through (*dia*) Abraham. How he did this, the Apostle goes on to show in the next verse.

10 **For he was yet in the loins of his father, etc.**—This declaration is given in proof of the previous allegation, that Levi himself was tithed by Melchisedec through Abraham. The fact then is indisputable; but the sense in which this was done is still a matter of legitimate inquiry. To say with some, that this is simply an "argumentum ad hominem" is to trifle with the word of God. Nothing short of an "argumentum ad rem" will at all satisfactorily meet the case and fulfill the design of the Apostle. His object is not to illustrate, but to prove; it is not to remove an objection, but to establish a fact. And hence any explanation of this difficult passage, founded on "Jewish prejudices" or "Rabbinical conceits," is

wholly out of the question. The context admits of no such evasion as this. And yet on the other hand there is danger of taking these words of the Apostle in too literal a sense; otherwise he would not have used the qualifying phrase, *"so to speak."* That Levi did not personally and by his own voluntary act pay tithes through Abraham, as his appointed agent, is very certain for as the Apostle says, Levi was not then born: he was yet in the loins of his great grandfather Abraham, when Melchisedec met him.

What then is the meaning of this passage? This will perhaps be best understood by considering a parallel case. Such a one occurs in Rom. 5: 12. Here the same Apostle says, "By one man sin entered into the world, and death by sin; and so death passed through upon all men, for that all sinned (*hemarton*)." That is, the fact that all men die, depends on the antecedent fact, that all men sinned. But how? "Not," says Paul, "after the similitude of Adam's transgression." He sinned in his own proper person; and the rest of mankind, so to speak, sinned in him. For the Apostle adds (verse 19), "by the disobedience of the one the many were made sinners." God created mankind in Adam (Gen. 1: 26, 27), and with him as the head and representative of the race he made a covenant, upon the keeping of which depended the life, not only of Adam himself, but also of his entire posterity. When he transgressed the covenant he died, and then also the race died in him; because, so to speak, they all sinned in him: for they were all still in the loins of Adam when he ate of the forbidden fruit. And hence it is that we are all by nature (*phusei*) under the curse of that broken law, and treated by God as children of wrath, until we are redeemed by the second Adam. Now just so it was with Abraham and his posterity. God made a covenant with him also, as the head and representative of his race. Their fortunes were therefore largely involved in his fortunes; their dignity, in his dignity; and their rights and privileges, in the honors which God bestowed on him as the father and founder of his own elect people. When Abraham therefore paid tithes to Melchisedec, Levi also and his posterity virtually paid tithes through him as their federal head and representative: for they were all yet in the loins of their father Abraham, when he met and honored Melchisedec as the Priest of the Most High God. This is the simple fact of the case, as it is here stated by the Apostle, and used by him as an essential element of his promises. And hence it should be received by all, as a fact, however incompetent we may be to understand the principle which underlies it in all its ethical and religious bearings. Infidels may scoff and sneer at this principle of federal representation as "unjust and absurd"; but it somehow happens that we cannot get rid of it, nor act independently of it even in secular matters. Individuals, corporations, and governments, are every day making arrangements, signing pledges, and sealing documents which involve largely the interests and fortunes of others, as well as of themselves. It would be much more becoming, then, in frail and fallible men, humbly to confess their ignorance in such cases, and to try to learn more of the infinite wisdom of God, as exhibited in the works of creation, providence, and redemption, rather than scoffingly and scornfully to reject as "unjust and absurd," matters about which they yet know but little, and into which the angels desire to look with reverence. (1 Pet. 1: 12.)

Without then making any further attempt at explanation, we simply admit the fact as here stated, that Levi himself, and of course his whole posterity including the house of Aaron, virtually paid tithes to Melchisedec through Abraham, on the principle of federal representation. And consequently it clearly follows from the premises submitted that the Levitical Priests were all inferior to Melchisedec, and still more to Christ, of whom Melchisedec was but a type.

## 2. THE LEVITICAL PRIESTHOOD AND THE LAW OF MOSES BOTH ABROGATED ON ACCOUNT OF THEIR INSUFFICIENCY; AND A BETTER GROUND OF HOPE BROUGHT IN THROUGH THE PRIESTHOOD OF CHRIST
### 7: 11-19

11 If therefore [1]perfection were by the Levitical priesthood, (for under it the people received the law,) [2]what further need was there that another priest should arise after the order of Melchisedec, and not be called after [3]the order of Aaron?

[1]Chap. viii. 7-13; x. 1-4; Gal. ii. 21; iii. 21; Col. ii. 10-17.
[2]Chap. viii. 7; Gal. iii. 21.
[3]Num. xvii. 1-11; xviii. 1-7.

11 **If therefore perfection, etc.**—The Greek word for *perfection* (*teleiosis*) means properly completion, consummation, perfection. It may therefore be used to denote the end or consummation

of any scheme, plan, or purpose. But here, it evidently means the full consummation of God's benevolent designs and purposes in reference to the redemption of mankind; including of course pardon, justification, sanctification, and whatever else is necessary in order to our enjoyment of full and perfect blessedness. All this, the Jews were wont to believe, would be finally secured to the seed of Abraham through the Levitical priesthood and the other provisions of the Old Covenant. And hence it was, that rejecting God's plan of justification by grace through faith in Christ, they went about to establish their own righteousness by the works of the Law. (Rom. 10: 3.) To those who were in danger of being misled by this delusion, the Apostle here addresses himself. If, he says, perfection were attainable through the Levitical priesthood, then whence the necessity that another priest should arise of a wholly different order? If God's honor could be promoted and man's salvation secured through the services of Aaron and his successors, then why did God say by David that he would raise up another Priest after the order of Melchisedec? Manifestly, this implies that there was imperfection in the Levitical priesthood: for otherwise, God would certainly not have abolished it, and established another. He never would have required that the blood of his own dear Son should be shed and offered for the sins of the world, if these sins could have been expiated by means of the Levitical offerings. So Paul reasons very forcibly in his letter to the Galatians. "If," he says, "there had been a law given which could have given life, then verily righteousness would have been by law." (Gal. 3: 21.) God would never have set aside the Law and introduced the Gospel, as a means of justification, had the Law been adequate to save men from their sins. "But now the Scripture hath concluded all under sin, that the promise by faith of Jesus Christ might be given to them that believe." (Gal. 3: 22.)

**for under it the people received the law.**—(*ho laos gar epi autes nenomothetetai*), *for upon it the people have received the law.* The idea is that the priesthood was, so to speak, the basis of the whole Mosaic economy. It was the main object with reference to which the law was given, and consequently it was also the ground on which the law properly rested. Had no priesthood been contemplated, then indeed no law would have been given. But as a priesthood was necessary in order to the accomplishment of

12 For the priesthood being changed, there is made of necessity ¹a change also of the law.

13 For he of whom these things are spoken pertaineth to another tribe, ¹of which no man gave attendance at the altar.

¹Ch. viii. 6-13; x. 1-18; Jer. xxxi. 31-34; Rom. iii. 21-28; vii. 1-6; 2 Cor. iii. 6-14; Gal. iii. 19-29; iv. 19-31; Col. ii. 10-17.
¹Num. xvi. 40; 2 Chron. xxvi. 16-21.

God's benevolent purposes, then it followed that the law was also necessary, not only to prescribe and regulate the several functions of the priesthood, but also to serve as a civil code, to convict men of sin, to restrain idolatry, and to support in various ways the worship of the true God, till the Seed should come to whom the promise was made. (Gal. 3: 19.) It is obvious, therefore, that the object of the Apostle in introducing this parenthetical clause, was simply to keep prominent before his readers the fundamental bearings of the Levitical priesthood; to remind them that it was in fact the foundation of the Old Economy, and that the whole law of Moses stood or fell with it.

12 **For the priesthood being changed, etc.**—This clearly follows from the premises submitted. Concede that the priesthood was the basis of the law, the ground on which it rested; and then it follows of necessity that any change in the priesthood must have an effect also on the whole law. Take away the foundation, and the superstructure must fall to the ground. Remove from any system that which is central and fundamental, and then all that depends on it falls at once for want of the necessary support. The abrogation of the Levitical priesthood was therefore not a matter of small moment. God would never have effected a change involving such consequences, for light and unimportant reasons. But this very change he has effected as our author now proceeds to show.

13 **For he of whom these things are spoken**—The Apostle assumes here what was doubtless conceded by all his readers, and of which he has, in fact, already spoken with sufficient fullness (see notes on 5: 5, 6), that Christ has been made a priest by the decree of him who said to him, "Thou art my Son, this day have I begotten thee." But this, our author insists, implies of necessity a transfer of the priesthood; and by consequence, the abrogation of the whole law. For it is evident, he says, that our Lord has sprung up as a branch out of the house of David (Jer. 23: 5), and from the tribe of Judah. But according to the law of Moses, none

14 For it is evident that ²our Lord sprang out of Judah; of which tribe
Moses spake nothing concerning |priesthood: *priests*|.

15 And it is yet far more evident: for that ³after the similitude of Melchisedec there ariseth another priest,

----

²Gen. xlix. 10; Isa. xi. 1-5; Jer. xxiii. 5, 6; Micah v. 2; Matt. i. 3-16; Luke ii. 23-
33; Rom. i. 3; Rev. v. 5.
³Psa. cx. 4.

----

but those of the house of Aaron were allowed to minister at the
altar. (Num. 16-18: 7.) And consequently it follows that in the
decree given in Psalm 110: 4, God contemplated a transfer of the
priesthood, and also the abolition of the whole Sinaitic Covenant.

14 **For it is evident that our Lord sprang out of Judah;**—
This is evident from the given references: see particularly the
genealogies of Christ as recorded by Matthew and Luke. In the
word "sprang" (*anatetalken*), there is a beautiful allusion to the
springing up of plants, as in Isa. 11: 1; Jer. 23: 5; 33: 15; and
Zech. 6: 12. Or it may be, as some have alleged, that the Apostle
draws his imagery from the rising of the sun, as does the prophet
Malachi (Mal. 4: 2) ; or from the rising of a star, as Balaam does
in Num. 24: 17. But as he has here in view the genealogy of
Christ, it is more natural to suppose that, in harmony with Hebrew
usage, he refers to Christ's springing up as a branch from the roots
of Jesse.

15 **And it is yet far more evident:**—What is far more evident?
In reply to this, it is alleged (1) that it is the distinction between
the Levitical priesthood and that of the New Testament (Chrysostom) ; (2) that it is the fact that our Lord sprang out of Judah
(Ebrard) ; (3) that the law of Moses is abrogated (Alford) ; (4)
that perfection was not attainable through the Levitical priesthood
(Delitzsch) ; and (5) that a change of the priesthood involves of
necessity a change also of the law (Tholuck). The passage is confessedly a very difficult one, and where there is so great a diversity
of views even among the ablest critics, it becomes us to be cautious and modest in giving our own judgment. I fully agree with
Alford, however, in this, that the view of Ebrard is wholly inadmissible, and that "his whole commentary on this verse is one of
those curiosities of exegesis which unhappily abound in his otherwise valuable commentary." But it seems to me that the more
judicious Alford has also failed to perceive the exact point of the
argument. The abolition of the law is indeed a necessary con-

16 Who is made, not after ¹the law of a carnal commandment, but after ²the power of an endless life.

¹Chap. ix. 9, 10; x. 1; Rom. iv. 1; Eph. ii. 15.
²Vers. 21, 24, 25, 28; Acts xiii. 34; Rom. vi. 9; Rev. i. 18.

sequence of what is here uppermost in the mind of the Apostle, but it is certainly not the main thought which he here endeavors to set forth and support by a twofold argument. This, according to my understanding of the passage, is the fact, not merely that the Levitical priesthood was insufficient; but more particularly that, in consequence of this, there had been made such a change in the priesthood as in effect to abolish both the Levitical order of priesthood, and also the law which was given in reference to it. This the Apostle proves (1) from the fact that Christ, though of the tribe of Judah, is now a priest, contrary to the provisions of the law (Num. 16: 40; 17: 1-9) ; and (2) from the fact that, according to the decree of Jehovah Christ's priesthood is of a wholly different *order* from that of the house of Aaron. This it is which makes the aforesaid change so very obvious. True, indeed, the transfer of sacerdotal functions from the tribe of Levi to the tribe of Judah, is very strong evidence of such a change, but not so strong as that which we gather from the transfer which was made according to the oath of Jehovah, from the order of Levi to that of Melchisedec. This thought our author now proceeds to develop more fully in the following verse.

16 **Who is made, not after the law of a carnal commandment,**—The Levitical priests were all so constituted. Their appointment was made, not on account of any superior excellence on their part, but solely on the ground of carnal descent. It was made, therefore, as Paul says, "according to the law of a carnal commandment," but Christ received his appointment "according to the power of an endless life." These two clauses are placed in contrast with each other, and they will therefore be best understood by comparing together the several antithetical words of which they are composed. Thus we find that *law* is opposed to *power; carnal,* to *endless;* and *commandment* to *life.* By the word *law* (*nomos*) in this connection, some understand the whole law of Moses (Chrysostom, Calvin, Bengel, Tholuck) ; but others, with more propriety, understand by it simply the rule of priestly succession as prescribed by the carnal commandment. This is the

17 For | he testifieth: *it is testified*|, [1]Thou art a priest forever after the order of Melchisedec.

[1]Psa. cx. 4.

---

view of Alford, T. S. Green, Moll, and others. In either case it had reference only to outward and perishable forms, and it was therefore wholly destitute of the internal power which commended Christ to the Father, and on the ground of which he received his appointment from the Father, as the high priest of our confession. The Levitical priests had all the form of godliness, but many of them were wholly destitute of its power. But in Christ dwelleth all the fullness of the Godhead bodily. (Col. 2: 9.) And hence he is able to save, even to the uttermost, all who come to God by him. The word *carnal* (*sarkinos*) may have reference (1) to anything composed of flesh; (2) to anything relating to the flesh; and (3) to whatever has the properties, characteristics, or accidents of the flesh, such as frailty, weakness, corruptibility, etc. As it is here used in contrast with "endless" or imperishable (*akatalutou*) it seems to indicate externality, frailty, or perishableness. The idea is that the commandment was outward and perishable, liable at any time to be changed or abrogated, but the life of Christ is inherent and imperishable. It is this intrinsic difference between the two orders of priesthood which makes them so very distinct from one another, and which, therefore, serves to make the aforesaid change so very obvious.

17 **For he testifieth, Thou art a priest forever after the order of Melchisedec.**—Or rather, *Thou shalt be a priest forever after the order of Melchisedec.* The verb is not expressed in either the Hebrew or the Greek, but the historical circumstances clearly indicate that the decree of Jehovah, as given in Psalm 110: 4, has reference to the future. Christ was not a high priest in the time of David, nor could he become a priest after the order of Melchisedec until after his death, burial, and resurrection. For if we draw a picture of the priesthood of Melchisedec, we see in it no beginning, no ending, no interruption by death or anything else. Nothing, in fact, appears in it but life—continued and uninterrupted life, crowned with royal and sacerdotal honors. And just so it must ever be with every correct representation of the priesthood of Christ. It must, in these respects, resemble the priesthood of Mel-

18 For there is verily [1]a disannulling of the commandment going before for the weakness and unprofitableness thereof.

[1]Ch. viii. 6-13; x. 1-9; Rom. vii. 1-6; 2 Cor. iii. 7-11; Gal. iii. 19, 25; iv. 19-31; Eph. ii. 14-16; Col. ii. 10-17.

chisedec, for they are of the same order, and are therefore similar in these essential points. That Christ acted, in some respects, both as a king and a priest while he was on earth we may readily grant. But such acts were only preparatory, and therefore extraordinary. His royal entrance into Jerusalem, for instance, and his giving himself up voluntarily to death, were but a shadow of what was to follow. The fact is, that the precise time when he was fully invested with the royal and sacerdotal honors and prerogatives of the new dispensation, is not known to mortals. The first manifestation of this was given on the day of Pentecost, just fifty days after his resurrection. But then he appeared, as Melchisedec appeared to Abraham, in all his royal and sacerdotal dignity, to bless all who would acknowledge his authority as the priest of the Most High God. And just so he ever lives, and reigns, and intercedes for his people. For like Melchisedec, he had no predecessor, and like him he will have no successor. As he is the only begotten Son of the Father, so also he is now the only king and high priest that is appointed by the Father; and as such he will sit as a priest upon his throne until the purposes of God in reference to the redemption of mankind shall have been fully accomplished. Then, and not till then, will he deliver up both the kingdom and the priesthood to the Father. But that epoch, like the beginning of his administration, is concealed from the eyes of mortals. In the representation of his priesthood, therefore, as given by the Holy Spirit, there is neither beginning nor ending. Like Melchisedec, he abides a priest perpetually. See note on verse 27.

18 **For there is verily a disannulling of the commandment** —In this verse and the next following, we have the argument of the paragraph amplified and brought out to its legitimate results. In the twelfth verse, the Apostle speaks simply of a change or transfer (*metathesis*) of the priesthood and the law. But that change, as he now proceeds to show, results of necessity in a complete abrogation (*athetesis*) or setting aside of the commandment relating to the priesthood, and also of the whole law, in order to make way for the bringing in of a better ground of hope, through

19 For ²the law made nothing perfect, but ³the bringing in of a better hope
did; by the which we draw nigh unto God.

²Ch. viii. 6-13; Rom. iii. 21; vii. 7-25; viii. 3; Gal. ii. 21; iii. 11, 21, 24.
³Chap. iv. 14-16; ix. 11-14; x. 19-22; Jer. xxxi. 31-34; Rom. iii. 21-31; x. 1-10; Gal.
iv. 21-31.

the Gospel of our blessed Lord and Savior Jesus Christ. The construction of the sentence is well given, and the main thought happily expressed by Delitzsch as follows: "For while there taketh
place, on the one hand, a disannulling of the foregoing commandment, because of its weakness and insufficiency (for the law had
perfected nothing), there is, on the other hand, a bringing in, over
and above, of a better hope, through which we draw nigh to God."

19 **For the law made nothing perfect,**—This parenthetical
clause is thrown in here for the purpose of explaining on what account the law was abrogated. It was an introductory arrangement, and had not the power to bring anything to perfection.
Had it been sufficient to meet and accomplish God's benevolent designs in reference to the justification, sanctification, and redemption of mankind, then indeed, as our author very clearly intimates
in the eleventh verse of this chapter, and also in Gal. 3: 21, perfection would have been by the law. In that event, Christ would
never have died for the salvation of the world (Gal. 2: 21), and
the New Economy would never have been inaugurated. But the
fact is, as here stated, that owing to the weakness and imperfection
of the flesh (Rom. 8: 3) the law perfected nothing. And hence
when God had accomplished his benevolent designs in giving it to
the Israelites, he then took it out of the way, and gave the Gospel
to the world as the only efficient means of purifying our "consciences from dead works," and fitting us for his service here, and
for the enjoyment of his presence hereafter. (9: 14.)

**but the bringing in of a better hope did;**—This is an erroneous construction, and serves to mislead the reader. The idea
which the Apostle wishes to convey to his readers is simply this:
that, on the one hand, there is a setting aside of the Old Economy
on account of its weakness and insufficiency; and on the other
hand, there is the bringing in of the New Economy, by which we
may all now, as priests, draw nigh to God and worship him in
spirit and in truth. So Alford, Green, and others, rightly construe
this passage, and this rendering is sustained by such other passages
as Rom. 5: 1, 2; Heb. 10: 19-22, and 1 Pet. 2: 5.

## 2. THE SUPERIORITY OF CHRIST'S PRIESTHOOD PROVED FROM THE FACT THAT, UNLIKE THE LEVITICAL, IT WAS INAUGURATED WITH AN OATH
### 7:20-22

20 And inasmuch as [1]not without an oath he was made priest:

[1]Psa. cx. 4.

---

20 **And inasmuch as not without an oath he was made priest:** —I have in the analysis of this, as in that of every other section, endeavored to assist the reader by indicating the extent and scope of each of the several paragraphs of which it is composed. The change of thought at the close of each of these may, I think, be readily perceived by all who read the Epistle with even ordinary care and reflection. Caution, however, is necessary lest perchance we make the breach of thought greater than what is really demanded or warranted by the construction and course of the argument. The connection of thought is very close throughout this entire section; and the several parts of it are all very intimately connected together, as links of the same chain. In the first paragraph, we have discussed and demonstrated very clearly, the superiority of the Melchisedecian order of priesthood. In the second, the Apostle shows that it was God's purpose of old, even in the time of David, to set aside the Old Economy and introduce the New; thereby proving indirectly from Psalm 110:4, the very great superiority of Christ's priesthood over that of Aaron. But as yet, the meaning of this oracle of Jehovah is but partially developed. It furnishes indeed the main line of thought throughout the remainder of the section, leading the Apostle to the sublime conclusion in which his whole argument finally culminates, that Jesus is now a High Priest and Minister of the Holy of holies, and also of the true Tabernacle which the Lord pitched and not man. The third phase of thought in this line of argument is given, as indicated, in verses 20-22; in which the Apostle further demonstrates the superiority of Christ's priesthood from the fact that it was confirmed and its perpetuity guaranteed by the oath of God. The reasoning of the Apostle, says Dr. Macknight, "is founded on the conceded fact that God never interposed his oath except to show the certainty and immutability of the thing sworn. Thus he swore to Abraham, Gen. 22:16-18, that in his seed all the nations of the

21 (For ¹those priests were made without an oath; but this with an oath by him that said unto him, ²The Lord sware and will not repent, Thou art a priest forever [after the order of Melchisedec] :)

¹Ex. xxviii. 1; Num. xviii. 1-7.
²Gen. xxii. 15-18; Ex. xxxii. 13; Psa. cx. 4; Isa. xlv. 23; Jer. xxii. 5; Micah vii. 20.

---

earth should be blessed; and to the rebellious Israelites, that they should never enter into his rest, Deut. 1: 34, 35; and to Moses, that he should not go into Canaan, Deut. 4: 21; and to David, that his seed should endure forever, and his throne unto all generations, Psalm 89: 4.   Wherefore, since Christ was made a priest, not without an oath that he should be a priest forever after the order of Melchisedec, that circumstance showed God's purpose never to change or abolish his priesthood; and never to change or abolish the covenant which was established on his priesthood. Whereas the Levitical priesthood and the Law of Moses being established without an oath, were thereby declared to be changeable at God's pleasure."

21 **For those priests were made without an oath:** *without the swearing of an oath.*—(*horkomosia* from *orchos* an oath and *omnumi* to swear).   God simply said to Moses, "Take unto thee Aaron thy brother and his sons with him, from among the children of Israel, that he may minister unto me in the priest's office, even Aaron, Nadab and Abihu, Eleazar and Ithamar Aaron's sons." (Ex. 28: 1.)   There was nothing extraordinary in the mode of their appointment.   They were consecrated merely in the way of ordinary legislation, with becoming rites and ceremonies.   See Ex. 24 and Lev. 8 and 9.   But the manner of Christ's appointment was altogether extraordinary.   God himself made oath on the occasion, as David testifies in Psalm 110: 4, "Jehovah has sworn and will not repent, Thou art a priest forever after the order of Melchisedec."   It is therefore clearly indicated that God will never set aside the priesthood of Christ, as he did that of Levi, in order to make way for another of a different order.   When God is said to repent, the meaning is that he simply wills a change; and when it is said that he will not repent, it means that he will never will a change.   And consequently there is nothing beyond the priesthood of Christ, to which it will ever give place, as a means of accomplishing God's benevolent purposes in the redemption of mankind. Christ himself will continue to officiate as a priest upon his throne,

22 By so much was Jesus made [3]a surety of [4]a better testament.

[3]Gen. xliii. 9; xliv. 32; Job xvii. 3; Prov. vi. 1; xx. 16.
[4]Chap. viii. 6-12; ix. 15-23; x ii.24; xiii. 20; Matt. xxvi. 28; Gal. iv. 21-31.

until the work of man's redemption shall have been fully consummated.

22 **By so much, etc.**—The Levitical priests received their appointment according to the law of a mutable and transitory Institution; an Institution which perfected nothing, because it was in its design wholly preparatory and introductory to a better state of things; and which was therefore finally set aside in order to make way for the inauguration of a new and better Institution, of which Christ is made the Surety. But as before intimated, this new arrangement embracing the priesthood of Christ and all else pertaining to the justification, sanctification, and redemption of mankind, can never be set aside in order to make room for anything else. God's oath is given as a pledge of this; and Christ himself being constituted a priest by the oath of God, now stands as security that this new covenant or arrangement will never be abrogated, until the benevolent designs of God shall have been accomplished in the salvation of all who believe and obey him. For as the Levitical priesthood was the basis of the Old Covenant (verse 11), so also is the priesthood of Christ the basis of the New Covenant; and as this will, according to the oath of Jehovah, endure to the final consummation of all that God has promised by his holy Apostles and Prophets, so also will the New Covenant of which Christ is made the Surety, continue until God's eternal government is magnified in the everlasting salvation of the righteous, and the eternal condemnation of the wicked. This, the oath of Jehovah clearly indicates showing, as Peter says, that this is the true grace of God in which we now stand. (1 Pet. 5: 12.) And hence the difference of being made a priest with or without an oath is very great; and just so great is the difference between the Old Covenant and the New.

The Greek word rendered *testament* (*diatheke*) means properly a disposition or an arrangement. And it is accordingly used (1) to denote any arrangement made by a superior for the benefit of an inferior; such, for example, as that which God made for the Israelites at Mount Sinai. And (2) it is used in the same sense as *suntheke* to denote a mutual agreement between equals; such as the covenant which Abraham made with Abimelech. (Gen. 21 : 22-32.)

In our text, it is evidently used in the former sense, to denote God's gracious arrangement made through Christ for the salvation of the world on given conditions. But what shall we call this *diatheke?* The word *arrangement,* or *disposition,* is too generic; and the word *will,* or *testament,* is specifically different. For as our author says (9: 16), before a testament can be carried into effect, there must of necessity take place the death of the testator. In this sense, which is very common in the Greek classics, the word *diatheke* can never of course be literally and strictly applied to any of God's arrangements for the benefit of mankind. And to the word *covenant* there is this objection, that in its usual acceptation it represents the parties as too much on an equality. It corresponds much better with the second meaning of *diatheke* than with the first. But as it is now used by our writers to represent *diatheke* in both senses, it is perhaps on the whole the best word that we can employ in this instance. This covenant is better than the old covenant in many respects (see notes, on 8: 6-13), but chiefly in this, that founded as it is on the everlasting and efficacious priesthood of Christ, it cannot fail to secure for all who accept of its conditions, free, full, and everlasting forgiveness.

Of this better covenant, Christ is made the Surety (*enguos*). But what is the meaning of this? Some think that the word is used in the same sense as *mediator* (*mesites*) in 8: 6; 9: 15; 12: 24; Gal. 3: 19, 20; and 1 Tim. 2: 5. But if this had been Paul's meaning, he would doubtless have used the word mediator as in other instances. The word *enguos* does not occur elsewhere in the New Testament; but in classic Greek, it means *a surety, a sponsor* or *a bondsman*: one who pledges his name, property, or influence that a promise shall be fulfilled, or that something else shall be done. In this sense it is manifestly used in our text. Jesus has become the surety, sponsor, or bondsman of the New Covenant. But in what sense, and for what purpose? "It can not be," says Albert Barnes, "that he is a bondsman for God that he will maintain the covenant, and be true to the promises which he makes; for we need no such security of the Divine faithfulness and veracity. It cannot be that he becomes responsible for the Divine conduct in any way; for no such responsibility is needed or possible. But it must mean that he is security, or bondsman on the part of man." This is plausible, but it does not well harmonize with the context.

The argument of the Apostle requires us to understand this security as given on the part of God for the greater encouragement and
consolation of his children; just as he gave the oath to Abraham
and to his seed after him. (6: 17, 18.) "Jesus," says Lünemann,
"is become the surety of a better covenant; that is, in his person
security is given to men that a better covenant is made and
sanctioned by God. For Christ, the Son of God, became man to
publish this covenant on earth; he has sealed it with his death and
sufferings; and by his resurrection from the dead, he was declared
with power to be sent by God as the founder of such a covenant."

## 4. THE FREQUENT CHANGES IN THE LEVITICAL PRIEST-
HOOD OCCASIONED BY THE DEATH OF THE HIGH
PRIEST, CONTRASTED WITH THE EVER-ENDURING
AND UNCHANGEABLE CHARACTER OF
CHRIST'S PRIESTHOOD
### 7 : 23-25

23 And they truly [1]were many priests, because they were not suffered to
continue by reason of death:
24 But this man, because [2]he continueth ever, hath an unchangeable priesthood.

[1] Chron. vi. 3-15; Neh. xii. 10, 11.
[2]Chap. vii. 16, 17, 25, 28; xiii. 8; Psa. cx. 4; Rev. i. 18.

23 **And they truly were many priests,**—The contrast made
here by the Apostle, is not between Christ and all the Levitical
priests, but, as we learn from the context, only between Christ and
the high priests. In this sense the word *priest* (*hiereus*), is often
used in the Holy Scriptures; as, for example, in Ex. 29: 30; 31:
10; Lev. 1: 7; 4: 3, 5, 6, 7, etc. The title *high priest* occurs first
in Lev. 21: 10. See note 4: 14. These high priests under the law
were not permitted to continue long in office, because they were
soon cut off by death. Thus, Joseph, surnamed Caiaphas, who
served from A.D. 26 to A.D. 35, was the sixty-seventh in the line
of Aaron, and Phannias, the last who wore the mitre, A.D. 70, was
the eighty-first in order, showing that mortality was a prominent
feature in the Levitical priesthood. See "Calmet's Dictionary of
the Holy Bible:" *Art. on the priesthood.*

24 **But this man, because he continueth ever, etc.**—Christ is
not subject to death like the Levitical priests. He continues in life
forever, and hence he has an unchangeable priesthood. This same

25 Wherefore [1]he is able also to save them to the uttermost [2]that come unto God by him, seeing [3]he ever liveth to make intercession for them.

[1]Chap. ii. 18; v. 9; Matt. xxviii. 18; John vi. 37-40; x. 29, 30; 2 Tim. i. 12.
[2]Chap. x. 19-22; xiii. 15; John xiv. 6; Rom. v. 2; Eph. ii. 18.
[3]Chap. ix. 24; Isa. liii. 12; John xiv. 13, 16; xvi. 23, 24; xvii. 9-16; Rom. viii. 34; 1 John ii. 1, 2.

point of contrast was slightly touched on by the Apostle in the eighth verse, and also in the sixteenth. But in the former instance, as Alford justly remarks, his object was to show the abiding nature of the superiority of the priesthood; its endurance in Melchisedec, and in Christ, Melchisedec's antitype, as contrasted with dying men who here receive tithes, and in the latter it was to bring out the differences between the ordinances which constituted the two priesthoods, the one, the law of a carnal commandment; the other the power of an endless life. Here, however, in the twenty-fourth verse, it is the *personal* contrast that is brought out and made prominent. The many change, but the one abides. And hence he has an unchangeable priesthood.

25 **Wherefore he is able also, etc.**—The object of the Apostle in this verse is very nearly the same as in Rom. 8: 28-31; viz.: to give to the ransomed sons and daughters of the Lord God Almighty strong assurance that if they continue faithful to the end of life, Christ will certainly save them from all the power and devices of their enemies. But here he does not embrace so wide a range of thought as he does in the eighth of Romans. There, he refers particularly to the decrees of God as indicating his benevolent designs and purposes with respect to all the faithful in Christ Jesus. But here, the ground of consolation is the fact that Christ ever lives "to make intercession for those who come unto God by him." The Apostle assumes, of course, that in order to redeem man Christ became flesh and dwelt among us; that for this purpose he died and made an offering of his own blood for the sins of the world, and that to this end he has been invested with all authority in heaven and on the earth. All this is implied in the argument. But the main ground of encouragement in this paragraph is the consoling fact that Christ, having died for our sins according to the Scriptures, and having also by the offering of his own blood made an atonement for the sins of the world, now *lives*, and *lives forever,* to intercede for those who come unto God by him, and so to perfect their salvation.

The word *intercede* (*eutunkano*) is used here in a very comprehensive sense, to denote all that Christ is now doing for the justification, sanctification, and redemption of his people. Seated, as he is, on the right hand of the Father, and clothed with omnipotent power and authority, he is ever ready to plead for those who have been cleansed by his blood, ever ready to defend them against all the assaults of their enemies, and, in a word, ever ready to make all things work together for their good.

## 5. THE SUPERIORITY OF CHRIST'S PRIESTHOOD PROVED AND ILLUSTRATED FROM HIS OWN PURE AND SPOTLESS CHARACTER, AND THE PERFECTION OF THE ONE OFFERING WHICH HE MADE FOR THE SINS OF THE WORLD
### 7 : 26-28

26 For [4]such an high priest became us, who is holy, harmless, undefiled, separate from sinners, and [5]made higher than the heavens;

[4]Chap. iv. 15; viii. 1; ix. 11-14; x. 12-14; 2 Cor. v. 21; Rev. i. 17, 18.
[5]Ch. i. 3; iv. 14; viii. 1; xii. 2; Eph. i. 20, 21; iv. 10; 1 Pet. iii. 22.

26 **For such an high priest became us,**—That is, we ourselves needed just such a high priest; such a one as the Apostle has described in this section, and such as he describes still further in this paragraph: one "who is holy, harmless, undefiled, separate from sinners, and made higher than the heavens." The word *holy* (*hosios*) means godlike, pious, devout, religious. It is used here to denote the pious and reverential bearing of Christ in his relations to God. *Harmless* (*akakos*) means without malice or ill-will to anyone. It indicates a person who is kind, benevolent, and gracious to all. *Undefiled* (*amiaitos*) means without spot, immaculate. It here denotes that Christ is never, like the Levitical priests, disqualified for the performance of his duties in consequence of any personal defilement. There is no defect or blemish about him. "He is the chief among ten thousand, and the one that is altogether lovely." He is constantly purifying others, but he is himself never defiled. And hence there is no necessity that he should, like the Levitical priests, bathe and purify himself before making purification for the sins of the people. He is moreover *"separate from sinners,"* not only because he is himself without sin (4 : 15), but also perhaps because he is exalted far above all sinners. *"And made higher than the heavens,"* or, as Paul says in Eph. 4 : 10, "He is

27 Who needeth not [1]daily, as those high priests, to offer up sacrifice, [2]first for his own sins, and [3]then for the people's: for [4]this he did once, when he offered up himself.

[1]Ex. xxix. 38-46; Num. xxviii. 1-10.
[2]Ch. v. 3; ix. 7; Lev. iv. 3-12; xvi. 6-14.
[3]Lev. iv. 13-21; xvi. 15-19.
[4]Ch. ix. 14, 25, 28; x. 10-13; Isa. liii. 4-12; Dan. ix. 26; Rom. vi. 10; Eph. v. 2, 25; Titus ii. 14.

exalted far above all heavens." This is, by some expositors, construed as indicating that Christ has gone literally above all created heavens, even the dwelling place of angels and of the spirits of the just made perfect, into "the place of God," the uncreated glory of the Divine presence and essence, "which," says Delitzsch, "is not essentially different from God himself, who is above all, and through all, and in all." (Eph. 4:6.) And again he says, "He [Christ] has passed away from the world and entered into God— and now he mediates for us in the Holy of holies of the Divine nature." This, it seems to me, is but "to darken counsel by words without knowledge." Delitzsch is an able critic, and, in the main, a judicious commentator, but occasionally his speculations savor more of the Hegelian philosophy than of the inspiration of the Holy Scriptures. I am not sure, however, that I myself fully understand the meaning of the Spirit in some of these apparently hyperbolical expressions. But I am inclined to think that nothing more is intended by the Apostle than to strongly indicate Christ's absolute supremacy over the whole created universe, as when he says to the brethren at Ephesus, "God hath put all things under his [Christ's] feet, and given him to be the Head over all things to the church, which is his body, the fullness of Him that filleth all in all." (Eph. 1: 22, 23.) See also 1 Cor. 15: 27, and 1 Pet. 3: 22.

27 **Who needeth not daily, etc.**—The high priest was officially the head of the Levitical priesthood, and to him was therefore committed, in a special manner, an oversight of all the services of the Tabernacle. He was not required by any law or statute to offer the daily sacrifice in person, but as the head of the priesthood, he was of course chiefly responsible for the offering of the daily sacrifice, and also all the other sacrifices of the year. And hence what was done by a subordinate priest might be said to be done by the high priest, on the principle that "what any one does by another he does himself."

For a like reason, being first in authority and first in responsibility, he was also relatively the first for whom the daily, weekly, monthly, and yearly sacrifices were offered. On the day of atonement he was therefore required to slay a young bullock and make an atonement for himself and his house, before he was allowed to make expiation for the sins of the people. (Lev. 16: 11-15.) But in the daily offerings, the distinction between himself and the people is not made so obvious, because, in this case, there was but one lamb offered in the morning and one in the evening. (Ex. 29: 38-46; Num. 28: 1-10.) It is obvious, however, from the nature of the case, as well as from the words of our text, that the high priest was relatively the first represented in the daily, as well as in the yearly offerings. He, like the rest of the Israelites, sinned daily, and hence the necessity that he should make a daily offering, either in his own proper person, or through a representative, first for his own sins and then for the sins of the people. For priority in point of privilege always implies priority in point of obligation. This is a law of the moral universe.

**For this he did once when he offered up himself.**—What did he do once? or rather, once for all (*ephapax*)? Evidently, he offered himself once, and once only, for the sins of the people. To say that the offering was for his own sins, as well as for the sins of the people, would be blasphemous, and plainly contrary to one of the most clearly illustrated laws of sacrifice under the Old Economy, that none but an innocent victim could suffer for the guilty. And besides, it is contradictory of what is taught elsewhere in this same Epistle. See notes on 4: 15 and 7: 26. Beyond all doubt then it was for the sins of the people, and for these only, that Christ offered himself once for all.

But when and where did he do this? Was it when he expired on the cross? Or was it when he "entered into that within the Vail," to make an atonement for the sins of the world? Or does the Holy Spirit in this remark refer to both of these events as together constituting the one great offering?

Under the Law, the victim was first brought to the north side of the altar of burnt-offerings, and there the sinner was required to lay his hand upon its head and kill it. (Lev. 1: 4, 5; 3: 2, 8, 13; 4: 4, etc.) If the whole congregation sinned, the Elders were required to act as their representatives. (Lev. 4: 15.) On the Day of Atonement, the High Priest performed this service for the people;

but not until he had first offered a young bullock for himself and his house. (Lev. 16: 11-16.) The slaying of the victim was not therefore, of necessity, a priestly act. This was only preparatory to the offering, and was usually performed by the sinner himself. But after this was done, the priests were required to dispose of the several parts of the victim, as prescribed in the Law. On the Day of atonement the High Priest took the blood of the victim with incense into the Most Holy Place; and there, while burning the incense before the Lord, he sprinkled of the blood seven times on and before the Mercy-Seat; making an atonement for the Most Holy Place itself, and also for all the people. In like manner he made an atonement for the Tabernacle of the congregation and for the Altar of burnt-offerings. The fat of the victim was then consumed on the Altar, and its flesh was burned without the camp. (Lev. 16: 15-28.)

This reference to the Old Economy may serve to illustrate in some measure the great atoning sacrifice of the Lord Jesus. He, like an innocent lamb, had no direct agency in putting himself to death. This was done by sinners. Jews and Gentiles united in laying their guilty hands on his sacred and consecrated head, and in hurrying him off to the cross. He was by them led as a lamb to the slaughter, "and as a sheep before her shearer is dumb, so he opened not his mouth." (Isa. 53 : 7.) True, indeed, he came from Heaven to Earth, and assumed our nature, so that he might by the grace of God taste death for every man. And for this purpose he went up to Jerusalem before the Passover (Mark 10: 32-34), and gave himself up to the people, knowing perfectly well all that was about to befall him there. It is not too much to say that he even sought death; went voluntarily to the cross, and gave up his life a ransom for the many. But in this there was no priestly offering. It was all preparatory to the great sin-offering that Christ was about to make in the Holy of holies for the sins of the world. That the Apostle may have some reference here to Christ's death on the cross, as well as the offering of his blood in Heaven, is quite probable. These two events are, of course, inseparably connected, but not I think as parts of the atoning act. The former of these, like his incarnation, is rather preparatory to this. And hence it seems most probable, that Christ did not begin to act in the full capacity of a Priest, till after his resurrection. Then, and not till

28 For ¹the law maketh men high priests which have infirmity; but ²the word of the oath, which was since the law, maketh the Son, ³who is consecrated for evermore.

¹Chap. v. 1, 2; Ex. xxxii. 21-24; Lev. iv. 3; Num. xii. 1-11; 1 Sam. ii. 27-36.
²Psa. cx. 4.
³Chap. ii. 10; vii. 21, 24; x. 12.

then, was he made a Priest forever after the order of Melchisedec. See note on verse 17.

This view of the matter is corroborated by what is further said of Christ's priesthood in this Epistle. In 8: 3, for instance, our author after saying that Christ is now a High Priest, and that as such he must have something to offer, goes on to state in substance, that he could not lawfully make his offering on Earth; and that he is therefore exalted to Heaven, and made "a Minister of the Sanctuary and of the true Tabernacle, which the Lord pitched, and not man." To the same effect is also his teaching in 9: 7, 12, 14, 24-26; 10: 10, 11, 14. From all of which it is, I think, manifest that Christ, as our great High Priest, entered into Heaven itself, and there once for all made an offering of himself unto God for us.

28 **For the law maketh men high priests who have infirmity;**—Such was the character of the Levitical High Priests. Some of them were very wicked, proud, vain, and ambitious men: and all of them, without exception, were subject to the common weaknesses and infirmities of our nature. Even Aaron himself, the first and doubtless one of the best of the order, made a golden calf and encouraged the people to worship the idol. (Ex. 32: 1-29.) And hence the necessity that these High Priests should daily offer up sacrifices for themselves as well as for the sins of the people. But not so with Jesus, the Son of God, who was made a High Priest by "the word of the oath" which was given after the Law. He has by the one offering of himself in the heavenly Sanctuary, not only made expiation for the sins of the people, but by the sufferings and trials which he endured on Earth he has himself been perfected (*teteleiomenos*) forevermore. See notes on 2: 10 and verse 9.

## 6. THE SUPERIORITY OF CHRIST'S PRIESTHOOD FURTHER DEMONSTRATED FROM THE HIGHER AND BETTER SPHERE OF HIS MINISTRY
### 8:1-5

1 Now of the things which we have spoken this is the sum: [1]We have such a high priest, [2]who is set on the right hand of the throne of the Majesty in the heavens:
2 [3]A minister of the sanctuary, and of [4]the true tabernacle, which the Lord pitched, [and] not man.

[1]Chap. vii. 26; ix. 11-14; x. 12-14.
[2]Chap. i. 3, 13; xii. 2; Rev. iii. 21.
[3]Chap. i. 7; ix. 8-12; x. 21; Ex. xxviii. 1, 35; Rom. xv. 8.
[4]Chap. iii. 6; ix. 11; x. 21; Matt. xvi. 18; Acts xv. 16, 17; 1 Cor. iii. 16; 2 Cor. vi. 16; Eph. ii. 20-22; 1 Tim. iii. 15; 1 Pet. ii. 5.

---

1 **Now of the things which we have spoken this is the sum.** Or more literally: *But the crown upon the things spoken [is this]; we have such a High Priest who sat down on the right hand of the throne of the Majesty in the heavens; a Minister of the Sanctuary and of the true Tabernacle which the Lord pitched and not man.*—The word rendered *sum* (*kephalaion*) means (1) that which is chief or principal; (2) the sum or result of numbers added together and set down at the head of the column; (3) the crown or that which gives completeness to anything, and (4) the division of a book, as a chapter or section. The object of the Apostle is not to give a summary of what was said before, for in the next verse, he states as an additional argument, the sublime fact that Jesus is now a Minister of the heavenly Sanctuary and of the true Tabernacle which the Lord pitched and not man. His idea therefore seems to be this: that in what follows we have not only the chief, but also the crowning point of the whole argument. It all culminates in the glorious and important fact that Jesus is now a High Priest and Minister, not of the typical economy, but of the real; not of the shadow, but of the substance.

**who is set on the right hand, etc.**—*Who sat down (ekathisen)*: that is, when he made his one offering in the heavenly Sanctuary. The best commentary on these words is given by the Apostle himself in 10: 11-13. "Every High Priest," he says, [belonging to the Levitical order] "standeth daily ministering and offering oftentimes the same sacrifices which can never take away sins. But this man after he had offered one sacrifice for sins, forever sat down on the right hand of God; from henceforth expecting till his enemies he made his footstool."

2 **A minister of the sanctuary,**—The word rendered *minister*
(*leitourgos*) means a public officer of high and honorable rank,
whether civil, military, or religious. It is here applied to Christ, as
the High Priest of the New Covenant. The word *sanctuary* (*ta
hagia*) means Heaven itself, the archetype of the Most Holy Place
of the ancient Tabernacle. In this sense, the same Greek words
are used in 9 : 8, 12, 24, 25 ; 10 : 19 ; 13 : 11.

**and of the true tabernacle,**—The adjective *true* (*alethinos*)
denotes not only the real as opposed to the false (as *alethes*), but
also, and more particularly, the perfect and substantial, as opposed
to the imperfect and unsubstantial. The Tabernacle of Moses was
a real structure, formed and fashioned according to the exact
model which was shown to him in the mount. But nevertheless it
was a mere shadow of the true ; the type of that in which Christ
now officiates as our High Priest. The former was made by
human hands, and was constructed of perishable materials ; but the
latter is the workmanship of God himself, a Bethel that will never
wax old.

What, then, is this true Tabernacle, of which Christ has become
the prime Minister ?

Some, as Moll and Kendrick, maintain that it is identical with
the Sanctuary ; and that the term *true tabernacle* is therefore but
another name for Heaven itself, into which Christ has for us entered. They argue that the rending of the Vail, when Christ was
crucified, was a virtual removal of all distinctions between the
Holy Place and the Most Holy ; and that henceforth they were to
be regarded as one and the same ; so that the name, *true tabernacle,*
is used here but as an explanatory synonym of the word *sanctuary.*

But to this it may be objected (1) that the rending of the Vail
did not in any way change the local relations and objects of the
two apartments. It only indicated that henceforth the way from
the Holy Place into the Most Holy was made manifest. See 9 : 8.
(2) Moll's view is inconsistent with the most natural construction
and obvious meaning of the sentence. The first impression of any
one on reading the text would be that the Apostle refers here to
two separate and distinct apartments. (3) It is opposed to the
*usus loquendi* of the Hebrews, for whose special benefit the Epistle
was written. Sometimes indeed the word *tabernacle* (*skene*) is
used as the name of the whole structure, including both the Holy

Place and the Most Holy; and sometimes it is used to denote either of these apartments. But when it is used, as here, in connection with the word *sanctuary* (*to hagion* or *ta hagia*) it means simply the east room of the Tabernacle, or that of which this was a type. See Lev. 16: 16, 17, 20, 23, 33, etc. And (4) in 9: 11, 12, our author evidently keeps up a distinction between the Tabernacle and the Holy of holies; for Christ, he says, according to the most approved rendering of the passage, passed through the true or more perfect Tabernacle into the Most Holy Place. For these and other like reasons, most expositors justly maintain that there is still a difference between the Sanctuary and the true Tabernacle. But if there is a difference, what is it?

Macknight, following Josephus and Philo, makes the whole Tabernacle a symbolical representation of the universe; alleging that the Most Holy Place was symbolical of Heaven, and that the Holy Place was a symbol of the whole Earth. See Jos. Ant. iii. 7. 7. This hypothesis originated in an attempt on the part of Josephus, Philo, and others, to make the symbolical system of Moses harmonize with the tenets and speculations of Gentile philosophy. It has no foundation whatever in the word of God.

Delitzsch maintains, as we have seen (7: 26), that the Sanctuary was a symbol of the uncreated Holy of holies of the Divine nature, into which Christ entered when he ascended from Mount Olivet; and that the Tabernacle proper or Holy Place was a symbol of the highest created heaven, where dwell the angels and the spirits of the just made perfect. But this again is too fanciful, and without scriptural support.

A more plausible hypothesis is that of Hofmann and others, who maintain that by the true Tabernacle is meant here the glorified body, or, as some say, the human nature, of Christ. In support of this hypothesis it is alleged (1) that in John 1: 14, it is said, "The Word was made flesh and dwelt (*eskenosen,* tabernacled) among us"; (2) that in John 2: 21, Christ himself speaks of his body as a tabernacle or temple (3) that in Heb. 10: 20, the Vail of the Temple is represented as a symbol of his flesh; and (4) that in Eph. 2: 19-22, Christ and the Church are together compared to a holy temple. All this is quite plausible, but by no means conclusive. That Christ's body may be properly compared to a tabernacle, no one, of course, doubts who believes the Bible to be the word of

God. But this is not the question. The point to be determined is, not whether there is any analogy between the body of Christ and a tabernacle, but whether it is the antitype for the symbolizing of which the Jewish Tabernacle was constructed. That it is not, seems probable for several reasons; but chiefly for this, that the true Tabernacle is here represented not as a part of Christ, but simply as the sphere in which he, in his full and proper personality performs his ministry.

Is then the Church of Christ the true Tabernacle?

In favor of this hypothesis it may be said (1) that the Church sustains the same relation to Heaven that the Holy Place of the Tabernacle and Temple did to the Most Holy. God's only revealed way of entering into Heaven is through the Church. (2) The Holy Place of the Tabernacle had ordinances corresponding with the ordinances of the Church. In it was the Table supplied constantly with the twelve loaves emblematical of the bread of life, of which we partake, not in, but through, the ordinances of the Church, particularly the Lord's Supper. See John 6: 33, 35, 48, 50, 53-56. There, too, was the Altar of incense, corresponding with the altar of prayer (Psalm 141 : 2; Luke 1 : 9, 10; Rev. 5 : 8; 8 : 3, 4) ; and there was the light of the seven lamps of the golden Candlestick, corresponding with the light of the Holy Spirit, by means of which the Church is made the light of the world (Isa. 60: 1; Matt. 5: 14; Rev. 1: 20). (3) The Church of Christ is compared in Acts 15: 16, 17, to a booth or tent (*skene*), so enlarged that the Gentiles, as well as the Jews, may find shelter and protection under it. Compare Isa. 54: 1-4. (4) In 1 Cor. 3: 16, Paul says to the Corinthian brethren, "Know ye not that ye are the Temple of God, and that the Spirit of God dwelleth in you?" And in 2 Cor. 6: 16, he says, "Ye are the Temple of the living God ; as God hath said, I will dwell in them, and walk in them, and I will be their God, and they shall be my people." And again the same Apostle says in his Epistle to the Ephesians (2: 19-22), "Now therefore ye are no more strangers and foreigners, but fellow-citizens with the saints and of the household of God ; and are built upon the foundation of the Apostles and Prophets, Jesus Christ himself being the chief cornerstone ; in whom all the building fitly framed together groweth into a holy Temple in the Lord : in whom ye also are builded together for a habitation of God through the Spirit." In like manner, writing to Timothy, he calls the Church the house of God (1 Tim. 3: 15) ; and so he does also in Heb. 3: 6; 10: 21. The same thought is also expressed in 1 Pet. 2: 5. From all of which we are constrained to believe that the true Tabernacle and the Church of Christ cannot be separated : they are certainly identical in whole or in part.

But to this view, it is proper to say, there is this apparent objection. The Church of Christ did not exist as a distinct organization till the Day of Pentecost, A.D. 34, about ten days after Christ's ascension. That God had a people even from the beginning, and that Christ had followers from the beginning of his public ministry, is of course conceded. But not till the Pentecost that next followed after his resurrection, was he publicly proclaimed the anointed Sovereign of the universe (Acts 2: 36) ; not till then was any one baptized by his authority into the name of the Father, and of the Son, and of the Holy Spirit (Acts 2: 38) ; and not till then was the Spirit given to animate the body (John 7: 37-39). And yet it is said in 9: 11, 12, that Christ entered through a greater and more perfect Tabernacle (than that of Moses) into the Most Holy Place. Now I think it must be conceded that this greater and more perfect Tabernacle is identical with the true Tabernacle of our text ; and if the true Tabernacle is identical with the Church, then how could it be said with propriety that Christ went up through the Church ten days before it had a distinct organic existence ?

Perhaps a reference to Christ's mode of teaching by parables may assist us in solving this confessedly difficult problem. At one time he compares the kingdom of Heaven to a grain of mustard seed ; at another, to leaven ; at another, to a drag-net ; at another, to ten virgins, etc. ; his object being in all these cases to illustrate only some one element or characteristic of his Kingdom. Seldom, if ever, does he include in his comparisons all that belongs to it as a complete and perfect organization. May not Paul then, in like manner, speak by synecdoche of the greater and more perfect Tabernacle, having reference at the same time to some of the elements of the Church of Christ? The Church is the same thing as the Kingdom of Christ on earth, only viewed under different aspects. It, as well as the Kingdom, has its essential elements. Christ is its head ; believers anointed with the Holy Spirit are its members : the

3 For ¹every high priest is ordained to offer gifts and sacrifices: wherefore ²it is of necessity that this man have somewhat also to offer.

¹Ch. v. 1; vii. 27; x. 11; Lev. ix. 7-21.
²Ch. ix. 12-14; x. 9-12; Gal. i. 4; Eph. v. 2; Titus ii. 14.

promise given to Abraham concerning Christ (Gal. 3: 17) may be regarded as its constitution; the rules and regulations given by the Apostles are its laws and ordinances; Apostles, Prophets, Evangelists, Elders, and Deacons, are its officers; the sanctified portion of the Earth is its territory, and the blue vault of heaven, covered with cherubim, may perhaps be regarded as an emblem of its canopy or inner curtain. Now as Christ so often speaks of his Church or Kingdom by synecdoche, putting a part for the whole; and as the inner curtain of the Tabernacle is often put for the Tabernacle itself (see, for instance, Ex. 40: 19), may we not with propriety regard the sky, covered as it is with the wings of angels and the protecting shield of God's providence, as emblematical of the greater and more perfect Tabernacle referred to in 9: 11? And is not this view corroborated by what is said in 4: 14? See notes on 9: 11.

If this view of the matter is correct, it may serve to explain that precept of the Law which required that no one should be in the Tabernacle while the High Priest went into the Holy of holies to make an atonement for the people. (Lev. 16: 17.) When Christ went up through the heavens (4: 14) into the Most Holy Place, on the fortieth day after his resurrection, he left behind him many sincere and devoted followers; but it was not until after that he had made expiation for the sins of the world, and came out to bless the people by his Spirit on the following Pentecost, that the Church was fully organized and prepared for a habitation of God through the Spirit. Then, for the first time, believers were received into it on condition of their repenting and being baptized into the name of the Father, and of the Son, and of the Holy Spirit.

3 **For every high priest is ordained, etc.**—The logical train of thought in this connection is well stated by Delitzsch as follows: "Christ is a priest in the heavenly archetypal Sanctuary (verses 1, 2), for there is no priest without some sacrificial function (verse 3); and if here on earth he would not be a priest at all (verse 4), where there are priests already who serve the typical and shadowy Sanctuary (verse 5). The priestly functions of Christ must there-

4 |For if: *if then*| he were on earth, [1]he should not be a priest, seeing that there are [priests] that offer gifts according to the law:

[1]Ch. vii. 11-15; Num. xvi. 40; xviii. 7; 2 Chron. xxvi. 18, 19.

fore be discharged in a higher sphere, and so it is." Or to express the same train of thought syllogistically, "A priest's office is to offer sacrifice; Christ is a priest; and therefore he must have something to offer. The sphere in which Christ's priestly office is discharged must be either an earthly or a heavenly one; but an earthly one it cannot be, inasmuch as on earth (in the material Tabernacle) there are other priests officiating according to the law, and therefore Christ's sphere of priestly operation must be a heavenly one."

To this view of the matter it has been objected that Christ is thus represented as making frequent and continual offerings like the Levitical priests, whereas our author says distinctly that he has made but one offering, and that this has been made once for all, never again to be repeated. See 7 : 27 ; 9 : 12, 26, 28 ; 10 : 12.

But the allegation does not logically follow from the premises, for the Apostle speaks here indefinitely with regard to time, and the whole expression may be rendered thus : "Wherefore it [was] necessary that this [Priest] should also have something which he might offer" (*prosenegke*). So the passage is translated by Beza, Bengel, Bleek, De Wette, Lünemann, Hofmann, Macknight, and others. And hence the reference may be simply to the one offering which Christ made of himself in the heavenly Sanctuary after his ascension. But as this one offering of Christ, by means of which he made an atonement for the sins of the world, is the ground of his continued ministry in our behalf, I am inclined to think with Delitzsch, Alford, Moll, and others, that the Apostle refers here particularly to the constant use and application of the one offering of Christ, as the only means of procuring our pardon, justification, and sanctification. Christ's one offering is, in fact, a continual offering; an offering the efficacy of which will endure forever. So that while he officiates as a minister in the heavenly Sanctuary, and in the true Tabernacle, he will always have to offer what is fully adequate to the justification and salvation of all who come unto God by him.

4 **For if he were on earth, he should not be a priest,**—The

5 Who serve unto ²the example and shadow of heavenly things, as Moses
was admonished of God when he was about to make the tabernacle: for,
³See, saith he, that thou make all things according to the pattern showed to
thee in the mount.

²Ch. ix. 9, 23, 24; x. 1; Col. ii. 17.
³Ex. xxv. 40; xxvi. 30; xxvii. 8; Num. viii. 4; 1 Chron. xxviii. 12, 19; Acts vii. 44.

meaning of this verse is quite obvious from what precedes.  As
Christ was not of the house of Aaron, he could not lawfully officiate as a priest on earth. (Num. 18: 1-7.)  True, indeed, as our author shows in 7: 11-19, the law had ere this been abolished.  As a
religious institution, it was abrogated when Christ was crucified.
(Col. 2: 14.)  But no other law creating a new order of earthly
priesthood had been enacted in its place.  And as, for wise and benevolent reasons, God allowed the law of Moses to continue for a
time as a civil institution, it was, in fact, the only existing law on
earth, of Divine appointment, according to which gifts and sacrifices could be rightfully offered.  This point of the argument was,
of course, well understood and appreciated by the Hebrew brethren.

5 **Who serve unto the example, etc.**—Or more literally and
correctly: *Who serve the delineation and shadow of heavenly
things.*  The word rendered *delineation* (*hupodeigma*) means (1)
a private sign or secret token, and (2) a delineation or copy of
anything.  Here, it denotes that the Jewish Tabernacle, with all that
pertained to it, was but a faint symbolical representation of the
heavenly Sanctuary and the true Tabernacle.  The word *shadow*
(*skia*) is added with the view of intensifying the thought; thus indicating that the given representation was wholly destitute of the
substance which is inherent in the heavenly realities.

**as Moses was admonished of God, etc.**—The Apostle now
submits as proof of the above allegation, the fact recorded in Ex.
25: 40, that when Moses was about to make the Tabernacle, God
directed him to frame it according to the exact pattern (*tupos*)
showed to him in the mount.  In order that this symbolical structure might exactly correspond in its shadowy outlines with the
heavenly archetypes, God, it seems, caused Moses to see in vision a
just representation of these on Mount Sinai, and then instructed
him to make the Tabernacle according to this pattern.  And hence,
according to the testimony of Moses, the Jewish Tabernacle was

not an original structure, but only a copy of the representation which God gave to him of the heavenly Sanctuary and of the true Tabernacle. From all of which it is evident that the sphere of Christ's ministry is greatly superior to that in which Aaron and his successors performed their services, and consequently that his priesthood is also greatly superior to theirs.

It is no objection to the view above taken of the true Tabernacle, that it is here ranked and classified with the "heavenly things," of which the Jewish Tabernacle was but a shadowy representation. For the Church of Christ is in no proper sense a worldly institution. It is in all its essential elements identical with the kingdom of heaven, and hence those who become members of it are said to sit down together "in heavenly places in Christ Jesus." See Eph. 1 : 3 ; 2 : 6 ; Heb. 9 : 23.

## REFLECTIONS

1. How true it is that the testimony of Jesus is the spirit of prophecy. (7 : 1-10.) Who, without the aid of the Holy Spirit, would have ever thought that the fourteenth chapter of Genesis has any reference to Christ? But it is even so. God who sees the end from the beginning, knows always by what means his ends and purposes can be best accomplished. To effect these, he often turns the hearts of kings as the rivers of water (Prov. 21 : 1), and makes the history of individuals and of nations fill up the exact measure of his benevolent intentions. Thus it was, for instance, that he made Hagar a type of the Old Covenant, and Sarah a type of the New (Gal. 4 : 21-31) ; and thus it was that he made Melchisedec a type of Christ; so that in the ages to come he might make it manifest to all that he is himself the author of the whole plan of redemption, and that his son, Jesus Christ, is the Alpha and Omega of the whole Bible.

2. As Jesus had no predecessor, so also he has no successor in office (verses 16, 17). Like Melchisedec, he remains a priest upon his throne perpetually. Not that he has to offer daily, weekly, monthly, and yearly sacrifices, like the Levitical priests ; for by one offering he has made full and complete expiation for the sins of the world. But as he ever lives to make intercession for us, so also he must of necessity be continually presenting the one offering of

himself to God, as the ground of his intercessions, and as the only means of our justification. This priestly function can never be transferred to another. And consequently the word of the oath which was since the Law maketh him a priest forevermore.

3. The Old Testament is not "a fable devised by learned and crafty Hebrews," but a revelation from God, given to us by holy men of old, as they were moved by the Holy Spirit. (2 Pet. 1: 20, 21.) What Jew would ever of his own accord have predicted the rise of another priest after the order of Melchisedec, and not after the order of Aaron? What, but the Spirit of the Almighty, could have ever induced David to utter a prophecy involving the abrogation of the whole Jewish economy? Truly, "all Scripture is given by inspiration of God."

4. None who believe in Christ need ever be dismayed at the approach of death or anything else, for he is both able and willing "to save to the uttermost all who come unto God through him, seeing he ever lives to make intercession for us" (verse 25). All other helps will fail, sooner or later. Our friends may now comfort us in many ways; and physicians by their skill and timely remedies may greatly relieve our present sufferings. But death will soon separate us all, and put an end to all our kind offices here in behalf of one another. For no man can redeem his brother from death, nor save him from the corruption of the grave. But Jesus never forsakes those who trust in him. (13: 5.) Having washed us from our sins in his own precious blood, he will not desert us in the hour of death, nor will he then allow any calamity to overcome us; so that we may say confidently with David, "Though I walk through the valley of the shadow of death, I will fear no evil; for thou art with me; thy rod and thy staff, they comfort me." (Psalm 23: 4.) And with Paul we may exclaim, "O Death, where is thy sting? O Grave, where is thy victory?" (1 Cor. 15: 55.) But what else than the religion of Jesus can fill the soul with such confidence and consolation? What has infidelity to offer in the hour of death to her many votaries? What has she ever done, and what can she do, to enlighten the understanding and fill the heart with confidence in reference to the future? What skeptic was ever known to say, as does Paul, "We know that if our earthly house of this tabernacle were dissolved, we have a building of God, a house

not made with hands, eternal in the heavens"? Who but the Christian can say with confidence, "To be absent from the body is to be present with the Lord"? And again, "It is better to depart and to be with Christ"? And still again, "There is a rest which remains for the people of God"? This is the language of him, and of him only, who knows in whom he has believed, and who is fully persuaded that he is able to keep that which he has committed to him. (2 Tim. 1: 12.)

5. The religion of the Lord Jesus is just such a religion as we all need (verses 26, 27). Notwithstanding all that infidels and scoffers have said against it, it so happens that the man who understands and obeys it most perfectly, is always, other things being equal, the most happy and the most useful member of society. And so, also, it is with whole communities and nations. Those that are most completely under the influence of the religion of Christ, are always the most happy and prosperous. The religions of the ancient Egyptians, Greeks, Romans, Celts, and Goths, all failed because of their incapacity to make men happy. There was nothing in them to satisfy the longing desires of the human heart. And for the same reason, Brahmanism, Buddhism, Mahometanism, and all other systems of false religion, are now waxing old and "are ready to vanish away." But Christianity is constantly gaining more power and influence over mankind, as civilization advances. And it is doing so simply because it presents to us a perfect Savior; one who is "holy, harmless, undefiled, separate from sinners, and made higher than the heavens." It reveals to us the only proper antidote for sin, the only atonement that is at all adequate to so meet and satisfy the claims of the Divine government, that God can be just in justifying those who believe in Jesus. It presents to us just such motives as best serve to make us hate sin, love holiness, do justice, and walk humbly, righteously, and godly in this present world. And, finally, it offers to us on the simple conditions of faith and obedience, just such a salvation as the heart of every man desires: a salvation from sin, death, hell, and the grave. And, in a word, it withholds from us nothing that is calculated to elevate, refine, and purify the heart; to make us like God; to fit us for doing his will here, and for enjoying his presence hereafter. Can such a religion be a falsehood? Judge the tree by its fruit.

6. How infinitely glorious and exalted is the great High Priest of our confession! (8:1, 2.) Having by the grace of God tasted death for every man, and made an atonement for the sins of the world, he now sits as a priest upon his throne, and officiates as a minister of the heavenly Sanctuary and the true Tabernacle. No wonder, then, that all heaven is filled with his praises, while the angels and the redeemed behold his glory and think of his condescending love in providing for the ransom of millions, who without his atoning sacrifice must have perished forever.

> "But angels can never express,
>     Nor saints who sit nearest his throne,
> How rich are his treasures of grace;
>     No, this is a secret unknown."

## SECTION SEVEN
### 8:6-13

#### ANALYSIS

In this short section, we have another partial digression from the main line of argument. Having stated in the closing paragraph of the last section that the sphere of Christ's ministry is the heavenly Sanctuary and the true Tabernacle, our author is naturally led to consider in the next place the superior efficacy of his ministry. And this point he actually introduces in the sixth verse of this (the eighth) chapter as the next subject for discussion. Christ, he says, has obtained a ministry as much superior to that of the Levitical priests, as the Covenant of which he is the Mediator is superior to the Old Covenant of which Moses and the Levitical priests were the mediators. But having mentioned the subject of the two covenants, his thoughts are at once wholly engrossed with this as his main theme. The ministry of Christ falls for awhile into the background, and the active and comprehensive mind of our author is wholly occupied with the superior excellencies of the New Covenant. He argues from Jer. 31:31-34, that it excels the Old Covenant in each of the following particulars:

I. The Old Covenant was faulty, but the New is faultless (verses 7, 8). That is, relatively so. In one sense, the Old Covenant was just as perfect as the New. Each of them was perfectly adapted to the end for which it was designed. But the former never did and never could justify, sanctify, or save anyone. In these respects it was relatively faulty, and the New is faultless.

II. The Old Covenant was written on stone, but the New is written on the understanding and the heart (verse 10. Compare 2 Cor. 3: 3, 7). And hence the latter is far more efficacious in forming the character and controlling the lives of its subjects than the former. It is of but little service that we have the truth written on marble or parchment, unless it is also put into the understanding and engraven on the hearts of the people.

III. The subjects of the Old Covenant were not all pious. Many of them were really aliens to God, while enjoying all the temporal and civil privileges of the Theocracy. But not so with the subjects of the New Covenant. They must all, of necessity, serve Jehovah as their God, for he says: "I will be to them a God, and they shall be to me a people" (verse 10).

IV. Most of the subjects of the Old Covenant became such by a birth of flesh (Gen. 15: 18; 17: 7, 8, etc.); but the subjects of the New Covenant must all be born of water and of the Spirit (John 3: 3, 5). They must all be begotten by the Holy Spirit through the word of truth, the good seed of the kingdom, before they can be admitted to the rights and privileges of the New Institution. (1 Cor. 4: 14, 15; James 1: 18, etc.) And hence they must all know the Lord, from the least of them even to the greatest of them (verse 11).

V. There was nothing in the Old Covenant that could really take away sin. (10: 4.) And hence, notwithstanding the many daily, weekly, and monthly sacrifices that were offered to make purification for the sins of the people, these sins were all called into remembrance again on the Day of Atonement. (Lev. 16.) But not so under the New Covenant. The blood of Christ procures for all its faithful and obedient subjects, free, full, and everlasting forgiveness. And hence, on the Day of Judgment, the faithful in Christ will all be treated as if they had never sinned (verse 12).

VI. The Old Covenant was abolished as a religious institution when Christ was crucified (Eph. 2: 14-17; Col. 2: 14; Heb. 7: 11-19); but the New Covenant will continue while time endures (verse 13).

## SUPERIORITY OF THE NEW COVENANT
### 8:6-13

6 But now hath he [1]obtained a more excellent ministry, by how much also he is [2]the mediator of a better covenant, which was established [3]upon better promises.

[1]2 Cor. iii. 6-11.
[2]Ex. xx. 19-21; xxiv. 1-12; Deut. v. 23-33; Psa. cvi. 23; Gal. iii. 19, 20; 1 Tim. 11-15.
[3]Rom. ix. 4; Gal. iii. 16-21; Titus i. 2; 2 Pet. i. 4.

---

6 **But now hath he obtained a more excellent ministry,**— That is, a ministry more excellent than that of the Levitical priests. The degree of this superior excellence is measured, as our author now proceeds to show, by the superior excellence of the new and better covenant of which Christ has become the Mediator. The word *mediator* (*mesitcs*) means one who intervenes or goes between two parties, as an interpreter, a reconciler, an internuncio, or an intercessor. "In all ages, and in all parts of the world," says Calmet, "there has constantly prevailed such a sense of the infinite holiness of the supreme Divinity, with so deep a conviction of the imperfections of human nature and the guilt of man, as to deter worshipers from coming directly into the presence of a being so awful; and recourse has therefore been had to mediators. Among the Sabians, the celestial intelligences were constituted mediators; among other idolaters, their various idols; and this notion still prevails in Hindostan and elsewhere. Sacrifices were thought to be a kind of mediator; and, in short, there has been a universal feeling, a sentiment never forgotten, of the necessity of an interpreter or mediator between God and man."

Under the Old Covenant, the office of mediator was filled primarily by Moses (Ex. 20: 19-21; 24; Gal. 3: 19, 20); and after him it seems that the high priest discharged the duties of a mediator, standing, as he ever did, between God and the people, especially on the Day of Atonement (Lev. 16). But under the New Covenant there is but "one mediator between God and man, the man Christ Jesus." (1 Tim. 2: 5.) He stands as security on the part of God, that he will graciously fulfill all his promises to man (7: 22); and on the part of man he appears before God, not only to plead our cause, but also to make purification for our sins, with his own blood, according to the Scriptures. Through him God can now be just in pardoning and justifying every obedient penitent

7 For ⁴if that first covenant had been faultless, then should no place have
been sought for the second.

⁴Ch. vii. 11, 18; Gal. iii. 21.

believer; and through him, unworthy as we are, we can now come
to God, as children to a father, and obtain mercy and find grace for
seasonable help. (4 : 16.)

The superior excellencies of the "better covenant" and the "better promises" will become more obvious as we proceed with the
exegesis of the following verses.

7 **For if that first covenant had been faultless, etc.**—The
form of the argument which our author uses here is the same
which he has employed in 7 : 11. If the first covenant had been
sufficient to accomplish God's purposes with respect to the salvation of man, then most assuredly he would never have set it aside
and made way for another. "For if," as Paul argues in his epistle
to the Galatians (3 : 21), "there had been given a law that was
able to give life, then, indeed, righteousness would have been by
law"; and the New Covenant in that event would never have been
inaugurated. But when it was fully demonstrated by the deeds
of law no flesh could be justified before God (Rom. 3 : 20; Gal. 2 :
16; 3 : 11); then it pleased God to give to his people a new and
better covenant, which is established on better promises.

Let it not be supposed, however, that God was in any way disappointed in his purposes with respect to the Old Covenant. He can
never be disappointed, as man is often disappointed; for known
unto him are all his works from eternity (*apo aionos*). Acts 15 :
18.) The fact is that the Law, or Old Covenant, was never given
for the purpose of justifying any man. It was added simply "on
account of transgressions, till the seed should come, to whom the
promise was made"; and it was intended to serve as a schoolmaster in bringing us to Christ. (Gal. 3 : 19, 24.) But the Holy Spirit
often speaks of things relatively, according to our conceptions of
them. See, for example, Matt. 19 : 17 and John 1 : 21. And just
so it is in this case. The Jews all looked upon the Old Covenant
as the power of God for the salvation of the seed of Abraham according to the flesh. And viewed in this light, it was of course
faulty; for by it no man ever was or ever could be saved. And
hence when God had accomplished his benevolent purpose in giv-

8 For finding fault with them he saith, ¹Behold, the days come, saith the Lord, when I will make ²a new covenant with the house of Israel and with the house of Judah.

¹Jer. xxxi. 31-34.
²Matt. xxvi. 28; 1 Cor. xi. 25; 2 Cor. iii. 6.

ing it to the people, he then took it out of the way, and gave to them a better covenant "established on better promises."

8 **For finding fault with them**—Or as it may be rendered in more exact harmony with the context: *For finding fault he saith to them.* God found fault with the Covenant, as above explained, and he also found fault with the people, for they were constantly transgressing the laws and requirements of the Covenant; and it, as a consequence, was constantly condemning them. Such an arrangement, therefore, however necessary as a preliminary measure, was never intended to accomplish fully God's benevolent designs and purposes with regard to the salvation of the world. And hence after the conquest of Jerusalem by the Chaldeans, about 588 B.C., while the captives were detained at Ramah, God revived the hearts of his disconsolate children by giving to them the very encouraging series of prophecies found in Jer. 30-31, from which our author makes the beautiful extract given in the following verses.

**Behold, the days come, saith the Lord, when I will make, etc.**—Or more literally: Behold, the days are coming, saith the Lord, when I will accomplish (*sunteleso*) upon the house of Israel and upon the house of Judah a new covenant. Man makes a covenant with his fellow-man; but God perfects his arrangements according to the counsel of his own will, and then bestows them on (*epi*) his people. And hence the idea of the prophet seems to be this: that in the last days, under the reign of the Messiah, God would himself complete and bestow upon the house of Israel and upon the house of Judah the arrangement (*diatheke*) which, though hid for ages, was really intended from the beginning for the benefit of mankind.

The name *Israel* means "He will be a prince with God." It was given (1) to Jacob himself, Gen. 32 : 28; (2) to all the descendants of Jacob taken collectively, Ex. 4 : 22; (3) to the ten tribes that revolted from Rehoboam, 1 Kings 12 : 19, 20; and (4) to all believers in Christ, Rom. 9 : 6. The term "house of Israel," as used in our text, means evidently the ten tribes that revolted from

the line of David, and made Jeroboam their king, 975 B.C.  Most
of them were carried away captive into Assyria by Shalmaneser,
721 B.C.  But some of them remained in Canaan (2 Chron. 30;
31: 5, 6; 34: 6-9; 35: 16-19, etc.) ; and others, it seems, returned
thither at different periods.  See Jer. 1: 4-7; Ezra 2: 70; 6: 16-
18; 8: 35, etc.

The name *Judah* means "praise," or he will be praised.  It was
given (1) to the fourth son of Jacob by Leah, Gen. 29: 35; (2) to
his descendants, called also the tribe of Judah, Num. 1: 7; (3) to
all who followed Rehoboam, including the tribes of Judah and
Benjamin and some also from the tribes of Simeon and Dan.  (4)
After the captivity the name *Jew* was applied indiscriminately to
all who were known to be of any of the tribes of Israel, and even to
Jewish proselytes.  And (5) it is used by Paul to denote any believer in Christ. (Rom. 2: 29.)

In our text the appellations "house of Israel" and "house of
Judah" are manifestly used, as in the time of Jeremiah, to denote
all the descendants of Israel.  With these and for these God promised by that prophet that he would, in the latter days, make a new
and better covenant than he had made with their fathers at Mount
Sinai.  But not with them as separate and distinct houses, nor
even as tribes; but simply as individuals.  All tribal and family
distinctions are now lost in Israel; and all who now enter into covenant with God become members of the one household of faith, in
which there is neither Jew nor Greek, neither bond nor free, neither male nor female; but all are one in Christ Jesus. (Gal. 3: 28.)

But why is this called a *new* covenant?  Is it not the same as
that of which Paul speaks in Gal. 3: 17; and which he says was
given to Abraham four hundred and thirty years before the law
was given from Mount Sinai?

In order to answer these questions properly it is necessary to go
back to the time when God called Abraham out of Ur of Chaldea,
and examine the promise which God then made to this illustrious
patriarch, in connection with all its subsequent developments.  The
first account of this promise is given in Gen. 12: 1-3, as follows:
"Now the Lord had said unto Abraham, Get thee out of thy country, and from thy kindred, and from thy father's house, unto a
land that I will show thee; and I will make of thee a great nation,
and I will bless thee, and make thy name great; and thou shalt be

a blessing: and I will bless them that bless thee, and curse him that curseth thee; and in thee shall all the families of the earth be blessed." The same promise is variously repeated and somewhat amplified in Gen. 13: 14-17; 15: 1-6, 18-21; 17: 1-8; 22: 15-18, etc.

Now, it is true that in these several passages we have given what may be regarded as four distinct promises. These are (1) a promise that Abraham should have a numerous offspring; (2) that God would be a God to him and to his seed after him; (3) that he would give to him and to his seed an everlasting possession; and (4) that he would bless all the nations of the earth through him and his seed. These may of course be considered as so many separate and distinct promises; but it is more in harmony with the design of the Spirit and the general tenor of the Holy Scriptures to consider them as but elementary parts of the one general promise (Eph. 2: 12); having, however, a double reference; the one side of it looking to what was carnal and temporal, and the other to what was spiritual and eternal. The first element of this promise, for instance, was a pledge to Abraham that he should have a numerous family; first, according to the flesh; and secondly, according to the Spirit: the second that God would be a God to both of these families, though in a far higher sense to the latter than to the former: the third, that each of them should become heirs of an everlasting inheritance: and the fourth, that through each of them the world would be blessed.

For awhile, the spiritual side of the promise was almost wholly concealed in the distance behind the carnal; which from time to time became more and more prominent by sundry new developments. The most important of these was the covenant of circumcision, given in Gen. 17: 9-14. This was a sign of the more general and comprehensive covenant which God made with Abraham in reference to his natural posterity. It served to distinguish the Hebrew race from all others; and it was to all of them, save those only who were excepted by special enactment, a pledge of the promised inheritance; while it had at the same time, like other elements of the carnal promise, a typical significance, looking to the spiritual circumcision of the family of the faithful. See Rom. 2: 28, 29; Eph. 1: 13, 14; Phil. 3: 3; Col. 2: 9-12.

At length, just four hundred and thirty years after the giving of this twofold promise to Abraham, the carnal side of it was fully developed into the Old or Sinaitic Covenant. In this were of course embraced many various and distinct elements, such as the laws and ordinances relating to the different kinds of sacrifices, the consecration of the Levites, the covenant of the priesthood, etc.; all serving, however, to form and perfect one great national Institution, answering all the ends and purposes of civil government; and serving at the same time to check the progress of idolatry, to illustrate the exceeding heinousness of sin and the necessity of holiness, and also to typify and adumbrate the glorious realities embraced in the spiritual side of the Abrahamic promise, which in due time was also to be developed into a far more gracious and comprehensive Institution. In the meantime the carnal was the stay and support of the spiritual, while the spiritual served also to preserve and sanctify the carnal. They were united, but not blended together: for "the Law is not of faith," says Paul (Gal. 3 : 12) ; and again he says in substance, Faith is not of the Law (Rom. 9 : 6).

So matters stood until Christ came, "made of a woman made under the Law, to redeem them that were under the law." (Gal. 4 : 4, 5.) For about three and a half years he instructed the people, and, by his personal ministry, developed to a great extent the beauties, riches, and superlative excellencies of the spiritual element of the Abrahamic promise. But still it was in an imperfect state, not yet having received its full and proper development. Nor could this be done really while the first Institution was standing. It was necessary that the Old Covenant should be abrogated before the New could be fully inaugurated. This was done at the death of Christ. Then the Law of Moses was taken out of the way, being nailed to the cross. (Col. 2 : 14.) After that it was no longer binding on any one as a *religious* Institution; though it was through the forbearance of God allowed to remain as a *civil* Institution, for about thirty-six years longer, until the destruction of Jerusalem by the Romans in A.D. 70. In the meantime the spiritual element of the Abrahamic promise was fully developed in the Church of Christ, which was set up as a separate and distinct Institution on the Day of Pentecost which next followed after his death, burial, and resurrection. Then, for the first time, he was publicly proclaimed to the world as the anointed Sovereign of the universe (Acts 2 : 36) ; and then also believing penitents were first required to be baptized by his authority into the name of the Father, and of the Son, and of the Holy Spirit. Compare Matt. 28: 19 with Acts 2: 38. From that time forward, the Church of Christ is repeatedly spoken of as an existing reality, a distinct and independent body, enjoying the many blessings and privileges of the New Covenant. See Acts 2: 47; 5: 11; 8: 1, 3; 9: 31; 11: 15; Col. 1: 13, etc.

It will now be an easy matter for the reader to reconcile Gal. 3: 17 with Jer. 31: 31. When Paul, writing to the Galatians, says, the covenant concerning Christ (*eis Christon*) was given to Abraham four hundred and thirty years before the giving of the Law upon Mount Sinai, he refers simply to the spiritual elements of the Abrahamic promise. But when with Jeremiah, he speaks of the constitution, laws, and ordinances of the Church of Christ, as a *new* covenant, he then manifestly refers to the full and perfect development of the spiritual side of the aforesaid promise under the personal reign and administration of the Lord Jesus. They were identical in the sense in which an oak is identical with the acorn from which it is produced; and in like manner they were also very different. But in no proper sense was either of them identical with the Old Covenant; the Old being to the New as the shadow is to the substance, or as the type is to the antitype. (Col. 2: 17; Heb. 10: 1.)

All this may perhaps be made still more evident to some of my youthful readers by means of the following diagram:

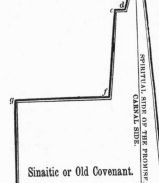

SPIRITUAL SIDE OF THE PROMISE.

CARNAL SIDE.

"Abraham believed God, and it was counted unto him for righteousness." (Rom. iv, 3.) In like manner were justified, not by works of law, but by faith in God, all the saved both of the Patriarchal and the Jewish age. See Gal. iii, 9; Heb. xi, etc.

The descendants of Abraham through Jacob were all by virtue of their natural birth made heirs of whatever blessings pertained to the carnal side of the promise : but it was only by faith that they were made partakers of such as belonged to the spiritual side.

### Sinaitic or Old Covenant.

"By the deeds of the Law there shall no flesh be justified in his sight." (Rom. iii, 20.)

"The Law is not of faith." (Gal. iii, 12.)

"The Law was our schoolmaster to bring us unto Christ, that we might be justified by faith." (Gal. iii, 24.)

Explanations.—ac Promise made to Abraham 1921 B. C.; de Circumcision ordained 1892 B. C.; fg Inauguration of the Old Covenant 1491 B. C.; hi The Law abrogated A. D. 34; jk Jerusalem destroyed A. D. 70; l Birth of Christ A. D. 1; mn Baptism of Christ A. D. 30; op Inauguration of the New Covenant fifty days after the resurrection of Christ A. D. 34. B. C. and A. D. have both reference to the year of Christ's birth, not to the erroneous epoch of Dionysius.

### THE NEW COVENANT.

(Jer. xxxi, 31.)

"By grace are ye saved through faith." (Eph. ii, 8.)

"If ye be Christ's, then are ye Abraham's seed, and heirs according to the promise." (Gal. iii, 29.)

9 Not according to ¹the covenant that I made with their fathers, in the day when ²I took them by the hand to lead them out of the land of Egypt; because ³they continued not in my covenant, and ⁴I regarded them not, saith the Lord.

10 For this is the covenant that I will make with the house of Israel after those days, saith the Lord; ⁵I will put my laws into their mind, and write them in their hearts: and ⁶I will be to them a God, and they shall be to me a people:

¹Ch. ix. 18-20; Ex. xxiv. 3-11; 2 Cor. iii. 5-18; Gal. iii. 15-19; iv. 19-31.
²Ex. xiii. 21, 22; xiv. 19, 20, 24; xix. 4, 5.
³Ex. xxxii. 8; Deut. xxix. 25-28; xxxi. 16-18; Josh. xxiii. 14-16; 2 Kings xvii. 13-23.
⁴Judges x. 13, 14; Amos v. 22.
⁵Ezek. xi. 19; xxxvi. 26, 27; Matt. xiii. 23; 2 Cor. iii. 3, 7, 8; Jas. i. 18, 21; 1 Pet. i. 23.
⁶Gen. xvii. 7, 8; Ex. xix. 5, 6; Jer. xxiv. 7; xxxi. 1, 33; xxxii. 38; Hos. ii. 23; Zech. viii. 8; 2 Cor. vi. 16.

9 **Not according to the covenant**—That is, the Sinaitic Covenant into which the carnal element of the Abrahamic promise was finally expanded. The word *day* is here used metaphorically for the period during which God led the people on their way from Egypt to Canaan. Certain pledges were of course given to them before they left Egypt, but the Covenant was made at Sinai. See references.

**because they continued not in my covenant,**—God here gives the reason why he was about to accomplish upon the house of Israel and the house of Judah a *new covenant*. It had now become manifest that by the Old Covenant no flesh could be justified before God: for the people were continually violating its requirements, and consequently God was under the necessity, so to speak, of rejecting them.

**and I regarded them not, saith the Lord.**—Because they rejected me and my covenant, saith Jehovah, I also rejected them. The Hebrew may be literally rendered as follows: *For they broke my covenant, and I was a lord to them.* That is, I treated them as a lord treats his unfaithful servants: I rejected them.

10 **For this is the covenant, etc.**—The Apostle now proceeds to state, according to the prophecy of Jeremiah, the several points of difference between the Old and the New Covenant: the first of which consists in the carnal externality of the former, and the spiritual internality of the latter.

**I will put my laws into their minds, etc.**—The ten fundamental precepts of the Old Covenant were written on two tables of stone (Ex. 34: 1, 28; Deut. 10: 1-5; 2 Cor. 3: 7), and the other laws and ordinances most likely on skins prepared for the purpose (Ex. 24: 7; Heb. 9: 19; 10: 7). Many of the pious Hebrews no doubt, like David, treasured up these laws in their minds and in their hearts (Psalm 119: 11) ; and, like Abraham, they were justified by faith through the covenant concerning Christ. But multitudes of those who lived under the Old Covenant never received the impress of God's law upon either their understanding or their hearts. And hence it was always to them but as a letter inscribed on stone, and not as an indwelling and life-giving power inscribed on their hearts. (2 Cor. 3: 6.) But not so under the New Covenant. For unless a man is begotten by the Spirit, through the word of truth, the good seed of the kingdom, he cannot become a member of it, nor can he be a partaker of its benefits. Compare John 3: 3, 5, with 1 Cor. 4: 15; James 1: 18; 1 Pet. 1: 23. God first enlightens the understanding by means of his inspired word, and then he inscribes it on the heart. Through the heart, the truth affects the will, and through the will it controls and sanctifies the life, so that all the members of the New Covenant are really "voluntary offerings," according to the promise of God to his Son. (Psalm 110: 3.) It is not therefore "the letter," but it is "the law of the Spirit of life in Christ Jesus" that constrains us to do the will of God from the heart.

**and I will be to them a God, etc.**—This is the second of the "better promises" on which the New Covenant is established. Under the Old Covenant, there were of course many true believers who, like Abraham, took Jehovah to be their God, all of whom he received and acknowledged as his people. (Ex. 19: 5; Lev. 26: 12.) But many, now knowing their right hands from their left, were of course incapable of so receiving him, and others were not willing to do so, preferring the worship of Baal, and other heathen idols, to the worship of the only living and true God. "The fact is," says Delitzsch, "there is no period in the history of Israel before the captivity, in which more or less idolatry was not united with the worship of Jehovah, except it be in the time of David and the first years of Solomon, during which the influence of Samuel continued to be felt. And when, by the captivity, idol worship was completely eradicated from the people, as far at least as regards that part of it which returned, it is well known that a hypocritical letter worship got the mastery over them, which was very little

11 And they shall not teach every man his |neighbor: *townsman,*| and every man his brother, saying, [1]Know the Lord: for [2]all shall know me, from the least to the greatest.

[1]2 Kings xvii. 27, 28; 2 Chron. xxx. 22; Ezra vii. 25.
[2]Jer. xxiv. 7; Ezek. xxxiv. 30; xxxix. 22; Hab. ii. 14.

better." But under the New Economy, no such state of things is at all possible. No one can really become a member of the New Covenant, except by faith and obedience (Mark 16: 16; Acts 2: 38, etc.), and no one can continue to be a member of it except on the same conditions (6: 4-6; 10: 26-31; 2 Pet. 1: 1-11). "Know ye therefore," says Paul, "that they who are of faith, the same are the children of Abraham, and heirs according to the promise." (Gal. 3: 7, 29.) To all such, God is now a God in even a higher sense than he was to the ancient patriarchs, for to none of them was the Holy Spirit given, as it is now given to all the subjects of the New Covenant, because that Jesus was not then glorified. (John 7: 37-39.) But now we are not only brought nearer to God by the offering of Christ, but we are also filled with his Spirit, through which we are enabled to cry "Abba, Father." (Gal. 4: 6.) Thus it is that Jehovah is now our God, and that we are his people "in truth and in righteousness." (Zech. 8: 8.)

11 **And they shall teach every man his neighbor, etc.**—The word *politēs* means a citizen, and with the possessive pronoun *his* (*autou*), as in our text, it means *a fellow-citizen.* And hence the whole verse may be properly rendered as follows: And they shall not teach every one his fellow-citizen, and every one his brother, saying, Know the Lord: for all will know me from the least to the greatest of them.

But of whom does the Lord speak when he says, They will all know me? Evidently, of the members of the New Covenant, and of these only. They must all know the Lord from the least of them even to the greatest of them. And hence we have given here a very striking point of contrast between the Old and the New Covenant. For if we except the few Gentile proselytes, who on condition of their being circumcised, were admitted to some of the rights and privileges of the Theocracy, all the subjects of the Old Covenant had to be taught to know the Lord. But not so under the New Covenant. No one, ignorant of Jehovah, can possibly become a member of it: "for he that cometh to God must believe that he is, and that he is the rewarder of them that diligently seek him." (11 : 4.)

The ground of this difference will become more obvious if we reflect for a moment on the relation which the Old Covenant sustained to the New, and also on the leading object for which the Old was instituted. Be it observed, then, that to communicate to mankind, in a clear and intelligible way, the whole plan of redemption through Christ, was a very difficult and intricate problem; difficult in itself on account of its unique and supernatural character; difficult on account of the many imperfections of the languages through which it had to be communicated; and difficult also on account of the preternatural blindness and depravity of the human heart. Now, in order to overcome these and other like obstacles, as far as possible, and to make the scheme of redemption plain and intelligible to all, it pleased God to explain and illustrate it by means of a series of material signs and symbols, which none of course but a Being of infinite knowledge was capable of inventing. For this purpose, he made Abraham the father of two families, the first embracing all his posterity according to the flesh, save such only as God himself saw fit to eliminate by special enactment, and the second embracing all who have the faith of Abraham. The first were made types of the second with respect to their birth, their circumcision, their inheritance, etc. The first became members of the Old Covenant, whether in its incipiency or in its fully developed state, by virtue of their natural birth, just as all mankind are by their natural birth made subject to the conditions of the Adamic covenant, and as the descendants of Levi were by virtue of their birth made subject to the conditions of the Levitical covenant. This is evident from such considerations as the following: (1) from the terms of the covenant which God made with Abraham respecting himself and his posterity (Gen. 17 : 7, 8) ; (2) from the fact that every male that was found to be uncircumcised after the eighth day was to be regarded and treated as a transgressor of the covenant (Gen. 17 : 14) ; (3) from the fact that all females of the stock of Abraham, through Jacob, were from their birth regarded as members of the Covenant (see, for instance, Num. 36) ; (4) from the fact that this is everywhere conceded by Christ and his Apostles, as well as by the ancient prophets (see Matt. 3 : 9; John 8 : 33, 37, etc.) ; and (5) from the existing analogies between the Old and the

12 For ¹I will be merciful to their unrighteousness, and their sins and their iniquities will I remember no more.

¹Ch. x. 17; Isa. xliii. 25; xliv. 22; Jer. xxxiii. 8; l. 20; Mic. vii. 19; 1 John i. 7-9; ii. 1, 2; Rev. i. 5.

New Covenant. As the family of the faithful now become members of the New Covenant by being born of water and of the Spirit (John 3 : 3, 5), so also the children of Abraham, by natural descent, became members of the Old Covenant by being born of the flesh.

Now this being so, one of the first lessons which the subjects of the Old Covenant had to learn was *to know the Lord*. But this necessity does not, and cannot, exist under the New Covenant, for its subjects are "born, not of blood, nor of the will of the flesh, nor of the will of man, but of God." (John 1 : 13.) God begets us, not by natural generation, but by means of "the word of truth, that we should be a kind of first-fruits of his creatures." (James 1 : 18.) And hence it is evident that all the subjects of the New Covenant must know the Lord. True, indeed, they are required to grow in knowledge, as well as in the grace of our Lord and Savior Jesus Christ. (2 Pet. 3 : 18.) Leaving the rudiments of the doctrine of Christ, we must go on to perfection, but not by learning again to know the Lord. This is the Alpha of the Christian Religion, without which no one ever did or ever can become a subject of the New Covenant, and a partaker of its benefits.

12 **For I will be merciful to their unrighteousness,**—This is given as the fourth of the "better promises" on which the New Covenant is established. The law having a mere shadow of the good things pertaining to the New Covenant, could never with its bloody rites take away the sins of the people. (10 : 4.) And hence, on the Day of Atonement all the sins of the year, for which many sacrifices had already been offered, were again called into remembrance. But under the New Covenant the case is wholly different, for the blood of Christ cleanses us thoroughly from all our sins. (1 John 7 : 7.) It is to the moral government of the universe what the blood of bulls and of goats was to the symbolical government of the Jews. It meets fully and satisfactorily the claims of the Divine government against every penitent believer, and procures for him, on given conditions, free, full, and absolute forgiveness. And hence it is that those who are justified by faith through the blood

13 In that he saith, A new covenant, ¹he hath made the first old. Now that which decayeth and waxeth old is ²ready to vanish away.

¹Ch. vii. 11, 12, 18, 19; ix. 9, 10.
²Matt. xxiv. 15-35.

of Christ, have no more consciousness of their past sins. God treats them as if they had never sinned, for he says: "Their sins and their iniquities will I remember no more." That is, he deals with the justified as if their sins were wholly forgotten, so that no one can ever successfully prefer a charge against the elect of God. See Isa. 54 : 17 ; Rom. 8 : 33.

13 **In that he saith, A new covenant, etc.**—The terms *old* and *new* are relative. And hence the Apostle argues that the use of the epithet *new* implies that the first had become old. Nay more, he further insists that the Old Covenant was even then "ready to vanish away." As a religious Institution, it was, as we have seen, abolished when Christ was crucified. He then took it out of the way, nailing it to his cross. (Col. 2 : 14.) And as a civil Institution it continued for only about seven years after the writing of this Epistle. God then took it entirely out of the way, forever abolishing at the same time the whole Tabernacle service in order to stay more effectually the hand of persecution, and correct the extreme judaizing tendencies that were then threatening to corrupt the simplicity of the Gospel, especially throughout Palestine.

## REFLECTIONS

1. What a blessed thing it is to be a subject of the new and better covenant: to enjoy its rights and privileges here, and its eternal honors and rewards hereafter (verse 6). To have Jehovah for our God, to have his laws and ordinances inscribed as a living power on our hearts, and to have our sins and iniquities all blotted out through the blood of Christ, knowing at the same time that if "our earthly house of this tabernacle were dissolved, we have a building of God, a house not made with hands, eternal in the heavens"— what more could we desire than this?

2. No irresponsible persons, whether they be infants or idiots, can become members of the New Covenant (verse 11). For God himself says of its subjects that they will all know him, from the least even to the greatest of them. But such knowledge is above the capacity of infants and idiots. And hence they can never be

lawfully received as members of the church of Christ. True, indeed, all who were of the seed of Abraham and of the stock of Israel, became members of the Old Covenant by virtue of their birth. But these were but types of those who by a birth of water and of the Spirit put on Christ and receive the sign and seal of the New Covenant. (Rom. 2: 28, 29; Phil. 3: 3; Col. 2: 9-12; Eph. 1: 13, 14.) The babes of the New Covenant are therefore the new converts who believe in Christ and obey his commandments. (Matt. 18: 6.)

3. Let it not be supposed, however, that those who die in their infancy are excluded from the benefits of Christ's death and mediation. By no means: for we say with truth, as did Paul (Rom. 5: 15-17), "In him the tribes of Adam boast more blessings than their fathers lost." Though infants are not proper subjects of the New Covenant, they are nevertheless all embraced in the more comprehensive arrangement of the Godhead, made for the benefit of all classes of mankind. Those, therefore, who die in their infancy will be saved, unconditionally on their part, through the sacrifice and mediation of the Lord Jesus. "For as by the one man's disobedience the many were made sinners, so by the obedience of the one shall the many be made righteous" (Rom. 5: 19); that is, so far as it respects the Adamic covenant. And hence it follows that all mankind will in due time be saved, through Christ, from the effects of the first transgression. And then will be fulfilled in its fullest sense the saying of the Psalmist, "Out of the mouth of babes and sucklings hast thou ordained strength, because of thine enemies, that thou mightest still the enemy and the avenger." (Psalm 8: 2.)

4. The New Covenant was framed for the benefit of those, and only those, who have attained to the years of responsibility. In it and through it we have given all that is really necessary to the attainment of life and godliness. He who believes, repents, and is baptized by the authority of Christ into the name of the Father, and of the Son, and of the Holy Spirit, has the fullest possible assurance that his past sins are all forgiven (Mark 16: 16; Acts 2: 38); and if, giving all diligence, he continue in well doing, he has then also the assurance that in the end he will receive an abundant entrance into God's everlasting kingdom (2 Pet. 1: 5-11). But he who, on the other hand, willfully neglects these laws and ordi-

nances of the New Covenant, will just as certainly be banished with an everlasting destruction from the presence of the Lord and from the glory of his power. (Mark 16: 16; 2 Thess. 1: 8, 9.) And hence it follows that everyone who has in his possession the Holy Scriptures, may even now read and understand his destiny. On this point there can be no mistake or failure so far as it respects God. "He is not a man that he should lie, nor is he the Son of man that he should repent." What a man sows, he will most assuredly reap: "He that soweth to his flesh shall of the flesh reap corruption; but he that soweth to the Spirit shall of the Spirit reap life everlasting." (Gal. 6: 8.)

5. But how is it with the millions who have no knowledge of God, nor of the gracious provisions of the New Covenant? Will they be saved, or will they be lost? If lost, it will not be on account of the Adamic transgression, for as we have seen, all will be finally saved from it through Christ. Nor will it be on the ground that they have rejected Christ, and the offer of salvation through him; for this they have not done. But it will be simply owing to their own personal transgressions, many of which they have all committed (Rom. 1: 18-32); and from which there is no salvation but through Christ (Acts 4: 12).

If saved at all, then, it must be by means of the Gospel. But how can they be saved by that of which they have no knowledge? Does not Paul say that the Gospel is the power of God for salvation to every one that believeth, because in it *is revealed* God's plan of justification by faith in order to faith? (Rom. 1: 16, 17.) And does not the commission given by Christ to his apostles, and through them to the church (Matt. 28: 18-20), clearly indicate that there is no salvation for those who are dead in trespasses and sins (Eph. 2: 1-3), except through the knowledge and faith of the Gospel? And did not the apostles act constantly under the influence of this conviction? When charged, as they doubtless often were, with being beside themselves in their great zeal to save the world from sin and death, the defense which Paul makes in his own behalf and also in behalf of his brethren is simply this; "The love of Christ constrains us; because we thus judge, that if one died for all, then were all dead; and that he died for all, that they who live should not henceforth live unto themselves, but unto him who died for them, and rose again." (2 Cor. 5: 14, 15.) On no other hypothesis can we explain the labors and teachings of the apostles than they looked upon the whole heathen world as lost, eternally and irrecoverably lost, unless saved by the Gospel. That some men may still, under extraordinary circumstances, be saved, as were the ancient patriarchs, with a very limited knowledge of God and of his Gospel, we may, I think, joyfully concede. But that any one who lives and dies in idolatry, can ever be admitted to a participation in the honors and privileges of God's everlasting kingdom, seems to me to be quite impossible; for "this is eternal life, that they might know thee the only true God, and Jesus Christ whom thou hast sent." (John 17: 3.)

7. We see, then, the wisdom and benevolence of God in making the church the pillar and ground of the truth (1 Tim. 3: 15); the golden candlestick that is to dispense the light of the Gospel to the benighted nations of the earth (Matt. 5: 14; Phil. 2: 15; Rev. 1: 20). Let her then faithfully fulfill her mission, as did the apostles, and very soon the idols of the heathen will be cast "to the moles and to the bats," and the whole earth will be filled with the knowledge and the glory of the Lord. (Isa. 11: 6-9.)

## SECTION EIGHT
### 9: 1 to 10: 18

#### ANALYSIS

The Apostle having sufficiently considered the superiority of the New Covenant, proceeds now to demonstrate more fully and particularly the superiority of Christ's ministry and sacrifice.

I. He begins the discussion by referring to the structure and furniture of the Jewish Tabernacle. (9: 1-5.) The first covenant, he says, had ordinances of Divine service and a worldly Sanctuary. This consisted of two apartments, each of which was also called a Sanctuary, in the first of which, commonly called the Holy Place, were the Candlestick, the Table of Shewbread, and the Altar of Incense; and in the second, known as the Most Holy Place, was the Ark of the Covenant, wherein were the golden vase that had manna, Aaron's rod that budded, and the Tables of the Covenant; and over the Ark were the Cherubim of glory overshadowing the Mercy-seat.

II. He notices, in the second place, the services which were performed in these two apartments, and also the typical and transitory nature of the several ordinances which appertained to the Old Economy (verses 6-10).

1. The priests went into the Holy Place every day, performing the required services.

2. But into the Most Holy Place, the High Priest went alone, once every year, to make an atonement for himself and for the errors of the people, by which arrangement was divinely indicated the comparative darkness of that dispensation. For

3. The Tabernacle was but a figure for the time being, reaching down to the period of renovation, according to which were performed many carnal rites and ceremonies which never could purify the conscience of any one. For

(1.) Reason could perceive no moral or natural connection between the means and the ends.

(2.) God had not yet given to mankind any satisfactory explanation of these matters. And hence the necessity of the Inner Vail during that dispensation, to indicate that the way into heaven was not yet made manifest.

III. But Christ having appeared as the High Priest of the New Economy, entered through a greater and more perfect tabernacle into the heavenly Sanctuary, not with the blood of bulls and of goats, but with his own blood, thereby procuring eternal redemption for us, and purifying our consciences also from dead works (verses 11-14). Thus is indicated the superiority of Christ's ministry in several ways. For

1. On his way into the heavenly Sanctuary, he passed through, not a material structure, such as the Holy Place of the Tabernacle and Temple, but through the true and spiritual Tabernacle of the new creation.

2. He went into heaven itself, and not into a mere symbol of it.

3. He went by means of his own blood, rendered infinitely efficacious by the eternal Spirit through which it was offered.

4. By means of this one offering he has procured for us eternal redemption, and purified our consciences from dead works, thereby qualifying us for the service of the living God.

IV. The Apostle next contemplates Christ as the Mediator of the New Covenant, procuring, by means of his death, full forgiveness for all the faithful of the Old Covenant, and securing at the

same time for the saints under both dispensations the right and
title of the eternal inheritance (verse 15). But in order to this, he
argues that it was necessary that Christ should first die for all.
This he illustrates

1. By the case of a testator. A will, he says, is of no force
whatever until after the death of the testator. And just so, it was
necessary that Christ should die before anyone could read his title
clear to mansions in the skies (verses 16, 17).

2. By the still more analogous case of the Old Covenant, which,
as the Hebrews knew, was inaugurated with the shedding and
sprinkling of blood (verses 18-24). And hence Paul argues, that
the death of Christ was necessary in order to the inauguration of
the New Covenant, and the full enjoyment of the eternal inheritance.

V. The Apostle would next caution his readers against pressing
these analogies too far (verses 25-28). It is true that the services
of Moses in the inauguration of the Old Covenant, and also those
of the high priest in its subsequent regular administration, resem-
bled, in some respects, the services of Christ as our mediator and
high priest. But it should be observed that there are also between
these sundry points of contrast as well as of resemblance. For

1. The priest of the Old Covenant offered simply the blood of
clean and innocent animals, but Christ offered his own blood
(verse 26).

2. Their offerings were numerous, but Christ made but one offering (verses 25, 26).

3. When the high priest had finished the work of one year on
the Day of Atonement, he came out of the Tabernacle still defiled
by sin, and he had therefore to repeat the same services year by
year. But not so with Christ. He died once and only once laden
with the sins of the world (Isa. 53: 6; 2 Cor. 5: 21; 1 Pet. 2:
24); after which he was declared righteous by the Supreme Judge
of the universe (John 16: 10; Acts 5: 32; Rom. 1: 4; Phil. 2: 9,
etc.). And hence when he again appears there will be no sin upon
him. He will then appear in glory for the salvation of those who
look confidently for his appearing.

VI. From these points of contrast, our author is next led to
consider the utter moral inefficacy of the Levitical offerings, and
the full and complete efficacy of the one offering of Christ. The

first of these points forms the scope of his argument in 10: 1-4. The Law, he says, having but a shadow, and not the exact image, of the good things to come, could never with its bloody sacrifices and carnal ordinances take away sins. This he proves from the fact that even those sins for which the daily, weekly, monthly, and yearly sacrifices had been offered, were again brought into remembrance on the Day of Atonement.

VII. But the sacrifice of Christ, fulfilling as it does the perfect will of God, enables him to be just in justifying every true believer. And hence it procures for all such free, full, and everlasting forgiveness (verses 5-18).

This section may be divided into the seven following paragraphs:

I. 9: 1-5. The structure, arrangement, and furniture of the ancient Tabernacle.

II. 9: 6-10. Symbolical services of the Tabernacle, indicating the comparative darkness of the Jewish age, and the insufficiency of its carnal rites and ordinances.

III. 9: 11-14. The higher, purer, and more perfect services of Christ.

IV. 9: 15-24. The eternal inheritance secured for the called and faithful of all ages, through the death and mediation of the Lord Jesus.

V. 9: 25-28. Further illustrations of the differences between the Levitical services and those rendered by Christ as the high priest of our confession.

VI. 10: 1-4. The utter moral inefficacy of the Levitical offerings.

VII. 10: 5-18. The all-sufficiency of the one offering of Christ shown (1) in its fulfilling the will of God; and (2) in the full and complete forgiveness which it procures for every obedient believer.

## 1. THE STRUCTURE, ARRANGEMENT AND FURNITURE
## OF THE JEWISH TABERNACLE
### 9 : 1-5

1 Then verily [1]the first covenant [2]had also ordinances of divine service, and [3]a worldly sanctuary.

[1]Ch. viii. 7, 13.
[2]Lev. xviii. 4, 30; xxii. 9; Num. ix. 12.
[3]Ex. xxv. 8; xxx. 13, 24; xxvi. 1, 3, 4; Lev. iv. 6; x. 4; xxi. 12.

---

1 **Then verily the first covenant**—The Apostle returns here to the line of argument from which he was led off in the sixth verse of the eighth chapter by a comparison of the two covenants. In the fifth verse of the same chapter he speaks of the high priest under the first covenant serving the Tabernacle of Moses, which, he says, was but a shadowy representation of the heavenly things belonging to the second covenant. And now he simply concedes what is really implied in 8: 5, that the first covenant had its "ordinances of Divine service, and a worldly sanctuary." His object is not in any way to disparage the Old Covenant, but to honor it as far as truth will permit. And hence he readily grants that it, as well as the New Covenant, was of Divine origin; that it had the ordinances of Divine service appointed by God himself, and a worldly sanctuary framed in every respect according to the pattern which God showed to Moses in the Mount.

The word *covenant (diatheke)* is not expressed in the original; but is manifestly implied, as may be seen from both what precedes and what follows. And it is, therefore, now generally conceded that the word *covenant,* and not *tabernacle (skene),* should be supplied in our English text. The word rendered *ordinances (dikaiomata)* is a verbal noun, and means (1) a righteous action, an act by which righteousness is fulfilled (Rom. 5: 18); (2) a righteous judgment, indicating that a sinner is made righteous through the righteousness of Christ (Rom. 5: 16); (3) a righteous decree or appointment, an ordinance, law, rule, or regulation relating to the worship of God. In this last sense, the word is manifestly used in our text and also in the tenth verse of this chapter. The word *sanctuary (hagion)* means here, as in Ex. 25: 8, a holy dwelling place, referring to the entire Tabernacle. It is called a *worldly (kosmikon)* sanctuary in contrast with the *heavenly (epouranion)* sanctuary of the New Covenant. (8: 2; 9: 23.) It was a material perishable structure made with hands, and pertained wholly to this

2 For there was ⁴a tabernacle made; ⁵the first, wherein was ⁶the candlestick, and ⁷the table, and ⁸the shewbread, which is called the sanctuary.

⁴Ex. xxvi. 1-30.
⁵Ex. xxvi. 33, 35; xl. 22-27.
⁶Ex. xxv. 31-40.
⁷Ex. xxv. 23-30.
⁸Lev. xxiv. 5-9.

perishable world. But not so with the heavenly sanctuary. It, including both apartments, is "a building of God, a house not made
with hands," and it will endure forever.

**2 For there was a tabernacle made;**—Our author now proceeds to illustrate and amplify the general statement made in the
first verse; viz.: that "the first covenant had ordinances of Divine
service and a worldly sanctuary." This, he insists, is true; for
there was a tabernacle prepared (*kateskeusthe*); that is, framed
and furnished according to the pattern which was showed to
Moses in the Mount. For particulars see Ex. 26: 1-30. The
word *tabernacle* (*skene*) as used here is but a synonym of *sanctuary* in the first verse. It includes both the Holy Place and the
Most Holy, each of which is also called a tabernacle in what follows.

**The first, wherein was the candlestick,**—That is, the first or
east room of the Tabernacle, called the Holy Place. It stood first
in position, because the high priest had always to pass through it
on his way into the Holy of Holies. On the south side of this
apartment stood the candlestick made out of a talent of gold. (Ex.
25: 31-40.) It consisted of an upright shaft (which the rabbis say
was four cubits high) and six branches, all ornamented with
"bowls, knops and flowers." On the top of the main stem and
each branch there was a lamp in which pure olive oil was kept constantly burning. (Ex. 27: 20, 21; Lev. 24: 1-4.)

This candlestick was a type of the Church of Christ not as a
dwellingplace like the Tabernacle, but as God's appointed means
for perpetuating and dispensing the light of the Gospel. (Zech. 4:
1-14; Rev. 1: 20.) And hence every Christian congregation
should be a light-supporter and a light-dispenser. (1 Tim. 3: 15.)
But observe, the candlestick served only to support and dispense
the light. It was the oil, not the candlestick, that produced it; and
throughout the Bible oil is used as the appropriate symbol of the
Holy Spirit. See, for example, Isa. 16: 1; Acts 10: 38; Heb. 1:

9; 1 John 2: 20, 27. The seven lamps seem to be symbolical of the perfect light of the Gospel.

GOLDEN CANDLESTICK

**And the table and the shewbread,**—On the north side of the Holy Place, opposite the candlestick, stood the table of shewbread, or bread of the face, so called because it always stood in the presence or before the face of Jehovah. This table was made of acacia wood overlaid with gold. It was two cubits long, one cubit broad, and a cubit and a half high. Around its upper edge was a cornice of gold, and on its sides were fastened four rings through which were placed two staves of acacia wood covered with gold, for the purpose of bearing it conveniently from place to place. Its dishes and cups were all of gold. (Ex. 25: 23-30.)

TABLE OF SHEWBREAD

On this table were placed every Sabbath day by the high priest

twelve cakes of fine flour, six in a row, and on each row a cup of
frankincense. (Lev. 24: 5-9.) Each cake was made of two-tenths
of an ephah of fine flour, consisting of about seven quarts. These
cakes were eaten by the priests, and were symbolical of the spiritual food of Christians, all of whom are made priests to God
through Christ. (1 Pet. 2: 5, 9; Rev. 1: 6; 5: 10.) The frankincense seems to have been emblematical of praise and thanksgiving.
(Rev. 5: 8.)

In the Holy Place immediately before the vail stood the altar of
incense. It, too, was made of acacia wood overlaid with gold, and
was two cubits high, and one cubit in length and breadth. Like
the table, it had a cornice of gold around its upper edge. It had
also four rings of gold through which were placed two staves of
acacia wood overlaid with gold, by means of which it was carried
by the Kohathites. It had also four horns, or projecting corners,
on which the high priest made an atonement once every year. (Ex-
30: 1-10.)

ALTAR OF INCENSE

On this altar the priests every morning and evening burned
sweet incense made out of equal parts of stacte, onycha, galbanum,
and frankincense. (Ex. 30: 34-38.) This incense when burned
sent forth a delightful perfume, and seems to have been typical of
the prayers of the saints. See Psalm 141: 2; Luke 1: 9, 10; Rev.
5: 8; 8: 3, 4. And hence we see the propriety of placing this altar
of prayer directly before the Ark of the Covenant, which in connection with the Mercy Seat was a symbol of God's throne. (Jer.
3: 16, 17; Heb. 4: 16.) Every priest in offering incense on this
altar drew near to the throne of grace.

3 And after ¹the second vail, ²the tabernacle which, is called the Holiest of all;

4 Which had ¹the golden censer, and ²the ark of the covenant overlaid round about with gold, wherein was ³the golden pot that had manna, and ⁴Aaron's rod that budded, and ⁵the tables of the covenant;

¹Ex. xxvi. 31-34; xxxvi. 35-38.
²Ch. ix. 8; x. 19; 1 Kings viii. 6.
¹Lev. xvi. 12; 1 Kings vii. 50; Rev. viii. 3.
²Ex. xxv. 10-16.
³Ex. xvi. 32-34.
⁴Num. xvii. 1-11.
⁵Ex. xxv. 16; Deut. x. 1-5; 2 Chron. v. 10.

3 **And after the second vail,**—The first vail (*kalumma*) was suspended at the doorway on the east end of the Tabernacle, from golden hooks attached to five pillars overlaid with gold, each of which rested on a socket of brass. (Ex. 26: 36, 37.) But the second or partition vail (*katapetasma*) divided the whole Tabernacle into two apartments: that on the east was called the Holy Place; and that on the west, the Most Holy. This vail, like the inner curtain of the Tabernacle, was beautifully variegated with colors of blue, purple, and scarlet; and curiously embroidered all over with figures of cherubim. It was suspended directly under the golden clasps of the inner curtain, from hooks of gold attached to four pillars of acacia wood overlaid with gold and resting on four sockets of silver. (Ex. 26: 31-34.) The Rabbis say that this vail was made of thread six double; and that after the erection of the Temple it was renewed regularly year by year.

4 **Which had the golden censer,**—It is still a question with the critics, whether the word which is here rendered *censer* (*thumiaterion* from *thumiao* to burn incense) is used by our author to denote the Golden Censer on which, according to the Mishna, the High Priest burned incense once a year in the Holy of holies (Lev. 16: 12), or the Golden Altar on which he burned incense every morning and evening (Ex. 30: 7, 8). In favor of the former rendering, it is alleged by Luther, Michaelis, Bengel, Böhme, Reland, and many others, (1) that this is more in harmony with Greek usage. The word commonly used in the Septuagint for the altar of incense is *thusiasterion*. Indeed the word *thumiaterion* occurs but twice in this entire work (2 Chron. 26: 19; Ezek. 8: 11), in both of which cases it evidently means a censer. It is, however, frequently used by later writers, as Joseph and Philo, for the Altar of Incense. (2) It is alleged that the con-

struction of our text favors the same hypothesis. For, from such passages as Ex. 30: 6-8, it is perfectly obvious that the Altar of Incense stood before the Vail in the Holy Place, and that incense was burned on it daily; but the *thumiaterion* of our text is classified with the Ark of the Covenant, and seems to be located behind the Vail in the Most Holy Place. In reply to this it is urged by Olshausen, Ebrard, Delitzsch, and others, that the Apostle does not say that the golden thumiaterion was *in* the Most Holy Place; but only that it *belonged* to it. He simply affirms that the Holiest of all had a golden thumiaterion and the Ark of the Covenant. But behind the second Vail, he says [was], the tabernacle which is called The Holiest of all, *having* (*echousa*) a golden thumiaterion, and the Ark of the Covenant overlaid on all sides with gold; which was the golden vase containing the manna, and the rod of Aaron which had budded, and the tables of the covenant. Now, as a house may be said to have many things which are really not in it, such as a sign, an awning, etc., it is alleged by some that our author means nothing more in the above expression than simply this: that though the Golden Altar was located in the Holy Place before the Vail, it was, nevertheless, in its significance more properly connected with the Most Holy. And this view is thought to be supported by 1 Kings 6: 22, which may be literally rendered as follows: And the whole house he overlaid with gold, until he had finished all the house; also the whole altar which [pertains] to the Oracle, he overlaid with gold.

The main reason alleged in support of the second rendering is found in what would otherwise seem to be an unaccountable omission by the author, in speaking of the symbolical furniture of the Tabernacle. It is urged that the Apostle would certainly not have overlooked so important an article as the Altar of Incense, and name one that is not even referred to in the Law of Moses, unless it be in Lev. 16: 12. But here, the vessel used for carrying the coals of fire from the Brazen Altar, is not called in the Septuagint a golden thumiaterion, but simply *a pureion*, a fire-pan. In the Hebrew it is called a *machtah* which also means a fire-pan; but the golden censer spoken of in the Mishna is called a *kaph*; that is a curved vessel, as a dish or a pan.

This objection to the common rendering is certainly not without force. The omission, if indeed it is such, is certainly a very remarkable one, and one that is not easily accounted for. It should, however, be remembered (1) that it was not the purpose of our author to enter into minute details in describing the furniture of the Tabernacle (9: 4) ; but only to give a general outline of its divisions, apparatus, etc.  (2) In the discussions which follow these introductory remarks, he has reference chiefly to the solemn services of the Day of Atonement; and as on that day, the most solemn and important part of the incense offering was made in the Most Holy Place, and in the Golden Censer, the Apostle may have deemed it unnecessary to speak further in detail of the less imposing services of the same kind that were performed in the Holy Place and on the Golden Altar.  (3) It is remarkable that Josephus makes the same omission both in his Jewish War and in his Antiquities. In speaking of the conquest of Judea and Jerusalem by the Romans, he says, "Pompey and those that were about him went into the Temple itself, whither it was not lawful for any to enter but the High Priest, and saw what was deposited therein: viz., the Candlestick with its lamps, and the Table, and the pouring vessels, and the censers, all made entirely of gold; as also a great quantity of spices heaped together, with two thousand talents of sacred money" (J. War. b. 1, 7, 6).

On the whole I agree with Alford, and I might say with the majority of commentators both ancient and modern, that "the balance inclines toward the censer interpretation; though I do not feel by any means that the difficulty is wholly removed; and I would hail with pleasure any new solution which might clear it still further."

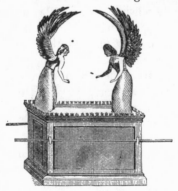

ARK OF THE COVENANT

5 And ¹over it the cherubim of glory shadowing ²the mercy-seat; of which we cannot now speak particularly.

¹Ex. xxv. 17-22; xxxvii. 6-9; Num. vii. 89; Ezek. x. 1; 1 Pet. i. 12.
²Ex. xxv. 17; xxxvii. 6; Lev. xvi. 2, 13; Heb. iv. 16.

**And the ark of the covenant**—This was a sort of chest, two and a half cubits long, a cubit and a half broad, and a cubit and a half high. It was made of acacia wood, overlaid on all sides with pure gold. Around the upper edge, was a cornice of gold; and on each side there were two rings of gold, through which were inserted two staves, for the purpose of bearing the Ark from place to place. (Ex. 25: 10-16.)

**Wherein was the golden pot, etc.**—In the Ark were placed a golden vase containing an omer (about seven pints) of manna (Ex. 16: 32-34); Aaron's rod that budded and brought forth almonds (Num. 17: 1-11); and the two tables of the covenant (Deut. 10: 1-5). It seems from 1 Kings 8: 9, that both the vase of manna and Aaron's rod had been removed from the Ark and most likely lost, before the building of the Temple; but our author speaks here of the original order and disposition of matters in the time of Moses. The Ark itself was in some way lost during the Chaldean catastrophe. It was never restored after the Babylonian captivity; but in its stead, there was placed in the second Temple a stone slab of three fingers in thickness, called by the Rabbis *Eben Sh'theyah* which means *a stone of drinking.*

5 **And over it, the cherubim of glory**—On the Ark was placed a cover (*hilasterion*) of pure gold; two cubits and a half long, a cubit and a half wide, and of unknown thickness. The original word *kapporeth* means simply a cover. But as from it, God was wont to give forth his gracious responses (Num. 7: 89), it hence obtained the name Propitiatory or Mercy Seat. On the ends of it were formed out of the same piece of solid gold from which the Propitiatory was made, two cherubim with wings extended, and having each his face turned toward the other, and also toward the Mercy Seat, as if anxious to look into the profound mysteries of the Ark upon which rested the Shekinah. (1 Pet. 1: 12.) The word *cherub* means a keeper, a guardian. These figures, as well as the cherubim of the vail and the linen curtain, were most likely symbolical of the angels who are sent to minister to the heirs of salvation. (1: 14.)

But of these matters, as our author says, it is not now necessary to speak particularly. I trust that enough has already been said on the general structure and the furniture of the Tabernacle to prepare the reader for the more profound and interesting themes which are discussed in the following paragraphs.

## 2. SYMBOLICAL SERVICES OF THE TABERNACLE INDICATING THE COMPARATIVE DARKNESS OF THE JEWISH AGE, AND THE INSUFFICIENCY OF ITS CARNAL RITES AND ORDINANCES
### 9 : 6-10

6 Now when these things were thus ordained, [1]the priests went always into the first tabernacle, accomplishing the service of God.

7 But [2]into the second went the high priest alone once every year, [3]not without blood, which he offered for himself, and for [4]the errors of the people:

[1]Ex. xxvii. 21; xxx. 7, 8; 2 Chron. xxvi. 16-19; Luke i. 8-11.
[2]Vers. 24, 25; Lev. xvi. 2-20.
[3]Lev. xvi. 11-16.
[4]Lev. iv. 2, 13, 22, 27; Num. xv. 22-29.

6 **Now when these things were thus ordained,**—The Apostle having described the Tabernacle with sufficient minuteness, proceeds now to show what was done in it. These things, he says, being thus arranged, the Priests enter constantly [every day] into the first tabernacle [the Holy Place] accomplishing [there] the services [of their order]. These services consisted in dressing the lamps and offering the incense every morning and evening; and of the change of the presence-bread on every Sabbath. The present tense (*eisiasin*) may be used here as the historical present, indicating merely what was customary; or it may denote that these services were still performed in the Temple when this Epistle was written in A.D. 63.

7 **But into the second went the high priest alone, once every year,**—That is, into the second apartment, the Most Holy Place, of the Tabernacle. Into this, none but the High Priest was allowed to enter; and he only once a year, on the tenth day of the seventh month. But on that day he entered the Most Holy Place at least three times, perhaps four. This will be best explained by indicating briefly the varied services of that most solemn of all the days of the year, as given in the sixteenth chapter of Leviticus. After the usual morning services and the offering of the sacrifices prescribed in Num. 29: 7-11, the High Priest was required (1) to

kill the bullock which he has provided for a sin-offering for himself
and for his house (Lev. 16: 11) ; (2) to carry a pan of coals from
the Brazen Altar and also a portion of sweet-incense into the Most
Holy Place, and there to burn the incense before the Lord (verses
12, 13) ; (3) to enter the second time with the blood of the bullock, and to sprinkle it seven times on and before the Mercy Seat
(verse 14) ; (4) to slay the goat of the sin-offering for the people
(verse 15) ; (5) to go the third time within the Vail, with the
blood of this goat, and to do with it as he had done with the blood
of the bullock; (6) to make an atonement for the Holy Place, the
tabernacle of the congregation, as he had done for the Most Holy,
by smearing with the blood of the two victims the horns of the
Golden Altar (Ex. 30: 10), and also most likely by sprinkling the
blood seven times with his finger on and before the Altar, as he
had before sprinkled it on and before the Mercy seat (verse 16,
compare Josephus Ant. iii. 10, 3) ; (7) to make an atonement for
the altar of burnt-offerings, by smearing its horns with the mingled
blood of the two victims, and by sprinkling of the mixture seven
times on it, as he had on the Altar of Incense (verses 18, 19).
The Rabbis say that for this purpose the blood of the two victims
was mingled in a basin. (8) After this the High Priest was required to send away the live goat to *azazel*, which means a state of
complete separation (verses 20-22) ; (9) to bathe himself and put
on his golden garments, which he had put off before entering the
Most Holy Place (verses 23, 24) ; and (10) to offer the burnt-offerings for himself and the people, and the fat of the sin-offerings;
and then to cause their flesh to be burned without the camp
(verses 24, 25). After this, according to the Mishna (Yoma v.
1 ; viii. 4), he again put off his golden garments, and entering the
Most Holy Place the fourth time, he brought out "the bowl and
the censer."

When, therefore, the Apostle says that the high priest went into
the Most Holy Place, "not without blood," he does not mean that
he was required to carry blood with him every time that he entered
it; but only that he had to do this on the day on which he went in
to make an atonement for himself and for the errors of the people.
The word rendered *errors* (*agnoemata*) means ignorance, involun-
tary error, etc.  But it here includes all sins, save those only which
were committed "with a high hand," and in open defiance and con-

8 [1]The Holy Ghost this signifying, that [2]the way into the holiest of all was not yet made manifest, while as the first tabernacle was yet standing:

[1]Chap. iii. 7; x. 15; Isa. lxiii. 11; Acts vii. 51, 52; xxviii. 25; 2 Pet. ii. 21.
[2]Chap. x. 19-22; John x. 7, 9; xiv. 6; Eph. ii. 18; See also Matt. xvi. 21, 22; Mark ix. 9, 10, 31, 32; Luke ix. 45; xviii. 33, 34; John xx. 9.

tempt of God's law. For such sins, no sacrifice was to be offered. (Num. 15: 30, 31; Heb. 10: 28.) See notes on 5: 2.

8 **The Holy Spirit this signifying,**—The Holy Spirit is here acknowledged to be the designer, as well as the interpreter of the Old Economy. It not only moved the ancient prophets to speak to the people the words and thoughts of God (see references), but it also breathed into the inanimate types of the Old Covenant a language which shows that they are all of God, and are designed to shadow forth and illustrate the sublime mysteries of redemption. And not only so,—not only were these types made shadows of good things to come, but they were moreover so framed as to indicate also in various ways the comparative darkness of the Jewish age. The fact, for instance, that none but the high priest was allowed to go behind the Vail, and that even he was allowed to do this but once a year, and then not without blood which he was required to offer for his own sins and for the sins of the people,—all this served to demonstrate that the way into Heaven, the antitype of the Most Holy Place of the Tabernacle (verses 12, 24), was still a mystery, a matter that was not fully understood by anyone but God himself while the Tabernacle and Temple worship was continued. That God did, in anticipation of the shedding of Christ's blood, justify and save believers, under both the Patriarchal and the Jewish age, is of course conceded. See Ex. 3: 6; 2 Kings 2: 1, 11; Dan. 12: 13; Luke 16: 22; 23: 43; Rom. 3: 25, 26; Heb. 6: 15; 11: 13-16, etc. But the ground on which they were so justified and made happy, was yet a mystery to men and angels; for none, it seems, but the Father, Son, and Holy Spirit yet understood that Christ must suffer and rise from the dead, and that repentance and remission of sins should be preached to all nations through him, as the way, the truth, the resurrection, and the life. See references under.[2] But when Christ's body was broken for our sins according to the Scriptures, then also was the Vail of the Temple "rent in twain from the top to the bottom" (Matt. 27: 51); and henceforth the way into Heaven, through the torn flesh

9 Which was ¹a figure for the time then present, |in: *according to*| which
were offered both gifts and sacrifices, ²that could not make him that did the
service perfect, as pertaining to the conscience;

¹Chap. viii. 5; ix. 24; xi. 19; Rom. v. 14.
²Gal. iii. 21; Heb. vii. 18, 19; ix 13, 14; x. 1-4, 11.

of Jesus, was made manifest.  Then also the Old Tabernacle, with
all that pertained to it fell to the ground; and on its ruins was
erected the true Tabernacle of which Christ has become the prime
Minister. (8: 2; 9: 11.)

**While as the first tabernacle was standing:**—First in what
respect?  Does the Apostle mean first in time, or first in place?
First in place or position say Ebrard, Delitzsch, Alford, Moll, and
others.  These able critics insist that the word *"first"* is used here,
as in verse sixth, to denote simply the Holy Place, standing as it
did in front of the Most Holy.  So long as it stood in that position,
it served of course to obscure the way leading through the Vail
into the Most Holy Place, which in the second verse is called the
second tabernacle.  All this is of course conceded as a matter of
fact.  But is this the meaning of the passage?  I think not.  It
seems to me that the Apostle has reference here to the entire Jewish Tabernacle, which however, he uses symbolically for the whole
system of Jewish worship, begun in the Tabernacle and continued
in the Temple; and that the second Tabernacle, with which the
first is contrasted, is the "greater and more perfect Tabernacle" of
the eleventh verse, together perhaps with the heavenly Sanctuary
into which Christ has for us entered.  Previous to Christ's entry,
the way into the Holiest of all was not made manifest to anyone.
Until the vail of Christ's flesh was rent (Heb. 10: 20), no man,
and perhaps no angel (1 Pet. 1: 12), understood how God could
be just in justifying any of Adam's race, and receiving them into
glory.  But when Christ died for our sins according to the Scriptures, then all was made manifest. (Rom. 3: 25, 26.)  Henceforth
Jesus was everywhere proclaimed as the way into the Holiest of
all.  See references.

9 **Which was a figure for the time then present,**—Or rather,
Which [tabernacle] was a figure [reaching down] to the present
time.  The idea of the Apostle seems to be this: that the Jewish
Tabernacle with all its rites was made a symbol (*parabole*) of the
good things of the kingdom of heaven; and that as the Law was

10 Which stood only ¹in meats and drinks, and ²divers washings, [and] ³carnal ordinances, imposed on them until ⁴the time of reformation.

¹Lev. xi. 1-45; Deut. xiv. 3-21; Acts x. 3-15; Col. ii. 16.
²Ex. xxix. 4; xxx. 19-21; Lev. xiv. 8, 9; xvi. 4, 24; xvii. 15; xxii. 16; Num. xix. 7-21; Deut. xxi. 6; xxiii. 11.
³Chap. vii. 16; Gal. iv. 3, 9; Eph. ii. 15; Col. ii. 20-22.
⁴Isa. lxv. 17-25; Matt. xix. 28; Gal. iv. 4; Eph. i. 10.

our schoolmaster to bring us to Christ (Gal. 3: 24), even so the symbolic worship of the Tabernacle was designed to continue until the beginning of the new dispensation under the reign of Christ. But no longer; for since the coming of Christ, we are no longer under the schoolmaster. (Gal. 3: 25.)

**In which were offered**—(*kathen*) according to which [figure] are offered both gifts and sacrifices. The present tense (*prospherontai*) seems to denote that the Levitical sacrifices were still offered by the Jews, according to the laws and ordinances of the ancient Tabernacle.

**That could not, etc.**—These bloody sacrifices procured for those who offered them a good relative standing with respect to the honors, rights, and privileges of the Old Covenant; but nothing more. They had no power to perfect anyone with respect to his own moral consciousness. They were, in fact, but shadows of the sacrifice of Christ (10: 1), and could therefore procure for neither priest nor people anything more than a mere symbolical pardon of sins.

10 **Which stood only in meats, etc.**—The construction of this sentence is somewhat obscure; and hence several different renderings have been proposed. The main trouble is to determine the proper antecedent member of the relation expressed by the preposition *epi,* the usual meaning of which is *on, upon,* or *in addition to.* What was on, upon, or in addition to meats, and drinks, and divers washings? "Gifts and sacrifices," say Delitzsch, Alford, etc.; "The service," say Luther and some of the more ancient commentators; "Carnal ordinances" representing gifts and sacrifices, say Green and Lünemann; "Perfect," say Ebrard and some of the Christian fathers: that is, they say, the gifts and sacrifices offered could not perfect anyone with respect to his conscience, but only with respect to meats, and drinks, and divers washings. On the whole, I agree in the main with Alford and Delitzsch. The object of the Apostle seems to be to connect the offering of sacrifices with

certain other matters relating to meats, and drinks, and divers washings,—all of which he characterizes as carnal ordinances, imposed on the people till the coming of Christ.

**And divers washings:**—(*diaphorois baptismois*) washings which were performed by immersing in water whatever was to be cleansed. These had reference (1) to the washing of the whole body (*louo*) ; as, for instance, the body of every Priest at the time of his consecration (Ex. 29:4) ; of the High Priest on the Day of Atonement (Lev. 16:4, 24) ; of a Priest defiled with any uncleanness (Lev. 22: 6) ; of the Priest who officiated at the services of the red heifer (Num. 19: 7) ; of the man who burned the red heifer (Num. 19: 8) ; of the person cleansed with the water of purification (Num. 19: 19) ; of the healed leper (Lev. 14: 8, 9) ; of any one who had eaten the flesh of an animal dead of disease (Lev. 17: 15) ; of the conductor of the scape-goat (Lev. 16: 26) ; of the man who burned the sin-offering without the camp on the day of atonement (Lev. 16: 28) ; of a person unclean from a running issue (Lev. 15: 13) ; of a person rendered unclean by coming in contact with anything defiled by a running issue (Lev. 15:8) ; of a person defiled by semen virile (Lev. 15: 16, 18) ; of a person defiled by female uncleanness (Lev. 15: 22, 27) : (2) to the washing of the hands and feet (*nipto*) ; as of the Priests (Ex. 30: 19, 20) ; of the Elders of the congregation (Deut. 21:6) : (3) to the washing of garments (*pluno*) ; as of the Levites at the time of their consecration (Num. 8:7) ; of the Priest who officiated at the sacrifice of the red heifer (Num. 19:7) ; of the man who burned the red heifer (Num. 19:8) : (4) to the washing of the inwards and legs of the burnt-offerings (*pluno*) ; see, for instance, Ex. 29:7; Lev. 1:9, 13: (5) to the washing of wooden vessels (*nipto*) ; see Lev. 15: 12: and (6) to such spoils of war as could not be made to pass through the fire (Num. 31:21-23). These washings were all but carnal ordinances, and had in themselves no efficacy beyond the purifying of the flesh; but in that age of types and shadows, these were all necessary to indicate and illustrate the moral purity that is required of all who would enjoy the benefits of the New Covenant.

**Until the time of reformation.**—That is, until the coming of Christ and the inauguration of the New Covenant. Then old things were to pass away, and all things become new. And hence the new era is called the period of the regeneration. (Matt. 19:28.)

### 3. THE HIGHER, PURER AND MORE PERFECTLY
### EFFICACIOUS SERVICES OF CHRIST AS THE
### HIGH PRIEST OF THE NEW ECONOMY
### 9:11-14

11 But [1]Christ being come [2]an high priest of good things to come, by [3]a greater and more perfect tabernacle, [4]not made with hands, that is to say, not of this building;

[1]Gen. xlix. 10; Matt. xi. 3; 1 John iv. 2, 3; v. 20; 2 John 7.
[2]Ch. ii. 17; iii. 1; iv. 15; v. 5, 6; vii. 26, 27; viii. 1.
[3]See refs. on viii. 2.
[4]Vs. 23, 24; Acts vii. 48.

---

11 **But Christ being come**—(*paragenomenos*) having come forward as a historical person. (Matt. 3: 1.) The Apostle makes the appearance of Christ (not his incarnation, but his historical manifestation) the grand turning point in the economy of redemption. Previous to his coming it was fit and right that all the Levitical ordinances should be carefully observed, and particularly that the high priest should go once every year into the most Holy Place to make a symbolical atonement for the people. But when Christ came forward as the high priest of the new institution, types and shadows were no longer necessary; and he, therefore, took them all out of the way, nailing them to his cross. (Col. 2: 14.)

**Through a greater and more perfect tabernacle,**—There is here, as well as in the following verses, a manifest reference to the services of the first Tabernacle. As the high priest passed through the Holy Place of this symbolic edifice on his way into the Most Holy; so also Christ passed through a greater and more perfect Tabernacle than the Holy Place of the ancient Tabernacle on his way into heaven.

But what is this greater and more perfect Tabernacle? The whole earth, says Macknight; the human nature of Christ, says Chrysostom; the holy life of Christ, says Ebrard; the glorified body of Christ, says Hofmann; the aerial and siderial heavens, says Bleek; the heaven of angels and of the just made perfect, says Delitzsch. The Apostle says here but little concerning it; he merely tells us that it is "a greater and more perfect Tabernacle" than was that of Moses; and furthermore that it is "not made with hands; that is, not of this creation" (*tautes tes ktiseos*). The Old Covenant had a wordly sanctuary (9: 1); but the Sanctuary of the New Covenant is not of this world (John 18: 36); it is heavenly. Its most Holy Place is heaven itself (9: 23, 24); and its Holy

12 Neither ¹by the blood of goats and calves, but ²by his own blood ³he entered in once into the holy place, ⁴having obtained eternal redemption for us.

¹Lev. xvi. 11-19.
²Ch. i. 3; x. 9-14; Acts xx. 28; Eph. i. 7; Col. i. 14; Titus ii. 14; 1 Pet. i. 19; Rev. i. 5; v. 9.
³Ch. iv. 14; vi. 20; ix. 24; Acts i. 9, 11.
⁴Ch. v. 9; ix. 15; Dan. ix. 24; 1 Cor. i. 30; Gal. iii. 13, 14; Eph. i. 7; Col. i. 14; 1 Thess. i. 10; Titus ii. 14.

Place is the house which God has established on earth for his people, and in which he himself condescends to dwell with them through his Spirit (Eph. 2: 20-22). It therefore manifestly includes the Church of Christ. Indeed the building was never complete until the Church was established as a distinct and independent body on Pentecost A.D. 34, ten days after Christ's ascension. We know, however, that God has been the dwelling-place of his people in all generations. (Psalm 90: 1.) He has always had a place of refuge and shelter for those who trust in him. Under the shadow of his wings the faithful have always reposed with confidence. But as the covenant concerning Christ was, for a time, in but an incipient state (see notes on 8: 8), so also it was with the house of God which is from heaven. For a long time it was but little more than a curtain, designed for the protection and shelter of those who reposed under it. But when our Solomon (*peaceable*), the Prince of Peace, became king, he converted the tent into a magnificent temple. See notes on 8: 2.

12 **Neither by the blood of goats, etc.**—The Apostle is still keeping up a comparison between the services of the high priest on the Day of Atonement and the services of Christ, when he, as our High Priest, entered for us "into that within the vail." The former gained admittance into the earthly sanctuary by means of (*dia*) the blood of a calf or young bullock (Sept. *moschos*) and that of a goat (Sept. *chimaros*); but Christ entered heaven itself as the high priest of the New Covenant by means of his own blood. It was, so to speak, the key by means of which the heavenly Sanctuary was opened, and Christ was allowed to enter, once for all in our behalf, into the immediate presence of the King eternal, immortal and invisible.

**Having obtained eternal redemption for us,** or rather, *obtaining eternal redemption for us.* That is, he obtained it by means of the offering which he then and there made. The verb *entered* (*eiselthen*) and the participle *obtaining* (*heuramenos*) are both aorists,

13 For if the blood of bulls and of goats, and [1]the ashes of an heifer sprinkling the unclean, sanctifieth to [2]the purifying of the flesh;

[1]Num. xix. 2-21.
[2]Num. viii. 7; xix. 12.

and express contemporaneous acts; so that it was not merely by means of his death, but by the offering of his blood in connection with his death, that he paid the ransom price of our redemption. The high priest under the Law first slew the victim and then carried its blood into the most Holy Place, where he offered it for the sins of the people, thereby procuring for them a sort of typical and relative pardon. But Christ, by means of his own blood offered in heaven itself, has procured for his people absolute and eternal redemption.

The word *redemption* (*lutrosis* or *apolutrosis*) involves the idea (1) of a ransom price (*lutron*) paid for the release of a slave or captive; and (2) the deliverance procured by means of the price that is paid for this purpose. In this case the price paid was the precious blood of Christ, in consequence of which God can now be just in justifying every true believer. See Matt. 20: 28; Acts 20: 28; Eph. 1: 7; 1 Tim. 2: 6; Tit. 2: 14; 1 Pet. 1: 18, 19. But in our text it is the *deliverance* that is made prominent, and that is said to be eternal; for "their sins and their iniquities," says God, "I will remember no more."

13 **For if the blood of bulls, etc.**—In this verse and the following our author proceeds to develop still further the amazing efficacy of the blood of Christ. For this purpose he again refers to the symbolical effects of the blood of bulls and goats by means of which purification was made for the sins of the people on the Day of Atonement.

**And the ashes of an heifer**—These ashes, as we learn from Num. 19, were prepared by burning without the camp of Israel a red or earth-colored heifer, together with cedar wood, hyssop, and scarlet. Out of these ashes was prepared the water of purification, by means of which were cleansed all who were symbolically defiled by the touch of a dead body, or by being in the same tent with a dead body. This was a solemn ordinance of Divine appointment, and as such had an efficacy, as well as the sprinkling of the blood of bulls and of goats, in symbolically cleansing the people and se-

14 How much more shall the blood of Christ, who through ³the eternal
Spirit ⁴offered himself ⁵without spot to God, ⁶purge your conscience from
dead works to serve the living God?

³Isa. li. 1; Matt. xii. 28; Acts x. 38; Rom. i. 4; 2 Cor. iii. 17; 1 Tim. iii. 16; 1
Pet. iii. 18.
⁴Ch. vii. 27; x. 6-12; Eph. v. 2; Titus ii. 14; 1 Pet. ii. 24.
⁵Lev. xxii. 20; Num. xix. 2.
⁶Ch. i. 3; ix. 9; x. 2, 22.

---

curing to them the continued enjoyment of their rights and privileges as members of a typical and carnal institution.

14 **How much more, etc.**—The form of the argument, used
here by the Apostle is what is technically called *a minori ad majus,*
from the less to the greater.  He concedes that the blood of bulls
and goats and the ashes of an heifer did secure for the members of
the Old Covenant a certain kind of purification; they sanctified to
the purifying of the flesh.  But now he says, "How much more
shall the blood of Christ, who through the eternal Spirit offered
himself without spot to God, purge [purify] your conscience from
dead works to serve the living God?"  The meaning evidently is
that the blood of Christ is far more efficacious in cleansing the
moral nature of man from all spiritual defilement than were the
aforesaid carnal ordinances in cleansing the flesh.  For the latter
cleansing was only temporary and symbolical.  There was no reality in it.  It served only to demonstrate the extremely polluting nature of sin, and the great necessity of that real spiritual cleansing
which can be effected only through the infinitely precious blood of
Christ. (1 John 1 : 7.)  This is a matter, however, which belongs
more properly to faith than to philosophy.  Nothing short of infinite knowledge would enable us to fully trace out and explain the
influence of the blood of Christ on the government of God, and on
the nature, character and destiny of mankind.  Without then attempting to be wise above what is written on this profound theme,
let us simply and joyfully accept the unequivocal declaration of the
Holy Spirit, that the blood of Christ is sufficient to cleanse our
consciences from all the works of the flesh leading to death (6 : 2),
and so to fit us for the service of God who is himself infinitely
holy.

But what is meant by *"the eternal Spirit"* through which Christ
offered himself without spot to God?

In reply to this query, we have given the following hypotheses:
(1) that the expression denotes the Divine nature of Christ (Beza,

Ernesti, Ebrard, Delitzsch, Alford) ; (2) that it means the Holy
Spirit (Bleek, Tholuck, Moll) ; (3) that it signifies the endless
and immortal life of Christ (Grotius, Limborch, Schleusner) ; (4)
that it has reference to the glorified and exalted person of Christ
(Döderlein, Storr) ; (5) that it represents the Divine influence by
which Christ was moved to offer himself up as a sacrifice for the
sins of the world (Kuinoel, Winzer, Stuart).  That something
may be said in favor of each of these hypotheses, is manifest from
the names by which they are supported.  But that the first is the
true one seems most probable for the following reasons: (1) It is
manifestly the design of the Apostle, in using this expression, to
heighten and intensify the value of Christ's offering.  And this he
could do in no more effectual way than by telling us that the offering was made and rendered perfect by means of his own Divine
nature.  It was the sacrifice of his perfect humanity, sustained and
supported by his own Divinity, that gave to his offering its infinite
value.  That it was made in some respect through the will and
agency of the Father himself, is proved by the fact that "the
Father sent the Son to be the Savior of the world" (1 John 4:
14) ; and that it was made also through the agency of the Holy
Spirit, is equally manifest from the fact that it was through the
Spirit that the Word became incarnate (Luke 1: 35), and that
Christ afterward performed his miracles (Matt. 12: 28, 31, 32).
God bestowed on him the gift of the Spirit without measure (John
3: 34), so that it may be truthfully said that under its influence he
went to the cross, rose from the dead, ascended to the heavens, and
there made an offering for the sins of the world.  All this is of
course conceded.  But it is not to any extraneous influence, but to
the personal dignity, glory, and Divinity of Christ himself that the
infinite value of his offering is to be ascribed.  (2) This seems to
be further indicated by the form of the expression.  It is not
"through the Holy Spirit," as we have given in a few manuscripts
(D, A, B, F, H, etc.) ; nor is it "through the eternal Spirit," as in
our English Version, but it is according to our best authorities (B,
D, K, L, etc.), simply, "through eternal Spirit," that Christ offered
himself without spot to God.  The eternal Spirit that is here spoken of, as Alford justly observes, "is Spirit absolute; Divine
Spirit; and thus it is self-conscious, laying down its own course,
purely of itself, unbounded by conditions.  The animals which

were offered had no will, no spirit (*pneuma*) of their own which
could concur with the act of sacrifice. Theirs was a transitory life,
of no potency or value. They were offered through law (*dia
nomou*) rather than through any consent or agency or counter-
agency of their own. But Christ offered himself, with his own consent assisting and empowering the sacrifice. And what was that
consent? The consent of what? Of the spirit of a man, such as
yours or mine, given in and through our finite spirit, whose acts
are bounded by its own allotted space and time, and its own responsibilities? *No:* but the consenting act of his Divine personality—his eternal Spirit (*pneuma aionion*), his Godhead, which
from before time acquiesced in, and wrought with the purpose of
the Father."

## 4. THE ETERNAL INHERITANCE SECURED FOR THE CALLED
## AND FAITHFUL OF ALL AGES, THROUGH THE DEATH
## AND MEDIATION OF THE LORD JESUS
### 9: 15-24

15 And for this cause ¹he is the mediator of ²the new testament, that by
means of death, ³for the redemption of the transgressions that were under
the first testament, they ⁴which are called might receive the promise of ⁵eter-
nal inheritance.

¹Ch. viii. 6; xii. 24; Gal. iii. 19, 20; 1 Tim. ii. 5.
²Ch. viii. 8; 2 Cor. iii. 6.
³Rom. iii. 24-26; Eph. i. 7; Rev. v. 9; xiv. 3, 4.
⁴Rom. viii. 28, 30; ix. 24; Gal. i. 15; 2 Thess. ii. 14.
⁵Rom. iv. 13; Gal. iii. 18; Eph. i. 11, 14, 18.

---

15 **And for this cause**—(*kai dia touto*) on this account; viz.,
that the blood of Christ has an inherent power and efficacy, such as
the legal sacrifices had not: a power to purify the conscience from
dead works, and to fit all who are purified and sanctified by it for
the service and enjoyment of the living God for this very reason.

**he is the mediator of the new testament,**—This clause is explained with sufficient fullness in our notes on 8: 6, 8, to which the
reader is referred. The word rendered *testament* (*diatheke*)
means here a covenant, and the "new testament" of this verse is
the same as the New Covenant of 8: 8.

**that by means of death, etc.**—Or more literally, *so that [his]
death having taken place for the redemption of the transgressions
grounded on the first covenant, those who have been called may
receive the promise of the everlasting inheritance.* The Apostle

here plainly declares that the death of Christ was necessary in order to the redemption of the transgressions which were committed under the Old Covenant during the Jewish age. But what was then true in this respect of the Jewish age, was also equally true of all previous ages. For as Hofmann says, our author here "regards the history of God's relations to mankind as one great whole, of which the religious history of Israel forms a typical part, exhibiting in one crucial instance the incapacity of the whole human race to satisfy the requirements of the Divine will. From this point of view, atonement for transgressions under the law will mean the same thing as the atonement of the sins of men in general, regarded as violations of the revealed will of God; and the death of Christ will be an atonement, not merely for sins in the abstract, but especially for sin in its most aggravated form, as conscious transgression of that revealed will. The special reference here made to transgressions under the covenant of Sinai has its ground not only in this, that that covenant had a real significance for mankind in general, but also that the point which the sacred writer has here mainly in view, is the transition from it and its failures to the saving dispensation of the Gospel. That transition could not take place without a death which would annihilate the transgressions of the former covenant." But the death of bulls and goats was wholly unavailing for the purpose. (10:4.) And hence the necessity that Christ should die for the people, before the "called" of any age could have an absolute right to the free and full enjoyment of the eternal inheritance.

But does it follow from this, as many suppose, that Abraham, Isaac, Jacob, and other faithful men of the Patriarchal and Jewish ages were still "under the dominion of sin and death," until Christ came, and by his death and alleged descent into Hades procured their deliverance? I think not, for the Scriptures everywhere teach that these holy men of old were justified by faith and obedience as well as we (Rom. 4:4; James 2:21-23, etc.), and this of course implies that they were received and treated by God as just persons, and that after their death they were immediately translated, if not directly to heaven, at least to a place and state of high spiritual enjoyment (Ex. 3:6; Dan. 12:13; Luke 16:23-26, etc.). And this is manifestly Paul's idea in Rom. 3:25, 26, where he says in substance that God had, as it were, passed by the sins of

16 For where a testament is, there must also of necessity be the death of the testator.

those faithful men for a time, and that in the end of the ages he had set forth Jesus Christ as a propitiatory sacrifice for a demonstration of his administrative justice in doing so. That no sin was ever forgiven absolutely, without the blood of Christ, is of course conceded, and so also no debt was ever paid absolutely by a mere paper currency. But nevertheless we know that thousands of obligations have been practically cancelled by notes, bonds, and other like documents. And just so God seems to have administered the affairs of his government during the Patriarchal and Jewish ages. He, too, so to speak, issued in the meantime a sort of promissory notes, based on the infinite value of the blood of Christ, which he knew was to be shed in due time. By means of these notes he was enabled (if I may say it with reverence) to meet, for the time being, all the claims of justice, and still to treat as just and righteous all who like Abraham, Isaac, and Jacob, became loyal subjects of his government. But no one could read his "title clear to mansions in the skies," until by the blood of Christ his sins were all cancelled absolutely, and the notes and bonds that had been issued in behalf of the sinner were all redeemed by the one great atoning sacrifice. See notes on 11 : 39, 40.

**they who are called**—That is, all in every age who by faith and obedience have become the children of God, "and heirs according to the promise." For all such, God has provided "an inheritance which is incorruptible, and undefiled, and that fadeth not away." (1 Pet. 1 : 4.) But before any could rightfully inherit it and claim it as their own, the covenant through which it has been provided had to be sealed and ratified with the blood of Jesus. The necessity of this the Apostle now proceeds to illustrate (1) by the analogous case of a will of testament; and (2) by example of the Old Covenant.

16 **For where a testament is, etc.**—That is, before a testament can have any legal force, the death of the testator must be known and publicly acknowledged as a fact. The reference which our author makes to "the eternal inheritance" at the close of the preceding verse, suggested to his mind the case of a testament, and this thought he now takes up, not for the purpose of proving, but simply of illustrating the necessity of Christ's death.

17 For [1]a testament is of force after men are dead: otherwise it is of no strength at all while the testator liveth.

[1]Gal. iii. 15.

17 **For a testament is of force after men are dead:**—This is a well known law of all civilized nations. So long as the testator lives, it is his privilege to change his will as he pleases, and nothing but his death can therefore immutably fix and ratify its various stipulations. Previous to this indeed, his intended heirs may be allowed to enjoy to any extent the benefits of his estate. But not until the will is ratified by his death, can they claim a legal right to the inheritance as their own. And so it was with respect to the eternal inheritance. "After Abraham had patiently endured, he obtained the promise." (6: 15.) That is, immediately after his death he was received into the enjoyment of the promised rest, as one of God's elect, and henceforth he was allowed to partake of the benefits of the inheritance so far as he was capable of enjoying them. (11: 10, 16.) And he also doubtless looked forward to the time when he and his children would be constituted the rightful owners of all things (Rom. 4: 13; 1 Cor. 3: 21-23), not excepting the redeemed and renovated earth. See notes on 2: 5-9. But it was not until the New Covenant was inaugurated by the death of Christ and ratified by his blood, that any one could claim, as we now claim, an absolute right to the eternal inheritance.

I see no reason for the protracted controversy that critics have kept up with respect to the meaning of the word *diatheke* in the sixteenth and seventeenth verses. It is quite evident that the *dia-themenos* of these verses is the maker of the diatheke, and that his death must of necessity take place before the diatheke can have any legal force. This is not true in the case of a covenant, but only in the case of a will or testament. And hence, beyond all doubt, the word *diatheke* in these verses means a will or testament. But on the other hand, it is equally obvious that this word cannot in this sense be literally applied to any of God's arrangements with men, nor does our author so intend to apply it. He refers to the well-known law of a will as an *analogous* case, merely for the purpose of illustrating his point, and of so impressing more deeply on the mind of his readers the necessity of Christ's death, before God could consistently bestow on the heirs of the promise a right in

18 Whereupon neither [1]the first testament was dedicated without blood.
19 For when Moses had spoken every precept to all the people according to the law, he took [2]the blood of calves and of goats, with water, and [3]scarlet wool, and [4]hyssop, and [5]sprinkled both the book and all the people,

[1]Ex. xxiv. 3-8.
[2]Ex. xxiv. 5.
[3]Lev. xiv. 4-6; Num. xix. 6.
[4]Ex. xii. 22; Num. xix. 18; Psa. li. 7.
[5]Ex. xxiv. 8.

---

fee-simple to the eternal inheritance. The word *diathemenos* means both a covenanter and a testator, and the word *diatheke* means in like manner both a covenant and a testament. And hence it was perfectly natural and legitimate that our author should, in this instance, pass from the first meaning of diatheke to the second, without however intending to apply the word to any of God's arrangements in a sense which would be altogether inapposite.

18 **Whereupon neither was the first testament dedicated without blood.**—Or more literally, *Wherefore neither was the first covenant inaugurated without blood.* The sixteenth and seventeenth verses are but an illustration of the fundamental principle submitted in the fifteenth, viz., that the death of Christ was necessary in order to redemption from the sins committed under the Old Covenant, and also to the rightful inauguration of the New Covenant, so that *all* the redeemed might have a legal right to the eternal inheritance. This thought the Apostle now proceeds to illustrate still further by referring to the way in which the Old Covenant was inaugurated. Since therefore it is thus and so in the case of a will, it is also analogically true of all the *diathekai* of God; they, too, must be inaugurated and ratified by means of death and the sprinkling of blood. And hence even the Old Covenant, which was but a type of the New, was not inaugurated without blood.

19 **For when Moses had spoken, etc.**—There is reference here to the solemn transactions that are recorded in Ex. 24: 1-8. When Moses had received from God the laws and ordinances recorded in Ex. 20-23, he recited them to the people, and they all answered with one voice and said, "All the words which the Lord hath said we will do." After this; he wrote all the words and commandments of the Lord in a book; and when he had again recited them to the people, and had received their second response, he then proceeded, as our author says, to ratify the covenant, by

20 Saying, [1]This is the blood of the testament which God hath enjoined unto you.

[1]Ex. xxiv. 8; Zech. ix. 11; Matt. xxvi. 28.

taking "the blood of calves and of goats, with water, and scarlet wool, and hyssop," with which he "sprinkled both the book and all the people." The account of these transactions, as given by both Moses and Paul, is very brief, each of them writing under the influence of plenary inspiration, like Matthew, Mark, Luke, and John, selected only such particulars as best served to accomplish his purpose. Moses makes no mention of the blood of goats, nor of the water, and scarlet wool, and hyssop, which were used on the occasion, nor does he speak of the sprinkling of the book of the covenant. And Paul, on the other hand, says nothing about building the altar and the twelve pillars, nor does he specify the particular kinds of offerings which were offered by the young men at the bidding of Moses. Like the Gospel narratives, however, these accounts are both true so far as they go, for on no fair principle of interpretation can mere omissions be construed as inconsistencies or discrepancies. The hyssop and scarlet wool were used on other occasions for the sprinkling of blood and water. See Ex. 12: 22; Lev. 14: 4-7; Num. 19: 18, 19, etc. Usually the bunch of hyssop was fastened to a stick of cedar wood, by means of a scarlet band, and then wrapped round with scarlet wool for the purpose of absorbing the blood and the water that were to be sprinkled.

20 **Saying, This is the blood of the testament**—That is, This is the blood by means of which the covenant is ratified, and you yourselves purified and consecrated to God, as his peculiar people. This shows that without the shedding and sprinkling of blood, the people could not be received into covenant relation with God: nay more, that without this blood, the covenant itself could have no validity.

**Which God hath enjoined unto you.**—The use of the word *enjoined* (*eneteilato*) shows very clearly that the Sinaitic Covenant was not a mere compact or agreement (*suntheke*), as made between equals. On the contrary, it was a solemn arrangement (*diatheke*) proposed by God himself to the people for their acceptance; and which when accepted unconditionally on their part, had to be ratified with blood.

21 Moreover ²he sprinkled with blood both the tabernacle, and all the vessels of the ministry.

²Ex. xl. 9-15; Lev. viii. 15, 19.

**21 Moreover he sprinkled with blood both the tabernacle, etc.**—This cannot have reference to the occasion spoken of in Ex. 24: 1-8; for the Tabernacle was not then constructed. But the Apostle must refer here to the consecration of the Tabernacle according to the directions given in Ex. 40: 9-11. True indeed there is no explicit mention made in these about the sprinkling of blood. God simply says to Moses, "Thou shalt take the anointing oil, and anoint the Tabernacle and all that is therein, and thou shalt hallow it and all the vessels thereof; and it shall be holy. And thou shalt anoint the altar of burnt-offerings and all its vessels, and sanctify the altar; and it shall be an altar most holy. And thou shalt anoint the laver and its foot, and sanctify it." In all this, there is nothing said about the sprinkling of blood on either the Tabernacle or its furniture. But neither is there anything said in the following verses (12-16) of the same chapter, about sprinkling blood on Aaron and his sons: and yet we know from Lev. 8: 30, that blood, as well as oil, was sprinkled on the Priests at the time of their consecration. The mere silence of Moses is therefore no evidence that the Tabernacle and all the vessels of the ministry were not purified with blood, as well as anointed with oil. We all believe on the testimony of Paul (Acts 20: 35), that Christ said on one occasion, "It is more blessed to give than to receive"; though this saying is not recorded in any of the Gospel narratives. And just so we reason in the case under consideration. The statement of Paul is quite sufficient on this point, without further evidence; though it is worthy of notice that the testimony of Josephus is to the same effect as that of Paul. Speaking of the consecration of the Priests he says, "And when Moses had sprinkled Aaron's vestments, himself, and his sons, with the blood of the beasts that were slain, and had purified them with spring water and ointment, they became God's Priests. After this manner did he consecrate them and their garments for seven days together. The same did he to the Tabernacle and the vessels thereto belonging,—both with oil first incensed, as I said, and with blood of bulls and rams slain day by day, one, according to its kind." (Ant. iii. 8, 6.) From this statement of Jo-

22 And [1]almost all things are by the law purged with blood: and [2]without the shedding of blood is no remission.

[1]Lev. xiv. 6, 7, 14, 25, 51, 52; xvi. 15-19.
[2]Lev. iv. 20, 26, 35; xvii. 11, 12.

sephus, as well as from the narrative of Moses (Ex. 40: 9-16), it seems most likely that the consecration of the Tabernacle and that of the Priest took place at the same time.

22 **And almost all things are by the law purged with blood:** —That is, the Law required that almost everything defiled in any way, should be purified by means of blood. In some cases, indeed, purification was made by means of water (Lev. 16: 26, 28; Num. 31: 24) ; and in others, by fire and water (Num. 31: 22, 23) ; but the exceptions to the general rule of purification by blood, were but few.

**And without the shedding of blood is no remission.**—To this law, there was no exception. Every sin required an atonement; and no atonement could be made without blood. The only apparent exception given in the Law is in the case of one who was too poor to bring "two turtle-doves or two young pigeons for a sin-offering." (Lev. 5: 11-13.) In that event, he was required to bring to the Priest the tenth part of a ephah (about seven pints) of fine flour, without oil or frankincense, a handful of which, the Priest was to burn as a memorial upon the altar. But that even in this case, the sin of the poor man was not forgiven without the shedding of blood, seems evident from what follows in the next verse of the same chapter, where it is said, "And the priest shall make an atonement for him for the sin which he hath sinned, and it shall be forgiven him." This atonement, it seems, could not be made without blood; for God says (Lev. 17: 11), "I have given it [the blood] to you upon the altar to make an atonement for your souls: for it is the blood that maketh an atonement for the soul." This law was regarded by the Jews as universal in its application: for in the Talmud it is said, "There is no atonement except in blood" (Yoma 5[1]). It is most likely therefore that in this case, the Priest was required to make an atonement for the sin of the poor man, at the public expense. The *memorial* was made with flour; but the *atonement* with blood.

23 It was therefore necessary that ¹the patterns of things in the heavens should be purified with these; but ²the heavenly things themselves with better sacrifices than these.

¹Chap. viii. 5; ix. 10, 24; x. 1; Col. ii. 17.
²Chap. viii. 2; ix. 11, 12, 24; Matt. iii. 2; xiii. 24, 31, 33, 44, 45, 47; Eph. i. 3; ii. 6.

23 **It was therefore necessary, etc.**—Without these sacrifices required by the Law, the Tabernacle and all its furniture would have been unclean; and the Priests themselves would have been unclean; so that no acceptable service could have been rendered to God in either the court or the Tabernacle. Nay more, without these sacrifices, the book of the covenant would have been unclean, and the covenant itself would never have been ratified. The very existence of the Theocracy depended, therefore, on the shedding and sprinkling of blood, without which the whole nation of Israel would have been cast off as an unclean thing.

**But the heavenly things themselves with better sacrifices than these;**—This profoundly significant phrase naturally suggests to our minds the following queries: (1) What are the "better sacrifices" with which the heavenly things are cleansed? (2) What are the heavenly things that are cleansed by means of these sacrifices? And (3) what is meant by the sacrificial cleansing of these heavenly things?

(1) By the better sacrifices is evidently meant the sacrifice of Christ himself. The plural is put for the singular by synecdoche, because of the plurality of the Levitical sacrifices which are spoken of in the same verse. See a similar case in Luke 16: 9.

(2) "The heavenly things" include all the antitypes of the Jewish Tabernacle, etc. The Holy Place had to be cleansed with the blood of bulls and goats, and so also had the Most Holy Place. (Lev. 16: 11-20; Heb. 9: 21.) But the former was a type of the Church, as God's dwelling-place on Earth; and the latter was a type of Heaven itself where God ever dwells with the spirits of the just made perfect. See notes on 8: 2, and also on 9: 11, 12. It is evident therefore that in the "heavenly things" are included both the Church on earth and the Church of the redeemed in Heaven. For as our author says, Christ has not entered into holy places made with hands, counterparts of the true, but into Heaven itself, now to be manifested in the presence of God in our behalf.

(3) The third query is confessedly one of great difficulty: and it

may perhaps be entirely above our present very limited attainments in the knowledge of Divine things. That the Church on Earth with all that pertains to it, needs the cleansing influence of the blood of Christ in order to make it a fit temple for the Holy Spirit, and to qualify its members severally for a place in the upper Sanctuary, is obvious enough. On this point, therefore, discussion is wholly unnecessary. But why should Heaven itself, or anything belonging to it, need to be cleansed by the atoning blood of the Lord Jesus? In reply to this question it is alleged (1) that the necessity arises from the sin of those angels who kept not their first estate, but who in consequence of their rebellion were cast down to Tartarus. (2 Pet. 2: 4; Jude 6.) But angels are not embraced in our premises; and must not therefore be forced into our conclusions. See note on 2: 16. (2) It is supposed that "in consequence of the presence of sin in us, the Holy of holies in the heavenly world could not be re-opened for our approach, until it was itself anointed with the blood of atonement" (Stier). In the verb *purified* (*katharizesthai*), says Bloomfield, "there is a metonymy, such as we often find when things partly similar and partly dissimilar are compared. For by the legal purifications, an entrance was afforded to the Sanctuary; so, by taking the effect as standing for the cause, Heaven is said to be purified or consecrated by the service of Christ, instead of saying that an entrance by it is given to that Heaven. So Rosenmüller and others. This is plausible; but to my mind it is not altogether satisfactory. It looks too much like making the substance conform to the shadow, rather than the shadow to the substance. Nothing short of a real purification of "the heavenly things" will, it seems to me, fairly meet the requirements of the text. And I am therefore inclined to think that for the present, at least, this is for us rather a matter of faith than of philosophy. When we can fully comprehend and explain how much more holy God is than any of the holy angels (Rev. 15: 4), and how it is that the very heavens are not clean in his sight (Job 15: 15), we may then perhaps understand more clearly than we do now, how it is that "the heavenly things," embracing even the city of the living God, the heavenly Jerusalem, should need to be purified with the atoning blood of the Lord Jesus. The fact itself seems to be clearly revealed in our text; but the reason of it is not so obvious. Can it be owing to the fact, that many of the

24 For Christ is not entered into ¹the holy places made with hands, which are ²the figures of the true; but ³into heaven itself, now to appear in the presence of God for us:

¹Ver. 11; Acts vii. 48; xvii. 24, 25; 2 Cor. v. 1.
²Ch. viii. 5; ix. 9, 23; Col. ii. 17.
³Ch. i. 3; vi. 20; vii. 26; viii. 2; ix. 12; Luke xxiv. 51; Acts i. 9-11; iii. 21; Eph. i. 20-22; Col. iii. 2.

saints were admitted into Heaven in anticipation of the death of Christ, and that though justified by faith, through the grace and forbearance of God, they nevertheless required the purifying application of the blood of Christ when shed, in order to make them absolutely holy. See notes on 9 : 15.

24 **For Christ is not entered, etc.**—In this verse the Apostle brings to a close the argument begun in the fifteenth, showing the necessity of Christ's death in order that the called might have an absolute right to the eternal inheritance. The services of the "wordly sanctuary" required the blood of bulls and of goats, without which the high priest could not enter the Holy of holies to intercede for the people. But now the sphere and object of Christ's ministry require better sacrifices than these. "For Christ," as our author says, "did not enter into holy places made with hands, mere counterparts of the true, but into heaven itself, now to be manifested in the presence of God in our behalf." And hence the necessity that he should have to offer a sacrifice sufficient to meet, to the fullest extent, all that is required by infinite Justice.

By the *"holy places"* (*hagia*) of our text are meant such as those into which the Jewish high priest entered in performing the services of the ancient Tabernacle. The word rendered *figures* (*antitupa*) means properly copies taken from a given pattern (*tupos*); such as counterfeit bills, etc. According to Scripture usage, the original heavenly realities are properly called *archetypes* (*archetupa*); the patterns shown to Moses in the Mount, the *types* (*tupos*); and the counterparts of these constructed by Moses, *antitypes* (*antitupa*). But in our modern usage we are wont to call the last of these *types;* and to apply both the names *archetypes* and *antitypes* to the original heavenly realities which the types were made to represent. The verb *appear* (*emphanisthenai*) is used in a forensic sense to denote that Christ is now manifested in the presence of God as our Advocate. "The whole comparison," says Prof. Stuart, "is taken from the custom of the Jewish high priest,

who when he entered the most Holy Place was said to appear before God or to draw near to God, because the presence of God was
manifested over the Mercy Seat in the Holy of holies; and God
was represented, and was conceived of by the Jews as sitting enthroned upon the Mercy Seat. Now as the high priest appeared
before God in the Jewish Temple and offered the blood of beasts
for expiation on the great Day of Atonement in behalf of the Jewish nation, so Christ in the heavenly Temple enters the most Holy
Place with his own blood to procure pardon (*aionon lutrosin*)
for us."

## 5. FURTHER ILLUSTRATIONS OF THE GREAT IMPORTANT DIFFERENCES BETWEEN THE LEVITICAL SERVICES AND THOSE THAT ARE PERFORMED BY CHRIST AS THE HIGH PRIEST OF OUR CONFESSION
### 9 : 25-28

25 Nor yet that he should [1]offer himself often, [2]as the high priest entereth
into the Holy Place every year with blood of others;
26 For then must he often have suffered since [1]the foundation of the world;
but now once [2]in the end of the world [3]hath he appeared to put away sin by
the sacrifice of himself.

[1]Ch. v.i. 27; x. 10, 12.
[2]Ver. 7; Ex. xxx. 10; Lev. xvi. 2-20.
[1]Ch. iv. 3; Matt. xxv. 34; Luke xi. 50; John xvii. 24; Eph. i. 4; 1 Pet. i. 20.
[2]Matt. xiii. 39, 40, 49; xxiv. 3; xxviii. 20.
[3]Ch. vii. 27; ix. 12; x. 10; John i. 29; 1 Pet. ii. 24; 1 John iii. 5.

25 **Nor yet that he should offer himself often,**—In the
preceding paragraph our author has forcibly proved and illustrated
the necessity of Christ's death as the only ground of redemption
from sin. In doing this he reasons mainly from the analogies of
the Old and New Covenant. Under the Old Covenant there was
no remission of sins without blood; and so he argues there can be
none under the New Covenant. But between these two institutions there are also many important points of contrast as well as of
similarity, one of which the Apostle has already stated in the twenty-
fourth verse; viz.: that Christ has not entered into the sanctuary
made with hands like that into which Aaron and his successors entered; on the contrary, he has gone into heaven itself, henceforth
to appear in the presence of God for us. In the twenty-fifth verse
he goes on to state another point of difference between the work of
Christ and that of the Levitical high priests. These had to offer
the same sacrifices year by year, but not so with Christ.

26 **For then must he often have suffered, etc.**—Every offer-

27 And as ⁴it is appointed unto men once to die, but ⁵after this the judgment :

---

⁴Gen. iii. 19; Job xiv. 5; Rom. v. 12.
⁵Eccl. xi. 9; xii. 14; Matt. xxv. 31-46; Acts xvii. 31; Rom. ii. 16; 2 Cor. v. 10.

---

ing of himself in heaven would of course imply an antecedent sacrificial death on earth.   If, then, an annual offering were necessary,
an annual sacrificial death would also be necessary.   But in that
event he must have often suffered since the foundation of the
world (*apo kataboles kosmou*) ; that is, since the epoch of the
Adamic renovation.   But this he has not done.   He has suffered
but one death, and has, therefore, made but one offering.

**But now once in the end of the world, etc.**—Or more literally : *But now once in the end of the ages (epi sunteleia ton aionon), he has been manifested for the putting away of sin by the
sacrifice of himself:* thus demonstrating that the one offering of
himself is sufficient to meet all the requirements of the case ; and
that it is not, therefore, necessary to repeat the offering as the high
priests were required to do under the Old Economy.   The one offering of Christ, therefore, reaches back in its meritorious effects to
the fall of man and forward to the end of time.

Another point of contrast made here by the Apostle consists in
this, that the high priest under the Law went into the Holy of Holies with alien blood (*en haimati allotrioi*) ; that is, invested, as it
were, with the blood of a young bullock and a goat; but Christ
went into heaven invested with his own blood, by means of which
he has paid the immense debt that was due to Divine Justice, and
so obtained eternal redemption for all who love and obey him.

27 **And as it is appointed unto men once to die,**—The Apostle still keeps up the contrast between Christ and the Jewish high
priest.   The latter, as we have seen, went once a year with the
blood of an innocent victim into the Holy of Holies, and there
having made an offering for himself and for the sins of the people, he came out of the sanctuary still defiled by sin ; and he had,
therefore, to repeat the same offerings year by year continually.
But not so with Christ.   His case, on the contrary, rather resembles, in some respects, the lot of all men.   They are all by the Divine sentence (Gen. 3 : 19) appointed to die once.

**But after this the judgment:** or, rather, "But after this, judgment" (*krisis* without the article).   The Apostle seems to refer

28 So Christ [*also*] [1]was once offered to bear the sins of many; and unto them [2]that look for him [3]shall he appear the second time without sin unto salvation.

[1]Isa. liii. 4-6; 1 Pet. ii. 24.
[2]Phil. iii. 20; 1 Thess. i. 10; 2 Tim. iv. 8; Titus ii. 13.
[3]John xiv. 3; Acts i. 11; 1 Thess. iv. 14-16; 2 Thess. i. 5-9; Rev. i. 7.

here more particularly to the judgment which is virtually pro-
nounced on every man immediately after death than to the general
judgment which will take place at the close of Christ's mediatorial
reign, though both of these may be included in his remark. But as
every one goes to his own proper place after death (Dan. 12: 13;
Luke 16: 22, 23; Acts 1: 25; 2 Cor. 5: 1, 8, etc.), it follows, of
course, that the true character of every individual is determined on
his exit from this world; and that his destiny is then also virtually
determined. And just so it was in the case of Christ, as our author now proceeds to show.

28 **So Christ [also] was once offered to bear the sins of many;**
—That is, he died once under the fearful load of human guilt, for
Jehovah laid on him the iniquities of us all. (Isa. 53: 4-6.) But no
sooner did he die than he was justified. The unrighteous decision
of Pilate and the Jewish Sanhedrin was immediately reversed in
the Supreme Court of the universe. God himself then acknowledged him as his Son, raised his body from the dead, and set him
at his own right hand in the heavenly realms, angels, and authorities, and powers being made subject to him. (Eph. 1: 20-22; 1 Pet.
3: 22, etc.)

**And unto them that look for him, etc.**—This refers to the second personal advent of Christ, when he shall come out of the Holy of
Holies, as did the High Priest under the Law, to bless those who
are anxiously waiting for his appearing. But he will not then
come like the High Priest still laden with sin. Once, indeed, he
bore the iniquity of us all; and so very great was the burden of our
guilt as we have seen (notes 5: 7), that it even crushed the blood
from his veins, and finally ruptured his heart. But the blood
which then flowed from his heart, under the tremendous pressure
of human guilt, has washed away from him, as well as from us, all
our iniquities, so that when he comes the second time there will not
be a trace of sin about his person. But robed in the habiliments of
righteousness, he will come in power and glory to redeem his
saints, and to take vengeance on them who know not God, and

who obey not the Gospel. Then we too will "be made the righteousness of God in him." (2 Cor. 5 : 21.)

### 6. THE UTTER MORAL INEFFICACY OF THE
### LEVITICAL OFFERINGS
### 10 : 1-4

1 For the law [1]having a shadow of good things to come, and not the very
image of the things [2]can never with those sacrifices which they offer year
by year continually make the comers thereunto perfect.

[1]Chap. viii. 5; ix. 9, 23; Col. ii. 17.
[2]Chap. vii. 18, 19; ix. 9.

1 **For the law having a shadow, etc.**—In this and the next following paragraph, we have, as Alford justly observes, the leading
thoughts of the whole section brought "together in one grand
finale, just as in the finale of a piece of music, all the hitherto scattered elements are united in one effective whole." But it is not a
mere summary of the thoughts and arguments of the section, that
is here presented. New thoughts are introduced, and others are
set forth in a fuller and more attractive light. In the last paragraph, for instance, it is fairly implied though not categorically expressed, that the blood of Christ and that alone "cleanses from all
sin." This thought the Apostle now proceeds to amplify and illustrate still further, by showing in the first place the utter insufficiency of the Levitical sacrifices. That they had no power to take
away sin, he argues from the nature of the sacrifices themselves
and the character of the services that were rendered under the Old
Covenant. For the Law, he says, having a mere shadow of the
good things to come, and not the very image of the things, can
never, with the same sacrifices which they offer year by year continually, perfect those who draw near [to God, by means of
them]. The word *shadow* (*skia*) is used here metaphorically to
denote that the Law, as a religious institution, was but a faint outline, a mere symbolical adumbration of the good things of the
Kingdom of Christ. And the word *image* (*eikoi*) means the true
bodily shape which belongs to the things themselves; the essential
form of the good things, in contrast with the shadowy representation of them as given in the Law. In the Gospel, we have both the
image (*eikon*) and the essence (*hupostasis*) : but in the Law we
have nothing more than a mere unsubstantial shadow of them.
And hence the Law had no power to take away sin; nor could it

2 For then would they not have ceased to be offered? **because that the** worshipers [3]once purged should have no more conscience of sins.

3 But in those sacrifices there is [4]a remembrance again made of sins every year.

---

[3]Chap. viii. 12; ix. 14.
[4]Ex. xxx. 10; Lev. xvi. 6-22; xxiii. 27, 29; Num. xxix. 7-11.

---

make any one perfect, except in a mere civil and symbolical sense.

**2 For then would they not have ceased to be offered?**—If these bloody sacrifices had been really efficacious in taking away the sins of the people, there would of course have been no need of repeating them with reference to the same sins; because, as our author says, the worshipers having been thoroughly cleansed once for all, would have no more consciousness of sins so forgiven. A debt that has been once fairly and fully cancelled, is not to be paid a second time. If a disease has been once thoroughly eradicated from the system, there is no further need of medicine. And just so, if a sin is once effectually blotted out, it is remembered no more.

**3 But in those sacrifices there is a remembrance again made of sins every year.**—For special sins, the Law required special offerings. "If any soul sin through ignorance," said God to Moses, "then he shall bring a she-goat of the first year for a sin-offering. And the Priest shall make an atonement for the soul that sinneth ignorantly, when he sinneth by ignorance before the Lord, to make an atonement for him; and it shall be forgiven him." (Num. 15: 27, 28.) See also Lev. 4: 3, 14, 23, 28. Besides these special offerings, others were offered daily (Ex. 29: 38-46); weekly (Num. 28: 9, 10); monthly (Num. 28: 11-15); and yearly at each of the three great festivals (Lev. 23). But nevertheless on the tenth day of the seventh month, all the sins of the past year were again called into remembrance; and an atonement was made, first for the sins of the Priests (Lev. 16: 11-14), and then for the sins of the people (Lev. 16: 15). Nor did even these sacrifices offered on the Day of Atonement, suffice to cover the sins of the worshipers, as any one may see from the following ordinance relating to the scape goat. "And when he [Aaron] hath made an end of reconciling the Holy Place and the Tabernacle of the congregation, and the altar, he shall bring the live goat; and Aaron shall lay both his hands upon the head of the live goat, and confess over him all the iniquities of the children of Israel and all their transgressions in all

4 For it is [1]not possible that the blood of bulls and of goats should take away sins.

[1]Chap. ix. 9, 13; Psa. l. 7-15; Isa. i. 11-15; Jer. vi. 20; vii. 21, 22; Hos. vi. 6.

their sins, putting them upon the head of the goat, and shall send him away by the hand of a fit man into the wilderness. And the goat shall bear upon him all their iniquities into a land not inhabited; and he shall let go the goat in the wilderness." (Lev. 16 : 20-22.) Thus it appears that what all the sacrifices of the year could not accomplish, was symbolically effected by the goat, on whose innocent head were laid the sins of the nation for the whole of the preceding year, to be borne away by it into a land of separation: "the Holy Spirit this signifying," that in due time Christ would, in like manner, bear away on his own person all our sins into a state of everlasting oblivion.

4 **For it is not possible, etc.**—Why not? Who can fully and satisfactorily answer this question? The fact is clearly and categorically stated by the Spirit that "searches all things, yea even the deep things of God." And some of the reasons are plain and obvious enough. It may be alleged, for instance, that every sinner is under condemnation; and that something is necessary in order to his redemption. And, furthermore, it may be shown that the sinner has really nothing to offer as a ransom for his soul: "for," says God, "every beast of the forest is mine, and the cattle upon a thousand hills." (Psalm 1 : 10.) All this, and much more, may be truthfully urged in support of the Apostle's declaration. But until we can estimate aright the exceeding sinfulness of sin and the just claims of the Divine Government on the sinner, I am inclined to think that all our speculations on this matter must fall short of a true and full solution of the question. It becomes us, therefore, to receive humbly and implicitly, as a matter of faith, what reaches far beyond the narrow limits of our speculative philosophy. That these sacrifices were of Divine appointment, is, of course, conceded by all who believe the Bible to be the inspired Word of God; and that they served to secure for the Israelites symbolical forgiveness, and, as a consequence of this, continued membership in the symbolical Church of the Old Covenant, is also equally obvious. But beyond this, they only served to direct the minds and hearts of the people to "the Lamb of God that taketh away the sin of the world."

## 7. THE ALL-SUFFICIENCY OF THE ONE OFFERING OF CHRIST SHOWN (1) IN ITS FULFILLING THE WILL OF GOD, AND (2) IN ITS PROCURING FOR ALL THE FAITHFUL, FREE, FULL, AND ABSOLUTE FORGIVENESS
### 10: 5-18

5 Wherefore ¹when he cometh into the world, he saith, ²Sacrifice and offering thou wouldest not, but a body hast thou prepared me:

¹Gen. xlix. 10; Deut. xviii. 15-18; Isa. ix. 6, 7; Jer. xxiii. 5, 6; Dan. ix. 24-26; Mic. v. 2; Hag. ii. 7; Zech. ix. 9; Mal. iii. 1; Matt. xi. 3; John x. 10.
²Psa. xl. 6-8.

5 **Wherefore when he cometh into the world,**—That is, since it is now manifest that the Levitical sacrifices had no power to take away sin, and since, therefore, a better sacrifice was needed for this purpose, Christ on coming into the world as God's chosen minister to redeem it, says:

**Sacrifice and offering thou wouldest not, etc.**—This citation is from the fortieth Psalm, and has reference primarily to David as a type of Christ; and secondarily to Christ himself as the antitype. See notes on 1: 5. In the first part of this Psalm, David praises God for deliverance from his persecutors, as well as for many other tokens of Divine grace. And then with an earnest desire to serve God and to do his will, he says, Sacrifice and offering thou hast not desired; ears hast thou digged out for me: burnt-offering and sin-offering thou hast not asked. Then said I, Lo, I come [I bring myself as a sacrifice] (in the volume of the book it is written of me); to do thy will, O my God I have delighted, and thy Law is in the midst of my bowels. In this remarkable utterance of David, we have clearly set forth the utter insufficiency of the legal sacrifices to accomplish the will of God; and also Christ's purpose to do this by the sacrifice of himself.

The general meaning of the passage then is plain enough. But how is the Greek rendering of our text, *"a body hast thou prepared me,"* to be reconciled with the Hebrew, *"ears hast thou digged out for me?"* It will not do to say with some that our author follows the Septuagint Version, without regard to the exact meaning of the passage. He never does this. When the Septuagint expresses correctly the meaning of the original, he then commonly quotes from it; otherwise, he either so modifies the rendering as to make it correct, or he gives us a new translation of the

6 [1]In burnt offerings and sacrifices for sin thou hast had no pleasure.

[1]1 Sam. xv. 22; Psa. l. 8, 9; Prov. xxi. 3; Isa. i. 11-17; Jer. vii. 22, 23; Hos. vi. 6; Amos v. 21-24; Mic. vi. 6-8.

Hebrew. Even in the few lines which are here cited, there are several slight departures from the Septuagint; but in the clause which we have now under consideration, he follows the Septuagint exactly; no doubt because it expresses exactly the mind of the Spirit.

But how is this? To the careless and superficial reader, there may at first seem to be no connection between digging out, or thoroughly opening the ears of any one, and providing a body for him. But the thoughtful reader will at once see that, in the case of Christ, the two expressions are nearly equivalent, and that the latter differs from the former chiefly in this: that it is rather more specific and expressive. To dig out the ears of a person means simply to make him a willing and obedient servant. (Ex. 21 : 6.) But in order to so qualify Christ as to make him a fit servant for the redemption of mankind, a body was absolutely necessary. Without this, there could have been no adequate sacrifice for sin, and without an adequate sacrifice, there could have been no suitable atonement, and without an atonement, the claims of Divine Justice could not have been satisfied, and without this, the will of God could never have been accomplished in the redemption of mankind. The Greek, therefore, though not an exact translation of the Hebrew, is nevertheless in perfect harmony with it, plainly indicating that both come from the same fountain of Divine inspiration. The only question of doubt, then, is simply this: Whence did the translators of the Septuagint obtain the specific idea which they have here so happily expressed? Or in other words, How came they to put such a construction on the original Hebrew? To me it seems most probable that they simply followed the current interpretation of the passage, as it had been explained by the ancient prophets. See 1 Cor. 14 : 1-4, and 1 Pet. 1 : 10-12.

6 **In burnt offerings, etc.**—This is but an echo of the sentiment expressed in the preceding verse, making with it a sort of Hebrew parallelism, in which "burnt offerings and sacrifices for sin" are made to correspond with sacrifices and offerings in general. Together, the two verses express with great emphasis the utter in-

**7** Then said I, Lo, ²I come (³in the volume of the book it is written of me,) to do thy will, O God.

²John iv. 34; v. 30; vi. 38.
³Gen. iii. 15; xxii. 18; xlix. 10; Deut. xviii. 15-19.

sufficiency of the Levitical sacrifices to accomplish the will of God in the redemption of mankind. For the law of the burnt offerings, see Lev. 1: 1-17, and for that of the sin offerings, see Lev. 4: 1-5: 13. The former was so called because it was wholly consumed on the altar, but the latter received its name from its having always special reference to sin and to the sin-offering of Christ. The former was instituted immediately after the fall of man, and in con- nection with the meat offering it constituted an important part of the Patriarchal worship. But the sin offering was instituted after the giving of the Law. It is first mentioned in Ex. 24: 14.

**7** **Then said I, Lo, I come**—The Septuagint rendering of this verse corresponds exactly with the Hebrew, and is as follows: Then said I, Lo, I come [to do thy will]: (in the volume of the book it is written of me); to do thy will, O my God, I have de- lighted. Our author, by omitting the latter part of the third clause, has changed in some measure the form of the whole verse, without affecting its meaning. He simply makes the phrase, *"to do thy will,"* in the third clause, depends directly on *"I come"* in the first. The second clause is thrown in parenthetically.

It is manifestly David that speaks in the Psalm from which the Apostle makes this citation. But, as Delitzsch says, "he speaks in typically ordered words which issue, as it were, from the very soul of the Antitype, the Anointed of the future, who will not only be the King of Israel, but also the Captain of their salvation, as well as of that of the whole world.—David speaks; but Christ, whose Spirit already dwells and works in David, and who will hereafter receive from David his human nature, now already speaks in him." See notes on 1: 5.

**in the volume of the book it is written of me,**—That is, in the roll or volume of the Law. "Anciently," says A. Clarke, "books were written on skins and rolled up. Among the Romans they were called *volumina* from volvo, *I roll*: and the Pentateuch in the Jewish synagogues is still written in the same way. There were two wooden rollers; on one they rolled *on,* and from the other they **rolled** *off,* as they proceeded in the reading." In the volume of the

8 Above when he said, Sacrifice and offering and burnt offerings and offering for sin thou wouldest not, neither hadst pleasure therein; which are
offered by the law;
9 Then said he, ¹Lo, I come to do thy will [O God]. ²He taketh away the
first, that he may establish the second.

¹Ch. v. 8; ix. 11-14; Phil. ii. 6-11.
²Ch. vii. 18, 19; viii. 7-13; xii. 27, 28; Col. ii. 14.

Pentateuch, which every king of Israel was required to transcribe
and carry with him as a *vade mecum* (Deut. 17: 14-20), there is
constant reference to Christ. Indeed, we may truly say of it, as
John has said of the Apocalypse, "The testimony of Jesus is the
spirit of the prophecy." (Rev. 19: 10.) This testimony is given
not only directly in such passages as Gen. 3: 15; 22: 17; 49: 10;
Deut. 18: 18; but also indirectly in all the types and shadows of
the Old Covenant.

8 **Above when he said,**—Our author now proceeds to explain
and apply the foregoing prophecy, and for this purpose he quotes it
again substantially in such a form as best serves to give point and
energy to his argument. But in doing so, he wholly overlooks the
type, and applies the words of the Psalm directly to Christ as their
true and proper author. It is no longer David, but Christ himself
who appears in front of the great drama of redemption, and who
comes forward to do the will of God, by giving his own life for the
salvation of the world. "Above," (that is in the former part of the
quotation,) "when he [Christ] saith, Sacrifices, and offerings,
and whole burnt offerings, and offerings for sin, thou wouldest not,
neither hadst pleasure therein; such as are offered according to the
law."

9 **Then said he, Lo, I come to do thy will**—The reader will
observe that in the preceding verse the Apostle has thrown together all the various kinds of Levitical offerings, no doubt for the
purpose of making the contrast between them and the one offering
of Christ, as strong and as pointed as possible. Numerous and
various as they were, they nevertheless all failed to fulfill the will
of God; but this, Christ has fully accomplished by the one offering
of himself.

**he taketh away the first, that he may establish the second.**
—The thing taken out of the way is not merely the Levitical sacrifices, but the whole arrangement under which they were offered,
and the thing established is the more gracious and perfect arrange-

10 By the which will [1]we are sanctified through the offering of the body of Jesus Christ once for all.

11 And every priest standeth [2]daily ministering and offering oftentimes the same sacrifices, [3]which can never take away sins:

[1]Ch. ii. 11; ix. 14, 26; xiii. 12; Zech. xiii. 1; John xvii. 19; 1 Cor. i. 30; vi. 11.
[2]Ch. vii. 27; Ex. xxix. 38, 39; Num. xxviii. 24; Dan. ix. 24, 27.
[3]Ch. ix. 9, 13; x. 4; Psa. xl. 6; l. 7-15; li. 6; Hos. vi. 6.

ment according to which the offering of Christ was made once for all. This is indicated (1) by the use of the abstract neuters, *"the first"* (*to proton*) and *"the second"* (*to deuteron*); and (2) by what follows in the next verse.

10 **By the which will we are sanctified through the offering, etc.**—From this clause taken in connection with what precedes, it is quite manifest that the thing taken out of the way, embracing the Old Covenant with all its rites and ceremonies, was not the will of God, but that the thing established and ratified by the sacrifice of Christ, is the will of God. "He taketh away the first," which was not the will of God; "that he may establish the second," which is the will of God. The term *"will,"* as used here, denotes God's redeeming purpose, conceived before the foundation of the world but gradually developed in the Holy Scriptures, and finally ratified by the atoning blood of the Lord Jesus. In the accomplishing of this will, embracing as it does the whole Gospel plan of salvation, "we are sanctified through the offering of the body of Jesus Christ once for all."

11 **And every priest standeth daily ministering, etc.**—The keynote of what follows is found in the last word of the tenth verse, (*ephapax*) *"once for all."* The Levitical sacrifices were not only numerous and various, but they were also often repeated: "Every priest standeth, day by day, ministering and offering oftentimes the same sacrifices which can never take away sins." "The same wearisome circle of ineffectual efforts," says Tholuck, "which has been shown to characterize the performances of the high priest on the Day of Atonement, is now exhibited as characteristic of the priestly institute in general." Several manuscripts and some of the ancient versions have *high priests* (*archiereus*) instead of *priest* (*hiereus*), but the balance of authority is in favor of the reading found in our English Version.

12 But ⁴this man, after he had offered one sacrifice for sins forever, sat down on the right hand of God;

13 From ¹henceforth expecting till his enemies be made his footstool.

14 For ²by one offering he hath perfected forever ³them that are sanctified.

⁴Ch. i. 3; viii. 1; Matt. xxii. 44; Acts ii. 33; vii. 56; Eph. i. 20-22.
¹Ch. i. 13; Psa. cx. 1; Luke xx. 43; 1 Cor. xv. 25.
²Ch. ix. 14.
³Ch. ii. 11; xiii. 12; Acts xx. 32; Rom. xv. 16; 1 Cor. i. 2; Eph. v. 26.

**12 But this man, after he had, etc.**—The main point of contrast here is, not between the one sacrifice and the many, but between the often repeated offerings of the many sacrifices of the Law, and the one offering of the sacrifice of Christ. For while every Levitical priest standeth daily ministering, as one who has never finished his work; Christ, on the other hand, having offered one sacrifice for sins, sat down perpetually on the right hand of God, as one who has accomplished his work; that is, the particular work to which our author here refers: the work of making an atonement for the sins of the world. This will never have to be repeated. The contrast that is here made by the Apostle is well presented by Menken as follows: "The priest of the Old Testament *stands* timid and uneasy in the Holy Place, anxiously performing his awful service there, and hastening to depart when the service is done, as from a place where he has no free access, and can never feel at home, whereas Christ *sits down* in everlasting rest and blessedness at the right hand of the Majesty in the Holy of Holies, his work accomplished, and he himself awaiting its reward."

**13 From henceforth expecting, etc.**—The Apostle refers again to Psalm 110: 1, where David by the Spirit says, Jehovah said to my Lord, Sit on my right hand till I make thy enemies thy footstool. Christ is represented in our text as calmly and patiently waiting for the fulfillment of this promise. Not that he has ceased to work for the redemption of mankind, for he must reign, and that, too, with infinite power and energy, until the last enemy, death, shall be destroyed. (1 Cor. 15: 25, 26; Rev. 19: 11-21, etc.) But his sacrificial work is done. The one offering which he made of himself is all-sufficient, as our author shows further in the following verse.

**14 For by one offering he hath perfected forever them that are sanctified.**—This is assigned as the reason why Christ has not to stand and daily repeat his offering, like the Levitical priests.

15 Whereof [4]the Holy Ghost also is a witness to us: for after that he had said before.

[4]Ch. ii. 3, 4; iii. 7; ix. 8; John xv. 26; Acts xxviii. 25; 1 Pet. i. 11, 12; 2 Pet. i. 21.

The one offering which he has made of himself is enough. By it he has forever perfected them that are sanctified. But who are they? Evidently the same as the sanctified in 2: 11; those who by faith and obedience have put on Christ (Gal. 3: 27), and who have risen with him from the baptismal grave to walk in newness of life (Rom. 6: 4; Col. 2: 12; 3: 1). All such have come to perfection *in Christ,* finding as they do in him all that pertains to life and godliness (2 Pet. 1: 3), so that they have only to persevere in well doing to the end of life, by abiding in Christ as the branch abides in the vine, and then with spirits as pure as the angels before the throne of God, they will join the redeemed millions "who have washed their robes and made them white in the blood of the Lamb."

15 **Whereof the Holy Ghost also is a witness to us:**—Our author now proceeds to prove and illustrate his position still further by referring to the inspired Hebrew writings. For this purpose he again quotes from the prophecy of Jeremiah (31: 33, 34), showing clearly that even under the Old Economy, it was God's purpose that through the blood of the New Covenant the sanctified in Christ Jesus should enjoy absolute and eternal forgiveness. But in making use of this passage, he quotes only so much of it as has a direct bearing on his argument, and by so abbreviating it, he has left the construction of it somewhat doubtful. The main point to be determined is simply this: Where does the protasis of the sentence end, and the apodosis begin? Most commentators, since Beza, make the division in the middle of the sixteenth verse as follows: "For after having said, *This is the covenant which I will make with them after those days,* the Lord [then] says, *Putting my laws into their hearts, I will also write them on their understanding; and their sins and iniquities will I remember no more.*" But some of our ablest expositors make the apodosis begin with the seventeenth verse, and render the whole passage as follows: "For after having said, *This is the covenant which I will make with them after those days, saith the Lord, putting my laws into*

16 ¹This is the covenant that I will make with them after those days, saith the Lord: I will put my laws into their hearts, and in their minds will I write them;
17 And their sins and iniquities will I remember no more.
18 Now ²where remission of these is, there is no more offering for sin.

¹Jer. xxxi. 33, 34.
²Chap. ix. 13, 14; Psa. ciii. 12; Isa. xliii. 25; xliv. 22; Mic. vii. 19.

*their hearts, I will also write them on their understanding,* [he then adds] *and their sins and iniquities will I remember no more."*

On the whole, I think with Beza, Delitzsch, and others, that the first construction is the most natural, and also most consistent with our author's free manner of quoting from the original text. It matters but little, however, which of these renderings is adopted. In either case, the main object of the writer is evidently to prove from the Old Testament Scriptures, that the subjects of the New Covenant enjoy, through the one offering of Christ, free, full, and absolute forgiveness.

18 **Now where remission of these is, there is no more offering for sin.**—That is, where there is absolute forgiveness of sins, there is no further need of a sin-offering. Another atonement would be wholly superfluous. This, as we have seen in commenting on 8: 12, is one of the leading points of contrast between the Old and the New Covenant. Under the former, the offerings were numerous, and were perpetually repeated; while they served to procure for the Israelites nothing more than a mere civil and ecclesiastical forgiveness. But under the latter, the one offering of Christ procures for all the sanctified absolute and everlasting forgiveness.

## REFLECTIONS

1. This is one of the most profoundly interesting sections in the whole Bible. Leading us back, as it does, to the original gracious purpose of God, conceived, of course, before the foundation of the world, but gradually revealed and illustrated from the fall of man until it was fully developed in the kingdom of Christ, it embraces within itself an outline of the whole remedial system. We see in it both the shadow and the substance in their true and proper relations to each other; and all looking to the one grand consummation, when the last enemy, Death, having been vanquished, the kingdom will be delivered up to God the Father. To understand

this one section, therefore, in all its legitimate bearings, is, in fact, to understand the whole economy of Divine grace.

2. Judaism, though in itself but a shadow, differs nevertheless in many respects from all false systems of religion; but chiefly in this, that it has in Christianity a real corresponding substance. The religious systems of the ancient Egyptians, Greeks, Romans, and other heathen nations, were nothing but shadows; mere counterfeits without any corresponding realities. The Romans, for instance, had their high priest or Pontifex Maximus, as well as the Jews. But while the Jewish high priest was a type of Christ, the Roman Pontifex Maximus was a type of nothing: a mere shadow of a shadow, without any corresponding substance. And this is true also of all the heathen temples, sacrifices, etc.; so that there is really no proper parallelism between Judaism and any other system of religion outside of the Bible. The one was given by God himself; but the other is wholly of human origin.

3. Christians should ever rejoice that the way into the holiest of all is now made manifest. (9:8; 10:19, 20.) Christ has made it so very plain, that all may now understand it and walk in it. Indeed he is himself the way, the truth, the resurrection and the life. The man who is in him, and who walks in him, cannot fail to enter, even as he himself did, into the holy of holies. Well, therefore, might Christ now say to us, as he once said to his disciples while on earth, "Blessed are the eyes which see the things that ye see: for I tell you that many prophets and kings have desired to see those things which ye see, and have not seen them; and to hear those things which ye hear, and have not heard them." Let us all then strive to walk worthy of our high and holy calling; "with all lowliness and meekness, with long-suffering, forbearing one another in love; endeavoring to keep the unity of the Spirit in the bond of peace."

4. The great end of all religion is to purify the conscience from all that is impure and unholy; and so to qualify us for the service of God here, and for the enjoyment of his presence hereafter. (9: 14.) Without this, all outward purifications are of no avail. The body will soon go to corruption, do as we may. "Dust thou art, and unto dust shalt thou return," is the irrevocable decree of God with respect to all flesh. But if by Divine grace the spirit is made like that of Christ, then also the body will in due time be made like

the body of Christ. (1 John 3 : 2.) And if we are like Christ, we will be with him (John 14 : 3), and be made heirs of the universe through him (1 Cor. 3 : 21-23).

5. There has ever been but one ground of pardon, justification, sanctification, and redemption. The conditions of enjoying the great boon of eternal life have varied somewhat in different ages and under different circumstances. Some things were required of the Jews, which are not now required of Christians; and some things are required of Christians, which were wholly unknown to the Jews. But neither Jews nor Christians ever did or ever can do anything by way of making an atonement for sin. This can be done only through the blood of the Lord Jesus Christ, which was just as necessary "for the redemption of the sins that were committed under the first covenant," as it is for the redemption of those that are now committed under the second covenant. (9 : 15; Rom. 3 : 25, 26.) This is the fountain which God by the mouth of Zechariah (13 : 1) promised that he would open "to the house of David for sin and for uncleanness"; and this is the fountain to which every penitent sinner is now invited to come and be cleansed.

6. How infinitely glorious will be the second advent of our blessed Lord. (9 : 28.) His first coming was in weakness, poverty, and suffering, because he was then "made of a woman, made under the law, to redeem them that were under the law; that we might receive the adoption of sons." (Gal. 4 : 4, 5.) He had then to be "made sin for us, though he knew no sin, that we might be made the righteousness of God in him." (2 Cor. 5 : 21.) But now his sacrificial work is done. His sufferings and sorrows are all over. He has borne away all our sins in his own person; and by the one offering of himself he has brought in everlasting righteousness. And hence when he comes again, it will be to redeem his saints, "and to convict all the impious concerning all their works of impiety which they impiously did, and concerning all the hard things which impious sinners spoke against him." (Jude 14, 15.) Then "all that are in their graves will hear his voice and come forth; they that have done good, to the resurrection of life; and they that have done evil, to the resurrection of damnation." (John 5 : 28, 29.) The judgment will sit, and the books will be opened. And then every man will be rewarded according to his works. (Rev. 20 :

11-15.) Sinner, are you prepared to meet him at his coming? If not, why not at once repent of your sins? Why not accept of the mercy which he now offers to you through the Gospel? "Behold, now is the accepted time; behold, now is the day of salvation." (2 Cor. 6: 2.)

7. God is not an arbitrary, but a just and righteous Sovereign. (10: 1-4.) Otherwise he might have accepted the blood of bulls and of goats as an atonement for sin; nay more, he might have even allowed all sin to pass with impunity. But this was impossible. God's own nature would not allow this. Justice, absolute and eternal justice, had to be satisfied before any sinner could be pardoned absolutely; for justice and judgment are the habitation of God's throne. (Psalm 89: 14.) But nothing it seems save the blood of Christ was sufficient to pay the ransom. And hence even this was not withheld by our ever gracious and merciful Father. For, as we are told, he "so loved the world that he gave his only begotten Son, that whosoever believeth on him should not perish, but have everlasting life." (John 3: 16.) But before this can be made available to the sinner, it must be humbly and thankfully accepted by him. He must reverently bow to the authority of Jesus, and receive him as the anointed Sovereign of the universe. (Phil. 2: 9-11.) To those who do so willingly, Christ has become the author of eternal salvation (5: 9); but to those who reject Christ, the Gospel is but a savor of death unto death (2 Cor. 2: 16). Better for all such that they had never been born; for by an eternal moral necessity they must be banished "with an everlasting destruction from the presence of the Lord and from the glory of his power, when he shall come to be glorified in his saints, and to be admired in all them that believe." (2 Thess. 1: 9, 10.)

8. How infinitely consoling is the assurance given to us in this section, that the one offering of Christ has so far satisfied the will of God, by meeting the claims of Divine justice against the sinner, that he can now be just in justifying every one who believes and obeys him. (10: 5-10; Rom. 3: 25, 26.) This is indeed to us as an anchor of the soul, both sure and steadfast, reaching even within the Vail. For, as our author says in his letter to the Romans (5: 10), "If when we were enemies to God by wicked works, we were reconciled to him by the death of his Son; much more being now reconciled, we shall be saved by his life." On this rock we may

now rest our hopes in confidence, feeling assured that "all things work together for good to them that love God" (Rom. 8: 28) ; and that "neither death, nor life, nor angels, nor principalities, nor powers, nor things present, nor things to come, nor height, nor depth, nor any other creature, shall be able to separate us from the love of God which is in Christ Jesus our Lord" (Rom. 8: 38, 39). May God help us then to renounce all self-righteousness and self-reliance, and to trust only in him "who of God has become unto us wisdom, and righteousness, and sanctification, and redemption."

## SECTION NINE
### 10: 19-39

#### ANALYSIS

In the first six chapters of our Epistle, exhortation follows exposition and argument in quick and rapid succession. But from 7 : 1 to 10: 18, we have one continued discussion of the priesthood of Christ, of the covenant of which he is the Mediator, and of the one great atoning sacrifice of himself which he once made for the sins of the world. At this point ends the doctrinal part of the Epistle; most of what follows being taken up with matters of exhortation, consolation, and encouragement.

In the first section of the hortatory part upon which we now enter, our author makes a practical application of some of the leading points involved in the preceding discussion, earnestly exhorting his readers to greater zeal and diligence in their Christian profession, warning them still further against the dangers and fearful consequences of apostasy, and encouraging them in various ways and by sundry motives to persevere with fidelity to the end of their Christian course. (10: 19-39.)

I. He begins by exhorting his Hebrew brethren (1) to draw near to God with true hearts and in the full assurance of faith, having their hearts sprinkled from an evil consciousness, and their bodies washed with pure water; (2) to hold fast the confidence of their well grounded hope; (3) to have a mutual watch-care over one another, so as to excite each other to love and good works, and (4) not to neglect the meetings appointed for social worship. (10: 19-25.) This exhortation he enforces.

1. On the ground that the way of access into the Holiest of all

had then been made manifest through the rent vail of the flesh of Jesus (verses 19, 20).

2. That they had a great high priest over the house of God, through whom they had at all times free access to the throne of heavenly grace (verse 21).

3. That God is faithful, and that he will certainly fulfill all his promises (verse 23).

4. That the day of trial was then near at hand (verse 25).

II. He again warns his readers against the dangers and fearful consequences of apostasy. Of these, he urges them to beware.

1. Because for the apostate even the sacrifice of Christ is no longer available, and consequently he can expect nothing but the awful horrors of the coming judgment (verses 26, 27).

2. Because his condemnation will be even more intolerable than was that of the presumptuous sinner under the Law, on the ground that wherever much is given, there also much is always required (verses 28, 29).

3. Because God will certainly execute his righteous vengeance on all the finally impenitent (verses 30, 31).

III. He urges and encourages them on the ground of consistency, to endure with meekness and resignation whatever trials and afflictions might come upon them (verses 32-34). They had, it seems, formerly endured much, and they had borne it all joyfully in view of the riches and honors that awaited them. And now the Apostle would have them persevere in the same course in which they had begun.

IV. He exhorts and encourages them to maintain their confidence, and to persevere in their begun course, (1) on the ground that their final recompense would be very great; and (2) on the ground that the coming of Christ was very near at hand, when the faithful would all be rewarded for their fidelity (verses 35-39). This the Apostle illustrates and enforces by referring to the overthrow of the Chaldean monarchy, and the deliverance of the faithful Israelites from its oppressive bondage.

The main points of this section may therefore be briefly summed up as follows:

I. 10: 19-25. An exhortation to greater diligence, purity, constancy, and fidelity in the worship and service of God.

II.  10 : 26-31.  A solemn warning against the dangers and fearful consequences of apostasy.

III.  10 : 32-34.  Exhortation and encouragement to the Hebrew Christians, drawn from their previous steadfastness and endurance.

IV.  10 : 35-39.  Further exhortation and encouragement to maintain their confidence, and to persevere through faith to the end, which to them was then very near at hand.

### 1. AN EXHORTATION TO GREATER DILIGENCE, PURITY, CONSTANCY, AND FIDELITY IN THE WORSHIP AND SERVICE OF GOD
### 10 : 19-25

19 [1]Having therefore, brethren, boldness [2]to enter into the holiest by the blood of Jesus,

[1]Ch. iv. 16; xii. 28; Rom. viii. 15; Gal. iv. 6, 7; Eph. iii. 12; 2 Tim. i. 17.
[2]Ch. ix. 7, 8, 12, 24; Eph. ii. 18.

19 **Having therefore, etc.**—In the preceding section the Apostle has shown (1) that the way into the Holiest of all, though dark and mysterious to the ancients, has now been made manifest to us through the shed blood of Christ; (2) that Christ has himself entered it by means of his own blood with which he has made an atonement for the sins of the world; (3) that he ever lives there as a priest on his throne to intercede for us and to bless us; and (4) that by virtue of his atoning blood, we, too, are allowed to follow him and to be with him as joint heirs of the eternal inheritance. All this, then, serves to inspire us, not exactly with "boldness," but rather with a joyful confidence (*parresia*) as regards our entrance into the Holiest of all, through the blood of Jesus. On this point there is really no longer any reason for doubting. We now *"know* that if our earthly house of this tabernacle were dissolved, we have a building of God, a house not made with hands, eternal in the heavens." (2 Cor. 5:1.) We are therefore no longer in bondage through the fear of death, having confidence that "it is better to depart and be with Christ." The phrase, *"by the blood of Christ,"* denotes the means by and through which this joyful access to heaven has been procured for us as illustrated in the preceding section.

20 ³By a new and living way, which he hath consecrated for us, through the vail, that is to say, his flesh;
21 And having ¹an high priest over ²the house of God;

³Ch. vii. 25; John x. 7, 9; xiv. 6; Acts iv. 12; Rom. v. 2.
¹Ch. ii. 17; iii. 1; iv. 14, 15; vi. 20; vii. 26; viii. 1.
²Ch. iii. 6; Matt. xvi. 18; 1 Cor. iii. 9-17; 2 Cor. vi. 16, 17; Eph. ii. 19-22; 1 Tim. iii. 15.

20 **By a new and living way,**—The meaning of this expression will be best understood when viewed in its proper relations to other parts of the sentence, the whole of which may be literally rendered as follows: Having therefore, brethren, confidence with respect to the entrance of the Holy of holies by means of the blood of Jesus, which [entrance or entranceway] he consecrated for us [as] a way fresh and living [leading] through the vail, that is through his flesh, etc. From this, it will be seen that our English Version gives the sense of the passage pretty accurately, without, however, giving the exact grammatical relation of the words as they stand in the original. The new and living way is the same as the entrance way. It is called new, fresh, or recent way, because it had but recently been initiated and consecrated by Christ, and it is called a living way, because like Christ himself it is ever fresh and living. "The way into the Sanctuary of the Old Testament," says Hofmann, "was simply a lifeless pavement, trodden by the high priest and by him alone. But the way that has been opened and consecrated for us by Jesus Christ, is one that really leads and carries all who enter it into the heavenly rest:—a living way, because one with the living person and abiding work of the Lord Jesus." It is also a way that leads through the vail; that is, through the rent flesh of Christ. As the vail was the only medium of access to God under the Old Economy, so also is the rent flesh of Christ the only medium of access to him under the New Economy. And hence when the heart of Christ was ruptured on the cross (see notes on 5 : 7), the vail of the temple was then also "rent in twain from the top to the bottom." (Matt. 27 : 51.) Then, and not till then, was the way of entrance into the Holies of all made manifest to men and angels.

21 **And having an high priest over the house of God;**—Literally, And having a great priest (*hierea megan*) over the house of God. True, indeed, in the Septuagint, as well as in the writings of Philo, these words (*hiereus megas*) are often used in the sense of

22 Let us ³draw near with ⁴a true heart ⁵in full assurance of faith, having ⁶our hearts sprinkled from an evil conscience, and ⁷our bodies washed with pure water.

³Ch. iv. 16; vii. 19; Jas. iv. 8.
⁴1 Chron. xxviii. 9; Jer. iii. 10; Acts viii. 21; Eph. vi. 5.
⁵Matt. xxi. 21, 22; Jas. i. 6.
⁶Ch. ix. 13, 14, 19; Ezek. xxxvi. 25; 1 Pet. i. 2; 1 John iii. 20.
⁷Ex. xxix. 4; Ezek. xvi. 9; Matt. iii. 11; John iii. 5; Eph. v. 26; Titus iii. 5; 1 Pet. iii. 21.

*archierus* (*archiereus*). But as they are not in any other instance so used by our author, it is most likely that he uses the word *great* in this instance, as in 4: 14, to denote Christ's personal dignity and royal highness. Like Melchisedec, he sits as a priest upon his throne, while he presides over the house of God, which is the church of the living God, the pillar and ground of the truth." (1 Tim. 3: 15.) The house of God may, however, in this instance, denote the church in heaven as well as the church on earth, for Christ is a minister of both the heavenly Sanctuary and the true Tabernacle. (8: 2.)

22 **Let us draw near**—Draw near to what? Evidently to God and to the throne of his grace, as we are exhorted to do in 4: 16. The priests of the Old Covenant drew near to God symbolically, whenever they approached the golden altar to burn incense, for between this altar and the Ark of the Covenant, on which God's presence was manifested, there was but little space. The vail, however, still intervened between the worshiped and the worshipers, and the whole scene was, in fact, one of mystery and terror to the priests, as well as to the people. But not so under the New Economy. "For as many as are [now] led by the Spirit of God, they are the *sons* of God." For as Paul assures us (Rom. 8: 15), we have not received the spirit of bondage again to fear, but we have received the spirit of adoption, whereby we cry, Abba, Father. And thus having a joyful confidence as respects the entrance into the Holiest of all, and having a great sympathetic high priest over the house of God, we may all now draw near to God as his redeemed children, and find grace for seasonable help.

But this near approach into the presence of our heavenly Father should always be made with becoming reverence and with due preparation of both head and heart. "I will be sanctified," says God, "in them that come nigh me." (Lev. 10: 3.) And accordingly the children of Israel were required to wash their clothes and

to purify themselves for three days, before they were allowed to
approach God at Mount Sinai. (Ex. 19: 10.) "God is spirit," says
Christ, "and they that worship him must worship him in spirit and
in truth." (John 4: 24.) This is just as necessary now as it ever
was. And hence while the Apostle would have all his Hebrew
brethren approach God in prayer and praise, he would have them
do so (1) with a true heart; (2) in the full assurance of faith; (3)
having their hearts sprinkled from an evil conscience; and (4)
having their bodies washed with pure water. Let us consider each
of these in order.

**with a true heart**—That is, with a heart that is free from all
guile, deceit, and hypocrisy. A heart made true by the knowledge
of itself and of the grace of God, through the enlightening and
sanctifying influences of the Holy Spirit. "When this knowledge
takes root," says Ebrard, "it will dispel the delusive fancy that God
needs no atonement; that God is only a dead idol, who knows not
the anger of holy love. It will dispel, too, the confidence in false
self-made atonements, including all merit of works, and it will destroy all self-deception about an atonement through any other sacrifices than the sacrifice of Christ." A true heart, then, is a heart
which, while renouncing all self-righteousness and every other
"refuge of lies," receives Christ and trusts in him as the way, the
truth, the resurrection, and the life.

**In full assurance of faith,**—That is, with a faith that dispels all
doubt with regard to God and his promises; a faith which enables
us to "take God at his word," and to do just what he commands,
feeling perfectly sure that all things work together for good to
them that love and serve him. That such a degree of faith is desir-
able no one can doubt; and that it is also attainable through the
grace of God is perhaps equally certain. And if so, then surely it
should be most earnestly sought for by all; for to approach God in
a doubtful state of mind is very dishonoring to him as well as injurious to ourselves.

**Having our hearts sprinkled from an evil conscience,**—The
word rendered *conscience* (*suneidesis*) may mean here, as in 9:9,
14, either conscience or consciousness; either the moral faculty of
the soul, or the state of mind resulting from the exercise of this
faculty. Every act that we perform contrary to the known will of
God defiles our conscience and also our consciousness; we have

them both an evil conscience and an evil self-consciousness. And this, so long as it continues, must seriously interrupt our union, communion and fellowship with God. The child that is suffering from an evil consciousness on account of its having transgressed the known will of its father cannot, so long as the feeling lasts, approach him with perfect confidence. But when it repents of the evil, confesses the wrong, and feels fully assured that the fault is forgiven, then what a change comes over it. It can then properly appreciate a father's love, and draw near to him with filial and joyful confidence. And just so it is with every child of God. So long as we feel conscious of guilt, so long we feel also that there is a strong barrier between us and our God. For if our heart condemns us, we know that God also condemns us. (1 John 3: 20.) But "if we confess our sins, he is faithful and just to forgive us our sins, and to cleanse us from all unrighteousness." (1 John 1: 9.) And this he does in all cases by applying to our hearts the blood of sprinkling; for it is this, and only this, that can cleanse from sin. (1 John 1:7.) And when our hearts are thus purified, we have then "confidence toward God" (1 John 3:21); and we can then approach him as his redeemed children and have sweet communion and fellowship with him. "Blessed are the pure in heart, for they shall see God."

**And our bodies washed with pure water.**—There is here a manifest reference to the bath of regeneration. (Titus 3:5.) It will not do to say with Calvin, Limborch, Owen, Bengel and others that this is a mere symbolical expression, having reference simply to the inward cleansing of the soul by the blood of Christ and the renewing influence of the Holy Spirit. The strong and pointed antithesis which the Apostle here makes between the sprinkling of the heart and the washing of the body forbids any such interpretation of the passage. This is conceded by Delitzsch, Alford, Moll and others. Indeed nearly all eminent expositors are now agreed that there is here a manifest reference to the ordinance of Christian baptism. Alford says, "There can be no reasonable doubt that this clause refers directly to Christian baptism. The bath of water (*loutron tou hudatos*) of Eph. 5:26, and the bath of regeneration (*loutron palingenesias*) of Tit. 3: 5, are analogous expressions; and the express mention of *body* (*soma*) here as distinguished from *hearts* (*kardias*) before, stamps this interpretation

23 Let us ¹hold fast the profession of our faith without wavering; (for ²he is faithful that promised;)

¹Ch. iv. 14; Matt. x. 22; Gal. vi. 9; Col. i. 23; Rev. iii. 11.
²Ch. vi. 18; 1 Cor. i. 9; x. 13; 1 Thess. v. 24; Titus i. 2.

---

with certainty. To the same effect are the remarks of Prof. Stuart. In commenting on our text he says, "It seems to me that there is a plain allusion to the use of water in the initiatory rite of Christian baptism. This is altogether consonant with the method of our author who is everywhere comparing Christian institutions with Jewish ones. So in the case before us he says, The Jews were sprinkled with blood in order that they might be purified so as to have access to God; Christians are internally sprinkled, that is, purified by the blood of Jesus. The Jews were washed with water in order to be ceremonially purified so as to come before God; Christians have been washed by the purifying water of baptism. So Ananias exhorts Saul to be baptized and wash away his sins. (Acts 22:16.) In this latter case and in that before us the phrase is borrowed from the legal rite of washing for purification." To these very judicious remarks I need only add that the obvious design of our author in using this expression is to indicate that the *whole man,* both soul and body, should be sanctified and consecrated to the service of God. See Rom. 12:1.

23 **Let us hold fast, etc.**—This would be better rendered as follows: Let us hold fast the confession of the hope (*homologian tcs elpidos*) without wavering. See notes on 3:1. I agree with Bloomfield that this is "a pregnant expression," and that its full meaning might be expressed thus: "Let us hold fast the faith which we have confessed and cling to the hope which it ministers." The idea is, that we are still but pilgrims here as all our fathers were. We have not yet reached the goal of our destiny. Eternal life is still with us an object of hope. And hence the necessity of clinging to this hope as the anchor of our souls.

**For he is faithful that promised;**—This clause is added by the Apostle for the purpose of encouraging his Hebrew brethren and all who might read this Epistle to hold fast the confession of their hope without wavering even to the end of life. To persuade them to do this was, indeed, his leading object in writing the Epistle; **and hence his** frequent reference to the fidelity of God, as well as to the glory and dignity of Christ. See notes on 6:18.

24 And let us [1]consider one another [2]to provoke unto love and good works;
25 [3]Not forsaking the assembling of ourselves together, as the manner of
some is; but exhorting one another: and so much the more, as ye see [4]the
day approaching.

[1]Rom. xv. 1, 2; 1 Cor. viii. 12, 13; ix. 22; x. 33; Gal. vi. 1, 2.
[2]Ch. vi. 10, 11; xiii. 1; Rom. xi. 14.
[3]Acts ii. 42; xx. 7; 1 Cor. xi. 17, 18, 20; xiv. 23; xvi. 1, 2; Jude 19.
[4]Ver. 37; Jer. xlvi. 10; Amos v. 18; Matt. xxiv. 33, 34; Jas. v. 8.

24 **And let us consider one another**—That is, Let us not be
selfish, caring merely for ourselves; but let us have constantly in
mind each other's wants and circumstances as members of the one
family of God; and that, too, for the purpose of exciting and encouraging one another to love and good works. The same sentiment is earnestly inculcated by Christ in his sermon on the Mount,
where he says to his disciples, "Let your light so shine before men,
that they may see your good works, and glorify your Father who is
in heaven." (Matt. 5: 16.) "How beautifully," says Delitzsch, "is
the exhortation here disposed of in conformity with the Pauline
triad of Christian graces. (1 Cor. 13: 13; Col. 1: 4; 1 Thess. 1: 3;
5: 8.) First, we have the injunction to approach in the full assurance of *faith*; then that to hold fast the confession of our *hope*; and
now, third, to godly rivalry in the manifestations of Christian *charity*."

25 **Not forsaking the assembling of ourselves, etc.**—The
Apostle refers here, not to apostasy from the Church, as some allege, but simply to the neglect of public and social worship. The
time when this letter was written was manifestly a time of persecution in Jerusalem and perhaps, throughout Palestine. (12: 4.)
Many of the Hebrew brethren were no doubt greatly discouraged;
and some of them had fallen into the habit of neglecting the regular
meetings of the Church. This was clearly wrong for several reasons. (1) Because by so doing, they neglected and set at naught
an ordinance of God. Nothing is more obvious in the history of
the primitive Church than that the members of the several congre-
gations were wont to meet together on every Lord's Day, and no
doubt also frequently during the week for public and social worship. (Acts 2: 42; 20: 7; 1 Cor. 16: 1, 2, etc.) And as these
meetings were held with the sanction of the Apostles, and for a
time under their immediate supervision, they had, as a matter of
course, all the force and obligation of a Divine ordinance. (2) Be-

cause by neglecting his ordinance of God, the disciples deprived themselves of many social and religious privileges.  The Church of Christ is a social institution designed for the edification and improvement of all its members.  And besides, Christ says that wherever even two or three are met together in his name he will be with them. (Matt. 18:20.)  But when Christ meets with his people it is of course to bless them, and to strengthen them for the many trials and conflicts of life.  No one can, therefore, properly estimate his loss in willingly absenting himself from the meetings of his brethren.  (3) The delinquent Hebrews were doing wrong, also, because of the bad example which they were setting before others.  Christ intends that every one of his disciples shall be a living witness for the truth.  No wonder, then, that the Apostle so earnestly exhorted the Hebrews, not to neglect the duty and privilege of meeting with their brethren for public and social worship.

**And so much the more, as ye see the day approaching.**—To what day does our author here refer?  To the day of judgment, say Delitzsch, Alford, Moll, and others; when Christ will come in person to raise the dead and reward every man according to his works. But this interpretation is manifestly erroneous.  To me at least it seems perfectly obvious that the Apostle refers here to a day which both he and his brethren were looking for as a day that was then very near at hand: a day that was about to come on that generation, and try the faith of many.  And hence I am constrained to think with Macknight, Scott, Stuart, and others, that the reference is most likely to the day of Jerusalem's overthrow.  Christ had himself foretold the near approach of that event (Matt. 24:34); he had also spoken of the signs of its coming and of the great calamities that would accompany it (Matt. 24:4-41).  No doubt, therefore, the Christians in Palestine were all looking forward with much anxiety to the time when this prophecy would be fulfilled.  They would naturally speak of it as "the day"; the day of trial; the day when seeing Jerusalem encompassed with armies, they would themselves have to flee to the mountains. (Luke 21:20-22.)

If this is not the meaning of the Apostle, I would then understand him as referring simply to the day when Christ comes in his providence to call on each individual to give an account of his stewardship.  In this general sense the passage may be regarded,

like the parable of the ten virgins (Matt. 25: 1-13), as an admonition and warning to all Christians in all ages and in all nations.
But to refer it exclusively to the day when Christ will come in person to judge the world is clearly inadmissible.  See notes on verse
37.

## 2. A SOLEMN WARNING AGAINST THE DANGERS AND
### FEARFUL CONSEQUENCES OF APOSTASY
### 10 : 26-31

26 For [1]if we sin willfully after that we have received the knowledge of
the truth, there remaineth no more sacrifice for sins,

[1]Chap. vi. 4-6; xii. 7; Num. xv. 28-31; Deut. xvii. 12; Psa. xix. 12, 13; Matt. xii.
31, 32; 2 Pet. ii. 20-22.

26 **For if we sin willfully, etc.**—To sin willfully after that we
have received the knowledge of the truth is the same as to apostatize from Christ, for which there is no forgiveness.  See notes on
6: 4-6.  The use of the present participle (*hamartanonton*) shows
that the sin is not one of error or inadvertence; not a sin of momentary excitement; but rather that it is a sin of *habit;* a sin that is
willingly and deliberately persisted in; a sin that is committed with
a high hand and in open violation and contempt of God's law.  For
the law in reference to these two classes of sins, see Num. 15: 22-
31.  The word rendered *knowledge* (*epignosis*) means more than
a mere objective knowledge (*gnosis*) of the truth.  It rather denotes a full experimental knowledge, such as we gain by the active
application of our minds to the study of the truth.  And hence it is
of "those who were once enlightened, and have tasted of the heavenly gift, and were made partakers of the Holy Spirit, and have
tasted of the good word of God and the powers of the world to
come," that our author speaks.  If such persons apostatize from
Christ—

**There remaineth no more sacrifice for sins,**—Or rather, there
remaineth *no longer* (*ouk eti*) a sacrifice for sins.  The idea of the
Apostle is not simply that those who presumptuously reject the
sacrifice of Christ can obtain salvation through no other; but further, he means to say that in the case of such high-handed transgressors, even the sacrifice of Christ is no longer available.  The
man who was once a Christian, a true child of God, and who as
such was made a partaker of the Holy Spirit, and yet falls away as

27 But a ²certain fearful looking for of judgment and ³fiery indignation, which shall devour the adversaries.

28 He that ¹despised Moses' law died without mercy ²under two or three witnesses :

²Isa. xxxiii. 14; Dan. v. 6; Hos. x. 8; Luke xxi. 6; xxiii. 30; Rev. vi. 15-17.
³Lev. x. 2; Num. xvi. 35; Mal. iv. 1; Matt. iii. 10, 12; xiii. 42, 50; xxv. 41; 2
Thess. i. 8; 2 Pet. iii. 7, 10, 12; Rev. xx. 15.
¹Num. xv. 30, 31, 36; Deut. xiii. 6-10.
²Deut. xvii. 6, 7; xix. 15.

---

an apostate from Christ, can obtain no more forgiveness in any way. "His desperate condition," as Delitzsch justly remarks, "is both the natural consequence of his willful error, and also a condign punishment inflicted by the Divine hand. He not only shuts out himself from grace, but the door of repentance is shut behind him; and he has before him only the prospect of a damnation from which there is no escape."

27 **But a certain fearful looking for of judgment**—This is the fearful condition of every apostate from Christ. Cut off from all hope of being saved, nothing remains for him but a certain fearful anticipation of coming judgment and a fervor of fire which will finally consume all the enemies of God. There seems to be an allusion here to the fire which came out from God and consumed the two hundred and fifty Levites who participated in the rebellion of Korah (Num. 16: 35) ; and perhaps also to the destruction of Nadab, Abihu, and other like rebels against the Divine government. See references. So, God himself is represented as a consuming fire (12:29), before whom all the wicked will finally perish (2 Thess. 1:8). This thought our author now proceeds to illustrate still further by a reference to the law of Moses.

28 **He that despised Moses' law, etc.**—The Apostle does not speak here of all manner of sins and transgressions committed under the Old Covenant, but only of such as were committed "with a high hand," and in open rebellion against God and in contempt of his government: such, for example, as the sin of idolatry; the law concerning which was inexorably laid down as follows: "If there be found among you, within any of thy gates which the Lord thy God giveth thee, man or woman, that hath wrought wickedness in the sight of the Lord thy God, in transgressing his covenant, and hath gone and served other gods, and worshipped them, either the sun, or moon, or any of the host of heaven, which I have not commanded; and it be told thee, and thou hast heard of it, and in-

29 Of ³how much sorer punishment, suppose ye, shall he be thought worthy, ⁴who hath trodden under foot the Son of God, and hath counted ⁵the blood of the covenant, ⁶wherewith he was sanctified, an unholy thing, and ⁷hath done despite unto the Spirit of grace?

³Chap. ii. 1-4; vi. 4-8; xii. 25; Matt. xi. 22-24; Luke x. 12-15; xii. 47, 48.
⁴2 Kings ix. 33; Isa. xiv. 19; xxviii. 3; Mic. vii. 10; Rom. xvi. 20; 1 Cor. xv. 25.
⁵Chap. ix. 20; xiii. 20; Zech. ix. 11; Matt. xxvi. 28.
⁶Chap. ii. 11; ix. 13.
⁷Isa. lxiii. 10; Matt. xii. 31, 32; Luke xii. 10; Acts vii. 51; Eph. iv. 30.

quired diligently, and behold, it be true, and the thing certain, that such abomination is wrought in Israel: then thou shalt bring forth that man or that woman, which have committed that wicked thing, unto thy gates, even that man or that woman, and shalt stone them with stones, till they die. At the mouth of two witnesses, or three witnesses shall he that is worthy of death be put to death; but at the mouth of one witness he shall not be put to death. The hands of the witnesses shall be first upon him to put him to death, and afterward the hands of all the people. So thou shalt put the evil away from among you." (Deut. 17: 2-7.)

This is the best possible commentary on our text. It proves beyond all doubt that for the apostate under the Old Covenant there was no forgiveness. And now he proceeds to show by an argument, *a minori ad majus*, that the case of the apostate under the superior light and privileges of the New Covenant, is even more intolerable.

29 **Of how much sorer punishment, etc.**—The lesson is taught by our Lord himself, that wherever much is given, there also is much always required. "That servant," he says, "who knew his lord's will, and prepared not himself, neither did according to his will, shall be beaten with many stripes. But he that knew not, and did commit things worthy of stripes, shall be beaten with few stripes. For unto whomsoever much is given, of him shall much be required; and to whom men have committed much, of him will they ask the more." (Luke 12: 47, 48.) And just so our author reasons in the case before us. If the apostate under the Old Covenant was punished with so great severity, much more shall the apostate, who under the superior light of the New Covenant has trampled under foot the Son of God, and accounted the blood of the covenant by means of which he was sanctified an unholy thing, and insulted the Spirit of grace, suffer the extreme penalties of the divine law. The threefold specification of his guilt is given here

30 For we know him that hath said, [1]Vengeance belongeth unto me: I

[1]Deut. xxxii. 35; Psa. xciv. 1; Isa. lxi. 2; Rom. xii. 19.

for the purpose of more clearly defining the desperately wicked and abandoned course of the apostate. Let us notice each of these in order:

(1) **Who hath trodden under foot the Son of God,**—The ineffably glorious and perfect Being who in infinite condescension became flesh and died to redeem him; who sent his good Spirit to enlighten, comfort, and sanctify him; and who, in a word, did all that Heaven could do to save him from his sins, and to make him an heir of honor, glory, and immortality;—this is the Being whom the apostate, as far as he can, now tramples under foot, and treats as an object of extreme hatred and contempt! What else can such a one expect but the extreme terrors and torments of the coming judgment.

(2) **And hath counted, etc.**—The word rendered *unholy* (*koinon*) means (a) what is common; and (b) what is unholy or impure. Its secondary meaning is to be preferred here as being more in harmony with the context. The apostate treats this blood, by means of which he was himself once sanctified, as an unholy and impure thing. The use of the word *sanctified* (*hegiasthe*) shows very clearly that the subject of the discourse was once a Christian, a true child of God, and prospectively an heir of glory. But now he is a child of the devil and an enemy of all righteousness.

(3) **Hath done despite unto the Spirit of grace?**—That is, to the Holy Spirit. It is here called the Spirit of grace, because through it God imparts all grace, comfort, and salvation to our helpless and sinful race. By it, Christ himself worked all his miracles (Matt. 12: 28); and by it, he convinces the world of sin, of righteousness, and of judgment (John 16: 8); and by it, he comforts his saints and helps their infirmities (John 7: 39; Rom. 8: 26). To insult this Spirit, then, as does the apostate, is manifestly the height of all wickedness, maliciousness, and impiety. And hence, as Christ says (Matt. 12: 32), for those who do so there is no forgiveness. Nothing remains for them but a certain fearful expectation of judgment, and a jealousy of fire which will devour all the adversaries of God.

30 **For we know him that hath said,**—The meaning is, we

will recompense, saith the Lord. And again, ²The Lord shall judge his people.
31 It is ¹a fearful thing to fall into the hands of the living God.

²Deut. xxxii. 36; Psa. l. 4; 2 Cor. v. 10.
¹Chap. xii. 29; Matt. x. 28.

know the character of God: we know him to be a God of truth; a
God of justice; and a God of infinite power and holiness.  We
know, therefore, that he will certainly execute all his threatenings
on his enemies, while he at the same time fulfills all his promises to
his children.

**Vengeance belongeth unto me, etc.**—This is a quotation from
Deut. 32: 35. It is cited in Rom. 12: 19, to show that vengeance
does not belong to us but to God.  Here, it is cited to prove that
God will certainly, in due time, render a just recompense to all his
enemies.

**And again, the Lord shall judge his people.**—This is a citation from Deut. 32: 36. The same expression is found also in Psalm
135: 14; but it is most likely that our author quotes from the law
as given by Moses.  The passage is variously explained by expositors.  Some take it to mean that the Lord will vindicate and avenge
his people, by executing just judgment on his and their enemies
(Delitzsch, Alford, Moll, Stuart); but others think that the object
of our author is rather to show that God is so very just and righteous, that he will not allow the sins of even his own children to
pass with impunity, much less the daring impiety of apostates
(Bleek, Lunemann, De Wette).  "For if the righteous scarcely be
saved, where will the ungodly and the sinner appear?"  (1 Pet. 4:
18.)  Perhaps both ideas may be included in the Apostle's argument.

31 **It is a fearful thing to fall into the hands of the living
God.**—This is plain enough from the scope of the passage and the
explanations already given.  For if God is infinitely just and infinitely holy, it must indeed be indescribably awful to fall into his
hands to be punished forever and ever.  True, indeed, David says,
"Let us fall now into the hands of the Lord; for his mercies are
great; and let us not fall into the hand of man."  (2 Sam. 24: 14.)
But David was not an apostate.  It was for correction, and not for
everlasting punishment, that he chose to fall into the hand of the
Lord, rather than into the hands of his enemies.  The cases are,
therefore, not at all parallel.  For it is not for the purpose of being

corrected during the short space of three days, or even three centuries, that the apostate falls into the hands of Jehovah; but it is that he may be "punished with an everlasting destruction from the presence of the Lord, and from the glory of his power." (2 Thess. 1: 9.) "These," says Christ, "shall go away into everlasting (*aionion*) punishment; but the righteous, into everlasting (*aionion*) life." (Matt. 25: 46.)

### 3. EXHORTATION AND ENCOURAGEMENT TO THE HEBREW CHRISTIANS, ON THE GROUND OF THEIR PREVIOUS ENDURANCE
### 10: 32-34

32 But call to remembrance the former days, in which, [2]after ye were illuminated, [3]ye endured a great fight of afflictions,

[2]Chap. vi. 4; John viii. 12; xii. 46; Acts xxvi. 18; Rom. xiii. 12; 2 Cor. iv. 6.
[3]Chap. xii. 4; Acts viii. 1-3; ix. 1, 2; xii. 1-4; Phil. i. 29, 30.

**32 But call to remembrance, etc.**—We are here reminded of the very happy and encouraging turn which our author gave to his argument in the sixth chapter. Having there treated of the alarming state of the apostate, he reminded his readers that though sadly delinquent in some respects, they were, nevertheless, still far removed from the sin of apostasy. "God," he says, "is not unrighteous to forget your work and labor of love, which ye have showed toward his name, in that ye have ministered to the saints, and do minister." And just so he proceeds in this instance. Having presented to the Hebrew brethren the awful doom of those who reject Christ and the great salvation purchased through his blood, he next encourages them by referring to their first love, and reminding them how heroically they had endured their former afflictions.

**After ye were illuminated,**—That is, after they had been translated from the kingdom of darkness into the Kingdom of him who is himself the light of the world (John 8: 12), the Sun of righteousness that has risen upon the nations (Mal. 4: 2). Those who follow him cannot walk in darkness. See notes on 6: 4.

**Ye endured a great fight of afflictions.**—These afflictions were such as occurred after the martyrdom of Stephen, when there was a great persecution against the Church which was at Jerusalem. (Acts 8: 1; 12: 1-3, etc.) All these, the Hebrew brethren of Jerusalem and Palestine had borne patiently and even heroically, as

33 Partly, whilst ¹ye were made a gazingstock both ²by reproaches and afflictions: and partly, whilst ³ye became companions of them that were so used.

34 For ¹ye had compassion of | me in my: *those in* | bonds, and ²took joyfully the spoiling of your goods, knowing | in: *for* | yourselves that ³ye have [in heaven] a better and an enduring substance.

¹Nahum iii. 6; 1 Cor. iv. 9.
²Chap. xi. 36, 37; xiii. 13; Psa. lxix. 9; Isa. li. 7; 2 Cor. xii. 10.
³Phil. i. 7; iv. 14; 2 Tim. i. 8, 16-18.
¹Matt. xxv. 36, 43; Acts xii. 5; xxiv. 23.
²Matt. v. 11, 12; Acts v. 41; Jas. i. 2, 10.
³Matt. vi. 19, 20; Col. iii. 1, 2; 1 Tim. vi. 19; 2 Tim. iv. 8; 1 Pet. i. 4.

faithful "soldiers of the cross." And now the Apostle would have them be consistent, and persevere in like manner even to the end.

33 **Partly, whilst ye were made a gazingstock, etc.**—The object of the Apostle in this verse, is to particularize and further illustrate the very severe nature and character of their former trials and afflictions; and also to remind them still further of the great readiness of mind with which they had endured them. They not only bore with patience and Christian fortitude the severe trials to which they themselves were subjected by their persecutors; but they also, it seems, voluntarily became the companions of others who were suffering in like manner. To be made a gazingstock (*theatrizomenoi*) is to be exposed to public abuse and insult, as criminals often were in the Greek and Roman theaters. (Acts 19: 29; 1 Cor. 4: 9.) Speaking of these barbarous exhibitions, Seneca says in his seventh epistle: "In the morning men are exposed to lions and bears: at midday, to their spectators. Those that kill are opposed to one another; and the victor is detained for another slaughter. The conclusion of the fight is death." The word *reproaches* (*oneidismoi*) has reference to the reproachful epithets which were heaped upon the Christians by their persecutors; and the word *afflictions* (*thlipseis*) denotes the various sufferings and calamities which they endured. All these they had borne with patience and Christian fortitude; and they had even voluntarily become the companions or *partners* (*koinonoi*) of those who were suffering from like reproaches and afflictions. This they did, no doubt, by contributing of their means for their support and comfort; and by doing all in their power to alleviate and remove their sufferings.

34 **For ye had compassion of me in my bonds,**—Or rather, according to the above critical note, *For ye sympathized with them*

*who were in bonds.* This reading is, on the whole, best sustained
by both the internal and the external evidence; and it is therefore
preferred by Grotius, Bengel, Semler, Wetstein, Michaelis, Griesbach, Scholz, Kuinoel, Bleek, Knapp, Ebrard, Delitzsch, and Moll,
as well as by the authorities cited in the above note. It is proper
to add, however, that the reading of the Textus Receptus is supported by the Codex Sinaiticus and several other valuable manuscripts. It is therefore a satisfaction to know that the difference of
these readings does not materially affect the sense of the passage;
the obvious purpose of the writer being in either case to praise and
encourage the Hebrews on account of their former sympathy for
those who were in bonds and afflictions.

**And took joyfully the spoiling of your goods,**—This may
refer (1) to the losses which the Hebrews sustained in consequence
of their becoming Christians; just as it sometimes now happens even in our own day. "When a Jew," says Ebrard, "shows
himself determined to become a Christian, he is disinherited by his
relatives; his share of the property is withheld from him; his credit
and every source of gain, withdrawn; and he falls into a state of
complete destitution." This same kind of injustice was extensively
practiced in primitive times by both Jews and Gentiles. But (2) it
is probable that the Apostle refers here more particularly to the
heavy losses of property which the Hebrew Christians had incurred in times of persecution. In either case, they bore all joyfully, just as the Apostles rejoiced that they were counted worthy
to suffer shame for the name of Jesus. (Acts 5: 41.)

**Knowing in yourselves, etc.**—Or, according to the most approved reading, *Knowing that ye have for yourselves a better possession, and one that is enduring.* Some valuable manuscripts, as
D, K, L, etc., retain the phrase *in heaven* (*en ouranois*). But
whether these words are spurious or genuine, the sense of the passage is in either case manifestly the same, as it is, no doubt, to the
heavenly inheritance that our author here refers. See 1 Pet. 1: 4.
The Hebrews, it seems, had joyfully submitted to being robbed of
their earthly possessions; because, like Abraham, Isaac, and Jacob,
they had constantly in view the heavenly country, and also the city
which had the foundations. (11: 10, 16.) "Thus," observes Delitzsch, "the sacred writer raises the hearts and minds of those
whom his previous language might have depressed. He had led

them to the brink of a terrible precipice of negligence and apostasy, down which they seemed in danger of falling; and now he leads them back from it to the contemplation of their own steadfast and favored past."

4. THE HEBREWS ARE FURTHER EXHORTED AND ENCOUR-
AGED TO MAINTAIN THEIR CONFIDENCE; AND TO PER-
SEVERE THROUGH FAITH EVEN TO THE END, WHICH
TO THEM WAS THEN VERY NEAR AT HAND, WHEN
THEY WOULD ALL BE ABUNDANTLY REWARDED
FOR THEIR FIDELITY
10 : 35-39

35 [1]Cast not away therefore your confidence, [2]which hath great recompense of reward.

[1]Chap. iii. 6, 14; iv. 14; Matt. x. 22; xiv. 13; Gal. vi. 9; Col. i. 23.
[2]Chap. xi. 6, 26; Psa. xix. 11; Matt. v. 12; Luke xiv. 14; 1 Cor. xv. 58; Gal. vi. 8-10.

35 **Cast not away therefore your confidence,**—There seems to be an allusion here to the conduct of weak and cowardly soldiers, who in the day of battle were wont to throw aside their shields and turn their backs on the enemy. This was regarded by the ancients as extremely dishonorable. And hence when the Lacedemonian women presented shields to their sons on going to battle, they were in the habit of saying to them, "Bring this back, or be brought back upon it." The same sentiment prevailed also among the ancient Germans. Tacitus says, that "to lose or cast away the shield in battle, was regarded by them as a matter of the greatest dishonor; and that those who acted so were not allowed to be present at the sacrifices, nor to attend the public assemblies of the people." (Germ. c. vi.) In allusion to this very prevalent feeling among the ancients, our author exhorts his Hebrew brethren not to act the part of cowardly soldiers by voluntarily casting away the shield of faith, or rather of that holy and joyful confidence (*parresia*) which faith inspires in the soul; but to quit themselves like men; "to be strong in the Lord and in the power of his might"; knowing that no one could ever deprive them of this most valuable weapon of their Christian panoply, unless they would themselves voluntarily cast it aside, and then turn about and act as cowards.

**Which hath great recompense of reward.**—This joyful and well grounded confidence gives us peace of mind here, and secures

36 For ³ye have need of patience, that, ⁴after ye have done the will of God, ⁵ye might receive the promise.

³Chap. vi. 15; xii. 15; Luke viii. 15; xxi. 19; Rom. ii. 7; v. 3, 4; xv. 4, 5; Jas. i. 3, 4; v. 7-11.
⁴Chap. xiii. 21; Matt. vii. 21; xii. 50; John vii. 17; Rom. xii. 2; Eph. vi. 6.
⁵Chap. vi. 12, 15, 17; ix. 15; xi. 9; 1 Pet. i. 9.

for all who possess it, "glory, honor, and immortality" hereafter. Great indeed, therefore, is the recompense of its reward. It should be remembered, however, that this reward is not bestowed on anyone as a matter of debt, but of grace. "For by grace are ye saved through faith; and that not of yourselves: it is the gift of God." (Eph. 2: 8.) This confidence is therefore but one of the legitimate fruits of God's gracious plan; and it serves as a means of enjoying the salvation that has been so freely purchased for us through the precious blood of the Lord Jesus.

36 **For ye have need of patience,**—Patience is necessary at all times, and especially in times of trial and affliction. For without it, God's gracious chastisements are unavailing; they only serve to irritate and excite our evil passions, and to make us more discontented. But with patience, they always give us a joyful and approving experience which fills us with an increase of hope and love. (Rom. 5: 3-5.) And accordingly James exhorts his brethren of the dispersion to let patience have her perfect work, that they "might be perfect and entire, wanting nothing." The man who does this, can always with Paul "glory in tribulations," knowing that "these light afflictions which are but momentary [serve to] work out for us a far more exceeding and eternal weight of glory." (2 Cor. 4: 17.)

**After ye have done the will of God,**—That is, after ye have done and suffered all that God requires of you. The Apostle does not mean to say that Christians should fulfill the will of God, as Christ did by means of his atoning sacrifice (10: 7, 9); but only that they should do and suffer patiently, in obedience to God's will, whatever he himself may appoint or permit for their own spiritual improvement, as well as for the welfare of others.

**Ye might receive the promise.**—The whole verse may be more literally and simply rendered as follows: For ye have need of patience; that having done the will of God, ye may receive the promise. By *"the promise"* is not meant *the word* of the promise; for that had been long previously given to Abraham and to his seed.

37 For ¹yet a little while, and he that shall come will come, and will not tarry.

¹Hab. ii. 3; Matt. xxiv. 27-34; Phil. iv. 5; Jas. v. 7-9; 1 Pet. iv. 7; Rev. ii. 5.

(Gal. 3 : 29.) But "the promise" here means the thing promised. It is the eternal life with all its accompanying blessings, upon the enjoyment of which the soul of every true believer enters immediately after death. (Luke 16 : 22; 2 Cor. 5 : 6, 8; Phil. 1 : 23, etc.) And so we read that after Abraham had patiently endured "he obtained the promise." (6 : 15.) The object of the Apostle, then, in the use of these words, is simply to persuade the Hebrew Christians to walk in the footsteps of their father Abraham; so that like him, when the toils and trials of life were all over, they too might obtain the promise, and enter on the enjoyment of the eternal inheritance.

37 **For yet a little while, etc.**—More literally: For yet a little little while [that is, a very little while], he who is coming (*ho erchomenos*) will come, and will not tarry. The coming One here spoken of is manifestly Christ himself. But what is meant by his coming? To what coming does our author here refer? Many say, "To his second personal coming." But this is plainly inconsistent with the scope of the Apostle's exhortation, as well as with the truth itself. His obvious design in the passage is to encourage the Hebrew brethren to persevere in their begun Christian course, on the ground that the coming of Christ was then very near at hand, when they would all be delivered from the snares, reproaches, and violence of their persecutors. But how could he consistently and truthfully encourage them to do this, on the ground that the second personal advent of Christ was then very near at hand? It will not do to say with some that the Apostles themselves so believed and so taught. They did neither, but just the reverse. For when some of the Thessalonian brethren so understood Paul's teaching (1 Thess. 4 : 15-17), he promptly addressed to them a second letter, in which he very emphatically corrected their mistake. "Now we beseech you, brethren," he says, "by the coming of our Lord Jesus Christ, and by our gathering together unto him, that ye be not soon shaken in mind, or be troubled, neither by spirit, nor by word, nor by letter as from us, as that the day of Christ [the Lord] is at hand. Let no man deceive you by any means: for

that day shall not come, except there come a falling away first, and that man of sin be revealed, the son of perdition," etc. (2 Thess. 2: 1-3.) This, then, is a clear and satisfactory refutation of the charge, that the Apostles believed and taught that the second personal coming of Christ was near at hand in their own day. And so also is the book of Revelation a refutation of it. Indeed, with this prophetic chart before us, no one can yet say understandingly that the second personal advent of Christ is even now near at hand. For after the destruction of Babylon, a long period of religious prosperity will intervene before the final judgment, which will take place immediately after Christ's second coming. See Matt. 13: 30, 41-46; 16: 27; 25: 31-46; John 5: 28, 29; Acts 17: 31; Rom. 2: 5-16; 1 Thess. 4: 15-18; 2 Thess. 1: 6-10; 2 Tim. 4: 1; 2 Pet. 3: 7-10; Rev. 20: 11-15. The coming of Christ, as referred to in our text, must therefore mean, not his second personal coming, but his coming in providence most likely, to destroy Jerusalem, and so to deliver his elect from the violent persecutions to which they had long been subjected by the unbelieving Jews. (Matt. 24: 29-41.) To this Christ himself refers encouragingly in Luke 21: 28; where, speaking of the signs of Jerusalem's approaching ruin, he says, "When these things begin to come to pass, then look up, and lift up your heads, for your redemption draweth nigh." The fall of Jerusalem put an end, of course, to Jewish persecution; and in this way and to this extent, it brought deliverance to the Christians of Palestine. And as this occurred in A.D. 70, about seven years after the writing of this Epistle, the evidence seems very clear that the Apostle has reference here to that ever memorable event. See note on the last clause of verse 25.

This view of the matter is also further corroborated by the fact that our author finds in the prophecy of Habakkuk, concerning the overthrow of the Chaldean monarchy, language so very appropriate to his purpose that he here takes and applies it as his own; thereby showing that the two cases are very analogous. The words of the prophecy may be literally rendered as follows, beginning with 2: 2, for the sake of the connection. And Jehovah answered me and said, Write the vision, and engrave it on smooth tablets, so that he may run [that is, read fluently] who reads it. For yet the vision is for an appointed time, and it will hasten to the end, and will not lie: if it tarry wait for it, for it will surely

38 Now | ¹the just: *my just one* | shall live by faith: but ²if any man draw back, ³my soul shall have no pleasure in him.

¹Hab. ii. 4; Rom. i. 17; Gal. iii. 11.
²Ch. vi. 4-6; Matt. xii. 43-45; xiii. 21; 2 Pet. ii. 18-22.
³Psa. v. 4; Isa. xlii. 1; Mal. i. 10; 1 Thess. ii. 15.

come; it will not be behind [the appointed time]. Behold his soul [which] is lifted up is not upright in him; but the just by his faith shall live. From this it will be seen that our author does not quote the exact words of God's reply to the Prophet; but as is usual in such cases of accommodation (see Rom. 10: 6-8), he so modifies the language as to adapt it to the case in hand. The main lesson is, however, the same in both Hebrews and Habakkuk; viz.: that God would certainly come and execute his purposes at the appointed time: and that while the proud and self-reliant would of necessity perish under the righteous judgments of God, the just man's faith, if it wavered not, would certainly support him under the severest trials.

This was all impressively illustrated in the fall of Jerusalem. The unbelieving Jews were all slain or taken captive; but not a Christian perished in the siege. Eusebius says, "When the whole congregation of the Church in Jerusalem, according to an oracle given by revelation to approved persons among them before the war, were commanded to depart from the city and inhabit a city which they call Pella, beyond the Jordan, to which when all those who believed in Christ had removed from Jerusalem, and when the saints had totally abandoned the royal city which is the metropolis of the Jews, then the Divine vengeance seized them who had dealt so wickedly with Christ and his Apostles, and utterly destroyed that wicked and abominable generation." (Eccl. Hist. iii. v.) To the same effect testifies also Epiphanius. He says, "The disciples of Christ being warned by an angel, removed to Pella; and afterward when Hadrian rebuilt Jerusalem and called it after his own family name, Ælia Colonia, they returned thither."

38 **Now the just shall live by faith:**—The following readings are submitted for the consideration of the thoughtful: (1) but the just by his faith shall live (Hebrew); (2) but the just by faith shall live (Rec.); (3) but the just by the faith of me shall live (Sept. Codex B); (4) but my just one by faith shall live (Sept. Codex A). In all these readings there is an ambiguity depending

39 But ¹we are not of them who draw back unto perdition; ²but of them that believe to the saving of the soul.

¹Ch. vi. 6; x. 26-29; 2 Pet. ii. 20-22; 1 John v. 16.
²Mark xvi. 16; John iii. 15, 16; v. 24; vi. 40; xx. 31; Acts xvi. 30, 31; Rom. i. 16; x. 9, 10.

on the grammatical relations of the phrase *"by faith"* (*ek pisteos*). But it is a satisfaction to know that these slight variations do not materially affect the sense of the passage. It is strictly true that the man who is justified by his faith, or by God's faith, shall live; and it is also true, that the just man, or God's just man, shall live by his faith. The former construction best suits the scope of the argument in Rom. 1: 17 and Gal. 3: 11; and the latter harmonizes best with the design of the writer both in our text and in Habakkuk 2: 4. But whichever reading and construction be preferred, the leading object of our author is substantially the same; viz.: to persuade and encourage his Hebrew brethren not to apostatize from Christ, but to be strong in the faith giving glory to God. This is rendered still more obvious by what follows.

**But if any man draw back, etc.**—The words *"any man"* are not in the original; and their introduction into the English version is unfortunate. It is not "any man," but the "just man," of whom God speaks. It is of the man who was once justified by his faith, and who lived by his faith, that the affirmation is made. The just man shall live by his faith; but if he [the just man] draw back [then] my soul shall have no pleasure in him.

39 **But we are not of them, etc.**—Here again the Apostle passes from what is threatening to what is encouraging. "But we are not of backsliding to perdition, but of faith to the saving of the soul." At this point the mind of our author becomes wholly engrossed with the saving and soul-sustaining power of faith; and leaving once more his direct line of thought, he makes this his main theme in the following section.

## REFLECTIONS

1. How transcendently great are the honors, birthrights and privileges of the children of God (verses 19-21). Having now free access to the Holiest of all by the blood of Jesus, and having a great high priest over the house of God, we need fear no evil so long as we walk worthy of our high and holy calling. All the

events of life must and will work together for our good while here (Rom. 8: 28) ; and death itself will but serve to elevate us to a higher state of glory, honor and blessedness hereafter (4: 10). "For we know that if our earthly house of this tabernacle were dissolved, we have a building of God, a house not made with hands, eternal in the heavens." (2 Cor. 5: 1.) Who then that has the faith and experience of Paul would not like him prefer to depart and be with Christ. (Phil. 1: 23.)

2. But let it not be forgotten that, after all, the enjoyment of heaven depends essentially, through Divine grace, on our own exertions (verse 23). "Work out your own salvation," says Paul, "with fear and trembling; for it is God that worketh in you both to will and to do of his good pleasure." (Phil. 2: 12, 13.) The blood of Christ is of no avail to the man who lives and dies in willful disobedience. Christ came to save men *from* their sins, not *in* them. And hence the force and propriety of the exhortation that we should draw near to God "with a true heart, in full assurance of faith, having our hearts sprinkled from an evil conscience and our bodies washed with pure water." God himself is infinitely holy ; and they only can enjoy his presence who purify their souls by obeying the truth, through the Spirit, unto unfeigned love of the brethren. (1 Pet. 1: 22.)

3. Obedience consists in doing from the heart the will of God, as it is revealed to us in his Holy Word (verse 23). It is, indeed, wholly useless for us to attempt to serve God in any other way. "In vain," says Christ, "they do worship me, teaching for doctrines the commandments of men." (Matt. 15: 9.) So he once said to the Jews, and so he still says to thousands today. For it must be confessed that many who profess to be the followers of Christ have departed quite as far from the letter and spirit of the New Covenant, as the Jews had departed from the Old. Indeed this spirit of will-worship is a weakness and proneness of human nature, not confined to any one age or people. The mystery of iniquity was at work even in Paul's time (2 Thess. 2: 7) ; and many have since departed still further and further from the faith and simplicity of the Gospel. How many thousands, for instance, who habitually desecrate the Lord's Day, are not superstitiously punctilious in observing days and festivals of their own creation. And to how many thousands might it still be said, as Paul once said to the Co-

rinthians, "When ye come together into one place, this is not to eat the Lord's Supper." O that God would raise up another Elijah to restore to the Church what the Man of sin has taken away; and to free her, at the same time, from the many oppressive burdens which he has arrogantly imposed on her.

4. Christians should never neglect the meetings appointed for public and social worship, especially on the Lord's Day (verse 25). Those who do so, show but a poor appreciation of their rights and privileges, and at the same time they set before others an example which often leads to the very worst of consequences. God has given to us a social nature, and he has also given to us a religion that is in all respects adapted to the wants of our nature: a religion that knows but "one body, one Spirit, one Lord, one faith, one baptism, one God and Father of all, who is above all, and through all, and in all." (Eph. 4: 4-6.) And hence we are required to bear one another's burdens (Gal. 6: 1); to exhort and admonish one another daily, lest any be hardened through the deceitfulness of sin (3: 13). The habit of going to meeting merely for the purpose of hearing some distinguished preacher has become entirely too common in the church of Christ. Indeed, it has become a very great evil. Christians should meet together to worship God, and to commemorate the death, burial, and resurrection of Christ, as did the primitive church, whether they have a preacher with them or not. If there is present anyone who is in all respects well qualified to instruct and edify the congregation, let us thank God for the favor and gratefully listen to the words of his servant. But if no such one is in the meeting, we have nevertheless the precious promise that Christ himself is present to bless all who meet in his name, and to honor him in the ordinances of his own appointment. (Matt. 28:20.) Let the Lord's Day, then, be wholly sanctified to the honor and glory of him who has inscribed his own name upon it, as a day that is most holy. Let it be a day of holy joy, and prayer, and praise, in the family, in the Sunday-school, in the social meeting, and in the public assembly of the saints, and very soon the happy consequences will be felt throughout all Christendom.

5. We have all reason to anticipate a day of trial, as well as the ancient Hebrews (verse 25). God has not called us to go to Heaven

"On flowery beds of ease,
   While others fought to win the prize,
   And sailed through bloody seas."

This world is preordained and arranged for our education and discipline, and it is therefore a great blessing to be allowed to suffer patiently for the sake of Christ and his church (Phil. 1:29.) But the danger is that in the hour of trial our faith may fail us, and that in consequence of our great weakness we may bring dishonor on the cause of Christ. Many have done so; some to their own shame and everlasting disgrace; and others, like Peter, to their deepest grief and mortification. We cannot, therefore, be too earnest in our supplications at the throne of grace, that God would help us, and not allow us to be tempted above what we are able to bear, but that he would enable us to come off more than conquerors through him who has so tenderly loved us. This, God will certainly do if we only trust in him and rely on him as we should. See 1 Cor. 10:13; Isa. 49:15.

6. It is well to remember our first love and to think often of the joy, comfort, and consolation which filled our hearts when we first put on Christ and were made partakers of the Holy Spirit (verses 32-34). Then, we had no thought of ever looking back to the flesh-pots of Egypt, or to anything else pertaining to "the lusts of the flesh, the lusts of the eye, and the pride of life." Jesus was to us "the chief among ten thousand, and the one altogether lovely." We then felt that we would gladly bear anything for the honor and glory of his name, and that we would never murmur or complain in the service of him who bore the cross for us. But, alas! how many become discouraged by the way, and are almost persuaded to turn back and walk no more with Jesus. Such persons need to be *encouraged*. The spirit is often willing when the flesh is weak. And it not unfrequently revives the hearts of these discouraged ones to talk with them of "the former days," when they willingly and joyfully bore much for the sake of Christ.

7. It is a consolation to know that the period of our earthly trials is of but short duration (verse 37). If we had to endure these trials and afflictions for even a few hundred years, many of us might faint by the way. But not so. Our blessed Lord says to each of us, "Behold I come quickly, and my reward is with me, to give to every man according as his works shall be" (Rev. 22:12).

"He that overcometh," he says, "shall be clothed with white raiment, and I will not blot out his name out of the book of life; but I will confess his name before my Father and his angels. He that hath an ear, let him hear what the Spirit saith unto the churches." (Rev. 3: 5, 6.)

## SECTION TEN
### 11: 1-40

#### ANALYSIS

In this section, we have another characteristic Pauline digression. Our author having touched, in the close of the tenth chapter, on the conservative nature and sustaining power of faith, his mind is at once seized with the importance and magnitude of the subject, and he accordingly devotes the whole of this section to its consideration and development.

I. He begins by giving us, not a logical definition of faith, but rather a plain statement with regard to its nature and province as an affection of the human mind, implying at the same time its great power and influence as a means and principle of enjoyment. It sustains and supports the soul of the believer, by enabling him to enjoy even now to some extent, as present realities, those things which are the objects of our hopes, and which lie far away beyond the narrow sphere of our corporeal senses. This is shown

1. From the fact that in consequence of their faith many of the ancients obtained a reputation which is as wide as the world, and as enduring as time (verse 2).

2. From the fact that through it we are enabled to rely with the utmost confidence on matters which lie far beyond the narrow limits, not only of our senses, but even of our philosophy; such, for instance, as the fact that "In the beginning God created the heavens and the earth" (verse 3).

II. Having thus stated, and in a general way verified his main thesis, the Apostle next proceeds to illustrate it at great length by citing some of the most remarkable examples that are found in Old Testament history. In doing so, he refers

1. To the case of Abel (verse 4);
2. To the case of Enoch (verses 5, 6);
3. To the case of Noah (verse 7);

4. To the case of Abraham, with regard to the promised inheritance (verses 8-10) ;

5. To the case of Abraham and Sarah with regard to the conception and birth of Isaac (verses 11, 12) ;

6. To the case of Abraham, Sarah, Isaac, and Jacob, with regard to the promises concerning Christ and the eternal inheritance through him (verses 13-16) ;

7. To the example of Abraham in offering up his son Isaac (verses 17-19) ;

8. To the example of Isaac, in blessing Jacob and Esau (verse 20) ;

9. To the case of 'Jacob, in adopting and blessing Ephraim and Manasseh, as his own sons (verse 21) ;

10. To the example of Joseph (verse 22) ;

11. To the conduct of Amram and Jochebed, the parents of Moses (verse 23) ;

12. To the example of Moses, (1) in preferring the reproach of Christ to the treasures of Egypt; (2) in leaving Egypt with the conviction that God would yet deliver the Israelites through him (Acts 7 : 25) ; and (3) in keeping the Passover (verses 24-28) ;

13. To the example of the Israelites, (1) in crossing the Red Sea; and (2) in compassing the walls of Jericho seven days (verses 29, 30) ;

14. To the example of Rahab, the harlot (verse 31).

III. From these special cases, our author next proceeds to give a summary of others too numerous to be mentioned in detail, all of which, however, serve to illustrate the great power of faith in sustaining the soul under the severest trials and afflictions. These heroic men and women, though in the world, were really not of it. Their affections were not set on the earth, but on heaven. And hence, while here, they regarded themselves but as strangers and pilgrims in a foreign land (verses 32-38).

IV. Finally, the Apostle reminds his readers that none of these illustrious ones lived to see Jesus, or to enjoy the superior blessings of his mediatorial reign (verses 39, 40). These matters were but partially revealed to the faithful ones of the Patriarchal and Jewish ages. And as Christians are now blessed with superior privileges, so also they are placed under greater responsibilities to remain steadfast even to the end of life.

The principal points of this section may therefore be summed up as follows:

I. 11: 1-3.  The nature, province, and sustaining power of faith.

II. 11: 4-31.  Sundry examples selected from the history of the ancients, illustrative of the nature, power, and influence of faith.

III. 11: 32-38.  Other general illustrations drawn from the exploits, deliverances, and heroic endurance of faithful men and women under the Old Covenant.

IV. 11: 39, 40.  Superior light and privileges of believers under the New Covenant.

## 1. THE NATURE, PROVINCE, AND SUSTAINING POWER OF FAITH
### 11: 1-3

1 Now faith is ¹the substance of things hoped for, ²the evidence of things not seen.

¹Chap. i. 3; iii. 14; 2 Cor. ix. 4; xi. 17.
²2 Cor. iv. 18; 2 Tim. iii. 16; 1 Pet. i. 8.

---

**1 Now faith is the substance of things hoped for,**—It is I think obvious from the context that the object of our author in this verse is, not to define faith, not to tell what it is in and of itself, but simply to describe it in its relations to the human soul, as a means of endurance and principle of enjoyment.  Having shown from Habakkuk, its marvelous conservative power, it was natural that he should next explain wherein its great strength lieth; and how it is that it wields so great an influence over the character, lives, and fortunes of those who possess it.  This he does with great clearness, beauty, and energy in the course of this section.  He begins by telling us that faith is the *hupostasis* of things hoped for.  This is all plain enough except the word *hupostasis*.  What does it mean?  In 1: 3, it evidently means *essence* or *substance,* in contrast with the outward manifestations of the Deity; and in 3: 14, it just as clearly means *confidence* in God and in the word of his grace.  In this latter sense, confidence in reference to the things hoped for, it is here taken by Luther, Melancthon, Grotius, Böhme, Tholuck, Bleek, DeWette, Bloomfield, McLean, Lünemann, Ebrard, Stuart, Delitzsch, Alford, Moll, and most other modern interpreters.  "There can be no reasonable doubt," says Alford, "that this is the true meaning here." But others, as Chrysostom, Ambrose, Augustine, Bengel, and the translators of our English Version, see in this word something more than "a well grounded confidence." They allege that, in the use of this term, the Apostle means to say that faith is in effect to the soul of the believer the very *substance* or *essence* of things hoped for : so that, by means of it, he is able to enjoy as present realities, what without faith would be to him in effect but as mere nonentities. It was faith, say they, that gave to the heavenly country such a substantive existence in the minds of Abraham, Isaac, and Jacob, as enabled them to enjoy it, in a measure, even while they were strangers and pilgrims on the Earth. That this is all implied in the use of the word *hupostasis,* is I think very clear from the several illustrations which follow in this chapter. But it is not so clear to my mind that the Apostle intends to express by this word anything more than a firm and well grounded confidence in reference to the objects of our hope. This confidence is of course followed by many joyful and encouraging effects, some of which are well illustrated by the remarks of Chrysostom and Augustine. For other instances of the use of this word, see 2 Cor. 9 : 4 ; 11 : 17.

**the evidence of things not seen.**—This, in connection with the preceding clause, forms a sort of constructive Hebrew parallelism. The expression, *"things not seen,"* comprehends more than "the things hoped for." The latter has reference only to future good ; but the former embraces all the invisible realities of the universe, past, present, and future, about which the Holy Spirit has borne witness. The word here rendered *evidence* (*elenkos*) is also used in different senses. It may denote (1) the proof or demonstration, by means of which any proposition is shown to be true or false ; and (2) the conviction or full persuasion wrought in the mind by means of this demonstration. Commentators are much divided as to the proper meaning of the word in this connection. Some, as Bengel, Böhme, Stier, Ebrard, Hofmann, Stuart, Delitzsch, and Alford, take it *objectively,* in the sense of proof or demonstration ; and others, as Kuinoel, Menken, Bleek, De Wette, Lünemann, etc., take it *subjectively,* in the sense of conviction or firm persuasion. For my own part, I think as in the former case, that both ideas are implied in the Apostle's use of the term ; but that it is the *subjective* element to which he has most direct refer-

2 For ¹by it the elders obtained a good report.

¹Vers. 4-38.

ence, and which he intends to express by the word *elegchos*. There can, of course, be no conviction without a sufficient proof; but it is not I think to the proof, but to its effect on the soul, that the Apostle here particularly refers. This is most in harmony with his main object throughout the entire chapter, which is manifestly to describe faith in its relations to the soul, both as a power of endurance, and a means and principle of enjoyment. He, therefore, begins the discussion with the simple affirmation, that faith is to the soul of the believer confidence with respect to things hoped for, and conviction with respect to things not seen.: that is, with respect to such invisible realities as are revealed to us in the word of God. For where there is no testimony there can be no faith. (Rom. 10: 17.) But when God speaks, his word is to the believer an end of all controversy. It is to the Christian what a demonstration is to the mathematician: it gives confidence with respect to whatever is promised; and it begets conviction with respect to the truth of whatever is affirmed. Do the Scriptures teach, for example, that "the hour is coming in which all that are in their graves shall hear his [Christ's] voice, and shall come forth; they that have done good to the resurrection of life; and they that have done evil to the resurrection of damnation?"—the Christian receives this testimony, believes it, and acts in reference to it with all confidence. Why so? Simply because *God says so*. No reasoning, no philosophy, and no demonstration of any kind, can ever go beyond this. And hence it is, that to the believer all the promises of God are yea and amen in Christ Jesus (2 Cor. 1: 20); and like Moses he endures as seeing him who is invisible (verse 27). The word *elenkos* occurs only here and in 2 Tim. 3: 16. In the latter case, it means conviction of sin, or of any erroneous notions or hypotheses.

2 **For by it the elders obtained a good report.**—Our author now proceeds with the proof and illustration of his main thesis, as submitted in the first verse. That faith is confidence with respect to the objects of our hope, and conviction with respect to those invisible realities which are revealed to us in the word of God, he argues (1) from the fact that by it (*en taute*) the elders obtained a

3 ²Through faith we understand that the worlds were framed by the word of God, so that ¹| things which are seen were: *that which is seen, was* | not made of things which do appear.

²Chap. i. 2; Gen. i. 1; Psa. xxxiii. 6; John i. 3; Rom. i. 19-21; Rev. iv. 11.
¹Isa. xl. 26; Jer. x. 11-16; John i. 1-3.

good name and a most enviable reputation from God as well as from his people; and (2) from the fact that by means of it we are convinced that the universe was framed by the word of God. These elders (*hoi presbuteroi*) were not only persons in official authority, but the term is used here to indicate all the heroic men of the Old Testament from Abel down to the Maccabees, as we learn from what follows. They were not generally distinguished for their wealth, their talents, their learning, or their worldly attainments of any kind; but they were men of faith. They believed God's word; and they were, therefore, constrained to look upward for life, health, and happiness. They set their affections on things that are above, and not on things that are on the Earth, knowing that they were but strangers and pilgrims in the world. This unwavering confidence in God and in the word of his grace, gave them even while here a realization of good things to come, and enabled them to endure with meekness and fortitude the severest trials and afflictions.

3 **Through faith we understand, etc.**—This is given by our author as an example of the "things not seen." The creation of the universe is a matter which we did not and which we cannot perceive by means of our corporeal senses: nor is it discernible by even the eye of reason through the medium of the light of nature. This, all must concede. But to the eye of faith it is just as plain that "In the beginning God created the heavens and the earth," as that Columbus discovered America, or that George Washington was once President of the United States.

The critics are not agreed as to the textual meaning of the word that is here rendered *worlds* (*aiones*). Literally, it means *ages;* and it is so rendered by Alford and most of the Greek Fathers. But it seems to me, judging from the terms of the context, that the Apostle intends to express here about the same general thought that Moses expresses in Gen. 1: 1; and I, therefore, agree with Delitzsch and others that *aiones* is used here by metonymy to denote at least the whole material universe. See note 1:3. This will become more obvious from the consideration of the following clause.

**so that things are seen, etc.:**—or rather, according to our best authorities, *So that that which is seen* [the visible universe] *has not come into being from visible materials,* as the heathen philosophers all believed and taught. Thales maintained that God made all things out of water or chaos. Plato concedes the eternity of three distinct principles, viz., God, matter, and ideas: meaning by the ideas a sort of incorporeal archetypes according to which God framed and fashioned all things. Aristotle held to the eternity of matter; and says, it was the common opinion of naturalists that "Nothing can be made out of nothing." This is as far as philosophy goes or can go. But our faith assures us that God alone is eternal; and that in the beginning he *created* the Heavens and the Earth. (Gen. 1:1.) It assures us moreover that through the eternal Word, who was with God and who was God, all things came into being (*egeueto*); and that without him not even one thing came into being which is in being (John 1:1-3). And just so in our text. The Apostle makes no attempt at explanation; but like Moses he simply affirms, by the authority of the Holy Spirit, that God did not make the universe, as an architect makes a house, or as an artist makes a steam engine out of pre-existing materials; but that in the beginning he *created* it by the word of his power. "He spake," and it was done; he commanded, and it stood fast."

2. SUNDRY EXAMPLES SELECTED FROM THE HISTORY OF
THE ANCIENTS, ILLUSTRATIVE OF THE NATURE,
POWER, AND INFLUENCE OF FAITH
11: 4-31

4 [2]By faith Abel offered unto God [3]a more excellent sacrifice than Cain, by which [4]he obtained witness that he was righteous, God testifying of his gifts: and [5]by it he being dead yet speaketh.

[2]Gen. iv. 3-5; 1 John iii. 11, 12.
[3]Prov. xv. 8; xxi. 27; Jude 11.
[4]Lev. ix. 24; Judges vi. 21; xiii. 20, 21; 1 Kings xviii. 38; 2 Chron. vii. 1; Psa. xx. 3.
[5]Chap. xii. 1, 24.

4 **By faith Abel offered, etc.**—Cain and Abel both brought offerings, but of different kinds. Cain brought of the fruits of the ground, but Abel brought of the firstlings and fatness of his sheep

or goats. (Gen. 4 : 3-5.) Wherein, then, did the superior excellence of Abel's offering consist? Not in its greater intrinsic value, for Cain's offering may have been quite as costly as that of Abel. Of this, we cannot judge positively from anything given in the inspired record. Nor can we determine in what the offering of Cain consisted, further than this: that it was purely a vegetable offering. True, indeed, it is called a *minchah,* a meat offering, and in Leviticus 2 : 1-16, the minchah is described as consisting of fine flour, or unleavened cakes, or parched corn, to which were added a portion of salt, oil, and frankincense. But in Gen. 4 : 3-5, the word *minchah* seems to be used, not in its legal and specific sense, but in its more general signification, to denote an offering of any kind, for in the fourth verse the offering of Abel is also called a minchah, though it consisted of lambs or goats; neither of which were included in the legal meat offering.

If, then, the superiority of Abel's offering did not consist in its greater intrinsic value, in what did it consist? Evidently, as our author says, in its being offered in faith, and in obedience to the command of God: for "To obey," says Samuel, "is better than sacrifice; and to hearken, than the fat of rams." (1 Sam. 15 : 22.) And Solomon says, "The sacrifice of the wicked is an abomination to the Lord, but the prayer of the upright is his delight." (Prov. 15 : 18.) That is, the most costly offering of the wicked man is hateful in the sight of God, while a mere prayer that costs nothing, if it be offered in faith and in obedience to God's will, is his delight. Cain, like King Saul, was a proud, haughty, and self-reliant rationalist. Instead of honoring God by bringing as he was required, a bleeding victim from his flock, he presumptuously substituted for it, what was more in accordance with his own blinded and perverted reason. But Abel was a man of faith; a man who trembled at the word of the Lord, and whose only question was, therefore, "Lord, what wilt thou have me to do?" In this, he and Cain had both been sufficiently instructed, for the Apostle says that Abel offered in faith. But this he could not do without a Divine warrant. In all such cases, faith must of necessity rest on the word of God. (Rom. 10 : 17.) Sacrifice is therefore, beyond all doubt, of Divine origin, and the superior excellence of Abel's offering consisted simply in this: that in making it, he acted strictly in compliance with the revealed will of God.

It does not follow, as Magee, Bloomfield, and others suppose, that Abel understood the typical import of his sacrifice, and that through it he showed his faith in the sacrifice of Christ, which was afterward to be offered for the sins of the world. That he may have had some faint conception of God's far-reaching designs in instituting sacrifice, is quite probable. Of this we cannot speak with certainty. All that is plainly and fairly implied in our text, is simply this: that Abel did what he did in consequence of his firm and unwavering faith in God. He knew God's will, and like Noah, Abraham, and others named in this chapter, he resolved to do it.

**by which he obtained witness, etc.**—The meaning is, not that he obtained this "witness" by his sacrifice, but rather by his faith in offering the sacrifice. Faith is the leading thought in the whole sentence, and to "faith" as the leading word, the pronouns *which* and *it* have both reference. But how and from whom did he obtain this witness? The answer to this question is given in the following clause.

**God testifying of his gifts:**—(*epi tois dorois*) with respect to his gifts. This God did, no doubt, in the usual way, by causing fire to come down and consume the victims which Abel offered. See references. So say the Jews as well as most Christian expositors. Abel's offering, like that of Elijah (1 Kings 18:38) was accepted by its being consumed on the altar, but Cain's offering, like the offerings of the false prophets, remained unconsumed, and of course unaccepted. This at once greatly excited and provoked the envy of Cain, and so he was moved to kill Abel, "because," says John, "his own works were evil, and his brother's righteous." (1 John 3:12.)

**and by it he being dead yet speaketh.**—The Textus Receptus, with the manuscripts, D, E, J, K, and the old Italic version, has the passive form of the verb (*laleitai*) *"is spoken of."* But some of the best manuscripts, most of the ancient versions, and several of the Greek Fathers, have the active voice (*lalei*), as in our English Version. This reading is also best supported by the internal evidence, and it is therefore now justly preferred by most expositors. The idea is not that Abel "is now spoken of" as a faithful man, and so commended for his piety, but rather that he, though dead, still speaks to us by his faith and example.

What, then, does he say? Most commentators, as Calvin,

5 By faith ¹Enoch was translated that he should not see death; and was not found, because God had translated him: for before his translation ²he had this testimony, that he pleased God.

¹Gen. v. 22-24; 2 Kings ii. 1, 11; Jude 14.
²Gen. v. 21-24; 1 John iii. 22.

---

Ebrard, Delitzsch, Alford, etc., maintain that there is here direct reference to Gen. 4: 10, and that in harmony with the record there given, Abel's blood still calls to God for vengeance. But it is not by his blood, but by his faith that he still speaks. And I therefore agree with Chrysostom, Stuart, and a few others, that what the Apostle means is simply this: that Abel by his faith and example still speaks to us, warning, admonishing, and encouraging us to obey God's will by doing just what he has commanded us to do, and giving us assurance, at the same time, that all things will certainly work together for the good of those who do this. His is the first example on record of just such an exercise of faith as God commends and approves, and hence it is, perhaps, that the Holy Spirit has given to it so great prominence.

5 **By faith Enoch was translated**—There is but little said in the Bible respecting this eminently pious man. In Gen. 5: 24, Moses says: "And Enoch walked with God; and he was not, because God took him." And from Jude (5: 14), we learn that he was a prophet, and that he warned his contemporaries that the Lord would finally come with "his holy myriads to execute judgment on all, and to convict all the impious concerning all the hard sayings which impious sinners spoke against him." Having thus, like Noah, been for a time a preacher of righteousness, the Lord rewarded him for his fidelity by translating him no doubt to Heaven, as he afterward translated Elijah. (1 Kings 2: 1, 11.) So the Psalmist expresses his confidence that, after death, the Lord would receive him to glory. (Psalm 73: 24.)

**that he should not see death;**—That is, that he should not experience death like other men. So the word *see* is often used in the Holy Scriptures. See, for example, Psalm 89: 48; Luke 2: 26; John 8: 51. Enoch did not experience death as men ordinarily do, but was miraculously delivered from it, perhaps in the same way that the living saints will be at the second coming of Christ. "Behold I show you a mystery," says Paul; "we shall not all sleep, but we shall all be changed, in a moment, in the twinkling of an

6 But [1]without faith it is impossible to please him: for [2]he that cometh to God [3]must believe that he is, and that [4]he is a rewarder of them that [5]diligently seek him.

[1]Mark xvi. 17; John iii. 18, 19; viii. 24; xvi. 9; Rom. viii. 8, 9; xiv. 23; Gal. v. 6; Rev. xxi. 8.
[2]Ch. vii. 25; Psa. lxxiii. 28; Isa. lv. 3; John vi. 44; xiv. 6.
[3]Rom. x. 14; xiv. 23.
[4]Gen. xv. 1; Prov. xi. 18; Matt. v. 12; vi. 1; x. 42; Luke vi. 35.
[5]Psa. cxix. 10; 2 Pet. i. 5; iii. 14.

eye, at the last trump: for the trumpet shall sound, and the dead shall be raised incorruptible, and we [the living saints] shall be changed." (1 Cor. 15: 51, 52.) All attempts at explanation in such cases, however, are wholly unwarranted by the word of God. See Deut. 29: 29.

**and was not found, because God had translated him:**—The meaning is, that he was not found on earth, because God had translated him from earth to heaven, as he afterward translated Elijah. After Elijah's removal, the sons of the prophets sent out fifty men, who sought for him three days diligently, but they did not find him, because God had taken him. (2 Kings 2: 17.) And so, also, it seems to have been in the case of Enoch. His friends no doubt made diligent search for him, but it was all in vain. "He was not found," because God had removed him from earth to higher and better climes.

**for before his translation, etc.**—The idea is that he pleased God before his translation, as is proved by the testimony. But this he could not have done without faith, as our author now proceeds to show.

6 **But without faith it is impossible to please him:**—Why so? The fact is clearly stated in our text, and it is even further emphasized in what follows: "He that cometh to God must believe that he is, and that he is a rewarder of them that diligently seek him." The same fundamental truth is also abundantly set forth in other passages. In Rom. 8: 8, for example, Paul says, "They that are in the flesh can not please God." And again in Rom. 14: 23, he says, "Whatsoever is not of faith is sin." There can be no doubt, therefore, that faith in God is essential to all acceptable worship and service of any kind.

But why is it so? Is it owing simply to an arbitrary arrangement on the part of God? or does it arise from a moral necessity? That the latter, and not the former, is true, will I think appear

7 By faith ¹Noah, being warned of God of things not seen as yet, moved with fear, ²prepared an ark to the saving of his house; by the which ³he condemned the world, and became heir of ⁴the righteousness which is by faith.

¹Gen. vi. 13-22; Matt. xxiv. 38, 39; 2 Pet. ii. 5.
²Gen. vi. 18; vii. 1, 23; viii. 16; 1 Pet. iii. 18.
³Matt. xii. 41, 42; Luke xi. 31, 32.
⁴Rom. i. 17; iii. 22; iv. 11; ix. 30; x. 6; Gal. v. 5; Phil. iii. 9.

---

manifest from a little reflection. Be it observed, then, (1) that there was a time when God was and nothing else beside him. By his own power he gave birth and being to all things. See Gen. 1: 1; John 1: 3; Col. 1: 16, etc. (2) He created all things according to the counsel of his own will, and in harmony with his own nature. See Eph. 1: 11; Rom. 11: 34, etc. (3) Hence it follows that whatever is in harmony with God's will is right, and that whatever is not in harmony with it is wrong—necessarily, immutably, and eternally wrong. (4) Every man, therefore, who acts from any other ruling motive than the known will of God, is so far a rebel against God and his government. What he does may of course serve to promote in many respects the interests of society. He may, for instance, feed the hungry, clothe the naked, instruct the ignorant, and if need be he may even die for his friends or his country. But unless, in all this, he acts from a supreme regard to the will of God, his conduct is wanting in one of the essential elements of virtue, and cannot, therefore, be otherwise than displeasing to God. (5) But no man can act in harmony with the will of God unless he has faith in God and in the revelation which he has made to us of himself, for his own glory and for the good of his creatures. This is self-evident. And hence it follows, as our author says, that he who would come to God and serve him acceptably, *"must* believe that he is, and that he is a rewarder of them that diligently seek him." Enoch did this. He walked with God. And the Apostle therefore justly argues that he had faith in God, and that his marvelous deliverance from death was both an attestation and a reward of his faith.

7 **By faith Noah, being warned of God, etc.**—From the brief record that is here given of Noah's faith, we learn (1) that he was divinely admonished (*chrematistheis*) with regard to the coming deluge. One hundred and twenty years before it occurred, God warned him of its coming, and directed him to go to work and prepare an ark for the saving of himself and his house. (Gen. 6: 3-18.)

(2) That he believed God and did just as he was commanded. Moved by a reverential fear (*eulabetheis*) through his belief in God's testimony, he prepared an ark for the saving of his house. This, under the circumstances, was a very remarkable instance of strong and unwavering faith in God. For (a) the time appointed was still far off in the future. (b) There were as yet no natural indications that such an event as the destruction of the world by a deluge would ever occur. (c) The experience of mankind was against it. For sixteen hundred years, the natural order of events had been uninterrupted, and no doubt many of the so-called philosophers of that age would be forward in proving to the people that such a catastrophe was physically impossible. (d) The profane and wicked scoffers of the age would also, as a matter of course, do all that they could by their wit, ridicule, and sarcasm, to destroy Noah's faith in the promise of God, and to dissuade him from his great undertaking. But nothing could move him from his purpose. Throughout the long period of one hundred and twenty years, he continued strong in faith giving glory to God. (3) By his faith and obedience he condemned the world, as Christ says the men of Nineveh and the queen of the south will, on the day of judgment condemn the unbelieving and disobedient men and women of his own generation. (Matt. 12: 41, 42.) Every man, in fact, who gives heed to God's warnings and admonitions, condemns by his faith and practice all who neglect to do so. Thus, Noah condemned his own disobedient contemporaries, and thus also he will, on the day of final reckoning, condemn millions of our own more highly favored generation. (4) By his faith, he also became heir of the righteousness which is according to faith. Several eminent expositors, as Cramer, Michaelis, Bisping, and Hofmann, make the phrase *"by which (dia hes)* depend on the word *ark (kibotos)*; that is, they say Noah condemned the world and became heir of the righteousness of faith by building the ark. But it is better with Bengel, Menken, Böhme, Bleek, De Wette, McLean, Ebrard, Lünemann, Delitzsch, Alford, and others, to make *"faith"* the antecedent of the relative *"which."* Faith is the leading thought of the whole sentence, and the word *faith* is therefore properly made the governing word in construction. It should be observed, however, that the building of the Ark is included in the word *faith*, for it is not of faith in the abstract, but of faith in all its practical bearings

8 By faith ¹Abraham, when he was called to go out into a place ²which he
should afterward receive for an inheritance, ³obeyed: and he went out, not
knowing whither he went.

¹Gen. xi. 31; xii. 1-4; Josh. xxiv. 3; Acts vii. 2-4.
²Gen. xii. 7; xiii. 15-17; xv. 7, 8; xvii. 8; xxvi. 3.
³Gen. xii. 4; xxii. 18; xxvi. 5.

that the Apostle is speaking. This is obvious from all the examples of faith that are given in this section. Indeed, the faith which
God commends and requires is, in no case, a mere cold, lifeless,
abstraction; it is a living, active, fruit-bearing principle, which is
constantly manifesting and developing itself in the life as well as in
the heart of the individual. Such was the faith of Abel; such was
the faith of Enoch; and such also was the faith of Noah, through
which he condemned the world, and became an heir of the righteousness which is according to the law of faith. (Rom. 3: 21-31.)

8 **By faith Abraham, when he was called**—In this verse we
have given (1) the fact that Abraham received a call from God;
(2) that by this call he was required to leave his home and kindred
in Ur of Chaldea, and go out into a strange land; (3) that this
land, though promised to his posterity, was wholly unknown to
him at the time; and (4) that he nevertheless obeyed God, and
went out of his own country, not knowing whither he went.

The original call is not recorded in the Scriptures; but in Gen.
12: 1-3 it is repeated in substance as follows: "Now the Lord had
said to Abram, Get thee out of thy country, and from thy kindred,
and from thy father's house, unto a land that I will show thee: and
I will make of thee a great nation, and I will bless thee, and make
thy name great; and thou shalt be a blessing: and I will bless them
that bless thee, and curse him that curseth thee; and in thee shall
all families of the earth be blessed." This call must have been a
very severe test of Abraham's faith. To leave a comfortable home
and friends and follow the call of another, at any time and under
any circumstances, shows a very strong degree of trust and confidence in the one who calls us. But this Abraham did, and did
promptly. Taking with him his father Terah, and Lot his nephew,
he immediately left Ur of Chaldea and came to Haran, where he
remained five years. But when his father was dead he left Haran
and passed over into Canaan, where he sojourned for one hundred
years.

These numbers may be easily verified as follows. We learn

9 By faith ¹he sojourned in the land of promise, as in a strange country, ²dwelling in tabernacles with Isaac and Jacob, ³the heirs with him of the same promise:

10 For ⁴he looked for a city which hath foundations, whose builder and maker is God.

¹Gen. xvii. 8; xxiii. 4; xxvi. 3; xxxv. 27; Acts vii. 5, 6.
²Gen. xii. 8; xviii. 1, 2, 9; xxv. 27.
³Gen. xxvi. 3, 4; xxviii. 4, 13, 14.
⁴Ch. xii. 22; John xiv. 2; Phil. iii. 20; Rev. xxi. 2, 10-27.

from Gal. 3: 17 and Ex. 12: 40, 41, that from the call of Abraham to the Exodus or giving of the Law was four hundred and thirty years; and from Gen. 15: 14 we also learn that from the birth of Isaac to the Exodus was four hundred years. Consequently thirty years intervened between the call of Abraham and the birth of Isaac. But when Isaac was born Abraham was a hundred years old (Gen. 21: 5); and hence he was seventy years old when he was first called and received the promise. But he was seventy-five years old when he came to Canaan (Gen. 12: 4); and he was a hundred and seventy-five years old when he died. (Gen. 25: 7.) And hence he sojourned five years in Haran and a hundred years in Canaan.

9 **By faith he sojourned in the land of promise, etc.**—It appears from this that Abraham never regarded Canaan as his *home*. He knew, of course, that when the Amorites should have filled up the cup of their iniquity in the fourth generation, the land would be given to his posterity for an everlasting possession (Gen. 15: 16). But until that time neither he nor his seed had any rights and privileges in Canaan beyond what might have been enjoyed by other strangers under like circumstances. "God," says Stephen, "gave him no inheritance in it; no, not so much as to set his foot on; yet he promised that he would give it to him for a possession, and to his seed after him, when as yet he had no child." (Acts 7: 5.) And hence Abraham had to purchase the cave of Machpelah as a burying-place from Ephron the Hittite (Gen. 23: 3-20); and hence, also, neither he, nor Isaac, nor Jacob, ever built a permanent residence in the country. They were satisfied to live in movable tents and fragile booths, feeling assured that, according to "the promise," they were all heirs of a better inheritance than any that was then to be found on this sin-stained earth.

10 **For he looked for a city, etc.**—This is given by the Apostle

as the reason why Abraham was satisfied to live as a stranger and
sojourner in Canaan.   He did so because he was looking for the
city (*ten polin*) which hath the foundations (*tous themelious*),
whose Architect and Builder is God.   From this and other like
passages we are constrained to think that God had given to the patriarchs information with regard to the heavenly country far beyond what is now recorded in Genesis or any other part of the Old
Testament.   What we find there at present was written for *our* instruction, as well as for the benefit of the ancients (Rom. 15: 4).
But much may have been said to them which would in no way benefit us; and which was, therefore, excluded from the Canon by
Moses, Ezra and other inspired writers.   The origin of sacrifice,
for instance, is nowhere expressly mentioned in the Old Testament; nor is there anything said in it respecting the origin of the
Patriarchal priesthood.   Information, clear, full, and explicit, on
all such matters, was of course needed by the ancients; but for us
the more general instructions of the Bible are quite sufficient.
And so, also, we think it was with respect to the heavenly country.
The Patriarchs seem to have received revelations concerning it
which have never been transmitted to us; for it is obvious that
Abraham, Isaac, and Jacob, lived in constant expectation of entering it at the close of their earthly pilgrimage. They were satisfied
to live here as strangers and pilgrims, knowing that they had in
heaven a city having permanent foundations whose Architect and
Framer is God. This city is manifestly the heavenly Jerusalem
(Gal. 4: 28; Heb. 12: 22; 13: 14), which for the present is located in heaven, but which will hereafter descend to the earth after
that it shall have been renovated by fire (Rev. 21).   Then will be
fulfilled in its full and proper sense the promise made to Abraham
that he and his seed should be the heirs of the world.   (Rom. 4:
13.) "The meaning of the whole verse," says Prof. Stuart, "most
evidently is that Abraham looked for a permanent abode in the
heavenly country; that is, his hopes and expectations were placed
upon the world to come." It was faith in this which was the demonstration of things not seen, and which moved him to obey the
commands of God, and to do and suffer whatever he required.
The fact then that the saints under the Old Testament were moved
in their conduct by considerations which had respect to the invisible world, or an immortal state of existence, is plainly implied here

11 Through faith also ¹Sarah herself received strength to conceive seed, | and was delivered of a child; *even* | when she was past age, ²because she judged him faithful who had promised.

12 Therefore sprang there even of one, ¹and him as good as dead, ²so many as the stars of the sky in multitude, and ³as the sand which is by the sea shore innumerable.

¹Gen. xvii. 15-21; xviii. 11-14; xxi. 1, 2.
²Chap. x. 23; Rom. iv. 20, 21.
¹Rom. iv. 19.
²Gen. xv. 5; xxvi. 4; Deut. i. 10.
³Gen. xxii. 17; xxxii. 12.

---

by the reasoning of the Apostle. God is here called the *architect* (*technites*) of the heavenly city, because he is the author of the plan; and he is also called the *builder* (*demiourgos*), because it is he himself who executes the plan. He is the master-builder as well as the projector of the heavenly Jerusalem.

**11 Through faith also Sarah herself received strength to conceive seed,**—Or more exactly, *By faith even Sarah herself received strength to conceive seed.* The emphatic manner in which this is expressed seems to indicate that there was something very extraordinary in the case of Sarah. But what was it? On this point the commentators differ. Some think that our author has reference merely to what he more fully and distinctly states in what follows, viz.: that Sarah, though now past the time of bearing, through faith received strength for the conception of seed (Schlichting, Schultz, Stuart, etc.). But the majority maintain that there is in these words an allusion also to the fact that, at the outset, Sarah herself was unbelieving. (Gen. 18: 9-15.) Thus Macknight: "By faith in God's promise, even Sarah herself, though at first she thought the matter impossible, received strength for the conception of seed, and brought forth a son when past the age of child-bearing; because she at length attained to the strongest persuasion of the faithfulness and power of Him who had promised her a son." So also Bleek, DeWette, Winer, Lünemann, and others. In this instance, the minority are probably right. It seems most likely that the Apostle makes no reference here whatever to the former incredulity of Sarah; but only to her past barrenness and advanced age. For at that time she was about ninety years old (Gen. 17: 17); far beyond the natural period of child-bearing. But nevertheless, through her strong faith in God, she obtained the promise.

**12 Therefore sprang there even of one, etc.**—The word *there-*

13 [1]These all died in faith, [2]not having received the promises, but [3]having

[1]Gen. xxiii. 1, 2; xxv. 8; xxxv. 29; xlix. 33.
[2]Ver. 39; Luke x. 23, 24; 1 Pet. i. 10-12.
[3]Gen. xlix. 10; Deut. xviii. 18; Job xix. 25; John viii. 56; xii. 41; 1 Pet. i. 10-12.

*fore* shows that what follows is to be taken as a result and consequence of the faith of Abraham and Sarah. They had both waited
long and patiently for the fulfillment of the promise: and now
when Abraham is about a hundred years old, and Sarah ninety,
their faith brought to them the promised reward. "Though it
tarry, wait for it; for it will surely come; it will not be behind the
appointed time." (Hab. 2: 4.) They did wait; and finally, as a reward for their faith in God and in the word of his promise, "there
sprang from one, and him as good as dead, so many as the stars of
Heaven in multitude; and as the sands of the sea shore innumerable." For Abraham, says Paul, "against hope believed in hope,
that he might become the father of many nations, according to that
which was spoken, So shall thy seed be. And being not weak in
faith, he considered not his own body now dead, when he was
about a hundred years old, neither yet the deadness of Sarah's
womb: he staggered not at the promise of God through unbelief;
but was strong in faith, giving glory to God; being fully persuaded
that what he had promised he was able also to perform." (Rom. 4:
18-21.) And therefore it was imputed to him for righteousness;
and not only so, but in consequence of this, Isaac was born, and his
descendants were multiplied as the dust of the earth. See references.

The bearing of this illustration of the main argument of the
Apostle is very obvious. Nothing could better serve to strengthen
the hands and encourage the hearts of the desponding and persecuted Hebrews, than this reference to the faith of their illustrious
ancestor. God himself makes a like reference to it, by the Prophet
Isaiah, for the purpose of encouraging the Israelites under the Babylonish captivity. "Hearken unto me," he says, "ye that pursue
righteousness, ye that seek Jehovah: look unto the rock whence ye
were hewn; and to the hollow of the cave whence ye were digged:
look unto Abraham your father, and unto Sarah who bore you; for
I called him, being a single person, and I blessed him, and I multiplied him." (Isa. 51: 1, 2.)

13 **These all died in faith,**—(*kata pistin*) *according to faith:*

seen them afar off, [and were persuaded of them,] and embraced them, and
⁴confessed that they were strangers and pilgrims on the earth.

⁴Gen. xxiii. 4; xlvii. 9; 1 Chron. xxix. 15; Psa. xxxix. 12; 1 Pet. i. 17; ii. 11.

that is, in the exercise of faith and in the enjoyment of its many
blessings. They died as they had lived, *in faith.* But of whom does
the Apostle here speak? Who are the *"all"* who died in faith?
Some, as Oecumenius, Theophylact, and Primasius, think that our
author refers here to the aforesaid faithful antediluvian Patriarchs,
as well as to the postdiluvian. But in this they are manifestly in
error. The context makes it quite obvious, that only Abraham,
Sarah, Isaac, and Jacob, are included in this remark. They are
the persons who received the promises (Gal. 3: 16), and who
might have returned to their father-land had they been inclined to
do so. But they all preferred remaining as strangers and pilgrims
in Canaan, because their hearts were set on the heavenly country
into which they hoped to enter soon.

**Not having received the promises,**—What promises?
Manifestly not the verbal promises; for these they did receive (Gal.
3: 16) : but the word *promises* (*epangliai*) is used here to denote the things promised. These they did not receive during their
earthly pilgrimage; they only saw them afar off, and "greeted them
as the wanderer greets his longed-for home, even when he comes
in sight of it at a distance; drawing to himself, as it were, magnet-
ically and embracing, with inward love, that which is yet afar off"
(*Del. in loc.*) But the important question still arises, What were
the things promised to Abraham, Isaac, and Jacob, which they did
not receive during their earthly pilgrimage, but which they only
saw by faith in the far distant future?

In order to answer this question properly it is necessary to refer
again to the inspired record and see what pledges were given by
God to these illustrious patriarchs. These, as we learn from Genesis, were (1) that Abraham should have a numerous offspring
(Gen. 13: 16; 15: 3-5; 17: 2, 4; 22: 16) ; (2) that God would be
a God to him and to his seed after him (Gen. 17: 1-8) ; (3) that
he would give to him and to his seed an everlasting inheritance
(Gen. 12: 7; 13: 15; 15: 18-21; 17: 8) ; and (4) that through
him and his seed, all the nations of the earth should be blessed
(Gen. 12: 3; 22: 18). To each of these God attached a double

14 For they that say such things ¹declare plainly that they seek a country.
¹2 Cor. iv. 18; v. 1-7; Phil. i. 23.

significance.  See notes on 8: 8.  They each consisted, so to speak, of two elements, one of which had reference to the carnal side of the covenant, and the other to the spiritual side: one to the type, and the other to the antitype.  Thus Abraham was made the honored father of two families; to each of which an inheritance was promised, and through each of which the world was to be blessed.

Now it is true that while Abraham, Isaac, and Jacob sojourned on Earth, their offspring was not very numerous; nor did they then receive the earthly inheritance; nor was the world as yet blessed by them.  And hence it is quite possible that there may be some allusion in our text to the temporal and typical blessings which were promised.  But certain it is, that our author refers here chiefly to the spiritual and antitypical blessings which God had promised to Abraham; and especially, as in the thirty-ninth verse, to the coming of Christ and the blessings of his mediatorial reign.  "Abraham," says Christ, "rejoiced to see my day, and he saw it, and was glad." (John 8: 56.)  To Christ, then, as the promised Seed, and to the inheritance redeemed by his blood (Eph. 1: 14), our author refers chiefly, if not exclusively, in the use of the word *"promises."*  These, the Patriarchs did not receive while here on earth; but through the telescope of faith they saw them afar off, and embraced them with joy and singleness of heart, confessing at the same time that they were strangers and pilgrims on earth.

14 **For they that say such things, etc.**—All men naturally desire a home.  To this they are prompted by one of the strongest and deepest natural instincts of the human heart.  And hence though many may, like Abraham, Isaac, and Jacob, wander about as pilgrims and sojourners for awhile, it is always with a view of securing a permanent home somewhere.  The case of these Patriarchs, as our author insists, was not an exception to this law of our nature. They declared very plainly, both in word and in deed that they were seeking after a home, *a father-land* (*patrida*), a fixed and permanent residence.

15 And truly, ²if they had been mindful of that country from whence they
came out, they might have had opportunity to have returned.

16 But now they desire a better country, that is, an heavenly: wherefore
¹God is not ashamed to be called their God: ²for he hath prepared for them
a city.

²Gen. xi. 31; xxiv. 6-9; xxxi. 17, 18.
¹Gen. xvii. 7, 8; Ex. iii. 15; Isa. xli. 8-10; Matt. xxii. 31, 32.
²Ch. xi. 10; xii. 22; Rev. xxi. 2.

15 **And truly, if they had been mindful, etc.**—If they had desired to return to Ur of Chaldea, or to Haran, there was nothing
to prevent their doing so. They had not been banished from their
father-land, nor have we any reason to think that God would have
so interfered as to prevent their return. He always prefers a willing service. And hence the Apostle argues that these Patriarchs
might all have returned to Chaldea had they been so minded. But
none of them ever showed any desire to do so. "Abraham in particular," says Macknight, "considered the very thought of returning into Chaldea as a renunciation of his interests in the promises
of God. And therefore he made his steward Eliezer swear to him
that on no pretense whatever would he carry Isaac into Chaldea."
(Gen. 24 : 5-8.)

16 **But now they desire a better country**—Better than either
Canaan or Chaldea. The course of the argument is well expressed
by Kuinoel as follows: "If these Patriarchs had sought a country
in those parts, or had regarded their native or ancestral land as
their true country, they might have found means to return thither.
But they did not consider Canaan as their country, nor did they
return to Chaldea, and therefore they desired not an earthly but a
heavenly country."

**wherefore God is not ashamed to be called their God:**—
Since it is true that these patriarchs sought no earthly home, but
set their hearts steadfastly on heaven as their permanent abode,
God is therefore not ashamed to be called their God, for he himself
says repeatedly, "I am the God of Abraham, and the God of Isaac,
and the God of Jacob" (Ex. 3: 6, 15; 4: 5, etc.), thus verifying
the promise which he had previously made to Abraham that he
would be a God to him and to his seed after him. (Gen. 17: 7.)

**for he hath prepared for them a city.**—This is given as evidence of the fact that God approved and rewarded the fidelity of
these his devoted servants. He did not allow them to dwell always

17 By faith ³Abraham, when he was tried, offered up Isaac: ⁴and he that
had received the promises offered up ⁵his only begotten son,

³Gen. xxii. 1-14; Jas. ii. 21-24.
⁴Ch. vii. 6; Gal. iii. 16.
⁵Gen. xxii. 2, 16.

in tents and booths, but according to "the promise" made to Abraham, he prepared for them a home in "the city which hath the
foundations," the heavenly Jerusalem.  See notes on 6 : 15 ; 9 : 15 ;
11 : 10.

Nothing could more clearly indicate the strong and abiding faith
of these patriarchs in a future state of rewards and punishments,
than does this passage (verses 13-16).  So fully convinced were
they of such a state, that like Paul (Phil. 3 : 8), they were willing
to suffer the loss of all things earthly, provided only that they
might attain to the rest which remains for the people of God.  The
*ground* of their justification was to them of course still a mystery.
See note on 9 : 8.  They did not yet understand that the very foundations of the heavenly city were laid prospectively in the blood of
the Lord Jesus, and that in the end of the ages, he would appear to
put away sin by the sacrifice of himself, so that God might be just
in justifying all true believers.  This was to them still a mystery,
as it was also to even the angels in glory.  (1 Pet. 1: 12.)
Nevertheless, they seem to have had no doubt whatever of the fact
that when their earthly house of this tabernacle were dissolved,
they would then have "a building of God, a house not made with
hands, eternal in the heavens."

17 **By faith Abraham, when he was tried, offered up Issac:**
—The account of this severest and last recorded trial of Abraham's
faith, is found in Gen. 22: 1-14.  Previous to this, God had tried
him in various ways and on various occasions.  He had called on
him to leave his home and his kindred, and to become a wanderer
in a foreign land during the rest of his life.  He had long delayed
the fulfillment of the promise which he had made with regard to
the birth of Isaac.  And he had furthermore put Abraham severely
to the proof when he required him to send away Ishmael and his
mother with a scanty supply of bread and water.  (Gen. 21 : 9-14.)
But all these trials were light and insignificant in comparison with
that to which reference is made in our text.  Hitherto God had
sustained him with the assurance that he would give him a son by
Sarah, and that in and through that son should in due time be ful-

filled all other promises. But now when Isaac, according to Josephus (Ant. I. 13, 2), was about twenty-five years of age, God says
to Abraham, "Take now thy son, thine only son Isaac, whom thou
lovest, and get thee into the land of Moriah, and offer him there
for a burnt offering upon one of the mountains which I will tell
thee of." (Gen. 22: 2.) How very strange and startling is this oracle! How many plausible reasons might have been alleged for
neglecting it! Had Abraham possessed the spirit of Cain or of
some of our modern rationalists, how easily he might have persuaded himself that there was some mistake or delusion in the
case; that the command could not be from God; that it was inconsistent with both his character and his promises. But no; nothing
of this occurred in the case of Abraham. He knew that the voice
of command was the voice of God, and that was enough. He "rose
up early in the morning, and saddled his ass, and took two of his
young men with him, and Isaac his son, and clave the wood for a
burnt offering, and rose up and went unto the place of which God
had told him. Then on the third day, Abraham lifted up his eyes
and saw the place afar off. And Abraham said unto the young
men, Abide ye here with the ass, and I and the lad will go yonder
and worship, and come again to you. And Abraham took the
wood of the burnt offering and laid it upon Isaac his son, and he
took the fire in his hand and a knife, and they went both of them
together. And Isaac spake unto Abraham his father and said, My
father; and he said, Here am I, my son. And he said, Behold the
fire and the wood; but where is the lamb for a burnt offering?
And Abraham said, My son, God will provide himself a lamb for a
burnt offering. So they went both of them together. And they
came to the place which God had told him of; and Abraham built
an altar there, and laid the wood in order, and bound Isaac his son
and laid him upon the altar on the wood. And Abraham stretched
forth his hand and took the knife to slay his son." (Gen. 22: 3-10.)
How very calm and deliberate is the good old patriarch in this
most trying and affecting scene. Nothing is done rashly or under
an impulse of momentary excitement. He had ample time and opportunity to reflect seriously and prayerfully on the whole matter,
and he did so. The distance traveled from Beersheba to Jerusalem, the land of Moriah, was about forty-two miles, and more than
two days were occupied in making the journey. In the meantime,

18 Of whom it was said, ¹That in Isaac shall thy seed be called :
19 ²Accounting that God was able to raise him up, even from the dead ;
from whence also he received him ³in a figure.

¹Gen. xvii. 17-21; xxi. 12; Rom. ix. 7.
²Gen. xxii. 5; Rom. iv. 17.
³Ch. viii. 5; ix. 9, 24; x. 1.

the presence and conversation of Isaac, as well as the quiet solitude
of the way, all served to bring the matter home to the heart of the
anxious father, and to make him feel most deeply the solemn and
awful import of what he was about to do. But nothing could move
him from his purpose to obey God. He builded an altar, laid the
wood in order, bound Isaac, and drew the fatal knife. The deed
was mentally done. In Abraham's purpose, Isaac was a slain victim. But while his arm was executing the volition, it was suddenly and unexpectedly arrested by a voice from heaven. The evidence of Abraham's loyalty and fidelity was sufficient, and God
then honored him by re-assuring him with an oath that in blessing
he would bless him, and in multiplying he would multiply him.

18 **Of whom it was said, etc.**—(*pros on*) to whom it was said
[that is, to Abraham] that *In Isaac shall thy seed be called*. This
clause is variously interpreted by expositors. But the meaning obviously is that Abraham's posterity with respect to the promised
Seed was to be reckoned in and from Isaac. In this sense he was
not only his son, but he was his *only* son. True, indeed, he had
other children beside Isaac, but by God's decree they were all elim-
inated from the regular line of descent, and the covenant was established with Isaac and his descendants through Jacob and with
them only. (Gen. 17: 17-21; 21: 12; 25: 4, 5.) The object of the
Apostle in adding this clause was, therefore, simply to illustrate
still further the great strength of Abraham's faith by showing that
even against hope he still hoped and believed that God would fulfill
his promise in yet giving him a son through Isaac, by raising him
from the dead.

19 **Accounting that God was able to raise him up, even from
the dead ;**—This was to Abraham the only possible solution of this
very mysterious and intricate problem. God had said to him, "My
covenant will I establish with Isaac" (Gen. 17: 21) ; and again,
"In Isaac shall thy seed be called" (Gen. 21: 12). But now he is
required to offer him up as a burnt offering ! How are the facts to

20 By faith ¹Isaac blessed Jacob and Esau concerning things to come.

¹Gen. xxvii. 26-40; xxviii. 2. 3.

---

be reconciled?  Abraham knew that the promise of God could not and would not fail, and as he could not anticipate that God would interfere, as he did, so as to prevent the actual immolation of his son, there was really left for him no other alternative than simply to conclude that God would restore Isaac to life.  This conviction seems to be implied in the remark which he made to his servants: "Abide ye here with the ass, and I and the lad will go yonder and worship, and come again."  The word rendered *come again* (*we will return*) is in the plural number, and seems to indicate a belief on the part of Abraham that God would immediately raise Isaac up again from the dead.

**from whence also he received him in a figure.**—On the meaning of this clause the commentators are much divided. Some of them as Hammond, Whitby, Newcome, Schultz, and Stuart, suppose that the Apostle refers here to the supernatural birth of Isaac. "The sentiment." says Stuart, "seems to be this: Abraham believed that God could raise Isaac from the dead, because he had as it were obtained him from the dead; that is, he was born of those who were as good as dead."  But if this had been the idea of the Apostle, he would most likely have used the pluperfect tense instead of the aorist. And besides, it would, as Alford suggests, be harsh and unnatural to make the phrase *"from the dead"* refer in this case to Abraham and Sarah.  I therefore think with Beza, Delitzsch, Alford, and others, that the reference is not to the birth of Isaac, but to his rescue from the altar. Abraham received him back from the altar, as one raised from the dead.  He had been *figuratively* (*en parabole*) sacrificed; and he was therefore now *figuratively* raised from the dead and restored to his father, as a reward for his fidelity.  For as Bloomfield says, "Isaac was in a manner dead in his father's opinion and in his own, and he was restored to his father from the gates of the grave."

20 **By faith Isaac blessed Jacob and Esau**—The idea is, that the blessing of Isaac was bestowed in faith.  Indeed, it could not be bestowed on any other ground, for at that time there were no natural indications that could in any way serve to define the fortunes of Jacob and Esau and their descendants.  See Gen. 27: 26-

21 By faith ²Jacob, when he was a dying, blessed both the sons of Joseph;
³and worshiped, leaning upon the top of his staff.

²Gen. xlviii. 8-22.
³Gen. xlvii. 31.

---

40. But relying on the promises of God, and guided by the spirit
of inspiration, Isaac blessed his sons concerning things to come.
"This blessing of Isaac," says Delitzsch, "had the wondrous power
of shaping and controlling the future of his posterity, because in
virtue of his faith his mind and will had become one with the mind
and will of God himself." (Compare Gen. 27: 37 with Jer. 1: 10
and other parallel passages.) And hence we find in the words of
Isaac a prophetic outline of the fortunes of the two races. "At
first, the elder seemed to prosper more than his brother Jacob.
There were dukes in Edom before there reigned any kings over the
children of Israel (Gen. 36: 31) ; and whilst Israel was in bondage
in Egypt, Edom was an independent people. But Saul defeated,
and David conquered the Edomites (1 Sam. 14: 47; 2 Sam. 8:
14) ; and they were, notwithstanding some revolts, constantly subject to Judah (1 Kings 11: 14; 2 Kings 14: 7, 22; 2 Chron. 28:
7). Judas Maccabaeus defeated them frequently. (1 Macc. 5; 2
Macc. 10.) At length his nephew, Hyracanus, completely conquered them, and compelled them to be circumcised, and incorporated them into the Jewish nation (Joseph. Ant. 13, 9, 1) ; though
finally under Antipater and Herod, they established an Idumean
dynasty, which continued till the destruction of the Jewish polity."
(Browne on Gen. 27: 40.)

21 By faith Jacob, when he was a dying, etc.—From the blessing of Jacob and Esau by their father, our author next passes to
the blessing of the two sons of Joseph, Ephraim and Manasseh, by
their grandfather. (Gen. 48: 1-22.) When Joseph heard that his
father was sick and near unto death, he took with him his two
sons, and went to see him. And when he arrived, Jacob said to
him, "God Almighty appeared to me at Luz in the land of Canaan,
and blessed me, and said unto me, Behold, I will make thee fruitful, and multiply thee, and I will make of thee a multitude of people; and I will give this land to thy seed after thee for an everlasting possession. And now thy two sons, Ephraim and Manasseh,
who were born unto thee in the land of Egypt, before I came into
Egypt, are mine; as Reuben and Simeon, they are mine." Thus

they were adopted as the sons of Jacob, and each of them was made the honored head of a separate and distinct tribe. After this, the old man in the exercise of a true and living faith, and guided by the spirit of inspiration, "wittingly put his right hand on Ephraim, and his left hand on Manasseh, and said, The God before whom my fathers Abraham and Isaac did walk, the God who fed me like a shepherd all my life long unto this day, the Angel who redeemed me from all evil, bless the lads; and let my name be named upon them, and the name of my fathers Abraham and Isaac; and let them grow into a multitude in the midst of the earth."

**And worshiped, leaning upon the top of his staff.**—This act of devotion did not occur at the same time that Jacob blessed Ephraim and Manasseh, but previous to it, when Joseph had sworn to his father that he would not bury him in Egypt. (Gen. 47: 31.) The chronological order of the two events is reversed, probably for the purpose of bringing together the blessings of the two patriarchs, Isaac and Jacob.

The reading in Genesis differs slightly from that which is here given by our author. According to the Masoretic text, followed by the Chaldee Targums, the Greek versions of Aquila and Symmachus, and the Latin Vulgate, the rendering is as follows: "And Israel bowed himself upon the bed's head;" but the Septuagint and the Syriac versions agree with our text in this Epistle. How, then, is this apparent discrepancy to be removed, and the Greek and Hebrew readings reconciled? Two ways have been proposed. (1) It is alleged that both readings are correct: that Jacob worshiped, leaning on the head of his bed and also on the top of his staff. And this is plausible, as well as possible; for it was customary among the ancients to set the staff of the chief and the spear of the warrior at the head of the bed. But (2) the alleged discrepancy may be owing wholly to a mistake of the Masorites. The Hebrew word may mean either *a bed* or *a staff,* depending simply on points which did not belong to the original text, but which were attached to it by the Masorites after the commencement of the Christian era. Thus *matteh* means a rod or staff, and *mittah* means a bed or couch. Now as these points were added by uninspired men, there is really no ground whatever for the allegation that there is a discrepancy between the readings of the original

22 By faith ¹Joseph, when he died, made mention of the departing of the children of Israel; and gave commandment concerning his bones.

23 By faith ²Moses, when he was born, was hid three months of his parents, because they saw he was a proper child; and ³they were not afraid of ⁴the king's commandment.

¹Gen. l. 24, 25; Ex. xiii. 19; Josh. xxiv. 32.
²Ex. ii. 2; Acts vii. 20.
³Chap. xiii. 6; Isa. xli. 10, 14; Dan. iii. 16-18; Matt. x. 28.
⁴Ex. i. 16, 22.

Hebrew and the Greek. For if the first explanation is not correct, then beyond all doubt the error lies with the Masorites and not with Paul; for on no condition can we concede, as some have done, that the Apostle has here followed an incorrect version of the original. He never does this; but always expresses the thoughts of the Holy Spirit in words which the Holy Spirit teacheth. (1 Cor. 2: 13.)

22 **By faith Joseph, when he died,**—(*teleuton*) *when drawing near to his end, made mention concerning the exodus of the children of Israel, and gave commandment concerning his bones.* "I die," he said, "but God will surely visit you, and bring you out of this land unto the land which he sware to Abraham, to Isaac, and to Jacob." (Gen. 50: 24.) His prosperity in Egypt had in no way impaired his faith in the promises of God; but feeling perfectly confident that his brethren would at the time appointed leave Egypt and return to Canaan, he made them swear that they would carry his bones up with them. And hence after his death, he was embalmed and put in a wooden chest, so that at the proper time his remains might be ready for removal.

23 **By faith Moses, when he was born, etc.**—The command of Pharaoh was, "Every son that is born shall be cast into the river." (Ex. 1: 22.) The penalty for neglecting this ordinance was no doubt very severe, depending perhaps on the arbitrary will of the wicked and despotic sovereign. But the parents of Moses, Amram and Jochebed, trusting in the promises of God, refused to obey the king's mandate. Deeming it proper, however, to use all lawful means for the preservation of the child's life, they first concealed him, most likely in their own house, for the space of three months; and then finding themselves unable to protect him longer, they cast him wholly on the care of Jehovah. This they did by constructing an ark of papyrus; and having made it water-tight with asphaltum and bitumen, they put the child in it, and placed it among the flags on the brink of the river. (Ex. 2: 3.) Thus when Moses was in a

24 By faith ⁵Moses, when he was come to years, refused to be called the son of Pharaoh's daughter;
25 ¹Choosing rather to suffer affliction with the people of God, than ²to enjoy the pleasures of sin for a season;

⁵Ex. ii. 10-12; Acts vii. 21-24.
¹Chap. x. 32; Psa. lxxxvi. 10; Matt. v. 10-12; Acts xx. 23, 24; Rom. v. 3; viii. 17. 18; 2 Cor. iv. 17; v. 10-12; Col. i. 24.
²Job xx. 5; Psa. lxxiii. 18-20; Luke xii. 19, 20; xvi. 25; Jas. v. 5; Rev. xviii. 7.

---

measure forsaken by his father and mother, then the Lord took him up (Psalm 27: 10) ; and under his care he was instructed in all the wisdom of the Egyptians, and was highly honored as the son of Thermuthis, the daughter of Pharaoh (Ex. 2: 5-10). The word rendered *proper* (*asteios*) means properly urbane, polite; fair, beautiful, comely. Stephen says that Moses was *fair of God* (*asteios to theo*) ; that is, very fair: and Philo says, "As soon as he was born he displayed a more beautiful and noble form than usual." (Vita Mos. i. 3.)

24 **By faith Moses, when he was come to years,**—(*megas genomenos*) *when he became great:* that is, when he had grown up; when he had attained to the years of manhood and responsibility. (Acts 7: 23.)

**refused to be called the son of Pharaoh's daughter;**—It is not necessary to suppose that he did this in any direct and formal way; but only that he felt and manifested a preference for his Hebrew brethren. (Ex. 2: 11, 12; Acts 7: 24.)

25 **Choosing rather to suffer affliction, etc.**—The Israelites are here called "the people of God" in contrast with the idolatrous Egyptians. The alternative offered to Moses was to remain, as he was, associated with the latter, where, as the adopted son of Pharaoh's daughter, he would be allowed to enjoy the honors and luxuries of a corrupt and licentious court; or to share in the future blessings of the Abrahamic covenant, by casting in his lot with the enslaved and despised Israelites. The contrasts were assuredly very great. The Egyptians were at that time among the most learned, powerful, and influential nations on Earth; and the Hebrews were among the most oppressed and degraded. But to the eye of faith, their future prospects were quite reversed. Moses knew perfectly well, that the pleasures of sin in the family and court of Pharaoh were to be enjoyed only for a season, and that in the end they would be as gall and wormwood to the soul: and he

26 Esteeming the [3]reproach of Christ greater riches than the treasures in Egypt: for [4]he had respect unto the recompense of the reward.

[3]Chap. x. 33; xiii. 13; Psa. lxix. 7, 20; lxxxix. 50, 51; Isa. li. 7; Acts v. 41; 2 Cor. xii. 10; 1 Pet. iv. 14.
[4]Chap. x. 35; xi. 6; Ruth ii. 12; Matt. v. 12; Luke xiv. 14.

knew just as well, on the other hand, that the blessings of God guaranteed to his people through the Abrahamic covenant would be sure and everlasting. On these points he was fully convinced. And hence he did not hesitate as to which he should choose; knowing that "the triumphing of the wicked is short, and that the joy of the hypocrite is but for a moment" (Job 20: 5), but that the good man "shall not be moved forever; and that the righteous shall be in everlasting remembrance." (Psalm 112: 6.)

26 **Esteeming the reproach of Christ, etc.**—This is given by the Apostle, in explanation of the conduct and preference of Moses, in leaving the court of Pharaoh. He chose to suffer affliction with the people of God, rather than to enjoy the pleasures of sin for a season; esteeming, as he did, the reproach of Christ greater riches than the treasures of Egypt. But what does Paul mean here by "the reproach of Christ"? In reply to this query, it is alleged (1) that the reproach of Christ is such reproach as Christ himself endured (Lünemann, Stuart); (2) that it is reproach suffered on account of Christ (Chrysostom, Ebrard); (3) that it is the reproach which fell on Moses as a type of Christ (Hofmann); and (4) that it is the reproach which Christ had to bear in his own person and also in the person of every true believer (Bleek, Delitzsch, Alford). The last of these explanations is preferable, because it is the most general and comprehensive. It is certainly true, that the reproach of Moses was similar to the reproach of Christ; and it is also true, that he suffered as a type of Christ and on account of his belief in Christ. But more than all this is manifestly intended by the Apostle. As Christ is the righteousness of all the redeemed (2 Cor. 5: 21), so also it may be truly said that all reproach suffered for righteousness' sake, since the world began, has been suffered for Christ's sake. And this is certainly the view which Paul takes of the matter, when he speaks of filling up "that which is behind of the afflictions of Christ." (Col. 1: 24.) See also 2 Cor. 1: 6-8; 4: 8-12; 11: 23-27; Phil. 3: 10; 2 Tim. 1: 8; 2: 9, 10. There is, then, as Paul says to the Philippi-

27 By faith ¹he forsook Egypt, not fearing the wrath of the king: for ²he endured, ³as seeing him who is invisible.

¹Ex. ii. 13-15; x. 28, 29; xii. 31; xiii. 17-21.
²Ch. vi. 15; x. 32; xii. 2; Jas. v. 11.
³Acts ii. 25; 1 Tim. vi. 16; 1 Pet. i. 8.

ans, a "fellowship" in the sufferings and reproaches of Christ, as well as in the enjoyment and privileges of the Gospel. This fellowship extended back even to the ancients, and was preferred by Moses to all the honors which he might have enjoyed in the court and family of Pharaoh.

**for he had respect unto the recompense of the reward.**—By faith he looked forward to the great and final recompense: the real and abiding pleasures of the heavenly country, and the rest which remains for the people of God. And with his eye fixed on these, he esteemed the reproach of Christ as of more value than all the treasures of Egypt; knowing that our present light afflictions which are but for a moment, serve to work out for us a far more exceeding and eternal weight of glory.

27 **By faith he forsook Egypt,**—When did he do this? Was it when he renounced his allegiance to Pharaoh, turned his back on all the honors and pleasures of Egypt, and fled for safety into Midian? Or was it when he led the children of Israel out of Egypt into the wilderness of Arabia? The latter view is supported by Calvin, Grotius, Böhme, Kuinoel, Bleek, Ebrard, Bisping, Scott, Clarke, Stuart, and others; because say they, when Moses fled into Midian, he certainly did fear the wrath of Pharaoh, as we learn from Ex. 2: 14, 15. But surely he did not fear him any more than did his parents, Amram and Jochebed, when they concealed their child three months, and then committed him to the care and providence of God by exposing him on the brink of the river, in an ark of bulrushes. And yet our author says of them, that "they were not afraid of the king's commandment" (verse 23). Manifestly, then, the Apostle uses the word *fear* in both these instances in a relative sense. Moses and his parents both feared the tyrant, so far that they thought it necessary to use all lawful means for their personal safety, but they did not fear him so far as to disobey God on his account, nor had they any fear that he would ever be able to nullify or set aside the decrees and purposes of God concerning Israel. In this sense, it may be truly said of both

28 Through faith [1]he kept the passover, and [2]the sprinkling of blood, lest [3]he that destroyed the firstborn should touch them.

[1]Ex. xii. 3-30.
[2]Ch. ix. 19; xii. 24; Ex. xii. 7, 13, 23.
[3]Ex. xii. 23, 29; Num. viii. 17.

Moses and his parents that they did not fear "the wrath of the king." And this being so, it is certainly more natural to understand the Apostle as having reference to the flight of Moses into Midian. This seems obvious for several reasons. (1) Because this is the only explanation which accords with the chronological order of the events recorded in our text. The Passover was instituted by Moses after his return from Midian, but not after the Exodus. (2) It seems to be implied in our text that this departure from Egypt was in opposition to the will of Pharaoh, and in defiance of his wrath; but the Exodus was made with his earnest and urgent request. (Ex. 12: 31-33.) (3) Had our author referred here to the Exodus, he would most likely not have spoken of Moses alone but of him in connection with those who forsook Egypt with him, as in verse 29. I therefore agree with Bengel, Michaelis, Schlutz, DeWette, Delitzsch, Alford, and most of the ancient expositors, that our author has reference, not to the Exodus, but to the previous flight of Moses into the land of Midian. (Ex. 2: 13-15.) Then it was that he renounced all connection with Egypt, and publicly avowed his purpose to suffer afflictions with the people of God, rather than to enjoy "the pleasures of sin for a season."

**for he endured, as seeing him who is invisible.**—By the eye of faith he saw the King eternal, immortal, and invisible, standing by him, ready to fulfill at the proper time all the promises that he had made to his chosen people. And hence he had no fears that Pharaoh would succeed in his diabolical attempts to hold Israel in perpetual bondage. He knew full well that by God's irrevocable decree, Canaan would in due time be given to the seed of Abraham for a possession, and that heaven itself was also prepared for as many of them as would walk in the footsteps of their illustrious ancestor.

28 **Through faith he kept the passover,**—The Passover was a positive ordinance instituted by God through Moses for the following purposes: (1) to commemorate the fact that the angel of death

29 By faith ¹they passed through the Red Sea as by dry land: which ²the Egyptians assaying to do were drowned.

¹Ex. xiv. 13-22; Josh. ii. 10; Neh. ix. 11; Psa. lxvi. 6.
²Ex. xiv. 23-29; Psa. lxxvii. 11-20.

passed over, and so spared the first-born of the Israelites, on the night on which he destroyed all the first-born of the Egyptians; (2) to educate the people in the knowledge and worship of the living and true God; and (3) to typify the sacrifice of Christ, who, as our passover, has been sacrificed for us. (1 Cor. 5:7.) Like the Lord's Supper, this ordinance was instituted in anticipation of the event which it was designed to commemorate; and the faith of Moses was shown in this instance in his doing and causing to be done just what the Lord himself had commanded. Under his directions, every Hebrew family (or two families in case they were small) was required (1) to select a lamb or a kid of the first year without blemish, on the tenth day of the month Nisan; (2) to kill it on the evening of the fourteenth; (3) to sprinkle its blood on the lintel and doorposts; and (4) to eat its flesh on the night following, with unleavened bread and bitter herbs, and this they were required to do with their loins girded, their shoes on their feet, and their staves in their hands, so that they might be ready at the appointed moment to begin their march of freedom. All this they did simply on the authority of God's word, as delivered to Moses, clearly showing that their faith was to them as a conviction or demonstration of things not seen. And in this, as in other instances, they were not disappointed. For while the Israelites were thus preparing for their exodus, even at the hour of midnight, "the Lord smote the first-born in the land of Egypt, from the first-born of Pharaoh that sat on his throne, unto the first-born of the captive that was in the dungeon, and all the first-born of cattle. And Pharaoh rose up in the night, he and all his servants, and all the Egyptians, and there was a great cry in Egypt; for there was not a house where there was not one dead." But when the destroying angel saw the blood on the lintel and doorposts of the houses of the children of Israel, he passed over and did not "touch them."

29 **By faith they passed through the Red Sea**—When the Israelites left their headquarters at Rameses, they came first to Succoth, thence to Etham; thence to Pihahiroth; and thence to the shore of the Red Sea. (Ex. 14:2.) Here they were overtaken by

30 By faith ¹the walls of Jericho fell down, after they were compassed about seven days.

¹Josh. vi. 8-21; 2 Cor. x. 4, 5.

Pharaoh with all his hosts; and to the eye of sense and reason, their ruin seemed inevitable. But God said to Moses, "Lift up thy rod, and stretch out thine hand over the sea and divide it." He did so; "and the children of Israel went into the midst of the sea upon dry ground; and the waters were a wall unto them on the right hand and on the left." (Ex. 14: 16.)

**which the Egyptians assaying to do were drowned.**—The Egyptians pursued the Israelites and went in after them into "the midst of the sea, even all Pharaoh's horses, his chariots, and his horsemen. And it came to pass, that in the morning watch the Lord looked upon the host of the Egyptians through the pillar of fire and of the cloud, and troubled the host of the Egyptians, and took off their chariot wheels, that they drave them heavily: so that the Egyptians said, Let us flee from the face of Israel, for the Lord fighteth for them against the Egyptians. And the Lord said unto Moses, Stretch out thine hand over the sea, that the waters may come again upon the Egyptians, upon their chariots, and upon their horsemen. And Moses stretched forth his hand over the sea, and the sea returned to his strength when the morning appeared; and the Egyptians fled against it; and the Lord overthrew the Egyptians in the midst of the sea. And the waters returned, and covered the chariots, and the horsemen, and all the host of Pharaoh that came into the sea after them; there remained not so much as one of them. But the children of Israel walked upon dry land in the midst of the sea, and the waters were a wall unto them on the right hand, and on the left." (Ex. 14: 23-29.) Here we have a very striking and impressive illustration of the power and saving efficacy of faith, on the one hand; and also of the ruinous effects of infidelity on the other. It was their belief in God and in his word that saved the Israelites, and it was the unbelief and persistent disobedience of the Egyptians that brought on their ruin.

30 **By faith the walls of Jericho fell down, etc.**—Here, again, it is the faith of the Israelites that secures for them the victory. When they came before Jericho, the Lord said to them, "Ye shall compass the city, all ye men of war, and go round about the city

31 By faith ²the harlot Rahab perished not with them that believed not, when she had received the spies with peace.

²Josh. ii. 1-22; vi. 22-25; Matt. i. 5; Jas. ii. 25.

once.  Thus shalt thou do six days.  And seven priests shall bear before the Ark seven trumpets of rams' horns.  And the seventh day ye shall compass the city seven times, and the priests shall blow with the trumpets.  And it shall come to pass, that when they shall make a long blast with the rams' horns, and when ye hear the sound of the trumpet, all the people shall shout with a great shout; and the wall of the city shall fall down flat, and the people shall ascend up, every man straight before him." (Josh. 6: 3-5.) All this they did, as they were commanded.  And it came to pass, on the seventh day, when the people heard the sound of the trumpet and shouted with a great shout, that "the wall fell down flat; so that the people went up into the city every man straight before him, and they took the city." (Josh. 6: 20.)  Thus, without the use of the usual implements of war, but simply by their faith in God and obedience to his will, they achieved a most important victory. How true it is that "in Jehovah is our strength," and in him also is "our salvation."  For if we would gain the victory through our Lord Jesus Christ, we must still say with Paul, "The weapons of our warfare are not carnal, but mighty through God to the pulling down of strongholds." (2 Cor. 11 : 4.)

31 **By faith the harlot Rahab perished not, etc.**—See Josh. 2: 1-22 and 6: 22-25.  This is a remarkable instance of faith on the part of a Gentile: a Gentile once dead in trespasses and sins, but who by her strong practical faith in God was not only saved from the common ruin which befell her unbelieving countrymen, but was also raised to a position of honor and distinction in Israel.  For though many of the Jews erroneously interpret the word rendered *harlot* (*porne*) so as to make it signify "a seller of food" or "an innkeeper," they all concede that she became the wife of Salmon and the mother of Boaz (Matt. 1: 5) ; both of whom stand in the direct line of our Lord's ancestry.  The name should be written *Rachab* as in Matt. 1: 5; but in the Septuagint as well as in our text it is *Raab*.  It means *large, wide, spacious;* but the name *Rahab* means *violence, pride, insolence.*

## 3. OTHER GENERAL ILLUSTRATIONS DRAWN FROM THE EXPLOITS, DELIVERANCES, AND HEROIC ENDURANCE OF FAITHFUL MEN AND WOMEN UNDER THE OLD COVENANT
### 11 : 32-38

32 And what shall I more say? for [1]the time would fail me to tell of [2]Gideon, and of [3]Barak, and of [4]Samson, and of [5]Jephthæ; of [6]David also, and [7]Samuel, and of [8]the prophets:

[1]John xxi. 25.
[2]Judg. vi. 11-viii. 32.
[3]Judg. iv. 1-v. 31.
[4]Judg. xiii. 1-xvi. 31.
[5]Judg. xi. 1-xii. 7.
[6]1 Sam. xvi. 1, 13; xvii. 1-58.
[7]1 Sam. i. 20; ii. 11, 18; iii. 1-xii. 25.
[8]Matt. v. 12; Luke xiii. 28; xvi. 31; Acts x. 43.

32 **And what shall I more say?**—The Apostle perceiving at this point of the discussion that the time and space allotted to his subject would not admit of further details, proceeds now to give in a general way such a summary of matters as he thought would best serve to illustrate the power of faith, and so to strengthen and encourage his brethren.

**for the time would fail me**—This form of expression is often used by classicial writers to denote simply that much that might be said on a given subject, has to be omitted for want of time.

**to tell of Gideon, and of Barak, etc.**—Chronologically, these names would stand as follows: Barak, Gideon, Jephthah, Samson, Samuel, David, and the prophets. But our author seems to place Gideon before Barak, and Samson before Jephthah, on account of the more prominent position which they hold in sacred history, and Samuel is placed after David, most likely for the purpose of directly connecting him with the prophets.

GIDEON, son of Joash, of the tribe of Manasseh, was the fifth Judge of Israel. He was surnamed Jerubbaal (*i.e.,* Let Baal plead) on account of his opposition to Baal in breaking down his altar and cutting down his grove. Afterward when the Midianites, the Amalekites, and "the children of the east country," were gathered together against Israel, "the Spirit of the Lord came upon Gideon, and he blew a trumpet," and there were gathered unto them thirty-two thousand men. The number was, however, reduced to three hundred, and with these Gideon by faith routed the assembled hosts, and "put to flight the armies of the aliens." See Judges 6: 11-8: 32.

BARAK was a leader of Israel, of the tribe of Naphtali. He became renowned for the great victory which he gained over the Canaanites. After the death of Ehud, the third Judge of the children of Israel, they did evil in the sight of the Lord, and he "sold them into the hand of Jabin, king of Canaan, that lived at Hazor, the captain of whose host was Sisera, who dwelt in Harosheth of the Gentiles. And the children of Israel cried unto the Lord: for he had nine hundred chariots of iron; and for twenty years he mightily oppressed the children of Israel." (Judges 4:2, 3.) And Deborah the prophetess, who was then judging Israel, sent and called Barak, and said to him, "Hath not the Lord God of Israel commanded, saying, Go and draw toward Mount Tabor, and take with thee ten thousand men of the children of Naphtali and of the children of Zebulun? And I will draw unto thee, to the river Kishon, Sisera, the captain of Jabin's army, with his chariots and his multitude, and I will deliver him into thine hand" (verses 6, 7). Trusting in God, he accepted the call on condition that Deborah would accompany him; and with his ten thousand men he joined in battle the immense host of Sisera at the foot of Mount Tabor. His victory was complete. Harosheth of the Gentiles was taken; Sisera was murdered; and Jabin was ruined. See Judges 4: 1-5: 31.

SAMSON was the thirteenth Judge of Israel, and lived as a Nazirite from his birth. The first manifestation of his great prowess was in the slaughter of a young lion which "he rent, as he would have rent a kid." After this, he smote the Philistines on several occasions with great slaughter; and finally, he destroyed himself and three thousand of them by overthrowing the temple of their god Dagon. See Judges 13: 1-16: 31. In this last act of his eventful life, as well as in many other things, we cannot but regard Samson as a very great sinner. And care must, therefore, be taken not to press into the words of the Apostle a meaning which he never intended. It is not his purpose to commend all that was done by even the best and most illustrious of these men of faith. Abraham sinned, and so did Moses, although their example was far more elevated than that of Samson. But when the Spirit of the Lord came upon him, he performed some feats, in the exercise of faith, which are without a parallel in human history. Indeed, it is quite obvious that many of the exploits ascribed in Greek mythol-

ogy to the renowned Hercules are drawn from the inspired memoirs of this illustrious descendant of Dan.

JEPHTHAE, the son of Gilead by a concubine, was the ninth
Judge of Israel. He was distinguished chiefly for his victories
over the Ammonites and the Ephraimites. (Judges 11 : 1-12 : 7.)
Like Samson, he was far from being perfect. The extremely rash
vow which he made unto the Lord previous to his engagement
with the Ammonites, indicates a spirit of daring recklessness,
which is far from being commendable. But even in this, he
showed his faith in God, and his reliance on the strong arm of Jehovah for the victory. And the subsequent sacrifice of his only
daughter, in compliance with his vow, shows also very clearly that
he ascribed his success in the war to the God of Israel. It is his
strong confidence in God, and this only, which our author so
highly commends here to his discouraged and disheartened Hebrew brethren.

DAVID, the well known son of Jesse, and second King of Israel,
was always distinguished for his trust and confidence in God.
This is shown in many of his beautiful lyric odes, as well as in the
whole course of his public administration. Speaking of his trials
and signal deliverances he says, "In my distress, I called upon the
Lord, and cried unto my God: he heard my voice out of his temple, and my cry came into his ears. Then the Earth shook and
trembled; the foundations also of the hills moved and were shaken,
because he was wroth.—He bowed the heavens also, and came
down, and darkness was under his feet. And he rode upon a
cherub, and did fly; yea, he did fly upon the wings of the wind.—
He sent from above, he took me; he drew me out of many waters.
He delivered me from my strong enemy, and from them that hated
me; for they were too strong for me." (Psalm 18 : 6, 7, 9, 10, 16,
17.)

SAMUEL was the fifteenth and last Judge of Israel. Even from
his childhood he was distinguished for his piety; "and all Israel
from Dan to Beersheba knew that he was established to be a
prophet of the Lord." (1 Sam. 3 : 20.) He stands, therefore, very
properly in this list of heroes, at the head of the prophets: among
whom are to be reckoned such faithful reformers as Elijah, Elisha,
Isaiah, Jeremiah, Ezekiel, Daniel, and the other inspired writers of
the Old Testament.

33 ¹Who through faith subdued kingdoms, ²wrought righteousness, ³obtained promises, ⁴stopped the mouths of lions,

¹2 Sam. v. 4-25; viii. 1-18; Psa. xviii. 32-34.
²1 Sam. xii. 4; 2 Sam. viii. 15; 1 Chron. xviii. 14; Jas. i. 20.
³Chap. vi. 12, 15; ix. 15; x. 36; 1 Pet. i. 9.
⁴Judges xiv. 5 6; 1 Sam. xvii. 33-36; Dan. vi. 20-23.

33 **Who through faith subdued kingdoms,**—The Apostle does not mean that Gideon, Barak, Samson, Jephthah, David, Samuel, and each of the prophets severally "subdued kingdoms, wrought righteousness, obtained promises, stopped the mouths of lions," etc.; but only that they did all these things as a class of men distinguished for their faith in God. Some of them through faith subdued kingdoms; some wrought righteousness; some obtained promises; some stopped the mouths of lions; some quenched the violence of fire; some escaped the edge of the sword; some out of weakness were made strong; some waxed valiant in fight; and some put to flight the armies of the aliens. Gideon, for instance, subdued the Midianites (Judges 8); Barak, the Canaanites (Judges 4); Jephthah, the Ammonites (Judges 11); and David, the Philistines, Moabites, Syrians, Edomites, and Ammonites (2 Sam. 5, 8, 10, etc.).

**wrought righteousness,**—This may denote all works of righteousness which are done in obedience to the known will of God; as Peter says, "In every nation, he that feareth God and worketh righteousness, is accepted of him." (Acts 10: 35.) But it is probable that our author refers here more particularly to the public and official acts of rulers in the administration of justice. Thus, for instance, when Samuel challenged all the people of Israel to bear witness against him; if he had in his whole public administration, taken any man's ass; or if he had defrauded or oppressed anyone; or if he had received a bribe from any; they all answered with one accord and said, "Thou hast not defrauded us, nor oppressed us; neither hast thou taken aught from any man's hand." (1 Sam. 12: 4.) So also it is testified of David, that "he reigned over all Israel, and executed judgment and justice to all the people." (2 Sam. 8: 15.)

**obtained promises,**—This may mean (1) that they obtained verbal promises or assurances from God, as did Abraham before he left Ur of Chaldea (Chrysostom, Bengel, Bleek, Stuart, Bloomfield); or (2) it may mean that they obtained the blessings prom-

34 ¹Quenched the violence of fire, ²escaped the edge of the sword, ³out of weakness were made strong, ⁴waxed valiant in fight, ⁵turned to flight the armies of the aliens.

¹Psa. lxvi. 12; Isa. xliii. 2; Dan. iii. 19-28; 1 Pet. iv. 12.
²2 Sam. xxi. 16 17; 2 Kings vi. 16-18; Jer. xxvi. 24.
³Judges vii. 19-25; 2 Cor. xii. 9 10.
⁴Psa. xviii. 32-45.
⁵1 Sam. xiv. 13-22; xvii. 51, 52; 2 Sam. viii. 1-8.

ised, as did the Israelites under Joshua, when they got possession of Canaan (Delitzsch, Alford, Moll). The latter view is most probable, as it harmonizes best with the use of the word rendered *obtained* (*epitunkano*), both in the Greek classics and in the New Testament. It occurs only in Rom. 11 : 7; Heb. 6 : 15; James 4 : 2; and in our text: in all of which it means the obtaining of the promised blessing. The Apostle does not mean, of course, that they obtained "the promise" of the Messiah's coming and reign; but only such subordinate promises as were often made to the Israelites. Isaiah, for instance, saw Jerusalem delivered from the invasion of Sennacherib; Daniel saw the end of the Babylonish captivity; and many others lived to see the erection of the second temple and the restoration of the Levitical services.

**stopped the mouths of lions,**—Several instances illustrative of this clause are mentioned in the Old Testament; as in Judges 14 : 6; 1 Sam. 17 : 34; 1 Chron. 11 : 22; and Dan. 6 : 20. Of these, the case of Daniel is the most remarkable. For fidelity to his God, he was cast into the den of lions; but his faith saved him.

34 **quenched the violence of fire,**—(*dunamin*) not merely the flame, but the power of fire. This is impressively illustrated by the case of Shadrach, Meshach, and Abednego. (Dan. 3.) And the same is, no doubt, true of other cases of persecution, under both the Old and the New Covenant. Rudelbach, for instance, relates of a martyr who was burned to death at Brussels, that when the flame rose up over his head, he cried out that he felt as if they were covering him with roses. His faith quenched the power of the fire, though it did not as in the case of Shadrach, Meshach, and Abednego, wholly arrest its effects.

**escaped the edge of the sword,**—As did David (1 Sam. 18 : 1; 19 : 10, 12), and Elijah (1 Kings 19 : 1-16), and Elisha (2 Kings 6 : 14-23, 31-33), and Jeremiah (Jer. 36 : 26). There is probably further reference here, as well as in each of the following clauses of this verse, to the heroic exploits of the Maccabaean period, when

35 ¹Women received their dead raised to life again: and ²others were tortured, not accepting deliverance; ³that they might obtain a better resurrection:

¹1 Kings xvii. 19-24; 2 Kings iv. 18-37; Luke vii. 11-17.
²Acts xxii. 24, 25, 29.
³John v. 29; Acts xxiv. 15; 1 Cor. xv. 54; Phil. iii. 11.

Mattathias and his seven sons, like Gideon, Samson, and David, became strong out of weakness, waxed valiant in battle, and put to flight the armies of the aliens. Judas Maccabaeus particularly distinguished himself by putting to flight, with comparatively small forces, the Syrian armies under Apollonius, Seron, Nicanor, Timotheus, and Lysias; and so finally succeeded in throwing off the Syrian yoke, and re-establishing the worship of the true God in Jerusalem. That these Maccabaean victories were achieved by faith is obvious from the whole tenor of their history. Of the truth of this, the following words of the aged and venerable Mattathias will serve as an illustration, and at the same time furnish to the reader the keynote of the whole Maccabaean movement. When he was about to die (166 B.C.), worn out as he was with the fatigues of the first campaign, he called his sons together and said to them, "Now, therefore, my sons, be zealous for the Law, and give your lives for the Covenant of your fathers. Call to mind what acts our fathers did in their time; so shall ye receive great honor and an everlasting name. Was not Abraham found faithful in temptation? and it was imputed to him for righteousness. Joseph in the time of his distress kept the commandment, and was made lord of Egypt. Phinehas, our father, in being zealous and fervent, obtained the covenant of an everlasting priesthood. Joshua, for fulfilling the word, was made a Judge in Israel. Caleb for bearing witness before the congregation, received the heritage of the land. David, for being merciful, obtained the throne of an everlasting kingdom. Elijah, for being zealous and fervent for the Law, was taken up into heaven. Hananiah, Azariah, and Mishael, by believing, were saved out of the flame. Daniel, for his innocency, was delivered from the mouth of the lions. And thus consider ye, that throughout all ages, none who put their trust in him [God] shall be overcome.—Wherefore, ye my sons, be valiant, and show yourselves men in behalf of the Law: for by it, ye shall obtain glory." (1 Macc. 2: 50-64.)

35 **Women received their dead raised to life again:**—There

is, no doubt, special reference here to the case of the widow of
Zarephath (1 Kings 17: 17-24) ; and to that of the Shunammite
(2 Kings 4: 18-37). The son of the former was restored to
life by Elijah ; and the son of the latter by Elisha. But according to our author, this was effected in part through the faith
of these women. Had it not been for their faith in God, the
miracles would not have been wrought.

**and others were tortured, not accepting deliverance;**—The
word rendered *tortured* (*etumpanistheson*) means properly to
stretch and torture upon the *tympanum* (*tumpanon*) ; an instrument of torture in the shape of a large drum or wheel, on which
criminals were stretched in order to be beaten to death with sticks
and rods. A case of this kind is recorded in 2 Macc. 6: 19-29.
During the persecutions of Antiochus Epiphanes, it was decreed
among other things that the Jews should abandon their religion,
and conform in all respects to the religious customs of the Syrians.
Many apostatized from the faith, and many suffered martyrdom.
Among these was one of the Jewish scribes, a man about ninety
years of age, called Eliazar. He was put to death on the tympanum for refusing to eat swine's flesh. "But when he was ready
to die with stripes, he groaned and said, It is manifest unto the
Lord who hath the holy knowledge, that whereas I might have
been delivered from death, I now endure sore pains in my body by
being beaten: but in soul I am well content to suffer these things,
because I fear him." Other instances of severe torture by flaying,
roasting, etc., are given, in the next chapter. (2 Macc. 7.) Here
we have an account of the martyrdom of a woman and her seven
sons, simply because they would not eat swine's flesh, and conform
to other heathen customs. They all chose death rather than life,
on the conditions offered by Antiochus.

**that they might obtain a better resurrection:**—Better than
what? To this query several answers have been given. (1) It is
alleged by many, that the contrast is between the final resurrection
of the just, and the resurrection that is spoken of in the first clause
of the verse. The sons of the widow of Zarephath and the Shunammite were raised from the dead to return again in a little while
to the dust: but these faithful ones were expecting a resurrection
to everlasting life (Chrysostom, Bengel, Schultz, Böhme, Bleek,
Stuart, Ebrard, Delitzsch, Alford). (2) Others suppose that the

contrast is between the final resurrection of the just and the deliverance from death which was offered to these faithful men and women, on condition that they would renounce their religion and worship the gods of the heathen. Like Isaac (verse 19), they were, so to speak, dead by the decree of their persecutors: but by apostatizing from the true religion, they might have obtained a deliverance similar, in some respects, to a resurrection. But in that event, they would have forfeited what they themselves esteemed a far greater boon than any deliverance from mere temporal death (Winer, Tholuck, Lünemann, Scott, Moll). And (3) others again think that the contrast is between the final resurrection of the just and that of the unjust. The former will be a resurrection to everlasting life; but the latter will be to everlasting condemnation (Œcumenius, Theophylact). The first hypothesis is supported by the weightiest authorities; but I am, nevertheless, constrained to think that the second view is most in harmony with the context and the special scope of the passage. For be it observed, that it is not our author who makes the comparison and expresses the given preference. Not at all. He merely states approvingly what, on due reflection, was the preference of the persons spoken of. They, it seems, after considering the whole matter, were unwilling to accept the proffered deliverance; because by their doing so, they knew they would forfeit what they themselves regarded as of infinitely more value than anything which their persecutors were able to offer.

This is impressively illustrated by the account which we have given of the martyrdom above referred to. When the second son, for instance, was about to expire, he said to Antiochus, "Thou like a fury takest us out of this present life; but the King of the world will raise us up, who have died for his laws, unto everlasting life." In like manner the fourth son, addressing his last words to the king, said, "It is good being put to death by men to look for hope from God to be raised up again by him. As for thee, thou shalt have no resurrection to life." (2 Macc. 7: 9, 14.) It seems clear, therefore, that the martyrs themselves made an estimate of what was offered to them by God, on the one hand, and of what was offered to them by their persecutors, on the other; and that it is simply their preference for the former in comparison with the lat-

36 And ¹others had trial of cruel mockings and scourgings, yea, moreover of ²bonds and imprisonment:

37 ¹They were stoned, they were sawn asunder, were tempted, ²were slain

---

¹Judges xvi. 25; 1 Kings xxii. 24; 2 Kings ii. 23; 2 Chron. xxx. 10; Jer. xx. 2, 7; xxxvii. 15.
²Gen. xxxix. 20; 1 Kings xxii. 27; Jer. xxix. 26; xxxii. 2, 3.
¹1 Kings xxi. 10, 13-15; 2 Chron. xxiv. 21.
²1 Sam. xxii. 17-19; Jer. ii. 30; xxvi. 23; Lam. iv. 13, 14.

---

ter which our author here designs to express. These faithful men and women chose death rather than life under the circumstances.

36 **And others had trial of cruel mockings, etc.**—A few instances of these sportive cruelties and scourgings, and also of bonds and imprisonments, are mentioned in the Old Testament. Mention is made, for example, of the mocking of Samson by the Philistines (Judges 16: 25); of the imprisonment of Micaiah by Ahab (1 Kings 22: 27); of Hanani's imprisonment by Asa (2 Chron. 16: 10); and of the mocking, beating, bonds, and imprisonment of Jeremiah by Pashur and others (Jer. 20: 2, 7; 32: 2, 3). But our author probably refers here more particularly to the persecutions and sufferings of the Jews at a later period: many instances of which occurred during the reign of the Persians, Greeks, Egyptians, and Syrians. Take, for example, the following incidents from the history of the martyrdoms previously mentioned: "It came to pass also that seven brethren and their mother were taken and compelled by the king [Antiochus Epiphanes] against the law to taste swine's flesh, and were tormented with scourges and whips." And when the first of the seven was mangled and tortured to death by the fiendish officers of Antiochus, they brought the second to make him a mocking-stock. And when they had pulled off the skin of his head with his hair, they asked him, "Wilt thou eat [swine's flesh] before thou be punished through every member of thy body? But he answered in his own language and said, *No*. Wherefore he also received the next torment in order, as the former did.—After him, the third was made a mocking-stock, etc." (2 Macc. 7: 1, 7, 8, 10.) These and other like statements made in the first and second books of Maccabees, are, no doubt, in the main correct. These writings are not inspired, as are the canonical books of the Old and New Testament; but they are as reliable as any other uninspired works of like antiquity.

37 **They were stoned,**—This was a common mode of capital punishment among the Jews, and hence it is quite probable that

with the sword: ³they wandered about in sheepskins and goatskins; ⁴being destitute, afflicted, tormented;

³2 Kings i. 8; Matt. iii. 4; Rev. xi. 3.
⁴1 Kings xvii. 2-6; Matt. viii. 20; 1 Cor. iv. 9-13.

---

many of the ancient martyrs suffered death in this way.  See Matt. 11: 35; 23: 37; Luke 13: 34.  Thus, for example, Zechariah the son of Jehoiada, was put to death by Joash, king of Judah (2 Chron. 24: 20-22), and thus also it is reported that Jeremiah was put to death by the Jews, at Daphne, in Egypt.

**they were sawn asunder,**—So, according to the Talmud, was Isaiah put to death by Manasseh, king of Judah.  The account that is given by the Jews of this barbarious act is most likely correct; it was so regarded by Justin Martyr, Tertullian, Origen, and other Christian Fathers.  Josephus, speaking of Manasseh, says, "He barbarously slew all the righteous men that were among the Hebrews, nor would he spare the prophets, for he every day slew some of them, till Jerusalem was overflown with blood." (Ant. 10, 3, 1.)

**they were tempted,**—This clause has given much trouble to the critics.  "It is difficult," says Ebrard, "to see what this jejune and general expression can have to do in this connection, and as sure as some word must have stood in this place, so sure it is that this (*epeirasthesan*) cannot have been the word."  So, also, Alford: "It is certainly surprising," he says, "to meet with so mild a word in the midst of torments and ways of dreadful death."  And hence it is conjectured (1) that this word (*epeirasthesan*) is an interpolation, and that it should be omitted as in the P. Syriac version. (2) It is alleged that it has been inadvertently substituted for some other word indicating death by fire (as *epurastheson*), or some other mode of torture.  But the word in our text is well supported by external evidence, and after all it is not so inconsistent with the context as many of the critics seem to imagine.  For as Prof. Stuart remarks, "Not only life, but wealth and honor were frequently proffered in the midst of torture most agonizing to the human frame, in order to tempt the martyrs to forsake their religion.  Such a temptation as this is by no means to be reckoned among the lighter trials of good men."  The temptations of Christ, both in the wilderness and Gethsemane (Matt. 4: 1-11; Luke 22: 40-46) seem to have given him very intense sufferings.

38 Of whom the world was not worthy: ¹they wandered in deserts, and in
mountains, and in dens, and in caves of the earth.

¹1 Sam. xxii. 1; xxiii. 15, 19, 23; 1 Kings xvii. 3; xviii. 4, 13; xix. 1-14.

---

**were slain with the sword:**—The prophet Urijah was brought
out of Egypt to king Jehoiakim "who slew him with the sword"
(Jer. 26: 23), and in the reign of Ahab, king of Israel, putting to
death with the sword seems to have been a common mode of punishment. Thus Elijah, in one of his complaints to God says, "The
children of Israel have forsaken thy covenant, thrown down thine
altars, and slain thy prophets with the sword, and they seek my life
to take it away." (1 Kings 19: 10.)

**they wandered about in sheepskins, etc.**—Driven away from
their homes, like Elijah the Tishbite (1 Kings 17: 3-9; 19: 3-14),
like him they wandered about in sheepskins and goatskins, being
"destitute, afflicted, tormented." It was the custom of the prophets to wear rough, hairy garments (Zech. 13: 4); and so in 2
Kings 1: 8, Elijah is described as "a hairy man," most likely from
the shaggy appearance of his dress, for in the Septuagint (1 Kings
19: 13, 19; 2 Kings 2: 8, 13, 14) his mantle is called a *melote;*
which means (1) a sheepskin, and (2) a garment made of any
rough woolly skin. Elijah may therefore be regarded as a fit type
of this class of men, who from the time that they entered on their
public ministry were subject to perpetual want, oppression, and
persecution.

38 **Of whom the world was not worthy:**—This seems to be a
sort of proverbial expression, and it is evidently thrown in here
parenthetically to denote (1) the eminent holiness of these good
men; and (2) the great wickedness of most of their contemporaries. Their mode of life showed very plainly that though in the
world they were not of it.

**they wandered in deserts, etc.**—The reference here seems to
be general, and includes no doubt those who for conscience's sake
suffered from the heathen, as well as from their own countrymen.
Indeed, this closing remark is peculiarly applicable to the Maccabaean period, when the mountains and caves of Judea were filled
with pious sufferers. For then the Syrians under Antiochus
"drove the Israelites into secret places, even wheresoever they
could flee for succor." (1 Macc. 1: 53.) And when Apollonious

entered Jerusalem with an army of twenty-two thousand, and commenced butchering the inhabitants on the Sabbath Day, "Judas Maccabaeus with nine others, or thereabout, withdrew himself into the wilderness, and lived in the mountains after the manner of beasts, with his company, who fed on herbs continually, lest they should be partakers of the pollution." (2 Macc. 5: 27.)

### 4. SUPERIOR LIGHT AND PRIVILEGES OF BELIEVERS UNDER THE NEW COVENANT
### 11: 39, 40

39 And these all, [1]having obtained a good report through faith, [2]received not the promise:

[1]Ver. 2; 1 Tim. v. 10.
[2]Gen. xxii. 18; xlix. 10; Deut. xviii. 18; Acts xiii. 23, 32, 33; Gal. iii. 16-19; Eph. i. 13; iii. 6.

---

39 **And these all, having obtained a good report through faith,**—That is, all the persons referred to in this chapter, whether named or unnamed, from Abel onward. All these, though they did not live to see fulfilled the promise relating to the personal coming of the Messiah, were nevertheless through their faith in God enabled to do and to suffer what has obtained for them a good report; a reputation for noble daring and patient endurance, which gives them a place in the first rank of moral heroes. The Apostle does not mean to say that they were all justified and saved by their faith in God and in the promise of a coming Redeemer. Not at all. His object is simply to illustrate the marvelous power and efficacy of faith in the word of God, whether that word relates to the building of an ark, the crossing of the sea, the compassing of a city with rams' horns, or anything else. These men all believed in God as the rewarder of them that diligently seek him; and through this faith they wrought many wonderful works, for which they have obtained a world-wide reputation. But with many of them God was not well pleased; for they were overthrown in the wilderness (1 Cor. 10: 5); and others were overthrown elsewhere on account of their impiety. Many of them, however, like Abraham, Isaac, and Jacob, persevered to the end in well doing; and so after they had patiently endured the toils and sufferings of this life, they obtained the promise of the heavenly rest. See note on 6: 15.

**received not the promise:**—They received many promises. Abraham, for instance, received the promise of a son by Sarah; the

40 God having provided some [3]better thing for us, that [4]they without us should not be made perfect.

[3]Ch. vii. 19, 22; viii. 6; ix. 23; xii. 24; Matt. xiii. 17; 1 Cor. ii. 9, 10; Eph. iii. 5, 6; 1 Pet. i. 10-12.
[4]Ch. ix. 8-15; x. 11-14; Rom. iii. 25, 26.

Twelve Tribes received the promise of the earthly inheritance; and Gideon, Barak, Samson, David, and Daniel, received many other promises during their earthly pilgrimage. But none of them lived to see the fulfillment of *"the promise"* relating to the personal coming and reign of the Messiah.

40 **God having provided some better thing for us,**—The "better thing" here spoken of is evidently the new and better covenant which was established on new and better promises, including all the superior blessings and privileges of the Gospel dispensation. This, the patriarchs saw afar off; for "Abraham," says Christ, "rejoiced to see my day; and he saw it, and was glad" (John 8: 56). But none of them saw it, as we now see it, and as the Hebrews in the time of Paul saw it; for "I tell you," says Christ, addressing his disciples, "that many prophets and kings have desired to see those things which ye see, and have not seen them; and to hear those things which ye hear, and have not heard them." (Luke 10: 24.) The Gospel economy could not be fully inaugurated until after the incarnation, death, burial, resurrection, ascension, and coronation of the Lord Jesus; and hence it was seen by the ancients, but "as through a glass darkly." For says Paul, quoting from the "evangelical Isaiah," "Eye hath not seen, nor ear heard, neither have entered into the heart of man the things which God hath prepared for them that love him." But he adds, "God hath revealed them to us by his Spirit; for the Spirit searches all things, yea the deep things of God." (1 Cor. 2:9, 10.) And hence even the least in the kingdom of heaven is said to be greater than John the Baptist, in this respect, that he now lives in the actual enjoyment of what John and the ancients perceived only by faith. (Matt. 11: 11.) "For the Spirit was not yet given, because that Jesus was not yet glorified" (John 7: 39)). Nor did even the Apostles yet understand that Jesus must suffer, and rise from the dead, in order that by the grace of God he might become unto us "wisdom, and justification, and sanctification, and redemption." See Matt. 16: 21, 22; Luke 18: 33, 34; John 20: 9.

**That they without us should not be made perfect.**—Without us in what respect? And perfect in what respect? These queries have been answered very differently by the commentators. It is alleged (1) that the Apostle refers here to the final consummation, when the spirits of all the saints, Patriarchal, Jewish and Christian, will, in their glorified bodies, enter together upon the full fruition of the eternal inheritance (Macknight, Moll). But against this interpretation it may be urged (a) that it does not well harmonize with the context. The object of the Apostle is manifestly to excite and arouse his Hebrew brethren to the exercise of more patience and greater diligence in their Christian course, by reminding them that their privileges and opportunities were greatly superior to those of the ancients. Nay more, the perfection of the ancients depended essentially on those very blessings which the Hebrew Christians were then enjoying through the incarnation, sacrifice, atonement and mediation of the Lord Jesus. It is therefore difficult to see what bearing an appeal to the final consummation could have on the Apostle's argument. (b) It seems to be inconsistent with what is said in 12: 23. Here, it is plainly taught that the spirits of all those faithful ones, who, like Abraham, had persevered in well-doing to the end of life, were even then perfect when Paul wrote this epistle. (2) Many able expositors maintain that previous to the death of Christ, the spirits of these ancient worthies were still in a state of condemnation, under the dominion of Death: and that their being made perfect consisted in their being delivered at that time by Christ himself from the power of Death, and so admitted to a participation of the joys, honors, and privileges of the heavenly Jerusalem. "Not without us," says Riger, "could they be made perfect; and with us, they have already been perfected. Christ went to them to open for them the gates of Death's kingdom, and thence to lead them forth with himself. And now henceforth, the souls of all who die in Christ go at once to him, and enter Heaven, there to await re-union with the body at his second coming." Such is also the view of Ebrard, Delitzsch, Alford, and many others. Alford says, "The result with regard to them is, that their spirits, from the time when Christ descended into Hades and ascended up into Heaven, enjoy heavenly blessedness, and are waiting with all who have followed their glorified

High Priest within the vail, for the resurrection of their bodies, the
regeneration, the renovation of all things."

That no sinner was ever made perfect without the blood of
Christ, is of course admitted. See notes on 9: 15. But that "the
spirits of the ancient saints were all shut up in the kingdom of
Death, until after the resurrection of Christ," is a hypothesis which
but illy accords with many passages of Scripture. Everywhere,
the Bible represents Abraham and his spiritual seed as being *"justified by faith"*; which implies of course that they were henceforth
treated by God as just and righteous persons. And in Rom. 3:
25, 26, we are told that God in the fullness of time, set forth Jesus
Christ as a propitiatory sacrifice for a demonstration of his justice
in passing by the sins of these faithful ones, and treating them as
if they had never sinned. And accordingly we read in 6: 15, that
after Abraham had patiently endured the toils and afflictions of
his weary pilgrimage, "he obtained the promise." For even while
here he was constantly looking forward to the heavenly city
(verses 10-16). That the happiness of these faithful ones may
have been increased by the work of Christ and the full developments of the Gospel is, I think, quite probable. (Rev. 5: 8-10.)
But if Elijah and Enoch were taken directly to the heavenly country (2 Kings 2: 1, 11), it seems most likely, that all the saints of
the Patriarchal and Jewish ages, were also, immediately after
death, transported to Heaven, or at least to a place of high spiritual
enjoyment. The Popish notion that Christ, after his death, went
down into Hades to convert anyone, is a mere figment of the imagination. When Dives died, he went to his own place, and so also
did Lazarus. And in his parable concerning them, Christ teaches
very plainly that any subsequent change in their allotment is morally impossible. (Luke 16: 19-31.) "If the tree fall toward the
south or toward the north, in the place where the tree falleth,
there it shall be." (Eccles. 11: 3.) The fact is, that when Christ
died, his spirit went, not into Hades, but into Paradise (Luke 23:
43); and Paradise, as Paul tells us, is identical with the third
Heaven (2 Cor. 12: 1-4). Christ does not say as in our Common
Version, "Thou wilt not leave my soul in Hell [Hades], but, Thou
wilt not leave my soul *to Hades* (*eis hadeu*); that is, thou wilt not
abandon my soul to Hades." Compare Matt. 16: 18; Rev. 20: 14,
etc.

The hypothesis of Ebrard, Delitzsch, and Alford, in regard to the intermediate state of the Old Testament saints, is therefore not correct. And even if it were, it could have no place in the solution of the question which we have under consideration. For it is manifestly of the relative privileges of the present state, and not of those of the intermediate or future state, that our author speaks. The ancients while here knew but little, and enjoyed but little of the economy of God's grace. They depended for salvation on what we now see and understand. But nevertheless they persevered in well-doing even to the end. And hence it is but reasonable that we should be at least equally faithful, under like trials and afflictions; seeing that we are now in possession of that *"better thing,"* to which they had all to look forward for salvation. The phrase *"without us"* may therefore be taken as equivalent to *without the religion which through Christ we now actually enjoy.* For Christ himself is the essential bond of union which binds together the saints of all ages. Those that are united to him are also united to one another. And as the ancients were not, and could not, be perfected without the cleansing efficacy of his blood, it may be truthfully said, that they were not perfected "without us" and the "better thing" which we by the grace of God now actually enjoy.

## REFLECTIONS

From this section, we may learn, with many other valuable lessons, the following:

1. We see in the first place the great value and importance of faith. This is shown (1) by the unusual amount of space which our author devotes to the discussion of the subject; and (2) by the great influence which faith has on the lives and fortunes of those who possess it. Reaching, as it does, far beyond the narrow limits of time and sense, it enables the soul to appropriate to itself, in a good degree, the riches, honors, glories, and blessings of the invisible world; and so qualifies it for the great trials, achievements, and conflicts of life. It makes a man feel confident that God is with him and for him; and that nothing can therefore successfully resist or oppose him, in his works of faith and service of love. He knows that so long as he remains faithful all things must work together for his good. And hence it is that the men of faith have always been the greatest of moral heroes. We search in vain,

among the world's most renowned heroes, for such men as Abraham, Moses, David, Daniel, Paul, and other kindred spirits, "who
through faith subdued kingdoms, wrought righteousness, obtained
promises, stopped the mouths of lions, quenched the violence of
fire, escaped the edge of the sword, out of weakness were made
strong, waxed valiant in fight, and turned to flight the armies of
the aliens."

> "Though dead they speak in reason's ear,
> And in example live:
> Their faith, and hope, and mighty deeds,
> Still fresh instruction give."

2. We learn also from this very instructive and encouraging
section what is the nature of faith, and also on what it rests as
its only true and proper foundation. Where there is no revelation
from God, there can be no faith. Without this, there may be en-
thusiasm and fanaticism, but no faith; for faith always rests ultimately on the word of God, and on nothing else. (Rom. 10: 17.)
The evidence, too, must be such as to produce conviction in the
understanding that such and such is the will of God; and that he
has thus and so commanded or promised. This is manifest from all
the examples that are given in this section. But more than this is
manifest. It is equally clear from these same examples, that the
faith which is here commended is not a mere conviction of the understanding. It begins with the understanding of course; but it
does not stop with it. Through the intellect, it pervades also
the heart; and through the heart, it moves and influences the
will; and through the will, it controls the life of its possessor,
bringing the whole man under subjection to the will of God.
The true believer may, like Saul of Tarsus, have to inquire of
the Lord what he would have him do; but having obtained an
answer from God, he deems this sufficient. He no longer confers with flesh and blood; but like Abel, he brings and offers
as a sacrifice just what God has himself prescribed; like Noah,
he builds such an ark as God has directed for the salvation of
himself and his house; like Abraham, he offers if necessary his
own son, or even his own life, in obedience to God's will; and
like Moses, he makes all things according to the pattern that
was showed to him in the mount. Faith then is a living, ac-

tive, all-pervading, and fruit-bearing principal, which, by uniting us to God through Christ, makes us partakers of the divine nature, and enables us to "escape the corruption that is in the world through lust." It is the appetite of the soul which brings us to the bread and water of life; and so enables us to eat and drink and live forever.

3. It seems evident from the examples and illustrations given in this chapter, as well as from many other parts of the Holy Bible, that the faith of many of the ancients was quite equal to that of the more highly favored moderns. In point of knowledge, we have as a matter of course greatly the advantage of both the Jews and Patriarchs. Christ has come: and by his resurrection, he has brought life and immortality to light. The mystery of redemption is now so fully revealed to us in the Gospel, that even the least in the kingdom of heaven knows more of the economy of God's grace through Christ, than did even Abraham or John the Baptist. (Matt. 11: 11.) But it is very evident that we cannot boast so much of the superiority of our faith. In this respect, those of the ancients who had a revelation from God, will compare favorably with the most enlightened Christians of the nineteenth century. We look in vain among the living for brighter and more illustrious examples of faith than those of Abel, Enoch, Noah, Abraham, Moses, Elijah, Jeremiah, Daniel, and even the Maccabaean heroes; many of whom suffered even unto death rather than violate what many would now regard as one of the very least of God's commandments.

Why is this? Without attempting to give an exhaustive reply to this question, which would carry us far beyond the proper scope of these reflections, we may I think safely conclude that it is owing largely to the influence of human traditions on the one hand, and of human philosophy on the other. By the former many have been led to trust more in the Man of sin than in the Lord of life and glory; and by the latter, many others have been induced to lean entirely too much on their own understanding, and so to walk by sight rather than by faith. This strange proclivity of human nature is as old as the fall of man. It was first manifested in the eating of the forbidden fruit. When the woman *saw,* or thought she saw, "that the tree was good for food, and that it was pleasant to the eyes, and a tree to be desired to make one wise, she took of the fruit thereof, and did eat; and gave also unto her husband with her, and he did eat." (Gen. 3:6.) This one melancholy illustration of the unspeakable folly of neglecting the plain teachings of God's word, and relying on anything else as the guide of life, we might reasonably hope would suffice as an example of warning and admonition to all subsequent generations. But not so. Soon after this, we see manifested in Cain the same rationalistic spirit which, through hs mother Eve, "brought death into our world and all our woe." He too thought he saw something better and more becoming than the sacrifice which God himself had prescribed and appointed. And instead of bringing a bleeding lamb as an offering to God, he brings no doubt a very handsome present of the fruits of the ground; ridiculing perhaps at the same time what he evidently regarded as a weakness on the part of his brother, who it seems was simple enough not to lean on his own understanding, but to bring just such an offering as God himself had commanded. So too the faith of Noah was no doubt a subject of ridicule among the proud, self-righteous, self-reliant, would-be philosophers of his day: while, at the same time, many of the more ignorant and superstitious would rely with more confidence on the silly tales of false priests and false prophets than on the inspired oracles of the living God. And just so it has ever been, in some measure, in all ages and in all nations. Tradition and philosophy have both served to undermine the authority of God's word, and so to weaken the faith of myriads. During "the dark ages," tradition had the ascendency. The Man of sin then sat in the temple of God, and issued his decrees to superstitious thousands who received them as the oracles of Jehovah. But with the reformation of the sixteenth century, the spirit of Rationalism again revived. And it gives us pleasure to know and confess that it has done much to free the human soul from the bondage and tyranny of the many forms of superstition which were then prevalent; for all of which we of course feel devoutly thankful. But the trouble is, that Rationalism, as well as Tradition, has transcended all the bounds of decency and propriety. Like the Man of sin, it claims for itself all the honors and prerogatives of the Deity. In its unbounded pride and arrogance, it deals with the inspired oracles of God, just as it deals with the absurd delusions and dogmas of the Mother of harlots. It is true, for instance, that the Bible says, "In the beginning God created the heavens and the earth." But what of that? Since Rationalism has discovered that "nothing can be made out of nothing," it must go! The word of God must be made to harmonize with the oracles of this new Divinity. And so it is, that the Bible is now divested of much of its power and authority in the popular consciousness: and its miracles are treated by many as the mere myths of ancient fable.

It is evident therefore that the great want of the present age, is a return to the simple faith and practice of father Abraham and the primitive Christians. Let Traditions and Rationalism be each confined to its own proper sphere, and let men everywhere bow to the authority of God's inspired word, and very soon the Church will appear without a spot, or wrinkle, or any such thing. (Eph. 5:27.)

## SECTION ELEVEN
### 12:1-29

### ANALYSIS

Having described the nature of faith, and illustrated by a great variety of examples its power and efficacy as a principle of human conduct, and also as a means of spiritual enjoyment, the Apostle now returns to his main line of thought, and proceeds to encourage still further his Hebrew brethren to persevere steadfastly in their begun Christian course. This he does,

I. By representing them as contestants in a race-course, surrounded by all the faithful ones referred to in the preceding chapter; who, as a cloud of witnesses for the truth, are represented as being also anxious spectators of the great contest for the crown of life (verse 1). The imagery is drawn from the foot-races then celebrated in Palestine, Greece, Italy, and other provinces of the Roman empire. In allusion to these, the Apostle exhorts his brethren

1. To make all due preparation for the race, by laying aside every weight that might in any way serve to impede their progress; and especially the besetting sin of unbelief, so paralyzing in its effects.

2. To run their race with patience, as in the presence of the aforesaid cloud of illustrious witnesses and sympathizing spectators.

II. He exhorts and encourages them to look off to Jesus in all their conflicts, and to follow him as their great Exemplar (verses 2, 3), remembering

1. That as the Author and Finisher of the faith, he had endured the cross:

2. That he had despised the shame; bearing calmly and meekly the most unjust and violent opposition of his enemies:

3. And that as a reward for all this, he has received a seat on the right hand of the Majesty in the heavens.

III. He encourages them to bear their trials and afflictions with patience (verses 4-11);

1. In consideration of their lightness. These Hebrew brethren had not, like Jesus and many other martyrs, resisted unto blood (verse 4).

2. He further urges them to bear their afflictions with patient resignation, in view of God's gracious designs in allowing them to come upon them (verses 6-11). They were all the chastisements of the Lord, intended to make them purer and better. In illustrating and amplifying this thought, the Apostle reminds his brethren,

(1.) That the simple fact of God's correcting them, was evidence of his love and care for them; that he was in fact dealing with them as his own beloved children (verses 6-8).

(2.) That they had borne patiently and even thankfully the corrections of their earthly parents; though they were, like themselves, carnal, and consequently ever liable to err in their discipline (verse 9).

(3.) That God never errs: but that being infinitely exalted above all the weaknesses and infirmities of the flesh, he always corrects his children in wisdom and in love; in order that they may be made partakers of his holiness.

(4.) That although all chastening is for the present grievous, it nevertheless, when wisely administered, always results in good to those who are properly exercised by it.

IV. In view of these facts, the Apostle further exhorts them,

1. To take fresh courage; and by removing every obstacle out of the way, to strengthen the weak, encourage the faint-hearted, and save if possible those who were even then ready to perish by the way (verses 12, 13).

2.  To follow peace with all men and holiness; without which none can have communion and fellowship with God (verse 14).

3.  To watch diligently that no root of bitterness should spring up among them, such as might cause many to fall from the grace of God; reminding them at the same time, by the case of Esau, that for the apostate there is no salvation (verses 15-17).

V.  He next encourages them by reminding them of their superior privileges and birthrights, as the favored subjects of the New Covenant, and members of the family of God (verses 18-24).

1.  The aspects of the Old Economy were full of terror and alarm (verses 18-21):

2.  But the New Economy is full of comfort and encouragement (verses 22-24).

VI.  But as it is a law of the Divine government, that wherever much is given, there also much is required, it follows that these superior privileges of the New Economy serve to increase very greatly the obligations of all who are permitted to enjoy them. And hence the Apostle again insists that the Hebrews should give the more earnest heed to the things which they have heard (verses 25-27);

1.  Because God himself was then speaking to them through his own Son from heaven; and not as he had formerly spoken to their fathers through Moses and angels from Mount Sinai (verse 25);

2.  Because they were then living, not under a preparatory dispensation, like the Jewish, but under the last dispensation of God's grace to fallen man; during which, God would so shake the world as to remove out of the way all antichristian powers, and make the Kingdom of Christ universal and perpetual (verses 26, 27).

VII.  Finally, he encourages them to persevere in serving God with reverence and godly fear,

1.  Because they had by the grace of God become citizens of a Kingdom which is immovable (verse 28).

2.  Because God himself is also unchangeable, and will prove to be a consuming fire to his enemies under the New Economy as well as under the Old (verse 29).

The first and second points of this analysis, though containing motives somewhat different, belong nevertheless to one and the same paragraph; and the same is also true of the fifth, sixth, and seventh points of division. And hence the whole section may be properly subdivided into paragraphs as follows:

I. 12: 1-3.—Exhortation and encouragement to the Hebrew brethren to persevere in their begun Christian course; (1) from the example and contemplated presence of the many faithful ones who had gone before them; and (2) from the example of Christ.

II. 12: 4-11.—Exhortation to endure their afflictions patiently; (1) in view of their comparative lightness; and (2) from the consideration that they were all the chastisements of God, designed for their own spiritual improvement.

III. 12: 12-17.—Exhortation to rouse themselves to more resolute and courageous perseverance in the Christian course; and following after peace and holiness, not to allow any cause of bitterness to spring up among themselves; lest some of them should, like the profligate Esau, discover too late the folly of renouncing their blood-bought privileges and birthrights.

IV. 12: 18-29.—Further warnings against apostasy, and exhortations to greater zeal and steadfastness in the Divine life; (1) from the superior honors and privileges of the New Covenant; (2) from the sovereign authority and righteous administration of Him who calls us; and (3) from the stability of the Kingdom which God has inaugurated for the salvation of those who love and serve him.

1. EXHORTATION AND ENCOURAGEMENT TO THE HEBREW BRETHREN TO PERSEVERE IN THEIR BEGUN CHRISTIAN COURSE; (1) FROM THE EXAMPLE AND CONTEMPLATED PRESENCE OF THE MANY FAITHFUL ONES WHO HAD GONE BEFORE THEM; AND (2) FROM THE EXAMPLE OF CHRIST
12: 1-3

1 Wherefore, seeing we also are compassed about with ¹so great a cloud of witnesses, ²let us lay aside every weight, and ³the sin which doth so easily beset us, and ⁴let us run with patience the race that is set before us,

¹Chap. xi. 2-38; Isa. lx. 8; Ezek. xxxviii. 9, 16.
²Matt. x. 37, 38; 2 Cor. vii. 1; Eph. iv. 22-32; Col. iii. 5-8; 1 Tim. vi. 9, 10.
³Chap. iii. 12, 19; iv. 1, 2, 11; x. 38; Matt. xiv. 30, 31; xvii. 20; John xvi. 9.
⁴1 Cor. ix. 24-27; Gal. v. 7; Phil. ii. 16; iii. 10-14; 2 Tim. ii. 4.

1 **Wherefore, seeing we also, etc.**—In the last section, the Apostle brought forward for the encouragement of his brethren, the example of many noble and faithful ones who, under the sever-

est trials, had run with patient endurance the race that was set before them.  And now returning to the line of exhortation commenced at 10: 19, but broken off at the close of the same chapter
(10: 39), he calls on his brethren in Christ to imitate the example
of those noble witnesses of the faith.  *Having,* he says; *such a
cloud of witnesses surrounding us, laying aside every superfluous
weight, and the sin which so easily besets us, let us also run with
patient endurance the race which is set before us.*

In this verse there is evident allusion to the games of the ancient
Greeks; or rather perhaps to those which Herod the Great had introduced into Palestine in imitation of the Grecian games.  See Josephus Ant. 15: 8; 15: 9, 6; 19: 7, 5; Bell. 1, 21, 8.  These games
consisted in such exercises as leaping, boxing, wrestling, throwing
the quoit, foot-races, horse-races, chariot races, etc.  The exercises
were performed in the arena of a vast amphitheatre, around which,
immense crowds of spectators, often amounting to from twenty-
five to one hundred thousand, were arranged on seats, rising high
one above another.  Corresponding with these assembled multitudes
of anxious spectators, is the "cloud of witnesses" by whom the Hebrew Christians are said to be surrounded while running their
race for the crown of life.  These crowned victors are here represented as a cloud on account of their immense numbers (Ezek. 38:
9, 16) as well perhaps as on account of their elevated position.

But why are they called *witnesses* (*martures*)?  Several answers have been given to this question.  (1) Some, as Lünemann,
supposes that they are so called simply from the fact, that in the
preceding chapter they all appear as "witnesses of faith."  They
have by their example borne honorable testimony with respect to
the nature, power, value, and sure rewards of faith. (2) Some, as
Bleek and Tholuck, take the word *witnesses* in the sense of *spectators* (*theatai*).  They think that these ancient worthies are called
witnesses simply because they are represented here as spectators of
the Christian conflict.  But (3) the majority of commentators
combine these two meanings.  They maintain that these faithful
ones are called witnesses (a) on account of the testimony which
they have ever borne as to the power and efficacy of faith and of
God's fidelity; and (b) on account of their being spectators of our
conduct in the arduous but honorable race which lies before us.
"Averse as we are in general," says Delitzsch, "to depart from the

simple sense of the text of Scripture, for the sake of making out a
multitude of meanings, so that 'the wood at last can hardly be seen
for the trees,' we feel that in the present case the double meaning
unmistakably obtrudes itself.  Those who were witnesses of faith
in the previous chapter, are turned by the word *surrounding* (*peri-
keimenon*) into witnesses of us in this: or rather the two applica-
tions of the word *martures* (witnesses) are in the writer's thought
and expression, inextricably combined."  I agree with Delitzsch,
Alford, Moll, and others, that the Apostle does represent these glorified saints, not only as witnesses of the faith, but also as spectators of our conduct.  But I think that in representing them as
spectators, gathered over and around us, he wishes to indicate that
these same champions of the faith will be witnesses for or against
us, according to the manner in which we deport ourselves in the
great conflict of life.  See Matt. 12: 41, 42.  The original word
(*martus*) never means merely a spectator (*theates*) ; it may, however, as in the case of the Apostle, denote one who sees and
hears with the view of bearing witness.

But in what sense are these witnesses of the faith and of our demeanor, spectators also of the Christian conflict? Is it in a literal
or in a metaphorical sense? On this question the commentators
are again divided. Alford says, "The words must be taken as dis-
tinctively implying community between the church triumphant and
the church below; that they who have entered into the heavenly
rest are conscious of what passes among ourselves. Any interpretation short of this leaves the exhortation tame and without point.
If they are merely quasi-witnesses, merely witnesses in a metaphor,
the motive, so far as this clause supplies one, is gone." The fact,
as here alleged by Alford, that the spirits of the just made perfect
are real witnesses of our conduct, is most likely correct. This is
certainly the most natural inference from our text, and it seems to
be supported by several parallel passages. See 1 Cor. 13: 12;
Heb. 13: 23; Rev. 6: 1, 3, 5, 7, etc. Still, I cannot agree with
this able, and in the main, judicious critic, that the metaphorical
interpretation supported by Macknight and others, is wholly pointless. It seems to me that even if the aforesaid ancient worthies
were wholly ignorant of our course and manner of life, the Apostle
might nevertheless by a bold rhetorical figure justly represent them
as quasi-witnesses of our conduct, in order to stimulate us to imi-

tate their noble example. See 1 Kings 22: 19-23; and Job 1: 6-12. I have not sufficient evidence, however, that any such figure is used in this case, and I therefore incline with Alford to the literal interpretation.

**let us lay aside every weight,**—In this clause the Apostle makes allusion particularly to those who run foot-races in the amphitheatre. These contestants laid aside everything that might in any way serve to impede their progress. The original word (*onkos*) means a weight, a burden, a swelling, an encumbrance, and it is evidently used here to denote whatever has a tendency to interrupt or retard our progress in the way of holiness; such as "the lusts of the flesh, the lusts of the eye, and the pride of life." All such hindrances the Apostle exhorts his brethren to lay aside, so that like the contestants in the Grecian games, they might be able to run with patient endurance the race that was set before them.

**and the sin which doth so easily beset us,**—That is, as the context plainly indicates, the sin of unbelief. This is the sin against which the Apostle warns his readers most particularly throughout the whole Epistle; and it is, moreover, the sin from which all other sins in a measure proceed, and by means of which they are ever more or less cherished and supported. When the Comforter is come, says Christ, he will convict the world "of sin, because they believe not on me." (John 16:9.) To put off the sin of unbelief is therefore in fact equivalent to putting off the old man with all his deceitful lusts, and putting on "the new man who, after God, is created in righteousness and true holiness." (Eph. 4: 22, 24; Col. 3: 9.) The qualifying epithet *euperistatos* does not occur elsewhere, either in the New Testament or in the Greek classics; but it is evident from the context as well as from the etymology of the word, that it means, as in our English version, easily besetting or surrounding. The temptations of the world, the flesh, and the devil, all serve to draw away our minds and hearts from God, and to make us trust more in the creature than in the Creator. And hence the constant tendency of unbelief to encircle us, and so to paralyze our spiritual energies as to make us faint by the way. That this is alarmingly true is abundantly evident from the history of God's ancient people and the church of Christ, as well as from our own daily experience and observation. The Apostle still draws his imagery from the race

2 [1]Looking unto Jesus [2]the author and [3]finisher of our faith; who [4]for the joy that was set before him [5]endured the cross, [6]despising the shame, and [7]is set down at the right hand of the throne of God.

[1]John i. 29; vi. 40; Titus ii. 13; 1 Pet. ii. 21.
[2]Ch. ii. 10; Acts. iii. 15; v. 31.
[3]Matt. xxv. 31-46; Phil. i. 6; Rev. xxii. 13.
[4]Ch. ii. 7-9; v. 9; Psa. xvi. 9-11; Isa. xlix. 6; John xii. 24-32; Phil. ii. 8-11; 1 Pet. i. 11.
[5]Ch. x. 5-12; Matt. xvi. 21; xx. 18, 19, 28; xxvii. 31-50.
[6]Psa. xxii. 6-8; lxix. 19, 20; Matt. xxvi. 67, 68; xxvii. 27-31, 38-44.
[7]Ch. i. 3; iv. 14; viii. 1; x. 12; Psa. cx. 1.

course, and seems to refer here to the custom of the contestants in laying aside even their inner garments, so that they might the more readily run with endurance the race that was set before them. So also the writer of our Epistle exhorts us to lay aside, in like manner, every superfluous weight, and especially the sin of unbelief, which, like a close-fitting garment, is ever liable to environ our whole persons, and so to paralyze our spiritual energies.

**let us run with patience the race that is set before us,**—The word rendered *patience* (*hupomone*) means here, endurance or perseverance. The object of the Apostle is not so much to exhort his brethren to bear the troubles and toils of life with patience, as it is to encourage them to persevere through all trials and difficulties even to the end. Since it is true he means to say in substance that so many illustrious patriarchs, prophets, kings, and martyrs, have preceded us in the way of holiness; and by perseverance in well-doing to the end of life have at length obtained the promised reward; therefore let us also, after their example, laying aside every superfluous weight, and especially the sin of unbelief run with patient endurance the Christian race, until, like our illustrious ancestors, we too reach the goal of victory and receive the crown of life.

2 **Looking unto Jesus, etc.**—The Apostle, in this verse, presents to his Hebrew brethren a second motive and ground of encouragement to persevere even to the end in their begun course. He exhorts them to run their race, not only as if in the presence of their illustrious ancestors, but while doing so he would have them also look off to Jesus the Leader and Perfecter of the faith; so that they might all be encouraged by his greatness and stimulated by his example. The word rendered *author* (*archegos*) means properly one who leads, or acts as principal in any given enterprise. It occurs in the New Testament only in Acts 3: 15; 5: 31; Heb. 2: 10, and in our text. In the first and also in the second instance,

it is rendered *prince;* in the third, *captain;* and in our text, *author.* The word rendered *finisher* (*teleiotes*) occurs nowhere else in the New Testament; but as its etymology indicates, it means a completer, perfecter, finisher; one who brings any scheme or enterprise to its full and perfect consummation. *"Our"* should be omitted and *the* inserted before the word *faith,* which is used here, as in many other parts of Scripture, to denote the Christian religion in its greatest fullness. See Acts 6:7; 13:8; Gal. 1:23; 3:23; and Jude 3. The object of the Apostle in introducing this clause is therefore manifestly twofold: (1) to encourage us by keeping constantly before our minds the fact that Jesus is himself the Leader and Perfecter of the faith, regarded as God's plan of justification, sanctification, and redemption; and (2) to fill us with his mind and temper, by keeping constantly before us his example as the very best possible illustration of the nature, power and efficacy of faith. For such was his trust in God and in the word of his grace, that he willingly endured the greatest sufferings and reproaches "for the joy that was set before him"; the joy of presently sitting down with the Father on his throne, and saving a world by means of his own death and mediation.

**endured the cross, despising the shame,**—It is difficult for anyone living in this age and country, to properly paraphrase this expression. We know indeed that the pains and sufferings of crucifixion must have been very great; but of the shame that was attached to it when Christ died for our sins, we can have no adequate conception. For as Mr. Barnes well remarks, "When we now think of the cross, it is not of the multitude of slaves, and thieves, and robbers, and rebels who have died on it, but of the one great victim, whose death has ennobled even this instrument of torture, and encircled it with a halo of glory. We have been accustomed to read of it as an imperial standard in war in the days of Constantine, and as the banner under which armies have marched to conquest. It is intermingled with the sweetest poetry; it is a sacred thing in the most magnificent cathedrals; it adorns the altar, and is even an object of adoration; it is in the most elegant engravings; it is worn by beauty and piety as an ornament near the heart; it is associated with all that is pure in love, great in self-sacrifice, and holy in religion." Before we can therefore feel and appreciate the full force of the Apostle's remark, we must remove

3 For ¹consider him that endured such contradiction of sinners against himself, ²lest ye be wearied and faint in your minds.

¹Ch. iii. 1; Matt. x. 24, 25; xii. 24; John viii. 46-49; 1 Pet. ii. 23.
²Deut. xx. 3; Prov. xxiv. 10; Isa. xl. 30, 31; 2 Cor. iv. 1, 16; Gal. vi. 9; 2 Thess. iii. 13.

---

from the cross "the halo of glory" which has so long encircled it, and we must place ourselves in such an attitude that we can see, and hear, and feel, as did the contemporaries of our blessed Lord: we must look upon it as an instrument of torture designed for the punishment and disgrace of only the lowest and vilest criminals. "There is," says the same pious author, "a degree of dishonor which is attached to the guillotine, but the ignominy of a death on the cross was greater than that: there is a disgrace attached to the block, but the ignominy of the cross was greater than that; there is a much deeper infamy attached to the gallows, but the ignominy of the cross was greater than that."    And yet such was Christ's zeal for the glory of God, and such was his regard for the recompense of the reward that was before him, that he willingly submitted to all the sufferings and reproaches through which he had to pass on his way to the throne of the Majesty in the heavens.   See notes on 1: 3 and 8: 1.

3 **For consider him that endured such contradiction, etc.**— "There is," says Bishop Sanderson, "scarce any other provocation to the performance of duty so prevailing with men as the example of such as have performed the same before them with glory and success."   Recognizing this well-attested fact, the Apostle would have his brethren, not only look off to Jesus as the Leader and Perfecter of the faith, but he would have them also carefully consider him as having meekly, patiently, perseveringly, and triumphantly borne "such contradiction of sinners against himself."   The word rendered *contradiction* (*antilogia*) means literally opposition by means of words and arguments, and it is so interpreted by some in this instance. But most expositors, as Chrysostom, Œcumenius, Theophylact, Delitzsch, and Alford, justly maintain that under this expression the Apostle includes all the opposition and persecution which Christ endured here from sinners, even to his agony on the cross.   For the contrary word often results in the contrary action; and hence it is that *antilogia* in its second intention means opposition of any kind. In John 19: 12, for instance, the cognate verb

(*antilegeo*) means not merely to contradict Caesar, but also to rebel against him. It is therefore to the suffering, bleeding, and dying Savior that Paul here especially calls the attention of his brethren.

**lest ye be wearied and faint in your minds.**—The Apostle has still in view the foot-races of the amphitheatre, and from them he continues to draw his metaphors. As the knees of the contestants in the ancient arena were apt to grow weary, so also it is with those who run in the Christian race. They, too, are apt to grow weary and faint in their minds. But as in the Greek stadium, a forward look to one who had won the prize, and who was then ready to crown other victors at the end of their race, was apt to inspire the athlete with fresh courage and energy, so also it is in our Christian race. When the soul is bowed down under the manifold trials and afflictions of this life nothing so much revives it as looking off to Jesus, and carefully considering him who endured such contradiction of sinner against himself. This, it seems, was one of Paul's chief means of gaining strength and support in all his trials and afflictions. He looked off constantly to Jesus, and became so inspired with his pious and heroic example, that he was even anxious to fill up in his own personal experience that which was "behind of the afflictions of Christ." (Col. 1 : 24.)

2. EXHORTATION TO ENDURE THEIR AFFLICTIONS
PATIENTLY, (1) IN VIEW OF THEIR COMPARATIVE
LIGHTNESS; AND (2) IN VIEW OF THE FACT
THAT THEY ARE ALL THE CHASTISEMENTS
OF GOD, DESIGNED FOR THEIR OWN
SPIRITUAL IMPROVEMENT
12 : 4-11

4 Ye have not yet [1]resisted unto blood, striving against sin.

[1]Ch. x. 32-34; Matt. xxiv. 9; John xvi. 2; Acts v. 33; vii. 56-60; viii. 1-3; ix. 1, 2; 1 Cor. x. 13; 2 Tim. iv. 6, 7.

4 **Ye have not yet resisted unto blood,**—There seems to be a change of metaphor here, as in 1 Cor. 9 : 24-27, from the agonistic race to the more severe contest of boxing. "In these games, the boxers were accustomed to arm themselves for the fight with the caestus. This at first consisted of strong leathern thongs wound around the hands and extending only to the wrist, to give greater solidity to the fist. Afterward, these were made to extend to the

5 And [1]ye have forgotten the exhortation which speaketh unto you as unto children, [2]My son, despise not thou the chastening of the Lord, nor [3]faint when thou art rebuked of him:

[1]Deut. iv. 9, 10; Matt. xvi. 9, 10; Luke xxiv. 6-8.
[2]Job v. 17, 18; xxxiv. 31; Psa. xciv. 12; cxix. 67, 71, 75; Prov. iii. 11, 12; Jer. xxxi. 18; 1 Cor. xi. 22; 2 Cor. iv. 17.
[3]2 Sam. vi. 7-10; 2 Cor. iv. 8, 9; xii. 9, 10.

elbow, and then to the shoulder, and finally they sowed pieces of lead or iron in them, that they might strike a heavier and more destructive blow. The consequence was that those who were engaged in the fight were often covered with blood and that resistance unto blood showed a determination, courage, and purpose not to yield" (A. Barnes). The contest of the Hebrews had not as yet assumed this severe form. They had not yet resisted unto blood, striving against sin. Their Christian profession had not yet cost them their lives. Stephen, James, and many others had resisted unto blood; but it is only of the living members of the Jerusalem Church that our author here speaks. The persons addressed in this Epistle had not yet been called on to suffer what Christ and many others had endured for the sake of the truth. And hence as their afflictions were yet comparatively light, they were the more inexcusable for their timidity and cowardice.

**striving against sin.**—Sin is here personified; and is supposed by many to be equivalent to sinners, the abstract being used merely for the concrete. But this is to sacrifice much both of the meaning and energy of the expression. It is not only of sin in others, but also of sin in ourselves that our author speaks. He himself found it necessary to strive against the depravity of his own nature, as well as against the enemies of the truth, in battling for the crown of life. (1 Cor. 9: 27.) And so also does everyone else, who like him would strive successfully in the arena of life.

5 **And ye have forgotten the exhortation, etc.**—Commentators are much divided on the question, whether this clause should be read affirmatively or interrogatively. See note on 3: 16. The former view is taken by all the ancient expositors, and also by many of the moderns; as, for instance, Bengel, Kuinoel, Tholuck, Ebrard, and Alford; and the latter is maintained by Calvin, Beza, Braun, Böhme, Lachmann, Delitzsch, Stuart, Bleek, Lünemann, Macknight, and others; chiefly on the ground that the declarative mode has an air of too great severity and harshness. But this expression

6 For ¹whom the Lord loveth he chasteneth, and ²scourgeth every son whom he receiveth.

¹Deut. viii. 5; Psa. lxxiii. 14, 15; Jas. i. 12; v. 11; Rev. iii. 19.
²2 Sam. vii. 14.

is no more harsh and severe than some others that occur in the Epistle; see, for instance, 5 : 11, 12. It is not to be supposed, however, that in either of these cases, the charge is preferred against all the members of the Church. See note on 5 : 12. Many of them may have remained faithful, and may have been striving earnestly for the faith which was once for all delivered to the saints. But that some of them had become very negligent in the study of God's word, and the discharge of their other Christian duties, is quite evident from what follows, as well as from other parts of the Epistle. "You have quite forgotten," says the Apostle, "the exhortation which discourses with you as with children." And in consequences of this neglect, he further intimates that the hands of some of them were hanging down; that their knees had become feeble; and that they were, in fact, in great danger of apostatizing from the faith.

**My son, despise not thou the chastening of the Lord,**—The Apostle quotes here from Prov. 3 : 11, 12, the Hebrew of which may be literally rendered as follows: My son, despise not the correction of Jehovah, and do not murmur at his reproof: for whom Jehovah loves he reproves, as a father a son in whom he delights. Our author quotes freely, but accurately, from the original. His object is to still further encourage his brethren, by showing from the Old Testament Scriptures, that the light afflictions which they were then enduring, were really evidences, not of God's anger, but of his love. They served to indicate that God had still a tender regard for them, and that he was dealing with them as with children. The word rendered *chastening* (*paideia*) means such correction and discipline as are necessary in the education of children, and such as the Lord himself uses for the spiritual improvement of his people. This chastening of the Lord, the Apostle exhorts his brethren not to despise or treat as a light matter; and on the other hand, not to be too much discouraged or dejected by it.

6 **For whom the Lord loveth he chasteneth,**—In this verse we have given the reason why we should not, on the one hand, treat lightly the chastening of the Lord; nor on the other be too

7 | If ye ³endure chastening: *At chastening be enduring* | , God dealeth with you as with sons; ⁴for what son is he whom the father chasteneth not?

³Job xxxiv. 31, 32; Prov. xxii. 15; xxiii. 13, 14; xxix. 15, 17; Acts xiv. 22.
⁴1 Sam. ii. 29; iii. 15; Prov. xxix. 15.

greatly dejected by it. The simple fact that this chastening is from God, makes it a very grave and momentous matter; and at the same time it gives us the assurance that the chastening is not the punishment of revenge but the discipline of love. "For whom the Lord loveth he chasteneth, and scourgeth every son whom he receiveth." Not that he does this arbitrarily or unnecessarily: for God does not willingly grieve nor afflict any of the children of men. (Lam. 3 : 33; Hos. 11 : 8.) But such is the common depravity and waywardness of our nature, that we all need this discipline; and God, therefore, as our ever-kind and gracious Educator metes out to us day by day such trials and afflictions as will best serve to humble and purify our hearts, and so to work out for us "a far more exceeding and eternal weight of glory." (2 Cor. 4 : 17.) No child of God need, therefore, expect to enter heaven without, on his way thither, passing through the furnace of afflictions. "We must through much tribulation enter into the kingdom of God." (Acts 14 : 22.)

7 **If ye endure chastening:**—That is, if it is a fact that you are suffering chastisement, this of itself is evidence that God is dealing with you as his children: for what son is there whom his earthly father does not chastise? How then can you expect, as the children of God, to escape his correction? Such is manifestly the meaning of the reading given in the Textus Receptus and our English Version: a reading which is supported by Reiche, Bleek, Lünemann, Stuart, Bloomfield, and Tischendorf in his latest editions; on the ground that it is best supported by internal evidence, and especially that it is required by the antithesis that is given in the seventh and eighth verses. The force of this will appear from the following paraphrase of these two verses as given by Kuinoel, and followed by Bloomfield and others: "If you have to conflict with trials and tribulations, you may thence infer that you are beloved of God, and that he takes care of you: but if you are exercised with no afflictions, you have reason to fear that God neglects you, as men neglect illegitimate children, of whose education and morals they take no care, leaving them wholly without chastisement."

8 But if ye be ¹without chastisement, whereof all are partakers, then are
ye bastards, and not sons.

9 Furthermore, we have had ²fathers of our flesh which corrected us, and
³we gave them reverence: ⁴shall we not much rather be in subjection unto
⁵the Father of spirits, and live?

¹Psa. lxxiii. 14, 15; 1 Pet. v. 9, 10.
²Gen. v. 3; vi. 3, 12; Job xiv. 4; Psa. li. 10; John iii. 6; Acts ii. 30; Rom. vii. 5, 18;
viii. 8; ix. 3, 5; Gal. v. 16-21; Col. ii. 11.
³Ex. xx. 12; Lev. xix. 3; Deut. xxi. 18-21; Prov. xxx. 17; Eph. vi. 1-4.
⁴Mal. i. 6; Jas. iv. 7, 10; 1 Pet. v. 6.
⁵Num. xvi. 22; xxvii. 16; Job xii. 10; Eccl. xii. 7; Isa. xlii. 5; lvii. 16; Zech. xii. 1.

This makes good sense, and harmonizes well with the context and
design of the writer. But it must be confessed that the external
evidence preponderates vastly in favor of substituting *eis* (*into,
for*) for *ei* (*if*). See critical note. But to make sense of this reading has somewhat perplexed the critics. T. S. Green renders the
phrase as in the amended text: *"At chastening, be enduring* (*eis
paideian hupomenete*); as with sons God is dealing with you;
for what son is there whom a father does not chasten? The Vulgate renders it thus: "With a view to chastening, endure patiently." And Alford, following Chrysostom, Delitzsch, and others, translates it as follows: "It is for chastisement that ye are enduring: as with sons God is dealing with you: for what son is
there whom a father chasteneth not?" The paraphrase of Chrysostom is to the point, and seems to indicate clearly the scope of the
passage. "It is for chastisement ye are enduring: not for punishment, not for torment, not for any evil purpose." This rendering
of the amended text differs but little in sense from the reading of
the Textus Receptus, and is most likely correct.

8 **But if ye be without chastisement, etc.**—If ye be without
that discipline of which all the children of God have ever been
partakers, it would follow that ye are really not his children: but
that ye are bastards (*nothoi*), an illegitimate offspring, whose education is commonly neglected, much to their own injury and disgrace. Instead, therefore, of murmuring and complaining at the
chastening of the Lord, you should rather feel encouraged by it,
knowing that it is evidence of your sonship, and of God's love for
you as his adopted children.

9 **Furthermore, we have had fathers of our flesh, etc.**—Or
thus: Then again, the fathers of our flesh we once had as chastis-
ers, and we reverenced them; shall we not much rather be in sub-

jection to the Father of Spirits, and live? See Deut. 21: 18-21, touching the penalty of the law for disobedience to parents.

The only matter that requires explanation in this verse, is the use of the words *flesh* and *spirit*. In what sense are our earthly fathers said to be the fathers of our flesh? and in what sense is God said to be the Father of spirits? In reply to this query, we have given the following hypotheses: (1) It is said that we receive our bodies from our parents by natural generation; but that our spirits are the direct gift of God, formed by his own immediate creative energy (Primasius, Calvin, Beza, Bengel, Wetstein, Delitzsch). This hypothesis requires us to use both these words, flesh and spirit, in too limited a sense. The Apostle does not say that God is the Father of *"our"* spirits merely, but *"of spirits"* in general. And there is nothing in either the text or the context which limits the word *"flesh"* simply to our bodies. This term is commonly used in a much wider sense in the Holy Scriptures. See references. (2) That God is the author and originator of our spiritual life, as our parents are of our natural life. "Flesh," says Ebrard, "denotes here as always the natural life produced by creature powers, in opposition to the life which is produced by the saving gracious act of God in regeneration. By natural generation we become carnal or fleshly men; but it is God who, by his Holy Spirit, causes our souls (*psuchai*) to be developed into sanctified spirits (*pneumata*). Such is also the interpretation of Cramer, Grotius, Bleek, De Wette, Lünemann, and others. But here again both the words are used in a sense which is not warranted by their usual acceptation in the Scriptures. (3) Others again, as Morus, Kuinoel, and Böhme, think that the word *father,* as used in this connection, means simply "an upholder" or "cherisher." God is called the Father of spirits, say they, "because he takes care of our spirits and provides for our spiritual wants, as our earthly parents provide for our physical wants." This is, of course, true, as far as it goes; but like the other hypotheses it falls far short of being an adequate explanation of the passage.

The words *flesh* and *spirits* must be understood and interpreted in harmony with the context and the special object of the writer, which is manifestly to give another reason why the Hebrew brethren should bear with patient endurance whatever trials and afflictions God might send on them: a reason which he draws from a comparison of God and his chastisements with our earthly parents and their chastisements. God, he argues, is infinitely perfect; and his chastisements are all like himself in this respect, that they are wise, and just, and good. But our earthly parents are like ourselves, frail, weak, and sinful; often erring in their attempts to educate us as well as in everything else. We, however, bore their imperfect chastisements with patience and reverence; much more then should we now bear with grateful resignation the wise and gracious chastisements of him who never errs, but who always corrects us for our own good, with the view of making us partakers of his holiness. This is manifestly the purpose of the author in the use of this passage; and hence it seems that he uses the words *flesh* and *spirits,* in this connection, after the manner of the Hebrews, chiefly as qualifying epithets. That in the use of the word *"father"* he intends to convey the idea of origin and also of guardianship is, I think, quite obvious. But like produces like. "Adam begat a son in his own likeness" (Gen. 5 : 3) ; and Christ says to the Jews, "If ye were the children of Abraham ye would do the works of Abraham" (John 8 : 39), clearly recognizing the relation of resemblance between the parent and the child, between the producer and the thing produced. Now as this principle was well understood by the Hebrews, it was perfectly natural that the Apostle should use these words, *flesh* and *spirit,* according to the well known Hebrew idiom, as genitives of quality, to express with energy and brevity the attributes of our earthly parents on the one hand, and of God on the other. For throughout the Bible, the word *flesh* is often used symbolically to denote what is depraved, weak, or sinful; and so also the word *spirit* is often used in contrast with it, to denote what is pure, holy, and perfect. "That which is born of the flesh," says Christ, "is flesh; and that which is born of the Spirit is spirit." (John 3 : 6.) See also Rom. 8 : 4-9; Gal. 5 : 16-25; 6 : 8, etc. The word *flesh,* then, in this connection is designed to indicate mainly that our earthly fathers are like ourselves, carnal, frail, sinful mortals; and like ourselves they are therefore ever liable to err in their discipline. But the word *spirits,* as here applied to God, denotes that he has none of the weaknesses and infirmities of the flesh (see note on 1 : 7) ; but that being himself, not only spirit (John 4 : 24), but also the Father of spirits, he cannot like our earthly fathers err in his chastisements. They are all the gifts and offspring of his

10 For they verily for a few days chastened us after their own pleasure, but ¹he for our profit, that we might be ²partakers of his holiness.

¹Psa. cxix. 67, 71, 75; 2 Cor. iv. 17.
²Eph. iv. 24; Col. i. 22; 1 Pet. i. 15, 16.

love, designed to make us wiser and better, so that we may become partakers of his holiness.

If I am right in this explanation, it follows that our text furnishes no grounds whatever for the doctrine of creationism, which many attempt to draw from it. It is not the purpose of our author to make known to us in this connection the origin of either the body or the spirit of man. God is as really the Creator of the one as he is of the other. At first they were both formed miraculously; but for aught that appears in our text, they may now be equally the product of natural generation, under the all-pervading, permeating, and gracious providence of Him in "whom we live, and move, and have our being." (Acts 17 : 28.)

10 **For they verily for a few days, etc.**—What does the author mean by the phrase, *"for a few days"* (*pros oligas hemeras*)? Does he mean the time during which our fathers, according to the flesh, exercised their authority over us; that is, during our minority? Or does he mean that their discipline had reference chiefly to the few days of our present earthly life; while the chastisements of God have supreme reference to our eternal welfare? The former, say Luther, Grotius, Bleek, Macknight, Stuart, Delitzsch, and Alford; the latter, say Calvin, Calmet, Bengel, Tholuck, and Ebrard. The construction is elliptical; and it is therefore difficult to determine with absolute certainty what are the exact points of the antithesis which our author intends to express. But to my mind the former view seems much more natural, and also more in harmony with the scope of the passage than the latter. Our earthly parents corrected us (1) for a little while, and then left us to our own erring judgment. But not so with God; he never leaves us; never forsakes us; but always watches over us, and when necessary corrects us. (2) Our fathers often erred during even the few days that we were subject to them; they corrected us according to what then seemed good in their own eyes. But God never errs: he always corrects us for our own good, with the view of making us partakers of his holiness.

We have then given in this paragraph three leading reasons why

11 Now ¹no chastening for the present seemeth to be joyous, but grievous: nevertheless afterward ²it yieldeth the peaceable fruit of righteousness unto them ³which are exercised thereby.

¹Psa. lxxxix. 32; Prov. xv. 10; xix. 18.
²Isa. xxxii. 17; Rom. v. 3-5; 2 Cor. iv. 17; Gal. v. 22, 23; Jas. iii. 17, 18.
³Chap. v. 14; 1 Tim. iv. 7, 8.

we should, with patient resignation, humbly submit to the Divine chastisements: (1) they all proceed from the love and benevolence of God: "Whom the Lord loves he chastens, and scourges every son whom he receives." (2) They come from one who is himself infinitely perfect, and who is in no respect subject to the weaknesses and imperfections of our carnal nature. (3) They are all intended for our highest good, and serve to make us partakers of the Divine nature, by helping us to escape the corruption that is in the world through lust. (2 Pet. 1:4.) This thought our author now proceeds to develop more fully in the following verse.

11 **Now no chastening for the present, etc.**—"This," says Ebrard, "is a precious verse, of which the only proper commentary is our own personal experience." Now all chastisement for the present seemeth to be a matter not of joy but of grief. This much the Apostle here concedes as a simple and acknowledged fact. All chastisement, both human and Divine, gives us present pain. This is its object; and without pain there can indeed be no chastisement. And hence it is for the time being, a matter not of joy but of grief. So we all feel and think.

**nevertheless afterward it yieldeth the peaceable fruit of righteousness**—Though it is at first bitter to the taste, it nevertheless afterward becomes a tree of life which yields constantly "the peaceable fruit of righteousness." That is, it produces righteousness as its fruit; and this fruit gives peace and consolation to the once grieved and troubled soul. "It is," says Tholuck, "fruit of righteousness to be enjoyed in peace after the conflict is over."

**unto them which are exercised thereby.**—Not to all; but only to those who are well exercised by it. The training of the ancient palaestra was of no service to such athletes as, deeming it a life of toil and drudgery, refused to submit to the rules and regulations of the contest. But to the victors in the games, the crown of olive pine, laurel, or parsley, was a boon of very great value. And just so it is in the school of Christ. To those who are of a perverse and rebellious spirit, the discipline of the Master is but "a savor of death unto death." Instead of softening and sanctifying the hearts of such persons, it only serves to make them more obstinate and rebellious. But to those who see in it the kind and gracious hand of God, it never fails to bring peace, joy, and consolation. So the purest and best of men have always testified. David says, "Before I was afflicted I went astray: but now I keep thy word." And again he says in the same connection, "It is good for me that I have been afflicted, that I might learn thy statutes." (Psalm 119: 67, 71.) To the same effect is also the testimony of Paul in several of his other Epistles. Writing to the Romans he says, "We glory in tribulations also: knowing that tribulation worketh patience; and patience, experience; experience, hope: and hope maketh not ashamed, because the love of God is shed abroad in our hearts by the Holy Ghost which is given unto us." (Rom. 5: 3-5.) And in his second Epistle to the Corinthians he says, "Our light affliction, which is but for a moment, worketh for us a far more exceeding and eternal weight of glory." (2 Cor. 4: 17.) This is all in harmony with our own blessed experience in the Divine life. We never feel that we have suffered too much or too severely from the hand of God.

3. THE HEBREW BRETHREN ARE EXHORTED TO ROUSE
THEMSELVES TO MORE RESOLUTE AND COURAGEOUS
PERSEVERANCE IN THEIR CHRISTIAN COURSE; AND
FOLLOWING AFTER PEACE AND HOLINESS, NOT TO
ALLOW ANY CAUSE OF BITTERNESS AND STRIFE
TO SPRING UP AMONG THEMSELVES, LEST PER-
ADVENTURE SOME OF THEM, LIKE THE PROF-
LIGATE ESAU, SHOULD DISCOVER TOO LATE
THAT THEY HAD FOREVER FORFEITED THEIR
BIRTHRIGHTS AS THE CHILDREN OF GOD.
12: 12-17

12 Wherefore ¹lift up the hands which hang down, and the feeble knees;

¹Job iv. 3, 4; Isa. xxxv. 3; Nah. ii. 10; 1 Thess. v. 14.

12 **Wherefore lift up the hands, etc.**—That is, since it is true that afflictions are the chastisements of the Lord, designed for your own greatest good, you should from this take courage and bring to their right position the relaxed hands and the paralyzed knees of the inner man. These words are cited from Isa. 35: 3, and may denote weariness arising from any cause whatever. Most exposi-

13 And ²make straight paths for your feet, lest that which is ³lame be turned out of the way; but ⁴let it rather be healed.

²Prov. iv. 26, 27; Isa. xxxv. 8-10; xl. 3, 4; Jer. xviii. 15; Luke iii. 5.
³Isa. xxxv. 6; Jer. xxxi. 8, 9.
⁴Gal. vi. 1; Jude 22, 23.

tors agree that there is an allusion here to the ancient palaestra. But as Isaiah in the prophecy quoted has reference (1) to the Jews on their return from Babylon to Jerusalem, and (2) to Christians on their way to the heavenly Jerusalem, it is more probable that Paul, in quoting and applying the words of the Prophet, draws his imagery simply from the case of weary travelers. His meaning is, however, in either case the same. He calls on the strong to strengthen and encourage the weak; and on the weak to take fresh courage and run their race with patient perseverance, in view of the fact that God is with them, caring for them, and sanctifying even their greatest afflictions to their good.

13 **And make straight paths for your feet,**—The writer has still before him the image of a company of persons marching onward to the heavenly Jerusalem. Some of them are lame, weak, and much disheartened by reason of the many obstacles in the way. And in order if possible to save such, the Apostle admonishes his stronger and more courageous brethren to make the paths of all straight and smooth, so that even the lame might be encouraged by the directness and evenness of the way, to persevere in it to the end. The same sentiment is forcibly presented in the fourteenth chapter of Romans; and it is also frequently and variously illustrated in the last great division of the prophecies of Isaiah (chapters 40-66). In this section the prophet has reference, as in the thirty-fifth chapter, (1) to the return of the Jews from Babylon to Jerusalem, under Zerubbabel; and (2) to the more sublime march of the redeemed, under Christ, from the captivity of sin and Satan to the free enjoyments of the heavenly Jerusalem. In this march, both Paul and Isaiah insist that there should be no meanderings in the ways of sin; and that no obstacles should be left as stumblingblocks in the way of the weak; but that the course of all should be straightforward in the King's highway of holiness. The voices of many harbingers should still be heard proclaiming before the King's army, "Prepare ye the way of the Lord; make straight in the desert a highway for our God." (Isa. 40: 3.) See also Isa. 43:

14 [1]Follow peace with all men, [2]and holiness, [3]without which no man shall see the Lord:

[1]Psa. xxxiv. 14; Rom. xii. 18; xiv. 19; Gal. v. 22, 23; Eph. iv. 1-8.
[2]Rom. vi. 22; 2 Cor. vi. 17; vii. 1; 1 Thess. iv. 7; 1 Pet. i. 15, 16.
[3]Matt. v. 8; Gal. v. 21; Eph. v. 5.

19, 20; 49: 9-12; 62: 10, 11. Such proclamations are strengthening and encouraging to all; and might serve to help even the weak and dejected to persevere in their onward march to the everlasting Zion.

14 **Follow peace with all men,**—There is no noun expressed in the orignal corresponding with the word *"men"*; and it may therefore be a question whether we should supply the word *"men,"* as in our English Version, or the word *"brethren,"* as is done by Michaelis, Storr, Tholuck, Bleek, Ebrard, Delitzsch, Alford, and others. "Individual believers," says Delitzsch, "are exhorted to cherish peaceful relations with all the members of the community, even with the lame, sick, and weak. The improvement of such is to be aimed at, not by carnal contention, harsh acts of judgment, and uncharitable avoidance of their society; nor yet by merely setting them a good example in the purity and decision of our own conduct, while coldly waiting for the first advance on their side towards mutual explanation or agreement; but by *pursuing peace* on our own part; that is, by earnest active endeavors after a good understanding, and pursuing or hunting after peace as a noble prey or object of search." This is all good and excellent as far as it goes. But I see no sufficient reason for limiting this course of action simply to "the brethren." The peace and prosperity of the Church may depend largely on the demeanor of its members toward those that are without, as well as toward one another. And I therefore think with Œcumenius, Theophylact, Böhme, Lünemann, Macknight, Clarke, and others, that the reference is to "all men," whether believers or unbelievers. The Apostle well knew that the Hebrew brethren, by living harmlessly and giving no unnecessary offense to either Jews or Gentiles, might greatly promote the peace and prosperity of the Church: and hence he exhorts them, as he does the Roman brethren, to live peaceably with all men as far as possible: that is, as far as the law of Christ will permit. He would have us imitate Christ in this respect, as well as in everything else.

**and holiness,**—The original word (*hagiasmos*) is a verbal

15 Looking diligently [1]lest any man fail of the grace of God; [2]lest any root of bitterness springing up [3]trouble you, and [4]thereby many be defiled;

[1]Chap. vi. 4-6; x. 26-29; Luke xxii. 32; 1 Cor. x. 1-12.
[2]Deut. xxix. 18; xxxii. 32; Isa. v. 4, 7; Jer. ii. 21; Matt. vii. 15-20.
[3]Josh. vi. 18; vii. 25, 26.
[4]Ex. xxxii. 21; Acts xx. 30, 31; 1 Cor. v. 6; 2 Tim. ii. 16, 17; 2 Pet. ii. 1, 2, 18.

noun, and denotes the putting on of the Divine holiness (*hagiotes*), or the becoming partakers of it, as indicated in the tenth verse. Our depraved nature is prone to resist the injurious; and in times of war and persecution, men are apt to follow after strife and contention. But the advice of the Apostle is quite different. Pursue peace, he says, and earnestly follow after a pure and holy life.

**without which no man shall see the Lord:**—That is, without which holiness or sanctity of life, no one shall be admitted into God's presence so as to enjoy his favor and fellowship. (Matt. 5: 8.) "For what fellowship hath righteousness with unrighteousness? and what communion hath light with darkness?" and what sympathy and concord can there be between an infinitely holy God and an impure human spirit? Like loves its like in Heaven, Earth, and Hell. And hence the earnest exhortation of God to all who would enjoy his fellowship: "Become ye holy, for I am holy." (1 Pet. 1: 16.)

15 **Looking diligently**—(*epispopountes*) *observing carefully*. This is an exhortation, not merely to the overseers (*episkopoi*) of the Hebrew Church, but also to all its other members. The Apostle calls on every one of them to carefully examine his own heart and life, while he at the same time exercises a prudent and judicious oversight over his brethren.

**lest any man fail of the grace of God;**—"The image," says Chrysostom, "is taken from a company of travelers, one of whom lags behind, and so never reaches the end of the long and laborious journey." Those who do so, fail of course to secure the promised reward: for they only who endure to the end shall be saved. Stuart very happily expresses the idea of the Apostle, in its proper connection, as follows: "See well to it, that no one fail of obtaining that Divine favor which is the result of holiness."

**lest any root of bitterness, etc.**—We have here given another example of Hebrew parallelism. In the preceding clause, the Apostle admonishes his brethren to take heed and watch carefully, lest any one by lagging behind on the King's highway of holiness,

16 Lest there be ¹any fornicator, or profane person, ²as Esau, who for one morsel of meat sold his birthright.

¹1 Cor. v. 1-6; vi. 15, 20; Gal. v. 19-21; 1 Tim. i. 9.
²Gen. xxv. 27-34; xxvii. 36.

---

should fail to reach the portals of the celestial city; and so fall short of the grace of God. But in this second member of the parallelism, he goes a step further, and cautions his brethren to see well to it, that no one, like Achan (Josh. 7 : 25, 26), by his evil example trouble and defile the whole Church. Our author seems to have reference here to Deut. 29 : 16-21, where Moses admonishes his brethren to beware of the sin of idolatry; "Lest," he says, "there should be among you man, or woman, or tribe, whose heart turneth away from the Lord our God, to go and serve the gods of those nations; lest there should be among you *a root that beareth gall and wormwood;* and it come to pass, when he heareth the words of this curse, that he bless himself in the heart, saying, I shall have peace, though I walk in the imagination of mine heart, to add drunkenness to thirst." Paul's root of bitterness, then, is one which, as Moses says, "beareth gall and wormwood." The metaphor is used here to denote anyone who is himself bitterly opposed to the faith of the Gospel, and who labors to turn others from its simplicity and purity. Such a man not unfrequently troubles and defiles a whole congregation by his evil example and false principles. In 1 Macc. 1 : 10, Antiochus Epiphanes is called a *sinful root (riza hamartolos)* because from him iniquity sprung up all over the land, as a luxuriant crop of vegetables.

16 **Lest there be any fornicator, etc.**—This is but an amplification of the admonitory lesson given in the preceding verse. See to it, says the Apostle, that no one by falling behind from any cause whatever, come short of the grace of God; and particularly, that no one apostatize from the faith, and so corrupt others by his bad example and false principles; and furthermore, that no one be so given up to the lusts of the flesh and to the neglect of spiritual things, that like the licentious and profane Esau, he will barter away his birthright as a child of God for a mere mess of pottage. The word *fornicator (pornos)* is to be taken in its literal sense, as denoting one who is given up to sensual lusts and pleasures; and the word *profane (bebelos)* means one who is regardless of God and of his religion. Both words are descriptive of one and the

17 For ye know how that afterward, [1]when he would have inherited the blessing, he was rejected: [2]for he found no place of repentance, though he sought it carefully with tears.

[1]Gen. xxvii. 31-41.
[2]Chap. vi. 4-6; x. 26-29.

same person, viewed from different standpoints: for the abandoned fornicator is always a profane person; and the man who throws off all the restraints of religion, is sure to indulge in all manner of carnal excesses. Esau was no doubt both a fornicator and a profane person. This view is most in harmony with the plain and obvious meaning of the text, as well as with the traditions of the Jews.

**who for one morsel of meat sold his birthright.**—The account of this is given in Gen. 25: 27-34, to which the reader is referred for a plain statement of the facts. Such was the abandoned and profligate state of Esau's mind, that for one meal he sold his rights of primogeniture (*ta prototokia heautou*). These may be best understood by a comparison of the fortunes of Jacob and Esau with their descendants. They evidently involve the rights and privileges of the Abrahamic covenants with respect to both the possession of Canaan and the birth of the Messiah.

17 **For ye know how that afterward, etc.**—Esau, as we have seen, sold his rights of primogeniture to his brother Jacob for a mess of pottage; and afterward, when he wished to obtain the blessing, which was really a part of what he had sold, he was rejected by both his father and his God (Gen. 27: 31-41): for the blessing of Isaac was in this case the blessing of God.

**for he found no place of repentance,**—What is the meaning of this? Does the Apostle mean repentance on the part of Esau, or on the part of his father Isaac? The *former,* say Luther, Calvin, Grotius, Bengel, DeWette, Hofmann, Delitzsch, Alford, and all the ancient Greek expositors: the *latter,* say Beza, Tholuck, Ebrard, Lünemann, Stuart, Macknight, and most of the other modern expositors. In either case the main lesson taught is about the same. For whatever construction be put on the several words of this sentence, it must be obvious that the object of the Apostle is to remind his readers, that the mistake of Esau, once committed, was committed forever: that no possible change of his mind could in any way effect a change in the mind and purposes of God. We might, therefore, without doing violence to the scope of the argu-

ment, refer the word *repentance* (*metanoia*) to either Esau himself
or to Isaac as God's representative. But with the ancient expositors, I prefer the reference to Isaac, (1) because this is required
by the literal meaning of the word *repentance,* which properly denotes a change of mind produced by sorrow for sin; and (2) because the phrase *"place of repentance,"* means properly a place
where the repentance of the sinner is made available. Whenever a
sinner believes and repents, he is brought within the sphere of
God's forgiving mercy. God can now, for Christ's sake, pardon and
justify him, because he has come within the sphere of true and genuine repentance. But to this place of repentance on the part of the
sinner, and of mercy on the part of God, the apostate has no access
(see notes on 6 : 4-6) ; and neither had Esau, so far as respects his
forfeited birthrights. That he may have afterward repented of his
sins, and so obtained forgiveness, is I think possible; but not so
with regard to his despised birthrights. These had by one foolish
and irreligious act, been irrecoverably lost. This, the Hebrews
well understood; and hence the Apostle holds up this case as an
example of warning to them, while he cautions them to beware lest
they too by their negligence and folly should forfeit their birthrights as the children of God, and so place themselves beyond the
divinely prescribed limits of repentance.

   **though he sought it carefully with tears.**—Sought what?
Many able expositors, as Chrysostom, Grotius, Luther, Ebrard,
and Alford, refer the pronoun *it* (*auten*) to repentance as its antecedent: but it is better with Calvin, Bengel, Bleek, Hofmann,
Macknight, Delitzsch, and others, to make *blessing* (*eulogian*) the
antecedent. Esau had his heart set on receiving the blessing; and
it was this that he sought so earnestly with tears. The whole sentence may therefore be construed and arranged according to our
English idiom, as follows: For ye know that even when afterward
he wished to inherit the blessing, though he sought it earnestly
with tears, he was rejected; for he found no place of repentance.
Or the order of the original may be preserved as in the English
Version, by simply enclosing the words, "for he found no place of
repentance" in a parenthesis.

4. FURTHER WARNINGS AGAINST APOSTASY, AND EX-
HORTATIONS TO GREATER ZEAL AND STEADFASTNESS
IN THE DIVINE LIFE, (1) FROM THE SUPERIOR HONORS
AND PRIVILEGES OF THE NEW COVENANT; (2) FROM
THE SOVEREIGN AUTHORITY AND RIGHTEOUS AD-
MINISTRATION OF HIM WHO CALLS US; AND (3)
FROM THE STABILITY OF THE KINGDOM WHICH
GOD HAS INAUGURATED FOR THE SALVATION
OF THOSE WHO SERVE HIM
12: 18-29

18 For ¹ye are not come unto | the mount that: *that which* | might be touched, and that burned with fire, nor unto blackness, and darkness, and tempest,

19 And ²the sound of a trumpet, and ³the voice of words; which voice ⁴they that heard intreated that the word should not be spoken to them any more:

¹Ex. xix. 12-19; xx. 18; xxiv. 17; Deut. iv. 11; v. 22-26.
²Ex. xix. 16, 19; 1 Cor. xv. 52; 1 Thess. iv. 16.
³Ex. xx. 1-17; Deut. v. 3-22.
⁴Ex. xx. 19; Deut. v. 24-27.

18 **For ye are not come, etc.**—*"For"* connects this verse with what precedes. Ye should, says the writer, look to it diligently that no one fall short of the grace of God; that no root of bitterness spring up to trouble you, and so to defile the many, and that there be among you no such licentious and profane person as Esau: for your privileges and responsibilities under the New Covenant are greatly superior to those of your fathers under the Old Covenant. For ye have not come near to the mountain that is tangible [material, and so capable of being touched], and that burned with fire; and to blackness, and darkness, and tempest, etc. The word mountain (*orei*) is not expressed in our best manuscripts, but it is manifestly understood.

Some expositors take the words *mountain, fire, blackness, dark-ness,* and *tempest,* as indicating so many separate and distinct ob-jects of approach. Thus, "Ye have not come near to a tangible mountain, and to a kindled fire, and to blackness, and to darkness, and to a tempest," etc. The construction is ambiguous, but the rendering of our English Version is more in harmony with the parallel passage given in Deut. 4: 11, to which our author here evi-dently refers. See also Deut. 5: 23; 9: 15. In all these parallel passages, "flaming fire" is taken as an attribute of the mountain, and not as a separate object.

19 **And the sound of a trumpet,**—The several clauses of this verse are best illustrated by the following brief extracts from the

20 (For they could not endure that which was commanded, [1]And if so much as a beast touch the mountain, it shall be stoned [or thrust through

[1]Ex. xix. 12, 13.

---

original narrative as given in Exodus: "And it came to pass on the third day [that is, say the Jews, on the sixth day of the month Sivan, just fifty days after the Exodus] in the morning, that there were thunderings and lightnings, and a thick cloud upon the mount, and the voice of the trumpet exceeding loud; so that all the people that was in the camp trembled. And Moses brought the people out of the camp to meet with God; and they stood at the nether part of the mount. And Mount Sinai was altogether on a smoke, because the Lord descended upon it in fire; and the smoke thereof ascended as the smoke of a furnace, and the whole mountain quaked greatly. And when the voice of the trumpet sounded long, and waxed louder and louder, Moses spake, and God answered him by a voice." (Ex. 19: 16-19.) After giving some further instructions to the people through Moses, God himself spoke to them from the top of Sinai, saying, "I am the Lord thy God, who brought thee out of the land of Egypt, and out of the house of bondage. Thou shalt have no other gods before me," etc. Thus, in an audible voice, he delivered to them all the words of the Decalogue; and in the meantime, "all the people saw the thunderings and the lightnings, and the noise of the trumpet, and the mountain smoking. And when the people saw it, they removed and stood afar off. And they said unto Moses, Speak thou with us, and we will hear; but let not the Lord speak with us, lest we die." (Ex. 20: 18, 19.) Thus they "entreated that the word should not be spoken to them anymore."

20 **For they could not endure that which was commanded,** —Our author now assigns parenthetically the reason why the ancient Hebrews felt so much terror and alarm, as they stood at the foot of Sinai, in the immediate presence of God, and heard from his own lips, in awful solemnity, the words of the Decalogue. "They could not bear that which was commanded, If even a beast touch the mountain, it shall be stoned." The original decree as given in Ex. 19: 12, 13, is as follows: "And thou shalt set bounds unto the people round about, saying, Take heed to yourselves, that ye go not into the mount, or touch the border of it;

with a dart] : 21 And so terrible was the sight that ²Moses said, I exceedingly fear and quake:)

²Ex. xix. 19; Deut. ix. 19; Isa. vi. 3-5.

whosoever toucheth the mount shall surely be put to death: there
shall not a hand touch it, but he shall surely be stoned or shot
through; whether it be a beast or a man, it shall not live." The
Apostle quotes freely from the Hebrews, giving in this, as in many
other instances, the substance but not the exact words of the original. The phrase *"thrust through with a dart,"* is manifestly an interpolation from the Septuagint, introduced into our text by some
post-apostolic writer. See critical note.

21 **And so terrible was the sight, etc.**—No such saying of
Moses, as that given in our text, is found in the Pentateuch. And
hence the question has been often asked and considered, "Whence
did our author obtain these words?" Some think that he obtained
them from Jewish tradition, while others suppose that this is a
mere inference of Paul, drawn from the appalling circumstances of
the case. But how very absurd and unsatisfactory are all such hypotheses! The only proper answer to such questions is to be
found in the promise which Christ gave to the Apostles touching
all such matters: "Howbeit," says he, "when the Spirit of truth is
come, he will guide you into all truth." (John 16: 13.) See also
John 14: 26, and 1 Cor. 2: 10-13. The Holy Spirit, then, was
Paul's infallible guide in writing every word and sentence of this
Epistle. From it, and not from Jewish tradition or logical inference, he learned whatever facts and principles were necessary for
our edification, as well as for the edification and encouragement of
his own persecuted and disheartened Hebrew brethren.

The occasion of this utterance was probably that to which Moses
himself refers in Ex. 19: 19: "Moses spake, and God answered
him by a voice." When Moses went up into the mount, and "drew
near to the thick darkness" out of which issued the thunders, and
lightnings, and the great fire which burned to the midst of heaven,
it seems that his courage failed, and he spoke tremblingly. But
when God answered him encouragingly, his fears were allayed.
The whole scene, however, was awful in the extreme, and served
to strike terror into the hearts of all Israel. "Their drawing nigh,"
as Delitzsch well observes, "was at the same time a shrinking back,

22 But [1]ye are come unto mount Sion, and unto [2]the city of the living God, the heavenly Jerusalem, [3]and to an innumerable company of angels,

[1]Psa. ii. 6; xlviii. 2; cxxxii. 13, 14; Joel ii. 32; Rev. xiv. 1.
[2]Ch. xi. 10, 16; xiii. 14; Psa. lxxxvii. 3; Gal. iv. 26; Rev. xxi. 2, 10; xxii. 19.
[3]Deut. xxxiii. 2; Psa. lxviii. 17; Dan. vii. 10; Jude 14; Rev. v. 11.

a remaining at a distance. The mount of Divine revelation was to them unapproachable; the Divine voice was full of terror; and yet it was only the visible and tangible forms of nature through which God then manifested, and behind which he hid himself. The true and inward communion with God had not yet been revealed. It was necessary that the law should first bring men to a painful consciousness of the hindrances opposed to such communion by sin, and their longing excited and intensified that such hindrances might be taken away. Under the New Covenant, we have no longer a tangible mountain, as the place of Divine revelation, and that made only from a distance; but heaven itself, a divine and supersensual world, is now thrown open, and we are permitted ourselves to approach there the very throne of God; it is thrown open for us by the Mediator of the New Covenant, and made approachable by us through his atoning blood." All this the Apostle now proceeds to explain and illustrate by a series of the most sublime and interesting specifications.

22 **But ye are come unto Mount Sion**—The exact topography of Mount Sion, or rather Mount Zion (*Sion*) is still a matter of inquiry. The name seems to have been at first limited to the mount in the southwestern part of the city of Jerusalem, but it was afterward made to embrace Mount Moriah; and in some instances, it seems to have included the site of the entire city, just as it is sometimes used by metonymy for the city itself. See, for example, 1 Macc. 4: 37, 60; 5: 54; 6: 48, 62; 7: 33. Being then the seat of both the royal and sacerdotal authority, it was properly called the "holy hill of Zion" (Psalm 2:6), and the chosen habitation of Jehovah (Psalm 132: 13). And hence it seems to be used in our text as a type of heaven itself, the mount of God, the site of the heavenly Jerusalem. To this intangible and glorious mountain, Christians have now come by virtue of their citizenship in the kingdom of heaven: "for our citizenship is in heaven; from whence also we look for the Savior, the Lord Jesus Christ." (Phil. 3: 20.)

**and unto the city of the living God, the heavenly Jerusalem,**

23 To ¹the general assembly and ²church of the first-born, ³which are written in heaven, and to ⁴God the Judge of all, and to ⁵the spirits of just men
made perfect,

¹Amos v. 21.
²Ex. iv. 22; xiii. 2; Jer. xxxi. 9; Jas. i. 18; Rev. xiv. 4.
³Psa. lxix. 28; Luke x. 20; Phil. iv. 3; Rev. iii. 5; xx. 15.
⁴Gen. xviii. 25; John v. 22; Acts xvii. 31; 1 Pet. ii. 23.
⁵1 Cor. xiii. 12; 2 Cor. v. 8; Phil. i. 21-23; iii. 1, 2; Col. i. 12; Rev. vii. 13-17.

—That is, the city where God dwells; the city of which he is the
Architect and Builder, and which is here called symbolically "the
heavenly Jerusalem." During the most prosperous period of the
Old Economy, under the reign of David and Solomon, Jerusalem
was the metropolis of the whole kingdom of Israel. Thither the
tribes of God went up to offer their sacrifices and to pay their
vows. (Psalm 122.) There stood the typical throne of David, and
there also was the Shekinah, the symbol of God's presence in the
Most Holy Place of the Tabernacle and Temple. And hence it
came to pass that this city was made typical of the metropolis of
the kingdom of the Messiah, the heavenly Jerusalem, "the city
which hath the foundations," whose site is the heavenly Mount
Zion, which abideth forever. See references. To this celestial
city, the antitype of the city of David, all now come who put on
Christ and become citizens of his kingdom. The Apostle does not
of course mean to say that those of us who are still in the flesh
have yet actually entered these celestial mansions, but as all foreigners who become citizens of these United States may, wherever
located, be said to have come to their metropolis; so, also, though
in a much higher sense, may all who are translated from the kingdom of darkness into "the kingdom of God's dear Son," be said to
have come to Mount Zion, and to the heavenly Jerusalem.

**and to an innumerable company, etc.**—The critics are much
divided with regard to the proper construction and punctuation of
this and the two following clauses. The words of the original are
plain enough, and may be fairly rendered without any marks of
punctuation as follows: *And to myriads of angels a festive assembly
and to the church of the first-born who are enrolled in heaven.* But
how is this to be punctuated? The following methods have been
proposed: (1) And to myriads, a festive assembly of angels; and
to the church of the first-born who are enrolled in heaven (Griesbach, Knapp, Böhme, Kuinoel, Moll); (2) And to myriads of angels, a festive assembly; and to the church of the first-born who are

enrolled in heaven (Œcumenius, Theophylact) ; (3) And to myriads of angels ; to the festive assembly and church of the first-born
who are enrolled in heaven (Elzevir, Beza, Lünemann, Hofmann,
English Version) ; (4) And to myriads, a festive assembly of angels and the church of the first-born who are enrolled in heaven
(Bengel, Lachmann, Ebrard, Deltizsch, Alford). I have thus
plainly indicated the several modes of punctuation, so that the
thoughtful reader may see and judge for himself. More than this
is, I think, unnecessary. A discussion of their relative merits would
be tedious and uninteresting to most readers. It seems to me,
however, that the choice lies between the first and the fourth, and
that of these, the first is the most simple and natural. For it is
manifestly the intention of the writer to introduce each of the leading members of this majestic sentence by means of the conjunction
*"and"* (*kai*), and to add such as are only explanatory without the
use of any connecting particle. Keeping this in view as one of our
distinctive landmarks, the whole sentence may, I think, be fairly
rendered as follows: But ye have come near to Mount Zion; and
to the city of the living God, the heavenly Jerusalem; and to myriads, a festive assembly of angels; and to the church of the first-
born who are enrolled in heaven; and to God the Judge of all; and
to the spirits of just ones made perfect; and to Jesus the Mediator
of the New Covenant; and to the blood of sprinkling which speaks
better [more encouragingly] than Abel. The word *myriads* is
often applied to the hosts of angels (Deut. 33: 2 ; Psalm 68: 17 ;
Dan. 7: 10 ; Jude 14 ; Rev. 5: 11), but as this is not its exclusive
use in the Scriptures, it was necessary to add the explanatory
phrase, *"a festive assembly of angels."* The word rendered *general assembly* (*paneguris*) means properly an assembly of all the
people, met to celebrate a public festival. Here, it denotes the joyful and multitudinous assembly of angels around the throne of
God, who there forever celebrate his praises (Rev. 5: 11 ; 7: 11,
12).

**and church of the first-born, which are written in heaven,—**
This has reference to the church of Christ on earth, all the members
of which are, on account of their high honors and privileges, called
"the first-born," just as Christ is himself called "the First-born of
every creature." (Col. 1: 15.) "Of his own will," says James,
"begat he us [all Christians] with the word of truth, that we

24 And to ¹Jesus the Mediator of the New Covenant, and to ²the blood of sprinkling, that ³speaketh | better things: *a better thing* | than that of Abel.

¹Chap. viii. 6; 1 Tim. ii. 5.
²Chap. ix. 14. 23; x. 22; Ex. xii. 7, 22; xxiv. 8; 1 Pet. i. 2.
³Chap. xi. 4; xii. 1.

should be a kind of first-fruits of his creatures." (James 1: 18.) These first-born of God are also still further honored by having their names all registered in heaven, as citizens of the New Jerusalem. See Luke 10: 20; Phil. 4: 3. "There is," says A. Clarke, "allusion here to the custom of enrolling or writing on tables the names of all the citizens of a particular city; and all those, thus registered, were considered as having a right to live there, and to enjoy all its privileges. All genuine believers are denizens of heaven: that is their country, and there they have their rights."

**and to God the Judge of all,**—God himself in his own proper person judges no one (John 5: 22); but he judges all by Jesus Christ (Acts 17: 31); and hence he is properly called "the Judge of all." "The Judge of all the earth will do right." (Gen. 18: 25.)

**and to the spirits of just men made perfect,**—That is, to the spirits of all the redeemed, from Abel downward to the present time. These just ones have finished their course and reached the goal of their destiny and, "therefore, they are before the throne of God, and serve him day and night in his Temple; and he that sitteth on the throne shall dwell among them. They shall hunger no more; neither thirst any more; neither shall the Sun light on them, nor any heat. For the Lamb who is in the midst of the throne feeds them, and leads them unto fountains of water of life; and God shall wipe away all tears from their eyes." (Rev. 7: 15-17.)

24 **And to Jesus the Mediator of the New Covenant,**—The Israelites at Sinai drew near to Moses, as the Mediator of the Old Covenant; but Christians now draw near to Christ, as the Mediator of the New Covenant. See note on 8: 6. He it is "who of God is made unto us wisdom, and righteousness, and sanctification, and redemption" (1 Cor. 1: 30), and through whom "we have access into this grace wherein we now stand, and rejoice in hope of the glory of God." (Rom. 5: 2.)

**and to the blood of sprinkling,**—This is the same as the blood of Jesus, by means of which the New Covenant was ratified (10: 14-18), and through which the hearts of all Christians have been sprinkled from an evil consciousness. (9: 14; 10: 22.) There is an allusion here to the ratification of the Old Covenant by the sprinkling of blood (Ex. 24: 8), and also to the sprinkling of the blood of atonement (Lev. 16: 14, 15).

**that speaketh better things than that of Abel:**—Or rather, *Which speaks better than Abel speaks (kreitton lalounti para ton Abel).* See critical note. Here again the critics are divided. The common opinion is that the blood of Christ calls for mercy; whereas the blood of Abel calls for vengeance (Calvin, Ebrard, Stuart, Scott, Bloomfield, Delitzsch, Alford). But as Adam Clarke says, "This interpretation reflects little credit on the understanding of the Apostle. To say that the blood of Christ speaketh better things than that of Abel, is saying little indeed. It might speak very little good to any soul of man, and yet speak better things than that of Abel, which speaks no good to any human creature, and only called for vengeance on him that shed it." The meaning of the passage then fairly construed is obviously this: Abel speaks well, but the blood of Christ speaks better. "By faith," says our author, "Abel offered unto God a more excellent sacrifice than Cain, by which he obtained witness that he was righteous, God testifying of his gifts; and by it [his faith] he being dead yet speaketh." (11: 4.) What then does he say? What did he say to the ancient Patriarchs, and what does he still say even to Christians? Evidently this and only this: that mercy has in some way been provided for every true believer; that God will in some mysterious way pardon, justify, and save all who believe and obey him. This he said by his faith and obedience in offering to God the required sacrifice. But he could say no more: for as yet the way, the truth, the resurrection, and the life, had not been made manifest (John 11: 25; 14: 6). The Word had not yet become flesh; and Jesus had not yet died for our sins according to the Scriptures. And, consequently, it was not yet understood how God could be just in justifying the believer. (Rom. 3: 25, 26.) But now all this is made manifest through the shedding and application of Christ's blood. And hence it is that God has reserved "some better thing (*kreitton*) for us" (11: 40); which thing is now fully revealed through the blood of sprinkling, which cleanses from all sin.

Such then is the contrast between the former and the latter dispensations; between the terrors of the Old Covenant and the more

25 [1]See that ye refuse not him that speaketh. For [2]if they escaped not who refused him that spake on earth, much more shall not we escape, if we turn away from him that speaketh from heaven:

[1]Prov. i. 24; Jer. xi. 10; Acts vii. 35.
[2]Chap. ii. 2, 3; iii. 17; x. 28, 29.

encouraging privileges of the New. But as it is a principle of the Divine government that "wherever much is given, there also much is always required," it follows, as our author now proceeds to show, that the superior privileges of the Hebrew Christians served very greatly to increase their obligations; and that there was, in fact, no possible way for them to escape the righteous vengeance of God, if they neglected the great salvation that was so freely offered to them in the Gospel. See notes on 2: 1-3.

25 **See that ye refuse not him that speaketh.**—The warning given in this verse is very plain, as well as very solemn and emphatic. . But who is he that speaketh? Certainly not Christ, as Mediator of the New Covenant (Chrysostom, Œcumenius, Ebrard, Stuart, Clarke, Bloomfield), but God himself in Christ, as in 1: 1 (Grotius, Bleek, Scott, Delitzsch, Alford, Moll). God anciently spoke from Sinai through Moses and the administration of angels, but now he speaks to us from Heaven through his own Son. It was the voice of Jehovah that once shook Sinai from its summit to its deepest foundations; and it is his voice which, according to Haggai (2: 6, 7), will once more shake both the Earth and the Heavens. The context will manifestly allow of no other interpretation. The same Almighty Sovereign who in the twenty-ninth verse is represented as "a consuming fire," is the speaker in both instances. The greater obligations of Christians do not, therefore, arise from the fact that they are now addressed by a speaker of greater dignity and authority; but simply from the fact that God himself now speaks to us through different media and under different circumstances. This is made plain by the reasoning of the Apostle in the beginning of the second chapter. "We ought," he says, "to give the more earnest heed to the things which we have heard, lest at any time we should be drifted away from them. For if the word spoken [by God] through angels was steadfast, and every transgression and disobedience [of that word] received a just recompense of reward, how shall we escape, if we neglect so great a salvation" which God has, in these last days, revealed to us in and through his own dear Son?

26 ¹Whose voice then shook the earth: but now he hath promised, saying,
²Yet once more I shake not the earth only, but also heaven.

¹Ex. xix. 18; Psa. cxiv. 6, 7.
²Isa. ii. 19; Joel iii. 16; Hag. ii. 6, 7.

26 **Whose voice then shook the earth:**—That is, when he
spoke to the Israelites from Mount Sinai. (Ex. 19: 18.) To this in
connection with the other stupendous miracles of the Exodus, the
Psalmist beautifully and encouragingly refers in Psalm 114: 1-4.
"When Israel," he says, "went out of Egypt, the house of Jacob
from a people of strange language; Judah was his sanctuary, and
Israel his dominion. The sea saw it, and fled: Jordan was driven
back. The mountains skipped like rams, and the little hills like
lambs."

**but now he hath said, Yet once more, etc.**—The reference
here is to the prophecy of Haggai 2: 6, 7, relating primarily to the
building of the second Temple by Zerubbabel; the historical circumstances of which may be briefly stated as follows: The Temple
of Solomon had been destroyed by the Chaldeans about 588 B.C.
(2 Kings 25: 1-17.) And in the year 536 B.C., Cyrus the Great,
king of Persia, issued a decree, permitting all Jews, who were willing, to return to Jerusalem and rebuild the Temple. (Ezra 1: 1-
11.) More than forty-two thousand of them gratefully accepted the
privilege, and set out immediately under Zerubbabel the governor,
and Joshua the High Priest. (Ezra 2: 46; Neh. 7: 66.) They
first, after their return, set up the altar of burnt-offerings and offered the required sacrifices (Ezra 3: 1-6) ; and on the second
month of the second year the foundation of the Temple was
laid with shoutings of joy and gladness on the part of the multitude. (Ezra 3: 8-11.) But some of the old men who had seen the
first Temple in all its glory, when they saw the great inferiority of
the second, wept with a loud voice. (Ezra 3: 12.) This, of course,
greatly discouraged the hearts of the people: and besides, the Sa-
maritans and other hostile tribes, by their violent opposition and
misrepresentations, so weakened the hands of the Jews that but little more was done during the short remnant of the reign of Cyrus
and the reign of his successor, Ahasuerus or Cambyses. And in
the reign of Artaxerxes (Smerdis the Usurper), the work was, by
his decree, wholly suspended. (Ezra 4: 24.) But in the second
year of the reign of Darius Hystaspes (519 B.C.), God stirred up

the minds of the people, by the prophecies of Haggai and Zechariah, to begin again the work of rebuilding the Temple. The first message of Haggai was delivered by Zerubbabel and Joshua on the first day of the sixth month of the second year of Darius, in which he severely reproves the people for neglecting the Temple. (Hag. 1:1-11.) His appeal was successful: for on the twentieth day of the same month, the work of rebuilding was commenced. But in order to comfort and encourage the hearts of those who were mourning over the manifest inferiority of this second Temple, Haggai was sent to them again on the twentieth day of the month following, and directed to say to them that God was with them to give them success in their labors; and to assure them that the glory of the second Temple would even surpass the glory of that which was builded by Solomon. "For thus saith the Lord of host, yet once, it is a little while, and I will shake the heavens, and the Earth, and the sea, and the dry land: and I will shake all nations; and the DESIRE of all nations shall come; and I will fill this house with glory, saith the Lord of hosts. The silver is mine, and the gold is mine, saith the Lord of hosts. The glory of this latter house shall be greater than that of the former, saith the Lord of hosts; and in this place will I give peace, saith the Lord of hosts." (Hag. 2:6-9.)

On this passage it may be well to remark (1) that the second Temple derived its chief glory from the presence of him who, as the Savior of the world, is here called "the DESIRE of all nations." In all other respects the temple of Zerubbabel even with the additions that were made to it by Herod the Great, was quite inferior to that of Solomon. For in it, as the Jews themselves confess, the chief glory of Solomon's Temple was wholly wanting. It had no Ark of the Covenant, no Mercy-seat, and no Shekinah. No symbol of God's presence was there manifested, until the Word became flesh and dwelt among his people. I know it is often said that "the desire of all nations" can have no reference to the Messiah; because, says the objector, "the word desires is in the plural number." But this is not the case in the Hebrew. In the Septuagint, the corresponding word is in the plural; the choice things (ta eklekta) of all the nations shall come: but in the Hebrew the word is singular; the desire of all the nations shall come. True, indeed, the verb come is in the third person plural, masculine, showing

27 And ¹this word, Yet once more, signifieth the removing of those things that are shaken, as of things that are made, that those things which can not be shaken may remain.

¹Psa. cii. 26, 27; Ezek. xxi. 27; Joel ii. 31; Matt. xxiv. 35; 2 Pet. iii. 10-13.

that the noun, though in the feminine singular, really conveys the idea of a masculine plural; indicating most likely the royal majesty of Christ and the superabounding fullness of the blessings of his mediatorial reign.   He is called the Desire of all nations (a) because he alone is capable of satisfying their desires; and (b) because for some time before the coming of Christ there was a very general expectation among the civilized nations that the Golden Age would soon be restored through the righteous administration of some great one who was about to be born in Judea, and who would give to the Jews the dominion of the world.  To this Tacitus refers as follows: "There was," he says, "in the minds of many a conviction that it was contained in the ancient writings of the Priests, that at that very time it would come to pass that the east would acquire strength, and that those who had gone forth from Judea would become the masters of affairs." (Hist. 5: 13.) Suetonius also testifies to the same effect: "Throughout the whole east," he says, "an old and firmly fixed opinion became prevalent that it was included in the decrees of fate, that those who had gone forth from Judea should at that time become the masters of affairs." (In Vesp. 100: 4.)  (2) It is obvious that the shaking of the heavens and the earth was to commence soon with the coming of the Messiah and the inauguration of the new era under him.  For says God by the Prophet, "It is yet but a little while, when I will shake once for all (*hapax*) the heavens, and the earth, and the sea, and the dry land; and I will shake all the nations; and the Desire of all the nations shall come, and I will fill this house with glory."  The shaking of the world is therefore chronologically connected with the coming of the Messiah; but the Prophet does not say explicitly how long this shaking of all things will continue.  This is more clearly indicated by the Apostle in what follows.

27 **And this word, Yet once more, etc.**—The Apostle now explains what is meant by the phrase, *Yet once more* (*eti hapax*). It denotes, he says, "the removal of the things shaken, as of things which have been made, so that the things which are not shaken may remain."  That is, since there is to be but one more shaking of

all things, it is implied in this phrase, *"Yet once more,"* that the shaking will continue until all things perishable shall be removed; so that nothing will remain but what is eternal and immutable. It will continue therefore until Judaism and all false systems of religion and philosophy are taken out of the way; until the kingdoms of the world shall become the kingdom of our Lord and of his Christ (Rev. 11:15); and until the heavens and the earth which are now shall be transformed into new heavens and a new earth, wherein nothing but righteousness will forever dwell. For Christ came not merely to remove the shadows of the Old Economy, and to introduce the sublime realities of the New; but he came also to destroy the works of Satan (2:14), and to establish a kingdom which will endure forever (2 Pet. 1:11). And consequently he must reign and shake the world until his mission shall be fully accomplished. (1 Cor. 15:24, 25.)

**as of things that are made:**—That is, made by art or man's device, and are therefore perishable. For "all flesh is grass, and all its glory as the flower of grass: the grass withereth, and the flower falleth away; but the word of the Lord endureth forever." (1 Pet. 1:24, 25.)

**that those things which can not be shaken may remain.**— These are all such as have their foundation in the nature and truth of God; having particular reference, however, to the kingdom of Christ. Judaism with all its splendid ritual was, like a work of art, made for a temporary purpose; and, like all things else of the same class, it was destined to pass away when its end was accomplished. But the kingdom of Christ is wholly different. Its object is not temporal but eternal. It was set up during the shaking of thrones and kingdoms, and it will continue when the heavens shall have passed away as a scroll. (1 Cor. 15:24; 2 Pet. 1:11.) And hence it follows that the kingdom of Christ can never, like Judaism, give place to anything better (Dan. 2:44); for "this," says Peter, "is the true grace of God wherein ye stand" (1 Pet. 5:12). God has nothing better to offer to any man than salvation through Christ. The man, therefore, who rejects Christ and his kingdom seals of necessity his own eternal condemnation.

28 Wherefore we receiving [2]a kingdom which can not be moved, let us have grace, whereby we may serve God acceptably with reverence and godly fear:

29 For [1]our God is a consuming fire.

[2]Isa. ix. 7; Dan. ii. 44; Matt. xxv. 34; 2 Pet. i. 11.
[1]Ch. x. 27; Lev. x. 1; Num. xi. 1; xvi. 35; Deut. iv. 24; Psa. 1, 3; xcvii. 3.

28 **Wherefore we receiving a kingdom, etc.**—Since it is true that we Christians have received a kingdom which cannot, like the Jewish Theocracy and false systems of religion and philosophy, be shaken and removed, let us hold fast our confession: let us by patiently and perseveringly submitting to the will of God in all things, obtain from him such measures of grace as will enable us to serve him with "godly fear and dread."

29 **For our God is a consuming fire.**—This is a quotation from Deut. 4: 24. It is cited here as furnishing an additional reason why we should serve God with "godly fear and dread." To the faithful in Christ Jesus, God is life, and light, and love: but to the willfully disobedient he has always been "a consuming fire." See references. Nothing, therefore, remains for the apostate and the finally impenitent but "a certain fearful looking for of judgment and fiery indignation which shall devour the adversaries."

### REFLECTIONS

1. It is pleasant to think of the many faithful witnesses for the truth, who having finished their course now stand to encourage us in our conflicts with the world, the flesh, and the devil. (verse 1). These by their own heroic example have clearly demonstrated that the way of duty, though strait and narrow, may nevertheless be trodden by all, as the way that leads to certain victory. This should encourage us to "lay aside every weight and the sin which so easily besets us," so that we too may run with patient endurance "the race that is set before us."

2. But our main ground of encouragement is to be found in the example of Jesus, the Leader and Perfecter of the faith, "who for the joy that was set before him endured the cross," and through it triumphed over all his and our enemies (verses 2, 3).

So full of instruction indeed is his whole life that it of itself serves us as a general directory, and gives us comfort and consolation under all the circumstances of our earthly conflict. When tempted, for instance, it will always assist us to say with Jesus, "It is written," "It is written," "It is written"; and when solely persecuted for righteousness' sake, the best we can do is to say in the spirit and temper of our great Exemplar, "Father, forgive them, for they know not what they do."

3. It is a good thing to be afflicted, (1) because it serves to mortify the flesh with its affections and its lusts; (2) because it serves to keep us humble and mindful of our mortality; and (3) because it serves to purify our hearts, and so to make us partakers of God's holiness (verses 4-11). Thus it is that our light afflictions which are but for a moment, serve in the providence of God to work out for us a far more exceeding and eternal weight of glory. To those who have their portion in this life, and whose daily concern is about what they shall eat, and, what they shall drink, and wherewithal they shall be clothed, I know all this appears very absurd. But not so to the true child of God who looks upon the present as but a preparation for the eternal world that is beyond. To him everything appears in the light of a blessing which serves to purify his heart, and so to prepare him for the high and holy destiny that is set before him. Let us then with Paul ever glory in tribulation, "knowing that tribulation worketh patience; and patience, experience; and experience, hope"; and that all things in fact "work together for good to them that love God."

4. Many for whom Christ died go to perdition through our inexcusable neglect (verses 12-17). This is true not only of many who are still in the world, and who if properly cared for might be converted and brought into the fold of Christ; but it is also equally true of many weak and sickly ones in the Church, whose hands are hanging down, whose knees have become feeble, and who are even now ready to perish for want of the proper aid, sympathy, and support of their brethren. This ought not so to be. And it would not be so did we but realize as we should our relations to each other, and our obligations to the one living and supreme head. But when, alas! will this lesson be duly learned by the professed followers of the Lord Jesus? "Brethren, if a man be overtaken in a fault, ye who are spiritual restore such a one in the spirit of meekness; considering thyself, lest thou also be tempted. Bear ye one another's burdens, and so fulfill the law of Christ." (Gal. 6: 1, 2.)

5. The object of God in providing and revealing to us the whole

economy of redemption, is to make us holy as he himself is holy (verse 14). Without this all else will be in vain: our confession will avail us nothing, nor will our baptism, nor our alms, nor our prayers. For "without holiness no man shall see the Lord"; and unless we see him, and have fellowship with him, Heaven itself will be no Heaven to us. In that event the hell within us would in fact only be made deeper and deeper by the infinite contrast of the Heaven without us. How earnestly then we should all strive after holiness of heart and purity of life; and how earnestly we should beseech God day by day to search our hearts and lead us "in the way everlasting."

6. The vail that now conceals God from the eyes of sinful mortals is "a vail woven by the hand of Mercy" (verses 18-21). If the children of Israel could not bear to look on even the natural phenomena through which God manifested himself on mount Sinai, what must have been the consequence if the vail had been wholly removed, and the full-orbed glory of Jehovah's power, and majesty, and holiness, had been allowed to burst forth in all its infinite splendor and fullness on the astonished eyes and trembling hearts of the multitude! Such a sight would have been too much for poor sinful mortals. (Ex. 33:20.) And hence we can never be sufficiently thankful, that even under the more benign influences of the New Covenant, God deals with us through the medium of a Mediator. We are not yet prepared for any higher and fuller manifestations of his glory than what we now see in the face of Jesus. But thanks be to God, that the time is coming when we shall see his face and when his name shall be on our foreheads. (Rev. 22:4.) Then we shall see as we are seen, and know even as also we are known. (1 Cor. 13:12.)

7. How very near and dear are our relations to God, to Christ, to holy angels, and to the spirits of the redeemed (verses 22-24). We are no longer strangers and foreigners, but fellow-citizens with the saints made perfect. For in covenant we have already come to mount Zion; and to the city of the living God, the heavenly Jerusalem; and to a countless host of angels composing as it were a joyful and festive assembly around the throne of God; and to the Church of the first-born whose names are registered in Heaven; and to God the judge of all; and to the spirits of the just made perfect; and to Jesus the Mediator of the New Covenant; and to

the blood of sprinkling which speaks more encouragingly than even Abel speaks by his faith and obedience. Who, then, would ever think of turning back to the weak and beggarly elements of this world? Who would renounce this holy society and these high and holy relations for the society and fellowship of Satan and his angels? May God save us all from such folly and madness.

8. Paul was not an advocate of either the Popish dogmas about purgatory, or of the doctrine of soul-sleeping (verse 23). With him it was a fundamental article of faith that "to be absent from the body is to be present with the Lord" (2 Cor. 5: 8); and to be present with the Lord is to be "made perfect." And hence he himself preferred to depart and to be with Christ. (Phil. 1: 23.)

9. Rejection of the highest grace is always followed by the severest punishment (verse 25). And consequently our destiny will be even more intolerable than that of the disobedient Israelites, if we neglect the overtures of mercy that are now offered to us in the Gospel.

10. The Gospel is God's last manifestation of mercy for the recovery of lost sinners (verse 28). When Christ comes the second time, it will not be to convert the world, but to judge it. It will be to raise the dead saints (1 Thess. 4: 16); to change the living (1 Thess. 4: 17); to renovate the world by fire (2 Thess. 1: 7, 8; 2 Pet. 3: 7-13); to raise the wicked out of the molten mass (John 5: 28, 29; Acts 24: 15); and then to reward every man according to his works (Matt. 16: 27; 25: 31-41; Rom. 2: 5-16; 2 Tim. 4: 1). It will not be to set up a new kingdom on earth, but simply to bring to an end his mediatorial reign, and then will he deliver up the Kingdom to the Father. (1 Cor. 15: 24, 25.) "Wherefore [since] we have received a kingdom which can not be moved, let us have grace whereby we may serve God acceptably with reverence and godly fear."

## SECTION TWELVE
### 13: 1-25

### ANALYSIS

The Apostle has now accomplished his main object in writing this unique epistle. In trains of profound thought and lofty sublimity, he has presented to us Jesus in all his varied relations and transcendent excellencies: with the hand of a master he has also traced the leading features of the economy of redemption; shown the infinite superiority of Christianity over Judaism; and most strikingly and impressively illustrated the obligations of all Christians to follow Jesus, if need be, "through floods and flames" on their way to the everlasting Zion. And now in conclusion, he simply exhorts his brethren to be faithful in the discharge of various personal and social duties: and particularly

1. To love one another as brethren in Christ (verse 1).

2. To be hospitable (verse 2).

3. To sympathize with those in bonds (verse 3).

4. To be faithful in their marriage relations (verse 4).

5. To be satisfied with their condition and circumstances (verses 5, 6).

6. To follow the example and imitate the faith of their departed leaders (verse 7).

7. To be firm and stable in the faith of Christ, who was offered up without the gate of Jerusalem, in order to lead our minds away from that which is symbolical and earthly to that which is real and heavenly (verses 8-15).

8. To be benevolent (verse 16).

9. To obey their overseers who had the care of their souls (verse 17).

10. To pray for himself and especially that he might soon be restored to them (verses 18, 19).

After delivering these several exhortations, our author brings the Epistle to a close as follows:

1. He offers up a brief but earnest prayer for their perfection (verses 20, 21).

2. He beseeches them to receive with favor what he had written for their encouragement and edification (verse 22).

3. He announces to them the fact that Timothy had been set at liberty; and that it was his purpose to see them in connection with Timothy very soon (verse 23).

4. He sends his own salutation and also that of his Italian brethren to the elders and saints in Jerusalem (verse 24).

5. Benediction (verse 25).

From this general analysis of the section, we see that it may be naturally and properly divided into the following paragraphs:

I. 13: 1-7. Exhortation to steadfast perseverance and fidelity in the discharge of sundry personal and social duties.

II. 13: 8-16. Exhortation to stability in Christian doctrine and practice; and to avoid being carried away from the faith of Christ by unprofitable discussions and controversies about such matters as clean and unclean meats.

III. 13: 17-19. Our duties to the overseers, and other public servants of the Church.

IV. 13: 20, 21. An earnest benedictory prayer in behalf of the Hebrews.

V. 13: 22-25. Closing remarks.

## 1. EXHORTATION TO STEADFAST PERSEVERANCE AND FIDELITY IN THE DISCHARGE OF SUNDRY PERSONAL AND SOCIAL DUTIES
### 13: 1-7

1 ¹Let brotherly love continue.

¹Chap. vi. 10, 11; x. 24; John xiii. 34, 35; xv. 17; Rom. xii. 9, 10; 1 Pet. i. 22; ii. 17.

1 **Let brotherly love continue.**—In the Greek classics, the word *philadelphia* means the natural love which brothers and sisters have for one another; but in the New Testament it means the love which all Christians should cherish for each other as members of the one family of God in Christ. See Rom. 12: 10; 1 Thess. 4: 9; 1 Pet. 1: 22; 2 Pet. 1: 7. This cardinal Christian virtue is one of the first fruits of that "faith which worketh by love:" and accordingly from the beginning it served to distinguish Christians from all others as the peculiar people of God. For we are told that immediately after the setting up of the Kingdom, "all that believed were together and had all things common." See Acts 2: 44-47. After this, when tribulations and persecutions began to abound, "because of the word," the love of many waxed cold. But it is evident from this Epistle (6: 10; 10: 32), as well as from Acts of Apostles (12: 5, 12; 15: 22, 25), that the Christians of Palestine continued to cherish for one another, a feeling of fraternal affection. And hence our author simply says to them, "Let brotherly love continue."

2 ²Be not forgetful to entertain strangers: for thereby ³some have entertained angels unawares.

²Lev. xix. 34; Deut. x. 18. 19; Matt. xxv. 35, 43; Rom. xii. 13; 1 Pet. iv. 9.
³Gen. xviii. 2-10; xix. 1-3; Judg. xiii. 15.

2 **Be not forgetful to entertain strangers:**—The duty of kindness to strangers was enjoined by the Law of Moses. "The stranger (*proselutos*) that dwelleth with you," said God to the Hebrews, "shall be unto you as one born among you, and thou shalt
love him as thyself; for ye were strangers in the land of Egypt."
(Lev. 19: 34.) Our author therefore assumes here, that his brethren understood their duty in this respect; and he simply admonishes them not to neglect it. The word (*philoxenia*) occurs only
here and in Rom. 12: 13; in both of which places it is supposed by
Delitzsch, Alford, and others, to denote a mere exercise of brotherly love. But I see no sufficient reason for so limiting it. It seems
rather to denote all exercise of that love which we owe to all men.
(2 Pet. 1: 7.) For this virtue, as well as for brotherly love, the
primitive Christians were very remarkable. Even Julian the apostate, in his forty-ninth Epistle, assigns "kindness to strangers" as
one of the means by which their religion was so rapidly propa-
gated.

**For thereby some have entertained angels unawares.**—There
is reference here no doubt to Abraham and Lot (Gen. 18: 2-10;
19: 1-3) ; and perhaps also to some other cases not recorded in the
Holy Scriptures. The idea of the Apostle is this; that the free and
liberal exercise of this social virtue may be of very great service to
ourselves as well as to others. Our guests may often be messen-
gers sent to us from God, for our own special benefit, as were the
angels who saved Lot and his family from the ruin of Sodom. At
all events, they give us an opportunity of showing to the world our
love for Christ, and our respect for his laws and ordinances. I
know it may be said, that the establishment of so many hotels and
the various other improvements of modern civilization, have somewhat lessened our obligations to receive and entertain strangers.
This is no doubt true to some extent. But it should not be forgotten that our mission is to do good to all men as we have opportunity (Gal. 6: 10) : and it is written for our encouragement that
"Whosoever shall give to drink to one of these little ones [who

3 [1]Remember them that are in bonds, as bound with them; and [2]them that suffer adversity, as being yourselves also in the body.

4 [3]Marriage is honorable in all, and the bed undefiled: but [4]whoremongers and adulterers God will judge.

[1]Chap. x. 34; Matt. xxv. 36, 43; Phil. iv. 14-19; Col. iv. 18; 2 Tim. i. 16-18.
[2]Rom. xii. 15; 1 Cor. xii. 26; 1 Pet. iii. 8.
[3]1 Cor. vii. 2; Eph. v. 22-33; 1 Pet. iii. 1-7.
[4]1 Cor. v. 1-11; vi. 9, 10; x. 8; 2 Cor. xii. 21; Gal. v. 19-21; Eph. v. 3-5.

believe in Jesus] a cup of cold water only, in the name of a disciple, shall in nowise lose his reward." (Matt. 10: 42.)

3 **Remember them that are in bonds,**—The reference here is no doubt chiefly to those who were in bonds on account of their religion; but the injunction may, and probably does, include prisoners of all classes. All such need our sympathy and our aid as far as it can be given. And as Christ himself came to preach glad tidings to the meek, to bind up the broken-hearted, to proclaim liberty to the captives, and the opening of the prison to them that are bound (Isa. 60: 1), so also we, as his disciples and co-workers, are required to sympathize with the prisoners, as if we ourselves were bound with them; remembering that so long as we are in the body we too are subject to like calamities.

The reader will observe that in these brief sententious admonitions, we have all the force, ardor, and characteristic haste of the great Apostle of the Gentiles. Most of what precedes is written with the care, dignity, and stateliness, which belong properly to a regular treatise on the sublime themes of redemption. But in this chapter we have some of Paul's most characteristic lifelike sketches.

4 **Marriage is honorable in all,**—Or rather, *Let marriage be honorable in all; and let the bed be undefiled: for fornicators and adulterers God will judge.* This verse, like the one preceding and also the one following, is hortatory, and should be rendered imperatively. It is so construed by Ebrard, Stuart, T. S. Green, Alford, Moll, and most other modern expositors. Polygamy and concubinage had long been more or less tolerated among the Jews; and all manner of uncleanness had been practiced among the Gentiles, often with the approval of their legislators and their most distinguished philosophers. And hence the necessity of this injunction: Let your marriage be held honorable in all respects, and let your marriage bed be undefiled: for (*gar*) fornicators and adulterers

5 Let your ¹conversation be without covetousness; and ²be content with
such things as ye have: for he hath said, ³I will never leave thee, nor forsake thee.

¹Ex. xx. 17; Mark vii. 22; Luke xii. 15-21; Eph. v. 3, 5.
²Matt. vi. 25, 34; 1 Tim. vi. 6-8.
³Gen. xxviii. 15; Deut. xxxi. 6, 8; Josh. i. 5; 1 Chron. xxviii. 20; Psa. xxxvii. 25.

God will judge. Or as rendered by T. S. Green: "Let marriage be
highly prized in all, and its bed be undefiled; but (*de*) whoremongers and adulterers will God judge." (1 Cor. 6: 9, 10.)

It is still a question with expositors, whether the phrase *"in all"*
(*en pasi*) means *in all persons* or *in all things*. The former view
is supported by Erasmus, Luther, Calvin, Beza, Stuart, and most
other Protestant commentators; and the latter, by Œcumenius,
Bleek, Delitzsch, Alford, and most of the Roman Catholic commentators. This is preferable (1) because it is the more general,
and, in fact comprehends the former: for if marriage is honorable
in all respects, then most assuredly it is also honorable among all
classes of men. (2) The latter is most in harmony with Greek
usage. Greek writers generally use the preposition *en* in reference
to things (1 Tim. 3: 11; 2 Tim. 4: 5; Tit. 2: 9, 10; Heb. 13:
18) and *para* in reference to persons (Matt. 19: 26; Acts 26: 8;
Rom. 2: 13; 2 Thess. 1: 6; James 1: 27).

5 **Let your conversation be without covetousness;**—The
word rendered *conversation* (*tropos*) means properly *a turning;*
and hence it is often used metaphorically to denote either a turn of
mind or a habit of life. Here it seems to include both. Let the
disposition of your minds and your habits of life be without covetousness. That is, let the whole tenor of your conduct clearly indicate that your hearts are not set on acquiring the riches of this
world. For "they that will be rich," says the same Apostle, "fall
into temptation and a snare, and into many foolish and hurtful
lusts, which drown men in perdition. For the love of money is the
[a] root of all evil; which while some coveted after, they have
erred from the faith, and pierced themselves through with many
sorrows." (1 Tim. 6: 9, 10.)

**and be content with such things as ye have:**—This does not
forbid all lawful endeavors to improve our own condition and that
of others. Such an injunction would be wholly inconsistent with
what is plainly taught in many other passages of Scriptures. See,
for example, Rom. 12: 11; Eph. 4: 28; 2 Thess. 3: 11. But the

meaning of the Apostle is simply this, that such should be our trust and confidence in God, that we would be satisfied with our condition, be it what it may; knowing that if we are only faithful God will cause all things to work together for our good. Be diligent in business; do all that you can lawfully and consistently to improve your own condition and to promote the happiness of others; and then with calmness and resignation leave all the consequences to God.

**for he hath said I will never leave thee, nor forsake thee.**— This is given as the reason why Christians should all be satisfied with their lot in life, and why they should be content with such things as they have. God has said to every one of his children, "I will never leave thee, nor forsake thee." Words almost identical with these are found in Deut. 31: 6; and they are afterward repeated with some modification in Josh. 1: 5; 1 Chron. 28: 20, etc. The original promise given by God to the Israelites through Moses is full of comfort and consolation; and it seems therefore to have become a sort of proverbial expression among the later Hebrews: for in Philo (Conf. Ling. Section 32) we have the identical words of our author as given in the Textus Receptus (*me se ano oude ou me se eukataleipo*): "an oracle," says Philo, "of the all-merciful God, full of gentleness, which shadows forth good hopes to those who love instruction." It is probable, therefore, that our author quotes here a Bible sentiment, proverbial among the Hebrews, without perhaps having direct reference to any one passage of Scripture. Be this as it may, the sentiment abounds in both the Old and the New Testament: in the sayings of Christ and his Apostles as well as in the writings of the ancient prophets. "Take no thought for your life," says Christ, "what ye shall eat, or what ye shall drink; nor yet for your body, what ye shall put on. Is not the life more than meat, and the body than raiment? Behold the fowls of the air; for they sow not, neither do they reap, nor gather into barns; yet your heavenly Father feedeth them. Are ye not much better than they?" And again he says, "Why take ye thought for raiment? Consider the lilies of the field, how they grow: they toil not, neither do they spin; and yet I say unto you that even Solomon in all his glory was not arrayed like one of these. Wherefore, if God so clothe the grass of the field which to-day is, and to-

6 So that we may boldly say, ¹The Lord is my helper, and ²I will not fear what man shall do unto me.

¹Gen. xv. 1; Deut. xxxiii. 29; Psa. cxviii. 6; Rom. viii. 31.
²Matt. x. 28; Luke xii. 4, 5.

---

morrow is cast into the oven, shall he not much more clothe you, O ye of little faith?" (Matt. 6: 25-30.)

What an infinite contrast we have given here between the consolations of God's word and such as are offered to us by even the wisest of the heathen philosophers.  In order to reconcile us to our present condition, some of them tell us "that our discontent only hurts ourselves, without being able to make any alteration in our circumstances; others, that whatever evil befalls us is derived to us by a fatal necessity, to which the gods themselves are subject; while others very gravely tell the man who is miserable that it is necessary he should be so, to keep up the harmony of the universe, and that the schemes of providence would be troubled and perverted were he otherwise.  These and the like considerations rather silence than satisfy a man.  They may show him that his discontent is unreasonable, but they are by no means sufficient to relieve it.  They rather give despair than consolation.  In a word, a man might reply to one of these comforters, as Augustus did to his friend who advised him not to grieve for the death of a person whom he loved, because his grief could not bring him back again. "It is for that very reason," said the emperor, "that I grieve" (Spectator, No. 574).  How utterly empty, then, are all such philosophical speculations compared with the precious promise of our text: "I will never leave thee, nor forsake thee."  The original form of expression is made as emphatic as possible.

6 So that we may boldly say,—Or rather, So that we say with confidence, The Lord is my helper; and I will not fear what man shall do unto me.  This is a quotation from Psalm 118: 6.  It forms a part of the great Hallel or collection of hymns which the Hebrews were wont to sing at the close of the feast of Tabernacles. And hence the manifest propriety of using the indicative form of expression; We say [*i.e.,* we are wont to say] with confidence, The Lord is my helper, etc.  The Hebrew may be literally rendered according to the Masoretic pointing, as follows: Jehovah is for me; I will not be afraid; what will man do to me?  Some critics, as Griesbach and Alford, following the Hebrew, place a mark

7 Remember them ³which have the rule over you, who have spoken unto you the word of God: ⁴whose faith follow, ⁵considering the end of their conversation.

³Matt. xxiv. 45; Acts ii. 42; vi. 3, 4, 8; xii. 2; Titus i. 5.
⁴1 Cor. iv. 6; xi. 1; Phil. iii. 17.
⁵Acts vii. 55-60.

of interrogation at the close of the verse. Thus, "The Lord is my helper; and I will not be afraid. What shall man do unto me?" But others allege with reason that the use of the conjunction *and* (*chai* omitted in some manuscripts), before the second clause, shows an intentional departure from the Hebrew construction; and they therefore prefer the declarative form of our English Version as being more suitable to the proverbial sentiment of our text. In both cases, however, the meaning is substantially the same. For "if God be for us, who can be against us? He that spared not his own Son, but delivered him up for us all, how shall he not with him also freely give us all things?" So that we may confidently say with David, "Though I walk through the valley of the shadow of death, I will fear no evil; for thou art with me: thy rod and thy staff they comfort me."

7 **Remember them which have the rule over you,**—Or more literally, Remember your leaders (*hegoumenon*) who spoke (*ela-lesan*) to you the word of God; carefully considering the issue (*ekbasin*) of their manner of life; imitate their faith. The reference is to such men as Stephen, James the brother of John, and other faithful preachers of the Gospel who had formerly proclaimed to the Hebrews the good word of God, and whose whole course of life, resulting as it did in a happy and triumphant death, was worthy of their admiration and imitation.

"After the author had thus held up the past as a mirror to the present, and had called to remembrance the gaps which death had made in the church of the Hebrews, what could be more appropriate," says Delitzsch, "than to raise his thoughts to the immutable Lord, exalted high above all change?" This he does in the following paragraph.

## 2. EXHORTATION TO STABILITY IN CHRISTIAN DOCTRINE AND PRACTICE; AND TO AVOID BEING CARRIED AWAY FROM THE FAITH OF THE GOSPEL BY UNPROFITABLE DISCUSSIONS AND CONTROVERSIES ABOUT SUCH MATTERS AS CLEAN AND UNCLEAN MEATS

### 13: 8-16

8 [1]Jesus Christ the same yesterday, and to-day, and forever.
9 [2]Be not carried | about: *aside* | with divers and strange doctrines. For [3]it is a good thing that the heart be established with grace; [4]not with meats, which have not profited them that have been occupied therein.

[1]Ch. i. 12; Jas. i. 17; Rev. i. 4, 8, 17, 18.
[2]Matt. xxiv. 4, 24; Acts xx. 30; Gal. i. 6-9; Col. ii. 4, 8; 1 Tim. iv. 1-3; vi. 3-5.
[3]Acts xx. 32; 2 Cor. i. 21; Eph. iii. 16-19.
[4]Rom. xiv. 17; Col. ii. 16; 1 Tim. iv. 3; Titus i. 14, 15.

8 **Jesus Christ the same yesterday, to-day, and forever.**— This expression is not in apposition with the phrase, "the end of their conversation," as our translators seem to have thought, but a proposition on a wholly distinct and separate subject. The object of the Apostle is to lead and encourage his brethren not to be carried away from "the faith which was once for all delivered to the saints," by various and strange doctrines; but to be firm and resolute in their Christian profession. And as the basis of his exhortation and argument, he reminds them that Jesus Christ, the Leader and Perfecter of the faith, is himself the same yesterday, today, and forever, without even the shadow of change. (James 1: 17.) And as is the Leader, so also he insists should be his followers.

9 **Be not carried about with divers and strange doctrines.**— The corrected reading of the critical note is more in harmony with the context, and is doubtless correct: "Be not carried away by various and strange doctrines." The admonition is general, and may refer to any doctrines, whether of Jewish or Gentile origin, that are inconsistent with the Doctrine of Christ, though the sequel shows that the former are particularly intended. The metaphor seems to be taken from a ship that is carried out of its course by means of violent winds.

**For it is a good thing that the heart be established with grace;**—That is, by means of the gracious truths and influences of the Gospel. This is good for us; and it is also good and acceptable in the sight of God our Savior; for being thus "rooted and grounded in love, we are no longer liable to be tossed to and fro, and carried about with every wind of doctrine by the sleight of

men, and cunning craftiness, whereby they lie in wait to deceive"
(Eph. 4: 14) ; but having a hope strong and steadfast "reaching
even into that within the vail," we can with it, as an anchor of the
soul, calmly smile on all the ills and misfortunes of life, knowing
that we have in heaven for ourselves a better and enduring possession.  This confirmation of the heart, then, by the grace of God,
gives us stability of character, fixedness of purpose, consolation in
our misfortunes, and makes us like Christ, kind, gentle, and benevolent to all.

**not with meats,**—What meats?  Those offered in sacrifice, and
of which the worshipers were allowed to partake, say Bleek, Lünemann, Macknight, Scott, Clarke, and some others: those which
were distinguished as clean and unclean merely as articles of food,
say Calvin, Tholuck, Delitzsch, Alford, and most other commentators.  But why make any such distinction as the above?  For my
own part I see no propriety in doing so.  That certain portions of
certain sacrifices were allowed to be eaten by certain persons, is
plain from such passages as Lev. 6: 26-30; 7: 11-15, etc.  These
rules were still rigidly observed and enforced by the Jewish Rabbis; and there was therefore danger that the judaizing party
among the Hebrew Christians would succeed in blending these
"divers and strange doctrines" with the plain and simple rules of
the Christian religion.  And it is equally obvious that, on the other
hand, the same judaizing party were then busily engaged in sowing
the seeds of discord among the churches, with regard to clean and
unclean meats. (Rom. 14.)  It was therefore necessary that the
Apostle should, as far as possible, correct all such mistakes about
meats and drinks, and other carnal ordinances which had been imposed on the people till the time of reformation; but which never
did and never could make anyone perfect, so far as respects his
moral consciousness. And consequently those who walked in them
were not profited by them.  See notes on 9: 9, 10.  Against all
such doctrines, therefore, in reference to meats and drinks, Paul
here earnestly cautions the Hebrew brethren.  For as he says to
the Romans, "The kingdom of God is not meat and drink; but
righteousness, and peace, and joy in the Holy Spirit." (Rom. 14:
17.)

10 ¹We have an altar, whereof they have no right to eat ²who serve the
tabernacle.

¹1 Cor. ix. 13; x. 17-20.
²Num. iii. 7, 8; vii. 5.

10 **We have an altar, etc.**—Two queries naturally arise with
regard to this verse. *First,* what is meant by the word *altar?* and
*second,* what connection has this verse with what precedes and
with what follows?

In reply to the first, it is alleged (1) that the word *altar* in this
connection represents no definite object whatever; but that the
Apostle uses it merely for the sake of the imagery, so as to give
consistency to the figurative expressions which he here employs
(Michaelis, Tholuck); (2) that it means Christ himself (Suicer,
Wolf); (3) that it means the Lord's Table (Böhme, Ebrard); (4)
that it denotes the heavenly place on which Christ now offers the
virtue of his own blood to the Father for us (Bretschneider); (5)
that it means the cross on which Christ was crucified (Delitzsch,
Alford); and (6) that it signifies the Divine nature of Christ on
which his human nature is supposed to have been offered, and by
means of which it was sanctified and made available. To me it
seems evident that the altar is here used by metonymy for Christ
himself, who was sacrificed for us; so that to partake of this altar
is simply to partake of the sacrifice of Christ. So Paul reasons in
reference to the sacrifices of the Old Economy. "Behold Israel," he
says, "after the flesh: are not they who eat of the sacrifices partakers of the altar?" (1 Cor. 10: 18.) And again he says, "Do ye not
know that they who minister about holy things live of the things of
the temple? and they who wait at the altar are partakers with the
altar?" (1 Cor. 9: 13.) To eat of the altar is therefore manifestly to
eat of the sacrifice which is offered on the altar. And that the sacrifice in this case was the sacrifice of Christ, is evident from the
context, as well as from many parellel passages. See, for example,
John 6: 53-55. Of this sacrifice, they have no right to eat who
serve the Tabernacle. For they who would partake of it must do
so in faith (John 6: 47; 20: 31; Acts. 16: 31); but those Jews
who served the Tabernacle, did not of course believe in Jesus as
the Lamb of God that taketh away the sins of the world; and consequently they had no right to partake of his sacrifice.

This, then, will enable us to understand readily the proper im-

11 For ¹the bodies of those beasts whose blood is brought into the sanctuary by the high priest [for sin], are burned without the camp.
12 Wherefore Jesus also, ²that he might sanctify the people with his own blood, ³suffered without the gate.

¹Lev. iv. 7, 11, 12, 18, 21; vi. 30.
²Ch. ii. 11; ix. 14; x. 29; 1 Cor. vi. 11; Eph. v. 26.
³John xix. 17, 18; Acts vii. 58.

port of the second query, touching the connection of this verse with what precedes and follows. The Jews boasted of their exclusive right to partake of their own consecrated sacrifices. This doubtless made a strong and deep impression on the minds of some of the weaker brethren; and they were in this way in danger of being misled by the false teachings of the judaizing party. But as an offset to all their vain speculations about meats and drinks, and carnal ordinances, Paul here reminds his brethren, that we Christians have also our exclusive rights and privileges; that we too have a sacrifice of which to partake as well as the Jews; a sacrifice of infinite value, and which is quite sufficient to satisfy the desires of all who lawfully partake of it. From this, however, the unbelieving Jews were all debarred according to their own ritual, as our author now proceeds to show.

11 **For the bodies of those beasts, etc.**—The point made by the Apostle is simply this; the Jews were not allowed to eat the flesh of any sin-offering whose blood was carried into the Sanctuary by the High Priest. The flesh of all such victims had to be carried without the camp, and there consumed by fire. "No sin-offering," says Moses, "whereof any of the blood is brought into the Tabernacle of the congregation to reconcile withal in the Holy Place, shall be eaten; it shall be burnt in the fire." (Lev. 6: 30.) According to this law, then, as the Apostle now goes on to show, the Jews, *as Jews,* were all prohibited from partaking of the sacrifice of Christ.

12 **Wherefore Jesus also, that he might sanctify the people, etc.**—To suffer without the gate was the same as to suffer without the camp; for Jerusalem was then the metropolis and camp of Israel. And as the blood of Jesus was taken by himself into the heavenly Sanctuary to make an atonement for the people, so also, according to the law of the sin-offering, it was necessary that he should bear our sins on his own body without the camp. All therefore who would partake of the benefits of his sacrifice, must

13 Let us go forth therefore unto him without the camp, [1]bearing his reproach.

14 [2]For here we have no continuing city, but we seek one to come.

15 [3]By him therefore let us offer [4]the sacrifice of praise to God continually, that is, [5]the fruit of our lips, [6]giving thanks to his name.

[1]Chap. xi. 26; xii. 3; Matt. v. 11; x. 24, 25; xvi. 24; xxvii. 39-44; 1 Pet. iv. 14.
[2]Chap. xi. 9, 10, 12-16; xii. 22; 2 Cor. iv. 17, 18; v. 1-8.
[3]Eph. v. 20; 1 Pet. ii. 5.
[4]Lev. vii. 12; Psa. 1, 14, 23; cxvi. 17-19; Eph. v. 19, 20.
[5]Hos. xiv. 2.
[6]Psa. xviii. 49; Matt. xi. 25.

do so without the gate. They must forsake the camp of Israel, leaving Judaism behind them, and take upon them the reproach of Jesus, if they would be made partakers of the benefits of his death.

13 **Let us go forth therefore unto him without the camp,**— Since it is true, that Jesus himself voluntarily suffered for our sake, without the gate of Jerusalem, all the pain, shame, and reproach of the cross; and since it is furthermore true that his sacrifice is really the only one that can meet and satisfy the wants and desires of our souls, let us therefore courageously follow him without the pale of Jerusalem, which is but as it were a temporary camp that will soon be broken up; and let us manfully bear the reproach of Christ whatever it may be. This he now proceeds to show will result in much gain and but little loss to us.

14 **For here we have no continuing city,**—It is vain to seek refuge in Jerusalem which, according to prophecy, will soon become a heap of ruins (Matt. 24); and in no other city on Earth, can we find a secure and permanent habitation. But if we leave Jerusalem with all its errors and corruptions, and follow Christ without the gate, we will thereby secure for ourselves a place in the heavenly Jerusalem, the city which hath the foundations, whose Architect and Builder is God. See notes on 11: 10, 16. "If then ye be reproached for the name of Christ, happy are ye." (1 Pet. 4: 14.)

15 **By him therefore let us offer, etc.**—Instead of falling back to Judaism, and offering sacrifices required by the Law, let us rather through (*dia*) Jesus, as the great High Priest of our confession, offer to God continually the sacrifice of praise and thanksgiving. For as Peter says to the strangers scattered throughout Pontus, Galatia, Cappadocia, Asia, and Bithynia, we are all "living stones, built up a spiritual house, a holy priesthood, to offer up

16 [7]But to do good and to communicate forget not: for [8]with such sacrifices God is well pleased.

[7]Matt. xxv. 35-40; Luke x. 30-37; Rom. xii. 13; Gal. vi. 6, 10; Eph. iv. 28.
[8]Chap. vi. 10; 2 Cor. ix. 12; Phil. iv. 18.

spiritual sacrifices, acceptable to God through Jesus Christ." (1 Pet. 2:5.) The sacrifice of praise in our text has reference particularly to the voluntary peace and thank offerings of the Law. (Lev. 7:11-25.) To these allusion is also frequently made in the Psalms of David. In Psalm 1:14, for example, Jehovah says to Israel, "Offer unto God thanksgiving, and pay thy vows unto the Most High." And in the twenty-third verse of the same beautiful ode, he says, "Whoso offereth praise glorifieth me; and to him that ordereth his conversation aright, I will show the salvation of God."

16 **But to do good, etc.**—It is not enough to praise God with our lips; we should also honor him with our substance, by doing good to all men as he gives us opportunity. We should, as far as in us lies, feed the hungry, clothe the naked, instruct the ignorant, and assist in converting the world to Christ. There seems to be a proneness in our selfish nature to neglect these practical duties, and hence the exhortation not to forget them. Imitate Christ who went about doing good. (Acts 10:38.)

**for with such sacrifices God is well pleased.**—Such sacrifices are pleasing to God (1) because they are in harmony with his own nature and administration. He opens his hand liberally, and supplies the wants of every living thing. (Psalm 145:16.) (2) Because they indicate in us a state of mind and heart, that is well pleasing in his sight; provided they proceed from proper motives. And hence on the day of judgment, our characters will be tested by this law of benevolence. (Matt. 25:34-35.) And (3) because they are of benefit to others. A very great change would soon be wrought in society, if all Christians would but act faithfully as good stewards of the manifold grace of God.

## 3. OUR DUTIES TO THE OVERSEERS AND OTHER
## PUBLIC SERVANTS OF THE CHURCH
### 13: 17-19

17 [1]Obey them that have the rule over you, and [2]submit yourselves: for [3]they watch for your souls, as they that must give account, that [4]they may do it with joy, and not with grief: for that is unprofitable for you.

[1]Acts vi. 3, 4, 8; xiv. 23; xx. 28; 1 Thess. v. 12; 1 Tim. v. 17; Titus i. 5.
[2]1 Cor. xvi. 16; Eph. v. 21; 1 Pet. v. 5.
[3]Ezek. iii. 17-21; xxxiii. 2-9; Acts xx. 28-31.
[4]Phil. i. 4; ii. 16; iv. 1; 1 Thess. ii. 19. 20; iii. 9, 10.

17 **Obey them that have the rule over you,**—(*tois hegoumenois humon*) *your leaders.* These were the Elders or Overseers of the Church, to whom were committed (1) the duty of instructing the members; and (2) the duty of watching over and governing them. So we learn from many passages in the New Testament. In the twentieth chapter of Acts, for instance, Paul says to the Elders of the Church of Ephesus, "Take heed to yourselves and to all the flock over which the Holy Spirit hath made you Overseers, to feed the Church of God (*tou kuriou,* the Lord) which he hath purchased with his own blood. For I know that after my departure shall grievous wolves enter in among you, not sparing the flock. Also of your own selves shall men arise speaking perverse things, to draw away disciples after them. Therefore watch, and remember that by the space of three years, I ceased not to warn every one night and day with tears." (Acts 20: 28-31.) So also in his first Epistle to Timothy, the same Apostle says, "Let the Elders that rule well be counted worthy of double honor, especially they who labor in word and doctrine." (1 Tim. 5: 17.) Compare also 1 Tim. 3: 1-7; Tit. 1: 5-9; James 5: 14, 15; 1 Pet. 5: 1-4.

**and submit yourselves:**—That is, submit to them so far as they teach and rule according to the Oracles of God. The obligations of the Church and of her officers, are mutually binding. If it is the duty of the Elders to teach, it is also manifestly the duty of the other members of the Church to receive their lawful instructions; and if it is the duty of the former to rule, it is equally the duty of the latter to submit to all their acts of discipline which are not in violation of the law of Christ.

**for they watch for your souls,**—This is a charge of fearful responsibility. "They watch for your souls as they that must give account!" "When I say to the wicked," says God in his instruc-

tions to Ezekiel, "thou shalt surely die, and thou givest him not
warning, nor speakest to warn the wicked from his wicked way,
to save his life; the same man shall die in his iniquity, but his blood
will I require at thy hand. Yet if thou warn the wicked, and he
turn not from his wickedness, nor from his wicked way, he shall
die in his iniquity; but thou hast delivered thy soul. Again when a
righteous man doth turn from his righteousness and commit iniquity, and I lay a stumbling-block before him [by allowing him to
be severely tried, as was Abraham, Gen. 22: 1-19], he shall die;
because thou hast not given him warning, he shall die in his sins,
and his righteousness which he hath done shall not be remembered;
but his blood will I require at thine hand. Nevertheless if thou
warn the righteous man, that the righteous sin not, he shall surely
live; also thou hast delivered thy soul." (Ezek. 3: 18-21.) Not unlike this is the solemn charge which Christ has given to every
shepherd of his flock. (Acts 20: 28.) And hence the solemn admonition which is here given to all the members: Obey your leaders,
and submit yourselves to their instruction and government; for
they watch for your souls, as they that must give an account of
their stewardship. It is no trifling matter, then, to watch over the
flock of Christ, which he has purchased with his own blood. How
few Pastors are doing this as they should; and how few of the
members of the flock have yet learned what it is to submit practically to their instruction and government.

**that they may do it with joy, and not with grief:**—Those
who under God "turn many to righteousness," and who succeed in
leading them to the end in the way of holiness, will of course render their final account with joy; but those who, though faithful
themselves, have the misfortune to see many of their flock perish
by the way, will do this with grief. And hence John says, "I have
no greater joy than to hear that my children are walking in the
truth" (3 John 4); and hence also Paul earnestly exhorts his
Thessalonian brethren to be faithful even to the end. "For what,"
he says, "is our hope, or joy, or crown of rejoicing? Are not even
ye in the presence of our Lord Jesus Christ at his coming? For
ye are our glory and our joy." (1 Thess. 2: 19, 20.)

**for that is unprofitable for you.**—That is, that your Pastors
and Teachers should have to render their final account concerning
you with grief. This would be even a greater misfortune to you

18 [1]Pray for us: for we trust [2]we have a good conscience, [3]in all things willing to live honestly.
19 But I beseech you the rather do this, [1]that I may be restored to you the sooner.

[1]Rom. xv. 30; Eph. vi. 19, 20; Col. iv. 3; 2 Thess. iii. 1.
[2]Acts xxiii. 1; xxiv. 16; 2 Cor. i. 12; 1 Tim. i. 5; 1 Pet. iii. 16. 21.
[3]Rom. xiii. 13; 1 Thess. iv. 12; 1 Pet. ii. 12.
[1]Rom. xv. 30-32; Phil. 22.

---

than to them.  As, therefore, your griefs in that event would be mutual, see to it that on the contrary your joys may be mutual.

18 **Pray for us:**—It is not enough that you obey your rulers, and submit to those who are directly over you in the Lord; you should also remember us the Apostles and Evangelists who have gone out from you to preach the Gospel to the Gentiles.

**for we trust we have a good conscience,**—Our admonitions to you, and our opposition to Judaism, proceed from no selfish or sinister motives: but simply from a desire to discharge conscientiously the duties which God has imposed on us with regard to both Jews and Gentiles; wishing in all things to act honestly in the sight of God.  Hence we claim an interest in your prayers.

19 **But I beseech you, etc.**—From this, in connection with the preceding verse, it is evident (1) that the writer of this Epistle was known to the persons addressed; (2) that he had been formerly with them, not necessarily as one of their Pastors, but in some respects as a co-worker; (3) that he was anxious to see them again, but was then prevented from doing so by some hindrances unknown to us; and (4) that he felt well assured that through the prayers of the Hebrew brethren in his behalf, these hindrances would be removed, and that he would be restored to them the sooner.  This, then, is a beautiful commentary on the efficacy of prayer; and it should encourage us to pray always for the success and welfare of all those who are laboring to convert the world to Christ, and to educate the converts for Heaven.  For "this is the confidence that we have in him, that if we ask anything according to his will he heareth us." (1 John 5: 14.) "Ask [then] and it shall be given you; seek, and ye shall find; knock, and it shall be opened unto you." (Matt. 7: 7.)

## 4. AN EARNEST AND COMPREHENSIVE PRAYER IN BEHALF OF THE HEBREW BRETHREN
### 13: 20, 21

20 Now ¹the God of peace, ²that brought again from the dead our Lord Jesus, ³that great Shepherd of the sheep, ⁴through the blood of the everlasting covenant,

¹Rom. xv. 33; xvi. 20; 1 Cor. xvi. 33.
²Acts ii. 24, 32; iii. 15; iv. 10.
³John x. 11, 14; 1 Pet. ii. 25; v. 4.
⁴Zech. ix. 11; Matt. xxvi. 28; Luke xxii. 20.

---

20 **Now the God of peace,**—God is here called "the God of peace," because all peace comes from him through Jesus Christ, who is himself "The Prince of peace." (Isa. 9:6.) The propriety of so designating "the Father of mercies" will be manifest when it is remembered that at the time of writing this Epistle, the Churches of Judea were threatened with many dangers, both from within and from without.

**that brought again from the dead our Lord Jesus,**—The resurrection of Christ is often ascribed to God the Father in the Holy Scriptures. See references. By raising him from the dead, God acknowledged him as his only-begotten Son (Rom. 1:4), and thus publicly demonstrated to the world that he was the promised Messiah of whom all the ancient Prophets had spoken (Acts 3:24). "This is the only passage," says Delitzsch, "in which the author mentions the resurrection. [He means, of course, the resurrection of Christ: see 11: 35.] Everywhere else he lifts his eyes from the depths of our Lord's humiliation, passing over all that is intermediate, to the highest point of his exaltation. The connection here suggests to him once at least to make mention of that which lay between Golgotha and the throne of God, between the altar of the cross and the heavenly Sanctuary, the resurrection of him who died as a sin-offering for us."

**that great Shepherd of the sheep,**—The Apostle had before spoken of the under shepherds of the flock (verse 17) and had enjoined obedience to them in all their lawful endeavors to edify the Church. Most appropriately, therefore, does he here call Christ himself the "great Shepherd of the sheep." To him both the under shepherds and the flock are alike responsible, purchased as they have been by his own blood. "I am the good Shepherd," says Christ; "the good Shepherd giveth his life for the sheep." (John

10: 11.) Every word in this benedictory prayer is well chosen, and serves to impress on our hearts more and more deeply the sentiments that have been inculcated.

**through the blood of the everlasting covenant,**—(*en haimati*) *in the blood,* or *by virtue of the blood* of the everlasting covenant. The New Covenant is here called "the everlasting Covenant" in contrast with the Old Covenant which was then abrogated (see notes on 8: 13) ; and the blood of this Covenant is the blood of Christ by means of which the Covenant was itself ratified. (Matt. 26: 28; Heb. 9: 23.) But what is the meaning and bearing of this clause? Does it stand connected with what precedes, or with what follows? Did God bring Christ from the dead and constitute him the great Shepherd of the sheep, by virtue of this blood? Or is it simply the wish and prayer of the Apostle that God would perfect the Hebrews by virtue of this blood? The latter view is taken by A. Clarke and a few others; but Delitzsch, Alford, and most other commentators justly support the former. Many of them, indeed, very unwarrantably limit the meaning of this phrase; some to the word *great,* implying that Christ's greatness as a Shepherd was owing to the shedding of his blood (Ebrard) ; and some to the words *"the great shepherd of the sheep,"* meaning that he was made a Shepherd of the sheep by virtue of the shedding of his blood (Lünemann, Moll). But all such restrictions are unnatural and arbitrary. The meaning of the passage fairly construed is manifestly and simply this; that by virtue of the blood of Christ, God raised him from the dead, and constituted him the great Shepherd of the sheep. The resurrection of Christ was the first in that series of triumphs which will result in the overthrow of Satan and the destruction of his works; all of which will be effected "by virtue of the blood of the everlasting covenant." For what but the efficacy of this blood could remove even from our blessed Savior that load of assumed guilt and responsibility, which ruptured his great heart, and crushed him down even into the dark chambers of death? See note on 5: 7. Manifestly it was the flowing of that blood from the heart of our Redeemer, which enabled God, as the righteous Sovereign of the universe, to raise Christ from the dead, and through him to offer salvation to all penitent believers. In this view of the matter only, can we comprehend the meaning of Jesus when he says, "I have a

21 [1]Make you perfect in every good work to do his will, [2]working in you that which is well pleasing in his sight, [3]through Jesus Christ; [4]to whom be glory forever and ever. Amen.

[1]John xvii. 23; Eph. iii. 16-19; 1 Thess. iii. 13; 2 Thess. ii. 17; 1 Pet. v. 10.
[2]Phil. ii. 13.
[3]Eph. ii. 18; Phil. i. 11; Col. iii. 17.
[4]Rom. xvi. 27; Gal. i. 5; Phil. ii. 11; 1 Tim. i. 17; vi. 16; 1 Pet. v. 11.

baptism to be baptized with, and how am I straitened till it be accomplished." (Luke 12: 50.)

21 **Make you perfect in every good work**—The word rendered *make perfect* (*katartizo*) means properly to make quite ready, to put in order, to make complete. Here, it means so to adjust, strengthen, and rectify the powers of the soul, as to thoroughly fit and prepare it for God's service. The Apostle saw among the Hebrew brethren lamentable evidence of mental, moral, social, and religious derangement. And he, therefore, earnestly prays that the God of all peace and order, who brought Jesus back from the dead, and so eminently qualified him for his work, would also through him fit and prepare them for doing his whole will, working in them by his Spirit, and by his truth "both to will and to do of his own good pleasure." (Phil. 2: 13.)

**to whom be glory forever and ever.**—This relative clause is by many expositors, as Calvin, Bleek, and Tholuck, referred to Jesus Christ; but others, as Bengel, Delitzsch, and Alford, more properly refer it to God the Father. *Doctrinally,* it may refer either to God (Rom. 16: 27), or to Christ (2 Pet. 3: 18); but *grammatically,* it refers properly to God, whose agency fills the whole sentence, and whose glory is, therefore, uppermost in the mind of the Apostle.

### 5. CLOSING REMARKS
### 13: 22-25

22 And I beseech you, brethren, [1]suffer the word of exhortation: for [2]I have written a letter unto you in few words.

[1]Matt. xvii. 17; Acts xviii. 14; 2 Tim. iv. 3.
[2]Gal. vi. 11; 1 Pet. v. 12.

22 **And I beseech you, brethren, suffer, etc.**—The word rendered *suffer* (*anechesthe*) means to bear patiently with, to receive with feelings of kindness and forbearance; and "the word of exhortation" is evidently the whole Epistle. By some, this is restricted to the thirteenth chapter (Beza); by others, to the last

23 Know ye that ¹our brother Timothy is set at liberty; with whom if he come shortly, I will see you.

¹1 Thess. iii. 2; Phil. 1.

great division of the Epistle, embracing all from 10: 18 to the close (Grotius); and by others, to the many exhortations which are interspersed throughout the Epistle (Kuinoel). But most commentators, as Delitzsch, Alford, and Moll, more properly apply it to the entire Epistle; the whole of which being eminently hortatory is by the author delicately called a word of exhortation. In this, as in many other instances, we see the very delicate, gentle, and masterly touches of Paul's pen; who being himself the Apostle of the Gentiles, and somewhat estranged from his Hebrew brethren, deals with these as gently as the nature of the case will permit.

**for I have written a letter unto you in few words.**—That is, in few words considering the importance and magnitude of the subjects discussed. He might have said much more on these momentous themes; but owing, perhaps, to the known prejudices of his brethren, he preferred making his communication as brief as possible: and this he assigns as a reason why they should receive and consider it kindly.

23 **Know ye that our brother Timothy is set at liberty;**— The Greek word for *know* (*ginoskete*) may be rendered either indicatively or imperatively: "You know that our brother Timothy has been set free; in company with whom, should he come speedily, I will see you" (T. S. Green); or "Know that our brother Timotheus is dismissed; with whom, if he come soon, I will see you" (Alford). Most commentators, however, justly as I think, prefer the latter. The word rendered *"set at liberty"* (*apolelumenon*) may signify either that Timothy was dismissed from prison, or that he had been sent away on some special errand. The latter view is supported by Euthalius, Mill, and Lardner on the following grounds: (1) "Because it appears from Phil. 2: 19-24, that Paul about this time purposed to send Timothy into Macedonia, with an order to return and bring him an account of the affairs of the brethren in that country; (2) because in none of Paul's Epistles written during his confinement in Rome, does he give the least intimation of Timothy's having been imprisoned, although he was with Paul the greater part of the time, as appears from Phil. 1: 1;

24 ²Salute all them that have ³the rule over you and ⁴all the saints. ⁵They of Italy salute you.

²Rom. xvi. 1-16.
³Ver. 17.
⁴2 Cor. i. 1; xiii. 13.
⁵Acts xviii. 2.

---

Col. 1: 1; and Philemon 1." In sentences so very brief and disconnected, as are these closing remarks, it is sometimes impossible to avoid ambiguity: but it is a significant fact that the great majority of commentators from Chrysostom to Alford have preferred the former rendering of this passage. The historical circumstances of Timothy's imprisonment and release are, however, wholly unknown to us.

"This twenty-third verse," as Delitzsch observes, "exactly harmonizes with the idea that Paul was the author of the Epistle: for no one stood in closer relation to Timothy than Paul; and this relation became more and more intimate towards the close of the Apostle's life."

24 **Salute all them that have the rule over you.**—That is, your Pastors and Teachers. See note on verse 17. As if he had said, Present to them my kindest regards and best wishes. Christianity enjoins on us all the proper courtesies and amenities of life. It is, indeed, itself the very soul and marrow of all genuine politeness; and no one, therefore, who has been thoroughly converted to God, can any longer be a man of rough and boorish behavior.

**and all the saints.**—That is, all within the limits of your acquaintance who are consecrated to Christ. See Acts 9: 13, 14; 26: 10; Rom. 1: 7, 8, etc.

**They of Italy salute you.**—From this expression, some have hastily inferred that when our author wrote this Epistle he could not have been in Italy; but that he must have been in some other place surrounded by Italians who had, perhaps been banished from Rome, like Aquila and Priscilla. (Acts 18:2.) But this inference is wholly unwarranted. "They of Italy" (*hoi apo tes Italias*) were simply Italians, just as "Jews of Thessalonica" (*hoi apo tes Thessalonikes Ioudaioi*) were natives or residents of that city. Whether they were then actually in Italy or out of it cannot be determined from the form of the expression. But as Delitzsch observes, "If the author was then in Italy, and at the same time was not a native

25 [1]Grace be with you all. Amen.

[1]Rom. xvi. 20, 24; Rev. xxii. 21.

of Italy, he could not have selected any more appropriate designation for the Italian Christians properly so-called."

25 **Grace be with you all. Amen.**—This is Paul's characteristic conclusion. See Rom. 16: 24; 1 Cor. 16: 23; 2 Cor. 13: 14; Gal. 6: 18; Eph. 6: 24; Phil. 4: 23; Col. 4: 18; 1 Thess. 5: 28; 2 Thess. 3: 18; 1 Tim. 6: 21; 2 Tim. 4: 22; Tit. 3: 15; Phile. 25. The word *grace* (*karis*) means favor: but with the article before it, as in this instance (*he karis*) it commonly means in the New Testament the special and peculiar favor of God to his children; that favor which supplies all that is good, and frees from all that is evil. No conclusion could therefore be more appropriate than is this beautiful and comprehensive benediction.

The subscription, *"Written to the Hebrews from Italy to Timothy,"* is postapostolic, and is manifestly incorrect for the following reasons: (1) it is inconsistent with what is said of Timothy in 13: 23. If Timothy was then absent from the place of writing, then how could he either write the letter or bear it to the Hebrews? (2) The forms of the subscription, like those of the title, vary very much both in the ancient versions and in the manuscripts. In D, M, L, M, there is no subscription whatever; in c, 17, it is simply *"To the Hebrews;"* in A, it is *"Written to the Hebrews from Rome;"* and in the Syriac, Coptic, K, D, followed by the Textus Receptus, it is as above given in our English Version.

### REFLECTIONS

1. Christianity is a *practical* system: a system which looks first to the life of the individual and then to the life of society (verses 1-7). True, indeed, it has its theory, as every system of doctrine must have, but the tendency of every element of this Divine scheme of philanthropy is to practically elevate, purify, and ennoble human nature. Having first washed away the sins of the believer, and filled his soul with the sweet influences of the Holy Spirit, it now requires and enables him to love his brethren; to be kind and hospitable to strangers; to sympathize with all who are in affliction; to avoid all uncleanness and covetousness; and to place his whole trust and confidence in God, feeling perfectly sure that all

things will work together for good to those who do so. In this respect it is without a parallel in all the religious and philosophical systems of earth and time. No other scheme of religion has, like it, been found adequate to expel the evil demons of the human soul, and to make men willing and even anxious to glorify God by doing good to all men as they have opportunity.

2. It must not be forgotten, however, that the power of the Christian Religion consists primarily in the nature and character of its doctrine (verses 8-16). It reveals to us Jehovah as a God of infinite justice, who will not allow even the slightest departure from his law to pass with impunity, but who is withal so full of love and compassion that he gave his own dear Son for the redemption of our race. It reveals to us this Son as being in the very image of his Father, and yet as laying aside his robes of glory, assuming our nature, voluntarily tasting death for every man, sending his good Spirit to convict sinners, comfort saints, and help their infirmities. These are the gracious media through which God operates on the human soul so as to destroy its selfishness, and elevate its aspirations from the things of earth to the things of heaven. How important it is, then, that we maintain the faith of the Gospel as it was once for all delivered to the saints. Here, there should be no halting and no vacillating. In matters of opinion we may and we should bear and forbear with one another, as God in his infinite mercy bears with us. (Rom. 14.) But faith is of a wholly different category. It admits of no compromise. Rob the Gospel, for instance, of the Divinity of Christ, or of the Scriptural doctrine of his atonement, and you at once rob it of its power to purify and govern the human soul. It is well then that "the heart be established with grace and not with meats."

3. Let us beware of trusting too much in outward forms and ordinances (verses 10-12). Men have always been prone to do this. Many of the Jews never looked beyond the type to the glorious realities of the antitype. They lived and died in vainly trying to satisfy their souls with the mere shadows of God's grace; and consequently they never enjoyed even a foretaste of "the heavenly gift." And just so it is still with many who profess to be followers of Christ. They glory in the so-called "sacraments" of the Christian religion, and talk much about "baptismal regeneration," "the real presence," and many other hallucinations that are equally vain

and chimerical. But though intent upon ordinances, they have never even tasted of the bread and water of life. The ordinances of God are of course not to be despised or neglected. They are all divinely appointed means to the attainment of a divinely appointed end. They are the media through which God pours into our hearts the rich treasures of his grace, which alone can satisfy the soul. The Lord's Supper, for example, is most admirably adapted to bring the soul into communion with Christ; but unless it really does so, and in this way makes us partakers of the bread of life, what does it profit? Baptism has also its advantages. It is well calculated to give us a realizing sense of our changed state and relations. But unless by introducing us "into the name of the Father, and of the Son, and of the Holy Spirit," it brings us into contact with that blood which cleanses from all sin, it profits us nothing. "For as the body without the spirit is dead," so the ordinances of the Christian religion without its essence are dead also.

4. Christians have been constituted a kingdom of priests to offer up spiritual sacrifices to God, and to serve as his ministers of mercy in doing good to all men (verses 15, 16). In this respect, as well as in everything else, we should as far as possible imitate Christ our Exemplar. We cannot, of course, like him, make an atonement for sin; but like him we can offer to God continually a sacrifice of praise and thanksgiving, and like him we can assist in doing good—in feeding the hungry, clothing the naked, instructing the ignorant, and preaching the Gospel to the poor, many of whom are even now perishing in the region and shadow of death. Why, then, are we not all more diligent in the work of our high and holy calling? Why allow selfishness, or the spirit of party, or anything else, to interfere with our mission of love? Christ did not do so. From his baptism to his cross he never wavered. The combined hosts of earth and hell did not and could not, in any instance, turn him aside, even for a moment, from the sublime object of his mission. And now that he sits on the throne of the universe, he is still the same, "yesterday, today, and forever"; always intent on the redemption of those for whom he died. O, that we all had the spirit and temper of Jesus; then, indeed, the world itself would soon become a temple of his praise.

5. How very near, dear, and interesting are the relations which the Pastors and other members of every Christian congregation

sustain to each other (verse 17). The former are held responsible for the souls of the latter; while the latter are held responsible for their demeanor towards the former. But where, alas, are these mutual obligations now practically acknowledged as they should be by either party? How few Pastors now go, like Paul, from house to house, and night and day with tears warn the people against the snares of the world, the flesh, and the devil? And on the other hand how few members of any congregation now submit, as they should, to the lawful authority of their Pastors and Teachers? The fact is, that the law of Christ is now too much ignored and set aside by all parties; and as a consequence, there is an alarming want of submission to rightful authority, in the church and in the family, as well as in the state. Let all be taught to reverence God's word and to bow to his authority; let parents so teach their children in the nursery; let Preachers, Editors, and Teachers of all grades and classes so instruct the rising generation; and soon the happy consequences of this change will be felt in every department of society. Parents will then be made to rejoice in seeing that their children are walking in the ways of wisdom; and Pastors of churches will be comforted in the assurance that the members of their respective charges are being nourished amid the green pastures and beside the still waters.

6. Why do men pray so little? Do they really believe Christ when he says, "Everyone that asketh receiveth, and he that seeketh findeth and to him that knocketh it shall be opened?" I fear they do not. If they did, there would surely not be so many prayerless individuals, prayerless families, and I may say comparatively prayerless churches. Did we all feel as Paul felt when he asked for the prayers of his brethren, that he might be restored to them the sooner (verse 19), it does seem to me that every meeting house in the land would become in a much higher sense than it is "a house of prayer."

7. How pleasant and full of comfort is the assurance that God is with us to help us in all our lawful endeavors to serve him (verses 20, 21); that we in fact live in him, move in him, and have our being in him; and that while we are called on to work out our own salvation with fear and trembling God himself also at the same time works in us both to will and to do of his own good pleasure. "Let us then not grow weary in well doing; for in due sea-

son we shall reap if we faint not." (Gal. 6:9.) And now, dear reader, may "the God of peace, that brought again from the dead our Lord Jesus, that great Shepherd of the sheep, through the blood of the everlasting covenant, make you perfect in every good work to do his will, working in you that which is well pleasing to his sight, through Jesus Christ; to whom be glory forever and ever. Amen."

END OF VOLUME 9

# ROBERT MILLIGAN

As the author of this volume was called to his eternal reward while the work was in course of publication, it was thought proper by the Publishers to append the following sketch of his life and character prepared by Prof. J. W. McGarvey, an intimate friend and associate in his labors. In making it a part of this volume, we entertain the hope that it will impress the virtues of a noble and well-spent life on the hearts of many, and that the heaven-born lessons which it is the purpose of this Commentary to unfold to the minds of its readers will be more readily received on account of the estimable character of the lamented author:

The deceased was born in the county of Tyrone, in the north of Ireland, July 25th, 1814, and died March 20th, 1875, in the 61st year of his age. When he was but four years old his parents emigrated to America, and settled in Trumbull County, Ohio. The country was then new, and the hardy farmers had severe toil in cutting away the timber and clearing their lands. While yet a boy, Robert was employed in this work, and even then it was characteristic of him to go at everything he did with all his might. While engaged in removing stumps from a field he received some internal injury which compelled him to give up this mode of life, and probably changed the current of his history. At seventeen years of age he was sent across the state line into Pennsylvania, and entered in a classical academy conducted by a Dr. Gamble, who was a noted teacher and a graduate of the University at Edinburgh. Here he acquired a knowledge of nearly the entire course of study usually pursued in colleges. At twenty-one years of age we find him again at his father's home, and becoming a communicant in the Reformed Presbyterian church. His father was a devoted member of that church, and a ruling elder; and he brought up his children with the strictness of religious training for which that body of people are distinguished.

Shortly after this he prepared to enter the chosen profession of his life, that of teaching. For the sake of a milder climate he sought a situation farther south; and in 1837, when twenty-three years of age, he opened a classical school in the little village of Flat Rock, Bourbon County, Kentucky. While thus engaged he began to be puzzled by questions which his pupils propounded to him concerning the meaning of passages of Scripture, and he then realized, as he has stated, for the first time, the responsibility of those who are called on to teach others the word of God. He went to work in the fear of God, and re-examined the entire ground of his religious convictions. The result was, that by the force of the Bible alone he was compelled to change his views in some important particulars, and soon afterward he was immersed by John Irvine, an elder of the church at Cane Ridge, Kentucky, and became a member of that congregation.

After teaching two years in Flat Rock, he determined to complete his own collegiate course, and for this purpose he started for Yale College. On his way he stopped at Washington, Pennsylvania, to visit some friends, and was persuaded by them to remain there and graduate in Washington College. The controlling inducement for this change of purpose was the fact that a mile or two from Washington there was a little band of Disciples who needed someone to teach them and to be a leader among them. He was told that if he would remain at Washington he could do those brethren great good by taking part in their meetings on the Lord's day, and that he could enjoy the privilege which he would not find at Yale, of worshiping with a congregation holding the same faith and order with himself. In consenting, he showed his characteristic devotion to Christ by sacrificing superior educational advantages for the sake of greater usefulness, and happiness in the service of God. In a single session he completed the course at Washington College, receiving his degree of Bachelor of Arts in 1840, when he was twenty-six years of age. But before he graduated, the rulers of that institution discovered in him such integrity, such aptness for teaching, and such proficiency in scholarship, that they elected him to a professorship which was vacant, and he assumed his new position at the beginning of the next session.

About this time the rising young scholar and professor formed the acquaintance of Miss Ellen Blaine Russell, whose father, Hon. James M. Russell, was at that time the representative in Congress from the district, and who received her name Blaine from the family of the popular and highly honored Speaker Blaine of the House of Representatives, who is her first cousin. To her he was married in January 1842, the twenty-eighth year of his age; and she remained his faithful companion until the day of his death.

In the same year, or the next after it, he was formally set apart as a preacher of the gospel, the hands of the venerable Thomas Campbell being laid upon him at the request of the church. From that time forward, although he never made preaching his chief employment, he was ever ready, as occasion required, to speak a word for his Master.

Twelve years of happiness and usefulness had been spent in Washington College, and in the excellent society of the town of Washington, when it was determined by the Trustees, in 1852, to make the College more strictly denominational. It had always been under Presbyterian control, but it was now determined to place it under the immediate management of the Synod. Prof. Milligan was assured by influential members of the Board that notwithstanding the contemplated change, he would be retained in his position if he desired it; but knowing that this would be distasteful to some other members who desired the institution to be strictly denominational, he handed in his resignation, and accepted a chair which was offered him in the State University of Indiana, situated at Bloomington in that State. His stay here was brief; for his family were so seriously afflicted with the miasmatic diseases which prevailed in that part of Indiana, that after two years he resigned his position and accepted a professorship, which had been repeatedly offered him, in Bethany College. Alexander Campbell had long known him, appreciated his worth, and desired his cooperation in the work of building up the institution over which he presided. Accordingly, in the fall of 1854 he entered on the duties of Professor of Mathematics in Bethany College, Va. He also became a co-editor with Alexander Campbell, W. K. Pendleton, and Robert Richardson, of the *Millennial Harbinger*. Here he remained for five years, discharging the duties of his professorship with his accustomed assiduity, and entering upon a work of personal religious labor among the students of the college, and the citizens of the community, such as had never before been known in that institution. His religious influence was distinctly felt by every young man in the College, and among the thousands who have heard with pain the news of his death, there are none who remember him with stronger affection than hundreds of men now occupying positions of honor and usefulness in the world, who were under his instruction, and who felt the impress of his goodness while they were students at Bethany College.

While these labors were going on, Kentucky University began to loom in prospect above our other institutions of learning, and to attract the wondering attention of the entire brotherhood. J. B. Bowman had gone forth among the generous brethren of Kentucky, and in an incredibly short time had secured an endowment fund of $200,000 for Bacon College, which was to be chartered as Kentucky University. When he and his advisers began to look around for a suitable President for their rising institution, they fixed their eyes on Prof. Milligan, of Bethany College, and determined, if possible, to secure him. It was a hard task for him to tear himself away from the field of usefulness which he was cultivating so successfully at Bethany, and he considered the question long and well before deciding. In a letter which he addressed to me in June, 1857, he uses these words: "Nothing but a sense of duty will induce me to dissolve my present relations; but I confess that it is difficult to withstand the generous appeals of our Kentucky brethren." To these appeals he finally yielded, and came to Kentucky, "to devote," as he said, "all the energies of body, soul, and spirit, to the building up, at Harrodsburg, of a literary institution free from all sectional and party jealousies, and devoted to the promotion of sound learning, and to the highest interests of our Redeemer's Kingdom." In the fall of 1859 he assumed the Presidency of the University, and labored with his accustomed zeal both for the institution and the church. With the faithful men who were his coadjutors there, he accomplished great good; but it was not until the institution was moved to Lexington, and the College of the Bible was organized, that he found himself engaged in a work perfectly suited to his taste. He had taught with zeal and earnestness, during his career as a Professor, all the branches of learning in the college course, and he was proficient in them all; but though he labored faithfully in these departments, they never enlisted his affections; it was not till he was permitted to devote his entire time to teaching the word of God, and teaching it to young men who desired to go forth and preach it to the world, that his soul reveled in delight as he went through his daily task. No man ever loved his work more devotedly, or labored in it with less regard to personal interest. Around the College of the Bible the deepest solicitude of his soul was gathered, and its interests were the greatest burden of his heart to the day of his death. During the delirium of his last sickness, he was conducting recitations in his classroom, and during his rational moments he persisted, in the face of remonstrances from his physicians, in holding some consultations about his classes.

We have now followed our beloved and venerable brother throughout his career of usefulness, and what an example does it furnish to the young men of America. We have seen the humble Irish farmer's boy of Northeastern Ohio becoming a country school teacher in Kentucky; passing thence through successive professorships in three different colleges, at each change advancing to a more honored position and acquiring a wider fame; then promoted to the presidency of an institution which promised to outstrip all those in which he had labored as professor; and finally, at the head of a college whose duties and honors were commensurate with the highest aim of his ambition, he died amid the affection and praises of a mighty multitude in this and other lands, who rise up to pronounce a blessing on his name.

A few words in reference to the results of his intellectual efforts may not be out of place here. As we have said before, he taught, during his career of thirty-five years as a college professor, through the entire range of literature and science usually taught in colleges, and in every department he was successful. Indeed, he was never so great anywhere else as he was in the classroom. No man knows how to appreciate his intellectual powers who has not seen him at work there. The hesitancy and apparent timidity which characterized him everywhere else, were not seen there, but he was master of the situation, and his demeanor was that of a king on his throne.

In addition to his labors in the college, and besides numerous contributions to periodical literature, he is the author of seven volumes on religious topics. The first of these was a small volume on Prayer. It was but a natural consequence that the first-fruits of authorship from one whose life was a life of prayer, should be devoted to this blessed theme. His next work was the one entitled Reason and Revelation, the prime object of which was to strike a blow at Rationalism, the contagion of which in institutions of learning was to the author a source of constant anxiety and apprehension. His third volume was his Scheme of Redemption, which is probably the greatest of all his works. His fourth was a Commentary on the Epistle to the Hebrews.

Soon after the completion of his manuscript on Hebrews, he published a small volume, which he entitled the Great Commission. It is an elaborate exposition of the last commission given by Jesus to the apostles. About eighteen months before his death he undertook the preparation of a complete analysis of the New Testament, intended as a textbook for the instruction of classes, one volume of which, including the Gospels and Acts, has been published; and the second volume, including the remainder of the New Testament, was not completed when his earthly labors were brought to a close. He also published a small volume entitled Grace and Good Works, intended to show the exact offices of grace and good works in our salvation.

These works, with the single exception of the tract on prayer, were all written during the ten years of his residence in Lexington. While we wondered from day to day, how, with his feeble health, he could live under the weight of his college duties, he added to those duties the prodigious labor involved in preparing these volumes for the press.

Of the moral and religious character of the deceased, we must take the liberty to speak freely. If we were to call on all who knew him to say what was the most prominent characteristic of the man, we would all very likely answer in the same words, and say that he was a *good* man. This is what all the people called him, and by this language they meant to designate his piety. When Luke undertakes to tell why Barnabas was selected from among the great spirits in the church at Jerusalem to go on an important mission to Antioch, he uses the words, "For he was a *good* man, and full of the Holy Spirit." This is the high encomium which first of all springs to the lips when we speak of President Milligan.

As a result of his goodness, he was pre-eminently a man of peace. It seemed to require no effort on his part to "seek peace and pursue it"; and that other precept of the apostle, "If it be possible, as much as lieth in you, live peaceably with all men," he observed with the most scrupulous care. And how well we all know that he was a peace-*maker!* Everywhere and at all times he was ready to do what he could to make peace among those who were at enmity. If the sentiment, "Blessed are the peacemakers; for they shall be called the children of God," expresses a true thought, how great the blessing that will rest on him!

He was also a conscientious man. We are sure we have never known a man more strictly so in regard to the very smallest matters pertaining to the service of God and to the rights and feelings of his fellowmen. Like Paul, he exercised himself to have always a conscience void of offense toward God and toward man. It was this which made him always so courteous and considerate in his bearing toward his colleagues in the University and in the church, so strict in his requirements of students under his care (for he was a strict disciplinarian both in the church and in the college), and so exact in maintaining good order and religious habits in his family.

If there was any one dominant feeling which might be called the ruling passion of life, it was his love for the word of God. He valued it above all things under the sun, and there was nothing that so nourished his soul as to study its blessed pages, to converse on its deep themes with others who were striving to understand it, and to impart a knowledge of it to willing minds. At one period of his studies, Pres. Graham and myself held a weekly interview with him at his request, for the purpose of comparing our views on difficult passages of Scripture, and on the profounder themes connected with the scheme of redemption. We met in his classroom, and at his suggestion our interviews were always opened with prayer. He would read to us something which he had written, and it would be subjected, word by word, and thought by thought, to the freest criticism. Well as we knew the care with which he had studied the word of God, and the laborious research with which he had gone through the Bible itself and the ponderous volumes of the theologians and the critics, we were often taken with surprise in these discussions by the thoroughness of his investigations, and by the skill with which he anticipated objections to his views and set them aside.

The gentleness and evenness of temper for which he had so great and so deserved a reputation, was not altogether natural to him. An Irishman by birth and ancestry, he inherited a large share of the impetuosity which belongs to his people; and it was the strict Presbyterian training of his childhood, the devout conscientiousness of his religious life, inciting him to a constant warfare against his passions; and doubtless also the debilitating effects of disease, which combined to curb his fiery temper, and to confine it within the channel in which God intended that it should flow. But let any man attack the Bible in his presence; let Rationalism dare to show its face; or let him be told of some inroad that infidelity was making on the territory of the Lord, and you would see in the twinkling of an eye that the lion within him was not dead, but only sleeping. Even in such moments, however, though you could see the flashing of a latent fire, you heard no foolish nor extravagant expressions.

His conscientiousness and his love of God made him a most industrious man. We have known a number of men of untiring industry, but we have never known one who labored so incessantly under so great disadvantages. Many a day have we known him to pass in his classroom, going through the entire routine of his daily labor, when he could not sit upright in his chair, but would be compelled to lean upon his desk, and rest his head on his hand. We remonstrated with him, but all in vain. There was his work before him, and it must be done. While he could creep to his room, and speak loud enough to be heard from one side of it to the other, go he would. And when his recitation hours were over, he was still in his classroom engaged in study or writing, and ready to hold all manner of interviews with students who called on him for consultation in regard to their studies, their religious difficulties, and their financial embarrassments. The intervals between these interruptions, together with the summer vacations, were employed in preparing the volumes of which we have spoken, so that the entire circle of the year was but a round of incessant labor.

If we were to say that President Milligan was a man of great decision of character, some would not receive the statement. It was the general opinion of his friends that he was lacking in decision. We concede the correctness of this opinion, yet in justice we must subject it to a certain limitation. On questions which were involved in some uncertainty, he always spoke with hesitation, even when his own judgment had been formed. So he did in reference to all theoretical questions, on which it appeared to his mind that there was room for any doubt. And in regard to questions of expediency, which involved the interests and the passions of men, he was never very decided, unless it was in the way of insisting on compromise and peace. But when the path of duty was clearly marked out before him, no man ever pursued it more fearlessly or with a firmer step: and when the truth, on any question, was so apparent to his mind as to admit of no reasonable ground for doubt, he was as decided in the expression of his convictions, and as persistent in maintaining them, as any man of my acquaintance. His indecision was the result of his extreme conscientiousness and his love of peace; and if, at times, any of us grew impatient with him, it was perhaps because we were rash and he was prudent.

For a long period he has borne that heavy burden of feeble health which so often excited our pity. It fell on him first in the year 1842, in the form of a violent attack of inflammatory rheumatism, which came near proving fatal, and which left his system enfeebled and exposed to other forms of disease. This was followed by neuralgia of the brain, which affected the optic nerve, and rendered his eyes exceedingly sensitive to the light. The sudden flashing of light upon them was like piercing them with a knife. It was this which caused him always, in conversation, to keep his eyes directed toward the floor, leading strangers to wonder why he did not look them in the face. For some years previous to his death, he did not pretend to read or write by gaslight or lamplight, but was dependent on the light of the sun for all his labor; and even in the daytime he spared his eyes as much as he well could by having members of his family to read to him. He was afflicted with frequent returns both of neuralgia of the brain and rheumatism; and besides this, his digestion was imperfect, and his throat and lungs were somewhat involved in the general prostration. He told us several years ago that he could not pass a day without the use of medicine, and this necessity continued until his last sickness.

In this connection we must mention a circumstance to which we invite the special attention of all young men. He consulted many eminent physicians in regard to his maladies, and he was repeatedly urged to drink daily a portion of strong whisky or brandy, with the assurance that it would add at least ten years to his life. But he steadfastly refused to do so, and said that he would rather die ten years earlier than to live by the daily use of intoxicating liquor. And this was not so much because he feared the effects on himself, as because he dreaded the influence it would have on others, and especially on young men, to know that from any cause he kept up such a habit.

When he was seized with his last sickness, he did not think it would be fatal, nor did he so conclude till he was informed by the consulting physician, that so it must be. He had fought the battle against his old diseases so long, that he felt confident of fighting it through a little longer. We know, however, from his own remarks to us in regard to his anxiety to push to completion the works on which he was engaged, that he did not expect to live very long, and he recently told his wife that he thought it probable that another year would bring his life to a close. He had his plans laid for that year, intending to take some rest, and to make a final visit to all his relatives and especial friends at a distance. But the new enemy proved too strong for him, and when it gained the mastery he sank under it very rapidly.

He talked much, during his illness, of the religious discipline of suffering, saying many beautiful things on the subject; but he said little concerning his death. When a friend during his illness, having spent the night with him, bade him farewell with some expression of doubt as to his recovery, he replied: "If the message were to come to me that I must set my house in order by noon today, I do not know how I would receive it," and here is his usual caution; "but I know how I ought to receive it, and how I think I would. I think I would say, the will of the Lord be done; I will be ready." And when, on the day of his death, the physician informed him that his case was hopeless, he answered, "Very well," as if he had been told something that had occurred in the household. In his last moments, he appeared to suffer but little. It was our privilege to sit by his side during the last hour or two, and watch his departure. Once or twice, as his breathing became less difficult because his lungs were ceasing to act, a slight shudder passed over his frame, as of one taken suddenly with a chilly sensation, but this, together with a slight rising and falling of his right hand, was the only motion or sign of pain that we discovered. The last moment came so quietly, that the family seemed hardly to know that it had come, until we looked at our watch to see the time, and remarked, "All is over."

It should be mentioned, for the purpose of giving completeness to the above representation of the character of the deceased, that he was always a liberal contributor to public religious enterprises; to the poor, and especially to poor students; and that in his last will he bequeathed out of his small estate one hundred dollars to the Kentucky Christian Education Society, to assist in educating poor young men for the ministry; one hundred dollars to the Kentucky Christian Missionary Convention, for the purpose of distributing the Holy Scriptures among the freedmen of the South; and the entire net proceeds of his New Testament Analysis, jointly to the Kentucky Female Orphan School and the Foreign Christian Missionary Society, which was organized at a recent meeting of the General Christian Missionary Convention.